Handbook for Teaching Introductory Psychology

Volume Three

(With an Emphasis on Assessment)

Handbook for Teaching Introductory Psychology

Volume Three

(With an Emphasis on Assessment)

Edited by

Richard A. Griggs
University of Florida

Ψ Psychology Press
Taylor & Francis Group

New York London

First published by Lawrence Erlbaum Associates, Inc., Publishers
10 Industrial Avenue
Mahwah, New Jersey 07430

Reprinted 2008 by Psychology Press

Psychology Press
Taylor & Francis Group
27 Church Road
Hove, East Sussex BN3 2FA

Library of Congress Cataloging-in-Publication Data

Handbook for teaching introductory psychology / edited by Ludy T. Benjamin, Jr., Robert S.
    Daniel, Charles L. Brewer.
    v. <1-2 > : ill. ; 28 cm.
    Vol. 2 edited by Michelle R. Hebl, Charles L. Brewer, Ludy T. Benjamin, Jr.
    Includes bibliographical references and index.
    ISBN 0-89859-561-4 (v. 1 : alk. paper) — ISBN 0-8058-3654-3 (v. 2 : alk. paper)
    ISBN 0-8058-3921-6 (v. 3 : alk. paper)
    1. Psychology—Study and teaching (Higher) I. Benjamin, Ludy T., 1945–   . II. Daniel,
Robert S.   III. Brewer, Charles L.   IV. Hebl, Michelle R. (Michelle Rae)
BF77.H26 1985
150′.7—dc19   85-006758

Printed in the United States of America
10 9 8 7 6 5 4 3 2 1

TABLE OF CONTENTS

Preface

PREFACE

In their prefaces to the first two volumes of the *Handbook for Teaching of Psychology*, the editors stressed two major points relevant to the development of these books. First, not only is introductory psychology one of the most popular courses for students, but it is also central in importance to the undergraduate psychology curriculum. Second, *Teaching of Psychology (ToP)*, the official journal of the Society for the Teaching of Psychology (Division 2 of the American Psychological Association), is recognized as one of the best pedagogical journals across disciplines and, as such, regularly includes excellent articles on teaching the introductory course. Thus, readily accessible, organized collections of articles from *ToP* on teaching the introductory course should be invaluable resources to introductory teachers, and indeed, this has proved to be the case for the first two volumes. My aim for Volume 3 is the same.

Whereas the first volume only sampled *ToP* articles for roughly a 10-year period from the last half of 1974 through 1984, Volume 2 had to attempt to cover a 15-year period (from 1985 through most of 1999) in which over 1,000 articles were published in *ToP*. Thus, both many valuable articles and entire topic subsections could not be included because of length constraints. For example, given the importance of testing and assessment to teaching the introductory course (and all courses), there was a clear need for more on these topics. The idea to produce Volume 3 so soon after Volume 2 arose to meet this need.

In preparing Volume 3, I examined articles published in *ToP* from 1985 through the first two issues of 2000, excluding the 85 articles included in Volume 2. Volume 3 contains 89 new articles presented in two main sections. Section I, Issues and Approaches in Teaching Introductory Psychology, consists of 52 articles in the following subsections: Approaches to the Introductory Course; Students' Interests, Perceptions, and Motives; Students' Knowledge About Psychology; Introductory Textbooks: Objective Features; Introductory Textbooks: Problems; Examinations: Questions; Examinations: Test Factors Affecting Exam Performance; Examinations: Student Factors Affecting Exam Performance; Examinations: Feedback; Extra Credit; and Academic Dishonesty. The articles in the first two subsections provide additional coverage of topics in Volume 2. The remaining nine subsections are new, with the last six providing thorough coverage of various topics related to testing and assessment.

Section II, Demonstrations and Activities in Introductory Psychology, consists of 37 more articles in subsections titled General, Research Methods and Statistics, Biopsychology, Sensation and Perception, Learning, Memory and Cognition, Developmental Psychology, Abnormal Psychology, and Social Psychology and Personality. The ordering of these subsections parallels that used in the first two volumes and in most introductory psychology textbooks. Articles in Section II present demonstrations, class and laboratory projects, and other techniques to enhance teaching and learning in both the introductory course and other more advanced courses. Most of these activities can be conducted in the classroom with little or no equipment.

As with the first two volumes in this series, this book contains the work of many dedicated teachers. I would like to thank all of them for sharing their ideas with us. All royalties from this book will go directly to The Society for the Teaching of Psychology to promote its activities for improving the teaching of psychology. If this volume helps introductory psychology teachers as much as the first two collections of *ToP* articles, then I will feel sufficiently rewarded.

Richard A. Griggs

References

Benjamin, L. T., Jr., Daniel, R. S., & Brewer, C. L. (Eds.). (1985). *Handbook for teaching introductory psychology*. Hillsdale, NJ: Lawrence Erlbaum Associates, Inc.

Hebl, M. R., Brewer, C. L., & Benjamin, L. T., Jr. (Eds.). (2000). *Handbook for teaching introductory psychology: Volume II*. Hillsdale, NJ: Lawrence Erlbaum Associates, Inc.

Handbook for Teaching Introductory Psychology

Volume Three

(With an Emphasis on Assessment)

Section I
Issues and Approaches in Teaching Introductory Psychology

1. APPROACHES TO THE INTRODUCTORY COURSE

Bringing Psychology to Life

Dale McAdam
University of Rochester

Bringing Psychology to Life (BPL) is a series of exercises that requires introductory students to find and discuss psychological explanations for their observations of behavior and mental life. It is the first set of recitations for students and teaching assistants (TAs).

The goals of BPL are: (a) to present an approach to psychology that will tap student energy and curiosity by allowing exploration of individual interests; (b) to introduce inexperienced TAs to the classroom with appropriate measures of structure, freedom, and self-reference to give them some teaching skills and confidence; and (c) to encourage students and TAs to become familiar with the textbook.

The first of these goals has been explored by Hettich (1976, 1980) who used a personal journal and by Brender (1982) who used a log-based term paper. Their approaches do not involve discussions, which can serve the goal of relating knowledge to experience (McKeachie, 1969).

In our one-semester introductory course, we provide the usual survey of psychology and training in the facile use of its language, procedures, and concepts. We offer individualized learning experiences through BPL and other guided involvements in matters close to students' lives and interests.

Undergraduate TAs are promised that they will learn psychology by teaching it. They are junior and senior psychology majors, "near-peers" of their students. Their backgrounds include a course in statistics and four or more courses in psychology. Most aspire to graduate work in psychology or related fields, and many are preparing for GREs.

The most important TA duty is the development of projects for small groups of students. At the beginning of the semester, TAs need time to construct their projects and BPL provides the time to do so. More important, BPL provides TAs with teaching experience in a context that includes active discussion, focused effort, the support of a structured lesson plan, and freedom to use their knowledge.

Introductory students develop questions about behavior and mental life before answers to them are covered in the course. This is especially true for their questions about social and clinical psychology, the savory and sweet offered last in most introductions. Furthermore, as we pass through the early material, I highlight its relevance to what will come later. I can do this more effectively if students are acquainted with the entire text. Because searches throughout the textbook are part of BPL, it develops early familiarity.

The BPL Assignment

The basic assignment for BPL is given in the syllabus. It is deceptively simple:

> Choose and explain three observations of behavior and mental life. Your report should include: (a) clear descriptions of the observations in simple, behavioral terms; (b) your (clearly noted) interpretations of the observations; and (c) most important, psychological explanations of the observations (and your interpretations of them) which are supported by (d) specific citations to your textbook. The critical presentation of alternative explanations is particularly encouraged.

All students receive that assignment and information about signing up and earning credit for BPL along with the following (imperfect) sample.

> My roomie is ordinarily a shy person who does not meet other people easily (especially girls) and who is usually very quiet in a group. However, his whole personality changes when he's partying. He flirts, and he's boisterous and funny. He says the alcohol "stimulates" him, and without it he's nerdy. But we know that alcohol is a depressant and, according to Carlson (p. 108), the apparent stimulation effects really are due to the depression of parts of the brain that are inhibiting behavior.

A critical approach to the sample is supported by several questions that are pointed at its imperfections:

> Which parts of the first sentence are observations, and which are interpretations? Does the report support the contention that the change after a few beers constitutes a "whole" personality change? What about other explanations for the observations; for example, those based in his roomie's expectations about drinking and about not drinking, or in the social facilitation provided by the party setting?

Procedures

There are three weekly meetings beginning the 3rd week of the semester. The first is an introduction, the second a workshop, and the third a presentation and discussion of student work. A written report is due the day after the third meeting. Each TA works with two BPL sections.

Efforts are made to keep meetings informal. Chairs or desks are set in a circle. The TAs begin the first meeting by introducing and telling something about themselves, including how and why they came to be TAs. Students are asked to introduce and say something about themselves, an important start in getting them to speak in recitations.

The syllabus example is discussed, and the questions posed are worked over, including those involving observation versus interpretation of behavior. The TAs present their own examples. The organization of the textbook is reviewed, and attention is called to the expanded table of contents and index as places to begin and to facilitate searches.

At the end of this meeting, students gather their observations. They are encouraged to begin to develop explanations, but not to worry if they have trouble because the next week's workshop will be a place to get help.

Students have three goals in the workshop: (a) to learn how to search skillfully through the textbook for explanations of their samples, (b) to seek alternative explanations (they should be highly suspicious of an observation with but a single unambiguous psychological explanation), and (c) to clarify matters about the written report and the nature of the final meeting.

The last meeting is more formal. Each student presents at least one sample that did not receive full discussion previously. The TA, now more chairperson than teacher, sees that everyone has an opportunity to speak, alternative explanations are explored, and there is a brisk progression across a wide sampling of topics.

The written reports are two to three pages. They are read and commented on by the students' TAs who also recommend grades. The recommendations can be influenced by students' participation in discussion. Final assignment of points is made by me and two graduate student graders.

The grading scale is as follows: honors (A+), very good (A), good (B), satisfactory (C), barely creditable (D), and no credit (F). These are associated with point values of 5, 4, 3, 2, 1, and 0, respectively. Compared to the total of 200 possible points on the examinations, BPL points do not usually determine students' final course grades, but a few points can sometimes make a critical difference.

TA Considerations

From the TAs' view, BPL is well supported. First, there is enough structure associated with it. Second, we talk about procedures and run through several examples in two meetings before recitations start. Third, we meet during the weeks that recitations are held, and TAs share their experiences. Fourth, TAs discover that they know, or can recover quickly, a good amount of psychology. Fifth, they gain support from the textbook as they use it.

However, this is the first time TAs have been responsible for teaching classes and they are anxious. This is a bear, and it matters not whether it's a James-Lange bear or a Cannon-Bard bear; the emotion and the behavior are both salient. The anxiety usually lifts when both TAs and students survive the first meeting with more grace than anyone had expected.

Experiences With BPL

In 1985, of the 370 students, 297 (80%) signed up for BPL and attended the first recitation. Of these, 262 (88%) participated in the meetings. Of this last group, 180 (69%) completed a written report and received points for the activity. There were 17 TAs. The mean group size was 7.7 students, and the range was from 5 to 11.

These levels of participation reflect a balance between extrinsic and intrinsic rewards. The project carried only a small number of points for the work it entailed. Some students attended because their friends did. Most students had fun thinking and talking about BPL; write-ups let them collect a few points for their time and energy.

Students like BPL because they find it easy, individual, creative, and more real than most other course experiences in their first 6 weeks of college; they are able to make academic use of something from their own lives. Some deduce the limited validity of their efforts in the context of our inexact science, which offers arguable and plausible explanations. Some do it because BPL carries credit.

My favorite set of observations from BPL concerns always being on time for meals in college, always taking too much food, always eating every bit of it, and always feeling too full and too dumb afterward. One finds explanations in parental practices, in social facilitation, in "nervous" needs to have something to do with one's hands, in extrinsic versus intrinsic criteria for eating behavior, and so on.

The TAs find BPL worthwhile. At the very least they see it as a valuable icebreaker. In general, those who are more freewheeling and more practiced feel that they are doing a better job and react more favorably to BPL. Their impressions are most positive when their students get turned on to psychology and its power to promote understanding of behavior and mental life.

I'm satisfied that BPL strikes a good balance between students' needs to earn grades and credit on one side, and to learn psychology on the other. Furthermore, BPL helps get my course off to a good and warm start.

References

Brender, M. (1982). The relevance connection: Relating academic psychology to everyday life. *Teaching of Psychology, 9,* 222–224.

Carlson, N. R. (1984). *Psychology: The science of behavior.* Boston: Allyn and Bacon.

Hettich, P. (1976). The journal: An autobiographical approach to learning. *Teaching of Psychology, 3,* 60–63.

Hettich, P. (1980). The journal revisited. *Teaching of Psychology, 7,* 105–106.

McKeachie, W. J. (1969). *Teaching tips: A guidebook for the beginning college teacher* (6th ed.). Lexington, MA: Heath.

Notes

1. The 17 TAs who brought life to BPL in 1985 were Tonja Acker, Liz Bryden, Karen deRidder, John Dumas, Jim Ferraro, Teresa Garcia, Janice Green, Dina Juffs, Peg Leary, Lin Lent, Elizabeth McDonald, Sharri Mercer, Jenny Olsson, Bill Reynolds, Deb Smith, Ted Trobaugh, and Karen Zelman. They earned my and their students' respect and gratitude.

Using *Psychology Today* Articles to Increase the Perceived Relevance of the Introductory Course

Drew C. Appleby
Marian College

One goal of the introductory course is to help students realize that psychology is a relevant field of study (i.e., it can contribute positively to their lives, and is not something to be merely memorized, regurgitated on tests, and then forgotten). Several authors have reported their attempts to increase students' perception of the relevance of psychology courses. Some attempts involve the opportunity to read popular books (Benel, 1975; LeUnes, 1974; McCollom, 1971) and articles (Wortman & Hillis, 1975) dealing with compelling psychological topics. Others concentrate on the application of psychological principles to explain or deal with everyday life incidences or problems (Brender, 1982; Grasha, 1974). Students have even replicated the "scientific" studies cited to lend validity to the claims made on television commercials (Solomon, 1979).

The concept of relevance has changed in the past 15 years. What was relevant to students in the past may seem irrelevant today. A question that occupies the minds of many contemporary students is: Will my undergraduate education provide me with the skills I need to get a good job after graduation? One way to capitalize on the motivation resulting from this question is to give students an opportunity to discover that a knowledge of psychological principles can benefit them in their academic majors and future careers. Students form strong loyalties to their academic majors and are ego-involved with their career choices. They perceive information that can help them to succeed in these areas to be highly relevant.

Students' eagerness to learn can be increased by an opportunity to improve their grade in the introductory course with extra credit projects. Such projects can facilitate learning more about psychology and about students' own academic major or career choices. Students are more highly motivated when they are allowed to write extra credit reports on articles related to their major and/or career choices, but their enthusiasm wanes if they are unable to locate such materials. This article includes a bibliography designed to alleviate this problem. It provides introductory students with a large amount of well organized and accessible literature that can simplify their search for relevant psychological information.

The first step in producing this bibliography was to assemble a list of the 27 academic majors and career areas offered by Marian College. Because there is a great deal of overlap in the subject matter in many of these areas, several list items were combined into single categories (e.g., Allied Health, Nursing, and PreMed), reducing the total number of categories to 18. The next step was to peruse the table of contents of each issue of *Psychology Today* published since 1967 to locate articles that contain information related to

one or more of these categories. This exhaustive search produced 407 articles. The mean number of articles per category was 22.6 and the range was 34 (7 to 41). Some areas were surprisingly well represented (e.g., theology—36 articles, English—31, and home economics—30); other areas were less popular (e.g., foreign languages—7 and computer science and math—8).

The response to this bibliography has been very positive. The number and quality of extra credit reports have increased. Students say that they enjoyed writing the reports because the articles they reviewed contained information that was personally relevant. An unexpected benefit was that many students used the list to find references for term papers and speeches in courses outside psychology. When copies of this bibliography and a memo explaining its purpose were distributed to the chairpersons of other academic departments, the response was very gratifying. Several stated that they had not realized how much their majors could learn about their own disciplines in the introductory psychology course. This bibliography is well suited to the introductory course in which students first encounter the diversity of psychological literature. Because most introductory psychology students never take another psychology course, it is important to expose them to as much relevant information as possible during their brief encounter with our discipline. This technique would not be appropriate for more advanced psychology courses in which the development of library research skills is valued, and students are expected to identify and find articles on their own.

The following list of *Psychology Today* articles and their publication dates is a sample from the complete bibliography. Two articles were chosen from each of the 18 major and/or career categories on the basis of their high level of interest for introductory students and the recency of their publication dates.

Allied Health, Nursing, and PreMed
  "Stress and Health" (8/85)
  "The Mystery of Alzheimer's" (1/84)
Art and Art-Therapy
  "Stalking the Mental Image" (5/85)
  "How the Mind Draws" (5/86)
Biology
  "Crime in the Family Tree" (3/85)
  "Genes, Personality, and Alcoholism" (1/85)
Business, Accounting, and Economics
  "What Makes a Top Executive?" (2/83)
  "To File, Perchance to Cheat" (4/85)
Chemistry

"Alcohol, Marijuana, and Memory" (3/80)
"The Chemistry of Craving" (10/83)
Computer Science and Mathematics
"The Human–Computer Connection" (3/84)
"Computer Games, Let the Kids Play" (8/85)
Education
"Challenging the Brightest" (6/84)
"Who's Intelligent?" (4/82)
English
"When is a Word a Word?" (11/85)
"A Conversation With Isaac Asimov" (1/83)
Foreign Languages
"Fear of Foreign Languages" (8/81)
"The International Language of Gestures" (5/84)
History and Political Science
"Reagan and the National Psyche" (1/82)
"Psychology and Armageddon" (5/82)
Home Economics, Dietetics, and Fashion Merchandising
"Clothes Power" (12/82)
"The Junk Food Syndrome" (1/82)
Music
"Music, the Beautiful Disturber" (12/85)
"The Music of the Hemispheres" (6/82)
Philosophy
"A Sense of Control" (12/84)
"Is it Right?" (6/81)
Physical Education
"Beating Slumps at Their Own Game" (7/84)
"The Playing Field of the Mind" (7/84)
PreLaw
"Beat That Lie Detector" (6/85)

"Mind Control in the Courtroom" (5/82)
Sociology
"Arresting Delinquency" (3/85)
"Marriages Made to Last" (6/85)
Theater and Speech
"The Language of Persuasion" (4/85)
"The Psychologist as TV Guide" (8/86)
Theology
"The Children's God" (12/85)
"Stages of Faith" (11/83)

References

Benel, R. A. (1975). Psychological thrillers: Thrilling to whom? *Teaching of Psychology, 2,* 176–177.

Brender, M. (1982). The relevance connection: Relating academic psychology to everyday life. *Teaching of Psychology, 9,* 222–224.

Grasha, A. F. (1974). "Giving psychology away": Some experiences teaching undergraduates practical psychology. *Teaching of Psychology, 1,* 21–24.

LeUnes, A. (1974). Psychological thrillers revisited: A tentative list of "master thrillers." *American Psychologist, 29,* 211–213.

McCollom, I. N. (1971). Psychological thrillers: Psychology books students read when given freedom of choice. *American Psychologist, 26,* 921–927.

Solomon, P. R. (1979). Science and television commercials: Adding relevance to the research methodology course. *Teaching of Psychology, 6,* 26–30.

Wortman, C. B., & Hillis, J. W. (1975). Some "thrilling" short articles for use in an introductory psychology class. *Teaching of Psychology, 2,* 134–135.

Encouraging Responsibility, Active Participation, and Critical Thinking in General Psychology Students

Norman B. L. Ferguson
Augsburg College

I recently made substantial changes in how I teach the General Psychology course. Part of my desire to change came from an observation that students seem readily inclined to adopt the role of passive learners, expecting me to dispense capsules of knowledge in coherent doses. They often demonstrate little propensity for accepting the responsibility of being active participants who are in charge of their own education. This is not surprising because, in my view, the vast majority of college students are the products of years of prior education that have typically emphasized assimilating facts, following orders, and pleasing others. They are treated as though they are vessels to be filled. (Interestingly, the word *educate* comes from the Latin *educere* = *e-*, out + *ducere*, to lead, draw, bring. Thus, the word means "to draw or bring out," *not* to "pump in.") In psychological terms, students have been rewarded for being passive recipients.

Although I have made changes in how I teach other courses (e.g., Brain & Behavior, Research Methods), I describe here only the modifications I made in the General Psychology course. The course, which is a liberal arts distribution option for all students, had an enrollment of 27 traditional college age students; 80% were sophomores.

Part of the plan for revising my teaching methods was to have students be more personally responsible for their own learning and, consequently, be more actively involved in the class process. Three individuals whose ideas formed the basis for many of my changes in methodology are William Glasser, Benjamin Bloom, and Socrates.

Glasser's (1969) book, *Schools Without Failure*, provided a major impetus for the changes. Glasser suggested that students sometimes lack motivation for learning because they see little relevance in what they learn and have little voice in determining how courses operate.

I used the methods of Socrates to implement some of the changes. Using the technique of the Socratic dialogue, I ask a series of questions with the intent of demonstrating what the students are able to reason out on their own. This process begins during the first meeting of the class. I ask, "What does it mean to be blind?" Through a series of questions, we move from considering the retina, to the visual cortex, to the split-brain phenomenon, to the meanings of consciousness and reality. Students do most of the talking.

At the end of the first class meeting, I explain that this is the main format I want to use in the course—question and answer. Students are given an initial reading assignment in their textbook and asked to develop questions for our next class. I specifically ask students to think about how the information relates to their own lives. In addition, they are given a set of my own discussion questions. I state that these will be referred to at appropriate times (e.g., if students run out of their own questions). Thus, the focus of the class meetings is changed so that students are actively involved in the class process. It was obvious from the outset, however, that the more assertive students and those more interested in psychology are the ones who respond most readily to these methods. To encourage greater participation by the less assertive students, I occasionally divide the class into small groups of 4 or 5 to discuss specific questions. Then, I ask someone from each group to report to the class what conclusions have been reached. Within this context, the reticent students appear more willing to participate. Overall, class discussions are facilitated by having students' chairs placed around the perimeter of the room in a large U-shape instead of in the more traditional rows.

During the first week of the course, I ask students to develop a list of expectations and responsibilities they have for themselves as students and for me as the instructor. We spend part of one class session discussing and coming to agreement on a list of such expectations and responsibilities. The list is typed and distributed to all students. Student responsibilities focus on attending class and participating, being prepared for class by reading and thinking, and getting assignments in on time. The instructor's responsibilities focus on being clear, being available for individual discussions, and treating students with respect.

Another procedure is implemented to give greater responsibility to students and to encourage class participation. Students are informed that, for evaluation purposes, each Monday they are to turn in four essay questions based on the information covered during the previous week. The questions cannot be taken from those in the textbook or from questions I have asked. Each question is written on a separate 3 × 5 in. card. Unclear or poorly worded questions are returned for rewriting. I select a subset of each student's questions for the course exams; each student's exams consist of only those questions that student has written. Evaluation

is based on (a) the quality of the questions developed and (b) the ability to give thoughtful responses to these questions. This procedure provides an incentive for individual students to ask these questions in class because they are likely to be on their exams.

In conjunction with this phase of the course, I introduce Bloom's (1956) taxonomy of educational objectives. Within the cognitive domain, Bloom identifies six levels or types of objectives: knowledge, comprehension, application, analysis, synthesis, and evaluation. Early in the term I describe each of these six types to the students and give examples of questions representing each type. The goal is to promote students' critical thinking. Most students have a clear initial preference for writing "knowledge"-level questions. This is not surprising because these questions are usually the easiest to write and to answer. They are also at the level which much of their previous education has tapped.

As the course progresses, I ask students to write questions at increasingly complex levels. I ask them to begin writing comprehension questions. Later, we move to analysis and synthesis. Some of these levels are difficult for some students to attain. Clearly, the instructor needs to be aware of individual differences in students' ability to move through the taxonomy. To facilitate the process of question writing, I have students evaluate their own questions. We develop a set of criteria for what constitutes a good question. Then, students are asked to evaluate their own questions on the back of each 3 × 5 in. card. Students give an overall rating to each question as *excellent*, *satisfactory*, or *unsatisfactory* and briefly defend their rating. This procedure produces an increase in the quality of the students' questions. Fewer questions are returned for rewriting and the high-achieving students are motivated to develop excellent questions.

An additional component to the question-writing phase of the course involves what I call "connection" questions. As the term progresses, I ask students to develop questions that "connect" information we are studying that week (e.g., social psychology) with information we discussed several weeks earlier (e.g., perception). This is a good vehicle for developing synthesis-type questions.

The vast majority of students made very favorable comments about the course on midterm and end-of-term anonymous course evaluation forms. The following quotes are typical of what most students said: "having to write our own tests made me feel more responsible for my thoughts and knowledge," "it [the course] made me open my eyes to see that I am learning for my *own* benefit," and "this course, for the first time in my experience, encouraged self-motivated learning."

Overall, I am pleased with the results of my new approach. I covered all the major topics in General Psychology that I had covered in previous years. There was some reduction in the total amount of content covered, but I believe the increase in student involvement in the class more than compensated for this slight reduction. This course was the most stimulating I have taught in 14 years as a college instructor. Implementing a process to give students more responsibility for their own education, to get them more actively involved, and to promote their critical thinking was an energizing experience for them and for me.

References

Bloom, B. (Ed.). (1956). *Taxonomy of educational objectives: Handbook 1. Cognitive domain.* New York: Longman, Green.

Glasser, W. (1969). *Schools without failure.* New York: Harper & Row.

Notes

1. I thank Diane L. Pike for reviewing an earlier version of this manuscript.

What Do Students Remember From Introductory Psychology?

Scott W. VanderStoep
Hope College

Angela Fagerlin
Kent State University

Jennifer S. Feenstra
Calvin College

Knowing what students remember from psychology courses provides descriptive information to teachers of psychology about what topics and what teaching techniques students remember well. Despite intuitive interest in what students remember, little research has been done. Rickard, Rogers, Ellis, and Beidleman (1988) found statistically significant differences between two groups of students who took an introductory psychology course and a control group that did not. The difference—measured by a multiple-choice test 4 months after the instructed students finished the course—seemed relatively small, with the concept-taught group scoring 72%, the traditionally taught group scoring 68%, and the control group (which received no psychology instruction) scoring 62%. Goldwater and Acker (1975) found that students in a standard lecture course scored only 55% correct on a final examination with objective questions. Similarly, Ellis and Rickard (1977) found students in two sections scored only 57% and 62% on a test when taught with traditional lecture. These same students scored only 33% on a test 4 months after completing the course. These studies suggest students' memory for psychology course material is quite poor. We used a noncourse measure of memory for class material and examined whether relevance in our free-recall technique correlated with in-class performance measures.

What will be the specific character of students' memory for course material? In two studies, Kintsch and Bates (1977) examined students' recognition memory of lectures from history of psychology and developmental psychology classes. They tested whether students recognized verbatim sentences from the lecture that were either related to the course or extraneous to course material. At both 2-day and

5-day intervals, students' recognition memory was better for extraneous material (e.g., jokes) than for course content (for a review of the research on memory for classroom material, see Conway, Cohen, & Stanhope, 1992). According to Kintsch and Bates (1977), students remembered extraneous items better because they were unique and stood out as separate from the standard lecture material. Therefore, we expected students to make frequent references to material not specifically related to course concepts.

Study 1

Method

Participants.   Participants were 71 students (37 women, 34 men) enrolled in two sections of Introductory Psychology at a 4-year, undergraduate, liberal arts college. Students enrolled in two different sections taught by the same instructor (first author). Eighty-one percent of the students attended on the administration day. No other administration times were used. Students received extra credit points for participating. They provided either their name or their social security number so that we could match their responses with course grades.

Procedure.   Students completed response sheets during the last week of the semester. The free-recall response sheet had 10 blank lines for students to complete. The following instructions were printed at the top of the page:

Table 1. Most Memorable Events From Study 1

Rank	Event	Students Citing[a]
1	Phineas Gage video (video from "The Brain" series, Heimenway, 1988)	46
2	Rat and desensitization (A rat was brought into the classroom, and phobic desensitization was described and briefly simulated)	36
3	"Psychic" demonstration (A series of magic tricks performed by the instructor designed to test critical thinking and debunk the notion of psychic powers)	30
4	Narcolepsy videos (One from ABC's *20/20* [Gaffin, 1994]; the other from an unknown source)	29
5	Milgram obedience video (From videodisc to accompany Myers's, 1996, *Social Psychology*)	
6[b]	Prism goggles (Perception demonstration using fresnel prisms made at a local optical shop)	24
	Attitude-behavior demonstration (Randomly assign students to write for and against controversial issue, then measure post-writing attitudes)	24
8[b]	Demonstration of neuron firing	23
	Classical conditioning/Pavlov	23
10[b]	Dissociative identity disorder/multiple personality	16
	Schizophrenia	16

Note. $N = 71$.
[a]Given in percentages. [b]Indicates tie.

As part of my research on college students' memory for course concepts, and also as a way to improve my teaching of Introductory Psychology, I am interested in what students remember from this course.

Let your mind wander freely as you do this assignment. Think back on the semester as a whole, and report to me the first 10 things that come to your mind as you answer the question: *What do you remember from this course?*

Don't "edit" your thinking as you report your memories; don't limit yourself in any way; don't worry about your memories being "correct." Simply review the course in your mind and report to me what you remember. It can be anything from the course or the text—stories told in class or in text, questions from tests, comments from other students, videos, activities—literally anything that comes to your mind.

Results and Discussions

Twenty-five (35%) of the students completed all 10 items ($M = 8.35$, $SD = 1.6$). Table 1 shows the most frequently remembered items. The commonality of these 11 (there was a tie for 10th highest frequency) events is their visual vividness or participatory character. Three items were direct references to videos. All three of these videos were dramatic presentations. The Phineas Gage video re-creates the famous tamping rod piercing Gage's skull. Students in this instructor's courses always react emotionally to this video clip. Both narcolepsy videos show cataplectic attacks in which people fall suddenly to the ground and lose muscle tone. The Milgram video is original footage from one of the Milgram experiments; the participant in the video displays noticeable anxiety. The video also shows the famous "shock board" and its incremental voltage labels. Three other items (schizophrenia, dissociative identity disorder, and classical conditioning) had a video presentation as the major instructional tool. The other five items (rat and desensitization, "psychic" demonstration, prism goggles, attitude-behavior demonstration, demonstration of neuron firing) were in-class demonstrations. Some or all of the students participated in each of these activities.

Students best remembered vivid videos and activities in which they (or their classmates) participated. The next question we asked was whether these videos and activities helped students remember the course concepts any better. We assigned each response a relevance score on a 3-point rating scale as a measure of the extent to which what students wrote down reflected an understanding of a course concept:

1. *Irrelevant:* No reference to a course concept or completely incorrect. Reference to a video or class activity, with no reference to the concept it meant to illustrate. ("The rod that went through the railroad worker's head.")
2. *Low/medium:*[1] Reference to specific course content, but course concept was mentioned only generally or incompletely. ("The man and the dog and the sleeping disorder where you fall.")
3. *High:* Clear understanding of principle; or reference to a technical, abstract, or specific concept. ("Schizophrenic on the film. Words and thoughts were so disjointed.")

The first author coded all 593 responses. The percentages of irrelevant, low/medium, and high responses were 43%, 42%, and 15%, respectively. A trend, albeit nonsignificant, toward linearly decreasing relevance scores from students' first to last response was present, $F(1, 24) = 2.25$, $p = .15$. It was somewhat surprising that this effect was not significant, as we conducted an identical study (unpublished) in which this trend was significant.

Correlations of relevance and quantity of responses with two achievement measures—final grade and test-score percentage—showed significant positive correlations. The students with more frequent or highly relevant memories did better in the course. Final grade correlated with both number of items recalled, $r(70) = .32$, $p = .007$, and average rele-

---

[1]In another study not reported here, we used a 4-point scale in which we separated low and medium. The rater (first author) found it difficult to distinguish lows from mediums, and therefore the 3-point scale was a better choice.

vance score, $r(70) = .54, p < .001$. Test-score percentage was also positively correlated with number of items recalled, $r(70) = .32, p = .006$, and average relevance score, $r(70) = .53, p < .001$.

Study 2

Study 1 provided a description of students' recollections of their experiences and the relation between these recollections and course achievement. It is interesting to note that all of the most frequently remembered events in Study 1 were either activities or videos. This finding illustrates the power of in-class activities. However, the large number of irrelevant responses suggests that students did not connect their recall of the activities with the concepts they illustrated. These findings are interesting especially to those instructors who use these activities and videos (many of which are probably well known to instructors).

However, the initial purpose of this investigation was to provide an account of students' memory for actual course topics; that is, which topics they best remembered. In an effort to get students to report more content, we changed the instructions in Study 2. The instructions in Study 1 may have created a mental set such that students were inclined to remember such activities more than they would have otherwise.[2] To obtain an account of what course concepts students remembered, Study 2 omitted references to specific events such as videos and activities.

Method

Participants. Participants were 68 students (35 women, 33 men) enrolled in two sections of Introductory Psychology at a 4-year, undergraduate, liberal arts college (different institution than Study 1). The same instructor who taught the Study 1 courses also taught these courses. Attendance was 89% on the day the form was administered. No other administration times were given. Students received extra credit points for participating. They provided either their name or their social security number so that we could match their responses with course grades.

Procedure. The procedure was the same as in Study 1, except that the instructions included no references to specific activities (e.g., videos). Students were simply asked to "think back on the semester as a whole, and report to me the first 10 things that come to your mind as you answer the question: What do you remember from this course?" The students completed the task at the end of the final full week of instruction class periods.

Results and Discussion

Thirty-four (50%) of the students completed all 10 items ($M = 8.18, SD = 2.3$). Table 2 shows the most frequently remembered items. Omitting the references to specific activi-

---

[2]We thank an anonymous reviewer for this suggestion.

Table 2. Most Memorable Events From Study 2

Topic	Students Citing[a]
Sleeping disorders	40
Freud/Freudian theory	38
Schizophrenia	38
Classical conditioning	37
Sexual orientation	29
Eating disorders	28
Major depression	21

Note. $N = 68$.
[a]Given in percentages.

Table 3. Frequencies of Responses by Chapter

Chapter	Chapter No.[a]	Total Responses[b]
Psychological Disorders	15	14.5
States of Consciousness	7	12.0
Motivation	12	11.8
Neuroscience, Genetics, and Behavior	2	10.7
Learning	8	7.9
Developing Child	3	7.2
Personality	14	6.2
Introduction/Thinking Critically With Psychological Science	1	6.0
Emotion	13	4.6
Memory	9	4.1
Perception	6	3.3
Sensation	5	3.1
Therapy	16	3.1
Intelligence	11	1.7
Thinking and Language	10	1.0

[a]Chapters from Myers (1998). [b]Given in percentages.

ties such as videos seemed to promote student responses that addressed more specific course content. A large majority of responses were to specific course topics (85%). However, although the references listed in Table 2 were mainly to specific course concepts, the teaching of five of the seven topics (sleeping disorders, schizophrenia, classical conditioning, eating disorders, and major depression) included a video. Often students cited a concept and also included reference to a video (e.g., "narcolepsy and the cool dogs," referring to a video of narcoleptic dogs). Although a comparison group is not available, we believe these topics are memorable largely because of their accompanying videos. We believe the findings from this study are consistent with Study 1; that is, students' memory is high for highly vivid instructional events such as videos.

Table 3 shows the distribution of recalled items by textbook chapter (Myers, 1998). Most of the chapters received between 2 and 3 days of coverage (50-min class). Students mentioned all chapters except for Adolescence and Adulthood.[3] The introduction is a short, unnumbered chapter, and in Table 3 it is combined with the first chapter.

---

[3]Social psychology is not included because in this study students completed this exercise before coverage of this chapter. Thus, the Milgram video did not appear as it did in Study 1.

Students cited the Psychological Disorders, States of Consciousness, and Motivation chapters most frequently. The high rate of recall for the States of Consciousness chapter may be a function of the high rate of recall of the topic of sleeping disorders. The high rate of recall for the Motivation chapter may be due to the memorable (and controversial, on this particular campus) discussion of sexual orientation. Students least often recalled Thinking and Language, Intelligence, Therapy, Sensation, and Perception. There was no correlation between the frequency of responses and the order of coverage for the chapters, $r_s(13) = .07$.

General Discussion

This research teaches psychology faculty at least two lessons. First, both studies (Study 1 directly) showed that students remembered vivid anecdotes and demonstrations. In Study 1 the seven most frequently remembered items (Table 1) were activities or videos. Also, of the most frequently remembered items from Study 2, all but Freud had some vivid instructional technique accompanying it—five had videos and one had a controversial lecture and subsequent discussion. The events in Table 1 refer to specific activities and those in Table 2 refer to more general concepts. Recall that our objective of Study 2 was to elicit more conceptual statements from students. We achieved this objective, but students still most frequently recalled those concepts with memorable pedagogical devices. This result adds to the claim that such vivid instructional techniques are the most remembered.

Given the small number of high-relevant ratings in Study 1, it does not appear students very easily connected these in-class activities with the relevant concepts. That better students may be more motivated to write better responses, which will in turn have higher quality ratings, cannot be ruled out. Whether the correlation between high ratings and high course achievement is a result of high skill or high effort (or both) cannot be determined. The fact the correlation exists, however, gives some evidence to the face validity of this free-response technique.

Second, students remembered atypical behavior such as sleeping disorders or schizophrenia. It is not clear whether atypicality increases remembering or simply that videos accompanied the atypical topics. Because atypical behavior lends itself well to teaching by video, escaping a correlation between vividness and teaching technique is difficult. A future study that can (somehow) unconfound topic and technique would clarify this methodological concern.

Many instructors have probably heard from their students that they are "visual learners." Given that students seem to remember highly visual material in this study, these data may lend support to this claim. The phrase *learning style* seems to imply that there are individual differences in the processing of information. For example, some students are visual learners, whereas others are textual learners. Regardless of whether that claim is true, it perhaps is more helpful to think of learning differences less in terms of styles and more in terms of strategies—effective learners adopt ways to handle different types of material based on their cognitive strengths, the performance requirements (e.g., test vs. paper), and the teaching style of the instructor. We urge caution in interpreting these data as indicating the presence of such individual differences in learning. Research suggests that students adopt different learning strategies depending, for example, on the nature of the discipline (e.g., Vander-Stoep, Pintrich, & Fagerlin, 1996).

For teachers of psychology, we see two ways in which these data are helpful. First, it is interesting to document what features of the introductory psychology course students remember. Of course, we recognize that between-subject variability in teaching style, course content, and so forth would make replication of these specific findings difficult. For example, not all instructors employ a "psychic" demonstration or show a schizophrenia video. Still, regardless of the specific activities used, it seems reasonable to assume the events students will most remember are the unique or vivid. We suspect this result will be true regardless of who teaches the course or what material they cover.

Second, instructors may be intrigued to know the correlations between relevance of memory and course performance were positive and significant. Few courses use such a free-recall response format. We suspect many introductory psychology courses, in fact, use recognition memory (e.g., multiple-choice tests) or cued recall (e.g., essay questions with several embedded cues). These studies demonstrated that when students were given no particular cues, their memory relevance correlated positively with achievement. It appears that those who remembered the course well are those who did well in class.

References

Conway, M. A., Cohen, G., & Stanhope, N. (1992). Very long-term memory for knowledge acquired at school and university. *Applied Cognitive Psychology, 6,* 467–482.

Ellis, N. R., & Rickard, H. C. (1977). Evaluating the teaching of introductory psychology. *Teaching of Psychology, 4,* 128–132.

Gaffin, R. C. (Producer). (1994, March 11). *20/20* (Segment 3: "Narcolepsy"). New York: American Broadcasting Company.

Goldwater, B. C., & Acker, L. E. (1975). Instructor-paced, mass-testing for mastery performance in an introductory psychology course. *Teaching of Psychology, 2,* 152–155.

Heimenway, J. (Producer). (1988). *The brain* (Teaching Module 2). New York: WNET.

Kintsch, W., & Bates, E. (1977). Recognition memory for statements from a classroom lecture. *Journal of Experimental Psychology: Human Learning and Memory, 3,* 150–159.

Myers, D. G. (1996). *Social psychology* (5th ed.). New York: McGraw-Hill.

Myers, D. G. (1998). *Psychology* (5th ed.). New York: Worth.

Rickard, H. C., Rogers, R., Ellis, N. R., & Beidleman, W. B. (1988). Some retention, but not enough. *Teaching of Psychology, 15,* 151–152.

VanderStoep, S. W., Pintrich, P. R., & Fagerlin, A. (1996). Disciplinary differences in self-regulated learning in college students. *Contemporary Educational Psychology, 21,* 345–362.

Student Perspectives on the First Day of Class

Baron Perlman
Lee I. McCann
University of Wisconsin Oshkosh

The first class meeting of any course is more important than many faculty realize. It sets the tone for what is to follow and can greatly influence students' opinions about the course and instructor for the remainder of the semester. Several authors have provided faculty-oriented guidance for a successful course beginning (e.g., Davis, 1993; Johnson, 1995; McKeachie, 1994; Nilson, 1998; Pica, Barnes, & Finger, 1990; Wolcowitz, 1984). They are unanimous on some recommended goals: setting a positive atmosphere, communicating course objectives, taking care of administrative details, grabbing the students' attention, and introducing yourself. Authors diverge on use of the entire hour for the first class meeting and in recommending covering course content.

Knowledge of students' preferences may lead faculty to modify the content and goals of their first class in ways that improve the first day and attend to students' needs and expectations, thus starting the class off on the right foot. A review of the literature revealed no data from students on these topics. The purpose of this study was to determine students' opinions of what is valuable for the first class meeting.

Method

Participants

All full-time faculty members ($N = 11$) in a regional public university sampled students in all of their undergraduate psychology course sections ($N = 31$) during the Spring 1998 semester. Participants were 570 students (361 first year and sophomores, 209 juniors and seniors; 381 women, 189 men). Over 95% of the students had completed at least one semester of college.

Procedure

Each instructor distributed index cards during the first class meeting and read the following:

Faculty in the Psychology Department are interested in maintaining and improving their teaching. To that end we are interested in the first class meeting of a course, what works well and what does not. If you have already done this exercise in a psychology class, leave the card blank. Label this index card Side A and Side B. On Side A put your class standing (first year, sophomore, junior, or senior), and gender (male or female). Based on your experiences as a student, what are the most useful things a faculty member can do during a first class meeting? Please list these on Side A. Based on your experiences as a student, what are your pet peeves about what faculty do during a first class meeting? Please list these on Side B.

Faculty members collected cards, thanked students, read and considered the comments during the next few days, and then gave the cards to the researchers.

Both authors met to read and code students' responses, beginning with a taxonomy based on the previously cited literature's recommendations. After reading 30 students' responses we modified the taxonomy and began anew. We resolved any disagreements on coding responses through discussion.

Results

Table 1 categorizes student responses based on important issues for the first day of class listed in the faculty-oriented literature. Students listed from zero to five positive comments and zero to six pet peeves. We entered a single tally when students provided two or more different responses that fit a particular category.

What Works Well

Students wanted a general course overview spelling out requirements and faculty expectations, both verbally and in a detailed syllabus (72%). A frequent response was that students (26%) wanted information on exams, assignments, grading, and what is necessary to earn a good grade. Eighteen percent liked instructors to describe their background and teaching style, and an accessible, approachable, and supportive (7%), relaxed (5%), fun (4%) tone was important for some students. Students (8%) stated that beginning course content is acceptable if the lecture or activity includes sufficient background that they can understand it without having read an assignment and it is put in a useful context. Some students wrote that they would like the instructor to describe why they should take the course and how they may profit from it (7%). Only 1% of the respon-

Table 1. The First Day of Class

Category	Works Well		Peeves[a]	
	n	%	n	%
General overview, syllabus, course nature and content, requirements, expectations	387	68	93	16
Teacher specifically describes exams, assignments, and grading	149	26	7	1
Introduces self (background, teaching style) to students	103	18	20	4
First day content is put in context and understandable without having read an assignment	43	8		
Describes why students should take the course and how they may profit from it	41	7		
Sets tone of being accessible, supportive	41	7		
Icebreakers (getting to know classmates)	39	7	54	9[b]
Meet full hour[c]	36	6	75	13
Sets relaxed, comfortable tone	30	5		
Sets a fun tone	23	4		
Beginning course content (lecture, etc.)	7	1	164	29
Poor use of class time (e.g., noncrucial information, read syllabus, unorganized)			177	31
Homework assignment			53	9
Instructor uncaring, intimidating			39	7
Poor teaching (instructor nervous, monotone, talks too fast, too much material)			28	15
Seating chart			15	3
Teacher late or absent			10	2

[a]Instructor fails to present this information on the first day of class, or does a poor job. [b]Icebreaker may be done well, these 54 students simply do not like them. [c]Assumes a class meeting for about 1 hr, not longer periods.

dents said beginning course content (e.g., lecture) makes for a good first class period and few students (6%) mentioned that keeping them the full class period works well.

To determine differences between demographic groups we computed chi-squares for what works well. A greater percentage of upperclass (n = 48, 23%) compared to underclass students (n = 55, 15%) wanted instructors to describe their background and teaching styles, $\chi^2(1, N = 570) = 5.34, p < .01$. Otherwise, under- and upperclassmen generally agreed on what makes for a good first meeting. There were no significant gender differences concerning what works well.

Pet Peeves

As expected, student peeves were the mirror opposite of their preferences (see Table 1). The greatest number of peeves dealt with poor use of class time (31%), beginning the course with content (29%), a poor overview (16%), or meeting the entire class hour (13%). More students (n = 54, 9%) disliked icebreakers than liked them (n = 39, 7%). Few students (4%) stated that they did not like faculty introducing their backgrounds. Other peeves included homework assignments the first day (9%); an uncaring, intimidating instructor (7%); poor teaching (5%); and a seating chart

(3%). Ten students (2%) wrote about instructors being late or absent for the first class.

A greater percentage of upperclass (n = 97, 46%) compared to underclass students (n = 66, 18%), $\chi^2(1, N = 570) = 51.3, p < .01$, and a greater percentage of men (n = 77, 41%) compared to women (n = 163, 23%), $\chi^2(1, N = 570) = 20.4, p < .01$, mentioned beginning course content (e.g., lecture) as a peeve. Also, a greater percentage of juniors and seniors (n = 28, 13%) compared to underclass students (n = 27, 7%) disliked icebreakers, $\chi^2(1, N = 570) = 5.32, p < .025$, whereas a greater percentage of women (n = 73, 19%) than men (n = 20, 11%), were concerned about a poor course overview, $\chi^2(1, N = 570) = 6.8, p < .01$.

Faculty Changes in Teaching

Ten of 11 faculty who participated in the research made at least one change in how they taught the first day of class the following semester. Five faculty took time to describe their background and professional experience, including 1 who put this information in his syllabus. Four faculty spent more time on course objectives and expectations, 2 decided not to begin course content, 2 who had always taught content the first day put it into more of a context, 1 emphasized a more relaxed atmosphere, 1 changed the amount of time devoted to topics, and 1 emphasized even more why studying statistics was important.

Discussion

Most student preferences are congruent with the faculty literature. From the student perspective, a good first class meeting includes a well-organized, focused presentation containing basic course information including requirements, expectations, and information on exams and assignments. Introduce yourself to the students (especially in courses with upperclass students), and set a tone of being accessible and supportive. Use icebreakers carefully, especially in upper-level courses. Students may not like them as much as faculty assume.

Many students want the class dismissed after administrative details are completed and significantly more upper- than underclass, and men rather than women, expressed this view. If a student has several courses starting on a given day the information overload may be enormous and this preference understandable. Faculty choosing to begin course content should assume that students have done no reading and make the lecture or in-class exercise understandable within that context. Telling students why the material is important, how it fits into the course, and how it assists students in beginning their course reading and assignments is good pedagogy. Conversely, students may be more motivated to attend to the material once they understand why it is being presented. The choice of waiting for the second course meeting before beginning to lecture, after students have done initial assignments, is a viable one and in some ways may be good teaching.

Many students may have had opinions that they did not think of, or care to, put down on the note card, which is a relative weakness of the open-ended format. The study could be replicated using a Likert-scale format using the categories identified herein to gather more valid data and allow better comparisons of the students' opinions.

Calling faculty attention to something all had done many times, holding a first class, led our colleagues to discussion and decisions on how to improve their teaching. Simple changes in first-day content or emphasis may have a positive effect on the course and student perceptions of the instructor.

References

Davis, B. G. (1993). *Tools for teaching*. San Francisco: Jossey-Bass.

Johnson, G. R. (1995). *First steps to excellence in college teaching* (3rd ed.). Madison, WI: Magna.

McKeachie, W. J. (1994). *Teaching tips: Strategies, research, and theory for college and university teachers* (9th ed.). Lexington, MA: Heath.

Nilson, L. B. (1998). *Teaching at its best: A research-based resource for college instructors*. Bolton, MA: Anker.

Pica, T., Barnes, G. A., & Finger, A. G. (1990). *Teaching matters: Skills and strategies for international teaching assistants*. New York: Newbury House.

Wolcowitz, J. (1984). The first day of class. In M. M. Gullette (Ed.), *The art and craft of teaching* (pp. 10–24). Cambridge, MA: Harvard University Press.

Notes

1. This article is based on a poster presented at the 21st Annual National Institute on the Teaching of Psychology, January 1999, St. Petersburg Beach, FL.
2. We gratefully acknowledge the assistance of our students and departmental colleagues.

What Introductory Psychology Students Attend to on a Course Syllabus

Angela H. Becker
Sharon K. Calhoon
Department of Social and Behavioral Sciences
Indiana University, Kokomo

Many published articles from many different disciplines discuss syllabus content. Most focus on which topics a course should cover, the order in which to cover those topics, or pedagogical considerations that underlie the syllabus (e.g., Lenthall & Andrews, 1983; Long & Crookes, 1992; Neumark, Mazor, Bellali, Kalujni, & Melamed, 1991). Many provide comprehensive lists of items of information that one could (or should) include and the rationales for inclusion (e.g., Altman & Cashin, 1992; Appleby, 1994; Matejka & Kurke, 1994; McDonnell-Harris, 1993). These reports are intended to help instructors produce comprehensive, informative syllabi, based mainly on the authors' observations and teaching experience or interviews with other faculty. Thus, these publications take the instructors' rather than the students' perspective.

There is relatively little information about how students view a course syllabus. As a reviewer of this article noted, long-time faculty have found that whereas the syllabus once was a single-page document mainly listing textbooks and assignments, it has evolved into a much longer document containing information about many course-related issues. Because faculty often consider the syllabus to be a contract with their students, and that contract is now rather complex, it behooves faculty to learn what aspects of that contract students pay attention to or consider important. We found only three sources that addressed this issue, none of which appeared in published forums commonly available to and accessed by psychology teachers.

In a symposium at an American Psychological Association meeting, Leeds (1993) discussed syllabus content from her perspective as a senior psychology major. She listed the following as important items for inclusion: exam and assignment dates; exam content; appropriate topics for papers and assignments; policies on academic dishonesty, attendance, missed exams, and late assignments; grading procedures; and the relevance of course material to students' lives outside the classroom. Zucker (1992) asked upper level psychology students to identify the first item they looked for when they received the syllabus. The three most frequently mentioned firsts were exam dates, number of exams, and course content and topics. Unfortunately, he collected the data after he had distributed and discussed the syllabus with the class, which may have influenced students' responses. Smith and Razzouk (1993) asked two groups of upper level business students to recall the part of the syllabus they referred to most. One group responded in the 3rd week of the academic quarter; the other responded in the 7th week. Students questioned early in the quarter frequently identified five items as most referred to: test dates (20%), course schedule (19%), chapter (16%), assigned reading (16%), and due dates

(11%; p. 217). These responses are similar to those given by Zucker's psychology students on the first day of class. Both sets of responses echo Leeds's informal observations. (Note that Smith and Razzouk's students generated their own labels when identifying the syllabus item they referred to the most. Therefore, Smith and Razzouk's report does not clarify the difference between "chapter" and "assigned reading." It is quite possible that the different students mentioning these two items were referring to the same syllabus item.)

Smith and Razzouk's (1993) study also explored whether the items students attended to changed as the term progressed. Students questioned later in the semester generally endorsed only four items as most referred to: course schedule (34%), assigned reading (21%), due dates (20%), and chapter (12%; p. 217). The largest differences between Smith and Razzouk's early- and late-term responders were how frequently students mentioned test dates, due dates, and course schedules. However, because the early and late data came from different students, it is difficult to tell whether differences reflect changes over time or simply differences between the two sets of students.

Zucker's (1992) and Smith and Razzouk's (1993) studies provide valuable information about students' perceptions of syllabus content. Both studies, however, surveyed students after the instructor had reviewed the syllabus with them. Thus, responses may reflect students' awareness of what the instructor considered important instead of the students' actual focus of attention. In addition, both studies surveyed students in upper-level courses. Students in introductory-level classes, many of whom are in their first semester and are new to university life, may have different views than more experienced students about which pieces of information are important. Also unclear is whether students change the importance they attach to various syllabus items as they gain experience with college courses over the course of a semester.

Students' success in a course may depend on their ability to attend to and use important syllabus information. For example, students new to college, and thus new to syllabi, may earn lower grades in part because they do not attend to critical syllabus information such as attendance or academic dishonesty policies. Even experienced students may not use syllabus information the way instructors expect. Knowing what beginning and continuing students attend to on a syllabus could help faculty members better design syllabi and better inform students about how to use syllabi to increase the chances of success in the courses those students take.

This study assessed the importance of different items of syllabus information to students in introductory psychology classes. Students completed our survey twice during a Fall semester: on the first day of class (prior to receiving or discussing the syllabus) and at the end of the semester. Although introductory courses generally contain students from all levels, first-semester students predominate in the Fall. Thus, by surveying students in introductory-level psychology courses we could focus on perceptions of first-semester students and compare them to those of more experienced students in the same class. We expected first-semester and continuing students' perceptions of syllabus content would differ, although we made no a priori assumptions about the nature of these differences. We also expected that first-semester students would change their ideas about syllabus content over the semester as they gained experience with what their instructors considered important.

Method

Participants

On their first day of class, 863 students in 19 sections of introductory psychology from four Midwestern colleges and universities completed the survey. Of these, 502 (58%) were students at Indiana University Southeast, 170 (20%) attended Indiana University Kokomo, 140 (16%) were students at Missouri Western University, and 51 (6%) attended Marian College. There were 520 (60%) first-semester freshmen, 154 (18%) continuing freshmen, and 176 (20%) upper level students (13 did not specify their class standing). There were 319 (37%) men and 527 (61%) women (17 did not report their sex). There were 722 (84%) traditional age students (ages 17–22, median = 18) and 136 (16%) nontraditional age students (ages 23–66, median = 30). Five students did not report their age.

At the end of the semester, 509 (59%) of the original 863 students completed the survey again. Although we had considerable attrition, these students appeared to be representative of the larger group who completed the initial survey in that there were no significant differences between the first group and the second group in which school they attended, their class standing, or their ages.

Materials

The students completed a questionnaire that listed 29 items likely to appear on a syllabus (see Table 1). We chose these items because several authors listed them as important to include in a syllabus (see Altman & Cashin, 1992; Appleby, 1994; Matejka & Kurke, 1994; McDonnell-Harris, 1993). Students rated how much attention they paid to each item on a Likert-type scale from 1 (*no attention at all*) to 7 (*a great deal of attention*).

Procedure

There were two phases in the study. We conducted the first phase at the beginning of the class period on the first day of class, before the students had seen or discussed the syllabus for the course. Students first signed a consent form stating that they understood the researchers wanted to know how much attention they paid to different pieces of information found on a course syllabus. We defined *syllabus* on the consent form as "an outline or brief statement of the main points of a . . . course of study" (*American Heritage Dictionary*, 1982, p. 1230). After receiving a participant number, the students completed the 29-item survey.

We conducted the second phase during the last week of classes. The students used their participant numbers from the first phase so we could pair responses from both phases. The 29 items on the survey were identical to those on the first. To avoid biasing the students' responses, the consent form for the second phase included the statement that "we do not know whether students change their minds about what they should attend to on a syllabus over the course of the semester or whether their perception of what they should attend to remains the same." We also instructed them not to worry about how they responded earlier in the semester but to answer the questions based on what they thought about each item "right now."

Results

Table 1 contains the means and standard deviations of the first-day-of-class ratings by all students for each of the 29 survey items, listed in order from the highest mean (most-attended-to item) to the lowest mean (least-attended-to item). Students reported paying little attention (i.e., gave ratings of less than 4) to only three items: titles and authors of textbooks and readings, withdrawal dates, and course information. They were neutral on one other item, academic dishonesty policy. All other items received a mean rating of five or higher.

We performed a four-way repeated measures ANOVA using class (first semester vs. continuing) and age (traditional vs. nontraditional) as grouping variables and time (beginning vs. end of semester) and item as within-subjects variables. ANOVA yielded main effects for class, time, and item as well as four two-way interactions: Class × Time, Class × Item, Age × Item, and Time × Item. The main effect for age and the other two-way interactions were not significant. We found no significant three- or four-way interactions.

We obtained a significant Class × Time interaction, $F(1, 436) = 5.21$, $p = .02$. There was no difference between the beginning-of-semester mean ratings of all items for first-semester students ($M = 5.58$, $SD = 0.66$) and continuing students ($M = 5.50$, $SD = 0.73$). First-semester students did not change their mean item ratings from the beginning of the semester to the end ($M = 5.49$, $SD = 0.73$). However, by the end of the semester the mean item rating for continuing students had decreased ($M = 5.29$, $SD = 0.82$), $t(943) = 2.87$, $p = .004$. These findings provide partial support for our hypothesis that first-semester students attend to syllabus content differently than more experienced students. Although first-semester and continuing students responded in similar ways at the beginning of the semester, they approached syllabus content differently by the end of the semester.

A significant Class × Item interaction also supported the hypothesis that first-semester students differ from continuing students, $F(28, 409) = 2.11$, $p = .001$. We performed t tests comparing the two class groups on item ratings collapsed across time. Because we had a large number of participants and made many comparisons, we used an alpha level of .005. First-semester students rated items pertaining to prerequisites, location of course materials, holidays, late assignment and academic dishonesty policies, and support services higher than did continuing students. Continuing students rated items pertaining to the type of exams and assignments higher than did first-semester students (see Table 2).

Repeated-measures ANOVA also yielded a significant Age × Item interaction, $F(28, 409) = 2.23$, $p < .0005$. To examine this interaction, we performed t tests comparing traditional-age students and nontraditional-age students, again using an alpha of .005. Table 3 shows that nontraditional-

Table 1. Means and Standard Deviations of Item Ratings on the First Day of Class

Item	M	SD	n
Examination or quiz dates	6.67	0.87	862
Due dates of assignments	6.63	0.86	862
Reading material covered by each exam or quiz	6.34	1.03	862
Grading procedures and policies	6.32	0.97	825
Type of exams and quizzes (e.g., multiple choice, essay)	6.29	1.16	863
Dates and times of special events that must be attended outside of class	6.25	1.15	862
Number of examinations and quizzes	6.21	1.21	863
Kind of assignments (e.g., readings, papers, presentations, projects)	6.12	1.03	860
Class participation requirements	6.05	1.13	824
Amount of work (e.g., amount of reading, length, and number of other assignments)	5.97	1.15	863
Whether extra credit can be earned	5.89	1.32	862
Makeup policy	5.87	1.32	826
Late assignment policy	5.80	1.31	826
Attendance policy	5.76	1.36	826
Schedule of topics to be covered	5.64	1.31	863
Course format (e.g., lecture, discussion, videos, classroom activities)	5.62	1.33	860
Where to obtain materials for the class (e.g., texts, readings, lab materials)	5.49	1.51	862
Days, hours, and location of class meetings	5.43	1.74	862
Prerequisite skills and course work	5.42	1.50	861
Course goals and objectives	5.38	1.45	859
Holidays	5.27	1.75	862
Course description	5.24	1.45	862
Instructor information (i.e., name, title, office location, phone number, e-mail address)	5.21	1.40	826
Available support services (e.g., tutoring, computerized study guides)	5.16	1.65	826
Instructor's office hours	5.12	1.44	826
Academic dishonesty policy	4.25	1.94	826
Course information (course number and title, section number, credit hours)	3.95	1.80	863
Drop (withdrawal) dates	3.68	1.83	862
Titles and authors of textbooks and readings	3.52	1.93	861

Note. Ratings were based on a 7-point scale ranging from 1 (*no attention at all*) to 7 (*a great deal of attention*).

Table 2. Items for Which Mean Ratings by First-Semester and Continuing Students Differed Significantly

Item	First-Semester Students			Continuing Students		
	M	SD	n	M	SD	n
Late assignment policy	5.85	1.14	502	5.56	1.35	316
Prerequisite skills and coursework	5.52*	1.27	518	5.09	1.39	320
Holidays	5.50	1.54	517	5.09	1.73	321
Where to obtain materials for the class	5.48	1.29	518	5.18	1.49	321
Available support services	5.13*	1.42	502	4.66	1.57	316
Academic dishonesty policy	4.34*	1.70	502	3.85	1.87	316
Type of exams and quizzes	6.23	1.06	518	6.48	0.91	321
Kinds of assignments	5.96	0.96	518	6.19	0.90	321

Note. Ratings are means of first-day-of-class and end-of-semester item ratings. Ratings were based on a 7-point scale ranging from 1 (*no attention at all*) to 7 (*a great deal of attention*). $p < .005$ unless otherwise noted.
*$p < .001$.

age students rated items pertaining to course goals, title and author of textbooks, and kind of assignments as more important than did traditional-age students. Younger students reported paying more attention to items pertaining to holidays and to late assignment and academic dishonesty policies than did older students.

A significant Time × Item interaction, $F(28, 409) = 2.86$, $p < .0005$, indicated that students changed their ratings of items from the beginning to the end of the semester. We performed individual t tests comparing item ratings and found that 18 of the 29 items' ratings changed. Ratings for the first 15 items in Table 4 decreased from the beginning to the end of the semester; the ratings for the final three items increased.

To examine our second hypothesis that first-semester students change their opinion about what is important on a syllabus after gaining experience with college courses, we

Table 3. Items for Which Mean Ratings by Traditional-Age and Nontraditional-Age Students Differed Significantly

Item	Age					
	Traditional			Nontraditional		
	M	SD	n	M	SD	n
Kind of assignments	5.99	0.95	722	6.29	0.91	136
Course goals and objectives	5.24	1.31	721	5.60	1.25	136
Titles and authors of textbooks and readings	3.38*	1.71	722	4.01	1.79	135
Late assignment policy	5.79	1.19	704	5.39	1.45	133
Holidays	5.51	1.53	721	4.42	1.78	136
Academic dishonesty policy	4.23*	1.74	704	3.65	1.89	133

Note. Ratings are means of first-day-of-class and end-of-semester item ratings. Ratings were based on a 7-point scale ranging from 1 (*no attention at all*) to 7 (*a great deal of attention*). $p < .005$ unless otherwise noted.
*$p < .001$.

Table 4. Items for Which Mean Ratings on the First Day of Class and at the End of the Semester Differed

Item	First Day of Class		End of Semester		
	M	SD	M	SD	n
Reading material covered by each exam	6.36*	0.98	6.15	1.11	509
Dates and times of special events	6.33	1.11	6.12	1.29	508
Kind of assignments	6.18*	0.99	5.91	1.17	504
Amount of work	6.04*	1.10	5.77	1.26	508
Class participation requirements	6.04*	1.53	5.74	1.31	475
Makeup policy	5.85	1.33	5.65	1.50	477
Late assignment policy	5.72	1.34	5.50	1.52	477
Schedule of topics to be covered	5.65*	1.30	5.32	1.45	508
Prerequisite skills and course work	5.49	1.51	5.25	1.49	508
Where to obtain materials for the class	5.48*	1.53	5.10	1.58	506
Course goals and objectives	5.38*	1.45	5.11	1.45	506
Instructor information	5.19	1.40	4.94	1.58	477
Available support services	5.18*	1.63	4.51	1.62	477
Instructor's office hours	5.10	1.42	4.83	1.59	477
Academic dishonesty policy	4.18*	1.93	3.79	1.91	476
Days, hours, and location of class meetings	5.43*	1.75	5.81	1.55	508
Holidays	5.32	1.71	5.56	1.69	509
Drop dates	3.68*	1.80	4.02	1.89	508

Note. Ratings were based on a 7-point scale ranging from 1 (*no attention at all*) to 7 (*a great deal of attention*). $p < .005$ unless otherwise noted.
*$p < .001$.

17

Table 5. Items for Which Mean Ratings by First-Semester Students on the First Day of Class and at the End of the Semester Differed Significantly

Item	First Day of Class		End of Semester		
	M	SD	M	SD	n
Type of exams and quizzes	6.16	1.31	6.41	0.97	312
Days, hours, and location of class meetings	5.68*	1.57	6.04	1.33	311
Holidays	5.52*	1.59	5.86	1.50	312
Drop (withdrawal) dates	3.68*	1.79	4.16	1.83	311
Kind of assignments	6.10	1.03	5.86	1.15	308
Class participation requirements	6.10	1.10	5.82	1.24	290
Amount of work	6.04	1.05	5.76	1.25	312
Where to obtain materials for the class	5.54	1.47	5.25	1.49	310
Available support services	5.43*	1.46	4.61	1.64	292
Course goals and objectives	5.35	1.39	5.08	1.41	311
Academic dishonesty policy	4.39	1.82	4.02	1.88	292

Note. Ratings were based on a 7-point scale ranging from 1 (*no attention at all*) to 7 (a great deal of attention). $p < .005$ unless otherwise noted. *$p < .001$.

compared their ratings on the first day of class to those at the end of the semester. A 2×29 (Time × Item) repeated-measures ANOVA yielded a significant effect for items, $F(1, 28) = 93.59$, $p < .001$, and a significant interaction, $F(1, 28) = 6.56$, $p < .001$. Thus, the second hypothesis was supported. Using matched-sample t tests, we found that the ratings of 11 items differed significantly from the beginning to the end of the semester (see Table 5). Ratings decreased for items pertaining to the course goals, where course materials may be found, the kind of assignments, amount of work, class participation requirements, available support services, and academic dishonesty policy. Ratings increased for items pertaining to when and where the class meets, the type of exams, withdrawal dates, and holidays.

Discussion

Faculty members currently view the syllabus as both a contract and a teaching tool (Altman & Cashin, 1992; Smith & Razzouk, 1993). Thus, it has become a longer, more comprehensive document of course content and policies. Instructors use the syllabus to communicate to their students their expectations of what students must do to be successful in the course. Therefore, it is important to know what students attend to when they read a course syllabus.

Based on our data, students do not attend equally to all information in a syllabus. Students in introductory-level psychology classes pay little attention to information they can find elsewhere (e.g., textbook information that is available at the bookstore and basic course information and withdrawal dates published in the schedule of classes). These same students pay a great deal of attention to dates of important course events such as exams and assignments.

In addition, we found that attention ratings differed depending on whether participants were first-semester or continuing students and whether they were of traditional age. For example, first-semester students paid more attention to prerequisites and support services than did continuing students. Perhaps first-semester students are more uncertain of their scholastic abilities and thus seek out syllabus information that would help them deal with these concerns. Similarly, first-semester students may pay less attention to items

about types of exams and assignments because they do not yet realize that different kinds of exams and assignments require different study strategies and different amounts of organization and work. Nontraditional-age students paid less attention to late assignment and dishonesty policies than did traditional-age students. Perhaps nontraditional-age students perceive themselves as having a strong work ethic and thus assume they will not need to make use of this information.

Given the effort instructors put into creating syllabi, what can you as a faculty member do to ensure that students use them effectively? First, consider placing information that students most attend to on the first page of the syllabus. When you review the syllabus with your students, this student-friendly order of information should increase the chances that you and your students attend to the same parts of the syllabus at the same time. Alternatively, if you wish to place information that you consider important on the first page but that students generally do not, give students time to find the information most important to them before going over the syllabus together. Consider using word-processor features such as different fonts, underlining, bold facing, or italicizing to draw attention to important information. You might also consider eliminating syllabus information that neither you nor the students find particularly useful. One would expect that students would be more likely to read a concise yet relevant syllabus than one that is overly lengthy and appears to contain irrelevant information.

Our data indicate that the syllabus alone is not an adequate communication tool because students do not attend equally to all information in a syllabus, and because there are differences in what they attend to depending on such factors as class standing, age, and time of semester. The instructor must facilitate communication at the beginning of the semester by focusing student attention on information, such as course withdrawal dates and academic dishonesty policies, that is important but to which students pay relatively little attention. Given the general trend for students, particularly continuing students, to pay less attention to syllabus items as the semester wears on, it would be wise to revisit portions of the syllabus in class with the students throughout the semester. For example, our data indicate decreased attention to makeup and late assignment policies near the end of the term, just when students often have many assignments due. They may be tempted to skip a quiz or turn an assignment in late for one class to complete some obligation for another class and assume they can complete the missed work without penalty later. Thus, a few weeks before the end of the semester would be a good time for instructors to remind students of makeup and late policies. Providing students with reminders of important syllabus items should encourage students to make wiser (or at least more informed) decisions throughout the semester.

References

Altman, H. B., & Cashin, W. E. (1992). *Writing a syllabus* (Idea Paper No. 27). Manhattan: Kansas State University, Division of Continuing Education, Center for Faculty Evaluation and Development.

American heritage dictionary (2nd college ed.). (1982). Boston: Houghton Mifflin.

Appleby, D. C. (1994). How to improve your teaching with the course syllabus. *APS Observer, 7,* 18–19, 26.

Leeds, J. D. (1993, August). *The course syllabus as seen by the undergraduate student.* Paper presented at the meeting of the American Psychological Association, Washington, DC. (ERIC Document Reproduction Service No. ED 356 747)

Lenthall, G., & Andrews, D. (1983). Psychological seduction: Effective organization of the introductory course. *Teaching of Psychology, 10,* 137–139.

Long, M. H., & Crookes, G. (1992). Three approaches to task-based syllabus design. *TESOL Quarterly, 26,* 27–56.

Matejka, K., & Kurke, L. B. (1994). Designing a great syllabus. *College Teaching, 42,* 115–117.

McDonnell-Harris, M. (1993). Motivating with the course syllabus. *The National Teaching & Learning Forum, 3,* 1–3.

Neumark, E., Mazor, E., Bellali, L., Kalujni, S., & Melamed, M. (1991). The evaluation of some 8th and 9th grade textbooks according to the English syllabus. *English Teachers' Journal, 43,* 54–61.

Smith, M. F., & Razzouk, N. Y. (1993). Improving classroom communication: The case of the course syllabus. *Journal of Education for Business, 68,* 215–221.

Zucker, E. L. (1992, April). *What students look for in course syllabi.* Poster presented at the meeting of the Southwestern Psychological Association, Austin, TX.

Notes

1. We are grateful to Drew Appleby of Marian College, Sally Radmacher of Missouri Western State College, and Diane Wille of Indiana University Southeast, who coordinated data collection at their schools. We also thank Cathy A. Grover for help during the development stage and Cynthia Fisher, Nadene Keene, Donna McLean, and Sue Sciame-Giesecke for help in preparing this article.

Students' Pet Peeves About Teaching

Baron Perlman
Lee I. McCann
University of Wisconsin, Oshkosh

There are often differences between how well faculty believe they teach and students' satisfaction with the delivery of instruction. Existing student perspectives (e.g., Eison & Stephens, 1988; Waters, Kemp, & Pucci, 1988) and a variety of simple and effective techniques (e.g., Angelo & Cross, 1993; Paulsen & Feldman, 1995) may help faculty identify such problems and, thereby, improve their teaching.

One such form of classroom assessment obtains student feedback on teaching quality by asking: "What are your pet peeves about college instructors?" (Rallis, 1994). This technique has several strengths: (a) students feel heard and appreciated, (b) instructors can make immediate changes in their teaching, (c) faculty can easily administer and read it, and (d) teachers can make adjustments without feeling they are responding to criticisms of their teaching.

The recent literature reports on students' perceptions of irritating faculty classroom behaviors in a small private college (Appleby, 1990) and lists pet peeves (N = 193) of teacher education students (Rallis, 1994) in a regional university. We wanted to (a) increase both studies' sample sizes with students attending psychology classes in a public university, (b) investigate differences in pet peeves between underclass and upperclass students, and (c) describe use of the pet peeves method as a cooperative venture by a psychology department for faculty teaching improvement.

Method

Participants

Faculty members (N = 13) in a public regional university sampled undergraduate students in all psychology course sections (N = 25) during the Spring 1997 semester. Faculty included 1 adjunct lecturer, 1 senior lecturer, 3 assistant professors, 4 associate professors, and 4 full professors. Participants were 671 students (377 first year and sophomores [underclass] and 294 juniors and seniors [upperclass]).

Procedure

Each instructor distributed index cards during the first class meeting and told students the following:

> Along with colleagues in the psychology department, I am interested in improving my teaching. To that end I want to learn your pet peeves (major likes/dislikes/annoyances, things which are unfair) about faculty whose courses you have taken (both in and out of psychology). Take a few minutes and write down your two or three major pet peeves about faculty when they teach. What bothers you or annoys you the most? All responses will be anonymous and confidential. Please provide me with your class standing and whether you have done this exercise in another class during the last few days.

Faculty members collected cards, thanked students, read their comments, and gave the cards to the authors.

Table 1 shows Rallis's (1994) categories and new ones (we added) to encompass all the responses. Students listed between zero and five pet peeves. Some provided two or more different responses for a single category. To avoid duplication, we discarded cards from students who had participated in previous classes.

Table 1. Student Pet Peeves About Teaching

	N	%[a]
Teaching		
Poor organization/planning	253	17
Poor teaching mechanics (e.g., speak too fast/slow/softly, poor use of board)	207	14
Lecture style and technique	154	11
Poor testing procedures/exams	121	8
Monotone voice	81	6
Grading process	50	3
Lack of interest/competence/depth, lack of course content	36	2
Unfair grading	24	2
Inappropriate humor	18	1
Total	944	65
Respect		
Intellectual arrogance/talk down	44	3
Don't respect students	42	3
Not approachable, unhelpful	41	3
Control/impose views	16	1
Intolerant of questions	8	1
Total	151	10
General		
Poor use of class time (coming late, stopping early)	76	5
Not in during office hours/hard to find	35	2
Poor syllabus	33	2
Forced class participation	28	2
Insensitive to student's time constraints	25	2
Too much work	20	1
Don't relate material to real life	12	1
Bias/sexism/racism	2	0
Other	34	2
Total	265	18
Negative mannerisms		
Negative mannerisms (e.g., attire, vocal, and nonverbal mannerisms)	95	7
Overall total	1,455	100

Note. Responses represent number of peeves. Students sometimes gave two different peeves coded into a single category. Total percentage may not equal sum of item percentages due to rounding.
[a]Percentage of number of peeves to the total (N < 1,455).

Results and Discussion

Student Pet Peeves

Despite some differences in data collection methods from Appleby (1990) and a different sample from both Appleby and Rallis (1994), students identified similar pet peeves about irritating faculty behaviors. Chi square analyses comparing the ratio of pet peeves from underclass and upperclass students in each category to each group's total responses were nonsignificant, signifying that student concerns apply to courses at all undergraduate levels. Six underclass and 4 upperclass students listed no peeves.

Table 1 categorizes 1,455 responses; 944 (65%) fell in one of the "teaching" categories, most emphasizing poor organization and planning, teaching mechanics, lecturing, testing procedures and exams, or a monotone voice. Some complained exams cover only the text and others only the lecture, others about use or nonuse of grading curves, or requiring or not requiring attendance. Obviously, teachers cannot please everyone.

"Respect" elicited 151 peeves (10%) and the "general" category elicited 265 peeves (18%). Lack of respect for students and poor use of class time elicited the most concerns.

Positively, few faculty members seemed to demonstrate a lack of interest, competence, or depth in their subject or teaching, and most seemed to grade fairly. Students rarely complained about too much work, sexism, or racism.

Of the many peeves (n = 95, 7%) in the negative mannerism category, a few were humorous (e.g., bad haircuts and wardrobes, sloppy dresser). Many simple peeves regarding vocal (e.g., repetitive verbal mannerisms such as "uhs") and nonvocal mannerisms (e.g., walking around too much) would, if remedied, easily improve teaching or the perception thereof.

Faculty Changes in Teaching

Of the 13 faculty participating, 11 (85%) made teaching changes during the first week of classes; all have maintained these changes two semesters later. Changes included enhancing lectures with more overheads, greater sensitivity to scheduling reading and assignments, extra care reviewing previous classes, reducing pauses ("uh") in lectures, a brief break in a 90 min class, more clarity in grading criteria, slower speech, and arriving to class earlier. Future research could investigate the differential effectiveness of student evaluations, peer review, and the pet peeves technique in facilitating changes in faculty teaching.

The study has limitations. The data represent a single public regional university campus with few minority students.

Lessons Learned

1. The concerns in Table 1 provide a starting point for improving instruction for any teacher.
2. Students know good teaching and are sensitive to not receiving it.
3. This is a simple technique faculty can use to improve pedagogy. If faculty wish, they can easily remedy many identified teaching concerns.

4. The lack of significant differences between underclass and upperclass students' peeves means instructors' teaching improvements need not be made differentially for lower- or upper-level undergraduate courses.

5. Separating evaluation of teaching for summative purposes (e.g., personnel decisions) from the formative purpose of improving one's pedagogy encourages faculty to become better teachers by responding to student concerns. Our colleagues at all ranks embraced improving their teaching willingly and energetically.

References

Angelo, T. A., & Cross, K. P. (1993). *Classroom assessment techniques: A handbook for college teachers* (2nd ed.). San Francisco: Jossey-Bass.

Appleby, D. C. (1990). Faculty and student perceptions of irritating behaviors in the college classroom. *Journal of Staff, Program, and Organization Development, 8,* 41–46.

Eison, J., & Stephens, J. (1988). Elements of instructional excellence: The views of university honors and non-honors students. *Forum for Honors, 18,* 35–47.

Paulsen, M. B., & Feldman, K. A. (1995). *Taking teaching seriously: Meeting the challenge of instructional improvement* (ASHE–ERIC Higher Education Rep. No. 2). Washington, DC: George Washington University, Graduate School of Education and Human Development.

Rallis, H. (1994). Creating teaching and learning partnerships with students: Helping faculty listen to student voices. *To Improve the Academy, 13,* 155–168.

Waters, M., Kemp, E., & Pucci, A. (1988). High and low faculty evaluations: Descriptions by students. *Teaching of Psychology, 15,* 203–204.

Notes

1. This article is based on a poster presented at the 1998 Annual National Institute on the Teaching of Psychology, St. Petersburg Beach, FL.
2. We acknowledge the assistance of our students and departmental colleagues.
3. A handout with examples of student pet peeves from the "teaching," "other," and "negative mannerisms" categories is available from the authors.

Effects of Topic Order in Introductory Psychology on Student Achievement, Interest, and Perceived Course Difficulty

Rondeau G. Laffitte, Jr.
Winthrop College

In describing the content organization of the typical introductory psychology course, Lenthall and Andrews (1983) suggested that student interest in course topics, as well as learning course material, might be enhanced by the earlier introduction of topics with which students are already familiar. They noted that insertion of the "hard" topics (e.g., psychology as a science, biological and perceptual processes, learning) should be followed alternately by subject matter that is intrinsically interesting to students (e.g., social psychology, levels of consciousness). Lenthall and Andrews's four alternative content arrangement options include Option A, the conventional order (i.e., psychology as a science, biological foundations, perception, learning, information processing, development, etc., to social psychology). Option B is simply the reverse of Option A. Option C, designed to engage the interest of the average student while avoiding the early establishment of false perceptions of psychology, begins with the study of personality theory and abnormal behavior, and provides a pattern of two consecutive "hard" content areas followed by a "soft" one. Option D begins with the topic psychology as a science, followed by the study of personality, learning, abnormal psychology, biological processes, and ends in a manner similar to the third option. Lenthall and Andrews cited no earlier research and reported no experimental comparison of the various topic organizations.

McKenzie and Cangemi (1978) provided evidence that students are more interested in some course topics than others. They administered a 90-item questionnaire to 678 introductory psychology students who ranked potential course topics for interest and importance. Among the lowest ranked topics were some of Lenthall and Andrews's "hard" content areas (i.e., history of psychology, nervous system structure, language, and research methods). The highest ranked items included human sexual behavior, love, suicide, and child psychology.

Various topic organizations of the introductory psychology course have been suggested by different writers. For a good example, see Dimond and Senter's (1976) suggestion that the course involve the examination of learning, perception, and motivation from the experimental, developmental, and clinical psychology points of view.

There have been few experimental tests of the efficacy of different topic organizations. In fact, Irion (1976) questioned the assumption that variance in the distribution of students' test scores in introductory psychology is a primary function of teaching variables and suggested that students' ability might have a greater influence. My study compared the effects of two different topic organizations on achievement test scores, student interest, and perceived course difficulty.

Method

Students in two sections of introductory psychology at a state-supported senior college served as subjects. Section I included 42 students and met at 11:00 a.m. on Monday, Wednesday, and Friday. Section II also included 42 students and met in the same classroom on the same days of the week at 12:00 noon. Both sections were taught by the same instructor, used the same textbook (Lahey, 1983), and contained comparable numbers of males, females, and upper- and lower-division students.

The students in Section I covered the topics as they appeared in the textbook (Option A), and students in Section II covered the same topics in an order similar to Lenthall and Andrews's (1983) Option D. Their Option B was not used because it seems to be unworkable in the classroom (i.e., students must understand social psychology experiments before studying research methodology, and they consider personality development and abnormal behavior before examining developmental, biological processes, and learning). For similar reasons Option C, although more promising than Option B, was not tested. The topic order provided for each section is listed below.

I	II	
1	1	What is Psychology? (History & Research Methods)
2	7	Biological Foundations of Behavior
3	10	Sensation and Perception
4	9	States of Consciousness
5	3	Basic Principles of Learning
6	4	Memory
7	5	Cognition, Language, and Intelligence
8	12	Infant and Child Development
9	13	Adolescence, Adulthood, and Aging
10	8	Motivation and Emotion
11	2	Personality Theories and Assessment
12	6	Stress and Abnormal Behavior
13	14	Therapies
14	11	Social Psychology
15	15	Psychology Applied to Business and Other Professions

The same number of class periods was devoted to the different topics in each section. Each course included four 50-min tests and an identical cumulative final examination. Scores on the final examination provided a direct comparison of the achievement of students in the two sections.

Attached to each of the four 50-min tests given to both sections was a brief questionnaire that included two 4-point scales. Students rated the course content on a continuum from *not interesting* to *very interesting*, and the course difficulty from *not difficult* to *very difficult*. Responses to this rating scale permitted a comparison of students' stated interest in and perceived difficulty of the course at each test time.

Results

Academic achievement of the two groups was compared by giving the same 150-item cumulative multiple-choice examination. There were no differences. The mean and standard deviation for Section I were 97.90 and 16.15, respectively, and for Section II, $M = 97.78$, $SD = 16.03$, $t(77) = .034$, $p > .05$.

The degree of interest in content expressed by students in the two sections was assessed by using the rating scale described earlier. This questionnaire was administered at each of the four 50-min tests and the results analyzed by computing chi-squares. In no case was a significant relationship found between the two topic orders and the degree of expressed interest.

Perceived course difficulty was also measured by a rating scale item at each 50-min test. Again, the four chi-squares failed to detect any significant degree of relationship between topic order and reported level of difficulty.

Discussion

These data fail to support Lenthall and Andrews's (1983) suggestion that a modification of the traditional topic sequence in introductory psychology courses might enhance students' achievement. There also seemed to be no relationship between topic order and students' expressions of interest and judgments of course difficulty at four different times during the semester. Of course there are some topic sequences that must be avoided. It is difficult, for example, to discuss behavior therapy before students understand operant and classical conditioning. Likewise, it makes little sense to study memory before covering learning processes. But, unless a teacher chooses a sequence that requires students to learn concepts for which they lack necessary knowledge, the topic order simply does not matter.

References

Dimond, R. E., & Senter, R. J. (1976). An organizational framework for the teaching of basic psychology. *Teaching of Psychology, 3*, 181–182.

Irion, A. L. (1976). A survey of the introductory course in psychology. *Teaching of Psychology, 3*, 3–8.

Lahey, B. B. (1983). *Psychology: An introduction*. Dubuque, IA: Wm. C. Brown.

Lenthall, G., & Andrews, D. (1983). Psychological seduction: Effective organization of the introductory course. *Teaching of Psychology, 10*, 137–139.

McKenzie, S., & Cangemi, J. P. (1978). What new students in introduction to psychology really want to learn: A survey. *Journal of Instructional Psychology, 5*, 5–7.

Student Belief and Involvement in the Paranormal and Performance in Introductory Psychology

Wayne S. Messer
Richard A. Griggs
University of Florida

There is adequate reason to believe that interest in the paranormal is a continuing aspect of American culture (e.g., Arndorfer, 1988; Crichton, 1988; Frazier, 1989; Kemp, 1988; McCarthy & Leikind, 1986). Recent examples include the Reagans' reliance on astrology (Regan, 1988) and Time–Life's new series called *Mysteries of the Unknown*, which features topics such as psychic powers and UFOs. The prevalence of paranormal belief and involvement among college students and whether such belief and involvement are related to academic performance are important issues for the educational community. Our study was designed to address these questions in the context of the introductory psychology course.

Several researchers have found a relation between paranormal belief and reasoning deficiencies. Alcock and Otis (1980) reported that, compared to skeptics, believers showed a relative lack of ability to evaluate evidence and a tendency to be more dogmatic in their approach to new situations. Blackmore and Troscianko (1985) observed greater shortcomings in probability judgments among believers, including the consistent underestimation of the likelihood of chance events. Wierzbicki (1985) found that believers performed less well on a syllogistic reasoning test and that the difference was manifested primarily on those syllogistic forms that required reasoning from statements of evidence to the validity of hypotheses.

Good probabilistic thinking skills, an open-minded approach, and the ability to evaluate evidence are skills particularly essential to competent performance in introductory psychology because many of the concepts are counterintuitive or concern matters about which many students already have developed strong beliefs. Students must be prepared to overcome their initial reaction and evaluate the evidence, nearly all of which is probabilistic, on its own merits.

Discussions of the paranormal are likely to arise in the introductory psychology course, and psychology professors have been found to have greater skepticism about the paranormal than professors in other academic disciplines (Wagner & Monet, 1979). Thus, any class discussions concerning the paranormal are likely to generate skeptical comments from the professor. If so, cognitive dissonance and selective learning might result for the believing student. Russell and Jones (1980), for example, found that when confronted with disconfirming evidence concerning ESP, believers showed significantly poorer recall of the evidence than did skeptics.

For many reasons, then, students who believe or are involved in the paranormal might experience more difficulty accepting, integrating, and learning the material in an introductory psychology course, resulting in lower course grades. Our study examined this hypothesis and assessed the extent of such belief and involvement.

Method

Subjects

Subjects were 176 first-term freshmen (84 men, 92 women) enrolled in the same section of introductory psychology. Participation partially satisfied the general research requirements of the course. The text was Myers's (1986) *Psychology*.

Materials

A 10-page paper-and-pencil questionnaire was designed to assess belief and involvement in each of 10 paranormal phenomena: out-of-body experiences, extraterrestrial visitation, reincarnation, precognition during dreams, astrology, biorhythm, ESP/psychokinesis, tarot cards, firewalking, and spiritualism/mediumistic communication. On one side of each page, subjects were given a brief description of one of the phenomena and were asked to circle the statement that best described their highest degree of involvement in that particular phenomenon. There were four statements:

Statement 1: "I have never heard of the phenomenon."
Statement 2: "I know what the phenomenon is, but do not concern myself with it."
Statement 3: "I personally know someone who participates in or has experienced the phenomenon."
Statement 4: "I myself have participated in or have experienced the phenomenon."

Responses to Statement 1 were scored as 1, responses to Statement 2 as 2, and so on. This comprised the individual's involvement score for that phenomenon.

On the reverse side of each page were two statements of belief pertaining to the phenomenon. Each statement was rated on a 5-point scale ranging from *strongly agree* (1) to *strongly disagree* (5). For the 5 phenomena of biorhythm, precognition during dreams, astrology, spiritualism/mediumistic communication, and ESP/psychokinesis, both statements were worded so that agreement signified belief in the phenomenon (e.g., "Evidence exists that intelligent beings from space have visited the earth and perhaps influenced the course of human civilization in times past."). For the remaining 5 phenomena, one of the two statements was worded so that agreement signified belief, and the other was worded so that agreement signified skepticism (e.g., "Coincidence and loose interpretation of the tarot symbols are sufficient to explain why some tarot readings seem accurate; no supernatural explanations are necessary.").

Strong agreement to a statement worded in the direction of belief was scored as 5 and *strong disagreement* as 1. Scoring of responses to the statements worded in the direction of skepticism was reversed so that *strong agreement* was assigned a 1 and *strong disagreement* a 5. Scores from the two statements were then totaled so that a number from 2 to 10 resulted, with 2 indicating *extreme skepticism*, 10 indicating *extreme belief*, and 6 indicating *uncertainty*. This number comprised the individual's belief score for that phenomenon.

Procedure

The questionnaire was administered during the first week of classes. Course grades and exam scores were obtained with students' permission from the instructor. Three 60-point exams were given, for a maximum total of 180 points. A point total of from 162 to 180 was graded as an A, with subsequent letter grades at 18-point decrements. For the upper 9 points of each of these 18-point intervals, a "plus" grade was given.

With students' permission, their SAT scores were obtained from the Registrar. Initial analyses of extent of belief and involvement and calculations of mean belief and involvement scores included all 176 subjects. Correlations between belief and involvement scores and course scores and subsequent analyses of covariance (ANCOVAs) involving SAT scores and course scores were calculated for 147 subjects, because SAT scores were unavailable for 29 individuals.

Results

Prevalence of belief and involvement in the 10 paranormal phenomena were examined first. Table 1 gives a breakdown of the percentages of the sample that expressed some belief (Score ≥ 7), strong belief (Score ≥ 9), and personal involvement (Circled Statement 4) in each of the 10 phenomena. Averaging the percentages of some belief, strong belief, and personal involvement across the 10 phenomena yielded 33.6%, 8.1%, and 11.9%, respectively.

Percentages of the sample that expressed some belief, strong belief, and personal involvement in different numbers of the phenomena were also calculated. Belief was extensive. Expressing some belief in all 10, in at least 6, and in at least 1 of the phenomena were 27.4%, 91.4%, and 99.4% of the sample, respectively. Expressing strong belief in at least 3, at least 2, and at least 1 of the phenomena were 9.7%, 15.4%, and 38.3%, respectively.

Personal involvement was more moderate but substantial. Personal involvement in at least 1 and at least 2 of the phenomena was indicated by 65.3% and 30.4% of the sample, respectively. Personal involvement in more than 5 of

Table 1. Percentages of Sample Indicating Some Belief, Strong Belief, and Personal Involvement in the 10 Paranormal Phenomena

Phenomenon	Some Belief[a]	Strong Belief[b]	Personal Involvement[c]
Out-of-body experience	23.8	9.1	5.1
Extraterrestrial visitation	32.4	7.9	4.0
Reincarnation	32.9	9.1	7.6
Precognition during dreams	52.3	9.1	39.2
Astrology	30.3	4.0	26.9
Biorhythm	22.2	7.4	11.9
ESP/psychokinesis	47.1	9.7	18.3
Tarot cards	6.8	1.7	1.1
Firewalking	53.5	16.5	0.6
Spiritualism/mediumistic communication	34.7	6.8	4.6

Note. N = 176.
[a]Subjects were considered to have some belief in a phenomenon if their belief score was ≥7. [b]Subjects were considered to have strong belief in a phenomenon if their belief score was ≥9. [c]Subjects were considered to be personally involved in a phenomenon if they circled Statement 4 for that phenomenon.

the phenomena was not indicated by any subject, and lack of personal involvement across all phenomena was indicated by 34.9%.

Table 2 presents the mean belief and involvement scores for each of the paranormal phenomena. A split-plot factorial analysis of variance (ANOVA) with gender as the between subjects variable revealed significant differences between the mean overall belief score of men (5.4) and women (5.8), $F(1, 171) = 4.07, p < .05$, as well as significant differences between the mean belief scores of different phenomena and a significant Phenomenon × Gender interaction, $F(9, 1,539) = 29.16, p < .05$, and $F(9, 1,539) = 3.05, p < .05$, respectively.

A multiple comparison follow-up, using Tukey's HSD, found that the belief score for firewalking, which ranked highest at 6.7, was significantly greater, $p < .05$, than the scores of all other phenomena, except for precognition during dreams and ESP/psychokinesis. The lowest scoring phenomenon was tarot cards, which at 4.2 was significantly lower than any of the other 9 phenomena. In all cases except extraterrestrial visitation, women had higher mean belief scores than men. As indicated in Table 2, some of these differences were significant.

A similar split-plot ANOVA was conducted for involvement. For both men and women, overall mean involvement score was 2.3. However, some of the differences between the mean involvement scores for different phenomena were significant, $F(9, 1,494) = 46.72, p < .05$. Involvement scores in precognition during dreams (3.0) and astrology (2.8), although not significantly different from each other, were higher than those for any of the remaining 8 phenomena, $p < .05$. There was a significant Phenomenon × Gender interaction, $F(9, 1,494) = 3.59, p < .05$. The significant differences in involvement scores between men and women are given in Table 2.

To investigate the relationships between belief and involvement and course performance, Pearson correlation coefficients were calculated between course score (point total for the three exams) and the belief and involvement scores

Table 2. Mean Belief and Involvement Scores for Each Paranormal Phenomenon

Phenomenon	Belief			Involvement		
	Both Sexes	Men	Women	Both Sexes	Men	Women
Out-of-body experience	5.5	5.3	5.6	2.1	2.1	2.0
Extraterrestrial visitation[a]	5.5	5.8	5.1	2.1	2.2	2.1
Reincarnation	5.8	5.5	6.1	2.3	2.2	2.3
Precognition during dreams	6.3	6.1	6.6	3.0	3.0	3.0
Astrology[a,b]	5.1	4.5	5.6	2.8	2.6	2.9
Biorhythm[a,b]	5.5	5.2	5.8	2.0	2.2	1.8
ESP/psychokinesis	6.2	6.0	6.3	2.5	2.6	2.5
Tarot cards	4.2	4.1	4.4	2.1	2.1	1.9
Firewalking[b]	6.7	6.8	6.7	2.0	2.1	1.9
Spiritualism/mediumistic communication[a]	5.7	5.4	6.0	2.2	2.2	2.3

Note. For both sexes, $N = 176$; for men, $n = 84$; for women, $n = 92$.
[a]Denotes sex difference in belief, $p < .05$. [b]Denotes sex difference in involvement, $p < .05$.

of men and women for each phenomenon. All significant correlations were negative. For men, course score was significantly correlated with belief score, $p < .05$, for the five phenomena of: precognition during dreams, $r = -.27$; astrology, $r = -.27$; biorhythm, $r = -.26$; ESP/psychokinesis, $r = -.24$; and tarot cards, $r = -.33$. No involvement score correlated significantly with course score for men. For women, course score was significantly correlated, $p < .05$, with belief score for precognition during dreams, $r = -.25$, and with involvement score for precognition during dreams, $r = -.28$.

Following up on these seven significant correlations, average course scores were computed and compared between skeptics (Score ≤ 5) and believers (Score ≥ 7) and, in one case, between the involved (Score = 4) and the uninvolved (Score < 4). Subjects with a score of 6, indicating uncertainty of belief about a phenomenon, were not included.

For men, of the 5 phenomena for which significant correlations existed between belief score and course score, significant differences, $p < .05$, were found between the mean course scores of skeptics and believers for all but tarot cards, $t(56) = 0.46$. Differences in mean course score were: 11.2 points for precognition during dreams, $t(57) = 2.48$; 8.9 points for astrology, $t(63) = 1.67$; 10.4 points for biorhythm, $t(49) = 1.98$; and 9.5 points for ESP/psychokinesis, $t(55) = 2.02$. In all four cases, the skeptics' performance was at least half a letter grade (8 points) higher than that of believers.

For women, skeptics of precognition during dreams scored significantly higher than believers by 12.6 points, $t(52) = 2.21$. For those women who were not personally involved in precognition during dreams, their mean course score was 14.4 points higher than that of women who were involved, $t(69) = 3.2$.

Significant differences in mean course score also appeared between skeptics and believers in two other phenomena for which there were near significant correlations between course score and belief, $p < .10$. These were firewalking for men, $t(54) = 2.49$; and ESP/psychokinesis for women, $t(52) = 2.34$. Mean course score differences were 12.6 and 13.3 for men and women, respectively, with skeptics scoring higher.

ANCOVAs were conducted to remove the influence of SAT score. For men, significant differences in course score between skeptics and believers for precognition during dreams, astrology, and biorhythm disappeared when the ef-

fect of SAT score on course score was taken into account, $F(1, 56) = 3.74$, $F(1, 62) = 0.92$, and $F(1, 48) = 1.72$, respectively, all $ps > .05$. For ESP/psychokinesis and firewalking, however, significant course score differences remained, $F(1, 54) = 4.08$ and $F(1, 53) = 4.14$, respectively, both $ps < .05$. For women, grade differences disappeared for belief in precognition during dreams and ESP/psychokinesis, $F(1, 51) = 0.75$, and $F(1, 51) = 1.54$, respectively, both $ps > .05$, but remained for involvement in precognition during dreams, $F(1, 68) = 10.36$, $p < .05$.

Discussion

Our results indicate a substantial extent of belief and involvement in the paranormal among college freshmen. Negatively correlated relationships between belief and involvement in certain paranormal phenomena and performance in introductory psychology are also indicated.

To what degree should educators be concerned? To the extent that belief and involvement are related to poorer performance in class, the psychology instructor has just cause for concern. Beyond this, however, psychology instructors should be aware that responsibility for helping make students knowledgeable consumers of scientific results tends to fall naturally on their shoulders. For better or worse, many paranormal claims are associated by the public with the science of psychology. As mentioned earlier, paranormal topics may come up often in the introductory psychology class. Many of the anomalies of experience often labeled *paranormal* result from processes of perception, memory, and imagery (Marks, 1986), which psychologists should be able to explain. Psychology has the methodology to deal with the phenomena that are put forth as paranormal events.

Reasons for belief in the paranormal are numerous: a personal experience; an experience that happens to somebody one knows; misinformation through the media, including uncritical reporting of events and pseudodocumentaries about paranormal phenomena; and personalities like Uri Geller, who popularize the paranormal. About half of those believing in paranormal phenomena give personal experience as the main reason for their belief (Blackmore, 1984; Evans, 1973; Jones, Russell, & Nickel, 1977). Otis and Alcock (1982) reported that college professors were most likely to cite personal experience, but undergraduates and members of the general public were more likely to base their beliefs on the print media and television programs. Either way, critical assessment skills and an understanding of memory and perceptual processes could serve to reduce levels of belief. The introductory psychology instructor can play a crucial role in fostering both the learning of critical thinking skills and reducing levels of unfounded belief.

We believe that there are two possible mechanisms accounting for the relation between paranormal belief and poorer performance in introductory psychology. Paranormal beliefs may provide an alternative explanatory system in direct conflict with psychologically based explanations. Given this view, paranormal belief would directly cause poorer performance. A more likely possibility is that underlying deficiencies in critical assessment skills contribute to both paranormal belief and poorer performance. Following are several approaches the psychology instructor can take to foster critical assessment skills. These examples all involve paranormal claims, but numerous examples that use fraudulent consumer, health, and psychological claims could be substituted.

Morris (1981) advocated debunking the paranormal by hoaxing a class into believing the instructor or a "psychic" guest has paranormal powers, then following up with a dehoaxing that reveals some of the stage tricks, and an anti-ESP lecture explaining "cold reading," the Barnum effect, and the methodological problems and poor track record of ESP research. He found such tactics particularly effective. Although hoaxing a class into accepting a "psychic" performance is purportedly very easy (Cornell, 1984; Marks, 1986), this may go beyond what most instructors are willing to do.

Such an extreme approach may not be needed, however. Although Morris found the hoax/dehoax plus lecture approach was most effective (and perhaps longer lasting) in creating skepticism toward ESP, he also found that the critical lecture, along with merely relating the example of the hoax was nearly as effective. In both cases, the resulting skepticism generalized to other paranormal phenomena.

A separate course in ESP was added to the curriculum at the University of Pittsburgh during a period of active student interest in the topic. The course resulted in heightened skepticism concerning paranormal claims (McBurney, 1976). A full-length course may not be necessary. Banziger (1983) found that a 1-week course on the paranormal at a summer Elderhostel resulted in significant and long-term changes in the direction of more skepticism about reported paranormal events.

Besides specific lectures and courses, numerous exercises, such as using a classroom demonstration in astrology to teach the basics of research methods (Ward & Grasha, 1986), can easily be incorporated into the introductory psychology course. Lectures can be reworked to provide examples of faulty critical thinking with direct relevance to traditional course content. Books by Hines (1988) and Stanovich (1989) are both excellent sources for material. We believe that such efforts would lead to greater skepticism about paranormal claims and to more critical assessments of scientific, consumer, and other claims. Students

would become better consumers of psychological and scientific information and their understanding of basic psychological principles and the scientific approach would be anchored in example.

For the interested teacher, Lamal (1989) provided further references and suggestions for attending to paraphenomena in the introductory psychology class. However, Lamal also pointed out that although belief in parapsychology seems widespread (as substantiated by our findings), most authors of introductory psychology textbooks ignore it and many psychologists are disinclined to deal with it. Given our results, we urge introductory psychology authors and teachers to reconsider their position. The development of critical thinking skills is an important goal for the introductory psychology course. As discussed earlier and by Lamal (1989), paraphenomena provide natural subject matter for exercises to develop these skills in the introductory psychology class. By taking this approach, psychology teachers may also help to decrease student belief in paraphenomena. Given the findings of our study, this is definitely needed.

References

Alcock, J. E., & Otis, L. P. (1980). Critical thinking and belief in the paranormal. *Psychological Reports, 46,* 479–482.

Arndorfer, B. (1988, May 24). In the stars: Is astrology a guide or a gimmick? *Gainesville Sun,* pp. 1d–2d.

Banziger, G. (1983). Normalizing the paranormal: Short-term and long-term change in belief in the paranormal among older learners during a short course. *Teaching of Psychology, 10,* 212–214.

Blackmore, S. J. (1984). A postal survey of OBEs and other experiences. *Journal of the Society for Psychical Research, 52,* 225–244.

Blackmore, S., & Troscianko, T. (1985). Belief in the paranormal: Probability judgments, illusory control, and the "chance baseline shift." *British Journal of Psychology, 76,* 459–468.

Cornell, J. (1984, March). Science vs. the paranormal. *Psychology Today,* pp. 28–34.

Crichton, M. (1988, May). Travels with my karma. *Esquire,* pp. 94–105.

Evans, C. (1973). Parapsychology: What the questionnaire revealed. *New Scientist, 57,* 209.

Frazier, K. (1989). Gallup poll of beliefs: Astrology up, ESP down. *Skeptical Inquirer, 13,* 244–245.

Hines, T. (1988). *Pseudoscience and the paranormal: A critical examination of the evidence.* Buffalo, NY: Prometheus.

Jones, W. H., Russell, D., & Nickel, T. W. (1977). Belief in the paranormal scale: An objective instrument to measure belief in magical phenomena and causes. *JSAS, Catalog of Selected Documents in Psychology, 7,* 100. (Ms. No. 1577)

Kemp, M. (1988, January). Beam us up, José. *Discover,* p. 90.

Lamal, P. A. (1989). Attending to parapsychology. *Teaching of Psychology, 16,* 28–30.

Marks, D. F. (1986). Investigating the paranormal. *Nature, 320,* 119–124.

McBurney, D. H. (1976). ESP in the psychology curriculum. *Teaching of Psychology, 3,* 66–69.

McCarthy, W. J., & Leikind, B. J. (1986, December). Walking on fire: Feat of mind? *Psychology Today,* pp. 10–12.

Morris, S. (1981). Believing in ESP: Effects of dehoaxing. In K. Frazier (Ed.), *Paranormal borderlands of science* (pp. 32–45). Buffalo, NY: Prometheus.

Myers, D. G. (1986). *Psychology.* New York: Worth.

Otis, L. P., & Alcock, J. E. (1982). Factors affecting extraordinary belief. *Journal of Social Psychology, 118*, 77–85.

Regan, D. T. (1988). *For the record: From Wall Street to Washington.* San Diego: Harcourt Brace Jovanovich.

Russell, D., & Jones, W. H. (1980). When superstition fails: Reactions to disconfirmation of paranormal beliefs. *Personality and Social Psychology, 6*, 83–88.

Stanovich, K. E. (1989). *How to think straight about psychology* (2nd ed.). Glenview, IL: Scott, Foresman.

Wagner, M. W., & Monet, M. (1979). Attitudes of college professors toward extra-sensory perception. *Zetetic Scholar, 5*, 7–16.

Ward, R. A., & Grasha, A. F. (1986). Using astrology to teach research methods to introductory psychology students. *Teaching of Psychology, 13*, 143–145.

Wierzbicki, M. (1985). Reasoning errors and belief in the paranormal. *Journal of Social Psychology, 125*, 489–494.

University, Community College, and High School Students' Evaluations of Textbook Pedagogical Aids

Wayne Weiten
Daniel Deguara
Erika Rehmke
Laura Sewell
Santa Clara University

Although pedagogical aids have been an important element in introductory texts since the 1970s (Weiten & Wight, 1992), they have been the subject of empirical research only recently. For example, in a study of 43 introductory psychology texts, Weiten (1988) found that the presence or absence of nine common learning aids failed to predict professors' evaluations of a text's overall pedagogical quality. In a subsequent study of students' perceptions, Weiten, Guadagno, and Beck (1996) found that 13 learning aids varied considerably in terms of their familiarity to students, their likelihood of being used, and their perceived value. Some common pedagogical devices, such as outlines and discussion questions, earned relatively low marks, prompting Weiten et al. to wonder whether the abundant learning aids in modern texts really meet students' needs. Weiten et al. also found that students' educational experience, as indexed by year in school, and their academic success, as indexed by grade point average (GPA), showed a remarkable lack of relation to their ratings of the pedagogical devices.

More recently, Marek, Griggs, and Christopher (1999) pursued two lines of inquiry. First, they set out to determine the extent to which introductory psychology texts incorporated various specific learning aids, producing an informative compendium of current textbook pedagogy. Second, following Weiten et al. (1996), they compared first-semester university students' and more advanced students' perceptions of 15 common learning aids.

The purpose of this study was to extend the research on student attitudes about pedagogy to community college and high school students. The previous two studies involved university students, who might depend less on pedagogical aids than community college and high school students. Within each group, we also examined correlations between

the attitude measures and students' GPAs and year in school to determine whether academic success and educational experience relate to feelings about textbook pedagogy.

Method

Participants

The participants consisted of 200 students (124 men, 76 women) from a selective regional university located in an urban area; 189 students (60 men, 129 women) from a large, urban community college; and 130 students (52 men, 78 women) from an urban high school. In all three cases, one of the researchers or a class teacher administered a brief, voluntary survey during a regularly scheduled class.

The university students reported a mean age of 20.04 years ($SD = 3.03$) and a mean GPA of 3.21 ($SD = 0.47$). The community college students reported a mean age of 25.30 years ($SD = 8.81$) and a mean GPA of 3.25 ($SD = 0.53$). The high school students reported a mean age of 16.64 years ($SD = 0.80$) and a mean GPA of 3.05 ($SD = 0.69$).

Materials

The survey, which was an expanded version of the instrument originally administered by Weiten et al. (1996), asked students to evaluate the 15 pedagogical aids listed in Table 1. To clarify the nature of these learning aids, the questionnaire included a prototypical example excerpted from an introductory psychology textbook. The survey asked participants to rate their familiarity with each pedagogical aid, to rate the probability that they would use each type of aid if it was available in a text they were studying, and to rate the overall educational value of each pedagogical device.

Results

Table 1 shows each group's mean familiarity rating for each of the 15 pedagogical aids, along with information on significant differences among the groups based on ANOVAs and post hoc *t* tests. The last row in the table reports a composite index of participants' overall familiarity with the learning aids, created by averaging each student's 15 familiarity ratings. The data show that students were most familiar with chapter summaries, boldface technical terms, discussion questions, running glossaries, italics for emphasis, and self-tests. Although we found a few significant differences (5 out of 48 possible pairwise contrasts), the three groups generally showed fairly similar familiarity rat-

ings. Reflective of this similarity, we found no significant differences among the groups on the measure of overall familiarity with the pedagogical devices.

Each group's mean ratings of the probability of using the 15 pedagogical aids appear in Table 2. The students indicated that they were most likely to pay attention to boldface technical terms, running or chapter glossaries, chapter summaries, and self-tests. We observed many (18) significant differences among the three groups in the reported probability of using specific learning aids. The main trend was for community college students to be more likely to use selected learning aids than either university or high school students. The other significant differences were that university students were more likely than high school students to use learning objectives, chapter summaries, and section summaries, whereas high school students were more inclined to use discussion questions and pronunciation guides. The ratings of the pedagogical aids' overall value were largely redundant

Table 1. Students' Mean Ratings of Familiarity With Pedagogical Aids by Student Level

Pedagogical Aid	Student Level			F(2, 516)	Significant Contrasts
	University (a)	Community College (b)	High School (c)		
Chapter outlines	4.75	4.98	4.55	2.57	
Learning objectives	5.04	5.15	4.65	4.08*	b > c
Chapter summaries	6.13	5.86	5.20	17.43***	a, b > c
Section summaries	4.44	4.41	4.30	0.24	
Boldfaced terms	6.32	6.56	6.42	2.24	
Running glossaries	5.54	5.25	5.82	5.00**	b < c
Chapter glossaries	5.36	5.30	4.91	2.71	
Pronunciation guides	4.68	4.75	5.04	1.57	
Italics for emphasis	5.60	5.49	5.40	0.85	
Chapter review exercises	5.41	5.38	5.60	0.99	
Learning checks	4.70	4.66	4.67	0.03	
Demonstrations	4.34	4.40	4.25	0.25	
Discussion questions	5.70	5.22	5.42	5.07**	a > b
Organizational questions	3.66	3.99	3.95	1.84	
Self-tests	5.56	5.39	5.44	0.70	
Overall	5.15	5.16	5.05	0.67	

Note. Ratings were based on a scale ranging from 1 (*unfamiliar*) to 7 (*very familiar*).
*p < .05. **p < .01. ***p < .001.

Table 2. Students' Mean Ratings of Probability of Using Pedagogical Aids by Student Level

Pedagogical Aid	Student Level			F(2, 516)	Significant Contrasts
	University (a)	Community College (b)	High School (c)		
Chapter outlines	3.94	4.26	3.98	2.25	
Learning objectives	4.37	4.61	3.82	10.30***	a, b > c
Chapter summaries	5.95	5.75	4.93	22.82***	a, b > c
Section summaries	5.40	5.25	4.70	10.19***	a, b > c
Boldfaced terms	6.14	6.55	6.28	7.83***	a < b
Running glossaries	5.97	6.20	6.09	1.86	
Chapter glossaries	5.59	6.05	5.77	6.64**	a < b
Pronunciation guides	4.45	5.16	5.09	11.84***	a < b, c
Italics for emphasis	5.20	5.32	5.10	0.99	
Chapter review exercises	4.66	5.26	4.91	7.22**	a < b
Learning checks	4.81	5.42	4.75	10.01***	a, c < b
Demonstrations	4.72	4.94	4.91	1.01	
Discussion questions	4.00	4.36	4.58	5.50**	a < c
Organizational questions	5.09	5.10	4.83	1.44	
Self-tests	5.57	5.99	5.33	9.37***	a, c < b
Overall	5.06	5.38	5.01	10.77***	a, c < b

Note. Ratings were based on a scale ranging from 1 (*unlikely*) to 7 (*very likely*).
**p < .01. ***p < .001.

with participants' probability of use ratings (average r = .84) and we do not report them here.

We correlated students' self-reported GPAs and year in school with the 45 ratings of pedagogy for each group, yielding a total of 270 correlations (90 for each group). Fortunately, the trends apparent in these voluminous data can be summarized more economically by collapsing the 45 pedagogy ratings into the three composite indexes that represent students' overall familiarity, probability of use, and value ratings, yielding just 18 correlations. These correlations indicate that students' GPAs and year in school were largely unrelated to their pedagogy ratings. However, there were three small, but significant (p < .05), positive correlations between students' GPAs and their ratings. Among both university, $r(200)$ = .17, and community college students, $r(189)$ = .16, there was a weak association between the overall probability of using the pedagogical aids and higher GPA. Among high school students, there was a weak relation, $r(115)$ = .22, between overall familiarity with the pedagogical devices and higher GPA.

Discussion

Are the pedagogical preferences of university, community college, and high school students similar? Our analyses turned up some significant differences that were informative, but the three groups' attitudes about pedagogy seem much more similar than different. For example, if you compile a list of the five pedagogical aids each group is most likely to use, the lists for university and community college students were identical and four of these five learning aids made the high school students' top five. Even more compelling, if you correlate each set of mean pedagogy ratings, the average correlation between the high school and university students' ratings was .82, the average correlation between the community college and high school students' ratings was .89, and the average correlation between the university and community college students' ratings was .94. The magnitude of these correlations indicates that the three groups' rankings of the pedagogical aids were largely in agreement.

Which pedagogical devices are students most likely to use? Comparing the ratings of our three groups, the two groups studied by Marek et al. (1999), and the single group examined by Weiten et al. (1996), the consensus across the six samples is striking. The five pedagogical devices that students depend on most clearly are boldface technical terms, running or chapter glossaries, chapter summaries, and self-tests. These five learning aids made each group's top five, with but two exceptions: Chapter summaries failed to make the top five among our high school students, and Weiten et al. did not include self-tests on their questionnaire. Thus, consistent with the conclusions of Marek et al., it appears that students are very test conscious and therefore highly pragmatic in their study efforts. They are most enthusiastic

about pedagogical aids that help them to master terminology (boldface technical terms, running and chapter glossaries), quickly review text content (chapter summaries), and practice for upcoming exams (self-tests).

Are favorable attitudes about pedagogy or greater use of pedagogy related to academic success or progress through school? Surprisingly, the answer to this question appears to be negative. We did find that GPA correlated positively with university and community college students' overall likelihood of using pedagogical aids and with high school students' overall familiarity with the 15 learning aids. These correlations provide the first evidence to date that greater reliance on textbook pedagogy might be associated with academic success. However, as a whole, the correlations between GPA and pedagogy ratings were weak and inconsistent.

What are our recommendations for future research on textbook pedagogical aids? The failure to find much evidence of a positive correlation between greater reliance on pedagogy and higher grades accentuates the need to put the educational value of specific learning aids to an empirical test. For example, it might be useful to ask students to study representative chapters from introductory texts with and without specific learning aids to determine whether these pedagogical devices have any impact on their mastery of the material in the chapters.

References

Marek, P., Griggs, R. A., & Christopher, A. N. (1999). Pedagogical aids in textbooks: Do college students' perceptions justify their prevalence? *Teaching of Psychology, 26,* 11–19.

Weiten, W. (1988). Objective features of introductory psychology textbooks as related to professors' impressions. *Teaching of Psychology, 15,* 10–16.

Weiten, W., Guadagno, R. E., & Beck, C. A. (1996). Students' perceptions of textbook pedagogical aids. *Teaching of Psychology, 23,* 105–107.

Weiten, W., & Wight, R. D. (1992). Portraits of a discipline: An examination of introductory psychology textbooks in America. In A. E. Puente, J. R. Matthews, & C. L. Brewer (Eds.), *Teaching psychology in America: A history* (pp. 453–504). Washington, DC: American Psychological Association.

Notes

1. The 15 examples of learning aids in the survey came from 12 introductory texts. None of the examples were taken from the first author's introductory text. Readers can obtain the list of examples and the survey instrument by writing to the first author.

2. The data on participants' ratings of the pedagogical aids' educational value, omitted from this report to save space, are also available from the first author.

Misconceptions Tests or Misconceived Tests?

Richard A. Griggs
Sarah E. Ransdell
University of Florida

Since Vaughan's (1977) study on misconceptions about psychology among introductory psychology students using her Test of Common Beliefs (TCB), numerous articles on this topic have appeared, especially in this journal. There were earlier relevant papers (e.g., McKeachie, 1960), but Vaughan's article seems to have had a greater impact. Later articles have dealt with several topics, including the relationship between the amount of misconception and subsequent performance in the introductory psychology course (Gutman, 1979), the amount of misconception as related to the number of accumulated college credits (Gardner & Dalsing, 1986), criticism of specific TCB items (Brown, 1984; Ruble, 1986), and faculty evaluations of items on the TCB (Gardner & Hund, 1983). Our article touches on all of these topics but focuses mainly on: (a) the effect of having taken a high school psychology course on the performance of college students on a misconceptions test and (b) a critical assessment of the test items that have been labeled *misconceptions*.

More and more high schools have added psychology to their curriculum, and enrollment in these courses has increased (Breland, 1978). For example, about 50% of our introductory psychology students at the University of Florida have had a high school psychology course. Two studies (Carstens & Beck, 1986; Hedges & Thomas, 1980) found that students who completed a high school psychology course began their college introductory course with a greater knowledge of psychology than students who had not taken a high school psychology course. In addition, studies from McKeachie (1960) to Gardner and Dalsing (1986) have usually reported statistically significant (although not large) reductions in the amount of misconception as a function of taking a college introductory psychology course. Thus, a high school course might have a similar effect; students who have had a high school psychology course might do better on the misconceptions test than students who have not.

If there is such an effect, the overall amount of misconception observed today might be less than the 39.5% overall initial level reported by Vaughan (1977). Consistent with this hypothesis, Gardner and Dalsing (1986) reported a 22.9% overall misconception level, which would represent a substantial decrease from Vaughan's 39.5%. However, in analyzing Gardner and Dalsing's raw data, we discovered that they reported their overall level incorrectly.[1] In their study, the mean number of true responses across 60 test items was 22.9. Thus, they observed an overall level of almost 38%, only slightly less than the 39.5% observed by Vaughan (1977).

Gardner and Dalsing (1986) used a 60-item version of the TCB and included a third response category in addition to true and false responses. They deleted items that they considered unclear or that previous studies had shown few students judged to be true, and they allowed students to respond with a question mark if they had no opinion on an item. For reliability assessment of the Gardner and Dalsing results, we used their version of the TCB.

If the corrected Gardner and Dalsing results are reliable, then the overall level of misconception has remained fairly constant over the decade since Vaughan's initial study. We decided to see if the particular test items labeled *misconceptions* have also remained relatively constant across studies. Because only Vaughan (1977) and Lamal (1979) reported test items for which at least 50% of their subjects responded true (Vaughan's definition of a misconception), our comparison involved these two studies, our study, and the study by Gardner and Dalsing, who provided us with their data. Thus, our analysis involved two studies from the late 1970s that essentially employed the original TCB and two recent studies that used a shorter version of the TCB with a third response category added. The results of this analysis, along with the subsequent critical assessment of the individual test items involved, are presented and used to argue that the misconception test itself may have been misconceived.

Method

The subjects were 273 undergraduates at the University of Florida; 198 were entering freshmen who had no college credits, and 75 had earned nine or more college credits; 135

---

[1]This mistake has been verified (R. M. Gardner, personal communication, September 26, 1986). It should be pointed out that the results in Figures 1 and 2 in Gardner and Dalsing (1986) are also incorrectly given as percentages of items marked true. However, this is only an error of labeling, and all of their results and conclusions pertaining to these two sets of data remain the same as originally reported.

Table 1. Intercorrelations Between Sex of Subjects, Number of College Credits, High School Psychology, Course Grade in Total Points, and Misconceptions Test Score

Variable	SEX	CREDITS	HSPSY	GRADE	MISC SCORE
SEX	–	–.10	–.17**	–.01	–.07
CREDITS		–	.23**	.16*	–.25**
HSPSY			–	–.02	.01
GRADE				–	–.18**
MISC SCORE					–

Note. The negative correlations are due to the coding scheme used. Male students were coded as 0; female students as 1. Students who had taken a high school course in psychology were coded as 2; students who had not taken such a course as 3. The misconceptions test score is the number of items marked true (errors).
*$p < .05$. **$p < .01$.

had taken a high school psychology course and 138 had not. The test was administered during the second class meeting in an introductory psychology class.

We used the 60-item modified form of Vaughan's (1977) TCB reported by Gardner and Dalsing (1986). As in Gardner and Dalsing's study, subjects were told that the items represented controversial statements about psychology and that we were interested in their opinions about them. Three responses were allowed: true, false, and ? (don't know/no opinion). Subjects also reported whether or not they had taken a psychology course in high school, their sex, and the number of college credits they had completed.

Results and Discussion

The number of students marking each statement true, false, and ?, as well as the number of true, false, and ? responses for each subject, were computed.

We computed correlations between the sex of the subjects (SEX), subjects' misconceptions test score (MISC SCORE) defined as the number of items marked true, completion or not of a high school psychology course (HSPSY), final grade in the college course (GRADE), and the number of college credits earned (CREDITS). Final grade in the course was coded as the total number of exam points earned in the course (0–180-point scale). The intercorrelations matrix is given in Table 1.

The correlation between HSPSY and MISC SCORE was not significant. The mean number of misconceptions for subjects who had taken a high school psychology course was 23.99; for those who had not, 24.12. Thus, taking a high school course in psychology did not improve performance on the misconceptions test.

However, the correlations between HSPSY and SEX and HSPSY and CREDITS were significant. These results are consistent with recent descriptions of the high school course. More female than male students take high school psychology (Goldman, 1983). Fifty-nine percent of our subjects who had taken a high school course in psychology were women. The relationship between HSPSY and CREDITS indicates that more beginning students had taken such a course. This too agrees with the recent trend toward more high school psychology courses and a growing enrollment in them (Breland, 1978).

The significant correlation between CREDITS and MISC SCORE reflects the fact that beginning students did significantly worse on the misconceptions test. Subjects with no college credits had a significantly higher mean number of misconceptions (24.68) than did subjects with some college experience (22.39), $t(271) = 2.41$, $p < .05$. This result is consistent with Gardner and Dalsing's finding that as the number of college credits increases, the amount of misconception decreases. However, it is clear that this reduction is not of much practical significance because the omega-squared score for this significant effect shows that only 1.74% of the variance in the misconceptions scores is accounted for by the number of college credits.

The significant correlation between CREDITS and GRADES is not surprising. Students with some college experience did better in the course. The mean number of points earned in the course for beginning students was 141.4, and for students with some college experience, 146.6, $t(260) = 2.15$, $p < .05$.[2] But, again, the practical significance of this finding is limited. The omega-squared indicates that only 1.29% of the variance in the students' grades is accounted for by the number of college credits.

The last significant correlation, GRADES and MISC SCORES, is consistent with Gutman's (1979) finding that students who received A or B grades in an introductory psychology course had fewer misconceptions at the beginning of the term than students who did poorly in the course. However, our results indicate that this finding may only apply to experienced students. When the correlation between GRADES and MISC SCORE was computed separately for beginning students and students with some college experience, it was only significant for the experienced students ($r = -.35$, $p < .01$); for beginning students, $r = -.05$.

With respect to overall level of misconception, 40% of the responses were marked true, 48% were marked false, and only 12% were marked ?. This last percentage is almost identical to that observed by Gardner and Dalsing (1986). In addition, the overall level of misconception is comparable to Vaughan's (1977) 39.5%, Lamal's (1979) 41% to 43%, and the 38% observed by Gardner and Dalsing (1986). Thus, it does not appear that the overall level of misconcep-

---

[2]Only 262 students received grades in the course. Thus, the number of degrees of freedom is lower in this case.

tion has decreased since Vaughan's initial study using the complete TCB.

Next we consider our analysis of the test items that have been labeled *misconceptions*. Vaughan (1977) defined a misconception to be any test item marked true by at least 50% of the subjects. Using this criterion, Vaughan observed 23/80 misconceptions; Lamal, 22/76; Gardner and Dalsing, 16/60; and we found 23/60. There is consistency across these four studies. If we look at the 60 items these four studies have in common, only 27 different items constitute misconceptions: Nine items were misconceptions in all four studies, 8 appeared in three studies, 4 were misconceptions in two studies, and 6 in only one study.

Using the criterion that in order to be classified as a reliable misconception a test item has to have been so categorized in at least two of the four studies, we are left with a group of only 21 items. Six of these 21 items have already been criticized in published articles (Brown, 1984; Ruble, 1986). If these criticisms are accepted, we are left with only 15 items. These 15 items are given in Table 2, along with the percentage of subjects responding true in each of the four studies being examined.

The items are ordered first according to how often they were categorized as a misconception. Then, within each of these groups (i.e., the items classified as misconceptions in all four studies, those classified as such in three studies, etc.), the items are ordered according to the average amount of misconception, from highest to lowest. Thus, Item 1 is the strongest misconception, and Item 15 is the weakest.

The fact that there are only 15 reliable misconceptions across the studies reviewed should not be too surprising.

Brown (1983) concluded that "widely shared misconceptions are rare indeed" (p. 209). Panek (1982) found that only 2 of 10 suspected misconceptions about the psychology of aging were believed by the majority of his undergraduate students. But what about the 15 items remaining in the present analysis? Are they all unquestionably misconceptions? It appears not.

Even psychologists do not rate several of these items as completely false. Gardner and Hund (1983) had psychologists and other scientists assign ratings to 20 items from the TCB on the following scale: *completely false* (1), *mostly false* (2), *partly false and partly true* (3), *mostly true* (4), and *completely true* (5). Ten (Items 1, 2, 3, 4, 6, 7, 8, 9, 12, and 14) of the 15 items in Table 2 were included. The ratings of psychologists for these 10 items ranged from 1.20 (for Item 7) to 2.59 (for Item 1) with a mean rating of 1.97 (mostly false on the 5-point scale). The means for six of the items were at least 2.00, and four were below 2.00. Thus, psychologists do not even agree that these items are completely false.

Further evidence of this lack of agreement is provided by Lamal (1979). He had seven introductory psychology instructors rate items from the TCB with respect to their agreement with each item's falsity. In addition, the instructors rated their concern with how their students answered each item. There were nine items that at least one instructor did not rate as false. Items 1, 6, and 9 were in this set of nine. In addition, for 7 (Items 1, 2, 3, 4, 6, 10, and 11) of the 11 items in Table 2 considered in Lamal's study, fewer than half of the instructors said they would be unhappy if their students missed the item. Thus, both the falsity and the im-

Table 2. Data for TCB Items With Proportion of True Responses .50 or Greater in at Least Two Studies

	Proportion of True Response			
TCB Item	Vaughan (1977)	Lamal (1979)	Gardner and Dalsing (1986)	Present Study
1. To change people's behavior toward members of ethnic minority groups, we must first change their attitudes.	.92	.91	.84	.76
2. By feeling people's faces, blind people can visualize how they look in their minds.	.83	.78	.70	.83
3. Children memorize much more easily than adults.	.66	.68	.52	.66
4. Unlike man, the lower animals are motivated only by their bodily needs—hunger, thirst, sex, etc.	.69	.53	.59	.62
5. "The study of the mind" is the best brief definition of psychology today.	.57	.54	.62	.57
6. The more you memorize by rote (e.g., poems), the better you will become at memorizing.	.50	.62	.50	.53
7. The best way to ensure that a desired behavior will persist after training is completed is to reward the behavior every single time it occurs throughout training (rather than intermittently).	.77	.70	—	.68
8. Fortunately for babies, human beings have a strong maternal instinct.	.73	—	.62	.77
9. The ability of blind people to avoid obstacles is due to a special sense that develops in compensation for their absense of vision.	.65	—	.63	.68
10. By giving a young baby lots of extra stimulation (e.g., mobiles and musical toys), we can markedly increase his intelligence.	—	.65	.60	.61
11. Psychiatrists are defined as medical people who use psychoanalysis.	.67	.57	—	.52
12. Boys and girls exhibit no behavioral differences until environmental influences begin to produce such differences.	.61	—	.56	.55
13. The high correlation between cigarette smoking and lung cancer proves that smoking causes lung cancer.	—	.55	.56	.66
14. Genius is akin to insanity.	.53	.56	—	—
15. In love and friendship, more often than not, opposites attract one another.	—	—	.51	.51

Note. Proportions not given are less than .50.

portance of several of the items have been questioned by psychology instructors.

It is also the case that a college-level introductory psychology course does not change many of these misconceptions. Lamal (1979) provided some pretest (at the beginning of the term) and posttest (at the end of the term) results for 11 of the 15 items in Table 2. Performance on 6 of the 11 items (Items 1, 2, 3, 5, 6, and 14) did not change much. There was a substantial decrease (greater than 5%) for three items (Items 7, 11, and 13) and a substantial increase (greater than 5%) for two of the items (Items 4 and 10). This lack of effect may be due partially to the fact that some of these misconceptions are not even addressed in introductory psychology texts. For example, Items 2 and 9 deal with blind people, a topic not covered in most current introductory texts.

Given that such problems exist even for these 15 test items, one begins to doubt the value of the misconceptions test. The number of misconceptions normally observed is already fairly low, and the problems described indicate that this low number is likely to be an overestimate. Many of these problems are probably due to the true–false test format, which is not a good way to assess students' knowledge. In his book on teaching tips for beginning college teachers, McKeachie (1986) did not advocate the use of true–false tests. He argued that "students can usually figure out reasons why any particular item can be either true or false" (pp. 90–91). Thus, it would appear that rather than assessing student misconceptions, the misconceptions test itself may have been misconceived. As Barnett (1986) argued, perhaps teachers of psychology should not be so concerned with assessing what beginning students know or misconceive to be true or false about psychology; but, rather, it is more important that we "help them to appreciate the complexities of human behavior that are rarely captured in simple true–false statements" (p. 64).

References

Barnett, M. A. (1986). Commonsense and research findings in personality. *Teaching of Psychology, 13,* 62–64.

Breland, N. S. (1978). A survey of precollege psychology in New Jersey. *American Psychologist, 33,* 959–961.

Brown, L. T. (1983). Some more misconceptions about psychology among introductory psychology students. *Teaching of Psychology, 10,* 207–210.

Brown, L. T. (1984). Misconceptions about psychology aren't always what they seem. *Teaching of Psychology, 11,* 75–78.

Carstens, C. B., & Beck, H. P. (1986). The relationship of high school psychology and natural science courses to performance in a college introductory psychology class. *Teaching of Psychology, 13,* 116–118.

Gardner, R. M., & Dalsing, S. (1986). Misconceptions about psychology among college students. *Teaching of Psychology, 13,* 32–34.

Gardner, R. M., & Hund, R. M. (1983). Misconceptions of psychology among academicians. *Teaching of Psychology, 10,* 20–22.

Goldman, J. J. (1983). Recent trends in secondary school psychology: The decade from Oberlin to the HBCP. *Teaching of Psychology, 10,* 228–229.

Gutman, A. (1979). Misconceptions of psychology and performance in the introductory course. *Teaching of Psychology, 6,* 159–161.

Hedges, B. W., & Thomas, J. H. (1980). The effect of high school psychology on pre-course knowledge, midterm grades, and final grades in introductory psychology. *Teaching of Psychology, 7,* 221–223.

Lamal, P. A. (1979). College students' common beliefs about psychology. *Teaching of Psychology, 6,* 155–158.

McKeachie, W. J. (1960). Changes in scores on the Northwestern misconceptions test in six elementary psychology courses. *Journal of Educational Psychology, 51,* 240–244.

McKeachie, W. J. (1986). *Teaching tips: A guidebook for the beginning college teacher* (8th ed.). Lexington, MA: Heath.

Panek, P. E. (1982). Do beginning psychology of aging students believe 10 common myths of aging? *Teaching of Psychology, 9,* 104–105.

Ruble, R. (1986). Ambiguous psychological misconceptions. *Teaching of Psychology, 13,* 34–36.

Vaughan, E. D. (1977). Misconceptions about psychology among introductory psychology students. *Teaching of Psychology, 4,* 138–141.

Notes

1. We thank Steve Lange for his assistance with the data analyses, and Rick Gardner and Peter Lamal for providing us with further information about their studies.

Some Retention, But Not Enough

Henry C. Rickard
Ronald Rogers
Norman R. Ellis
William B. Beidleman
University of Alabama

Early researchers reported poor retention of factual classroom materials (Eurich, 1934; Greene, 1931; Tyler, 1933). One investigator (Wert, 1937) stated that if achievement in a course in zoology was measured 3 years later, "practically all students would 'flunk' unless the passing standards were shifted" (p. 139). Retention of psychology material was examined in two more recent studies published in this journal. Students in a human growth and development course taught by the Personalized System of Instruction (PSI) were found superior to traditionally taught students on a retention test taken 5 weeks later (Lu, 1976). Goldwater and Acker (1975) compared PSI and traditional instruction for introductory psychology students. In a follow-up test during the first week of classes of the next school year, PSI students retained course material significantly better than those traditionally taught.

Noninstructed students were not included in either of these studies, and there is no way to estimate the possible contribution of extraclassroom learning. Ellis and Rickard (1977) included a noninstructed control group in their effort to measure students' retention of introductory psychology factual content. They found that 4 months after the course ended, instructed students retained significantly more information than the control group. However, the mean differences in retention scores were surprisingly small. A 10-year review (1975–1985) of *Teaching of Psychology* identified no articles with titles indicating a focus on the retention of psychology coursework, although at least three included retention data (Ellis & Rickard, 1977; Goldwater & Acker, 1975; Lu, 1976). Some studies with imbedded retention data may have been overlooked, but it appears that the topic has received little attention from psychologists who contribute to this journal.

Our follow-up to the Ellis and Rickard (1977) investigation occurred in the practical framework of ongoing classroom teaching. The subjects were 74 lower division undergraduate students at the University of Alabama. Twenty-nine subjects received traditional classroom instruction (TT), 30 received instruction that emphasized the teaching of concepts (CT), and a control group (C) of 15 received no instruction. A retention test was administered approximately 4 months after subjects in the instructed groups had completed their introductory psychology course. Only instructed subjects who were not enrolled in a second psychology course were included. Subjects in the control group had never taken a psychology course.

The retention test consisted of 60 multiple-choice items, 30 from the instructor's manual and 30 constructed for this study. A textbook (Lefton, 1979) was required; a student workbook (Valvatne, 1978) was optional. In the CT condition, instructors emphasized concepts and illustrated these with examples. In the TT condition, the instructors' lectures centered around the materials contained in the text. Concepts were not emphasized.

Grades were assigned on a percentage basis (A = 90%, B = 80%, etc.), and there were no significant grade differences between the instructed groups, $F < 1.00$. The two instructed groups and the control group were compared on self-estimated overall college grade point average achieved to date. Again, no significant differences were found. The percentages of the 60 items correct for the three groups on the retention test were: CT = 68%, TT = 72%, and C = 62%. The analysis of variance applied to the retention scores for the three groups was significant, $F(2, 71) = 4.87$, $p < .01$. The textbook items, treated separately, yielded $F(2, 71) = 3.11$, $p < .05$; the constructed items yielded $F(2, 71) = 5.28$, $p < .01$. Further analyses indicated that scores for the instructed groups were not significantly different, but that both were significantly higher than those for the control group.

At first glance, 70% retention of introductory psychology material 4 months later seems reasonable enough. However, the uninstructed control group, in a finding similar to that reported by Ellis and Rickard (1977), answered 62% of the questions correctly. In our study and the Ellis and Rickard investigation, statistically significant differences in retention were found in favor of the instructed groups, but the percentage differences were small. There is evidence, of course, that students who take a large number of psychology courses do eventually retain a substantial amount of psychological information (e.g., graduate students admitted to PhD programs score well on the Graduate Record Examination in Psychology). Various comprehensive examinations administered by psychology departments may also be cited as evidence for retention. But at what point may students demonstrate retention? It would be of interest to follow undergraduate students as they progress through the psychology major, plotting retention of general psychology content as a function of accumulated psychology coursework.

The unexpectedly high performance of our control group must reflect learning from other sources, because those subjects had never taken a college psychology course. Apparently, the retention tests we used contained many items of common knowledge. Because of the inadequacies of the retention test, our conclusions must be viewed as preliminary and tentative. Clearly, future research must begin with the development of a more adequate test of retention.

References

Ellis, N. R., & Rickard, H. C. (1977). Evaluating the teaching of introductory psychology. *Teaching of Psychology, 4,* 128–132.

Eurich, A. D. (1934). Retention of knowledge acquired in a course in general psychology. *Journal of Applied Psychology, 18,* 209–219.

Goldwater, B. C., & Acker, L. E. (1975). Instructor-paced, mass-testing for mastery performance in an introductory psychology course. *Teaching of Psychology, 2,* 152–155.

Greene, E. B. (1931). The retention of information learned in college courses. *Journal of Educational Research, 24,* 262–273.

Lefton, L. A. (1979). *Psychology.* Boston: Allyn & Bacon.

Lu, P. H. (1976). Teaching human growth and development by the personalized system of instruction. *Teaching of Psychology, 3,* 127–128.

Tyler, R. W. (1933). Permanence of learning. *Journal of Higher Education, 4,* 203–204.

Valvatne, L. (1978). *Keeping pace: An active reading study guide to accompany Psychology.* Boston: Allyn & Bacon.

Wert, J. E. (1937). Twin examination assumptions. *Journal of Higher Education, 8,* 136–140.

Notes

1. William B. Beidleman is now at the University of Alabama in Birmingham.

Commonsense and Research Findings in Personality

Mark A. Barnett
Kansas State University

Several authors have expressed concern that beginning psychology students enter the classroom with numerous misconceptions about the subject matter (Gutman, 1979; Lamal, 1979; McKeachie, 1960; Panek, 1982; Vaughan, 1977). However, a review of these reports suggests that this concern may be largely unfounded. For example, despite the fact that investigators have used true–false tests (e.g., Vaughan's (1977) Test of Common Beliefs), that are purposely designed to "catch" students' misconceptions, most students are typically found to reject a majority of the presumed misbeliefs. Moreover, the number of students characterized as holding misconceptions may be inflated because several items included on these misconception tests are subject to qualification and, therefore, are not entirely false (Brown, 1984). As Brown (1983) concluded, "it turns out that widely shared misconceptions are rare indeed" (p. 209).

It is likely that the extent and importance of the "misconception problem" will be debated continually. However, by focusing attention on instances of student misbelief, investigators may be encouraging the impression that undergraduates know less psychology than they actually do. Indeed, much of what we attempt to teach students about human behavior may already be known to them through informal everyday experiences. That is, the findings of many research investigations presented in textbooks and in lectures may be commonsensical. Some support for this notion comes from a study reported by Gordon, Kleiman, and Hanie (1978). In this investigation, "empirical evidence is presented which suggests that much of the research literature in industrial-organizational psychology is material already familiar to those without training in the field and, hence, that this discipline appears preoccupied with commonsense matters" (p.

894). If this is true in other topic areas as well, it would appear to have important implications not only for researchers but for those who teach psychology.

My study assessed the extent to which research findings in psychology of personality textbooks are known to individuals varying in academic achievement levels and degree of formal training. Although group differences were of some interest, the primary concern in this investigation was to determine whether students with limited or no training in psychology can score above the chance level on a test of research findings in personality.

Method

Subjects

The subjects were 127 high school students (56 males and 71 females; mean age = 16.22 years) enrolled in five sections of an introductory psychology course at Manhattan High School (Manhattan, KS), 178 undergraduates (87 males and 91 females; mean age = 19.52 years) enrolled in a general psychology course, 21 undergraduates (6 males and 15 females; mean age = 18.33 years) enrolled in an honors general psychology course, 29 undergraduate members of junior and senior general academic honor societies (16 males and 13 females, mean age = 21.03 years), and 22 undergraduate members of the Psi Chi psychology academic honor society (8 males and 14 females; mean age = 22.64 years). All of the undergraduates attended Kansas State University. The students in general psychology, honors general psychology, and

35

Table 1. Sample Items From the PRT

2. The presence of objects associated with aggression (e.g., weapons) tends to cause angry people to be less aggressive than they otherwise would have been. (False, Aggression)
55. People who are in a "good mood" tend to be less helpful than people who are experiencing a neutral mood. (False, Altruism)
38. In elementary school textbooks, males are often portrayed as active and competent, while females are portrayed as passive and conforming. (True, Sex Roles and Sex Differences)
30. When people are frightened or anxious they prefer to avoid other people rather than seeking the company of others who are facing the same kind of situation. (False, Anxiety and Stress)
50. A good way to improve the health of many institutionalized patients is to give them an opportunity to make some choices and decisions. (True, Self-Control and Perceived Control)
42. Children's scores on standardized intelligence tests tend to be unrelated to how well they do in school. (False, Intelligence)
37. People with low self-esteem are typically more easily persuaded by others than are people with high self-esteem. (True, Self-Concept and Self-Esteem)

Note. Item answer and topic area appear in parentheses.

the junior/senior honor societies were majoring in a variety of disciplines.

Materials and Procedures

The Personality Research Test (PRT) is a 60-item true–false exam developed by the author for use in this study (see sample items in Table 1). The items on the test were derived from statements of research findings in personality as presented in several leading undergraduate textbooks in the area. Many of the research findings included on the test were reported by more than one author (if an inconsistency was found in two authors' presentations of a particular finding, the item was not included on the test). Items on the test were drawn from several personality research topics, including aggression, altruism, sex roles and sex differences, anxiety and stress, self-control and perceived control, intelligence, and self-concept and self-esteem. The topics and test items selected for inclusion on the PRT represented a broad

sampling of research presented in personality textbooks rather than an exhaustive review of all research in the area. The statements on the test were written to minimize the use of psychological jargon. Half of the items were "true" as stated; half were phrased to reflect the opposite of the reported finding (i.e., for half, "false" was the correct answer). Two personality psychologists reviewed each statement for accuracy, clarity, and avoidance of jargon. Items were eliminated or rewritten until they satisfied all three of these criteria.

The PRT was administered to the high school students in their regular classroom during the second day of class. The undergraduates were tested in small groups during the first few weeks of the semester. In addition to the PRT, all of the subjects completed a brief information sheet on which they indicated their sex, age, and grade point average (undergraduates enrolled in general psychology and honors general psychology were asked to provide their high school grade point average because a majority were in their first year at Kansas State University).

Results

Table 2 presents the mean scores and percentage correct on the PRT by student group and sex of subject. A 5 × 2 (Subject Group × Sex of Subject) analysis of variance (ANOVA) performed on the test scores revealed a significant main effect of student group, $F(4, 367) = 22.23$, $p < .001$. A Newman-Keuls test indicated that students in Psi Chi had significantly higher scores than did undergraduates in honors general psychology or junior/senior academic honor societies. The latter two groups had significantly higher scores than did the undergraduates in general psychology who, in turn, had significantly higher scores than did the high school students. No significant main or interaction effects involving sex of subject were found.

A series of t tests comparing each group's scores with the performance level expected by chance (i.e., 30 correct answers or 50%) was also conducted. All the groups scored well above chance, all $ts > 20.00$, $ps < .001$.

Scores on the PRT and the students' self-reported grade point averages were found to be related for both the high school students, $r(125) = .35$, $p < .01$, and general psychology undergraduates, $r(176) = .21$, $p < .01$. No significant relationship was found for the three honors groups (i.e.,

Table 2. Mean Scores and % Correct on the PRT by Student Group and Sex of Subject

Sex of Subject	Student Group				
	High School	General Psychology	Honors General Psychology	Junior/Senior Honors	Psi Chi
Males					
Mean Score	38.76	42.58	44.83	46.31	51.50
Percentage Correct	64.60%	70.97%	74.72%	77.18%	85.83%
Females					
Mean Score	40.21	43.62	48.79	47.61	50.42
Percentage Correct	67.02%	72.70%	81.32%	79.35%	84.03%
Total					
Mean Score	39.57[a]	43.11[b]	47.67[c]	46.90[c]	50.82[d]
Percentage Correct	65.95%	71.85%	79.45%	78.17%	84.70%

Note. Mean scores that do not share a common superscript differ at $p < .05$ as determined by the Newman-Keuls test.

honors general psychology, junior/senior honor societies, and Psi Chi), presumably because of a restricted range in self-reported grade point average for these students.

Discussion

The major result of this study is that students with little or no training in psychology scored well above the chance level on a test of research findings selected from personality textbooks. This result is consistent with the notion that the findings of research in this area may, to a considerable extent, be commonsensical. Perhaps textbook authors, concerned with clarity and conciseness in their writing, inadvertently choose to report the less complex and controversial findings, thereby underrepresenting research results that are less consistent with intuition. It should be noted, however, that in a similar demonstration of the commonsensical nature of research findings in psychology (Gordon et al., 1978), the test of research findings was drawn directly from refereed journals rather than from textbooks.

The students' scores on the PRT were found to be influenced by their academic achievement levels. Specifically, for the high school students and the undergraduates enrolled in general psychology, a significant relationship was found between self-reported grade point averages and scores on the PRT. Moreover, members of general academic honors groups consistently outperformed non-honors students, although their formal training in psychology was generally no more extensive. These findings are consistent with another report (Gutman, 1979), which suggested that better students may "know" more psychology and be better able to intuit research results than students with poorer academic standing. The finding that Psi Chi psychology honors students did significantly better than all of the other students tested is not surprising and indicates that formal training in psychology enhances one's knowledge of the subject matter (see Lamal, 1979).

In sum, the results of this study suggest that much of what personality textbooks purport to teach undergraduates about research findings in the area may already be known to them through common, informal experiences. The extent to which research findings in other areas, such as social psychology and developmental psychology, are commonsensical has yet to be determined. But, as teachers of psychology, perhaps we should not be overly concerned with assessing what undergraduates already know (or misconceive) to be true or false about psychology. It would seem to be more important to help them to appreciate the complexities of human behavior that are rarely captured in simple true–false statements.

References

Brown, L. T. (1983). Some more misconceptions about psychology among introductory psychology students. *Teaching of Psychology, 10,* 207–210.

Brown, L. T. (1984). Misconceptions about psychology aren't always what they seem. *Teaching of Psychology, 11,* 75–78.

Gordon, M. E., Kleiman, L. S., & Hanie, C. A. (1978). Industrial-organizational psychology: Open thy ears o house of Israel. *American Psychologist, 33,* 893–905.

Gutman, A. (1979). Misconceptions of psychology and performance in the introductory course. *Teaching of Psychology, 6,* 159–161.

Lamal, P. A. (1979). College students' common beliefs about psychology. *Teaching of Psychology, 6,* 155–158.

McKeachie, W. J. (1960). Changes in scores on the Northwestern Misconceptions Test in six elementary psychology courses. *Journal of Educational Psychology, 51,* 240–244.

Panek, P. E. (1982). Do beginning psychology of aging students believe 10 common myths of aging? *Teaching of Psychology, 9,* 104–105.

Vaughan, E. D. (1977). Misconceptions about psychology among introductory psychology students. *Teaching of Psychology, 4,* 138–141.

Notes

1. I thank Janet Cazier for her assistance in the development of the PRT, and E. Jerry Phares and William B. Griffitt for reviewing the test items. I am also grateful to the members of the various student groups for their participation in this study.

Research Findings in Developmental Psychology: Common Sense Revisited

Mark A. Barnett
Jill Knust
Tiffany McMillan
Jane Kaufman
Christina Sinisi
Kansas State University

Beginning with the efforts of McKeachie (1960) and Vaughan (1977), researchers have attempted to assess what undergraduates know (or misconceive) to be true about the subject matter in psychology. Barnett (1986) concluded that "much of what personality textbooks purport to teach undergraduates about research findings in the area may already be known to them through common, informal experiences" (p. 64). As an extension of Barnett's investigation, this study was designed to assess the extent to which research findings in developmental psychology textbooks are known to students with limited training in psychology. Moreover, we sought to determine whether the research findings that authors report in certain topic areas (e.g., personality and social–emotional development) are more commonsensical than the research findings reported in other areas.

Method

Subjects

The subjects were 137 high school students (53 males and 84 females; M age = 16.56 years) enrolled in six sections of an introductory psychology course at Manhattan High School (Manhattan, KS), 132 undergraduates (62 males and 70 females; M age = 20.77 years) enrolled in a general psychology course at Kansas State University (KSU), 25 undergraduate members of a senior general academic honor society at KSU (14 males and 11 females; M age = 21.56 years), 105 undergraduates (14 males and 91 females; M age = 26.95 years) enrolled in a human development course at California State University at Stanislaus, and 16 advanced undergraduate members of the Psi Chi psychology academic honor society at KSU (6 males and 10 females; M age = 22.38 years). The undergraduates in general psychology, human development, and the senior general academic honor society were majoring in a variety of disciplines. The students enrolled in the human development course had already completed the general psychology prerequisite and, in some cases, several other courses in psychology.

Materials and Procedure

The CART is a 90-item true–false exam developed by the authors for use in this study. The items were derived from statements of research findings in 13 leading undergraduate developmental psychology textbooks published in 1986 or 1987. A majority of research findings included on the test were reported in more than one textbook. The statements were written to minimize the use of psychological jargon. Forty-eight of the items were true as stated; 42 were false. Two developmental psychologists reviewed each statement for accuracy, clarity, and avoidance of jargon. Items were eliminated or rewritten until they satisfied all three of these criteria.

The 90 items were categorized into one of three major topic areas: (a) personality and social–emotional development (PSE); (b) cognitive and language development (COG); and (c) physical development, abilities, and needs (PD). For 61 of the 90 items (67.8%), four of the authors and another individual uninvolved in any other part of the study were in perfect agreement in their independent assignment of items to categories. For another 17 items (18.9%), four of the five judges agreed in their assignment. Disagreements in categorizing the remaining 12 items (13.3%) were resolved through brief group discussion. This procedure placed 44 items on the PSE subtest, 16 items on the COG subtest, and 30 items on the PD subtest. (In selecting and editing items for the CART, many research findings concerning cognitive and language development were deemed inappropriate because they required knowledge of psychological jargon. The elimination of these potential test items appears to account for the relatively small number of items on the COG subtest.) Table 1 presents two sample items from each subtest.

The CART was administered to the high school students in their regular classroom during the first week of the introductory psychology course. The undergraduates were tested in small groups during the first few weeks of the semester.

Results and Discussion

Table 2 presents the percentage correct on the CART by student group. Initially, t tests comparing each group's scores with the performance level expected by chance (i.e., 50%) were performed. All of the groups were found to score well above chance level on all of the subtests and on the overall test, all ts > 8.0, ps < .001. These results are consistent with the notion that the research findings presented in

Table 1. Sample Items From the CART Subtests

Subtest		Sample Item
PSE	19.	Spanking a child for acting aggressively tends to be an effective method for decreasing the child's general level of aggressiveness. (False)
PSE	75.	Overweight children tend to be less popular with peers than do normal weight children. (True)
COG	40.	A child tends to say his or her first word at about 1 year of age. (True)
COG	66.	Children from large families tend to have higher intelligence test scores than do children from smaller families. (False)
PD	17.	An infant's length at birth tends to be a good predictor of his or her height at maturity. (False)
PD	57.	Adolescents today tend to achieve their full adult height at a later age than adolescents did 100 years ago. (False)

Note. PSE = Personality and Social-Emotional Development subtest; COG = Cognitive and Language Development subtest; PD = Physical Development, Abilities, and Needs subtest. Answers appear in parentheses.

Table 2. Percentage Correct on the CART by Student Group

Student Group	CART			
	PSE	COG	PD	TOTAL
High School				
Males	72.3	74.5	65.6	70.5
Females	76.4	76.4	68.2	73.7
General Psychology				
Males	77.8	78.2	69.4	75.1
Females	76.9	79.7	70.3	75.2
Senior Honor Society				
Males	78.7	83.9	72.1	77.4
Females	80.8	74.4	71.2	76.5
Human Development				
Males	76.0	76.8	69.8	74.1
Females	81.3	78.7	76.8	79.3
Psi Chi				
Males	81.1	86.5	72.8	79.3
Females	85.2	85.0	79.7	83.3
Total	77.7	78.1	70.9	75.5

Note. PSE = Personality and Social-Emotional Development subtest; COG = Cognitive and Language Development subtest; PD = Physical Development, Abilities, and Needs subtest.

developmental psychology textbooks may, to a considerable extent, be commonsensical.

A $2 \times 5 \times 3$ (Sex of Subject $\times$ Student Group $\times$ Subtest) analysis of variance (ANOVA) revealed a significant effect of student group, $F(4, 405) = 10.93$, $p < .001$. A Newman-Keuls test indicated that students in Psi Chi ($M = 81.8\%$) and the human development course ($M = 78.6\%$) had significantly higher total scores on the CART than did the high school students ($M = 72.5\%$) and the undergraduates enrolled in the general psychology course ($M = 75.2\%$). Total scores of the undergraduates in the senior honor society ($M = 77.0\%$) were at an intermediate level and did not differ significantly from the scores of any other group. The heightened performance of the Psi Chi and human development groups appears consistent with the observation that formal training in psychology enhances one's knowledge of the subject matter (Gardner & Dalsing, 1986; Lamal, 1979). However, variables other than "formal training in psychology" may have contributed to the effect of student group. For example, the heightened performance of subjects in the older groups may reflect the fact that these individuals have had more time than subjects in the younger groups to interact with and learn about children in informal settings. Alternatively, older students may simply be more "test wise" and better able to intuit research results than their younger counterparts (the correlation between age and total CART scores for the entire sample was .33, $p < .001$).

Females ($M = 76.5\%$) had somewhat higher total scores on the CART than did males ($M = 73.8\%$), $F(1, 405) = 2.97$, $p < .09$. This sex difference may reflect the tendency of females to spend more time interacting with and learning about children (e.g., as babysitters) than do males (Kourany & LaBarbera, 1986).

Finally, the students consistently scored higher on the PSE ($M = 77.7\%$) and COG ($M = 78.1\%$) subtests of the CART than on the PD ($M = 70.9\%$) subtest, $F(2, 810) = 48.20$, $p < .001$. In comparison to the items on the other subtests, statements on the PD subtest appear to tap knowledge concerning children and adolescents that is: (a) less available through informal sources of information (e.g., television and magazines) and (b) less likely to be learned through personal experience and observation (see Table 1). It should be noted, however, that even on the PD subtest, the students' level of performance was still well above chance.

Conclusion

The major finding of this study is that many of the research results presented in leading developmental psychology textbooks, like many of those presented in leading personality textbooks (Barnett, 1986), may already be known to individuals with limited training in psychology. Although the results concerning the subtests suggest that there may be considerable variability in the extent to which research findings in particular areas of psychology are commonsensical, additional investigation across a broad range of topics within psychology is needed to address this issue.

How do we account for the major finding of our study? As suggested in the earlier report (Barnett, 1986), perhaps textbook authors are so concerned with clarity and conciseness in their writing that they "inadvertently choose to report the less complex and controversial findings, thereby underrepresenting research results that are less consistent with intuition" (p. 63). One alternative explanation (suggested by an anonymous reviewer) posits that by rewriting or eliminating potential test items that require knowledge of psychological jargon, we have made the CART easier than it otherwise would have been. There is no doubt that a test filled with jargon is more difficult than a test written in clear and understandable language. In writing items for the CART, our goal was to have incorrect answers reflect a student's failure to intuit a particular research result rather than a failure to comprehend what we were stating. Although the language unique to a discipline may indeed be an important indicator of the discipline's separation from common sense, jargon may also be used to obscure information that is otherwise understandable and, perhaps, commonly known.

Another explanation for the major finding (suggested by another anonymous reviewer) is that although complex and controversial research findings are probably contained in these textbooks, we may have tended not to write true–false items concerning such results because of the difficulty in doing so. Our only response to this contention is that it is unfounded. Although the CART was certainly not intended to be an exhaustive review of all the research findings presented in leading developmental psychology textbooks, we believe that the CART represents a broad and fair sampling of the research findings presented in these textbooks.

One important implication of our findings for teachers of developmental psychology is to use innovative teaching techniques that encourage students to appreciate the complexities of human development that often go far beyond common sense. Some promising procedures include classroom debates of controversial developmental issues (Moeller, 1985), discussion of videotaped demonstrations of developmental principles (Balch, 1986; Poole, 1986), and writing assignments that encourage students to critically review their own development as well as the results of research presented in developmental journals (Beers, 1985).

References

Balch, W. R. (1986). The use of student-performed developmental exercises in the classroom. *Teaching of Psychology, 13,* 140–142.

Barnett, M. A. (1986). Commonsense and research findings in personality. *Teaching of Psychology, 13,* 62–64.

Beers, S. E. (1985). Use of a portfolio writing assignment in a course on developmental psychology. *Teaching of Psychology, 12,* 94–96.

Gardner, R. M., & Dalsing, S. (1986). Misconceptions about psychology among college students. *Teaching of Psychology, 13,* 32–34.

Kourany, R. F. C., & LaBarbera, J. D. (1986). Babysitting: A milestone of early adolescence. *Journal of Early Adolescence, 6,* 197–200.

Lamal, P. A. (1979). College students' common beliefs about psychology. *Teaching of Psychology, 6,* 155–158.

McKeachie, W. J. (1960). Changes in scores on the Northwestern Misconceptions Test in six elementary psychology courses. *Journal of Educational Psychology, 51,* 240–244.

Moeller, T. G. (1985). Using classroom debates in teaching developmental psychology. *Teaching of Psychology, 12,* 207–209.

Poole, D. A. (1986). Laboratories and demonstrations in child development with unedited videotapes. *Teaching of Psychology, 13,* 212–214.

Vaughan, E. D. (1977). Misconceptions about psychology among introductory psychology students. *Teaching of Psychology, 4,* 138–141.

Notes

1. We thank Sandra McCoy for her assistance in developing the CART and Laura King and Susan Wanska for reviewing the test items. We are also grateful to the members of the various student groups for their participation in this study.

College Students' Misconceptions About Behavior Analysis

P. A. Lamal
University of North Carolina at Charlotte

One important goal of undergraduate psychology teachers should be to dispel students' misconceptions about psychology. One area that seems to be particularly fertile ground for misconceptions is behavior analysis. Unfortunately, misconceptions about behavior analysis are not limited to students; they are also found among writers of textbooks (Lamal, 1993; Morris, 1985; Todd & Morris, 1983; Wyatt, 1993) and among psychology faculty (DeBell & Harless, 1992). Some members of the Association for Behavior Analysis formed a special interest group in 1991, the main purpose of which is to try to increase the accurate characterization of behavior analysis in psychology textbooks as well as the popular media. Members of the group have reviewed many widely adopted introductory psychology textbooks to evaluate the extent and accuracy of their treatment of behavior analysis. Some members have also written to textbook authors and publishers, endorsing accurate characterizations of behavior analysis and calling attention to inaccurate portrayals. A symposium describing results of a review of introductory textbooks was presented at the 1993 meeting of the Association for Behavior Analysis.

DeBell and Harless (1992) described what they called five myths about the views held by Skinner. These myths were that Skinner (a) discounted the role of physiology and genetics in behavior, (b) believed that any behavior can be conditioned, (c) neglected uniqueness of the individual, (d) viewed punishment as a preferred method of behavior control, and (e) denied the existence of internal states. DeBell and Harless described the basis of each of these myths and constructed a 14-item, true–false questionnaire to determine the prevalence of these myths. Seven of the items addressed these myths, and the others surveyed different knowledge about Skinner's views. The questionnaire was administered to several groups.

DeBell and Harless (1992) found that advanced undergraduates, beginning graduate students, advanced graduate students, and psychology faculty missed significantly more myth items than general knowledge items. DeBell and Harless also found no significant differences in the number of myth items missed by the beginning graduate students, the advanced graduate students, and psychology faculty. However, advanced undergraduates missed significantly more myth items than the beginning and advanced graduate students and the psychology faculty. The purpose of my study was to partially replicate DeBell and Harless's (1992) study with advanced undergraduates from a different university and with a somewhat different instrument. I studied advanced undergraduates because they appear to believe more myths than other students (DeBell & Harless, 1992). Unlike DeBell and Harless, I used a pretest–posttest design with an academic course as the intervention. Previous studies have used this procedure to evaluate changes in misconceptions about other topics in psychology (e.g., Lamal, 1979; McKeachie, 1960; Vaughan, 1977).

Method

Subjects

Subjects were students in the Introduction to Behavior Modification course I teach at the University of North Carolina at Charlotte. All psychology majors in the course had completed an introductory psychology course. The course met for three 5-min lectures and one 2-hr laboratory per week. The textbook was Martin and Pear's (1992) *Behavior Modification: What It Is and How to Do It.*

For the spring 1992 semester, complete data were collected on 13 of the 16 students who finished the course. Complete data were collected for 10 of the 16 students who finished the course during the spring 1993 semester. Twelve of the 16 students in the 1992 class were psychology majors; 14 of the 16 students in the 1993 class were psychology majors. All students in both classes were juniors or seniors. They were told that participation was voluntary and that their responses would have no effect on their course grade.

Instrument

A 13-item, true–false questionnaire was used. Twelve of the items were taken from the instrument used by DeBell and Harless (1992), with one important change. Rather than referring to Skinner in each item ("According to Skinner . . ." and "Skinner believes . . ."), reference is made to be-

havior analysts or behavior analysis ("Behavior analysts believe . . ." and "Behavior analysis is . . ."). This change was made to counteract what seems to be another myth, namely, that Skinner wrote everything that constitutes the corpus of behavior analysis. Also, my questionnaire did not include DeBell and Harless's Items 7 ("Skinner is well known for his work with pigeons") and 11 ("Skinner recognizes the existence of human consciousness"). For DeBell and Harless's Item 7, I substituted "Behavior analysts showed that principles of learning apply better to animals than humans." The purpose was to tap a possible misconception of wider scope than that captured by DeBell and Harless's Item 7. The fact that Skinner was well-known for his work with pigeons does not necessarily imply that principles of learning do not apply to humans; my Item 7 is meant to elicit that misconception, if present. Also, for DeBell and Harless's Item 11, I substituted "Behavior analysts focus on behavior that is observable and measurable." The concept of human consciousness continues to be a topic of disagreement and debate, even among some behavior analysts. The importance of focusing on observable and measurable behavior is not a contentious topic among behavior analysts. Also, I added Item 13 ("Behavior analysis is a popular viewpoint in American society"). This addition resulted from my observation that many people hold the misconception that behavior analysis has had a major impact on American society (Lamal, 1989). Item 8 was revised ("Behavior analysts support the use of physical [added] punishment in controlling human behavior") because many behavior analysts support the use of punishment in some situations. The instrument was administered on the second class day (pretest) and penultimate class day (posttest) in both the 1992 and 1993 classes.

Results and Discussion

The 1992 and 1993 class means of number of questionnaire items answered correctly on the pretests were 8.38 (range = 6 to 11, SD = 1.34) and 9.20 (range = 8 to 11, SD = 0.98), respectively; posttest means were 8.77 (range = 6 to 11, SD = 1.31) and 9.00 (range = 5 to 11, SD = 1.48), respectively. There are no meaningful differences.

Analysis of the individual items by year and pretest–posttest revealed clear differences among some items, as presented in Table 1. Students were most misinformed about the species limits on conditioning, behavior analysts' belief in the importance of genetics, and the impact of behavior analysis on American society (Items 2, 4, and 13, respectively). Furthermore, the course had no significant effect in changing these misconceptions. The misconceptions about conditioning and genetics are consistent with DeBell and Harless's (1992) findings. Given Todd and Morris's (1983) finding that textbooks commonly presented misconceptions of behavior analysis as being totally environmentalistic, it is not surprising to find that students are misinformed about the role of genetics.

My students' most common misconceptions (Items 2, 4, and 13) were immune to change, even after a course in behavior analysis. Clearly, I need to work at correcting these misconceptions in future courses. Although Items 2, 4, and 13 were addressed in class and Items 4 and 13 were covered

Table 1. Number of Undergraduates Correctly Responding on Pretest and Posttest

| | Year | | | |
| | 1992[a] | | 1993[b] | |
Item	Pretest	Posttest	Pretest	Posttest
1. According to behavior analysts, negative reinforcement is another term for punishment. F	13	13	8	9
2. Behavior analysts believe that any behavior can be conditioned.[c] F	1	3	0	0
3. Behavior analysts believe that theories that attempt to explain psychological phenomena through hypothetical constructs are useful to psychology. F	7	7	6	7
4. Behavior analysts believe genetics play an important role in behavior.[c] T	3	5	4	4
5. Behavior analysts use rigorous statistical analyses in examining data from their studies.[c] F	7	3	8	4
6. Behavior analysts recognize the uniqueness of the individual.[c] T	5	11	9	10
7. Behavior analysts showed that principles of learning apply better to animals than humans. F	8	13	8	7
8. Behavior analysts support the use of physical punishment in controlling human behavior.[c] F	13	11	9	7
9. Behavior analysts demonstrated that shaping has minimal impact in teaching new behaviors. F	12	13	10	10
10. In general, behavior analysts believe positive reinforcement is more effective than punishment.[c] T	12	12	9	10
11. Behavior analysts focus on behavior that is observable and measurable. T	13	13	9	10
12. Behavior analysis discusses secondary reinforcers; one example of these is money. T	13	13	9	10
13. Behavior analysis is a popular viewpoint in American society. F	3	2	4	3

Note. T = true; F = false.
[a] $n = 13$. [b] $n = 10$. [c] Designated a myth by DeBell and Harless (1992), substituting "Skinner" for "behavior analysts."

in the course textbook (Martin & Pear, 1992), that information was demonstrably insufficient. With respect to Item 2, I said in class a few times that behavior analysts do not claim that any behavior can be conditioned. The textbook, however, does not explicitly make this point. Item 4 is addressed in a note on one page at the end of the first chapter of the textbook. The authors stated that behaviorists, starting with Watson, have not denied the importance of the role of genetics in behavior. In class, I listed on the board the individual's genetic endowment as one of the important categories of causal factors determining behavior. Martin and Pear addressed Item 13 in a note at the end of the second chapter where they abstracted an article (Lamal, 1989) in which the author concluded that behavior analysis had little impact on American culture and that only a small minority of psychologists identify themselves as behavior analysts. I also said in class a couple of times that behavior analysis is not a popular view.

A point about my revision of the item referring to physical punishment (Item 8) is warranted. Some behavior analysts support the use of physical punishment, at least in certain circumscribed situations. But, as a blanket statement without a context, it is misleading to assert that behavior analysts support the use of physical punishment. This item should probably be revised if used again.

The advanced undergraduates in this study performed about the same as those in DeBell and Harless's (1992) study; DeBell and Harless's advanced undergraduates answered a mean of 4.33 out of 7 myth questions incorrectly. Those in my study answered mean numbers of 4.62 (1992 pretest) and 3.70 (1993 pretest) out of 13 myth questions

incorrectly, for an overall mean of 4.22. Results from students at other institutions are needed for a more accurate picture of the extent of misconceptions about behavior analysis.

Although my items referred to behavior analysts or behavior analysis rather than to Skinner (as in DeBell & Harless's, 1992, study), this difference in wording does not seem to have made much difference. Nevertheless, I advocate using the terms *behavior analysts* or *behavior analysis* to avoid the emergence of a new misconception, namely, that all of behavior analysis is encompassed in Skinner's writings.

In summary, few of these students held many of the common misconceptions about behavior analysis, but the few misconceptions they held were resistant to change. What to do? One technique known to many teachers is simple repetition. To overcome misconceptions, relevant accurate statements probably must be repeated numerous times throughout a course. Also, during the last class day and before the final exam, I now discuss the students' most widely held misconceptions. One benefit of giving a pretest is that it enables the teacher to identify misconceptions at the outset. A teacher may also conduct a contest that would reward those who obtain the best pretest–posttest gain scores.

References

DeBell, C. S., & Harless, D. K. (1992). B. F. Skinner: Myth and misperception. *Teaching of Psychology, 19*, 68–73.

Lamal, P. A. (1979). College students' common beliefs about psychology. *Teaching of Psychology, 6*, 155–158.

Lamal, P. A. (1989). The impact of behaviorism on our culture: Some evidence and conjectures. *The Psychological Record, 39,* 529–535.

Lamal, P. A. (1993, May). Behavior analysis: What students learn about it in *Understanding Psychology* (2nd ed.), by Robert S. Feldman, and other introductory texts. In W. J. Wyatt & B. Newman (Chairs), *Killing us softly? Representations and misrepresentations of behavior analysis in popular introductory psychology texts.* Symposium conducted at the meeting of the Association for Behavior Analysis, Chicago.

Martin, G., & Pear, J. (1992). *Behavior modification: What it is and how to do it* (4th ed.). Englewood Cliffs, NJ: Prentice Hall.

McKeachie, W. J. (1960). Changes in scores on the Northwestern Misconceptions Test in six elementary psychology courses. *Journal of Educational Psychology, 51,* 240–244.

Morris, E. K. (1985). Public information, dissemination, and behavior analysis. *The Behavior Analyst, 8,* 95–110.

Todd, J. T., & Morris, E. K. (1983). Misconception and miseducation: Presentations of radical behaviorism in psychology textbooks. *The Behavior Analyst, 6,* 153–160.

Vaughan, E. D. (1977). Misconceptions about psychology among introductory psychology students. *Teaching of Psychology, 4,* 138–141.

Wyatt, W. J. (1993, May). A review of *Psychology: Themes and variations* (2nd ed.), by Wayne Weiten. In W. J. Wyatt & B. Newman (Chairs), *Killing us softly? Representations and misrepresentations of behavior analysis in popular introductory psychology texts.* Symposium conducted at the meeting of the Association for Behavior Analysis, Chicago.

Counterattitudinal Advocacy as a Means of Enhancing Instructional Effectiveness: How to Teach Students What They Do Not Want to Know

Richard L. Miller
William J. Wozniak
Marci R. Rust
Beverly R. Miller
Jennifer Slezak
University of Nebraska at Kearney

A survey of 1,236 adult Americans (Gallup & Newport, 1991) reported that 49% believed in ESP and another 22% were not sure whether there is such a phenomenon. The survey further revealed that substantial percentages of the population either believe in or are unsure about many phenomena for which there is little or no scientific support, including paranormal explanations of déjà vu, subliminal perception, and the existence of extraterrestrial beings.

Teaching a college course can be challenging when students come into the classroom with preconceived notions such as those addressed in the Gallup poll. This challenge is especially noteworthy in the field of psychology when university instructors are pitted against the purveyors of pop psychology who proclaim many dubious, if not patently false, ideas as truth.

Students' commitment to unfounded beliefs about psychological processes is not a new phenomenon. Nixon (1925) noted "The beginning student especially, while willing to admit ignorance on many technical questions, comes to psychology with certain concepts of causation in human behavior quite firmly fixed" (p. 418). His research revealed that the prevalence of belief in nonscientifically sanctioned ideas about human behavior was 41.1% for women and

35.1% for men. Other researchers have reported similar results. For example, Lehman and Fenton (1930) found the percentage of misconceptions about psychological topics among college students to be about 50%. Psychologists' concern about students' unfounded beliefs was reflected in a review by Caldwell and Lundeen (1931) that included an annotated listing of 23 studies, conducted between 1887 and 1930, of superstitious beliefs among college students.

Have things changed since these studies were conducted? Not really. In fact, some forms of unfounded beliefs, especially belief in the paranormal, have increased (see Singer & Benassi, 1981; Woods, 1984). In a study of undergraduates, Messer and Griggs (1989) found that 99% of those surveyed expressed belief in at least 1 of the 10 paranormal phenomena listed on their questionnaire.

The record of success of traditional classroom approaches in overcoming students' unfounded beliefs has been discouraging (Lamal, 1979). Tobacyk (1983) documented a reduction in paranormal belief attributable to a course specifically designed to examine evidence of the paranormal critically. Using the Belief in the Paranormal Scale, which ranges from a high of 125 to a low of 25 (Jones, Russell, & Nickel, 1977), Tobacyk found that students entered with a belief score just above the median (78), which was reduced to a score of 60 after completing the course. Unfortunately, many unfounded beliefs still remained. Similarly, Woods (1984) found that, after students had completed a reading program designed to reduce beliefs in the paranormal, scores on the Belief in the Paranormal Scale fell from the precourse mean of 71 to a posttest mean of 51. Again, many unfounded beliefs remained. Similarly, Banziger's (1983) 1-week course on parapsychology taught to participants in an elderhostel program resulted in a reduction of 8 points on the Belief in the Paranormal Scale. Finally, Gray (1985), whose one-semester course emphasizing methodological issues resulted in some reduction in unfounded beliefs, stated: "Should we be pleased that belief in ESP can be brought down from 85% to about 50%, or should we be seriously concerned that 50% of those tested still believe in ESP, UFOs, and Reincarnation?" (p. 269).

When students arrive on the first day of class with a preconceived notion about the content of the class, instructors cannot assume that simply laying out the facts will cause them to change their minds. In fact, students will more likely persevere in their false beliefs than readily renounce them, even when confronted with disconfirming evidence (Nisbett & Ross, 1980). Anderson, Lepper, and Ross (1980) reported that changing a false belief can be surprisingly difficult once an individual has generated ideas to support it. Thus, the assumption that students walk into the classroom with an open mind that can be easily swayed by the classroom experience is clearly not true. Indeed, students may inoculate themselves from potential cognitive changes by various techniques, some of which may even preserve good grades. Students may superficially process the arguments to the extent that reasonable test performance can be achieved; assume that the arguments apply only in a limited context (such as the classroom); or, at worst, simply ignore arguments that run counter to their present beliefs. The problem of how to change a student's mind seems to be more difficult than how to fill a student's mind.

Given the lack of dramatic change in students' paranormal beliefs produced by traditional teaching methods, it seems that college-level instruction should impart up-to-date factual information designed to counter students' erroneous beliefs and be a forum for attitude change. This is not a new goal for higher education. However, the view that the university instructor should institute specific techniques designed to change students' attitudes is relatively new.

One promising method for changing attitudes is derived from the induced compliance paradigm (Festinger & Carlsmith, 1959) and involves the use of counterattitudinal advocacy. A variant of counterattitudinal advocacy was used by Lord, Lepper, and Preston (1984) and Anderson and Sechler (1986) to reduce belief perseverance. In these studies, participants were required to explain why the opposite of their own beliefs might be true. This approach resulted in a less biased consideration of the evidence. A procedure for eliciting counterattitudinal advocacy that is easily implemented in the classroom was developed by Cohen (1962). It requires individuals to write an essay advocating a position that is counter to their privately held opinions. When the subjects' opinions are reassessed, those who have written a counterattitudinal essay show more atti-

tude change toward the advocated position than those who have written a neutral essay.

Results of these studies may be accounted for by Festinger's (1957) concept of cognitive dissonance. According to Festinger, beliefs and attitudes must maintain a degree of consistency. Inconsistent or contradictory beliefs and attitudes create a state of dissonance, which is said to be an unpleasant and highly motivational state. While in a state of cognitive dissonance, participants are driven to reduce the cognitive tension by somehow resolving the conflict among cognitions. In the earlier example, one's privately held opinion concerning an issue and the fact that he or she just wrote an essay espousing the opposite position puts the participant in a state of dissonance. If the essay was not written for a strong reason (e.g., the payment of money), the participant must somehow reduce the cognitive dissonance. Because the participant cannot deny writing the essay, the remaining dissonance-reducing option is to change the original opinion.

Various factors have been shown to be important to the success of counterattitudinal advocacy in changing attitudes. Linder, Cooper, and Jones (1967) noted the importance of free choice. Students who were asked to write an essay and promised a small incentive exhibited significant change, but those who were required (no-choice condition) to write a counterattitudinal essay exhibited very little change. Zanna and Sande (1986) examined the effects of writing alone or in a group and demonstrated that diffusion of responsibility in a group-writing situation can lessen the dissonance effects. Zimbardo (1965) noted that the amount of effort expended in the counterattitudinal advocacy can increase the amount of attitude change, and Axsom (1989) reported that mere anticipation of high effort is sufficient to arouse dissonance.

In our study, we applied the technique of counterattitudinal advocacy to teaching introductory psychology. A pre- and posttreatment assessment of attitudes concerning a set of psychology topics was the design we used. The topics were selected on the basis of their potential for irrational (and wrong) opinions concerning these topics by students. The treatment was an in-class assignment requiring that students write an essay espousing a position opposite to their own or read such an essay written by another student. The design also permitted assessment of the effects of different means of covering the material (i.e., lecture, book, lecture and book, or no coverage).

Method

Participants

Participants were 71 introductory psychology students (41 women and 30 men) enrolled in one of two sections taught by the same instructor during the fall 1993 semester at the University of Nebraska at Kearney. Participants completed the study as part of their regular course routine. Fifteen participants in the pretest were not present in class at the time of the posttest; thus, their data were discarded from the analysis.

Materials

The pre- and posttreatment questionnaires were composed of the same 48 items. Each item was a declarative statement concerning a psychological phenomenon (e.g., "Under hypnosis, people can be induced to perform feats that they would otherwise find impossible"). The initial population of such items was taken from Bolt's (1989) *Instructor's Resources for Use With Myers: Psychology* (2nd ed.). The instructor of the introductory psychology classes reviewed a list of 190 statements from Bolt's *Instructor's Resources* and indicated the type of coverage each topic would receive. Because the instructor used a book other than the Myers text, each item was rated as to whether it would be covered (a) in the textbook only, (b) in a lecture only, (c) in both the book and lecture, or (d) in neither the book nor the lecture. From the entire list of items, a four-person panel of senior undergraduate psychology students selected 12 items from each category of coverage on the basis of how likely introductory psychology students would be to hold an incorrect opinion about the topic. Preference was given to topics related to paranormal phenomena.

On the pre- and posttreatment questionnaires, each of the 48 items thus selected was accompanied by a 6-point scale ranging from 1 (*strongly agree*) to 6 (*strongly disagree*). The items were balanced with respect to which end of the scale represented the answer that was scientifically supported.

Procedure

The pretreatment questionnaire was administered by the instructor during the third week of the semester. All students enrolled in the courses completed the questionnaire, which also requested demographic data and their name. Completed questionnaires were assessed by the experimenters so that two topics could be assigned to each subject. The topics were selected on the basis of whether the participant's response agreed or strongly agreed with the position contrary to existing scientific evidence. One of the topics was assigned to the participant so that he or she could write an essay supporting the opposite position; the other topic was assigned so that the participant could read an essay, supporting the opposite position, which would be written by another participant.

Participants were instructed to complete an in-class writing assignment 3 weeks before the end of the semester. At this time, each participant was given the preassigned writing topic and the following instructions:

> The Psychology Department is assessing a number of introductory psychology classes with regard to their knowledge of psychological issues. Your task is to write a persuasive essay supporting the position listed below. You will have 30 minutes to organize your thoughts and write your essay. Support the position with as many valid arguments as you can think of. This essay will be graded by a student reader as well as a professor in the Psychology Department. Raise your hand when you are done; do not leave your seat.

Participants were not given specific information on how the writing assignment would be graded or what portion of their course grade the assignment would represent. After 30

min, the essays were collected and redistributed to the participants. Each participant was given an essay written by another participant that supported an alternative position the reader also opposed. Participants received the following instructions about reading the essay:

> Please read over the essay and assess it on how persuaded you are by the arguments in the essay. Assign a letter grade (A–F, no plusses or minuses). You have 10 minutes to do this task. Raise your hand when you are done; do not leave your seat.

All essays were then collected by the experimenters. The entire task fit into one class period of 50 min. The posttest questionnaire was administered during finals week by the instructor 3 weeks after the writing assignment had been completed.

Design

The three independent variables were advocacy condition, time of testing, and type of coverage. Advocacy condition consisted of writing an essay, reading an essay, or neither reading nor writing an essay. To obtain scores for the latter condition, comparison items that met the criteria for being chosen for writing/reading were randomly selected from the pretest questionnaire. Students' beliefs were assessed on the full set of items both before and after counterattitudinal advocacy. The four levels of topic coverage were book only, lecture only, book and lecture, and material not covered in either the book or the lecture. Equal numbers of participants from each level of topic coverage were assigned to each level of advocacy condition.

Results

Half the ratings were transformed so that, in all cases, a high rating indicated a high degree of agreement with the scientifically accepted position. Subjects' scores indicating the extent to which they agreed with the correct scientific position were analyzed using a 3 (advocacy condition) × 2 (time: pre- vs. posttest) repeated measures analysis of variance (ANOVA). A significant main effect for the advocacy condition was found, $F(2, 285) = 21.30$, $p < .001$, along with a significant main effect of time, $F(1, 285) = 816.24$, $p < .001$. The advocacy condition × time interaction was also significant, $F(2, 285) = 19.54$, $p < .001$.

Figure 1 presents the effects of the different advocacy conditions. All participants, regardless of advocacy condition, showed significant change toward an opinion more consonant with the scientific view. However, the extent of change differed depending on the type of counterattitudinal behavior in which students engaged. Simple effects analysis of the posttest means indicated that students who wrote counterattitudinal essays (M = 4.46) showed the greatest change at the posttest in comparison to those who read (M = 3.29) counterattitudinal material, $F(1, 143) = 31.53$, $p < .001$, as well as with those in the control condition who neither read nor wrote (M = 3.79) about such material, $F(1, 205) = 10.78$, $p < .001$. Students who only read a counterattitudinal essay showed the least amount of change, scoring

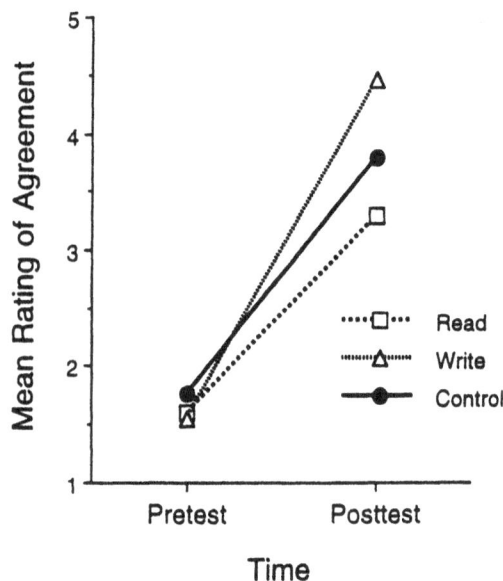

Figure 1. Mean agreement scores as a function of counterattitudinal advocacy condition and time of testing.

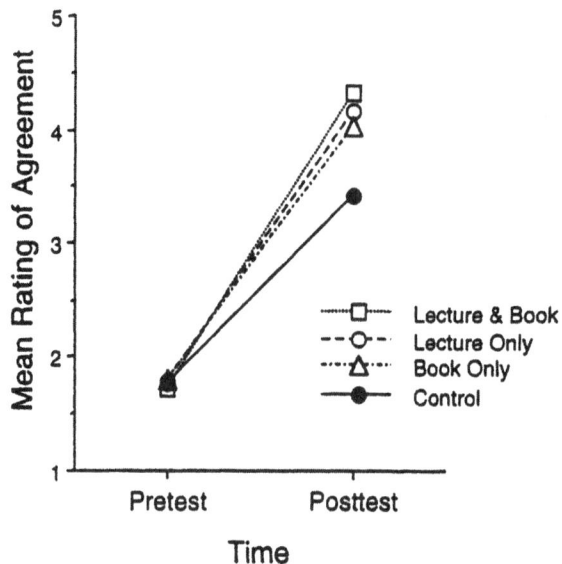

Figure 2. Extent to which participants agreed with the scientifically accepted position as a function of type of coverage and time of testing.

significantly lower than those in the control condition, $F(1, 204) = 16.77$, $p < .001$.

To examine the relative effectiveness of different ways of covering the instructional material, participants' scores on the control group items (i.e., those about which the participant neither read nor wrote) were analyzed using a 4 (type of coverage) × 2 (time: pre- vs. posttest) repeated measures ANOVA. Significant main effects for type of coverage, $F(3, 126) = 5.73$, $p < .001$, and time, $F(1, 126) = 601.08$, $p < .001$, were found. Also, the type of coverage × time interaction was significant, $F(3, 126) = 5.32$, $p < .01$. Figure 2 presents these means.

Simple effects analysis of the posttest means indicated that coverage of the material by lecture (M = 4.15), $F(1, 145) = 5.39$, $p < .05$, and by lecture plus textbook (M = 4.31), $F(1, 131) = 7.37$, $p < .01$, were both effective in causing a belief change as compared to scores on the posttest items not covered during the course (M = 3.40). Reading material in the textbook (M = 4.02) was not significantly different from no coverage, $F(1, 145) = 3.11$, $p < .08$. None of the three pedagogical methods differed from one another in effectiveness, $Fs < 1$.

Discussion

Counterattitudinal advocacy in the form of writing an essay supporting an accepted scientific position was shown to be effective in changing students' erroneous beliefs about psychological phenomena. Reading another student's persuasive essay was not as effective in overcoming erroneous beliefs. In fact, there was less change concerning issues on which students read someone else's essay than there was on issues that were simply covered in the course using ordinary pedagogical methods (i.e., lectures and/or textbook).

Why does writing a counterattitudinal essay change students' erroneous beliefs? One possible explanation is that

writing requires a certain amount of effort. However, the process of reading and grading another student's paper also requires some effort, but this proved to be considerably less effective in producing change. A second explanation is that arguments that individuals generate for themselves are the most convincing—at least to those individuals. As Greenwald (1968) pointed out, self-persuasion is more effective than listening to the arguments of others because it is more salient, more personally relevant, and more memorable.

Reading, which showed significantly less change in comparison to writing or even noncoverage of the topic, may lose effectiveness partly due to the lack of self-persuasion effects. In addition, readers may perceive the quality of arguments generated by another student in a single class period as particularly weak. Thus, students may reason that if this is the best case that can be made for renouncing their beliefs, then they are not convinced. Moreover, even in the case of a well-written essay, students may dismiss another student's arguments based on a judgment of source credibility without giving serious consideration to the content of the essay. At any rate, students demonstrated less change on the items they read about than on the items not even covered in the course. Reading arguments that can easily be dismissed may allow students to resist efforts to correct their erroneous beliefs and may run the additional danger of inoculating them against other change efforts.

Numerous studies concerned with changing students' erroneous beliefs have examined the effectiveness of taking a course in psychology (e.g., Gray, 1985; Tobacyk, 1983; Woods, 1984). An additional finding in our study was that exposure to psychological information through course work reduced students' erroneous beliefs, but the particular pedagogical technique used made little or no difference. Students were just as likely to accept the scientific position as a result of listening to a lecture, reading the textbook, or doing both, although simply reading the textbook was the least effective. Data reported in Figure 1 suggest that, to some extent, students discarded erroneous beliefs about psychological phenomena that were not covered in the course at all. This result may be due to some sort of transfer effect. However, this apparent change was more likely due to a regression artifact because all of the items used in the tests were, by selection criteria, ones on which students initially scored very low. Thus, the control group means could be best viewed as a baseline with which to compare the relative effectiveness of the different instructional techniques.

In summary, our results demonstrate that (a) students' attitudes and beliefs are frequently inconsistent with current scientifically supported positions and (b) writing an essay that argues for the counterattitudinal position (i.e., the current scientific position) produces greater change in students' erroneous beliefs than normally occurs during a regular college class. Future research should compare the relative importance of effort versus self-generation of arguments in producing counterattitudinal advocacy effects.

Use as a Classroom Technique

To make effective use of counterattitudinal advocacy as a classroom technique, one should ensure that several conditions are met. First, the instructor must maintain the appearance that the student has a degree of free choice in the assignment. This can be done by making the essay-writing task optional (e.g., done for extra credit) or by allowing students to choose freely from the many topics about which they have erroneous beliefs. Second, the advocacy task should be one in which the student is clearly responsible for the arguments he or she generates. Therefore, group assignments are not recommended. Third, the greater the amount of effort expended in the advocacy task, the greater the amount of change one may expect. However, overexposure to counterattitudinal messages should be avoided, given Cacioppo and Petty's (1979) finding that maximum change occurred with three exposures to a counterattitudinal message but that five exposures reduced the amount of change.

Finally, note that we applied the advocacy technique toward the end of the course after students had been introduced to the scientific method, critical thinking, and relevant content. Our assessment of their essays indicated that the students' arguments reflected this grounding in the scientific literature. Thus, the timing of this exercise may be important in ensuring meaningful change. Also, within the constraints listed earlier, advocacy tasks are not limited to essay writing but could include debates, oral presentations, or other activities that provide a forum for self-persuasion.

References

Anderson, C. A., Lepper, M. R., & Ross, L. (1980). Perseverance of social theories: The role of explanation in persistence of discredited information. *Journal of Personality and Social Psychology, 39,* 1037–1049.

Anderson, C. A., & Sechler, E. S. (1986). Effects of explanation and counterexplanation on the development and use of social theories. *Journal of Personality and Social Psychology, 50,* 24–34.

Axsom, D. (1989). Cognitive dissonance and behavior change in psychotherapy. *Journal of Experimental Social Psychology, 25,* 234–252.

Banziger, G. (1983). Normalizing the paranormal: Short-term and long-term change in belief in the paranormal among older learners during a short course. *Teaching of Psychology, 10,* 212–214.

Bolt, M. (1989). *Instructor's resources for use with Myers: Psychology* (2nd ed.). New York: Worth.

Cacioppo, J. T., & Petty, R. E. (1979). Effects of message repetition and position on cognitive response, recall, and persuasion. *Journal of Personality and Social Psychology, 37,* 97–109.

Caldwell, O. W., & Lundeen, G. E. (1931). Students' attitudes regarding unfounded beliefs. *Science Education, 15,* 246–266.

Cohen, A. R. (1962). An experiment on small rewards for discrepant compliance and attitude change. In J. W. Brehm & A. R. Cohen (Eds.), *Explorations in cognitive dissonance* (pp. 73–78). New York: Wiley.

Festinger, L. (1957). *A theory of cognitive dissonance.* Palo Alto, CA: Stanford University Press.

Festinger, L., & Carlsmith, J. M. (1959). Cognitive consequences of forced compliance. *Journal of Abnormal and Social Psychology, 58,* 203–210.

Gallup, G. H., & Newport, F. (1991). Belief in paranormal phenomena among American adults. *The Skeptical Inquirer, 15,* 137–146.

Gray, T. (1985). Changing unsubstantiated belief: Testing the ignorance hypothesis. *Canadian Journal of Behavioral Science, 17,* 263–270.

Greenwald, A. G. (1968). Cognitive learning, cognitive response to persuasion, and attitude change. In A. G. Greenwald, T. C. Brock, & T. M. Ostrom (Eds.), *Psychological foundations of attitudes* (pp. 147–170). New York: Academic.

Jones, W., Russell, D., & Nickel, T. (1977). Belief in the paranormal scale: An objective instrument to measure belief in magical phenomena and causes. *JSAS Catalog of Selected Documents in Psychology, 7,* 100 (Ms. No. 1577).

Lamal, P. A. (1979). College students' common beliefs about psychology. *Teaching of Psychology, 6,* 155–158.

Lehman, H. C., & Fenton, N. (1930). The prevalence of certain misconceptions and superstitions among college students before and after a course in psychology. *Education, 50,* 485–494.

Linder, D. E., Cooper, J., & Jones, E. E. (1967). Decision freedom as a determinant of the role of incentive magnitude in attitude change. *Journal of Personality and Social Psychology, 6,* 245–254.

Lord, C. G., Lepper, M. E., & Preston, E. (1984). Considering the opposite: A corrective strategy for social judgment. *Journal of Personality and Social Psychology, 47,* 1231–1243.

Messer, W. S., & Griggs, R. A. (1989). Student belief and involvement in the paranormal and performance in introductory psychology. *Teaching of Psychology, 16,* 187–191.

Nisbett, R. E., & Ross, L. (1980). *Human inference: Strategies and shortcomings of social judgment.* Englewood Cliffs, NJ: Prentice Hall.

Nixon, H. K. (1925). Popular answers to some psychological questions. *American Journal of Psychology, 36,* 418–423.

Singer, B. F., & Benassi, V. A. (1981). Occult beliefs. *American Scientist, 69,* 49–55.

Tobacyk, J. J. (1983). Reduction in paranormal belief among participants in a college course. *The Skeptical Inquirer, 8,* 57–61.

Woods, P. J. (1984). Evidence for the effectiveness of a reading program in changing beliefs in the paranormal. *The Skeptical Inquirer, 9,* 67–70.

Zanna, M. P., & Sande, G. N. (1986). The effects of collective actions on the attitudes of individual group members: A dissonance analysis. In M. P. Zanna, J. M. Olson, & C. P. Herman (Eds.), *Social influence: The Ontario Symposium* (Vol. 5, pp. 151–163). Hillsdale, NJ: Lawrence Erlbaum Associates, Inc.

Zimbardo, P. (1965). The effect of effort and improvisation in self-persuasion produced by role playing. *Journal of Experimental Social Psychology, 1,* 103–120.

Notes

1. We thank Theresa Wadkins, who provided us access to her General Psychology classes; Victor Benassi, who assisted us in locating numerous references related to this research; and Sandra Peterson, who assisted in data collection. Also, we thank Charles L. Brewer, Joseph J. Benz, and three anonymous reviewers for their critical reading of an earlier draft of this article. Preparation of this article was supported by a Research Services Council Grant provided by the University of Nebraska at Kearney.

4. INTRODUCTORY TEXTBOOKS: OBJECTIVE FEATURES

Introductory Psychology Textbooks: Assessing Levels of Difficulty

Richard A. Griggs
University of Florida

"There is no substitute for detailed review of the competing texts for the course you are teaching. . . . Research on teaching suggests that the major influence on what students learn is not the teaching method but the textbook" (McKeachie, 1994, p. 14). Given this importance of textbooks, informed textbook evaluation and selection are crucial, especially for the introductory course with its estimated annual enrollment of 1.5 million students (Griggs, Jackson, & Napolitano, 1994). With a large number of introductory texts available, it is difficult for any teacher to know many of the books well. Weiten's (1988) instructor survey data attested to this difficulty. Weiten asked a large sample of professors who taught introductory psychology to rate each of 43 textbooks, but only 4 of 43 textbooks were rated completely by 50% or more of the respondents. Griggs and Jackson (1989) found that introductory psychology text editors and authors, like the psychology teachers, were also not very familiar with many of the available introductory texts. Much of this difficulty stems from the sheer number of texts available for the introductory course. Although the number of introductory texts has dramatically decreased during the past two decades (Griggs, 1990), there are still more than 40 full-length textbooks, along with brief versions of 14 of the texts, available for course adoption (Griggs, Jackson, Marek, & Christopher, 1998).

The large number of texts available leads to obvious problems in the text selection process. This situation is further complicated by the fact that little information is available on how to assess one of the most important dimensions in selecting an introductory text—level of difficulty (e.g., Dewey, 1995; Whitford, 1996). Matching the level of the text with the level of your students' ability is not an easy task. The purpose of this study is to help alleviate such problems and thus facilitate the text selection process for introductory psychology teachers.

Three levels targeting lower, middle, and higher level students are usually employed to classify introductory textbooks (e.g., Cush & Buskist, 1997; Dewey, 1995; Griggs & Jackson, 1989). Based on input from psychology authors and editors, Griggs and Jackson made the following distinctions between the three levels:

1. Higher level texts provide great depth and breadth of content coverage and are closely tied to the experimental literature. These texts seem most appropriate for honors classes and students of above average ability.
2. Middle level texts usually have the breadth, but not the depth, of the higher level texts. The writing is

more engaging for average students, but the treatment is still scientifically rigorous.
3. Lower level texts represent another step down in depth of coverage and, on average, include far more pedagogical aids and more often provide chapter coverage of nontraditional topics (e.g., applied psychology, sex, and gender). Such texts also tend to be more heavily illustrated.

Griggs and Jackson (1989) reported that psychology text authors and editors chose the Gleitman, Myers, and Coon textbooks as most representative of the higher, middle, and lower levels, respectively.[1] These choices agree with the level exemplars posited by others (e.g., Cush & Buskist, 1997). Objectively derived information on the levels of these texts and the numerous other textbooks presently in the introductory psychology textbook market, however, is essentially nonexistent. Even subjective information is scarce. Introductory textbook reviewers sometimes comment on text level (e.g., Vázquez, 1989), but usually they do not. Also, reviews of introductory texts typically appear a year or two, if at all, after the text is published, lessening the immediate value of the reviews to teachers. Publishers comprise another possible source for text level information. Due largely to the used book market, however, publishers need adoptions of the current year's introductory text(s) regardless of the appropriateness of the level for a particular school or course and thus may not be reliable sources for objective information on text level.

In an attempt to develop an objective database on text levels for the introductory textbooks in the current market, I examined the previous empirical literature on introductory textbooks and found three factors that one might use to determine the level of an introductory textbook. First, Weiten (1988) found that the eminence of the textbook author(s) (per citation counts in the *Social Science Citation Index* [SSCI]) was positively related to introductory psychology teachers' perception of text level.[2] Teachers perceived texts written by authors with higher SSCI counts to be

---

[1] The latest editions of these three texts are Coon (1998), Myers (1998), and Gleitman (1995).

[2] Weiten (1988) also found that text length was positively related to introductory psychology teachers' perception of text level. I did not use text length, however, because it was not as amenable to making comparative judgments between texts as the other three factors.

higher in level. Second, Griggs and Jackson (1989) found that psychology textbook authors and editors tended to differentiate level partially on the basis of the inclusion of chapter coverage of nontraditional research topics (e.g., applied psychology), with more such coverage in lower level texts. Third, Marek, Griggs, and Christopher (1999) found a strong negative correlation, $r = -.82$, between the number of pedagogical aids in a textbook and its perceived level.

My main goal in this study was to collectively use these three factors to derive level evaluations for the 37 introductory psychology textbooks published in the past 3 years (1995 to 1997). I used this publication period because (a) it was the latest revision cycle for introductory texts at the time of this study, and (b) the texts published during this period have been the subject of other recent studies by my research group (e.g., Griggs, Jackson, Christopher, & Marek, 1999). Thus, these findings will also extend the database for this set of current texts. My secondary goal was to develop a relatively simple, informal judgmental heuristic based on these three factors for assessing the level of new introductory psychology textbooks. Thus, the results of this study should be valuable for introductory teachers in making text selections both now and in the future.

Method

I already had copies of the 37 full-length introductory psychology textbooks published from 1995 through 1997 (for complete references of the 37 texts, see the Appendix).

I derived the eminence of the text authors by making an *SSCI* cumulative citation count for each textbook author for the 9-year period from 1988 (the year Weiten's study was published) up to 1997 (the year this study began). Two research assistants made all counts and resolved any discrepancies by recounts. Because Weiten (1988) summed the counts for multiauthored texts, I did also.[3] Data on the number of pedagogical aids in these 37 texts were already available in Marek et al. (1999), who checked for the presence of 15 pedagogical aids.[4] I indexed data on nontraditional chapter coverage by counting the number of chapters in each text devoted to the following topics: sex and gender, cultural diversity, and industrial/organizational or applied psychology. Data on this factor for the 37 texts were also available (Griggs et al., 1999).

To classify each text according to the three-levels scheme (higher, middle, and lower levels), I used the data for each factor. After I made the individual text classifications for

each factor, I combined the three classifications for each textbook into an overall classification. (The details of these two classification steps appear with the results.) Finally, I converted the overall level classifications for the 37 textbooks to a five-level classification scheme for comparison to Whitford's (1996) judgments based on his many years of experience with introductory psychology texts and the introductory course. I also compared all 37 predicted classifications to experientially derived level judgments based on my two decades of experience with introductory texts in both teaching and research. To control for experimenter effects, I made my judgments before I derived the objective classifications and independently of Whitford's judgments.

Whereas I realize that the two sets of experientially derived judgments, although independent, do not comprise the best criterion to assess the reliability of the predicted level classifications, no other set of levels data for these texts is available. Given the failure of Weiten (1988) and Griggs and Jackson (1989) to find many introductory psychology teachers, editors, or introductory text authors sufficiently familiar with many introductory texts to rate such text characteristics as level, I judged using the available experientially derived data sets to be the most reasonable course of action.

Results and Discussion

The number of pedagogical aids varied from 4 to 10 (see Table 1) with a mean of 6.92 and a median of 7. Given these range and central values, I classified texts with 4 or 5 aids as higher level, those with 6 to 8 as middle level, and those with 9 or 10 as lower level. This classification resulted in 10, 18, and 9 texts, respectively, at each level.

The number of SSCI citations varied greatly across the 37 texts (see Table 1), from 0 to 3,039 with a mean of 443.59 and a median of 147. The distribution was obviously skewed by the 6 texts with citation counts over 1,000. To classify the texts with respect to level, I used the rate of 10 or less citations per year (total count of 90 or less citations) to operationally define lower level, greater than 10 to 50 citations per year (total count of 91 to 450 citations) to define middle level, and greater than 50 citations per year (total count greater than 450 citations) to define higher level. These definitions seemed reasonable given the citation count distribution and resulted in 13 lower, 15 middle, and 9 higher level text classifications.

The number of nontraditional chapters ranged from 0 to 3 (see Table 1) with a mean of 0.68 and a median of 1. Because only one text had 3 such chapters, the most straightforward assignment scheme was to classify texts with no nontraditional chapters as higher level, those with 1 chapter as middle level, and those with 2 or 3 as lower level. This classification resulted in 17, 14, and 6 texts, respectively at each level.

To derive an overall level classification for each text, I made the following numerical assignments for each of the three factors: 1 (*higher level*), 2 (*middle level*), and 3 (*lower level*). Table 1 gives the total numeric value for each text. Because totals could range from 3 to 9, I classified texts with a total of 3 or 4 as higher level; those with a total of 5, 6, or 7

---

[3]It might seem more appropriate to use the average *Social Science Citation Index* (SSCI) count for multiauthored texts. Therefore, I calculated the average SSCI count for each multiauthored text and recomputed the predicted levels for these texts. The results were almost identical to those using total *SSCI* counts, as the predicted level of only two texts changed.

[4]The 15 pedagogical aids examined by Marek, Griggs, and Christopher (1999) were chapter outlines, learning objectives, questions as organizers, section and chapter summaries, bold and italic type styles, running and chapter glossaries, pronunciation guides, learning checks, discussion questions, review exercises, self-tests, and demonstrations.

Table 1. Classification Data on Three Factors and Overall Classification Total for 37 Introductory Psychology Texts

	Number of Pedagogical Aids[a]	1988–1996 Number of SSCI Citations[b]	Number of Nontraditional Chapters[c]	Overall Numeric Total[d]
Atkinson et al.	4	3,039	0	3
Baron[e]	7	488	1	5
Bernstein et al.	5	1,152	0	3
Carlson & Buskist	6	99	0	5
Coon[e]	10	19	2	9
Davis & Palladino	8	108	1	6
Dworetzky	5	10	0	5
Feldman[e]	8	139	2	7
Fernald	5	0	0	5
Gerow[e]	10	9	1	8
Gleitman[e]	4	135	0	4
Halonen & Santrock	7	276	3	7
Hockenbury & Hockenbury[e]	7	0	1	7
Huffman et al.[e]	10	12	2	9
Kagan & Segal	10	1,872	0	5
Kalat	7	92	1	6
Kassin	5	37	1	6
Lahey	9	489	2	7
Lefton	8	30	1	7
Matlin	6	153	0	5
Morris[e]	9	36	1	8
Myers[e]	7	284	1	6
Nairne	6	181	0	5
Peterson	6	1,111	1	5
Plotnik	8	16	0	6
Rathus[e]	7	168	1	6
Roediger et al.	6	2,676	1	5
Santrock	7	263	0	5
Sdorow	5	5	0	5
Sternberg[e]	6	2,020	0	4
Wade & Tavris[e]	7	321	1	6
Wallace & Goldstein	9	147	1	7
Weiten[e]	5	82	0	5
Westen	4	241	0	4
Wood & Wood	10	4	2	9
Worchel & Shebilske	9	229	0	6
Zimbardo & Gerrig[e]	4	470	0	3
Average	6.92	443.59	0.68	5.76

Note. The full references for the textbooks appear in the Appendix. *SSCI = Social Science Citation Index.*
[a]These data come from Marek, Griggs, and Christopher (1999). [b]An *SSCI* citation count was made for each textbook author from 1988 through 1996. Individual authors' figures were summed for multiauthored texts. [c]These data come from Griggs, Jackson, Christopher, and Marek (1999). [d]This total represents the sum of the numerical assignments: 1 (*higher*), 2 (*middle*), and 3 (*lower*) for each of the three factors. [e]Brief versions of these texts are available. There is also a brief version of the Lefton text (Lefton & Valvatne, 1992), but it has not been revised recently.

as middle level; and those with a total of 8 or 9 as lower level. This classification resulted in 6 higher level, 26 middle level, and 5 lower level texts. The middle level category is much larger than the other two categories because it includes texts appropriate for all students except the two extremes. Therefore, further differentiation within this category was necessary. Whitford (1996) used three subcategories: high–middle, middle, and low–middle. These three subcategories map directly to the range of values for the middle level category: 5 (*high–middle*), 6 (*middle*), and 7 (*low–middle*). Thus, I divided the 26 middle level texts into these three subcategories. Twelve were classified as high–middle level, 8 as middle level, and 6 as low–middle level.

To validate this procedure, I examined the reliability of these objective level classifications. I first checked the predicted levels for the prototypical higher, middle, and lower level texts cited earlier. These predictions were correct with numeric totals of 4, 6, and 9 for the editions of the Gleitman,

Myers, and Coon texts, respectively, used in this study. I next compared the predicted levels to Whitford's (1996) experientially derived levels assignments for 30 of the 37 texts. To make this comparison, I assigned the numbers 1 to 5 to indicate the higher, middle–high, middle, low–mid, and lower levels, respectively, to each text in each data set. These comparison data appear in Table 2. The fit was excellent, $r(29) = 0.79$, $p < .001$. To further examine the reliability of the procedure, I compared the predicted levels classifications to my own experientially derived judgments for all 37 texts (see Table 2). Again the fit was excellent, $r(36) = 0.81$, $p < .001$. The fit between the two experientially derived sets of levels classifications was even better, $r(29) = 0.95$, $p < .001$. Twenty-four (80%) of the 30 classifications were identical, and the other 6 (20%) were different by only one level.

To facilitate using the three sets of levels classifications, I computed the overall mean level classifications. These data appear in Table 2. Thirty-four of the 37 sets of level classifi-

Table 2. Level Classifications and Mean Level Classifications for 37 Introductory Psychology Texts

Textbook	Three-Factor Classification[a]	Whitford's Classifications[b]	My Classifications	Mean Classifications	Mean Level Classifications[c]
Atkinson et al.	1	1	1	1.0	Higher
Baron	2	3	3	2.7	Middle
Bernstein et al.	1	2	2	1.7	High–Middle
Carlson & Buskist	2	1	1	1.3	Higher
Coon	5	5	5	5.0	Lower
Davis & Palladino	3	3	4	3.3	Middle
Dworetzky	2	3	2	2.3	High–Middle
Feldman	4	4	4	4.0	Low–Middle
Fernald	2	NA	2	2.0	High–Middle
Gerow	5	4	5	4.7	Lower
Gleitman	1	1	1	1.0	Higher
Halonen & Santrock	4	4	4	4.0	Low–Middle
Hockenbury & Hockenbury	4	NA	5	4.5	Lower
Huffman et al.	5	5	5	5.0	Lower
Kagan & Segal	2	5	5	4.0	Low–Middle[d]
Kalat	3	3	3	3.0	Middle
Kassin	3	NA	3	3.0	Middle
Lahey	4	5	5	4.7	Lower
Lefton	4	4	3	3.7	Low–Middle
Matlin	2	NA	3	2.5	Middle
Morris	5	4	4	4.3	Low–Middle
Myers	3	3	3	3.0	Middle
Nairne	2	NA	2	2.0	High–Middle
Peterson	2	4	3	3.0	Middle
Plotnik	3	5	5	4.3	Low–Middle[d]
Rathus	3	4	4	3.7	Low–Middle
Roediger et al.	2	2	2	2.0	High–Middle
Santrock	2	2	2	2.0	High–Middle
Sdorow	2	3	3	2.7	Middle
Sternberg	1	1	1	1.0	Higher
Wade & Tavris	3	3	4	3.3	Middle
Wallace & Goldstein	4	NA	5	4.5	Lower
Weiten	2	2	2	2.0	High–Middle
Westen	1	NA	2	1.5	High–Middle
Wood & Wood	5	5	5	5.0	Lower
Worchel & Shebilske	3	3	3	3.0	Middle
Zimbardo & Gerrig	1	1	1	1.0	Higher
Average	2.78	3.17	3.16	3.02	

Note. The full references for the textbooks are given in the Appendix. Classifications are as follows: 1 (*higher level*), 2 (*high–middle level*), 3 (*middle level*), 4 (*low–middle level*), and 5 (*lower level*). [a]These classifications were derived from the overall numeric totals of 3 to 9 in Table 1 by using the following assignment scheme: Totals of 3 or 4 = 1, 5 = 2, 6 = 3, 7 = 4, and 8 or 9 = 5. [b]NA = not applicable because textbook was not included in Whitford's (1996) analysis. [c]Mean classifications were rounded to the nearest whole number to assign mean level classifications. [d]As explained in the Results and Discussion section, these two texts are most accurately described as lower level.

cations are internally consistent (the three level judgments are identical or within one). This high consistency and the three strong positive correlations observed for the pairwise comparisons provide strong evidence for the efficacy of the three-factor procedure. Because I recommend using the overall mean level classifications, the three inconsistent cases do not present a real problem. Only the overall classifications of two of the three texts need to be slightly changed. The Kagan and Segal and the Plotnik texts should be classified as lower instead of low–middle level.

The strong correlations between the levels classifications based on the three-factor procedure and the two sets of experientially based judgments indicate the reliability of the overall mean level judgments given in Table 2 for the 37 texts. Thus, teachers should be confident in using this information in their text selection process. However, a question does arise about the relation between the levels of a full-length text and the brief version of the text. Are they different? The 14 texts with brief versions are indicated in Table 1.

A good rule of thumb for answering this question is that the brief version is usually a level or so below that of the full-length text unless the full-length text is already lower level. I based this rule on the typical differences between the two versions: (a) less depth of coverage and (b) more pedagogical devices in the brief versions (Griggs et al., 1994). Because 7 (50%) of the 14 texts that have brief versions are low–middle or lower level, their level cannot change much. The drop in level is more apparent in the higher, high–middle, and middle level texts. They usually drop a level, but possibly two if more pedagogical devices are added. There is one exception—Tavris and Wade (1997). Because it employs an atypical organizational structure centering around the five major theoretical perspectives in psychology and emphasizes depth at the expense of breadth of coverage, this brief version, in my opinion, does not go down in level but rather up a level.

To make the three-factor evaluation procedure more readily useable by teachers for future introductory texts, I converted it into a simple, three-part judgmental heuristic. First, consider your familiarity with the author(s) with respect to their research and scholarship. Use three levels of familiarity. If the author is very familiar (someone like Sternberg or Roediger), it is most likely a higher level text on this dimension; if familiar but not overly so, it is probably a middle level text; if hardly familiar at all, then it is a lower level text. As with the *SSCI* counts, the clearest cases are the extremes. For multiauthored texts, use an average familiarity rating.

Second, check the table of contents for nontraditional chapters. In this case, you use the same classification scheme as in the three-factor procedure—if there are none, classify the text as higher level on this dimension; if there is only one, classify it as middle level; and if there are two or more, classify it as lower level. Third, check the prevalence of pedagogical aids in the text. An exact count is not necessary. If hardly any, then judge the text as higher level on this dimension; if there are some, judge it as middle level; if there are many, judge it as lower level. Finally, combine the three judgments into an overall classification total using a 1 to 3 numeric scale as in the three-factor procedure. You can then map this total to the 3- or 5-level scheme, giving you a good idea about the level of the text and whether it is appropriate for your students.

To informally check the efficacy of this heuristic, I used it to judge the level of one of the three new 1998 introductory texts, Smith (1998). The other texts, Bourne and Russo (1998) and Schlinger and Poling (1998), were not available at the time of this study. To me, Smith is moderately familiar. For those not familiar with his research, he would probably have lower familiarity. Thus, based on familiarity, the text level would be judged middle or lower. The text has some pedagogical aids (6 of the 15 examined) but not a large number. This number would lead to a higher or middle level judgment. There are no nontraditional chapters, indicating a higher text level. Overall, the total could range from 5 to 7, depending on one's familiarity with Smith and the level classification of the number of pedagogical aids. Regardless, the heuristic indicates a middle level text. This classification agrees with my personal judgment after a more careful examination and with the publisher's marketing of the text. My more specific judgment is that it is a high–middle level text.

In conclusion, the levels classifications for the 37 texts in Table 2, along with the rule of thumb for judging brief texts and the informal judgment heuristic for classifying new texts, should greatly assist introductory psychology teachers in the text review process. This information not only provides levels data for almost all of the texts presently available but also makes the teacher aware of the specific texts available at the particular level(s) under consideration. Both aspects should help teachers to make better text selections.

References

Bourne, L. E., Jr., & Russo, N. F. (1998). *Psychology: Behavior in context*. New York: Norton.

Coon, D. (1998). *Introduction to psychology: Exploration and application* (8th ed.). Pacific Grove, CA: Brooks/Cole.

Cush, D. T., & Buskist, W. (1997). Future of the introductory psychology textbook: A survey of college publishers. *Teaching of Psychology, 24*, 119–122.

Dewey, R. A. (1995, March). Finding the right introductory psychology textbook. *APS Observer, 8*, 32–33, 35.

Gleitman, H. (1995). *Psychology* (4th ed.). New York: Norton.

Griggs, R. A. (1990). Introductory psychology texts: Survival of the fittest. *Contemporary Psychology, 35*, 659–662.

Griggs, R. A., & Jackson, S. L. (1989). The introductory psychology textbook market: Perceptions of authors and editors. *Teaching of Psychology, 16*, 61–64.

Griggs, R. A., Jackson, S. L., Christopher, A. N., & Marek, P. (1999). Introductory textbooks: An objective analysis and update. *Teaching of Psychology, 26*, 182–189.

Griggs, R. A., Jackson, S. L., Marek, P., & Christopher, A. N. (1998, February). *Introductory psychology textbooks: A feature analysis.* Paper presented at the meeting of the Southeastern Conference on Teaching of Psychology, Atlanta, GA.

Griggs, R. A., Jackson, S. L., & Napolitano, T. J. (1994). Brief introductory psychology textbooks: An objective analysis. *Teaching of Psychology, 21*, 136–140.

Lefton, L. A., & Valvatne, L. (1992). *Mastering psychology* (4th ed.). Needham Heights, MA: Allyn & Bacon.

Marek, P., Griggs, R. A., & Christopher, A. N. (1999). Pedagogical aids in textbooks: Do college students' perceptions justify their prevalence? *Teaching of Psychology, 26*, 11–19.

McKeachie, W. J. (1994). *Teaching tips* (9th ed.). Lexington, MA: Heath.

Myers, D. G. (1998). *Psychology* (5th ed.) New York: Worth.

Schlinger, H. D., Jr., & Poling, A. (1998). *Introduction to scientific psychology*. New York: Plenum.

Smith, B. D. (1998). *Psychology: Science and understanding*. New York: McGraw-Hill.

Tavris, C., & Wade, C. (1997). *Psychology in perspective* (2nd ed.). New York: Longman.

Vázquez, C. A. (1989). Pedagogy versus substance. *Contemporary Psychology, 34*, 470–473.

Weiten, W. (1988). Objective features of introductory psychology textbooks as related to professors' impressions. *Teaching of Psychology, 15*, 10–16.

Whitford, F. W. (1996). *Teaching psychology: A guide for the new instructor* (2nd ed.). Englewood Cliffs, NJ: Prentice-Hall.

Appendix
Full-Length Introductory Psychology Texts
Used in This Study

Atkinson, R. L., Atkinson, R. C., Smith, E. E., Bem, D. J., & Nolen-Hoeksema, S. (1996). *Hilgard's introduction to psychology* (12th ed.). Fort Worth, TX: Harcourt Brace.

Baron, R. A. (1995). *Psychology* (3rd ed.). Needham Heights, MA: Allyn & Bacon.

Bernstein, D. A., Clarke-Stewart, A., Roy, E. J., & Wickens, C. D. (1997). *Psychology* (4th ed.). Boston: Houghton Mifflin.

Carlson, N. R., & Buskist, W. (1997). *Psychology: The science of behavior* (5th ed.). Needham Heights, MA: Allyn & Bacon.

Coon, D. (1995). *Introduction to psychology: Exploration and application* (7th ed.). St. Paul, MN: West.

Davis, S. F., & Palladino, J. J. (1997). *Psychology* (2nd ed.). Upper Saddle River, NJ: Prentice Hall.

Dworetzky, J. P. (1997). *Psychology* (6th ed.). Pacific Grove, CA: Brooks/Cole.

Feldman, R. S. (1996). *Understanding psychology* (4th ed.). New York: McGraw-Hill.

Fernald, D. (1997). *Psychology*. Upper Saddle River, NJ: Prentice Hall.

Gerow, J. R. (1997). *Psychology: An introduction* (5th ed.). New York: Addison Wesley Longman.

Gleitman, H. (1995). *Psychology* (4th ed.). New York: Norton.

Halonen, J. S., & Santrock, J. W. (1996). *Psychology: Contexts of behavior* (2nd ed.). Dubuque, IA: Brown & Benchmark.

Hockenbury, D. H., & Hockenbury, S. E. (1997). *Psychology*. New York: Worth.

Huffman, K., Vernoy, M., & Vernoy, J. (1997). *Psychology in action* (4th ed.). New York: Wiley.

Kagan, J., & Segal, J. (1995). *Psychology: An introduction* (8th ed.). Fort Worth, TX: Harcourt Brace.

Kalat, J. W. (1996). *Introduction to psychology* (4th ed.). Pacific Grove, CA: Brooks/Cole.

Kassin, S. (1995). *Psychology*. Boston: Houghton Mifflin.

Lahey, B. B. (1995). *Psychology: An introduction* (5th ed.). Dubuque, IA: Brown & Benchmark.

Lefton, L. A. (1997). *Psychology* (6th ed.). Needham Heights, MA: Allyn & Bacon.

Matlin, M. W. (1995). *Psychology* (2nd ed.). Fort Worth, TX: Harcourt Brace.

Morris, C. G. (1996). *Psychology: An introduction* (9th ed.). Upper Saddle River, NJ: Prentice Hall.

Myers, D. G. (1995). *Psychology* (4th ed.). New York: Worth.

Nairne, J. S. (1997). *Psychology: The adaptive mind*. Pacific Grove, CA: Brooks/Cole.

Peterson, C. (1997). *Psychology: A biopsychosocial approach* (2nd ed.). New York: Addison Wesley Longman.

Plotnik, R. (1996). *Introduction to psychology* (4th ed.). Pacific Grove, CA: Brooks/Cole.

Rathus, S. A. (1996). *Psychology in the new millennium* (6th ed.). Fort Worth, TX: Harcourt Brace.

Roediger, H. L., III, Capaldi, E. D., Paris, S. G., Polivy, J., & Herman, C. P. (1996). *Psychology* (4th ed.). St. Paul, MN: West.

Santrock, J. W. (1997). *Psychology* (5th ed.). Dubuque, IA: Brown & Benchmark.

Sdorow, L. M. (1995). *Psychology* (3rd ed.). Dubuque, IA: Brown & Benchmark.

Sternberg, R. J. (1995). *In search of the human mind*. Fort Worth, TX: Harcourt Brace.

Wade, C., & Tavris, C. (1996). *Psychology* (4th ed.). New York: HarperCollins.

Wallace, P. M., & Goldstein, J. H. (1997). *An introduction to psychology* (4th ed.). Dubuque, IA: Brown & Benchmark.

Weiten, W. (1995). *Psychology: Themes and variations* (3rd ed.). Pacific Grove, CA: Brooks/Cole.

Westen, D. (1996). *Psychology: Mind, brain, and culture*. New York: Wiley.

Wood, S. E., & Wood, E. G. (1996). *The world of psychology* (2nd ed.). Needham Heights, MA: Allyn & Bacon.

Worchel, S., & Shebilske, W. (1995). *Psychology: Principles and applications* (5th ed.). Englewood Cliffs, NJ: Prentice Hall.

Zimbardo, P. G., & Gerrig, R. J. (1996). *Psychology and life* (14th ed.). New York: HarperCollins.

Notes

1. I thank Sherri Jackson, Randolph Smith, and three anonymous reviewers for valuable comments on an earlier version of this article and Pam Marek and Andrew Christopher for their help with data collection.

Introductory Textbooks and Psychology's Core Concepts

Jeanne S. Zechmeister
Eugene B. Zechmeister
Loyola University of Chicago

> Core knowledge is transmitted in textbooks, not in teachers' opinions. (Joseph D. Matarazzo, 1987, p. 893)

According to Matarazzo (1987), not only is the core knowledge of a discipline found in its textbooks, but an examination of psychology's textbooks reveals "there has been a consensus of the core content of psychology in every generation since 1890" (p. 895; the publication date of William James's classic, *The Principles of Psychology*). In defense of his claim, Matarazzo contrasted the chapter titles of major introductory psychology textbooks written between 1890 and 1985. Four major content areas were represented in psychology textbooks over this 100-year period: biological bases, cognitive-affective bases, social bases, and individual differences (p. 895; Table 1, p. 896). It seems that not only do introductory psychology textbooks "reveal much about psychology's discourse about the world," as Morawski (1992,

p. 161) commented, but what they reveal since at least the 1890s has been rather consistent.

Weiten and Wight (1992) characterized the evolution of the introductory textbook during the 1970s and 1980s as the "Era of Artwork, Pedagogy, and Homogenization" (p. 469). These aspects of textbook creation, along with the dramatic increase in average textbook size in recent decades, led many critics, according to these authors, to view contemporary textbooks as "too long, too similar, and too gimmicky" (p. 488). Few introductory psychology instructors escape the impression when examining the row of publishers' copies wedged on their shelves that they all look alike. Several impressive content analyses of introductory psychology textbooks by Quereshi (1993; Quereshi & Sackett, 1977; Quereshi & Zulli, 1975) appeared to validate this impression. These analyses compared terms appearing in the indexes of 60 textbooks published in the early 1970s with those of 52 books published in the 1980s. Quereshi (1993) concluded that more recent texts were "more comprehensive and more similar to each other" (p. 220) and he predicted that the "basic core of introductory psychology vocabulary will maintain its coherence and stability for the foreseeable future" (p. 222).

Such glowing accounts of psychology's coherent and stable core vocabulary are at odds with results of other analyses. Landrum (1993), for instance, performed a page-by-page content analysis of "important" terms appearing in six introductory psychology textbooks published in the late 1980s and early 1990s, which yielded 2,742 different terms. Of these, 1,600 (58%) were unique and just 126 (6%) were common to all six books. Landrum's conclusion was remarkably at odds with Quereshi's (1993): "From these data, it appears that introductory psychology textbooks are much more different from one another than similar" (p. 663).

Evidence for incoherence rather than coherence, instability as opposed to stability, also can be found by closely examining the data provided by Quereshi (1993). In his analysis of 52 textbook indexes, 3,813 different terms appeared. Of these, 887 (23%) appeared in only one textbook index and were dropped from the factor analysis seeking to define principal components. When Quereshi looked for common terms among the 52 indexes, only 3 terms appeared in all of them. As few as 141 terms were common to three fourths of the books. In other words, hardly any terms were common to all books in his sample and fewer than 4% appeared in three fourths of the books.

Although the content areas of psychology textbooks have remained remarkably consistent over the years, as Matarazzo (1987) suggested, consensus is clearly lacking among textbook authors as to psychology's core vocabulary. This state of affairs presents a disturbing dilemma for teachers of introductory psychology. In many ways the introductory course is like a first language course, asking students to begin to learn the vocabulary of the discipline. We would like to think that students who have completed the typical introductory psychology course share a significant vocabulary, a common discourse. At the same time, we believe many instructors would concur with a recent report of members of the American Psychological Association's (APA) Committee on Undergraduate Education:

> The critical goal of teaching is to help students develop a conceptual framework that embraces relevant facts and concepts rather than isolated bits of knowledge, and to help them achieve a base for lifelong learning rather than a static, encyclopedic knowledge of the current state of the field. Because knowledge in the field and in parallel disciplines grows so rapidly, teachers need to recognize the principle that less is more in coverage of content knowledge in individual courses and in the curriculum as a whole. (McGovern, Furumoto, Halpern, Kimble, & McKeachie, 1991, p. 601)

If less is more, then what should that "less" be? One answer, at least for teachers of introductory psychology, may be found in the identification of the key concepts and terms found in introductory textbooks. Yet, as Landrum's (1993) and Quereshi's (1993) data reveal, identifying such a list appears problematic.

Before acceding to the conclusion that introductory textbooks do not provide students a common core vocabulary, we sought evidence from yet one more content analysis of introductory textbooks. In our first study, we performed a content analysis of the key terms and concepts in the glossaries of 10 full-length introductory textbooks. Boldfaced items appearing in a glossary take on particular importance. The textbook author has clearly identified these "key" terms as essential to understanding the textbook message and students expect these items to appear on examinations of the book's content. Landrum's (1993) raters conducted a page-by-page analysis of textbook content, whereas Quereshi (1993) analyzed textbook indexes. By focusing on textbook glossaries we sought to more quickly identify (and operationalize) what textbook authors considered to be key to the textbook's message. This information is not available in previous content analyses.

In a second study, we asked a national sample of introductory psychology instructors to judge whether key terms and concepts found in the glossaries of textbooks should be considered part of the basic or core knowledge of the field of psychology. This study is similar in some respects to surveys carried out by Landrum (1993, Study 2) and Boneau (1990) and provides an opportunity to compare results from several studies investigating psychology's core vocabulary and to seek converging validity among the findings.

Study 1

From a student's point of view, one of the most formidable tasks associated with the introductory psychology course is mastering key terms and concepts. Just how formidable this task is can be ascertained by examining glossary sizes. The average glossary size was 628.43 items in Weiten's (1988) analysis of 42 glossaries from full (i.e., not brief) introductory psychology texts. Griggs, Jackson, and Napolitano (1994) performed a similar analysis of brief versions of introductory psychology texts and found glossary sizes to be even larger ($M = 701.73$). They explained this rather nonintuitive finding by suggesting that briefer versions typically rely more on pedagogical aids than fuller texts.

Glossary sizes are also extremely variable. The range of glossary items in Weiten's (1988) analysis of full-length textbooks was 173 to 1,355 ($SD = 225.85$). Griggs et al. (1994) reported a range of 362 to 1,261 items ($SD = 295.56$) in briefer textbook versions. Glossary sizes differ no doubt for a number of reasons, including the breadth and depth of topic coverage in the textbook, the pedagogical philosophy and style of the authors, and other peculiarities associated with textbook development. Nevertheless, we asked whether there was a significant core of key terms and concepts that every introductory psychology text includes.

Method

Sample of textbooks. We used a purposive sample of 10 full-length introductory textbooks that were (a) recently published (i.e., 1994–1997), (b) approximately the same size (more than 600 pages), and (c) not first editions (see Appendix). Although we did not systematically sample introductory textbooks, the resulting sample gave every appearance of being roughly representative of the unabridged (somewhat higher level) introductory textbook market, with editions ranging from 2nd to 12th and including some of the most recommended texts in our field (see Weiten & Wight, 1992). Average total number of text pages was 796.2 (range = 683–930); mean number of chapters (not including appendixes) was 17.9 (range = 16–19).

Identification of glossary terms. With one exception, we determined the glossary sizes by counting boldfaced items in the glossary (or index). The exception was to tally different definitions within the same glossary heading as separate items when authors clearly differentiated the meanings. The average number of glossary items in the 10 books in our sample was 725.2 (range = 512–1,056; SD = 181.11).

To determine the number of terms and concepts shared by the various texts, we began by listing key items from the largest glossary and then checked entries that also appeared in other texts and added new items to our list when necessary. Obstacles immediately arose, however, when comparing key terms and concepts across various texts because there is significant variation in the way that the same or similar concepts are identified. We had to make decisions as to (a) when two (or more) literally different terms meant the same (or almost the same) thing (e.g., *depression* and *depressive disorder[s]*) and should be considered synonymous and (b) when different meanings of the same literal term (e.g., *discrimination* for operant and classical conditioning) were similar enough to warrant being collapsed and treated as one concept. Glossary entries also differed because authors used completely different terms for the same concept (e.g., *modal model of mind/multistore theory of memory* and *cocktail party effect/lunch-line effect*) and we combined such terms whenever a check of item definitions indicated that textbook authors were addressing essentially the same concept.[1] Both authors worked together to make judgments and settled disagreements before proceeding (or at least before the final draft). After reviewing the task of imposing order on what at times seemed to be psychology word salad, more objective criteria appeared impossible.

Results

We initially tallied 7,252 glossary items in the 10 books of our sample. We then combined items we judged to be essentially the same concept. Collapsing terms and concepts affected counts both within and across books. For example, one author listed simply the term *sex chromosomes* whereas three authors listed *X chromosome* and *Y chromosome* separately, and one author listed all three terms. We subsumed these terms under the single concept *sex chromosomes* (*X chromosome, Y chromosome*), which we judged to appear in five different books.

After collapsing similar terms and concepts *within* each glossary the total number of glossary items found in all 10 books dropped from 7,252 to 6,911 (M glossary size = 691.1, SD = 150.26). As might be predicted, our procedure reduced

most those glossaries with the largest numbers of items. Thus, one factor that contributes to large glossary size is inclusion of abbreviations and synonyms.

Our next step was to address the extent of overlap across the 10 glossaries. From the list of 6,911 items we identified 2,505 literally different key terms and concepts represented in the 10 glossaries. The 10 glossaries differed in how many terms and concepts were unique to the glossary. Unique terms represent the items within our final tally of 2,505 different items that appeared in only one glossary. Proportion of unique terms in the glossaries of our sample ranged from .08 to .24. The correlation between number of unique terms and glossary size was .97, indicating that the contribution of unique terms to the total pool of key items was directly related to glossary size.

Table 1 shows the number (and proportion) of times a term appeared in 1 or more of the 10 books. Approximately half (.49) the 2,505 terms and concepts appeared in only 1 textbook glossary; in fact, as the cumulative proportions in Table 1 show, approximately three fourths (.74) of the terms and concepts appeared in just 1, 2, or 3 books. At the other end, 197 (.08) terms and concepts appeared in 8, 9, or 10 books. Only 64 of the 2,505 terms and concepts (.03) appeared in all 10 books. In the book with the largest glossary, this figure represented 6% of the total glossary items; in the book with the smallest glossary, only 12.5% of the terms were common to all 10 books.[2]

Discussion

As instructors, we frequently accept the choice of key terms and concepts by textbook authors as reflecting the most important ideas in the field. Our results question these assumptions that both instructors and students make about introductory psychology textbooks. On one hand, we regularly encountered terms and concepts that we judged to be too esoteric (e.g., *trephining*), trivial (e.g., *group*), abstruse (e.g., *opinion molecule*), specific (e.g., *glucocorticoids*), or tangential to psychology (e.g., *Title VII of the 1964 Civil Rights Act*), to be called key terms in psychology. Nevertheless, we recognize that authors put their own stamp on a presentation and, as noted, glossaries serve as a pedagogical aid to students' understanding of an author's presentation. Not every glossary item, therefore, should be seen as helping to define the basic core of psychology. Yet, even allowing for the idiosyncrasies of presentation, the obvious lack of agreement among authors as to what constitutes a key term or concept for the introductory psychology student is discomfiting. Is the field well defined by 64 key terms and concepts?

We should emphasize that the issue is what makes a term or concept key and not whether it appeared in a particular

---

[1]This procedure to collapse synonyms differs from previous content analyses that included all terms encountered.

[2]Percentage agreement among the 10 textbooks is limited by glossary size. For example, after eliminating synonyms and abbreviations, the smallest glossary had 504 terms and the largest glossary had 932 terms (Table 1). Therefore, the maximum possible agreement for these two glossaries was 54% (504/932), and this calculation would require that the smaller glossary contribute no unique terms. Similarly, the smallest glossary sets a limit on the number of terms that may be common to all 10 books. If all 504 terms in the smallest glossary appeared in all of the remaining glossaries, then 20% (504/2,505) of the terms would be common to all glossaries.

Table 1. Frequencies and Proportions for the Number of Times a Term–Concept Appeared in 1 or More of the 10 Glossaries (Study 1) and Mean Ratings and Standard Deviations as a Function of Number of Glossaries (Study 2)

	No. of Glossaries									
	1	2	3	4	5	6	7	8	9	10
Study 1										
Frequency	1,227	399	224	151	98	115	94	65	68	64
Cumulative frequency	1,227	1,626	1,850	2,001	2,099	2,214	2,308	2,373	2,441	2,505
Proportion	.49	.16	.09	.06	.04	.05	.04	.03	.03	.03
Cumulative proportion	.49	.65	.74	.80	.84	.88	.92	.95	.97	1.00
Study 2										
M	2.71	3.09	3.32	3.49	3.66	3.82	3.88	3.92	4.10	4.40
SD	.74	.75	.71	.63	.64	.60	.56	.52	.49	.43

Note. Mean ratings are based on a scale ranging from 1 (*not important*) to 5 (*very important*). Frequency = how many terms and concepts appeared in a book; cumulative frequency = the sum of frequencies across the 10 books (by the 10th book all terms and concepts are counted); proportion = the proportion of terms and concepts in our table that appear in a book; cumulative proportion = the sum of the proportions across the 10 books (e.g., .74 of the terms and concepts appeared in 1, 2, or 3 books).

textbook. Our data speak only to what authors deemed important enough to emphasize as key in a glossary of key terms and concepts (cf. Landrum, 1993; Quereshi, 1993). There are no doubt more than 64 terms and concepts that appear (somewhere) in all 10 books in our sample; however, only 64 were called key by all the authors. On the other hand, many key terms and concepts were (as much as we could determine) unique to a book in that they did not appear anywhere in another book (e.g., *nuclear arms freeze* and *zeitgebers*).

We had hoped an analysis of textbook glossaries would help to identify a basic vocabulary that every introductory student should learn. Although 64 terms and concepts hardly seem enough to capture psychology's essence, perhaps we should not look for unanimity. By accepting a vote of 8 out of 10 authors (Table 1), we find what are introductory psychology's key 197 key terms and concepts according to the authors in our sample. Perhaps this is not such a small number. Some may be surprised that we could find that many terms and concepts on which 8 of 10 textbook authors agree.

Boneau (1990) identified what he referred to as "Psychology's 'Top 100' Terms/Concepts" (p. 894) through a survey of textbook authors in 10 subfields of psychology. His goal was to provide a measure of psychological literacy or, as he suggested, "a set of materials that psychology majors might be expected to master before their graduation" (p. 891). More than 150 textbook authors rated approximately 200 to 250 terms and concepts in their specialty areas. The scale ranged from 5 (*very important*) to 1 (*overly specialized*). He based his final "Top 100" on the 10 highest rated items from each specialty area. Only 22% of Boneau's 100 were in all 10 glossaries in our sample, 39% were in 8 or more books, and 10% did not appear in any glossary in our sample.

Content analyses by Quereshi (1993) and Landrum (1993) also speak to these questions, although using different approaches. Quereshi's (1993) analysis of textbook indexes (not glossaries) yielded 137 terms used by 39 or more of the 52 books in his sample. Of these terms, only 40% were among the 197 most frequent terms and concepts in our sample. Landrum's (1993) undergraduate judges found 126 terms in all six books of his sample. Less than half (44%) appeared in our list of 197. These numbers are based on rather literal comparisons and would no doubt change

slightly were we to collapse related items. Nevertheless, the lack of convergent validity is obvious and troubling. To rephrase Morawski (1992), these results reveal much about introductory psychology textbooks' lack of common discourse about the world.

Study 2

In the second study we asked a national sample of experienced introductory psychology instructors to evaluate the terms and concepts we found in introductory textbook glossaries. Respondents rated the importance of these terms and concepts for introductory psychology students.

Method

Survey procedure. We identified (with two restrictions) a random sample of 250 four-year colleges and universities in *Peterson's Guide to Four-Year Colleges* (1998). We included schools with undergraduate enrollments of more than 1,000 students that offered a psychology major. We mailed two survey packets to departmental chairs requesting the packets be distributed to two experienced introductory psychology instructors and sent a reminder 1 month later.

Questionnaire. We generated questionnaires using an alphabetical listing of the 2,505 glossary items obtained in Study 1. Each respondent provided ratings for three short alphabetical lists of approximately 60 items (created using a block randomization procedure) or about 180 items overall. The first page of the questionnaire asked respondents for information regarding (a) highest degree, (b) year degree earned, (c) major field, (d) number of times taught introductory psychology, and (e) whether respondent had authored an introductory textbook or supplement (e.g., study guide). Next, instructions asked respondents to "rate how important it is to introduce students to a term/concept in their first or introductory course in psychology." The rating scale ranged from 1 (*not important*) to 5 (*very important*). A note beneath the scale advised respondents not to rate terms and concepts that were unfamiliar.

Final sample. We received 194 questionnaires from 140 (56%) of the 250 departments surveyed. We discarded nine surveys because respondents had taught introductory psychology only once or twice (*n* = 8) or rated less than 10 items (*n* = 1). We distributed 6 additional questionnaires to colleagues (from two additional schools) who we knew to be experienced introductory psychology instructors to obtain a minimum of 11 judges per item. Thus, our final sample, after drops and additions, consisted of 191 respondents (and 135 schools). At least 11 experienced instructors rated each of the 2,505 terms and concepts (*M* = 13.64).

The 191 respondents in our final sample were generally highly experienced teachers of the introductory psychology course. Half (49.7%) had taught the introductory course 21 or more times; three fourths (72.3%) had taught this course 11 or more times. Seven introductory textbook authors and 13 authors of ancillary materials were represented in the final sample. More than 93% held a PhD (*n* = 176) or EdD (*n* = 2); the remaining held master's degrees or the equivalent. Approximately two thirds of the respondents (68.1%) obtained their degree prior to 1990, with about one third (31.4%) receiving their degree prior to 1975. Respondents taught at institutions in 41 different states; 51% of the institutions in the final sample had enrollments of more than 5,000.

Results

The mean rating of the 2,505 terms and concepts in our sample was 3.12 (*SD* = .85). Only 6 terms were unanimously rated 5.00 (*learning, memory, nature–nurture issue [debate], scientific method [science], unconditioned stimulus, unconditioned response*); 146 terms (5.8%) received mean ratings of 4.50 or greater; and 56 terms (2.2%) had mean ratings less than 1.50.

Mean ratings and frequency of appearance in 10 textbook glossaries (Study 1) for the 2,505 terms and concepts were moderately related *r* = .56). Table 1 presents the mean ratings (and standard deviations) as a function of the number of textbook glossaries in which terms appeared. Of the 146 terms rated 4.50 or greater, 21.9% (32 terms) appeared in 10 books, 30.8% (45 terms) appeared in 9 or 10 books, and 37% (54 terms) appeared in 8 or more textbook glossaries. The mean rating for the 197 terms and concepts appearing in 8 or more glossaries was 4.14 (*SD* = .52). Eleven percent (16) of the 146 terms rated 4.50 and above appeared in only 1 glossary; 27.4% (40 terms) appeared in 3 or fewer books.

Discussion

A total of 146 items received ratings of 4.50 or greater, suggesting they definitely should be included in the core of basic psychology concepts. However, only 54 of these terms were judged important enough by textbook authors (Study 1) to be identified as key terms and concepts in 8 of the 10 glossaries. Although there was less than unanimous agreement between instructors and authors, the correlation between glossary frequency and ratings was moderately strong. On average, judges rated the 197 key terms and concepts appearing in four fifths of the textbooks as "important." These results provide some degree of converging validity for what is an important term or concept.

We compared our results with those of two other studies with similar goals. Boneau (1990) provided ratings for 1,000 terms and concepts, the 100 highest rated items in each of 10 specialty areas. Although he referred judges (specialty textbook authors) to knowledge possessed by graduating psychology majors, we presumed that the highest rated terms would be important even for introductory students. Of the 2,505 terms and concepts in our sample, 612 terms were also in Boneau's 1,000-item list.[3] Despite the different selection procedures (for both selection of terms and selection of raters), there was a modest correlation between ratings across the two samples for the 612 terms (*r* = .40).

There were 212 terms in Boneau's (1990) list that did not appear in our glossaries and 18.5% of Boneau's top 1,000 terms appeared in only 1 textbook glossary. At the other end, only 8.8% of Boneau's terms appeared in all 10 glossaries, and 23.8% of his 1,000 top terms appeared in 8 or more glossaries. The correlation between Boneau's ratings and the number of textbook glossaries in which each term appeared was .31 (*n* = 612).

Landrum (1993) asked introductory psychology instructors to rate the importance of 2,742 items obtained from a content analysis of six introductory textbooks. At least five instructors, surveyed following their participation in an undergraduate teaching conference, rated each item. We compared mean ratings for a stratified (according to chapter) random sample of 472 terms from Landrum's list with the ratings of these same items made by our raters. Of the 472 items, 312 terms (66.1%) were on our list of 2,505 glossary terms. The ratings provided by our raters and Landrum's raters for the 312 overlapping items correlated .55, indicating moderately strong agreement in raters' judgments about the importance of these items for introductory psychology.

Conclusions

The results of our studies and those of others suggest that if psychology has a common language, there are many dialects. In our first study, only 64 terms and concepts (< 3%) appeared in all 10 glossaries of our textbook sample. Approximately half of the 2,505 glossary items appeared in just one textbook. Among the 197 terms and concepts appearing in 8 of 10 glossaries, less than half were among the most frequent items in Landrum's (1993) and Quereshi's (1993) content analyses of textbooks. Only 39% of Boneau's (1990) top 100 psychology terms were in this list. Although importance ratings by introductory psychology instructors correlated fairly well with glossary frequency (.56), more than one fourth of the highest rated terms appeared in 3 or fewer glossaries. What we, as instructors, tell psychology students is an important concept varies significantly from textbook to textbook and from classroom to classroom.

The lack of agreement among textbook authors and introductory psychology instructors as to what constitutes a

---

[3]These 612 terms do not represent 61.2% of Boneau's list (i.e., 612/1,000) because many terms in Boneau's list were repeated across categories (e.g., *ego* appeared in the abnormal and personality categories). When a term was repeated we entered into our analyses the highest rating reported for the term.

core set of terms for the first course in psychology is further revealed when we combined results of the several published studies on this topic. We identified those terms that (a) appeared in 39 or more textbooks in Quereshi's (1993) analysis of textbook indexes; (b) appeared in at least eight textbook glossaries of our Study 1; and (c) achieved a mean rating of 4.50 or greater in our survey, as well as in Landrum's (1993) survey and Boneau's (1990) survey. Only 14 terms or concepts made it into this elite group: *attachment, attitude(s), behavior therapy, central nervous system, classical conditioning, conditioned stimulus, long-term memory, mood disorder(s), operant conditioning, personality, punishment, sympathetic nervous system, unconditioned response,* and *unconditioned stimulus.*[4] Such a list fails even the most cursory test of face validity for psychology's key concepts.

We believe the difficulty that is evident when attempting to define a core vocabulary in psychology is part of a larger problem in the field. Indeed, many writers have questioned whether psychology has a core emphasis (e.g., Bakan, 1995; Bower, 1993; Koch, 1971, 1993; Miller, 1992; Yanchar & Slife, 1997). Miller (1992) said psychology is an "intellectual zoo" (p. 40). Bakan (1995) expanded on the same point: "There is no problem or set of problems on which psychology focusses. There is hardly any common language. There is no clear center" (p. 78). Yanchar and Slife (1997) flatly stated, "Psychology possesses no coherent, unified body of knowledge" (p. 237). We suggest that our analyses, and those of others, reveal that obvious signs of psychology's core problem are found in introductory psychology textbooks.

For teachers of introductory psychology this core problem poses a dilemma when attempting to follow the prescription that less is more in content coverage in the introductory course. Just what should that less be? One response is found in the suggestion made by the APA Committee on Undergraduate Education (McGovern et al., 1991), specifically, to emphasize the "conceptual framework that embraces relevant facts and concepts rather than isolated bits of knowledge" (p. 601). As Matarazzo (1987, p. 895) pointed out, the "core content" (if not the core vocabulary) of psychology has remained the same for more than 100 years. As instructors, our challenge is to teach a conceptual framework in the midst of the fragmentation and incoherence that characterizes psychology's core vocabulary in introductory psychology textbooks.

References

Bakan, D. (1995). The crisis in psychology. *The General Psychologist, 31,* 77–80.

Boneau, C. A. (1990). Psychological literacy: A first approximation. *American Psychologist, 45,* 891–900.

Bower, G. H. (1993). The fragmentation of psychology? *American Psychologist, 48,* 905–907.

Griggs, R. A., Jackson, S. L., & Napolitano, T. J. (1994). Brief introductory psychology textbooks: An objective analysis. *Teaching of Psychology, 21,* 136–140.

James, W. (1890). *The principles of psychology.* New York: Holt.

Koch, S. (1971). Reflections on the state of psychology. *Social Research, 38,* 669–709.

Koch, S. (1993). "Psychology" or "the psychological studies"? *American Psychologist, 48,* 902–904.

Landrum, R. E. (1993). Identifying core concepts in introductory psychology. *Psychological Reports, 72,* 659–666.

Matarazzo, J. D. (1987). There is only one psychology, no specialties, but many applications. *American Psychologist, 42,* 893–903.

McGovern, T. V., Furumoto, L., Halpern, D. F., Kimble, G. A., & McKeachie, W. J. (1991). Liberal education, study in depth, and the arts and sciences major—Psychology. *American Psychologist, 46,* 598–605.

Miller, G. A. (1992). The constitutive problem of psychology. In S. Koch & D. E. Leary (Eds.), *A century of psychology as science* (pp. 40–45). Washington, DC: American Psychological Association.

Morawski, J. G. (1992). There is more to our history of giving: The place of introductory textbooks in American psychology. *American Psychologist, 47,* 161–169.

Peterson's guide to four-year colleges. (1998). Princeton, NJ: Peterson.

Quereshi, M. Y. (1993). The contents of introductory psychology textbooks: A follow-up. *Teaching of Psychology, 20,* 218–222.

Quereshi, M. Y., & Sackett, P. R. (1977). An updated content analysis of introductory psychology textbooks. *Teaching of Psychology, 4,* 25–30.

Quereshi, M. Y., & Zulli, M. R. (1975). A content analysis of introductory psychology textbooks. *Teaching of Psychology, 2,* 60–65.

Weiten, W. (1988). Objective features of introductory psychology textbooks as related to professors' impressions. *Teaching of Psychology, 15,* 10–16.

Weiten, W., & Wight, R. D. (1992). Portraits of a discipline: An examination of introductory psychology textbooks in America. In A. E. Puente, J. R. Matthews, & C. L. Brewer (Eds.), *Teaching psychology in America: A history* (pp. 453–504). Washington, DC: American Psychological Association.

Yanchar, S. C., & Slife, B. D. (1997). Pursuing unity in a fragmented psychology: Problems and prospects. *Review of General Psychology, 1,* 235–255.

Appendix
Reference Information for Texts Used in This Study

Atkinson, R. L., Atkinson, R. C., Smith, E. E., Bem, D. J., & Nolen-Hoeksema, S. (1996). *Hilgard's introduction to psychology* (12th ed.). Fort Worth, TX: Harcourt Brace.

Carlson, N. R., & Buskist, W. (1997). *Psychology: The science of behavior* (5th ed.). Needham Heights, MA: Allyn & Bacon.

Davis, S. F., & Palladino, J. J. (1997). *Psychology* (2nd ed.). Upper Saddle River, NJ: Prentice Hall.

Feldman, R. S. (1996). *Understanding psychology* (4th ed.). New York: McGraw-Hill.

Gleitman, H. (1995). *Psychology* (4th ed.). New York: Norton.

Gray, P. (1994). *Psychology* (2nd ed.). New York: Worth.

Lefton, L. A. (1997). *Psychology* (6th ed.). Needham Heights, MA: Allyn & Bacon.

Myers, D. G. (1995). *Psychology* (4th ed.). New York: Worth.

Peterson, C. (1997). *Psychology: A biopsychosocial approach* (2nd ed.). New York: Addison Wesley Longman.

Roediger, H. L., III, Capaldi, E. D., Paris, S. G., Polivy, J., & Herman, C. P. (1996). *Psychology* (4th ed.). St. Paul, MN: West.

---

[4]A longer list of key terms and concepts may be obtained from the authors.

Notes

1. Results from the first study were presented at the annual meeting of the American Psychological Association, San Francisco, August, 1998.

2. We thank all who responded to our survey and acknowledge Steve Kimmons for helping to administer the survey and enter the data. We thank Emil Posavac and anonymous reviewers for their comments on earlier drafts of this article and our colleagues with whom we discussed the findings.

Pedagogical Aids in Textbooks: Do College Students' Perceptions Justify Their Prevalence?

Pam Marek
Richard A. Griggs
Andrew N. Christopher
University of Florida

Weiten, Guadagno, and Beck (1996) found that students' perceptions of the value of pedagogical aids varied considerably across different aids. Summaries, glossaries, and the use of boldface terms were more highly rated aids than chapter outlines, learning objectives, discussion questions, and demonstrations. Devices that took little time to read or complete and that seemed to be most directly related to aiding exam performance were most highly valued. These results led Weiten et al. to question whether including certain types of learning aids that add to the length and perhaps cost of texts is justified by their probability of use and perceived helpfulness.

This issue is not a new one. Weiten and Wight (1992) traced the growth and the diversity of pedagogical aids over several decades. As the average number of these features grew, so did questions about their substantive value (e.g., Hines, 1985; Vázquez, 1989). These questions remain unanswered.

What determines pedagogical quality? Although publishers project that an increase in the overall quality of introductory psychology texts will accompany a decline in the number of available offerings in the immediate future (Cush & Buskist, 1997), the definition of quality remains elusive. As a starting point, regression analyses of professors' ratings of 43 introductory texts revealed an inverse relation between perceived pedagogical quality of a text and the number of references, $r = -.41$, and authors, $r = -.29$ (Weiten, 1988). In contrast, text length, $r = .37$, and the number of figures per chapter, $r = .36$, were directly linked to perceptions of pedagogical quality. Where do pedagogical devices fit into this picture? The number of pedagogical aids present in a text did not have a significant predictive influence on professors' impressions of pedagogical quality.

Professors' perceptions, however, may not be as relevant as those of students. Texts include pedagogical aids to help student readers. Thus, Weiten et al.'s (1996) study on the value of such learning aids from the student perspective was a crucial first step in examining the utility of pedagogical aids in texts. However, as Weiten et al. pointed out, their sample did not have enough beginning students (only five first-year students in a sample of 134) to test reliably for relations between year in school and attitudes toward pedagogical devices. Their students were also from a relatively small school.

The research reported here aimed to determine whether Weiten et al.'s (1996) findings generalize to first-semester and advanced students at a large public research university. Additionally, given the typical 3-year revision schedule for introductory psychology texts (Griggs & Jackson, 1989) and the time lapse since the publication of Weiten's (1988) study, our research provides an update to Weiten's baseline data for full-length introductory texts. As instructors select textbooks for approximately 1.5 million introductory psychology students annually (Griggs, Jackson, & Napolitano, 1994), this information will permit instructors to consider student perceptions of pedagogical aids and their availability in competing texts.

Method

Our study included two phases. First, we undertook an analysis to determine the extent to which pedagogical aids are available in full-length introductory psychology textbooks published between 1995 and 1997, the current textbook 3-year revision cycle at the time of this study (June 1997). Second, we administered a survey to both first-semester and advanced University of Florida (UF) undergraduates to assess their ratings of pedagogical aids on the dimensions of familiarity, probability of use, and value.

Textbook Analysis

We obtained copies of all full-length introductory psychology texts with copyright dates from 1995 through 1997 from their publishers for a study on critical thinking in introductory textbooks (Griggs, Jackson, Marek, & Christopher, 1998). There are 37 (see Appendix for listing). At least two of us examined each text to determine which of the 15 pedagogical aids included in the student survey were present (see survey materials section).

Student Survey

We administered a survey to 411 students in psychology courses at UF during regularly scheduled class periods at the beginning of the second summer session. We chose this term because the majority of the enrolled students are first-semester freshmen, the type of student underrepresented in Weiten et al.'s (1996) sample. Of the 409 students who answered classification questions on the cover sheet of the survey, 256 (103 men and 153 women) were beginning their first semester of college, and 153 (55 men and 98 women) had completed at least one semester of college. In our results, we label the former group first-semester and the latter group advanced.

Participants. First-semester students reported an average Scholastic Assessment Test (SAT) score of 1147, an average unweighted high school grade point average (GPA) of 3.37, and an average weighted high school GPA of 3.76. The advanced students reported an average GPA at UF of 2.91. Twenty-four were first-year students (30 or fewer college credits), 47 were sophomores (31–60 credits), 45 were juniors (61–90 credits), and 37 were seniors (91 or more credits).

Survey materials. We used the 13-item pedagogical aids survey originally administered by Weiten et al. (1996), but expanded it to 15 items (W. Weiten, personal communication, June 1997). The two additional aids were use of questions as organizational devices and end-of-chapter self-tests. As in Weiten et al. (1996), the instructions on the cover page of the survey explained the purpose of the study. For each survey item, participants read a brief description of the device and examined an illustration to reinforce the description. Then they used three 7-point scales to indicate their familiarity with the learning aid, the probability that they would use it in the future, and its value to them. The three scales were anchored as follows: familiarity ranged from 1 (*unfamiliar*) to 7 (*very familiar*), probability of use ranged from 1 (*unlikely*) to 7 (*very likely*), and value ranged from 1 (*not helpful*) to 7 (*very helpful*). We told participants that they should base their ratings on general experience with each aid and not the quality of the specific illustrations.

Results and Discussion

Pedagogical Aids in Introductory Psychology Textbooks

Except for demonstrations, the pedagogical aids were readily classified into five categories: those related to text organization, summaries, type style, glossaries, or questions. Thus, we used this categorization scheme for data presentation in Table 1, which gives the frequency data for each of the 15 aids and the total number of aids in each textbook.

Boldface and italic type, chapter outlines, and chapter summaries were the most prevalent instructional devices. Relatively few books contained learning objectives or questions as organizers in the text body.[1] Among books with either chapter or running glossaries, 27% also included pronunciation guides.[2] All but three texts (Carlson & Buskist, 1997; Kagan & Segal, 1995; Wallace & Goldstein, 1997) had an end-of-text glossary (not included on our survey). Most texts (78%) employed at least one of the four question types, with five books containing at least three question styles. Demonstrations were seldom used as a regular feature, although virtually all texts inserted demonstrations in the perception chapter.

Overall, the number of pedagogical aids in introductory psychology textbooks has increased during the past 10 to 15 years. Weiten (1988) determined the extent to which 9 of the 15 pedagogical devices included in our analysis were present in full-length introductory psychology texts published from 1982 to 1985.[3] Of the 43 books included in his study, 13 (30%) have survived and are also in our sample.

---

[1]We credited a text with the questions-as-organizers feature if it regularly included any of the following: (a) a single question prior to a section, answered by material in the section; (b) a single question prior to a paragraph, answered by material in the paragraph(s) immediately following; or (c) a single question in the margin, answered by material that immediately followed. Four books (Feldman, 1996; Hockenbury & Hockenbury, 1997; Kalat, 1996; Myers, 1995) regularly included more than one question (typically two or three) at the beginning of sections. These questions appeared to us to serve a previewing rather than an organizing function. Additionally, the Roediger, Capaldi, Paris, Polivy, and Herman (1996) text began each chapter with five questions pertaining to five psychological perspectives. The Huffman, Vernoy, and Vernoy (1997) text began each chapter with the same questions subsequently used as organizers, grouped together to provide a preview. Although these previews are akin to learning objectives, we interpreted them as being illustrative of content rather than goal statements; thus, we did not classify them as learning objectives. Because we did not include preview questions in our survey, Table 1 does not reflect their presence.

[2]We credited a text with a running glossary only if the glossary appeared in the marginal area, corresponding to the example in the student survey. Thus, texts that integrated definitions with the narrative did not receive credit for a running glossary. Because of the considerable variability in the extent to which pronunciation guides accompany key terms throughout the texts, we adopted a liberal criterion for crediting books with this feature. We credited a text with a pronunciation guide if at least 30% of the key terms in the biological chapter were accompanied with pronunciation information and if pronunciation guides appeared in other chapters as well. We credited the Plotnik (1996) text with a pronunciation guide even though technical terms were not organized in a running or chapter glossary. We did so because the definitions, although not in the margins or at the end of the chapter, were distinguished from the surrounding text and met our criteria for a pronunciation guide.

[3]Weiten (1988) specified the following criteria for inclusion in his study:

> (a) being listed in the most recent Directory of Introductory Psychology Texts in Print (Rogers & Bowie, 1984), (b) not being a brief edition of a longer book or one intended for use in high schools, and (c) having an edition published in 1982 or later when the study began in May 1985. (p. 10)

Table 1. Pedagogical Aids in Individual Books

Textbook	Organization			Summaries		Type Style		Glossaries			Questions				Demonstrations	No. of Pedagogical Aids
	Chapter Outlines	Learning Objectives	Questions as Organizers	Chapter	Section	Bold	Italic	Running	Chapter	With Pronunciation	Learning Checks	Discussion	Review Exercises	Self-Test		
Atkinson et al.	•			•		•	•									4
Baron	•			•	•	•	•	•				•				7
Bernstein et al.	•				•	•	•	•								5
Carlson & Buskist	•			•	•	•	•	•								6
Coon	•	•	•	•		•	•	•		•	•	•				10
Davis & Palladino	•		•	•		•	•	•			•				•	8
Dworetzky	•			•		•	•	•								5
Feldman	•			•	•	•	•	•			•	•				8
Fernald	•			•		•	•					•				5
Gerow	•			•	•	•	•	•			•	•	•		•	10
Gleitman	•			•		•	•									4
Halonen & Santrock	•			•	•	•	•		•			•				7
Hockenbury & Hockenbury	•			•		•	•	•		•	•					7
Huffman et al.	•	•		•		•	•	•		•	•	•			•	10
Kagan & Segal	•	•[a]		•		•	•	•		•		•	•	•		10
Kalat	•				•	•	•		•[b]		•	•				7
Kassin	•			•		•	•	•								5
Lahey	•			•	•	•	•	•		•	•	•				9
Lefton	•				•	•	•	•		•	•	•				8
Matlin	•				•	•	•					•			•	6

	100	14	19	84	35	100	97	54	16	22	46	70	11	8	16	Total
Morris	•			•	•	•	•	•			•	•		•		9
Myers	•		•	•		•	•			•		•	•			7
Nairne	•			•	•	•	•			•		•				6
Peterson	•			•		•	•				•	•	•			6
Plotnik	•	•		•		•	•			•	•	•	•			8
Rathus	•			•		•	•			•	•	•				7
Roediger et al.	•			•	•	•	•	•				•				6
Santrock	•			•	•	•	•	•	•			•				7
Sdorow	•			•		•	•	•				•				5
Sternberg	•		•	•		•	•	•				•				6
Wade & Tavris	•			•		•	•	•			•	•				7
Wallace & Goldstein	•	•		•		•	•	•	•		•	•		•		9
Weiten	•			•		•	•	•			•					5
Westen	•			•		•	•									4
Wood & Wood	•		•	•		•	•	•		•	•	•		•	•	10
Worchel & Shebilske	•	•		•		•	•	•			•	•			•	9
Zimbardo & Gerrig	•			•		•	•									4
% of texts including aid	100	14	19	84	35	100	97	54	16	22	46	70	11	8	16	

Note. The full references for the textbooks are in the Appendix. A bullet indicates the presence of a pedagogical aid in a specific textbook. [b]In the Kalat text, there is a glossary at the end of each section. In the Kagan and Segal text, learning objectives appear at the end of each chapter.

Current editions of these texts include a mean of 3.5 of the 9 pedagogical aids originally tabulated, compared to 2.2 in the earlier editions, $t(12) = 2.89$, $p = .01$, two-tailed.

Weiten (1988) found that the number of learning devices in texts was not predictive of professors' ratings of pedagogical quality or level of discourse. Although we realize that texts change in ways other than the number of pedagogical devices, we correlated the number of pedagogical aids in the current editions of these 13 texts with professors' ratings of the texts' pedagogical quality and discourse level given in Weiten (1988). Number of pedagogical aids did not correlate significantly with ratings of pedagogical quality, $r(12) = -.18$, $p = .55$. Number of pedagogical aids was, however, significantly and inversely correlated with ratings of level of discourse, $r(12) = -.82$, $p = .001$, indicating that professors perceived texts with an abundance of pedagogical aids as being less difficult than texts with fewer devices. These relations suggest to us that texts with more devices "lose" in the arena of perceived level of discourse without a concomitant gain (and possibly a loss) in perceived pedagogical quality.

This inverse relation between the number of pedagogical aids in a textbook and its judged level of discourse is further substantiated by an examination of the relation between the distribution of aids in current textbooks and existing schemes for classifying textbooks at different levels. For example, the number of pedagogical aids contained in the current editions of introductory textbook authors' and editors' judged prototypes of high-, middle-, and low-level texts (Griggs & Jackson, 1989) decreased with level. The prototypical high-level text (Gleitman, 1995) included 4 devices, compared to 7 for the middle-level text (Myers, 1995) and 10 for the low-level text (Coon, 1995).

This pattern of results also held for the 30 of 37 texts in our sample (all except the texts by Fernald, 1997; Hockenbury & Hockenbury, 1997; Kassin, 1995; Matlin, 1995; Nairne, 1997; Wallace & Goldstein, 1997; Westen, 1996) that appeared in Whitford's (1996) five-level classification scheme. The 5 texts at the highest level in Whitford's classification had a mean of 4.8 aids, compared to 5.8 for the 4 upper middle-level texts, 6.9 for the 8 middle-level texts, 7.7 for the 7 lower middle-level texts, and 9.5 for the 6 low-level texts. To further examine this relation, we assigned a number to each level from 1 (*low*) to 5 (*high*) and correlated text level with the number of aids. Mirroring the correlation we found between number of aids and judged discourse level, we observed a strong inverse relation, $r(29) = -.82$, $p < .0001$, between number of aids and text level. Thus, this relation appears to be reliable. As the number of pedagogical aids in texts increases, perceived level of discourse decreases.

Students' Perceptions of Pedagogical Aids

The mean ratings for the 15 pedagogical aids for both first-semester and advanced students appear in Table 2. All significant differences between the mean ratings of first-semester and advanced students are indicated in the table.

Focusing on familiarity ratings, boldface type and chapter summaries were among the three most familiar aids for both first-semester and advanced students, whereas questions as organizers were the least familiar. These familiarity ratings

parallel the relative presence of these particular aids in introductory psychology texts. Other familiarity ratings did not mirror prevalence. For example, end-of-chapter self-tests, found in only 8% of the introductory psychology texts, received high familiarity ratings from both first-semester and advanced students. First-semester students exhibited greater familiarity with these devices and with pronunciation guides, perhaps reflecting the presence of these aids in high school textbooks. In contrast, advanced students were more familiar with chapter outlines, chapter summaries, chapter glossaries, and demonstrations.

On the probability-of-use dimension, the top three aids for both groups included boldface type and running glossaries. There was also a consensus on the three aids that were least likely to be used; namely, chapter outlines, discussion questions, and chapter learning objectives. Although learning objectives seldom appear in introductory psychology texts, all texts include outlines, and a majority offer discussion questions. Advanced students reported they were less likely to refer to these questions than were first-semester students. Advanced students were also significantly less likely than spanning the categories of organization, type style, glossaries, and questions.

Consistent with the probability-of-use findings, boldface type and running glossaries were among the top three most valued aids for both groups. Similarly, discussion questions and outlines were among the three least valued aids for both groups. Further echoing probability-of-use ratings, advanced students considered seven pedagogical aids to be significantly less helpful than did first-semester students.

Overall, the rating patterns for first-semester and advanced students are very similar. The major difference is that the advanced students' ratings for probability of use and value are significantly lower. First-semester students are slightly more receptive to the assistance pedagogical aids might provide them. This difference between groups suggests to us that college experience leads students to rate the value of an aid based on its perceived relevance to exam preparation. For example, the use of boldface type and running glossaries facilitate the learning of definitions, and chapter summaries and review questions assist in the learning of the major content points of a chapter.

This conclusion and our findings in general are consistent with those of Weiten et al. (1996) for their sample of mainly advanced students. The mean ratings for the 13 aids examined by Weiten et al. appear in Table 2. In both surveys, students were at least neutral toward the aids encountered, with virtually all ratings at or above the midpoint of the scale. Boldface type and chapter summaries were among the top three most familiar, most likely to be used, and most valued aids, whereas learning objectives and outlines were among the least likely to be used and least valued aids. Thus, it seems that students seldom take advantage of authors' efforts to organize textual material. Rather, readers appear to demonstrate greater interest in aids that provide a comprehensive but concise range of cues to material that they perceive as test related.

This pattern is also consistent with findings by Nitsche (1992) in his study of social studies textbook evaluations by high school seniors in introductory psychology and economics classes. These students rated glossaries as most help-

Table 2. Mean Ratings of Pedagogical Aids by Student Level

Pedagogical Aid	% of Texts Including Aid[a]	Familiarity			Probability of Use			Value		
		First-Semester Students	Advanced Students	Weiten et al. (1996)[b]	First-Semester Students	Advanced Students	Weiten et al. (1996)[b]	First-Semester Students	Advanced Students	Weiten et al. (1996)[b]
Organization										
Outline	100	4.75	5.18**	5.00	4.16	3.93	4.14	4.23	3.99	4.14
Learning objectives	14	5.38	5.42	4.87	4.49	3.86**	4.08	4.75	4.06**	4.33
Questions as organizers	19	4.16	4.33	NA[c]	5.13	4.80*	NA[c]	5.22	4.89*	NA[c]
Summaries										
Chapter	84	6.10	6.39*	6.26	5.80	5.77	5.94	5.82	5.76	5.96
Section	35	5.10	5.06	4.29	5.59	5.36	5.09	5.55	5.35	5.19
Type style										
Boldface	100	6.52	6.62	6.51	6.36	6.30	6.26	6.18	6.16	6.09
Italics	97	5.84	5.70	5.52	5.39	5.06*	4.90	5.23	4.86*	4.70
Glossaries										
Running	54	5.70	5.90	5.60	6.18	5.99	5.88	6.13	6.06	5.87
Chapter	16	5.86	6.16*	5.45	6.13	5.68*	5.43	6.20	5.76**	5.55
With pronunciation	22	5.59	5.23**	4.38	4.94	4.42**	3.93	5.12	4.53**	4.06
Questions										
Learning checks	46	5.27	4.97	4.18	5.15	4.76*	4.43	5.38	5.08*	4.81
Discussion	70	6.02	5.86	5.78	4.25	3.90*	3.88	4.58	4.27	4.41
Review exercises at chapter end	8	5.93	5.76	5.13	5.05	4.74	4.28	5.40	5.19	4.82
Self-test at chapter end	8	6.19	5.83**	NA[c]	5.83	5.53*	NA[c]	6.04	5.67*	NA[c]
Demonstrations	16	4.34	5.08**	4.16	4.60	4.72	4.64	4.62	4.90	4.72
Overall		5.52	5.57	5.16	5.27	4.99**	4.84	5.29	5.06**	4.97

Note. Students made ratings on 7-point scales anchored as follows: familiarity ranged from 1 (*unfamiliar*) to 7 (*very familiar*),, probability of use ranged from 1 (*unlikely*) to 7 (*very likely*), and value ranged from 1 (*not helpful*) to 7 (*very helpful*). NA = not applicable.
[a]These prevalence figures offer a framework in which to interpret student ratings. [b]Sample included 5 first-year students and 129 students beyond their first year. [c]item not included on Weiten et al. (1996) survey.
*p < .05 for mean difference between first-semester and advanced students. **p < .01 for mean difference between first-semester and advanced students.

ful, followed by chapter summaries and review questions. The students rated chapter overviews and objectives as least helpful.

Paralleling Weiten et al.'s (1996) analysis of their student rating data, we also explored individual differences by examining correlations of self-reported indexes of academic ability and educational experience with ratings of pedagogical aids. Given our large sample, we found some significant differences among both first-semester and advanced students, but no interpretable pattern emerged from these results.

We note, however, that for advanced students, the number of UF credits correlated negatively with the overall probability-of-use ratings of pedagogical aids, $r(148) = -.18$, $p = .03$. This significant inverse relation extends our finding that advanced students' overall ratings of the probability of use of pedagogical aids were significantly lower than the ratings of first-semester students. Similarly, for advanced students, the number of UF credits correlated negatively with probability-of-use and value ratings for learning objectives, $r(148) = -.22$, $p = .006$ and $r(148) = -.23$, $p = .004$, respectively, and for discussion questions, $r(148) = -.18$, $p = .02$ and $r(148) = -.19$, $p = .02$, respectively. These significant inverse relations are consistent with our finding that advanced students' ratings for these specific items were lower than those of first-semester students.

Conclusions

Students differentially value the plethora of pedagogical aids, and this value does not consistently coincide with the prevalence of these devices in introductory psychology texts. Generally, in our opinion, students' evaluation of aids seems driven by the perceived relevance of the aids to test preparation. For example, students give higher ratings to aids associated with learning definitions (e.g., boldface type and glossaries) or consolidating material (e.g., chapter summaries). Although these aids frequently appear in introductory psychology texts, another highly valued feature, the end-of-chapter self-test, does not.

On the other hand, students are relatively less enthralled by aids designed to promote more elaborative study patterns. Students indicate that they are relatively less likely to use (and value less highly) devices such as outlines (present in all of the introductory psychology texts in our sample) and discussion questions (present in more than two thirds of the books) that are usually described as a means of enhancing retention and developing critical thinking. Hence, it appears that given test-conscious students, the promotion of in-depth learning is dependent on the demands of the instructor, rather than flowing from the inclusion of particular pedagogical devices in textbooks. For example, students preparing for multiple-choice tests may rely more exclusively on aids such as glossaries and summaries, whereas students preparing for essay examinations may recognize the value of outlines and discussion questions. Additionally, the availability and accessibility of supplementary materials such as study guides may influence students' choices of which textbook aids to use.

Overall, first-semester and advanced students are about equally familiar with the pedagogical aids surveyed, but advanced students are less likely to use them and do not consider them as helpful. Thus, although our pattern of results generally replicates that of Weiten et al. (1996), we extend their work by demonstrating that first-semester students are somewhat more receptive to the pedagogical assistance these aids offer than the more advanced group surveyed by Weiten et al. Considering the inverse relation between college experience and use of pedagogical aids, student benefits from these features may not offset the cost of the growing number of aids on the increased length of textbooks, at least for introductory psychology students.

However, there are other avenues for addressing the prevalence issue. From a publisher's viewpoint, pedagogical aids may represent marketing devices to boost textbook adoptions, with prevalence being justified by increased sales. More important, from an educator's perspective, we might justify the prevalence of these aids by their potential contribution to learning. Together with Weiten et al. (1996), we emphasize the need for empirical investigation of whether the presence and use of pedagogical aids enhances learning and retention of key ideas and supporting facts. This information will provide crucial input for judging whether the value of pedagogical aids justifies their prevalence.

References

Cush, D. T., & Buskist, W. (1997). Future of the introductory psychology textbook: A survey of college publishers. *Teaching of Psychology, 24,* 119–122.

Griggs, R. A., & Jackson, S. L. (1989). The introductory psychology textbook market: Perceptions of authors and editors. *Teaching of Psychology, 16,* 61–64.

Griggs, R. A., Jackson, S. L., Marek, P., & Christopher, A. N. (1998). Critical thinking in introductory psychology texts and supplements. *Teaching of Psychology, 25,* 254–266.

Griggs, R. A., Jackson, S. L., & Napolitano, T. J. (1994). Brief introductory psychology textbooks: An objective analysis. *Teaching of Psychology, 21,* 136–140.

Hines, T. M. (1985). Four introductory texts. *Contemporary Psychology, 30,* 487–489.

Nitsche, C. G. (1992). A teacher and his students examine textbooks. In J. G. Herlihy (Ed.), *The textbook controversy: Issues, aspects and perspectives* (pp. 113–120). Norwood, NJ: Ablex.

Rogers, A., & Bowie, J. A. (1984). Directory of introductory psychology texts in print: 1984. *Teaching of Psychology, 11,* 59–62.

Vázquez, C. A. (1989). Pedagogy versus substance. *Contemporary Psychology, 34,* 470–473.

Weiten, W. (1988). Objective features of introductory psychology textbooks as related to professors' impressions. *Teaching of Psychology, 15,* 10–16.

Weiten, W., Guadagno, R. E., & Beck, C. A. (1996). Students' perceptions of textbook pedagogical aids. *Teaching of Psychology, 23,* 105–107.

Weiten, W., & Wight, R. D. (1992). Portraits of a discipline: An examination of introductory psychology textbooks in America. In A. E. Puente, J. R. Matthews, & C. L. Brewer (Eds.), *Teaching psychology in America: A history* (pp. 453–504). Washington, DC: American Psychological Association.

Whitford, F. W. (1996). *Teaching psychology: A guide for the new instructor* (2nd ed.). Upper Saddle River, NJ: Prentice Hall.

Appendix
Full-Length Introductory Psychology Texts
Used in This Study

(Since the publication of the current editions of these 37 textbooks, more publishing companies have merged; there are now only 10 companies publishing introductory textbooks. The most important changes for identifying the new publishers of some of the textbooks in this study are that Brown & Benchmark is now part of McGraw-Hill, Harper-Collins is now part of Addison Wesley Longman, West is now part of International Thomson Publishing with Brooks/Cole and Wadsworth, and Worth is now part of the Scientific American/St. Martin's College Publishing Group.)

Atkinson, R. L., Atkinson, R. C., Smith, E. E., Bem, D. J., & Nolen-Hoeksema, S. (1996). *Hilgard's introduction to psychology* (12th ed.). Fort Worth, TX: Harcourt Brace.

Baron, R. A. (1995). *Psychology* (3rd ed.). Needham Heights, MA: Allyn & Bacon.

Bernstein, D. A., Clarke-Stewart, A., Roy, E. J., & Wickens, C. D. (1997). *Psychology* (4th ed.). Boston: Houghton Mifflin.

Carlson, N. R., & Buskist, W. (1997). *Psychology: The science of behavior* (5th ed.). Needham Heights, MA: Allyn & Bacon.

Coon, D. (1995). *Introduction to psychology: Exploration and application* (7th ed.). St. Paul, MN: West.

Davis, S. F., & Palladino, J. J. (1997). *Psychology* (2nd ed.). Upper Saddle River, NJ: Prentice Hall.

Dworetzky, J. P. (1997). *Psychology* (6th ed.). Pacific Grove, CA: Brooks/Cole.

Feldman, R. S. (1996). *Understanding psychology* (4th ed.). New York: McGraw-Hill.

Fernald, D. (1997). *Psychology.* Upper Saddle River, NJ: Prentice Hall.

Gerow, J. R. (1997). *Psychology: An introduction* (5th ed.). New York: Addison Wesley Longman.

Gleitman, H. (1995). *Psychology* (4th ed.). New York: Norton.

Halonen, J. S., & Santrock, J. W. (1996). *Psychology: Contexts of behavior* (2nd ed.). Dubuque, IA: Brown & Benchmark.

Hockenbury, D. H., & Hockenbury, S. E. (1997). *Psychology.* New York: Worth.

Huffman, K., Vernoy, M., & Vernoy, J. (1997). *Psychology in action* (4th ed.). New York: Wiley.

Kagan, J., & Segal, J. (1995). *Psychology: An introduction* (8th ed.). Fort Worth, TX: Harcourt Brace.

Kalat, J. W. (1996). *Introduction to psychology* (4th ed.). Pacific Grove, CA: Brooks/Cole.

Kassin, S. (1995). *Psychology.* Boston: Houghton Mifflin.

Lahey, B. B. (1995). *Psychology: An introduction* (5th ed.). Dubuque, IA: Brown & Benchmark.

Lefton, L. A. (1997). *Psychology* (6th ed.). Needham Heights, MA: Allyn & Bacon.

Matlin, M. W. (1995). *Psychology* (2nd ed.). Fort Worth, TX: Harcourt Brace.

Morris, C. G. (1996). *Psychology: An introduction* (9th ed.). Upper Saddle River, NJ: Prentice Hall.

Myers, D. G. (1995). *Psychology* (4th ed.). New York: Worth.

Nairne, J. S. (1997). *Psychology: The adaptive mind.* Pacific Grove, CA: Brooks/Cole.

Peterson, C. (1997). *Psychology: A biopsychosocial approach* (2nd ed.). New York: Addison Wesley Longman.

Plotnik, B.. (1996). *Introduction to psychology* (4th ed.). Pacific Grove, CA: Brooks/Cole.

Rathus, S. A. (1996). *Psychology in the new millennium* (6th ed.). Fort Worth, TX: Harcourt Brace.

Roediger, H. L., III, Capaldi, E. D., Paris, S. G., Polivy, J., & Herman, C. P. (1996). *Psychology* (4th ed.). St. Paul, MN: West.

Santrock, J. W. (1997). *Psychology* (5th ed.). Dubuque, IA: Brown & Benchmark.

Sdorow, L. M. (1995). *Psychology* (3rd ed.). Dubuque, IA: Brown & Benchmark.

Sternberg, R. J. (1995). *In search of the human mind.* Fort Worth, TX: Harcourt Brace.

Wade, C., & Tavris, C. (1996). *Psychology* (4th ed.). New York: HarperCollins.

Wallace, P. M., & Goldstein, J. H. (1997). *An introduction to psychology* (4th ed.). Dubuque, IA: Brown & Benchmark.

Weiten, W. (1995). *Psychology: Themes and variations* (3rd ed.). Pacific Grove, CA: Brooks/Cole.

Westen, D. (1996). *Psychology: Mind, brain, and culture.* New York: Wiley.

Wood, S. E., & Wood, E. G. (1996). *The world of psychology* (2nd ed.). Needham Heights, MA: Allyn & Bacon.

Worchel, S., & Shebilske, W. (1995). *Psychology: Principles and applications* (5th ed.). Englewood Cliffs, NJ: Prentice Hall.

Zimbardo, P. G., & Gerrig, R. J. (1996). *Psychology and life* (14th ed.). New York: HarperCollins.

Notes

1. We thank all the publishers of introductory psychology texts for providing us with copies of their texts; Wayne Weiten for providing us with a copy of his survey; and Randolph Smith, Wayne Weiten, and two anonymous reviewers for invaluable comments on an earlier version of this article. We are also indebted to Cecile Chapman and David Sherman for their assistance in preparing the materials for this research.

Critical Thinking in Introductory Psychology Texts and Supplements

Richard A. Griggs
University of Florida

Sherri L. Jackson
Jacksonville University

Pam Marek
Andrew N. Christopher
University of Florida

"Psychology is about critical thinking; life is about critical thinking" (Smith, 1995, p. v). Smith's thoughts were echoed by McBurney (1996) who said, "the main goal of a psychology course should be to get students to think like psychologists, to apply the same critical thinking skills to human behavior that scientists do" (pp. vii–viii) and by Stanovich (1998) who said, "Psychology, probably more than any other science, requires critical thinking skills that enable students to separate the wheat from the chaff that accumulates around all sciences" (p. xvii). An entire issue of *Teaching of Psychology* focused on teaching critical thinking in psychology (Halpern & Nummedal, 1995). In their introduction to this issue, Nummedal and Halpern (1995) pointed out that although critical thinking has long been an important objective of higher education, only recently have psychologists understood that learning to think critically is not an inevitable outcome of instruction. Research shows that, without specific instruction in critical thinking, only a small proportion of college students will develop such thinking skills (e.g., Arons, 1979).

Given its importance as an educational goal and the need to teach it explicitly, critical thinking should be an essential component of introductory psychology texts. In fact, critical thinking began appearing in introductory psychology texts in the late 1980s (Bell, 1997). Wade and Tavris (1987) led the way by incorporating critical thinking into the pedagogical structure for their introductory text. In a recent collection of textbook authors' philosophies for teaching introductory psychology, 9 of 11 authors discussed critical thinking (Griggs, 1997). Bell estimated that almost all introductory psychology texts either discuss critical thinking or have supplements involving critical thinking. Because the introductory psychology course annually enrolls about 1.5 million students (Griggs, Jackson, & Napolitano, 1994), psychology teachers should be interested in how critical thinking is manifested in introductory psychology texts and supplements. This study provides this information.

The number of publishers of introductory texts has shrunk from 20 (Griggs & Jackson, 1989) to 13 (Cush & Buskist, 1997) in the past decade. Since Cush and Buskist's article, the number has dropped from 13 to 10, and 2 of these companies publish only one full-length text. Predict-

ably, there also has been a decrease in the number of introductory texts published. In addition, introductory psychology texts typically are revised on a 3-year (and in some cases, a 2-year) schedule (Griggs & Jackson, 1989).

Given this revision cycle and the shrinking numbers of publishers and texts, we examined all full-length college introductory psychology texts published in the United States with copyright dates from 1995 through 1997. There were only 37 texts in this group, revealing a sharp decline in the number of textbooks during the past decade. When Griggs and Jackson (1989) surveyed introductory texts with copyright dates from 1985 through 1987, they identified 61 full-length texts. In this study, we excluded the 13 brief introductory texts copyrighted from 1995 through 1997 because full-length versions were available. Thus, our analysis included virtually all books currently viable in this text market.

Our study also included all text supplements (excluding study guides) that explicitly claimed to involve critical thinking. We did not, however, include critical thinking books designed for more general use rather than as supplements to introductory texts (e.g., Levy, 1997) because we analyzed these books in a companion article (Marek, Jackson, Griggs, & Christopher, 1998).

Method

We contacted the publishers of introductory psychology texts and obtained copies of the 37 introductory texts (listed in Appendix A) and copies of text supplements explicitly involving critical thinking (listed in Appendix B).

Phase 1

First, we analyzed the critical thinking coverage in the introductory texts. We checked the preface, glossary, index, text chapters, and any special introductory text sections (not formally numbered as chapters) for mention of "critical thinking," noting multiple locations. We compiled these data for comparison with similar data collected by Bell (1997). Next, we examined the texts for definitions of critical thinking and descriptions of the critical thinking process and, if present, computed the extent of coverage by counting the number of words in the relevant discussions. At least two of us counted, and we averaged the counts for each text. The difference between the counts for each text was less than 1%. We also noted the locations of these discussions. In addition, disagreement among psychologists on a definition of critical thinking (e.g., Bell, 1997; Halonen, 1995) led us to content-analyze the critical thinking definitions and process descriptions and determine which components of critical thinking were most prevalent to develop a summary definition.

Second, we examined the specific pedagogical devices used to teach critical thinking and found two main approaches: (a) critical thinking features and (b) critical thinking questions. The critical thinking features involved either the application of a particular model of critical thinking detailed elsewhere in the text (which we refer to as *model* discussions) or material in a boxed insert that authors critically discussed (which we refer to as *topic* discussions). Frequently, the material encompassed in topic discussions in some books was standard textual material in others. We also noted whether the texts incorporated questions (and answers). For critical thinking questions not included in discussions, we determined their location and whether answers were provided.

Third, we examined pedagogical features that focused specifically on research methodology (scientific thinking). For texts that included methodological features, we determined whether these features (a) modeled the research process or focused on topic discussion and (b) included questions (and answers). We also noted whether the main discussion of the research process was given chapter-length coverage or was embedded in the first chapter.

Fourth, we examined coverage of difficulties in general thinking (e.g., confirmation bias) and in statistical thinking (e.g., gambler's fallacy). Whereas critical thinking features often focus on the evaluation of arguments and scientific thinking discussions highlight sound research procedures, awareness of general biases in people's thinking also impacts the ability to appropriately gather and interpret information. Similarly, in thinking critically about research, knowledge of statistical sampling and analytical procedures is crucial. Discussion of general and statistical thinking biases and shortcomings can help students discriminate between acceptable versus inadequate claims and make more rational choices beyond the classroom.

Phase 2

The second phase of our study reviewed critical thinking coverage in the text supplements. We aimed to (a) make teachers aware of what supplements are presently available and (b) provide them with an objective overview of each offering that would help them to decide which supplements they might want to examine more closely for possible use in their introductory courses. Thus, our reports are more descriptive than evaluative.

Results and Discussion

This section contains two subsections that correspond to the phases of our research. The first section presents findings from our analysis of the introductory psychology texts, and the second includes our descriptive summaries of the critical thinking supplements.

Analyses of Introductory Psychology Texts

We present the results of our textbook analyses in four parts: (a) critical thinking, (b) scientific thinking, (c) general thinking, and (d) statistical thinking.[1]

Critical Thinking

We determined that 65% of the texts in our sample mentioned "critical thinking" in either the glossary, index, or the first two chapters. This percentage closely replicates the 69% estimate from Bell (1997), although his sample of introductory texts was different from our sample. In our sample, 65% also included critical thinking as a goal in the preface. Only 8% did not mention critical thinking at all. These percentages, however, are somewhat deceiving because some of the texts that included critical thinking in the index or as a goal in the preface did not specifically define or describe critical thinking in the text. Thus, we credited a text with mentioning critical thinking only if the text defined or described critical thinking in the text proper, a special prechapter, or an appendix. Table 1 indicates that 25 (68%) texts met this criterion.

There was much variability among the 25 definitions of critical thinking. To create a summary definition, we extracted individual phrases and concepts from the definitions and process descriptions, tallied the frequency of occurrence for each phrase and concept, combined the phrases and concepts into broader categories, and then developed the following summary definition from the most frequently occurring categories.

> Critical thinking is a process of evaluating evidence for certain claims, determining whether presented conclusions logically follow from the evidence, and considering alternative explanations. Critical thinkers exhibit open-mindedness; tolerance of ambiguity; and a skeptical, questioning attitude.

Although this prototypical definition does not correspond exactly to any of the 25 definitions, it does capture their essence.

---

[1] We sent the original of this article to at least the first author of each of the 37 introductory texts for their feedback on our treatment of their text. Our reply rate was over 50%. We corrected specific errors pointed out and considered all comments in subsequent revisions of the manuscript. We note that two authors thought that our operationalization of critical thinking was too surface-structural and ironically seemed itself to go against the construct of critical thinking. We certainly agree with their claim that critical thinking is about developing students' way of thinking about psychology, which is more than featured discussions, questions, coverage of certain biases, and so forth. Our goal, however, in this study was only to provide an analysis of the objective critical thinking features of the texts and not to evaluate the authors' teaching of critical thinking via their individual writing styles. Such evaluation would clearly involve subjective assessment.

The length of these 25 definitions and descriptions of critical thinking varied greatly. For example, Table 1 shows word counts varied from 84 words to almost 4,200 words.[2] Most descriptions appeared in the first chapter or the methods chapter but some appeared in other chapters (e.g., the chapter on thinking), in a special prechapter introductory section, or in an appendix.

Table 1 shows that 16 of the 37 texts (43%) included model or topic discussion features, mainly the latter. The three texts that applied a specific model of critical thinking (Bernstein, Clarke-Stewart, Roy, & Wickens; Carlson & Buskist; Halonen & Santrock) allow students to practice critical thinking in a step-by-step manner. Half of the 16 texts (Davis & Palladino; Dworetzky; Halonen & Santrock; Hockenbury & Hockenbury; Huffman, Vernoy, & Vernoy; Morris; Santrock; Wade & Tavris) included questions within the discussions to encourage further thought about the material, although none provided answers to the questions.

Table 1 indicates that almost two thirds of the texts (23 of 37, 62%) introduced questions involving critical thinking that were not associated with featured textual discussions. Of these, 12 (52%) positioned the questions at the end of chapters, 10 (43%) at the end of chapter sections, and 4 (17%) in the text margins. These numbers exceed 23 because some texts (Coon; Sternberg; Wade & Tavris) included questions at multiple locations. Most (16, 70%) of these 23 texts did not provide answers for any of their questions, in part because many critical thinking questions do not have a single correct answer.[3] However, if instructors do not specifically review this material with students, it is unlikely that students will have a yardstick for measuring their critical thinking skills. Possible sample answers provided in the text would help in such cases. Unfortunately, if instructors neither discuss answers to these questions nor include related material on examinations and tests, students may choose to ignore the questions entirely.

Scientific Thinking

Coverage of research methods appeared in the general introductory chapter in 16 texts, in a separate chapter on methodology in 20 texts, and only in the statistical appendix in one text. Table 2 shows 12 (32%) of the texts offered special features focusing on research methodology. More texts employed topic discussions (7) than model discussions (4), and 1 included some discussions of both types. The modeling approach, which typically involves tracing the research process from hypothesis formation to appropriate conclusions, serves as a technique to reinforce scientific thinking. Two texts (Baron; Plotnik) used questions as organizers within methodology discussions, and both provided

answers. There was little overlap between texts with methodology featured discussions and those with critical thinking featured discussions. Only three texts (Bernstein et al.; Davis & Palladino; Sdorow) had both types.

General Thinking

Table 3 provides information about 14 biases and difficulties in general thinking processes. Each appeared in at least 5 of the 37 texts. These discussions were usually located in the chapter on thought, although Carlson and Buskist included them in the social psychology chapter. All but 2 of the texts also discussed the "false consensus effect" in the social psychology chapter; Myers and Wade and Tavris included it in the methods chapter. Four biases appeared in the vast majority of texts: functional fixedness (89%), mental set (84%), the availability heuristic (81%), and the representativeness heuristic (81%). The representativeness heuristic typically served as the context for discussions about the base rate fallacy and the conjunction fallacy.

Table 3 reveals the 11 texts that covered more than half of the 14 biases are (in order of percentage of biases covered) Myers (93%); Baron and Kassin (both 79%); Weiten (71%); Bernstein et al. and Matlin (both 64%); and Gleitman; Hockenbury and Hockenbury; Nairne; Rathus; and Roediger, Capaldi, Paris, Polivy, and Herman (all five, 57%).

Statistical Thinking

Except for possibly mentioning the correlation coefficient when presenting methodology, most texts (25) discussed statistical thinking only in an appendix. Four (Carlson & Buskist; Kalat; Nairne; Peterson) discussed it only in the methods chapter, and seven (Baron; Bernstein et al.; Fernald; Matlin; Sdorow; Wade & Tavris; Weiten) included presentations in both places. One text (Westen) used a separate supplement to the methods chapter to introduce statistics.

Table 4 groups seven elements of statistical reasoning included in introductory psychology texts into three broad categories: (a) sampling, (b) analysis, and (c) statistical biases. We excluded one element of statistical reasoning (the inappropriateness of making causal inferences from correlational data) because it is covered in all 37 texts and another element (regression to the mean) because it is covered in only one text (Myers).

Almost all texts (36, 97%) discussed the importance of representative or unbiased sampling, and 26 (70%) referred to the influence of sample size on interpretation of research findings. About two thirds of the texts (25, 68%) covered both of these items. Information related to sampling generally appeared in either the methods section (chapter) or in the statistical appendix.

Most texts (34, 92%) indicated how the mean, median, and mode provide different measures of central tendency in skewed distributions. Ten (Atkinson, Atkinson, Smith, Bem, & Nolen-Hoeksema; Feldman; Morris; Myers; Nairne; Peterson; Plotnik; Sternberg; Wade & Tavris; Weiten) supplemented this discussion with graphical illustrations labeling the three measures of central tendency, reinforcing the relation between skewness and central tendency. Only six

---

[2]Word counts of critical thinking descriptions included only sections that explicitly referred to critical thinking or critical evaluation of research results. The counts did not include sections that described the scientific method without explicit reference to critical evaluation of the finished product.

[3]Although answers to some questions in some texts (e.g., Lefton and Plotnik) appear in an accompanying instructor's manual rather than in the text proper, our analysis did not extend to instructor's manuals.

Table 1. Comparative Data on Critical Thinking Features of 37 Introductory Psychology Textbooks

Textbook	Length of Critical Thinking Explanation (in Words)[a]	Critical Thinking Pedagogical Features			
		Discussion Format		Questions (Other Than in Discussions)	
		Model	Topic	With Answers	Without Answers
Atkinson et al.			•		
Baron	1,048				•
Bernstein et al.	1,991	•			
Carlson & Buskist	444	•			•
Coon	672		•	•[b]	•
Davis & Palladino	1,678		•		
Dworetzky			•		
Feldman	1,819		•		•
Fernald					•
Gerow					•
Gleitman					
Halonen & Santrock	2,690	•	•[c]		
Hockenbury & Hockenbury	825		•		
Huffman et al.	925		•		
Kagan & Segal				•	
Kalat	142				•
Kassin	1,296				
Lahey	1,396				•
Lefton	1,421				•
Matlin	84				•
Morris	714		•	•	
Myers	1,125		•	•	
Nairne					•
Peterson				•	
Plotnik				•[b]	•
Rathus	2,335				•
Roediger et al.	4,195		•		•
Santrock	2,734		•		
Sdorow	719		•		
Sternberg	355				•
Wade & Tavris	3,951		•	•	
Wallace & Goldstein					•
Weiten					
Westen	1,276				
Wood & Wood	616				•
Worchel & Shebilske					•
Zimbardo & Gerrig	783				

Note. The full references for the textbooks are in Appendix A.
[a]Word counts include both definitions of critical thinking and descriptions of the critical thinking process. [b]The Coon text includes immediate answers to questions at the end of sections but does not include answers to questions at the end of chapters. The Plotnik text includes answers to some questions but not to others. Thus, both the with answers and without answers boxes are marked for these texts. [c]In the Halonen and Santrock text, boxes are topic discussions, but each is specifically linked to one of their 10 critical thinking skills in psychology. Thus, model discussion is marked as well.

Table 2. Comparative Data on Methodological Features of 37 Introductory Psychology Textbooks

Textbook	Location of Main Coverage		Pedagogical Features Discussion Format	
	General Introductory Chapter	Separate Methods Chapter	Model	Topic
Atkinson et al.	•			
Baron	•			•
Bernstein et al.		•		•
Carlson & Buskist		•		
Coon		•		
Davis & Palladino	•			•
Dworetzky	•			
Feldman		•		
Fernald		•		
Gerow	•			
Gleitman[a]				
Halonen & Santrock		•		
Hockenbury & Hockenbury	•			
Huffman et al.	•			
Kagan & Segal	•			
Kalat		•	•	
Kassin	•		•	
Lahey	•			
Lefton	•		•[b]	•[b]
Matlin		•		•
Morris	•			
Myers		•		
Nairne		•		
Peterson		•		•
Plotnik		•		•
Rathus		•		
Roediger et al.	•			
Santrock		•		
Sdorow		•	•	
Sternberg		•		
Wade & Tavris		•		
Wallace & Goldstein	•			
Weiten		•	•	
Westen		•		
Wood & Wood	•			
Worchel & Shebilske	•			
Zimbardo & Gerrig		•		•

Note. The full references for the textbooks are in Appendix A.
[a]In the Gleitman text, information about methods appears only in the statistical appendix. [b]In the Lefton text, some features include a series of steps, modeling the research process, whereas others are topic discussions.

Table 3. Comparative Data on General Thinking Biases and Difficulties for Individual Textbooks

Textbook	Anchoring and Adjustment	Availability Heuristic	Base Rate Fallacy	Belief Bias	Belief Perseverance	Confirmation Bias	Conjunction Fallacy	False Consensus Effect	Framing	Functional Fixedness	Hindsight Bias	Mental Set	Over-confidence	Representativeness Heuristic
Atkinson et al.					•[a]		•							•
Baron	•	•	•	•[a]		•		•	•	•	•	•		•
Bernstein et al.	•	•		•		•				•		•	•	•
Carlson & Buskist		•	•			•		•						•
Coon			•	•[a]		•			•	•		•		
Davis & Palladino		•				•			•	•				•
Dworetzky										•		•		
Feldman		•		•[a]		•				•		•		•
Fernald		•				•			•	•		•		•
Gerow		•	•							•		•		•
Gleitman		•	•		•	•			•	•		•		•
Halonen & Santrock										•		•		
Hockenbury & Hockenbury		•	•[a]	•	•	•				•		•		•
Huffman et al.										•		•		
Kagan & Segal		•			•	•[a]				•		•	•[a]	•[a]
Kalat		•	•		•	•[a]			•		•	•	•	•
Kassin		•	•	•[a]	•	•			•		•	•	•	•
Lahey		•							•	•[a]		•		•
Lefton		•						•	•	•				•

(Continued)

Table 3. (Continued)

Textbook	Anchoring and Adjustment	Availability Heuristic	Base Rate Fallacy	Belief Bias	Belief Perseverance	Confirmation Bias	Conjunction Fallacy	False Consensus Effect	Framing	Functional Fixedness	Hindsight Bias	Mental Set	Over-confidence	Representativeness Heuristic
Matlin	•	•	•				•		•	•		•	•	•
Morris		•				•				•		•	•	•
Myers		•	•	•	•	•	•		•	•	•	•	•	•
Nairne	•	•	•				•		•	•		•		•
Peterson		•	•[a]					•		•				•
Plotnik		•								•		•		
Rathus	•	•							•	•	•[a]	•	•	•
Roediger et al.		•		•[a]					•	•		•		•
Santrock		•	•[a]					•		•		•		•
Sdorow		•							•			•		•
Sternberg		•	•			•				•		•	•	
Wade & Tavris		•				•		•	•		•			•
Wallace & Goldstein										•		•		
Weiten		•	•		•	•	•		•	•		•	•	•
Westen		•				•				•				•
Wood & Wood										•		•		
Worchel & Shebilske		•	•[a]			•				•		•		•
Zimbardo & Gerrig	•		•						•	•		•		•

Note. The full references for the textbooks are in Appendix A.
[a]Describes bias or difficulty, but does not label it with specific term.

Table 4. Comparative Data on Statistical Thinking Biases and Difficulties for Individual Textbooks

Textbook	Sampling		Analysis		Statistical Biases		
	Representative or Unbiased Sample	Importance of Sample Size	Selection of Central Tendency Measure	Misleading Graphs	Gambler's Fallacy	Illusory Correlation	Misperception of Randomness
Atkinson et al.	•		•			•	•
Baron	•	•	•	•			
Bernstein et al.	•	•	•		•	•	
Carlson & Buskist	•	•	•			•	
Coon	•		•		•		
Davis & Palladino	•		•		•		•
Dworetzky	•		•				
Feldman	•	•	•				
Fernald	•	•	•	•			
Gerow	•	•	•				
Gleitman	•	•	•			•	
Halonen & Santrock	•		•				
Hockenbury & Hockenbury	•	•	•				
Huffman et al.	•	•					
Kagan & Segal	•		•				•
Kalat	•	•	•	•	•	•	•
Kassin	•	•			•		•
Lahey	•	•	•				
Lefton	•	•	•				
Matlin	•	•	•				•
Morris	•		•				
Myers	•	•	•	•		•	•
Nairne	•		•			•	
Peterson	•	•	•				
Plotnik		•	•				
Rathus	•	•	•		•		•
Roediger et al.	•	•	•	•	•	•	•
Santrock	•		•		•		•
Sdorow	•		•				•
Sternberg	•	•	•		•	•	•
Wade & Tavris	•	•	•	•	•	•	•
Wallace & Goldstein	•		•				
Weiten	•	•	•		•	•	•
Westen	•	•	•				
Wood & Wood	•		•				
Worchel & Shebilske	•	•					
Zimbardo & Gerrig	•	•	•				

Note. The full references for the textbooks are in Appendix A.

texts (Baron; Fernald; Kalat; Myers; Roediger et al.; Wade & Tavris) extended their coverage of data analysis to include a caveat regarding misleading graphs (e.g., misrepresenting the scale of measurement on the ordinate).

Approximately half (19, 51%) discussed at least one of the three biases related to the interpretation of numerical data. Eleven (30%) considered the gambler's fallacy, most typically in the context of thinking and the illusion of control, rather than in a statistical appendix or methods section. Although 11 (30%) discussed illusory correlation, this discussion was often linked to stereotyping and perception of minority groups, topics outside the realm of statistical reasoning. Fifteen (40%) made at least some reference to the tendency to misinterpret random events, attributing order to situations in which order may not exist. This reference typically appeared in the chapter on thinking, often in connection with the representativeness heuristic.

Critical Thinking Supplements

We classified the 11 critical thinking supplements into three categories: (a) workbooks emphasizing review and application of textbook material, (b) workbooks emphasizing the evaluation of arguments and research, and (c) readers with discussion topics for classroom use or thought paper assignments. We placed the Prentice-Hall auditory cassette on critical thinking, a "talking" workbook, in the second category. Although most of the supplements are linked to specific introductory texts, the supplements are amenable for general use given the homogeneity of textbook coverage. Thus, we do not mention these links.

Given the diverse style and organization in these supplements, we could not effectively consolidate descriptive information in a table. Instead, we provide a brief narrative overview of each book. Within each category, we present our summaries in alphabetical order by first authors' surnames. Appendix B provides complete reference information.

Workbooks Emphasizing Review and Application of Textbook Material

Coats, Feldman, and Schwartzberg. This 205-page workbook begins with a 30-page discussion of critical thinking, which includes background information on critical thinking and education, different sources of knowledge, an explanation of four major critical thinking components (identifying and challenging assumptions, checking for factual accuracy and logical consistency, considering the importance of context, and imagining and exploring alternatives), and guidelines on applying critical thinking to evaluate research. Following this discussion, the workbook provides three to six case studies for each of 19 topics (e.g., learning), which are usually chapters in introductory textbooks. Each presents a scenario, then two to five questions that require students to apply critical thinking principles and information from the text to the story. The book does not contain answers to any questions.

Diogenes and Vestal. This 74-page workbook contains a series of exercises and activities keyed to 12 chapter topics typically covered in introductory textbooks. For each topic there are at least three types of exercises including space to

write answers. The first, "Thinking Critically About . . . ," generally includes four questions emphasizing recall and some elaboration of text material. The second, "Critical Thinking Exercises," includes four to seven application questions. The third, "Critical Thinking Activity," offers an opportunity for active involvement in research-related activities, guiding users through the process of designing materials, recruiting participants, and conducting and analyzing surveys. Six topics also include questions about human diversity. The book contains answers for all "Critical Thinking About . . . " and "Critical Thinking Exercises" questions.

Halonen. This 130-page workbook begins by explaining six types of critical thinking skills: pattern recognition, practical problem solving, creative problem solving, scientific problem solving, psychological reasoning, and perspective taking. This discussion is followed by 14 chapters on topics usually covered in introductory texts. Each chapter contains two to four exercises providing practice in a specific skill. The components of each skill are clarified prior to the initial exercise in which the skill is modeled. Some of the exercises involve brief scenarios followed by questions, whereas others require charts or rating scales. The number and format of questions vary. The book contains an answer key for all questions except a few that involve personal opinions. A concluding chapter summarizes the expected cognitive and metacognitive changes in students upon completion of the introductory course and exposure to the critical thinking process of psychologists.

Rathus. This 140-page workbook aims to stimulate writing about psychology. It is based on the premise that learning how to write also teaches you how to think. It begins with a 2-page discussion of critical thinking, then devotes the next 33 pages to writing processes and skills. The material covered includes kinds of writing (e.g., expository), types of psychology papers (e.g., reports of empirical studies), and guidelines for good writing. It then provides 100, generally 1-page, writing exercises linked to 17 topics typically covered in introductory textbooks (about 6 to 9 exercises for each major topic). Many of the writing topics use an "agree or disagree" prompt, whereas others ask for explanations. Students are encouraged to use critical thinking principles (be skeptical, examine definitions, weigh premises, examine evidence, and consider logic) in preparing their answers. Each exercise includes preliminary questions to focus students' attention on critical analysis.

Tishman. This 24-page workbook begins with a 4-page introductory section that explains how critical thinking can improve retention and suggests how students might optimize their benefits from using the workbook. It is designed for use outside the classroom by individuals or small groups. It contains from 6 to 10 questions keyed to each of 15 topics typically given chapter coverage in introductory texts. The questions extend textbook material by asking students either to apply what they have read, think of further examples, compare different perspectives, or design research. The book does not provide answers. This supplement is briefer than the others, probably because it is one of five booklets comprising a study kit accompanying a companion text.

Workbooks Emphasizing the Evaluation of Arguments and Research

Bell. This 74-page workbook helps students learn a six-step critical thinking process to use when reading secondary sources in psychology—identifying the source, reading to understand, analyzing definitions, identifying research evidence, evaluating research evidence, and evaluating the rest of the source (e.g., nonscientific evidence, missing information, and reasoning). This workbook is for individual use outside of the classroom, after students read the methodology section (chapter) in their textbook. The first two chapters introduce the critical thinking process and provide a review of the terminology of scientific research, respectively. The next three chapters introduce the six critical thinking steps in more depth, and the final chapter integrates the entire process. Each chapter contains several exercises giving practice for each skill presented. The book provides answers for most exercises, but each chapter contains at least one exercise without an answer.

Mayer and Goodchild. This 70-page workbook contains two sections—discovering strategies for critical thinking and applying strategies for critical thinking. The preface indicates that students can complete the reading and exercises in a total of 6 hr. After explaining critical thinking, the first section of the book discusses different types of assertions, evidence, and theoretical explanations and then provides strategies for understanding and evaluating arguments. The second section of the book provides five opportunities to apply the skills covered earlier, with each exercise linked to a topic typically given chapter coverage in introductory texts. Exercises include graphs and diagrams, and answers appear at the end of each exercise.

The Prentice-Hall Critical Thinking Audio Study Cassette. This 1-hr tape includes examples and opportunities for listener participation. It contrasts two styles of learning—passive absorption and active filtering—and then presents four questions regarding the structure of an argument: identifying the issues and conclusions, supporting reasons, ambiguous words and phrases, and underlying assumptions and value conflicts. Four additional questions pertain to evaluating the evidence: determining if the sample is appropriate, if the statistical reasoning is flawed, if there are logical fallacies, and if significant information is omitted. The tape also offers caveats concerning argumentative techniques including personal attacks, creating false dilemmas, detracting attention from an issue, and begging the question. The final part is devoted to study skills, focusing on the SQ3R technique. Much of the content on this cassette is adapted from an earlier edition of a critical thinking book (Browne & Keeley, 1994) published by the same company.

Readers With Discussion Topics

McBurney. This 111-page reader offers 46 selections keyed to topics typically covered in introductory psychology. Each selection is about 2 pages long and is linked to a principle of psychology and the scientific method. Each se-

lection ends with one or two questions or exercises that entail critical thinking via discussing material from a textbook, explaining relationships, thinking of examples, linking material to personal experience, and other activities. The book does not provide answers.

Smith. This 128-page reader begins by explaining seven guidelines for critical thinking: tolerating ambiguity, identifying biases, maintaining a skeptical attitude, separating facts from opinion, avoiding oversimplification, using logical inferences, and examining available evidence before drawing conclusions. It also provides caveats for interpreting reports about psychology in the popular media and for dealing with "seductive statistics" (intentionally misleading statistics). It then offers 10 selections, each keyed to a different topic typically covered in introductory psychology. Each selection concludes with sections that point out violations of critical thinking guidelines, preconceptions that might bias thinking, and a paragraph summarizing the conclusions that may be appropriately drawn from the reading. For each selection, there are four to six critical thinking questions or exercises that may involve limited library research, developing counterarguments, linking material to personal experiences, seeking items from the popular media, and designing experiments or stimulus materials. The book does not provide answers.

Tavris. This 86-page reader offers 19 selections by Tavris—slightly edited opinion essays and book reviews originally published in *The Los Angeles Times* or *The New York Times Book Review*. The readings are broadly categorized into three sections: science versus pseudoscience, mental disorders and mental health, and applying psychology to social issues. The selections are on controversial topics, each explicitly linked to at least one chapter typically included in introductory texts. The book begins by presenting eight guidelines for critical thinking: asking questions, defining the problem, examining the evidence, analyzing assumptions, avoiding emotional reasoning, rejecting oversimplifications, considering other interpretations, and tolerating uncertainty. A summary of key points and questions precedes each selection.

Summary Comments

The choice of a supplement depends primarily on the rationale for introducing it. If a teacher aims to stimulate classroom discussion, one of the readers may be the best choice. The McBurney, Smith, and Tavris books all contain thought-provoking questions for each topic. Within this group, selection may depend on specific topics covered, desired depth of coverage, and inclusion of guidelines for critical thinking.

If a teacher intends to supplement textbook material with an emphasis on the general skill of evaluating arguments, there are two workbooks and an auditory tape from which to choose. Of the three, the Bell workbook is directed more specifically at evaluating articles written in scientific format. The Mayer and Goodchild workbook is geared toward understanding and evaluating arguments in general, as is the Prentice-Hall cassette.

If a teacher prefers a vehicle for review of material presented in the text, there are five choices. The Rathus workbook uniquely emphasizes writing techniques and opportunities for practicing writing skills. The Coats, Feldman, and Schwartzberg workbook is distinguished by its extensive coverage of critical thinking. The Halonen workbook provides a specific model of critical thinking involving six distinct skills, each practiced in several exercises. Both the Diogenes and Vestal and the Tishman workbooks include some exercises that involve research design. Thus, in selecting a supplement, a teacher might initially choose among the three broad categories of offerings based on class format and goals, then discriminate within the selected category by focusing on specific content and presentation style.

As stated earlier, although most of the supplements are linked to specific introductory texts, they are all relatively well-suited for general use. We realize, however, that selecting a supplement from a publisher other than the one offering your text might increase the overall cost to students because no shrinkwrap discount offer could apply. Other than this possible drawback, we endorse evaluating the supplements on their own merits and compatibility with instructor aims.

General Discussion

Because the population of introductory psychology texts is continually changing, this flux remains an inevitable shortcoming of any textbook study. However, given the recent consolidations of publishers of these texts, we expect that the number of new introductory texts appearing in the near future will be minimal. In addition, we reduced the impact of this shift on our findings by examining all of the currently viable introductory texts and supplementary materials.

Our approach to this analysis was clearly quantitative rather than qualitative. We recognize that critical thinking extends beyond word counts and checklists. Some authors opt for an integrated approach, interweaving a critical thinking theme throughout the narrative. Acknowledging that any evaluation of such a technique would be highly subjective, we chose to focus our content analysis on features readily amenable to objective measurement (see also footnote 1). We also recognize that students' attention to and benefit from critical thinking features are highly dependent on instructors' demands. We surmise that students may bypass such devices as boxed inserts and discussion questions unless the instructor specifically incorporates this material into classroom discussions or assessment measures.

Given these caveats, what can we conclude about the present set of textbooks and supplementary materials? The majority of introductory psychology textbooks discuss critical thinking, but they differ greatly both in the manner and extent of their coverage. Textbooks also vary considerably in their focus on methodology beyond the basic coverage as well as in their discussion of general and statistical biases and difficulties in thinking. Similarly, textbook supplements devoted to critical thinking approach the topic from different perspectives. Some are specifically tailored to

classroom discussion, whereas others are designed as workbooks for individual use. Some emphasize review of textbook material, whereas others focus on evaluating arguments. Thus, teachers who choose to actively incorporate critical thinking into their introductory course have an array of options, and the findings of this study should facilitate their decision process.

Given the current emphasis on critical thinking in psychology and the academic community in general, we also note that introductory psychology textbook coverage in this area is far from asymptotic. Only about two thirds of the texts define and discuss the critical thinking process, and only a small minority actually model critical thinking in features throughout the text. Some texts rely primarily on thought-provoking questions to promote critical thinking, although the effectiveness of this technique among student readers seems dependent on teacher emphasis. We view these findings from an optimistic "cup half full" perspective, suggesting room for growth in new texts and future editions of current introductory textbooks.

References

Arons, A. B. (1979). Some thoughts on reasoning capabilities implicitly expected of college students. In J. Lochhead & J. Clements (Eds.), *Cognitive process instruction: Research on teaching thinking skills* (pp. 209–215). Philadelphia: Franklin Institute Press.

Bell, J. (1997, January). *Teaching students to think critically using active and cooperative learning techniques.* Workshop at National Institute on the Teaching of Psychology, St. Petersburg Beach, FL.

Browne, M. N., & Keeley, S. M. (1994). *Asking the right questions: A guide to critical thinking* (4th ed.). Englewood Cliffs, NJ: Prentice-Hall.

Cush, D. T., & Buskist, W. (1997). Future of the introductory psychology textbook: A survey of college publishers. *Teaching of Psychology, 24,* 119–122.

Griggs, R. A. (1997). Prologue. In R. J. Sternberg (Ed.), *Teaching introductory psychology: Survival tips from the experts* (pp. 1–5). Washington, DC: American Psychological Association.

Griggs, R. A., & Jackson, S. L. (1989). The introductory psychology textbook market: Perceptions of authors and editors. *Teaching of Psychology, 16,* 61–64.

Griggs, R. A., Jackson, S. L., & Napolitano, T. J. (1994). Brief introductory psychology textbooks: An objective analysis. *Teaching of Psychology, 21,* 136–140.

Halonen, J. S. (1995). Demystifying critical thinking. *Teaching of Psychology, 22,* 75–81.

Halpern, D. F., & Nummedal, S. G. (Eds.). (1995). Psychologists teach critical thinking [Special issue]. *Teaching of Psychology, 22*(1).

Levy, D. A. (1997). *Tools of critical thinking: Metathoughts for psychology.* Needham Heights, MA: Allyn & Bacon.

Marek, P., Jackson, S. L., Griggs, R. A., & Christopher, A. N. (1998). Supplementary books on critical thinking. *Teaching of Psychology, 25,* 266–269.

McBurney, D. H. (1996). *How to think like a psychologist: Critical thinking in psychology.* Upper Saddle River, NJ: Prentice-Hall.

Nummedal, S. G., & Halpern, D. F. (1995). Introduction: Making the case for "Psychologists teach critical thinking." *Teaching of Psychology, 22,* 4–5.

Smith, R. A. (1995). *Challenging your preconceptions: Thinking critically about psychology.* Pacific Grove, CA: Brooks/Cole.

Stanovich, K. E. (1998). *How to think straight about psychology* (5th ed.). New York: Addison Wesley Longman.

Wade, C., & Tavris, C. (1987). *Psychology*. New York: Harper & Row.

Appendix A
Full-Length Introductory Psychology Texts Used in This Study

(Since the publication of the current editions of these 37 textbooks, more publishing companies have merged; there are now only 10 companies publishing introductory textbooks. The most important changes for identifying the new publishers of some of the textbooks, supplements, and supplementary books in this study are that Brown & Benchmark is now part of McGraw-Hill, HarperCollins is now part of Addison Wesley Longman, West is now part of International Thomson Publishing with Brooks/Cole and Wadsworth, and Worth is now part of the Scientific American/St. Martin's College Publishing Group.)

Atkinson, R. L., Atkinson, R. C., Smith, E. E., Bem, D. J., & Nolen-Hoeksema, S. (1996). *Hilgard's introduction to psychology* (12th ed.). Fort Worth, TX: Harcourt Brace.

Baron, R. A. (1995). *Psychology* (3rd ed.). Needham Heights, MA: Allyn & Bacon.

Bernstein, D. A., Clarke-Stewart, A., Roy, E. J., & Wickens, C. D. (1997). *Psychology* (4th ed.). Boston, MA: Houghton Mifflin.

Carlson, N. R., & Buskist, W. (1997). *Psychology: The science of behavior* (5th ed.). Needham Heights, MA: Allyn & Bacon.

Coon, D. (1995). *Introduction to psychology: Exploration and application* (7th ed.). St. Paul, MN: West.

Davis, S. F., & Palladino, J. J. (1997). *Psychology* (2nd ed.). Upper Saddle River, NJ: Prentice-Hall.

Dworetzky, J. P. (1997). *Psychology* (6th ed.). Pacific Grove, CA: Brooks/Cole.

Feldman, R. S. (1996). *Understanding psychology* (4th ed.). New York: McGraw-Hill.

Fernald, D. (1997). *Psychology*. Upper Saddle River, NJ: Prentice-Hall.

Gerow, J. R. (1997). *Psychology: An introduction* (5th ed.). New York: Addison Wesley Longman.

Gleitman, H. (1995). *Psychology* (4th ed.). New York: Norton.

Halonen, J. S., & Santrock, J. W. (1996). *Psychology: Contexts of behavior* (2nd ed.). Dubuque, IA: Brown & Benchmark.

Hockenbury, D. H., & Hockenbury, S. E. (1997). *Psychology*. New York: Worth.

Huffman, K., Vernoy, M., & Vernoy, J. (1997). *Psychology in action* (4th ed.). New York: Wiley.

Kagan, J., & Segal, J. (1995). *Psychology: An introduction* (8th ed.). Fort Worth, TX: Harcourt Brace.

Kalat, J. W. (1996). *Introduction to psychology* (4th ed.). Pacific Grove, CA: Brooks/Cole.

Kassin, S. (1995). *Psychology*. Boston: Houghton Mifflin.

Lahey, B. B. (1995). *Psychology: An introduction* (5th ed.). Dubuque, IA: Brown & Benchmark.

Lefton, L. A. (1997). *Psychology* (6th ed.). Needham Heights, MA: Allyn & Bacon.

Matlin, M. W. (1995). *Psychology* (2nd ed.). Fort Worth, TX: Harcourt Brace.

Morris, C. G. (1996). *Psychology: An introduction* (9th ed.). Upper Saddle River, NJ: Prentice-Hall.

Myers, D. G. (1995). *Psychology* (4th ed.). New York: Worth.

Nairne, J. S. (1997). *Psychology: The adaptive mind*. Pacific Grove, CA: Brooks/Cole.

Peterson, C. (1997). *Psychology: A biopsychosocial approach* (2nd ed.). New York: Addison Wesley Longman.

Plotnik, R. (1996). *Introduction to psychology* (4th ed.). Pacific Grove, CA: Brooks/Cole.

Rathus, S. A. (1996). *Psychology in the new millennium* (6th ed.). Fort Worth, TX: Harcourt Brace.

Roediger, H. L., III, Capaldi, E. D., Paris, S. G., Polivy, J., & Herman, C. P. (1996). *Psychology* (4th ed.). St. Paul, MN: West.

Santrock, J. W. (1997). *Psychology* (5th ed.). Dubuque, IA: Brown & Benchmark.

Sdorow, L. M. (1995). *Psychology* (3rd ed.). Dubuque, IA: Brown & Benchmark.

Sternberg, R. J. (1995). *In search of the human mind*. Fort Worth, TX: Harcourt Brace.

Wade, C., & Tavris, C. (1996). *Psychology* (4th ed.). New York: HarperCollins.

Wallace, P. M., & Goldstein, J. H. (1997). *An introduction to psychology* (4th ed.), Dubuque, IA: Brown & Benchmark.

Weiten, W. (1995). *Psychology: Themes and variations* (3rd ed.). Pacific Grove, CA: Brooks/Cole.

Westen, D. (1996). *Psychology: Mind, brain, and culture*. New York: Wiley.

Wood, S. E., & Wood, E. G. (1996). *The world of psychology* (2nd ed.). Needham Heights, MA: Allyn & Bacon.

Worchel, S., & Shebilske, W. (1995). *Psychology: Principles and applications* (5th ed.). Englewood Cliffs, NJ: Prentice-Hall.

Zimbardo, P. G., & Gerrig, R. J. (1996). *Psychology and life* (14th ed.). New York: HarperCollins.

Appendix B
Critical Thinking Supplements for Introductory Psychology

Bell, J. (1995). *Evaluating psychological information: Sharpening your critical thinking skills* (2nd ed.). Needham Heights, MA: Allyn & Bacon.

Coats, E. J., Feldman, R. S., & Schwartzberg, S. (1994). *Critical thinking: General principles & case studies*. New York: McGraw-Hill.

Diogenes, R., & Vestal, L. (1994). *Prentice-Hall critical thinking resource manual for psychology*. Englewood Cliffs, NJ: Prentice-Hall.

Halonen, J. (1995). *The critical thinking companion for introductory psychology*. New York: Worth.

Mayer, R., & Goodchild, F. (1995). *The critical thinker* (2nd ed.). Dubuque, IA: Brown & Benchmark.

McBurney, D. H. (1996). *How to think like a psychologist: Critical thinking in psychology*. Upper Saddle River, NJ: Prentice-Hall.

The Prentice-Hall critical thinking audio study cassette. (1989). Englewood Cliffs, NJ: Prentice-Hall.

Rathus, S. A. (1997). *Thinking and writing about psychology* (2nd ed.). Fort Worth, TX: Harcourt Brace.

Smith, R. A. (1995). *Challenging your preconceptions: Thinking critically about psychology*. Pacific Grove, CA: Brooks/Cole.

Tavris, C. (1995). *Psychobabble and biobunk: Using psychology to think critically about issues in the news*. New York: HarperCollins.

Tishman, S. (1997). *Critical thinking in psychology*. New York: Addison Wesley Longman.

Notes

1. We thank all of the publishing companies that provided copies of the textbooks and critical thinking supplements for our use, three anonymous reviewers, Jim Bell, and Randolph Smith for their invaluable comments on an earlier version of this manuscript.

Köhler's Insight Revisited

George Windholz
P. A. Lamal
The University of North Carolina at Charlotte

Wolfgang Köhler's two-stick experiment—involving a chimpanzee joining two sticks and then raking in a bait placed outside its cage—was published about 60 years ago (Köhler, 1917/1925). This particular study is still described in many American psychology textbooks (e.g., introductory, learning, and history and systems). It is almost invariably presented as an example, par excellence, of the Gestalt notion of insight, as opposed to Edward L. Thorndike's idea of trial-and-error learning. The student reading the textbook accounts of Köhler's insight studies might conclude that the concept of insight was well established and thoroughly confirmed. We contend that textbook writers' dissemination of such a conclusion is unwarranted. We also note that the issue of insight is still alive, as in the current reinterpretation of the notion by radical behaviorists (e.g., Epstein, 1981; Epstein, Kirshnit, Lanza, & Rubin, 1984).

Citation of Köhler's Insight Studies

An unsystematic survey of 19 recently published introductory psychology textbooks indicated that Köhler's insight studies are referred to in 17 of them; the two-stick experiment was mentioned in 8 of the books. Of the 10 learning textbooks examined, Köhler's insight studies are referred to in 8; the two-stick experiment is cited in 5. Köhler's insight studies are mentioned in every one of the 7 history and systems texts that were sampled, with the two-stick experiment cited in 5.

Köhler's Two-Stick Study: The Original Description and Interpretation

Köhler's two-stick study was first performed between 1913 and 1917 as part of the general research project on the intelligence of anthropoid apes at the Anthropoid Station in Tenerife, Canary Islands. Köhler's *Intelligenzprüfung an Menschenaffen* was published first in 1917, and its English version, *The Mentality of Apes*, appeared in 1925.

The description of the two-stick study was mainly based on the observation of the behavior of a chimpanzee named Sultan by Köhler and the animal's keeper. The problem confronting Sultan was to obtain a bait located outside his cage with the aid of two bamboo sticks of equal length but different thickness. Problem solution required that the thinner stick be inserted in the hollow end of the thicker stick making a stick long enough to reach the bait. At first, a number of unsuccessful behaviors were observed. These included pushing a box toward the bars, using one stick to touch the bait, and pushing one stick with another toward the bait. According to the keeper's report, Sultan finally sat on the box, played with the two sticks, held a stick in each hand, pushed the thinner one in the hollow end of the thicker one, moved to the bars, and pulled in the bait with the joined sticks.

Köhler interpreted the solution in terms of an insight that, on a perceptual level, took into consideration the relation of the elements to each other. This interpretation contrasted with Thorndike's understanding of problem solutions as the outcome of a fortuitously successful behavior out of many other behaviors the animal had exhibited. The main behavioral distinction between Köhler's insightful solution and Thorndike's trial-and-error explanation was seen in the relative suddenness with which Sultan solved the problem (about 5 min), as contrasted with the relatively slow solution typically obtained in trial-and-error learning.

The insight interpretation of the two-stick experiment is justified provided there is sufficient evidence to show that chimpanzees solve the problem according to the criteria of insightful learning, such as suddenness of the solution. Before concluding that the chimpanzee had demonstrated insight, Köhler's experiment should be replicated and controlled. Our aim is to consider whether subsequent studies supported Köhler's interpretation of the two-stick experiment.

Replications and Reinterpretations of the Two-Stick Experiment

In an attempt to resolve the issue of whether the solution of complex problems is insightful or achieved by trial-and-error, Pechstein and Brown (1939) replicated the two-stick experiment. The subject, Romeo, was a male chimpanzee, about 4½ years of age. The first trial of the two-stick problem lasted 30 min and ended with failure. It was observed that Romeo tried to pull in the bait using either stick separately, and that he played with the two sticks attempting to insert one stick into the other.

Romeo solved the problem 17 min after the beginning of the second trial. Romeo's behavior showed two patterns: joining the two sticks, and attempting to reach the bait with one stick. The solution was accomplished when the two patterns were combined; the ape joined the two sticks together and used the single long stick to rake in the bait. Pechstein and Brown concluded that at the end of the experiment, which consisted of 11 trials over 4 days, the ape achieved a solution that satisfied the criteria of insight but achieved it through trial-and-error behavior.

Wazuro's (1962) controlled replication of the two-stick experiment was a continuation of Ivan P. Pavlov's work with apes at the Koltushi Biological Station in the U.S.S.R. during the 1930s. Pavlov replicated Köhler's building experiment, which involved chimps piling up boxes to reach a suspended bait, and interpreted the results within his theory of higher nervous activity. According to Pavlov's theory, the solution is achieved through trial-and-error behavior, which results in the formation of associations on the cortical level. Köhler considered the ape's inactive period to be the visual survey of the entire situation preceding the insightful solution, but Pavlov considered it to be a period of mere rest (Windholz, 1984).

Wazuro became the director of the Primate Laboratory at Koltushi in 1937, a year after Pavlov's death (Kvasov & Fedorova-Grot, 1967). Wazuro (1962) replicated Köhler's two-stick experiment using Pavlov's male chimpanzee named Raphael as his subject (Ladygina-Kots, 1959). The controlled aspect of the experiment consisted of giving the ape two sticks. The thicker stick had a hole at one end, and several similar holes made along the side of the stick. The insertion of the thinner stick into the hole at the end of the thicker stick would produce a stick long enough to rake in the bait. The insertion of the thinner stick into one of the holes at the side of the thicker stick would form a "T" figure, which would not enable the ape to reach the bait.

The ape was first given the two sticks without the bait; he then put the thinner stick in the holes of the thicker stick (which one was not reported). Subsequently a bait was placed outside the cage. The ape put the thinner stick into the holes of the thicker stick forming the T figure (that was insufficiently long) and tried to rake in the bait. Then Raphael took apart the sticks and attempted to rake in the bait using only one stick. After numerous trials the ape placed the thinner stick into the hole at the end of the thicker one and used the construction to pull in the bait.

Schiller (1952) found that chimps fitted sticks together as part of their play behavior, and that age was an important variable as older chimps were more likely to join the sticks. He concluded that the chimps' fitting the sticks together and using the resulting longer stick as a tool to obtain food were independent activities. The chimps often joined the sticks and pulled them apart without using the joined sticks to obtain the bait. "In none of the animals tested was there any evidence of the immediate perception of a relation between the united sticks and the distance of the food to be reached" (Schiller, 1952, p. 185). Although Schiller concluded that specific experiences were a prerequisite to insightful behavior, he also pointed out the need for research conducted with animals whose histories have been controlled, which was not true of Köhler's chimps.

Conclusion

The replication studies of Köhler's two-stick experiment, using chimpanzees as subjects, provide little support for their interpretation in terms of insight. Ultimately, most apes joined the two sticks and raked in the bait, but the process was not sudden and the importance of prior experience cannot be dismissed.

Köhler interpreted the solution of the problem on the perceptual level, where the ape obtains insight by restructuring the entire field. However, the results indicate that the solution of the problem was reached on the behavioral level as a result of experience with the relevant aspects of the problem situation (Birch, 1945; Epstein, 1981; Epstein et al., 1984; Harlow, 1951). According to this interpretation, the chimpanzee emits various overt responses when confronted with the problem. Those responses that fail to obtain the bait are extinguished, and those that obtain the bait are more likely to recur when the chimpanzee is again confronted with the same problem. This behavioral interpretation eschews speculation about unobservable processes occurring in the chimpanzee, such as the chimpanzee's perceptual restructuring of the field.

This alternative interpretation suggests a change in the presentation of the two-stick experiment interpretation in psychology textbooks. We have seen that Köhler's two-stick experiment is frequently used to illustrate the concept of insight in contradistinction to the concept of learning by trial-and-error. This one-sided conclusion is by no means warranted. The presentation in textbooks of Köhler's two-stick experiment is, of course, justifiable. The interpretation of the experiment solely in terms of insight, however, is unwarranted because it may create the misleading impression that Köhler's insight interpretation is the only one possible.

References

Birch, H. G. (1945). The relation of previous experience to insightful problem-solving. *Journal of Comparative Psychology, 38,* 367–383.

Epstein, R. (1981). On pigeons and people: A preliminary look at the Columban Simulation Project. *The Behavior Analyst, 4,* 43–55.

Epstein, R., Kirshnit, C. E., Lanza, R. P., & Rubin, L. C. (1984). "Insight" in the pigeon: Antecedents and determinants of an intelligent performance. *Nature, 308,* 61–62.

Harlow, H. F. (1951). Primate learning. In C. P. Stone (Ed.), *Comparative psychology* (3rd ed., pp. 183–238). Englewood Cliffs, NJ: Prentice-Hall.

Köhler, W. (1925). *The mentality of apes* (2nd rev. ed.) (E. Winter, Trans.). London: Routledge & Kegan Paul. (Original work published 1917)

Kvasov, D. G., & Fedorova-Grot, A. K. (1967). *Fiziologicheskaia shkola I. P. Pavlova* [The physiological school of I. P. Pavlov]. Leningrad: Izdatel'stvo Nauka.

Ladygina-Kots, N. N. (1959). *Konstruktivnaia i orudiinaia deiatelnost' vysshikh obezian (shimpanze)* [The constructive and tool-making activities of higher primates (chimpanzees)]. Moskva: Izdatel'stvo Akademii Nauk SSSR.

Pechstein, L. A., & Brown, F. D. (1939). An experimental analysis of the alleged criteria of insight learning. *Journal of Educational Psychology, 30,* 38–52.

Schiller, P. H. (1952). Innate constituents of complex responses in primates. *Psychological Review, 59,* 177–191.

Wazuro, E. G. (1962). *Die Lehre Pawlows von der Höheren Nerventätigkeit* [Pavlov's teachings on the higher nervous activity]. Berlin: Volk und Wissen Volkseigener Verlag.

Windholz, G. (1984). Pavlov versus Köhler: Pavlov's little-known primate research. *Pavlovian Journal of Biological Science, 19,* 23–31.

Notes

1. We thank W. C. McGrew for his comments on an earlier draft of this article.

Who Is Mrs. Cantlie and Why Are They Doing Those Terrible Things to Her Homunculi?

Richard A. Griggs
University of Florida

If you teach introductory psychology or have some introductory psychology texts at hand, choose one at random. Examine the section on the brain. Look for *homunculi*—those strange drawings of distorted human anatomy in which the size of the body part is proportional to its area in the motor or somatosensory cortex and not its actual size. If homunculi are used to illustrate both the motor and somatosensory cortical areas, check their accuracy. It is very likely that you will find an error (e.g., the left hemisphere will be indicated, but the homunculus will be for the left side of the body instead of the right side).

Why is there such a high error rate for these illustrations? My interest in this question was piqued when in the second printing of Myers's *Psychology* (1986), several errors in the physiological illustrations were corrected, but the errors in the homunculi were not. Before this happened, I had the subjective feeling that many of the homunculi in introductory texts were inaccurate, but I had not conducted a very objective study of this problem. Myers's text is excellent and one of the most popular for the introductory course. If the homunculi in this text are incorrect, then inaccurate homunculi might be a problem in other introductory texts. So I decided to conduct a more objective study.

Because my copies of the 1987 batch of introductory psychology texts were conveniently located in a stack ready for transfer to a closet in preparation for the onslaught of 1988 introductory texts, I decided to use the 1987 texts for my study. I had 21 such texts (some new editions; some new texts). This set of texts is probably close to an exhaustive sample of the introductory texts for 1987.

Of the 21, 7 did not include homunculi and 2 used only a motor homunculus, which was correct in both cases. However, in the texts that used both motor and somatosensory homunculi, 11 of the 12 contained errors! Five had one side of the body paired with the opposite side of the face within the same homunculus, and 6 indicated a particular hemisphere but depicted the wrong side of the body and face for that hemisphere.

Having more firmly established the existence of these errors, I decided to attempt to identify their origin. When a reference source was cited for the homunculi, invariably it was Penfield and Rasmussen (1950). After a brief search, I found a copy of this book in my university's medical school library. I discovered that the original source for these homunculi was a certain Mrs. H. P. Cantlie, who had provided a combined sensory and motor homunculus for an earlier article by Penfield and Boldrey (1937). Because of some inaccuracies in the earlier combined homunculus, Mrs. Cantlie provided the separate sensory and motor homunculi for the Penfield and Rasmussen (1950) book (see Figures 17. and 22, respectively; they are also repeated in Figures 114 and 115).

Mrs. Cantlie's two homunculi appear to be for the same hemisphere but from postcentral (for the sensory homunculus) and precentral (for the motor homunculus) gyral views of the left hemisphere. However, they are not explicitly labeled as such in the figure captions. Thus, the precentral gyral view of the left hemisphere might be misinterpreted as the right hemisphere. Such a misrepresentation is enhanced by the fact that Penfield and Rasmussen invite the reader to compare these two figures with an earlier figure (Figure 9) in which both left and right hemispheres are depicted. The authors' purpose for this comparison was to examine size and sequencing for the various body parts in each type of cortex and had nothing to do with particular hemispheres.

Clearly, adaptation of the homunculi found in the Penfield and Rasmussen book for introductory psychology texts could lead to errors. However, it does not seem plausible that the Penfield and Rasmussen presentation is responsible for all of the various types of errors that have appeared. It is more likely that some of the errors (especially those in which one side of the body is paired with the opposite side of the face within the same homunculus) have resulted from adaptations from secondary sources, such as other introductory texts. The resulting inaccurate homunculi comprise a good example of what not to do in writing texts. Adapting secondary sources may not only perpetuate an error but may also compound it. Also, such use of secondary sources probably plays a major role in the commonality of topics and illustrations across introductory psychology texts. It almost seems that the primary sources for any new introductory text are the existing introductory texts.

Another matter that I have not resolved but wish to share with you concerns the appearance of a seemingly female breast in some of the homunculi, usually a left breast in the motor homunculus. It did not appear in Mrs. Cantlie's original homunculi. It did, however, appear in about 25% of the 1987 texts depicting both homunculi. There is nothing in Mrs. Cantlie's original motor homunculus that would lead to this addition (Penfield & Rasmussen, 1950). I did find such a breast in Geschwind's 1979 *Scientific American* article on the brain (cited in Hebb & Donderi, 1987). (Even Geschwind has the errors described earlier in his homunculi.) Thus, Geschwind's article is a likely source of the breast (and maybe the errors) appearing in the 1987 texts.

Geschwind probably adapted his homunculi from some earlier source, but provides no reference. However, I would like to think that somewhere along the way Mrs. Cantlie has ghostdrawn these homunculi with breasts in order to reduce the sexual bias prevalent in her earlier drawings. (Have you ever noticed the male genitals in them?) And why not? Her homunculi have come a long way.

References

Geschwind, N. (1979). Specializations of the human brain. *Scientific American, 241*, 180–199.

Hebb, D. O., & Donderi, D. C. (1987). *Textbook of psychology* (4th ed.). Hillsdale, NJ: Lawrence Erlbaum Associates, Inc.

Myers, D. G. (1986). *Psychology*. New York: Worth Publishers.

Penfield, W., & Boldrey, E. (1937). Somatic motor and sensory representation in the cerebral cortex of man as studied by electrical stimulation. *Brain, 60*, 389–443.

Penfield, W., & Rasmussen, T. (1950). *The cerebral cortex of man: A clinical study of localization of function*. New York: Macmillan.

The Portrayal of Child Sexual Assault in Introductory Psychology Textbooks

Elizabeth J. Letourneau
Department of Corrections
United States Air Force

Tonya C. Lewis
Beckwith Mental Health Center
Greenwood, South Carolina

For the past 15 years, scientist–practitioners in clinical and social psychology and related fields have documented the high prevalence rates of child sexual assault (CSA). A recent survey of adolescents (Boney-McCoy & Finkelhor, 1995) reported that 15% of adolescent girls and 6% of adolescent boys had experienced contact sexual assault (fondling and rape) or serious noncontact sexual assault (exhibitionism, voyeurism, and requests to engage in sexual activities). Robust findings indicate that victims of CSA are at increased risk for a variety of psychological disorders, including depression (e.g., Conte, 1988), posttraumatic stress disorder (e.g., Boney-McCoy & Finkelhor, 1995), other anxiety disorders (e.g., Saunders, Villeponteaux, Lipovsky, Kilpatrick, & Veronen, 1992), and increased use and abuse of alcohol and other substances (e.g., Briere, 1988).

These findings led to increased awareness of and improved treatment for CSA victims. Finkelhor (1995) noted the movement toward a better understanding of sexual assault victimization has been successful and has reached some of its goals earlier, with less opposition, than have other movements (e.g., the movement to reduce tobacco

use). Given these successes, Finkelhor argued that it was perhaps predictable that some opposition would form against victims of sexual crimes and those professionals who help them. In particular, opposition has formed against survivors of CSA who pursue legal redress as adults (Enns, McNeilly, Corkery, & Gilbert, 1995; Finkelhor, 1995). Central to this opposition is controversy surrounding delayed recall of CSA memories (Enns et al., 1995).

Several theories propose mechanisms for delayed recall of traumatic events. The False Memory Syndrome Foundation (FMSF) both proposed and popularized the theory that a substantial proportion of CSA victims has *false memory syndrome*, a term coined by the FMSF (1995). The FMSF, with the assistance of its scientific advisory board, proposed that false memories of CSA are formed when therapists (or others) persist in identifying certain symptoms with a history of CSA, even when clients deny such a history. Berliner (1997) provided an up-to-date review of alternate theories regarding delayed recall of CSA. One of the most widely cited theories is psychoanalytically oriented and suggests that children repress upsetting memories until they are better

83

equipped to handle conscious recollections of abuse. Another theory is that memories of abuse are subject to the same vagaries as nontraumatic memories including problems with memory encoding, storage, and retrieval. Despite the latter theory, previously inaccessible memories of CSA are often labeled "repressed" memories by researchers (e.g., Loftus, 1993a, 1993b) and special interest groups (e.g., Freyd, 1996).

The debate between supporters of the false memory theory and supporters of the repressed memory theory has been controversial and highly publicized (e.g., Brokaw, 1997). In response to concerns raised by this debate, the American Psychological Association (APA) formed a working group to investigate memory of childhood abuse (Alpert et al., 1996). In brief, the APA working group concluded that there is insufficient research at present to provide answers to many of the questions raised by the memory debate. However, it also concluded that most experts in the field of memory and trauma believe (a) memories of childhood abuse can be forgotten and then accurately remembered, (b) it may be possible for adults to form false memories of childhood abuse, and (c) at this point it is impossible to distinguish a true memory from a false one in the absence of corroborative evidence. Thus, it seems clear that any discussion of memory issues should be tentative and should provide information from both sides of the controversy.

The FMSF credited itself with providing a "corrective to a run-away belief system" (Freyd, 1996, p. 3) and noted that its views are now presented in numerous media sources, including psychology textbooks. College textbooks reach a large population, yet they represent a source of information on CSA that has gone unstudied to date. For many college students, introductory psychology provides their only collegiate exposure to topics such as CSA. In this article, we examine the manner in which introductory psychology textbooks present CSA-related issues.

Method

Sample

We identified recently published introductory psychology textbooks by querying faculty in the psychology department at a small public university in the southeast and by reviewing *Books in Print* (1996). This search resulted in the identification of over 50 introductory psychology textbooks. We were able to procure 24 of these texts, all published between 1994 and 1997 (see the Appendix).

Procedure

The review of each textbook consisted of reading sections that contained any of the following key words or topics from subject indexes: (a) abuse or abuse prevention, (b) child abuse, (c) child sexual assault, (d) depression, (e) eyewitness testimony, (f) false memories, (g) false memory syndrome, (h) rape, (i) reconstructed or recovered memories, (j) repression, (k) repressed memory or repressed memory syndrome, and (l) sexual assault. We also read sections referring to Elizabeth Loftus or Linda Williams, two prominent memory researchers.

We established five distinct but broad categories of overgeneralizations pertaining to unbalanced presentations of CSA. We then independently reread and placed the textbook sections into zero, one, or more of these categories. We resolved all discrepancies on category placement through review of the material in question. To avoid focusing on individual authors, we note quoted material from individual textbooks by chronological number of the text and by publication year (see Table 1).

Table 1. Overgeneralizations by Authors

Authors	None	1	2	3	4	5	No Mention	Total
1. Baron (1996)				•				1
2. Bernstein et al. (1997)			•					1
3. Coon (1994)		•	•	•				3
4. Davis & Palladino (1995)							•	NA
5. Dworetzky (1997)	•							0
6. Feldman (1996)				•				1
7. Gerow (1995)				•				1
8. Gleitman (1996)				•	•			2
9. Goldstein (1994)							•	NA
10. Halonen & Santrock (1996)				•				1
11. Hockenbury & Hockenbury (1997)				•		•		2
12. Huffman et al. (1997)						•		1
13. Kalat (1996)			•		•			2
14. Lefton (1997)	•							0
15. Matlin (1995)	•						•	NA
16. Morris (1996)	•							0
17. Myers (1996)			•	•	•	•		4
18. Plotnik (1996)	•							0
19. Rathus (1996)							•	NA
20. Wade & Tavris (1996)					•	•		2
21. Weiten (1995)		•	•		•			3
22. Westen (1996)	•							0
23. Wood & Wood (1996)			•	•				2
24. Zimbardo & Weber (1994)		•						1

Note. None = no overgeneralizations; 1 = false memory syndrome is a valid diagnosis; 2 = false memories occur frequently; 3 = memories of abuse are easily implanted in adults; 4 = memories of abuse frequently lead to litigation and conviction; 5 = memories of abuse cannot be forgotten; no mention = no discussion of child sexual assault.

Results

Four texts (17%) made no mention of any issue related to CSA (see Table 1). Of the remaining textbooks, the vast majority of information about CSA issues concerned memory. Within this information we identified five overgeneralizations, including (a) false memory syndrome is a valid diagnosis, (b) false memories occur frequently, (c) memories of abuse are easily implanted in adults, (d) memories of abuse are frequently associated with unwarranted litigation, and (e) traumatic memories cannot be forgotten. Table 1 indicates those texts mentioning CSA issues with or without making any of these overgeneralizations.

False Memory Syndrome Is a Valid Diagnosis

Although the terminology implies scientific endorsement, false memory syndrome is not currently an accepted diagnostic label by the APA and is not included in the *Diagnostic and Statistical Manual of Mental Disorders* (4th ed.; American Psychiatric Association, 1994). Seventeen researchers (Carstensen et al., 1993) noted that this syndrome is "a non-psychological term originated by a private foundation whose stated purpose is to support accused parents" (p. 23). These authors urged professionals to forgo use of this pseudoscientific terminology. Terminology that implies acceptance of this pseudodiagnostic label may leave readers with the mistaken impression that false memory syndrome is a bona fide clinical disorder supported by concomitant empirical evidence.

In discussing CSA, half the 20 textbooks suggested that false memories of CSA might occur, although the texts did not mention a related syndrome. However, 3 textbooks (15%) portrayed false memory syndrome as a valid clinical diagnosis (see Table 1). For example, one text asserted that "the **false memory syndrome** is a pattern of thoughts, feelings, and actions based on mistaken or distorted recollection of experiences the rememberer claims to have previously repressed" (No. 24, 1994, p. 272). These textbooks generally failed to identify the FMSF as the source of this terminology. This omission hampers students' ability to evaluate information critically on the false memory syndrome.

False Memories Occur Frequently

One of the central questions surrounding the debate on memories of CSA is how often false or repressed memories actually occur. The APA working group (Alpert et al., 1996) and other experts (e.g., Loftus, 1993a) noted that no reliable method can distinguish between accurate and inaccurate memories. Therefore, no one can determine the prevalence of false or repressed memories. Nevertheless, six texts (30%) implied that false memories occur frequently (see Table 1). Of these, three included the opinionated suggestion that a "witch hunt" may be occurring in which innocent parents are routinely falsely accused of, and then severely punished for, CSA. Two texts suggested that false memories of CSA must occur because an entire support group (the FMSF) has been formed for falsely accused parents. These authors apparently failed to consider that some

members of the FMSF may actually have sexually assaulted children but are motivated to appear innocent.

A concern related to the frequency of false memories is the prevalence of therapists who utilize techniques that may lead to false memories. Four texts (20%) discussed the prevalence of therapists who help clients recover memories in the absence of an acknowledged abuse history. Three texts referenced a study by Poole, Lindsay, Memon, and Bull (1995). Poole et al. concluded that 70% of the therapists sampled used hypnosis or other techniques to help clients recover memories of CSA. However, Pope (1996) noted that the items in Poole et al.'s survey assessed whether therapists had used techniques such as hypnosis, not whether they used these techniques in conjunction with clients who initially denied having been sexually assaulted.

At this time little evidence substantiates the claim that false memories of CSA occur frequently or that large numbers of therapists implant false memories in clients. Furthermore, a recent study of a random sample of adults (Elliott, 1997) indicated that, of survivors who have experienced delayed recall of a traumatic event, the least likely trigger or cue for the recall was psychotherapy (17%), whereas the most common cues included some form of media presentation (54%) or an experience similar to the traumatic event (37%).

Students who read about witch hunts against innocent parents may become predisposed to doubt claims of CSA. Furthermore, textbooks that include unsupported information about inappropriate therapy techniques may serve to entrench already prevalent stigmas against mental health professionals. Of course, students and other potential consumers of psychotherapy deserve to be apprised of appropriate standards of care. It is not standard practice for therapists to search for a history of sexual abuse once a client has discounted that possibility. The APA working group publicized some suggested guidelines for individuals seeking therapy for childhood memories of abuse or other issues (Alpert et al., 1996, p. 230). The American Professional Society on the Abuse of Children (APSAC) has published several guidelines on evaluating suspected abuse in children and adolescents (e.g., APSAC, 1990).

Memories of Abuse Are Easily Implanted in Adults

Loftus and her colleagues (e.g., Loftus, 1993b; Loftus & Ketchum, 1994) demonstrated that adults may form false childhood memories in some situations, such as when an older, trusted relative insists that something occurred early in childhood. Thus, it seems at least plausible that some therapy clients could form false memories of abuse in some situations. It is equally plausible that several conditions would need to be present before a false memory of CSA would occur in adult clients. One such condition might include explicit, repeated suggestions made by a trusted therapist over the course of long-term therapy.

Eight texts (40%) gave the impression that it is relatively easy to implant false memories of CSA in adults (see Table 1). Several texts suggested that a person could form a false memory of abuse simply by listening to televised portrayals of people who have recovered abuse memories. Other texts suggested clients might be primed to form false memories following a single statement made by a therapist, such as, "You know, I've seen many cases like yours and often find that the person was abused or molested as a child. Do you suppose anything like that ever happened to you?" (No. 7, 1995, p. 268).

The implication that memories of abuse are easily implanted in adults may cause readers to overestimate the likelihood that their own memories (or the memories of others) are inaccurate. Claims that memories are easily implanted may also serve to deter students who are (or will be) victims of sexual assault from seeking assistance in dealing with the abuse or reporting their abuse. Finally, the typical description of someone who might form false memories is a young woman who forms memories of sexual abuse. Concerns about the development of false memories have not arisen with regard to other forms of childhood trauma. This focus on sexual abuse may be due to the influence of the FMSF, which is concerned primarily with accusations of sexual assault. There also seems to be a lack of concern about the development of false memories in men. It may be easier to imagine women forming false memories of CSA because girls are more likely than boys to be sexually assaulted (Boney-McCoy & Finkelhor, 1995; Finkelhor, Hotaling, Lewis, & Smith, 1990). It may also be easier to imagine women forming false memories given biases against women's mental and cognitive abilities (e.g., Coltrane & Adams, 1996).

Memories of Abuse Frequently Lead to Litigation

It is well documented that sexual assault is rarely reported to authorities and, when it is, rarely leads to conviction. For example, the National Institute of Justice (NIJ) estimated that 432,700 rapes, attempted rapes, and other sexual assaults occurred in 1994 (Maguire & Pastore, 1995, 1998). In that same year 137,310 people were arrested for rape or other sexual assaults, and only about 20,000 sex offenders were sentenced to prison or probation (these figures do not include plea bargains). The inadequacy of these arrest and prosecution rates is even more apparent considering that national surveys of women indicate twice as many victimizations as does the NIJ (e.g., Kilpatrick, Edmunds, & Seymour, 1992). Information on civil litigation in the United States is not readily available. However, Loftus (1993b) stated that academicians have estimated that hundreds of cases involving delayed recall of CSA are being considered in the courts. Although "hundreds" of cases may represent an increase from 20 years ago, it is not a large increase.

Despite these findings, a recurrent theme among the textbooks reviewed is that repressed or false memories of CSA frequently lead to litigation. Six of the reviewed texts (30%) made statements suggesting that prosecution is common in instances of past CSA (see Table 1). One text included the following: "The 1990s have brought a rash of lawsuits in which adult plaintiffs have sued their parents, teachers, and neighbors for alleged child abuse decades earlier, based on previously repressed memories" (No. 21, 1995, p. 280).

Certainly, false accusations and inappropriate arrests do occur. In fact, approximately 8% of allegations of CSA are unfounded (*Crime in the United States*, 1995). Besharov (1993) reviewed literature suggesting that 4% to 10% of

child sexual assault reports are knowingly false. Such false accusations result in highly intrusive investigations, during which friends and family members may be interviewed. Thus, the damage to falsely accused individuals, their reputations, and their families is likely to be substantial. However, in the same chapter, Besharov reviewed literature suggesting that 40% of CSA cases known to professionals remained unreported. This information, coupled with the NIJ crime statistics, suggests that occurrences of CSA are far more likely to remain unreported or unprosecuted than to result in legal action. None of the textbooks provided a sufficient discussion of the problem of underreporting of CSA.

The suggestion that repressed or false memories often result in litigation may cause readers to overestimate their own likelihood of being falsely accused of CSA and could make them fearful of interacting with children. This suggestion may also lead readers to believe that prosecution of alleged child molesters occurs too frequently (or too rashly), when the data suggest exactly the opposite problem.

Memories of Actual Abuse Cannot Be Forgotten

Several retrospective studies (Briere & Conte, 1993; Elliott, 1997; Feldman-Summers & Pope, 1994; Loftus, Polansky, & Fullilove, 1994) and one prospective study (Williams, 1994) indicated that between 19% and 59% of sexual assault victims experience some period of time during which they forget all or part of the abuse. Despite evidence to the contrary, four texts (20%) suggested that true abuse memories cannot be forgotten and then remembered (see Table 1). For example, one text stated that "no one forgets that they were in a concentration camp or a war" (No. 20, 1996, p. 365) to support the idea that CSA victims would not forget their abuse experiences. However, these authors did not include references to support this statement. Another text included the statement that "there just isn't evidence . . . that an event can be repressed for years, and then accurately reproduced. With rare exceptions, most negative emotional events are actually remembered well" (No. 17, 1996, p. 249).

Textbooks presenting the inaccurate view that forgetting abuse is rare may cause students who have experienced both abuse and periods of forgetting to doubt their own memories. Furthermore, these texts may contribute to the view that recovered memories are generally false when, in fact, no data link periods of forgetting with systematic changes in the veracity of CSA memories.

Summary

Of the 24 textbooks reviewed, 4 made no mention of CSA or any related issues. Of the 20 that described CSA, all discussed issues related to the memory debate. Only 9 (45%) discussed CSA outside the context of memory issues, and all but 1 devoted substantially more text to memory issues than to issues related to other aspects of CSA. As shown in Table 1, 5 of the 20 texts (25%) that addressed issues related to CSA did so without making any of the overgeneralizations identified previously. Seven of these 20 texts (35%) made one overgeneralization, 5 texts (25%) made two overgeneralizations, 2 texts (10%) made three overgeneralizations, and 1 text (5%) made four overgeneralizations.

Recommendations

For students, textbooks are an important medium for obtaining critical information. Many college students complete only limited formal education on psychological topics. Thus, topics presented in these courses must be portrayed in the least biased and most accurate manner possible. Furthermore, an accurate presentation of the scientific basis for claims about psychological issues provides students with the ability to critically evaluate noneducational presentations of psychological issues such as appear on popular talk shows, the Internet, and in newspapers. Unfortunately, texts that did not overlook CSA altogether tended to focus on the single most controversial aspect of CSA. Delayed recall of CSA memories is a relatively new area of research and clinical focus. Thus, authors should be tentative and inclusive in their discussion of memory issues. In addition, it is imperative that authors include coverage of CSA that involves issues outside the memory debate. Recently, concerns about the prevalence and welfare of CSA victims appear to have taken a back seat to the memory debate. Issues on prevalence rates and increased risk for psychological disorders have been extensively researched and are well within the purview of most introductory psychology textbooks. Professors whose textbooks lack information or present CSA-related issues inadequately have several courses of action. One solution is to address textbook inadequacies in the classroom and use these problems as starting points for discussion. This solution not only teaches students about CSA, but it also encourages students to develop and use critical thinking skills. Another strategy is for professors to contact textbook authors, who will likely appreciate receiving constructive criticism and who can respond with improved coverage of CSA in revisions of their texts. Finally, professors can contact textbook publishers and insist on accurate, relevant coverage of important topics. All publishers of the reviewed texts have World Wide Web sites or toll-free numbers that facilitate this type of contact.

Controversy in science is not new and often provides the impetus for more and better research in unknown areas. We agree with Finkelhor (1995) that scrutiny of the treatment received by CSA victims may have positive effects such as reducing the use of inappropriate treatment techniques. However, we also agree with Finkelhor that professionals must be vigilant against nonscientific, biased, or one-sided coverage. This vigilance is particularly important for coverage of CSA issues in college textbooks.

References

Alpert, J. L., Brown, L. S., Ceci, S. J., Courtois, C. A., Loftus, E. F., & Ornstein, P. A. (Eds.). (1996). *Working group on investigation of memories of childhood abuse: Final report.* Washington, DC: American Psychological Association.

American Professional Society on the Abuse of Children. (1990). *Guidelines for psychosocial evaluation of suspected sexual abuse in young children.* Chicago: Author.

American Psychiatric Association. (1994). *Diagnostic and statistical manual of mental disorders* (4th ed.). Washington, DC: Author.

Berliner, L. (1997). Introduction to the special commentary: The memory wars: Detente, anyone? *Journal of Interpersonal Violence, 12,* 629–631.

Besharov, D. J. (1993). Overreporting and underreporting are twin problems. In R. J. Gelles & D. R. Loseke (Eds.), *Current controversies on family violence* (pp. 257–272). Newbury Park, CA: Sage.

Boney-McCoy, S., & Finkelhor, D. (1995). Psychological sequelae of violent victimization in a national sample of youth. *Journal of Consulting and Clinical Psychology, 63,* 726–736.

Books in print. (1996). New York: Bowker.

Briere, J. (1988). The long-term clinical correlates of childhood sexual victimization. *Annals of the New York Academy of Sciences, 528,* 327–334.

Briere, J., & Conte, J. (1993). Self-reported amnesia for abuse adults molested as children. *Journal of Traumatic Stress, 6,* 21–31.

Brokaw, T. (1997, April 14). In G. Prince (Producer), *NBC nightly news with Tom Brokaw.* New York: National Broadcasting Company.

Carstensen, L., Gabrieli, J., Shepard, R., Levenson, R., Mason, M., Goodman, G., Bootzin, R., Ceci, S., Bronfrenbrenner, Edelstein, B., Schober, M., Bruck, M., Keane, T., Zimmering, Oltmanns, T., Gotlib, I., & Ekman, P. (1993, March). Repressed objectivity. *APS Observer,* p. 23.

Coltrane, S., & Adams, M. (1996). Work-family imagery and gender stereotypes—Television and the reproduction of difference. *Journal of Vocational Behavior, 50,* 323–347.

Conte, J. (1988). The effects of sexual abuse on children: Results of research project. *Annals of the New York Academy of Sciences, 528,* 310–226.

Crime in the United States. (1995). Washington, DC: U.S. Department of Justice.

Elliott, D. M. (1997). Traumatic events: Prevalence and delayed recall in the general population. *Journal of Consulting and Clinical Psychology, 65,* 811–820.

Enns, C. Z., McNeilly, C. L., Corkery, J. M., & Gilbert, M. S. (1995). The debate about delayed memories of child sexual abuse: A feminist perspective. *The Counseling Psychologist, 23,* 181–297.

False Memory Syndrome Foundation. (1995, June 7). *The False Memory Syndrome Foundation.* [Announcement posted on the World Wide Web]. Philadelphia, PA: Author. Retrieved February 25, 1997 from the World Wide Web: http://iquest.com/~fitz/fmsf/aboutFMSF.html

Feldman-Summers, S., & Pope, K. S. (1994). The experience of "forgetting" childhood abuse: A national survey of psychologists. *Journal of Consulting and Clinical Psychology, 62,* 636–639.

Finkelhor, D. (1995, Fall). "The backlash" in sociological perspective. *The APSAC Advisor, 8(3),* 1–22.

Finkelhor, D., Hotaling, G., Lewis, I. A., & Smith, C. (1990). Sexual abuse in a national survey of adult men and women: Prevalent characteristics, and risk factors. *Child Abuse & Neglect, 14,* 19–28 .

Freyd, P. (1996, March 1). FMSF Newsletter 5.3. *FMS Foundation Newsletter, 5(3),* 1–36. Retrieved December 17, 1997 from the World Wide Web: http://advicom.net/~fitz/fmsf/articles/news5_03.html

Kilpatrick, D. G., Edmunds, C. N., & Seymour, A. K. (1992). *Rape in America: A report to the nation.* Washington, DC: National Victim Center.

Loftus, E. F. (1993a). The reality of repressed memories. *American Psychologist, 48,* 518–537.

Loftus, E. F. (1993b, July 5–11). A trip down memory lane: How reliable are "repressed" memories? *Washington Post National Weekly Edition*, p. 25.

Loftus, E. F., & Ketchum, K. (1994). *The myth of repressed memory: False memories and allegations of sexual abuse*. New York: St. Martin.

Loftus, E. F., Polansky, S., & Fullilove, M. T. (1994), Memories of childhood sexual abuse: Remembering and repressing. *Psychology of Women Quarterly, 18,* 67–84.

Maguire, K., & Pastore, A. L. (1995). *Sourcebook of criminal justice statistics, 1995*. Washington, DC: U.S. Department of Justice, Bureau of Justice Statistics.

Maguire, K., & Pastore, A. L. (1998). *Sourcebook of criminal justice statistics, 1997*. Washington, DC: U.S. Department of Justice, Bureau of Justice Statistics.

Poole, D., Lindsay, D., Memon, A., & Bull, R. (1995), Psychotherapy and the recovery of memories of childhood sexual abuse: U.S. and British practitioners' opinions, practices, and experiences. *Journal of Consulting and Clinical Psychology, 63,* 426–437.

Pope, K. S. (1996). Memory, abuse, and science: Questioning claims about the false memory syndrome epidemic. *American Psychologist, 51,* 957–974.

Saunders, B. E., Villeponteaux, L. A., Lipovsky, J. A., Kilpatrick, D. G., & Veronen, L. J. (1992). Child sexual assault as a risk factor for mental disorders among women: A community survey. *Journal of Interpersonal Violence, 7,* 189–204.

Williams, L. M. (1994). Recall of childhood trauma: A prospective study of women's memories of child sexual abuse. *Journal of Consulting and Clinical Psychology, 62,* 1167–1176.

Appendix
Introductory Psychology Textbooks Reviewed

Baron, R. A. (1996). *Essentials of psychology*. Boston: Allyn & Bacon.

Bernstein, D. A., Clarke-Stewart, A., Roy, E. J., & Wickens, C. D. (1997). *Psychology* (4th ed.). Boston: Houghton Mifflin.

Coon, D. (1994). *Essentials of psychology: Exploration and application* (6th ed.). St. Paul, MN: West.

Davis, S. F., & Palladino, J. J. (1995). *Psychology*. Englewood Cliffs, NJ: Prentice-Hall.

Dworetzky, J. P. (1997). *Psychology* (6th ed.). Pacific Grove, CA: Brooks/Cole.

Feldman, R. S. (1996). *Understanding psychology* (4th ed.). New York: McGraw-Hill.

Gerow, J. R. (1995). *Psychology: An introduction*. New York: HarperCollins.

Gleitman, H. (1996). *Basic psychology* (4th ed.). New York: Norton.

Goldstein, E. B. (1994). *Psychology*. Pacific Grove, CA: Brooks/Cole.

Halonen, J. S., & Santrock, J. W. (1996). *Psychology: Contexts of behavior* (2nd ed.). Madison, WI: Brown & Benchmark.

Hockenbury, D. H., & Hockenbury, S. E. (1997). *Psychology*. New York: Worth.

Huffman, K., Vernoy, M., & Vernoy, J. (1997). *Psychology in action* (4th ed.). New York: Wiley.

Kalat, J. W. (1996). *Introduction to psychology* (4th ed.). Pacific Grove, CA: Brooks/Cole.

Lefton, L. A. (1997). *Psychology* (6th ed.). Boston: Allyn & Bacon.

Matlin, M. W. (1995). *Psychology* (2nd ed.). Fort Worth, TX: Harcourt Brace.

Morris, C. (1996). *Understanding psychology* (3rd ed.). Englewood Cliffs, NJ: Prentice-Hall.

Myers, D. (1996). *Exploring psychology* (3rd ed.). New York: Worth.

Plotnik, R. (1996). *Introduction to psychology* (4th ed.). Pacific Grove, CA: Brooks/Cole.

Rathus, S. A. (1996). *Psychology in the new millennium* (6th ed.). Fort Worth, TX: Harcourt Brace.

Wade, C., & Tavris, C. (1996). *Psychology* (4th ed.). New York: HarperCollins.

Weiten, W. (1995). *Psychology: Themes and variations* (3rd ed.). Pacific Grove, CA: Brooks/Cole.

Westen, D. (1996). *Psychology: Mind, brain, and culture*. New York: Wiley.

Wood, S. E., & Wood, E. G. (1996). *The world of psychology* (2nd ed.). Boston: Allyn & Bacon.

Zimbardo, P. C., & Weber, A. L. (1994). *Psychology*. New York: HarperCollins.

Notes

1. We thank Ann Elliott and Julie Lipovsky for their thoughtful comments on previous drafts of this manuscript. We also thank the Department of Psychology at Augusta State University for support during the initial portion of this project. Lastly, we appreciate the comments from several anonymous reviewers.

The Quiz Game: Writing and Explaining Questions Improve Quiz Scores

Dennis D. Kerkman
Kay L. Kellison
Marites F. Piñon
Donna Schmidt
Sharon Lewis
Southwest Texas State University

Since Socrates's time, asking good questions has been regarded as a strong indicator of knowledge and intelligence. Does asking good questions merely indicate knowledge, or does it increase knowledge? Many introductory texts recommend writing questions as a study technique (e.g., Atkinson, Atkinson, Smith, & Hilgard, 1987; Dworetzky, 1990; Hebb & Donderi, 1987). Denner and Rickards (1987) found that students who wrote questions as they studied a passage recalled more facts than those who read the same passage without writing questions. However, writing questions did not improve performance on conceptual test questions. Frase and Schwartz (1975) found that students tend to write factual rather than conceptual questions. They also found that the effect of writing questions was content specific: Question writers had higher scores on test items that were directly related to the questions that they had written. Foos (1989) suggested that writing questions improves students' ability to recall facts because students' multiple-choice questions usually require recalling facts. He hypothesized that writing essay questions would improve performance on essay tests, whereas writing multiple-choice questions would improve performance on multiple-choice tests. However, he found that those who wrote either type of question had significantly higher scores than the control group who did not write questions, whether one looked at performance on multiple-choice or essay tests. As Frase and Schwartz (1975) noted with respect to multiple-choice questions, Foos noted that students' essay questions tended to focus on facts rather than concepts.

In a pilot study, we noticed that undergraduates in a developmental psychology course tended to write multiple-choice questions that were factual rather than conceptual, even though conceptual questions were awarded 2 points and factual questions were awarded only 1. Typically, students copied a sentence directly from the text, omitted a critical word or phrase, then used that phrase plus three others as the four response options. They often wrote questions with more than one correct answer. Under these conditions, the effect of writing questions was inconsistent.

To rectify the tendency to write questions with more than one correct answer, we began encouraging students to write a brief explanation of why each response was correct or incorrect. Improvements in the quality of their questions were striking, and test scores also improved. We undertook this study to examine the effects of writing questions with explanations on students' quiz performances.

Craik and Lockhart's (1972) levels of processing theory emphasized that success in recalling information critically depended on the nature and number of mental operations carried out while the individual was learning the information. Anderson and Reder's (1979) elaboration hypothesis extended this line of reasoning by proposing that material was easier to remember when it was associated with many other items in memory than when it was an isolated fact. The mental operations involved in composing multiple-choice questions and explaining why each response option is correct or incorrect should induce a deeper level of processing than the typical strategy of simply reading the text repeatedly. In particular, requiring students to explain why each response option is correct or incorrect should elaborate the student's associative network because the student must formulate an explicit statement of the relation between the concept in the question stem and those in each of the response options. This elaboration should improve recall of any concept in the network.

Our study tested three major hypotheses. All three were derived from the idea that writing questions with explanations elaborates the conceptual network and, thus, should improve recall. First, assigning students to write multiple-choice questions with explanations should cause them to have higher quiz scores than a control group who did not write questions.

Second, in the experimental class, students whose questions met all the minimum requirements should have higher quiz scores than those whose questions were not correctly formed. Writing questions should increase quiz scores to the extent that the network of associations it generates clearly and accurately represents the nature of the relations among the concepts. Questions that are ill formed (e.g., verbose, grammatically incorrect, two correct answers, no correct answer, or lacking an accurate explanation for one or more responses) are less likely to facilitate recall during the quiz because the conceptual network is not clearly articulated.

Third, the conceptual quality of students' questions also should be correlated with their quiz scores. Questions that require either application of a general principle to a situation or the integration of information from more than one part of the assignment should indicate deeper processing and, thus, result in better quiz performance than simply writing a formally correct question on that assignment.

Method

Participants

Ninety-six undergraduates enrolled in an introductory developmental psychology class participated. One section of 47 students was randomly assigned to be the experimental group. The other, containing 49 students, was the control group. Students were unaware of the hypotheses until the study was complete.

Procedure

On the first day of class, students in both groups were given a syllabus containing the daily reading assignments (approximately 20 pages per class meeting), course requirements, and grading scale. Grades were based on the percentage of points earned (A = 90% to 100%, B = 80% to 89%, etc.), including a comprehensive multiple-choice midterm examination (50 points), 10 pop quizzes (10 points each), and a comprehensive final examination (100 points). The classes met on Tuesdays and Thursdays in adjacent time periods. Both classes had the same lectures, films, quizzes, and examinations.

The experimental class was also given instructions for the quiz game. They were required to submit one multiple-choice question daily, based on that day's reading assignment. Minimum requirements for writing questions were that each question should (a) be grammatically correct; (b) be less than 40 words long; (c) have four response options, each with 10 words or less; (d) have only one correct answer; and (e) have a brief (one-sentence) explanation as to why each response was correct or not. They were also instructed to avoid questions that involved the names or dates associated with particular experiments and to avoid responses such as "a and b" or "none of the above."

Any question that met all the requirements received 2 points; otherwise, it received a 0. Hereafter, these scores are referred to as the *correctness scores*. Correctness scores constituted 20% of the experimental group's semester grade. Two seniors who previously received an A in the course were trained to score questions. Interrater agreement for correctness scores was 95%.

Students had no advance warning or any way of predicting when they were going to have a pop quiz. We used no particular pattern in deciding when to give a pop quiz, except that (unbeknownst to the students) we never gave quizzes on more than two consecutive class meetings. Quizzes were composed of the 10 best questions submitted at the previous class meeting. Raters recommended 15 to 20 questions for each quiz, and the professor selected the final 10.

Students in the experimental group were told that if their question appeared on the quiz and more than one half of their classmates (in the experimental group) answered it incorrectly, then the submitter would receive 10 bonus points—the equivalent of a perfect score on a pop quiz. The purpose of the bonus points was to encourage students to write challenging questions. We attempted to give each student an opportunity to have at least one question on a quiz, so that all would have an equal chance to win bonus points. Of the 47 students in the experimental group, 35 (75%) had at least one question on a quiz (21 had one, 13 had two, and 1 had three). Seven students won bonus points; none won more than once.

Students traded papers and graded each quiz immediately after it was administered. In the experimental group, the number of students who answered each question correctly was determined by a show of the graders' hands so that bonus points could be awarded. All quiz scores were converted to percentage correct scores, so that the scores of those who contributed a question could be computed on the basis of the nine questions that had not been written by that individual.

For purposes of computing course grades, students who missed a quiz or failed to turn in a question received a 0 on that assignment. However, it seemed unreasonable to include these 0s as data for purposes of statistical analysis because the absence of a quiz score does not necessarily reflect a complete absence of knowledge of the material and, thus, would misrepresent the student's knowledge. Alternatively, treating these as missing data would drastically restrict the generalizability of the results to that subset of students who never missed a single class meeting—a decidedly atypical subsample. To resolve this dilemma, we computed average scores for each variable by summing the "nonmissing" scores for each student and dividing by the number of nonmissing values for that variable.

After the experiment was completed, it was suggested that we score the questions' conceptual quality. Questions that involved applying a principle to a real-world situation or integrating information from more than one part of the reading received 1 point; those that did not received a 0. Agreement between the two raters was 100%.

The experiment was originally planned to span the entire semester. However, a preliminary analysis was conducted just before spring break to prepare for a conference (Kellison, Kerkman, & Piñon, 1992). The results were sufficiently strong that we felt ethically compelled to advise the control group of the efficacy of question writing. The control group was also given an extremely easy quiz that the experimental group was not given, so that being in the control group did not adversely affect anyone's semester grades.

Results and Discussion

First, we tested the hypothesis that writing questions caused superior quiz scores. Analysis of variance showed that the experimental group had significantly higher average quiz scores than the control group, $F(1, 94) = 7.09$, $p < .01$. Means for the experimental and control groups were

72.4% and 66.0%, respectively. This difference cannot be attributed to any preexisting differences in academic skill because it persisted even when grade point average was covaried, $F(1, 93) = 5.27$, $p < .05$. Adjusted means for the experimental and control groups were 71.4% and 66.9%, respectively. Writing questions increases quiz performance.

Students quickly learned to write questions correctly. The average correctness scores increased from 72% passing (Questions 1 to 3) to 87% passing (Questions 9 to 11), $F(1, 46) = 8.72$, $p < .01$. Conceptual quality scores increased from 15% (Questions 1 to 3) to 33% (Questions 9 to 11), $F(1, 46) = 11.58$, $p < .01$. This improvement in conceptual quality is surprising because students were not being graded on the conceptual quality of their questions. Perhaps this improvement was the result of being awarded bonus points for writing a question that half the submitter's classmates missed.

Next, we tested the hypotheses that the questions' formal correctness and conceptual quality would predict quiz performance. Average correctness of questions was significantly correlated with average quiz score, $r(45) = .29$, $p < .05$, but average conceptual quality of questions was not.

In summary, both the experimental and the correlational findings converge on the same conclusion: Writing formally correct questions improved quiz performance. We are not certain why the questions' conceptual quality was not significantly correlated with quiz performance. Perhaps our measure of conceptual quality, though reliable, was not a valid indicator of depth of processing. Alternatively, writing conceptual multiple-choice questions may improve comprehension in ways that are not readily measured by the multiple-choice questions that students write. Nonetheless, from a pedagogical perspective, we are intrigued with the prospect of a study technique that is easy to learn and significantly improves performance. We recommend that future research examine the conceptual quality issue experimentally, rather than correlationally, and include other measures of performance (e.g., essays, term papers, and practicum performance) to assess more thoroughly the potential value of composing conceptual questions. Future research should also examine

whether the effect of question writing is primarily due to generalized test-wiseness improvements or to content-specific improvements in comprehension and/or recall of the material to be learned.

References

Anderson, J. R., & Reder, L. M. (1979). An elaborative processing explanation of depth of processing. In L. S. Cermak & F. I. M. Craik (Eds.), *Levels of processing in human memory* (pp. 385–403). Hillsdale, NJ: Lawrence Erlbaum Associates, Inc.

Atkinson, R. L., Atkinson, R. C., Smith, E. E., & Hilgard, E. R. (1987). *Introduction to psychology* (9th ed.). New York: Harcourt Brace.

Craik, F. I. M., & Lockhart, R. S. (1972). Levels of processing: A framework for memory research. *Journal of Verbal Learning and Verbal Behavior, 11*, 671–684.

Denner, P. R., & Rickards, J. P. (1987). A developmental comparison of the effects of provided and generated questions for text recall. *Contemporary Educational Psychology, 12*, 135–146.

Dworetzky, J. P. (1990). *Introduction to child development* (4th ed.). New York: West.

Foos, P. W. (1989). Effects of student-written questions on student test performance. *Teaching of Psychology, 16*, 77–78.

Frase, L. T., & Schwartz, B. J. (1975). Effect of question production and answering on prose recall. *Journal of Educational Psychology, 67*, 628–635.

Hebb, D. O., & Donderi, D. C. (1987). *Textbook of psychology* (4th ed.). Hillsdale, NJ: Lawrence Erlbaum Associates, Inc.

Kellison, K., Kerkman, D. D., & Piñon, M. F. (1992, April). *ISIS: An Interrogative Student Instructional System for teaching developmental psychology.* Poster presented at the biennial meeting of the Southwestern Society for Research in Human Development, Tempe, AZ.

Notes

1. We thank the students who participated in this research and our departmental colleagues, the reviewers, and Ruth Ault for their comments, criticisms, and suggestions.

Effects of Student-Written Questions on Student Test Performance

Paul W. Foos
Florida International University

Students use a variety of techniques when preparing for an exam (e.g., recitation, making an outline, and rote memorization), and instructors use a variety of techniques to help improve student performance (e.g., giving sample questions and holding review sessions). One technique that is frequently recommended for students is writing test questions. This recommendation is found in introductory psychology textbooks (e.g., Atkinson, Atkinson, Smith, & Hilgard, 1987; Hebb & Donderi, 1987) and in books on how to succeed in college (e.g., Lyng & Gerow, 1986). My experiment was designed to investigate the effects of student-written test questions on student test performance to determine whether such question writing is beneficial and whether any derived benefits depend on the type of questions written.

Many studies have shown that students who answer questions while studying a text perform better than students who do not (see Hamaker, 1986; Hamilton, 1985, for reviews). In these studies, however, the questions were prepared by the researcher; few studies have examined the effects of student-generated questions.

Denner and Rickards (1987) compared experimenter- and student-generated question groups to a no-question control group for students in the 5th, 8th, and 11th grades. Recall of facts and concepts was examined. The question groups performed better than the control group. No difference was found between groups that received experimenter-generated questions and those that generated their own, when recall of facts was tested. For recall of concepts, the groups that received experimenter-generated questions performed better than the no-question group. Those who generated their own questions performed between these extremes. This latter result was also obtained by Lehman and Lehman (1984). It appears that student-generated questions are beneficial for recall of specific facts but less beneficial for the recall of concepts.

Frase and Schwartz (1975) compared high school and college students who wrote questions while reading a text to those who only studied the text. Question writers performed better on a recall test but only on those items that were directly related to the questions they had written. Other work (Frase & Schwartz, 1975; Martin, 1985) indicates that the majority of student-written questions pertain to specific facts in a text rather than to general concepts and applications of concepts. It should be no surprise, then, that Denner and Rickards (1987) found better performance by question writers only on recall of facts. Students who write their own questions perform better on the recall of facts, because the questions that they write usually pertain to the recall of facts.

My experiment encouraged students to write questions pertaining to general concepts, as well as to specific facts, by varying the type of questions they were instructed to write. Half of the question writers were told to write multiple-choice questions, which may encourage questions about specific facts, and half were told to write essay questions, which may cover general concepts rather than specific facts.

Method

Participants

Participants were 94 students enrolled in Introductory Psychology at Florida International University. Forty-nine other students were eliminated because they did not volunteer to participate or they failed to follow instructions.

Materials

The textbook used was Myers (1986). Three tests were given during the semester, each consisting of 40 multiple-choice and 2 essay questions.

Procedure

Two weeks before each scheduled test, randomly assigned students were told to write either multiple-choice or essay questions for the upcoming test. For the first test, 14 students wrote essay questions, 16 wrote multiple-choice questions, and 64 did not write questions; these sample sizes for the second and third tests were 11, 11, and 72, and 21, 21, and 52, respectively. Throughout the semester, students participated only once in a question-writing group (i.e., essay or multiple-choice) but twice in a no-question group. All questions were due at the penultimate class meeting before the scheduled test. Questions were examined to ensure that they had been written in the correct form (i.e., multiple-choice or essay) and that they covered the material assigned for that test. Student-written questions were compared with actual test questions to ensure that no student questions would be included on the test. All students took the same test at the scheduled time.

Results and Discussion

Table 1 shows the mean number of points earned out of 100 (each of 40 multiple-choice questions was worth 2 points and essays were worth 15 and 5 points) for students who wrote essay questions, multiple-choice questions, and no questions on each of the three tests. There were no significant differences between students who wrote essay questions and those who wrote multiple-choice questions on any of the tests, all $Fs < 1$. Students who wrote essay questions did not perform significantly better on essay test questions than did students who wrote multiple-choice questions, and students who wrote multiple-choice questions did not perform significantly better on multiple-choice test questions than did students who wrote essay questions, all $Fs < 1$.

On the first and second tests, students who wrote questions performed significantly better than those who did not, $F(1, 91) = 4.67, p < .05$, and $F(1, 91) = 6.65, p < .05$, respectively. On the third test, this difference was marginally significant, $F(1, 91) = 3.59, p < .10$.

It appears that writing questions before an exam does aid performance. Perhaps the failure to find a significant differ-

Table 1. Average Performance for Question Writers and Nonwriters on Three Tests

Test Number	Questions Written		
	Essay	Multiple-Choice	None
1	76.00	76.75	71.56
2	77.82	78.00	71.88
3	82.19	79.76	77.52

ence on the last exam was due to many students adopting the question-writing strategy for themselves after having tried it on one of the first two exams. This adoption of the question-writing strategy by individuals in the no-question group would then improve the overall performance of the no-question group. Unfortunately, no data are available to test this hypothesis. It is also possible that students who wrote questions benefited from the additional review required to write the questions. It may be this extra review of the text material, rather than the generation of questions, that led to better performance for question-writing groups. Further research is needed to address this possibility.

The failure to find a difference in performance between students who wrote essay questions and those who wrote multiple-choice questions appears to be due to the fact that most student-written essay questions asked for specific facts just as most of their multiple-choice questions did. Specific instruction or training in question writing may be needed to produce student-generated conceptual questions.

Students who wrote questions performed better on the overall tests and not simply on items of the same type (i.e., essay or multiple-choice) as those they had written. This result supports the claim that writing questions is a useful technique for students reading a text and preparing for an exam. Question writing should be encouraged by instructors who discuss study techniques in their classes.

References

Atkinson, R. L., Atkinson, R. C., Smith, E. E., & Hilgard, E. R. (1987). *Introduction to psychology* (9th ed.). New York: Harcourt Brace Jovanovich.

Denner, P. R., & Rickards, J. P. (1987). A developmental comparison of the effects of provided and generated questions on text recall. *Contemporary Educational Psychology, 12*, 135–146.

Frase, L. T., & Schwartz, B. J. (1975). Effect of question production and answering on prose recall. *Journal of Educational Psychology, 67*, 628–635.

Hamaker, C. (1986). The effects of adjunct questions on prose learning. *Review of Educational Research, 56*, 212–242.

Hamilton, R. J. (1985). A framework for the evaluation of the effectiveness of adjunct questions and objectives. *Review of Educational Research, 55*, 47–85.

Hebb, D. O., & Donderi, D. C. (1987). *Textbook of psychology* (4th ed.). Hillsdale, NJ: Lawrence Erlbaum Associates, Inc.

Lehman, J. R., & Lehman, K. M. (1984). The relative effects of experimenter and subject generated questions on learning from museum case exhibits. *Journal of Research in Science Teaching, 21*, 931–935.

Lyng, R. D., & Gerow, J. R. (1986). *How to succeed in college* (2nd ed.). Glenview, IL: Scott, Foresman.

Martin, M. A. (1985). Students' applications of self-questioning study techniques: An investigation of their efficacy. *Reading Psychology, 6*, 69–83.

Myers, D. G. (1986). *Psychology*. New York: Worth.

Oral Application Questions as a Teaching Strategy

Ernest B. Gurman
W. Bruce Holliman
University of Southern Mississippi

Kay Camperell
Utah State University

Instructors assume that introductory courses provide students with factual and practical content, but are often disappointed when test results reveal that students are unable to apply this information to new situations. Since Rothkopf's (1965, 1966) work, many investigators have studied the effect of using adjunct questions to facilitate learning new material. Adjunct questions typically require the student to use newly learned factual information, such as a definition of *reinforcement*, to answer more applied questions (e.g., Describe the learning of superstitious behavior). Independent variables in such research have usually been the cognitive level of test questions (factual vs. higher order), relation between the adjunct questions and test questions (repeated or different questions), and position of the questions (whether questions occur before, during, or after the presentation of new information).

Watts and Anderson (1971), Felker and Dapra (1975), Hamilton (1985), and Wollen, Quackenbush, and Hamlin (1985) found that students who were questioned on instructional material performed better than students who were not. Others (Bing, 1982; Hamilton, 1986) found no significant effects of the questioning procedure. All of the studies reviewed investigated the effects of written questions on retention of prose material in controlled laboratory conditions, rather than under classroom conditions (Hamaker, 1986). Andre (1979) reviewed research on the effects of using adjunct questions on instruction and concluded that they were not well understood. Following the suggestions of Richards and Denner (1978), Duchastel (1983), and Hamilton (1985), we examined the effect of using application questions presented orally in a classroom situation. Dependent variables were the numbers of factual and application questions answered correctly on regularly scheduled exams.

Method

Subjects were 154 undergraduates (70 men and 84 women) in the general psychology course at the University of Southern Mississippi. The textbook used was Lahey (1986). A team teaching approach was used; students attended two 1-hr lectures and one small-group discussion section per week. In small-group sections, students discussed, performed experiments, clarified lecture material, participated in role-play, and viewed films.

Procedure

During the eighth and ninth weeks of the semester, students in selected small-group discussion sections were exposed to one of two instructional approaches in classical and operant conditioning during two 1-hr class periods. Discussion sections were conducted by three psychology graduate students enrolled in a teaching seminar and supervised by two of the authors. Two of the discussion leaders were women; one was a man. The man conducted one experimental and two control groups; one woman conducted two experimental and one control group; and the other woman conducted two experimental and two control groups. Students in the treatment groups (32 men and 45 women) practiced answering adjunct questions that required application of basic principles and information from lecture and readings to the prediction of behavior. Control students (38 men and 39 women) viewed films during both sessions. All students attended the same lecture sections.

For the first week, subjects in the treatment group were shown a training film containing 40 vignettes emphasizing application of the concepts of: (a) positive reinforcement, (b) negative reinforcement, (c) punishment, and (d) extinction in interpersonal dyadic situations. Brief discussion followed the presentation of each vignette identifying the specific behaviors constituting the concept portrayed, possible alternative behaviors, and their effects. During the second week, discussion leaders read questions that required application of learning principles and conducted discussion about the application of course material to everyday life situations. Students were monitored closely to ensure a high level of participation and were directed to write their responses before the discussion. Written responses were collected and checked to determine if students were, in fact, active participants.

Students in the control groups were shown a film on classical and operant conditioning each week. Although the material in both films covered the same topics that were covered by the experimental group, no attempt was made to apply, clarify, or otherwise discuss material in either film unless students asked specific questions.

Dependent Variable

An examination, the second in the course, covering the topic of learning was administered the following week. The exam was a 50-item multiple-choice test, 30 items of which pertained to classical and operant conditioning. Of the 30 items, 10 were factual, or identification questions (e.g., "the term *stimulus* may be defined as __"), and the remaining 20 were questions requiring sufficient understanding of the concept to apply principles of learning to predict behavior (e.g., "The angel fish in your aquarium get excited when you close the freezer door where their brine shrimp are kept. What causes their excitement?").

Results

Because subjects could not be randomly assigned to treatment and control groups, both hypotheses were tested by a one-way analysis of covariance (ANCOVA) using scores on the first exam as the covariate. The hypothesis that treatment subjects would correctly answer more factual questions was confirmed, $F(1, 151) = 4.79$, $p < .02$. On the 10 factual questions, mean scores for treatment and control groups were 7.60 and 5.05, respectively.

Treatment subjects did not perform better than controls on the 20 questions requiring application, $F < 1.00$. Means for treatment and control groups were 13.32 and 13.80, respectively.

In order to determine whether treatment varied with student ability, subjects were placed into quartiles according to American College Testing Program (ACT) scores and data were submitted to a Treatment × Levels (2 × 4) ANCOVA. As expected, differences were observed between quartile levels, but no interaction effect was noted, indicating that level of ability did not differentially affect treatment outcome.

Discussion

The purpose of this study was to investigate the effect of having students discuss application of learning principles on subsequent test behavior. Treatment subjects scored higher than controls on factual questions, but not on application questions.

Asking students to apply principles was beneficial only to the extent that it helped make questions more personally relevant, leading to improved retention of factual material. Although the goals of learning usually go beyond recall of the material to include the application of information to other situations, the record of instruction in achieving these higher goals is far from a resounding success. The superior performance of the treatment group on factual questions is encouraging. Although the difference was quite small (2.55 questions), it represented 25% of items measuring this variable.

These findings are contrary to those of Watts and Anderson (1971) and Wollen et al. (1985) who concluded that training through the use of application questions and examples led to superior performance on new application questions. Although there was general improvement in test performance, we did not observe transfer of principles from training to test. Because subjects, material, and procedures were different, it is difficult to speculate on the source of discrepant findings. Learning is a difficult topic for our students. It is possible that the task of selecting a particular response from such a large and confusing array of choices (e.g., negative reinforcement vs. punishment or classical vs. operant conditioning) is more difficult than the Wollen et al. task of defining and applying two or three basic variables. In addition, the study-to-test interval was 1 week in our study, whereas testing in the previous studies was immediate.

We are not discouraged by these results. The fact that treatment subjects correctly identified 25% more factual items than did controls is encouraging. Any instructional approach that can improve retention of factual material by 25% should not be ignored. Brown (1983) suggested that much of the content of the introductory course is devoted to developing a vocabulary in psychology. Perhaps we should only ask beginning students to develop a vocabulary and reserve applications of facts and principles for advanced students.

References

Andre, T. (1979). Does answering higher-level questions while reading facilitate productive learning? *Review of Educational Research, 49,* 280–318.

Bing, S. (1982). Role of adjunct questions and reading ability levels on rote and conceptual learning from prose. *Instructional Science, 11,* 129–138.

Brown, L. T. (1983). Some more misconceptions about psychology among introductory psychology students. *Teaching of Psychology, 10,* 207–210.

Duchastel, P. C. (1983). Interpreting adjunct question research: Processes and ecological validity. *Human Learning, 2,* 1–5.

Felker, D. B., & Dapra, R. A. (1975). Effects of question type and question placement on problem-solving ability from prose material. *Journal of Educational Psychology, 67,* 380–384.

Hamaker, C. (1986). The effects of adjunct questions on prose learning. *Review of Educational Research, 56,* 212–242.

Hamilton, R. (1985). A framework for the evaluation of the effectiveness of adjunct questions and objectives. *Review of Educational Research, 55,* 47–85.

Hamilton, R. (1986). Role of adjunct questions and subject ability levels on the learning of concepts from prose. *American Educational Research Journal, 23,* 87–94.

Lahey, B. B. (1986). *Psychology: An introduction* (2nd ed.). Dubuque, IA: Brown.

Richards, J. P., & Denner, P. R. (1978). Inserted questions as aids to reading text. *Instructional Science, 7,* 313–346.

Rothkopf, E. Z. (1965). Some theoretical and experimental approaches to problems in written instruction. In J. D. Krumboltz (Ed.), *Learning and the educational process* (pp. 193–221). Chicago: Rand McNally.

Rothkopf, E. Z. (1966). Learning from written instructive materials: An exploration of the control of inspection behavior by test-like events. *American Educational Research Journal, 3,* 241–422.

Watts, G. H., & Anderson, R. C. (1971). Effects of three types of inserted questions on learning from prose. *Journal of Educational Psychology, 62,* 387–394.

Wollen, K. A., Quackenbush, R. L., & Hamlin, C. K. (1985). The use of literal and applied test questions to assess understanding of concepts. *Teaching of Psychology, 12,* 136–139.

Multiple-Choice Questions With an Option to Comment: Student Attitudes and Use

Anthony F. Nield
Maxine Gallander Wintre
York University

Large enrollments in college classes present teachers with a conflict between the restrictions on the time available for grading tests and papers, and their desire to employ valid and compassionate evaluation procedures. This situation has caused many teachers, who would prefer to use short-answer or essay tests, to turn to multiple-choice tests. Well-constructed multiple-choice items can be valid measures of student performance, but some students complain that these tests do not effectively tap their knowledge. Those who complain might not represent the opinions of all students, and we have found no information in the literature concerning students' actual preferences. Most articles on testing concentrate more on the validity and rigor of the tests than on the problems of the students who take them.

Student feelings about the appropriateness of the testing method are a legitimate concern of the tester. If students are indignant, anxious, or frustrated in the test situation, then the validity of the test is in question. Also, a good relationship between the students, teaching assistants, and faculty is enhanced when the students feel that they are being tested fairly. In a preliminary survey, 343 Introductory Psychology students were asked to rate the statement "If I have to take a test in the social sciences I would prefer to take a __ test" on a scale ranging from *strongly agree* (1) to *strongly disagree* (5). The results indicated that they preferred short-answer tests, followed in order by multiple-choice, essay, fill-in-the-blank, and true/false tests.

Student complaints about multiple-choice tests center on the frustration and lack of control they feel in the test situation. They feel anxious, helpless, and stressed when forced to select one "best" answer. Although many teachers read and evaluate comments on objective tests, we have found only a few students who claim to have been given this explicit option in either college or high school. Books and articles on test-taking skills often recommend that students comment on objective tests (e.g., Feder, 1979); however, they may be reluctant to do so.

A number of studies have shown that performance on multiple-choice tests improves when the students are explicitly given an opportunity to comment. This improvement is assumed to stem from a decrease in anxiety and is greatest in highly test-anxious students (Calvin, McGuigan, & Sullivan, 1957; McKeachie, Pollie, & Speisman, 1955; R. E. Smith, 1971; W. F. Smith & Rockett, 1958). The largest effect is produced when the students perceive the opportunity to comment as indicating a permissive, nonthreatening atmosphere (McKeachie, 1984; McKeachie et al., 1955). If students are told that the comments will not be taken into account in the grading, the opportunity to comment seems to make them more anxious (Wittmaier, 1976), possibly due to uncertainty as to the purpose of the comments.

There is considerable evidence that even when other aspects of a stressful situation remain unchanged, perceived control leads to a decrease in feelings of stress and anxiety (Thompson, 1981). We believe that the option to comment provides students with an increased sense of control in the test situation, which leads to a corresponding reduction in both anxiety and frustration.

For several years, we have been using four-alternative, multiple-choice tests in large Introductory Psychology classes. In addition to selecting the "best" answer to each question, the students have been explicitly allowed to comment on the questions by marking their preferred answer and an additional alternative (E), with space provided for their comments. This strategy allows rapid stencil or computer grading and alerts the grader to the presence of written responses. Student feedback has been useful in exposing students' misconceptions and in evaluating new questions. When we discuss the tests in class, we can more easily distinguish students who genuinely recognize a difficulty with a question from those who jump on the bandwagon after the more competent students have pointed out a problem.

In this study, we questioned students in two large classes to assess their attitudes toward our test format versus other formats they have experienced—regarding both their preferences and their reasons for them—and we asked how often they had encountered similar modifications of multiple-choice tests in other classes. We also collected data on how they used their opportunity to comment, how much they used it, how their grade was affected when they did use it, and the effect on the work load of the graders.

Method

Subjects

The subjects were students enrolled in two, large, full-year sections of Introductory Psychology at York University—each section taught by one of the authors. The data on attitudes were collected from 201 students who were present on the day that the questionnaire was administered

and who stayed to complete it. The data on usage came from an analysis of the use of the E-option by all the students who took each test. The numbers of students taking Tests 1 to 4 were 416, 399, 386, and 379, respectively.

Procedure

In both sections, grades were based on the students' performance on four multiple-choice tests, each covering a separate unit of material, and each comprising 25% of the grade. The questions were different for the two sections, in that they reflected the different emphases of the instructors. However, more than two thirds of the questions came from the test file accompanying *Introduction to Psychology* by Atkinson, Atkinson, and Hilgard (Breland, 1983). On each test, the students were provided with an answer sheet, and the following instructions were both written at the top of the test and read aloud by the instructor.

> Answer the questions on the answer sheet provided by marking an "X" on the letter identifying the best answer to each question. If you want to explain your answer, you should also mark an "X" on the choice "E," and write your explanation on the back of the answer sheet.

The tests were graded using a stencil overlay, and the students received 1 point for each correct answer. The students' comments were then read and evaluated to decide whether the grade should be changed. The students gained 1 point for a good explanation of a wrong answer and lost 1 point for a bad explanation of a right answer. Otherwise, their grade remained unchanged. Each use of the E-option was also scored as to type of use—a criticism of the question, an explanation of an answer, or "other" (which meant that the student had either misunderstood the question or had misused the E-option).

During a lecture period following the third test, the students were asked to fill out a questionnaire anonymously. In the questionnaire, we asked them about their attitudes toward the E-option format and the degree to which they had taken advantage of it. In addition, we asked about the students' attitudes toward multiple-choice (with no opportunity to comment), true/false, fill-in-the-blank, short-answer, and essay questions. Students responded on a 5-point scale with the following responses: *strongly agree* (1), *agree* (2), *no opinion* (3), *disagree* (4), and *strongly disagree* (5). The items on preference, anxiety, and frustration were: "When writing a test in the social sciences I would prefer to write this type of test"; "I tend to feel anxious when writing this type of test"; and "I often find this type of test frustrating." We also asked the reasons for their attitudes.

Results and Discussion

Student Attitudes

The preference ratings were provided by 191 students and the anxiety and frustration ratings by 176 students. The decrease from the 201 students who answered the questionnaire was due to a misuse of the rating scales by some students. Because of the wording of the questions, a low mean rating indicates greater preference, but a high mean rating indicates greater anxiety and frustration.

Three repeated-measures analyses of variance showed a highly significant effect of test format on ratings of preference, $F(5, 945) = 32.7, p < .001$; anxiety, $F(5, 875) = 8.23, p < .001$; and frustration $F(5, 875) = 21.52, p < .001$. Short-answer questions were most preferred ($M = 2.13$), followed by the E-option ($M = 2.41$), essay ($M = 2.77$), multiple-choice ($M = 3.22$), fill-in-the blank ($M = 3.40$), and true/false ($M = 3.51$) questions. The E-option was rated as least anxiety provoking ($M = 3.10$), followed by short answers ($M = 2.93$), multiple-choice ($M = 2.72$), essays ($M = 2.59$), fill-in-the-blank ($M = 2.54$), and true/false ($M = 2.52$). The students rated the E-option as least frustrating ($M = 3.44$), followed in order of increasing frustration by short-answer ($M = 3.32$), essay ($M = 2.77$), true/false ($M = 2.67$), fill-in-the-blank ($M = 2.58$), and multiple-choice ($M = 2.50$) questions.

The preference for short-answer questions, even though they are more frustrating and anxiety producing than the E-option, implies that preferences are based on more than the avoidance of anxiety and frustration. However, no differences between the E-option and the short-answer formats were significant. A Tukey post-hoc test comparing the E-option with the other formats showed it to be significantly better ($p < .05$) than all except short answers for preference, anxiety, and frustration.

In describing the advantages of the various formats, the students liked true/false and multiple-choice because the answers were provided (which allowed them to guess), and because these formats, along with fill-in-the-blank questions, required little mental or physical effort. The E-option provided the advantages of multiple-choice, along with the possibility of explaining their answer (a point mentioned by 70% of the respondents). The students liked essay and short-answer formats because they could fully indicate what they had learned, show their ability to organize the material, and earn partial credit. In addition, the short-answer format did not assign too many points to any one question.

When asked about disadvantages, 32% of the students stated that the E-option offered no disadvantages, compared with 16% for short-answer questions and 5% or fewer for each of the other formats. They considered true/false, multiple-choice, and fill-in-the-blank questions to be tricky, picky, and confusing, and hence anxiety producing. The E-option questions were considered potentially too time consuming, with the added risk of losing a point for an inappropriate explanation of a correct answer. Both essay and short-answer questions were considered too easy to misinterpret and too reliant on writing skills. In addition, essay questions were considered too long and worth too many points per question, and short-answer questions required the students to be concise and to the point. In rating both essay and short-answer questions relative to the objective formats, students considered effort to be a major cause for concern.

In previous classes, when one of the authors (A. F. N.) provided students with a choice between answering short-answer questions and E-option questions, only about 10% of them chose the short-answer questions. This may seem surprising in light of our students' expressed preferences, but our data may provide a possible explanation. When the students are answering a questionnaire, and weeks away from the next test, the positive preference values may dominate, causing them to prefer short-answer questions. However, in the anxiety-arousing test situation, the relatively greater effort, anxiety, or frustration associated with the short-answer questions may lead them to choose the E-option questions. This view would be consonant with the traditional findings on conflict (Miller, 1959).

Stated Use of the E-Option

Of the students who answered the questionnaire, only 15% claimed to have previously encountered a similar option in either college or high school. Forty percent stated that they liked the availability of the E-option and had used it at least once during the year. Of those who did not use it, 50% gave no explanation, 40% said they had no need for it (25% of these volunteered that they were glad the option was available), and 10% gave as their reasons for not using it either their fear of being wrong or their concern that it would take too much time. One student thought the whole exercise a stupid waste of time.

Because we assumed that anonymity would lead to less biased responding, the students were asked neither to identify themselves on the questionnaires nor to tell us their current grade in the course. We were, therefore, unable to match the students' stated usage of the E-option with their actual usage.

Actual Use of the E-Option

The E-option was used at least once by 173 (41%) of the 416 students who took one or more of the four tests. Almost twice as many students used the E-option on the first test as on any succeeding test, with 118 students (28%) using the option on Test 1, 63 (15%) on Test 2, 64 (16%) on Test 3, and 65 (17%) on Test 4. Repeat users represented 73% of the users on Test 2, 67% on Test 3, and 74% on Test 4. The top half of the class contributed 99 users and the bottom half 74, but this difference was not significant, $\chi^2(1, N = 173) = 3.36$.

The drop in usage from Test 1 to Test 2 cannot be accounted for by students dropping the course, because only one of the 17 who dropped the course between the two tests had used the E-option on Test 1. Over the four tests, there was no apparent relationship between test difficulty, as measured by class average (%), and E-option use. It may be that an initial enthusiasm for the E-option produced an inflated usage on Test 1. When few points were gained as a result of their comments, and some were lost, the students may have used the option more selectively on future tests.

The average usage on each test was between 1.5 and 2 times per user. These means are slightly inflated because a few students used the E-option liberally, with one student using it 11 times on one test. A correlation of number of uses during the course with the users' final grades yielded a nonsignificant Pearson correlation coefficient, $r = .08$.

Table 1. Number and % of E-Option Uses by Category and User Class Position

Class Position	Category of Use			
	Criticize	Explain	Other	Total
Above median	93 (28.3)	226 (68.7)	10 (3.0)	329 (100.0)
Below median	58 (26.4)	149 (67.7)	13 (5.9)	220 (100.0)
Total class	151 (27.5)	375 (68.3)	23 (4.2)	549 (100.0)

Note. Percentages in parentheses.

Overall, the average use per user was 3.17 times during the course, or less than one use (0.79) per test. The average number of uses per student in the course was 1.31, or .32 explanations per student per test—not an onerous amount of reading for the graders.

The ways in which the E-option was used are shown in Table 1, which summarizes the number and percentage of students using each response category. Both the better and poorer students used the option to explain their answers more than twice as often as to criticize the question.

The effect of the use of the option on the students' grades is shown in Table 2. The use of the E-option had little effect on student grades overall, and the outcome was independent of a student's position in the class.

Overall, only 30 points were gained and 5 points lost during the course. Students in the top half of the class gained more points than those in the bottom half. Interestingly, they were also the ones who lost the 5 points. The net gain for both groups was about the same, 13 points for the better students, and 12 points for the poorer students. As might be expected, in the two "no change" categories the better students produced a higher proportion of right answers than the poorer students. The continued use of the E-option in the face of this lack of success reinforces our belief that the students find it useful for reasons other than obtaining extra points—presumably to relieve frustration and anxiety.

Although grades changed little as a direct result of student comments, they might have been improved by a reduction in anxiety due to the option to comment (Calvin et al., 1957; McKeachie et al., 1955; R. E. Smith, 1971; W. F. Smith & Rockett, 1958). However, we suspect that in our case this effect would be small due to the nature of our instructions. McKeachie et al. (1955) found that, although nonspecific instructions ("feel free to comment") produced a considerable improvement in the performance of test-anxious students, specific instructions ("please state your explanation of how you arrived at your particular answer") produced only a slight improvement.

We conclude that a multiple-choice format with a formal option to comment can be a useful alternative to short-answer questions. Grading effort is increased minimally by the addition of this option, and the instructor can retain the advantages of objectivity and rapid grading inherent in objective tests, yet still provide students with an opportunity to express themselves. Our students liked the E-option, even though they rarely used it, and it had little impact on their grades. Many students claimed that the option to comment relieved their anxiety and frustration in the test situation. Usage was kept low partly because of the penalty for inappropriate explanations. Presumably, the removal of this penalty would increase usage and decrease anxiety further. Nevertheless, we believe that this feature reflects a concern for a fair and accurate assessment of the students' knowledge of the material.

When students are encouraged to comment, their responses provide us with feedback, permitting us to change our grading scheme and revise our coverage of troublesome topics. Because both instructors have taught this course often, this feature was not well tested in this study. Nevertheless, student comments enabled us to identify, and compensate for, three unsatisfactory new questions.

Since adopting this test format, much less grader and instructor time is taken in confrontations with students, and we find rapport between the students and teachers to be improved. In short, we recommend multiple-choice with the E-option as an efficient and humane approach to testing large classes.

References

Breland, N. S. (1983). *Test file for Atkinson, Atkinson, and Hilgard's Introduction to Psychology* (8th ed.). New York: Harcourt Brace Jovanovich.

Calvin, A. D., McGuigan, F. J., & Sullivan, M. W. (1957). A further investigation of the relationship between anxiety and classroom examination performance. *Journal of Educational Psychology, 48,* 240–244.

Feder, B. (1979). *The complete guide to taking tests.* Englewood Cliffs, NJ: Prentice-Hall.

McKeachie, W. J. (1984). Does anxiety disrupt information processing or does poor information processing lead to anxiety? *International Review of Applied Psychology, 33,* 187–203.

McKeachie, W. J., Pollie, D., & Speisman, J. (1955). Relieving anxiety in classroom examinations. *Journal of Abnormal and Social Psychology, 50,* 93–98.

Miller, N. E. (1959). Liberalization of basic S–R concepts: Extensions to conflict behavior, motivation, and social learning. In S.

Table 2. Number and % of E-Option Uses by Effect on Grade and User Class Position

Class Position	Effect on Grade				
	Gain Point	Lose Point	No Change (Right)	No Change (Wrong)	Total
Above median	18 (5.5)	5 (1.5)	188 (57.1)	118 (35.9)	329 (100.0)
Below median	12 (5.5)	0 (0.0)	103 (46.8)	105 (47.7)	220 (100.0)
Total class	30 (5.5)	5 (1.0)	291 (53.0)	223 (40.5)	549 (100.0)

Note. Percentages in parentheses.

Koch (Ed.), *Psychology: A study of a science* (Vol. 2, pp. 196–292). New York: McGraw-Hill.

Smith, R. E. (1971). Humor, anxiety, and task performance. *Journal of Personality and Social Psychology, 19*, 243–246.

Smith, W. F., & Rockett, F. C. (1958). Test performance as a function of anxiety, instructor and instructions. *Journal of Educational Research, 52*, 138–141.

Thompson, S. C. (1981). Will it hurt less if I control it? A complex answer to a simple question. *Psychological Bulletin, 90*, 89–101.

Wittmaier, B. C. (1976). Low test anxiety as a potential indicator of underachievement. *Measurement and Evaluation in Guidance, 9*, 146–151.

Notes

1. This research was partially funded by a York University Faculty of Arts Minor Research Grant to the second author.
2. The authors acknowledge the contributions of Demo Aliferis, Paul Chernabrow, Charlotte Copas, Myra Radzins, and Sara Persaud—our teaching assistants who graded all the tests and categorized the students' comments; and Dannielle Poirier and Lorraine Chiasson who coded the data. We also thank the Introductory Psychology students who were good enough to fill out the questionnaires.

Answer Justification: Removing the "Trick" From Multiple-Choice Questions

David K. Dodd
Linda Leal
Eastern Illinois University

Students' perceptions that multiple-choice exams contain "trick" questions may contribute to test anxiety and lead them to view the instructor as an adversary rather than an advocate. Over the past several years, we have developed and used a technique called *answer justification* (AJ) that allows students to convert any multiple-choice item perceived as being "tricky" into a short-answer essay. While an earlier version of our manuscript was under journal review, Nield and Wintre (1986) described and evaluated a similar procedure. The purposes of this article are to compare and contrast our technique with that of Nield and Wintre, to present our own evaluation data, and to summarize the specific benefits of the technique for students and instructors.

Similarities and Differences

With both our technique and that of Nield and Wintre (1986), students have the opportunity to write a brief explanation of their answers for any multiple-choice question that is perceived to be ambiguous or confusing. Students select one "best" alternative and then explain their answer on the back of their answer sheet (Nield and Wintre's method) or on forms provided (our method). A convincing explanation earns credit for a missed question. The most fundamental difference between Nield and Wintre's (1986) technique and ours is that their students can also lose credit for a faulty explanation of a correct answer, whereas our students are not penalized.

We have evaluated our technique in introductory psychology courses (3 sections of 50 to 110 students each), a sophomore–junior level course in human-interaction skills (2 sections of 25 students each), and a junior–senior level course in prejudice and discrimination (35 students). Collectively, our analyses included 345 students and 17 different exam administrations, with exam length varying from 27 to 50 multiple-choice questions. From a total of 44,370 opportunities to use AJ, students used it 505 times (1%). On a typical exam, 25% of the class used AJ; most of those using it did so only once (mode = 1, M = 1.9, range = 1 to 7). Scoring was unnecessary 67% of the time because the student had selected the correct alternative; of the remaining justifications, 24% received full credit, 6% partial credit, and 70% no credit. Justifications tended to be brief and easily scored; on a typical 50-item exam given to a class of 50 students, total scoring time, including modifications to grades, was about 20 min.

Nield and Wintre (1986) evaluated the usage of their technique on a sample of 416 introductory psychology students. Like us, they found usage to be between 1.5 and 2 times per user, and they also did not find the amount of extra grading to be excessive. Over the entire course, 41% of Nield and Wintre's students explained at least one answer, compared to 56% of our students. There are two probable explanations for our apparently higher usage rate: Most obviously, our students had nothing to lose by using AJ, whereas their students could be penalized for incorrect explanations. In addition, we were apparently more lenient in scoring. Among students who explained incorrect answers, 30% of our students received full or partial credit, whereas only 12% of their students received credit.

Evaluation

We administered a brief, anonymous questionnaire to our students near the end of the semester to evaluate satisfaction with the technique. Of 259 respondents, 94% "liked having AJ available" and 93% recommended its use in other classes. No differences in satisfaction were found between the 56% who reported using AJ versus the 44% who reported never using it. Comments included: "heck of a good idea," "persuade other departments to use it," "lets the instructor know you understand the material," and "even though I haven't used it, it is very reassuring to know it is available if I do need it."

Benefits

Answer justification yields several important benefits for instructors and students. For instructors, AJ makes administration of exams easier because it helps eliminate "hint hunting" by students during exams. Most student questions can be handled by encouraging the use of AJ. Second, complaints about ambiguous questions that typically arise when students receive exam feedback are nearly eliminated; students know they will be given a fair chance to express their concerns and justify their answers during the exam. Third, AJ creates a "dialogue" between students and instructors. Identification of misleading or ambiguous exam questions, as well as unusual student interpretations of text or lecture material, is facilitated. Fourth, AJ eliminates both the need to rescore exams when bad exam items are "thrown out" and the temptation to give everyone "free points" to offset poor exam items. Instead, extra points are earned only by those students who know the course material well enough to detect an ambiguous question and write a convincing justification for their answer.

For the student, the most obvious benefit of AJ is the opportunity to improve one's exam score. However, there are several other possible benefits. Students may perceive an increased sense of control over ambiguous or difficult items. They may be encouraged to evaluate item alternatives more carefully and to review their knowledge of items. In fact, students have often been observed to begin their justification, stop and ponder, and then become so confident of their answer that they do not use AJ.

Finally, AJ may help modify students' perceptions of the instructor from someone who may be trying to trick them into mistakes to someone who is genuinely concerned about assessing their knowledge. To test this hypothesis, we administered a 7-item questionnaire to 234 students who had the opportunity to use AJ and to 303 students who did not have the opportunity to use AJ. Factor analysis of the questionnaire data revealed two factors: instructor concern for fairness and student performance (e.g., "multiple-choice exams fairly measure how much I know" and "instructors are concerned that students perform well on their exams"), and perceived "trickiness" of exam questions and instructors (e.g., "multiple-choice exams contain at least a few 'trick' questions" and "instructors purposely include a few 'trick'

questions on exams to keep students 'on their toes' "). After statistically removing variance due to instructor and expected final grade, it was found that students who had the opportunity to use AJ had more favorable attitudes on the Trickiness factor than did those who did not have the opportunity, $F(1, 524)$ 16.46, $p < .001$. Among students who had the AJ opportunity, users and nonusers did not differ in their attitudes toward "trickiness." There were no differences on the Fairness factor between users and nonusers nor between those who did and did not have the AJ opportunity.

Conclusions

Providing students with the opportunity to explain multiple-choice answers yields several important benefits for students and instructors. Nield and Wintre's (1986) students liked the procedure better than the traditional multiple-choice format and rated it as less frustrating and anxiety producing. Among our students, both users and nonusers liked having the technique available and perceived their exams and instructor as being "less tricky."

Instructors who are considering the justification procedure must decide whether to penalize incorrect explanations. Nield and Wintre (1986) acknowledged that with their technique "usage was kept low partly because of the penalty for inappropriate explanations. Presumably, the removal of this penalty would increase usage and decrease anxiety further" (p. 199). We agree and also believe that our technique is easier on instructors. Even though more of our students use the technique, our scoring time is probably much less. Our users select the correct answer 67% of the time, and because these justifications do not need to be evaluated for possible penalty points, they can be skimmed very quickly. With the Nield and Wintre procedure, every comment must be evaluated.

In sum, the benefits of allowing students to justify their multiple-choice items are impressive and the costs are minimal. The technique has become a standard component of our multiple-choice exams, and we highly recommend it.

Reference

Nield, A. F., & Wintre, M. G. (1986). Multiple-choice questions with an option to comment: Student attitudes and use. *Teaching of Psychology, 13,* 196–199.

Notes

1. An earlier version of this article was presented at the annual convention of the American Psychological Association, Washington, DC, August 1986.

The Use of Literal and Applied Test Questions to Assess Understanding of Concepts

Keith A. Wollen
Robert L. Quackenbush
Clint K. Hamlin
Washington State University

The goal of this article is to provide an empirical demonstration of the importance of the type of test questions used to assess knowledge. Several taxonomies of comprehension have been developed, the most famous of which is that of Bloom, Englehart, Furst, Hill, and Krathwohl (1956). We are concerned with two of these levels, literal factual knowledge, and application. Each of these types of comprehension can be assessed with specific types of questions that have been described most clearly by Anderson (1972).

Anderson (1972) pointed out four different types of literal questions–verbatim, transformed verbatim, paraphrase, and transformed paraphrase. *Verbatim questions* use the exact wording of the passage, and the student is typically asked to recall or recognize missing information. For example, after reading "The smallest unit of meaning is a morpheme," the student could be asked a verbatim question such as "The smallest unit of meaning is a ____?" *Transformed-verbatim questions* use the same words but reorder phrases. *Paraphrase and transformed-paraphrase questions* correspond to verbatim and transformed verbatim, respectively, except that major words are paraphrased.

Even if students answer verbatim questions correctly, we cannot be sure that they understand the concepts; instead, students might simply recognize the wording and remember the appropriate responses without really comprehending the material. Paraphrased questions suffer from the same criticism, although the paraphrasing means that students must at least understand enough to recognize the alternative wording.

Another type of question that provides a more convincing index of comprehension has variously been referred to in existing test banks as conceptual (e.g., Dunn, 1983; Wollen & Wright, 1978) or applied (e.g., Costin, Slaw, Ory, & Landesman, 1983). The form of such questions that are discussed here requires students to recognize or recall a concept name or to identify a new instance of a concept. For example, the question, "Identify the morphemes in the word 'uneventful,'" would represent application of the concept "morpheme," provided the passage did not specify the morphemes in this particular word. This type of question is called "applied" because it involves the application of knowledge to new situations. If students can apply knowledge to new situations, we can be much more confident that they comprehend the material better than if they were merely to answer literal questions.

The type of questions used in tests is often dictated, at least in part, by the type of questions found in test banks provided by publishers of textbooks. Introductory psychology texts in particular are accompanied by test banks, and the temptation to use them is high, especially given the heavy demands on our time. Unfortunately, many existing test banks provide more literal than application questions, although the trend is changing.

The present research used a type of passage known to produce superior performance on application questions. The passage consisted of definitions of concepts followed by several instances of those concepts. Providing instances of a concept together with its definition results in better performance on application-type questions than does merely providing a definition without instances (e.g., Klausmeier & Feldman, 1975; Merrill &. Tennyson, 1971). A problem with these experiments is that they did not examine the effect of concept examples on literal questions. Johnson and Stratton (1966) did compare literal and applied tests, but their data are unusual in that the typical superiority of application questions over literal was not obtained. The lack of a difference, however, might be attributed to a ceiling effect.

The major question investigated herein is whether the superior performance of subjects who have both definitions and examples will show up as higher scores on tests consisting of literal questions. Accordingly, some students were given both definitions of concepts and examples of those concepts, whereas others were given the definitions only. Performance was then compared on tests involving literal and applied questions.

Method

Subjects

The subjects were 59 males and 69 females; participation partially fulfilled a course requirement of Introductory Psychology. To reduce students' pre-experimental familiarity with the material, the experiment was restricted to students taking their first course in psychology, and the introductory course they were taking did not explicitly cover the concepts tested in the experiment. All subjects used English as their first language. Subjects were run in small groups of about eight.

Materials

The materials were four passages written by the experimenters in a style similar to that used in introductory texts. Each passage introduced and defined two or three concepts:

Passage A (phonemes and morphemes), Passage B (reinforcement, extinction, and differential reinforcement), Passage C (classical and instrumental conditioning), and Passage D (kinesics and proxemics). For half of the subjects, each passage was accompanied by two or three examples of each concept. Thus, there were two versions (definitions or definitions plus examples) for each of four passages. The number of words in definitions-only passages and in definitions-plus-examples passages were: A = 86 and 251, B = 108 and 402, C = 167 and 344, and D = 248 and 495. Passage A, with examples, follows:

> *The Basic Units in Language.* The fundamental sounds of each language are called *phonemes.* English has 45 phonemes, and other languages have from 13 to 71. Languages have many more phonemes than letters, and each letter may consist of several phonemes. Phonemes can be combined to make *morphemes.* Morphemes are the smallest units of meaning in a language. In some cases, morphemes can be words, but often morphemes are word parts—such as prefixes, suffixes, and stems of words—that have definite meanings.

> *Examples.* Examples may help to clarify the difference between phonemes and morphemes. The phonemes for the vowel "a" include the "a" sounds in *tan* and *tall.* Similarly, the phonemes for the vowel "o" are illustrated by the "o" sounds in *boot, foot,* and *sore.* Many letters are made up of combinations of phonemes; for example, "pub" and "ee" sounds are combined in our pronunciation of the letter "p," and "buh" and "ee" sounds are combined in the letter "b." Letters such as "w" have several phonemes.

> Morphemes are sometimes single words such as *house* or *book.* Often, however, words contain several morphemes, as in the word *typewriter,* which has three morphemes (*type, write,* and *er*). Each of these contributes to the meaning of the word. Similarly, the word *running* consists of the morpheme *run* and a second morpheme *ing* (meaning "at the present time"). Sometimes the morpheme can be a single letter, as in the word *dogs,* which contains the morpheme *dog* and a second morpheme *s* (indicating plural).

Each subject was given one pair of passages, either A and B or C and D. Within each pair, the passage that appeared first was counterbalanced across subjects.

Design and Procedure

The design included two between-subject variables and one within. The between-subject variables were passage type (concept definition only or concept plus examples) and reading condition (read through once or read for 4 min). The time variable was included as a control to determine if the total amount of study time were a critical variable. Passages with examples were obviously longer, and so subjects with examples might do better simply because they spent more time studying rather than because they were or were not given examples. Accordingly, half of the subjects were told to read each passage until they heard a bell indicating that the 4-min study session was over. The other half of the subjects were instructed to read each passage just once. The within-subject variable was test question type (literal or applied).

The passages were placed face down on desks before the subjects entered the experimental room. The subjects were told that their task was to read two passages and to try to learn the passages so that they could answer questions about them later. They were informed that the first page of their booklets would have more specific instructions.

The specific written instructions asked subjects (a) to read the first passage once and then to read the second passage once, or (b) to read the first passage until they heard the bell (4 min) and then to read the second passage until they heard the bell again (also 4 min). The instructions asked subjects to turn to the next page after the reading period and to take the test they saw there.

The test consisted of 10 blanks requiring brief written answers of one word or phrase. The test over each passage had 5 literal questions requiring answers directly stated in the passage. The questions were either verbatim with the passage (e.g., "The fundamental sounds of a language are called ___") or paraphrases/transforms (e.g., "About how many phonemes are there in English?"). The 5 literal questions were followed by 5 questions requiring subjects to apply the concept (e.g., "What are the morphemes in the following word? bathrooms ___"). After completing a 10-item test on the first passage, the subjects turned the page and took another 10-item test on the second passage.

Immediately after the second test, subjects completed a 16-item questionnaire to determine how they rated the passages in terms of clarity, difficulty, interest, and, where applicable, helpfulness of the examples. The only purpose of this questionnaire was to occupy subjects who finished early (those who read each passage only once) and to prevent them from disrupting those who had not yet finished. Consequently, data from the questionnaire are not reported.

Results

The percentage correct was approximately equal for the four passage topics, as was the percentage correct for the first and second passages. Hence, the data were collapsed over these variables. The result was two scores for each subject: the total correct for the 10 literal questions and the total correct for the 10 applied questions. However, half of the subjects had only 8 literal questions because the first 2 questions of Passage C had to be discarded due to an experimenter error that was not discovered until after all subjects were run. The error arose before the experiment began; the wording of the passage was changed, but appropriate modifications were not made for 2 questions. This meant that 2 questions could not be classified as either applied or literal. There is no reason to expect the elimination of questions to have any effect on the outcome because the remaining 8 questions would be no more biased than if all 10 were present. Also, the overall mean for subjects who had 8 questions was not significantly different from those who had 10, $t(126) = 1.45$, $p > .10$. The scores were converted to percentages of the maximum possible (either 8 or 10, as the case might be). In all, there were 12 verbatim questions and 6 that were paraphrased or transformed-paraphrased.

The means of the percentages correct were subjected to a mixed-design analysis of variance, with reading time and presence or absence of examples as between-subject vari-

Table 1. Mean Percentage Correct on the Test as a Function of Question Type and Presence or Absence of Concept Examples

Passage Studied	Question Type	
	Literal	Applied
Definitions Only	54.25	46.25
Definitions + Examples	54.20	62.05

ables and with question type as a within variable. Reading each passage for 4 min produced significantly higher percentages correct (59.3) than simply reading each passage once (49.0), $F(1, 124) = 13.00$, $p < .001$. However, no interactions involving reading time approached significance, and so the data are collapsed over reading time in the subsequent analyses.

The data of major interest pertain to the interaction between type of question and presence or absence of examples. These means are shown in Table 1. The interaction was significant, $F(1, 124) = 13.85$, $p < .001$, and so the simple effect of examples was examined at each level of question type. Considering the applied questions, subjects who had both definitions and examples recalled significantly more than those who had only definitions, $t(124) = 7.41$, $p < .001$. On literal questions, however, the addition of examples to definitions of the concepts had no effect; subjects performed just as well with the concept definitions only.

Discussion

The primary question was whether the superior understanding that subjects gained from having examples along with concept definitions would be evidenced on literal questions as well as on applied ones. The superiority was present on the applied questions, which replicates previous findings that providing both definitions of concepts and examples of those concepts facilitates test performance relative to a group that is given definitions only. The key finding was that this increased understanding was not evidenced on the literal portion of the test. These results were obtained both when subjects read each passage just once and when they read a passage for a 4-min period. Thus, tests having only literal questions may well miss assessing portions of students' knowledge.

Another interesting result is that the relative difficulty of applied and literal questions depends on the nature of the passage. If a passage defines concepts without providing examples, applied questions become more difficult. But if a passage also provides examples, applied questions become easier. Thus, it seems that text authors should take care to present sufficient examples of defined concepts.

The present data suggest that we should use questions such as the application type in the present study if we want to determine the extent to which our students understand concepts (as opposed to simply recalling explicitly presented information). Fortunately, a few publishers have made conceptual questions a significant part of their test banks (e.g., Costin et al., 1983; Dunn, 1983; Wollen & Wright, 1978), and the frequency of such questions is definitely on the rise. However, care must be exercised; many test banks are still comprised primarily or totally of literal questions. Hence, instructors are urged to be cautious in the selection of test materials and to encourage publishers to provide more questions that tap understanding.

References

Anderson, R. C. (1972). How to construct achievement tests to assess comprehension. *Review of Educational Research, 42,* 145–170.

Bloom, B. S., Englehart, M. D., Furst, E. J., Hill, W. H., & Krathwohl, D. R. (1956). *Taxonomy of educational objectives. Handbook I: Objectives.* New York: McKay.

Costin, F., Slaw, K. M., Ory, J. C., & Landesman, A. (1983). *Test item file for* Psychology. Glenview, IL: Scott Foresman.

Dunn, W. (1983). *Test item file for* Psychology Today. New York: Random House.

Johnson, D. M., & Stratton, R. P. (1966). Evaluation of five methods of teaching concepts. *Journal of Educational Psychology, 57,* 48–53.

Klausmeier, H. J., & Feldman, K. V. (1975). Effects of a definition and a varying number of examples and nonexamples on concept attainment. *Journal of Educational Psychology, 67,* 174–178.

Merrill, M. D., & Tennyson, R. D. (1971). *The effect of types of positive and negative examples on learning concepts in the classroom* (Final Report on Project No. 0-H-14). Provo, UT: Brigham Young University, Department of Instructional Research and Development. (ERIC Document Reproduction Service No. ED 113 660)

Wollen, K. A., & Wright, J. W. (1978). *Test bank for Lindzey Hall Thompson: Psychology.* New York: Worth.

Affective Cues and Processing Strategy: Color-Coded Examination Forms Influence Performance

Robert C. Sinclair
Alexander S. Soldat
University of Alberta

Melvin M. Mark
Pennsylvania State University

Considerable research has demonstrated that affective states influence processing strategy and judgmental accuracy (e.g., Sinclair, 1988; Sinclair & Mark, 1992, 1995). Generally, happy moods lead to nonsystematic, less detail-oriented, and more heuristic processing; whereas sad moods lead to more systematic, more detail-oriented, and less heuristic processing. Consistent with this position, Sinclair (1988) and Sinclair and Mark (1995) demonstrated that happy people were less accurate on performance appraisal and statistical judgments than were sad people. Cognitive response analyses demonstrated that these effects occurred because of the differential processing strategies associated with happy versus sad moods.

One explanation for these differential processing strategy effects is the cognitive tuning extension of the affect-as-information hypothesis (Clore, Schwarz, & Conway, 1994; Sinclair, Mark, & Clore, 1994). According to this hypothesis, affective states provide informational signals about situations and the conduct of tasks. Happy moods signal that situations are benign and that no extra cognitive resources are necessary for processing and judgment, whereas sad moods signal that situations are threatening or important, and that detailed processing is necessary (for empirical evidence supporting this position, see Sinclair et al., 1994).

Recently, Soldat, Sinclair, and Mark (1997) extended the cognitive tuning branch of the affect-as-information hypothesis to environmental affective cues (e.g., color) that do not directly influence perceivers' moods. In particular, they argued that colors serve as affective cues, thereby signaling the degree of processing required in a particular situation. For example, although red conveyed positive affect and blue conveyed negative affect, color had no actual impact on mood. This pattern of effects emerged in a study in which participants rated their current affective state or the affect conveyed by the paper. Paper color did not influence reported affective state (cf. Jacobs & Blandino, 1992; Jacobs & Suess, 1975) but did influence ratings of the affect conveyed by the paper. An additional study replicated this effect and demonstrated that white fell between red and blue

on the measure of conveyed affect (again, no effects emerged on affective states; see Soldat et al., 1997). In Soldat et al., another group of participants completed both simple and complex Graduate Record Exam-like questions, involving analytic problem solving, on either red or blue paper and evaluated their current affective states and the difficulty of reading the materials on Likert scales. Blue paper led to greater accuracy, especially for complex questions. However, paper color did not influence mood or reading difficulty. Furthermore, analyses of covariance controlling for arousal (as reported on the arousal component of the measure of current affective state) demonstrated no effects of arousal.

The Soldat et al. (1997) findings, replicated in a second study that included a white-paper control group that fell between the performance levels of blue and red, appear to have implications for testing situations. For example, instructors may create different forms of multiple-choice examinations to prevent cheating. Generally, instructors present questions in different orders on the different forms. Furthermore, instructors may print different forms on differently colored paper to make it clear that there are different forms, and to provide a straightforward visual check that copies of the same form are not adjacent to one another. In this situation, students whose examination forms are on colors that convey more positive affect may process information less systematically, leading to differential performance on the examination. Of course, in these naturally occurring situations, exam form is confounded with paper color, so whether form effects are due to color or question order is unclear. Soldat et al. conducted their research demonstrating differential accuracy as a function of paper color in laboratory settings with volunteer participants. Thus, it is unclear whether a similar pattern of effects would emerge in an actual examination setting, where motivation levels should be higher than in a laboratory situation.

We conducted a study to assess the generalizability of the extended cognitive tuning hypothesis to the real-world setting of the classroom. Students completed their midterm examination on either red or blue paper, with random assignment of paper color. Following Soldat et al. (1997), we expected that the blue paper would lead to greater accuracy, especially for difficult questions.

Method

Participants

Participants were 45 introductory psychology students at the Grant MacEwan Community College, who received no remuneration. There were 14 men and 31 women.

Procedure

We collected the data during a regularly scheduled examination in the participants' usual classroom. Under the auspices of presenting two different forms of a midterm examination, participants completed identical forms of the examination (with identical item orders) printed on either red (i.e., Wausau Papers Astrobrights Rocket Red) or blue (i.e., Wausau Papers Astrobrights Lunar Blue). Assignment to conditions was random within gender. The examination consisted of 75 multiple-choice questions that assessed factual knowledge and ability to apply and integrate concepts. Following the examination, we fully debriefed the participants and assured them that we would adjust scores to control for any color effects.

Results

We conducted an item analysis and categorized questions as simple if 65% or more of the participants responded correctly. There were 30 simple and 44 difficult questions. We deleted 1 difficult question because it was a bad item. Inclusion of this question did not change the pattern of effects or levels of significance.

The percentage of the simple and of the difficult questions correctly answered served as two levels of a within-subjects factor (Question Difficulty) in a Color × Question Difficulty mixed-model ANOVA, with Color the between-subjects factor. There was a main effect of color, $F(1, 43) = 5.84$, $p < .03$, with participants completing the blue examination ($M = 66.63$, $SD = 15.35$) outperforming those taking the red examination ($M = 56.45$, $SD = 12.73$), and a main effect of question difficulty, $F(1, 43) = 324.71$, $p < .0001$, with a lower percentage of difficult questions answered correctly ($M = 46.41$, $SD = 15.42$) than of simple questions ($M = 76.89$, $SD = 16.63$). These effects occurred in the context of a Color × Question Difficulty interaction, $F(1, 43) = 5.08$, $p < .03$, illustrated in Figure 1. As is apparent in Figure 1, for simple questions, red ($M = 73.64$, $SD = 14.94$) led to poorer performance than blue ($M = 80.00$, $SD = 17.89$); the color effect accounted for 3.74% of the total sum of squares for simple questions. This effect was more pronounced for difficult questions ($M = 39.26$, $SD = 12.05$ and $M = 53.26$, $SD = 15.38$ for red and blue, respectively), where color accounted for 21.08% of the total sum of squares. Adjusted

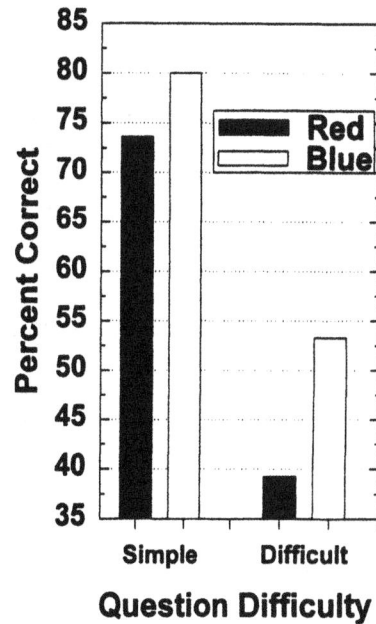

Figure 1. Percentage correct as a function of color and question difficulty.

least significant difference tests indicated that all means differed at the .05 level. We point out that there were 7 men per color condition, and 15 women and 16 women in the red and blue conditions, respectively. A Color × Sex × Question Difficulty mixed-model ANOVA revealed no effects for sex and no interactions with sex. All other effects reported previously remained significant.

Discussion

The results extend the cognitive tuning branch of the affect-as-information hypothesis to actual testing situations. Blue paper led to better performance than red paper, particularly for difficult questions. Given that Soldat et al. (1997) demonstrated that red paper conveyed positive affect and blue paper negative affect, we believe that the present results occurred because red paper signaled that the situation was relatively more benign and that systematic processing was less necessary, whereas blue paper signaled that the situation was relatively more serious and that systematic processing was more necessary. Given that previous research showed that paper color did not affect the perceivers' experienced moods (Soldat et al., 1997), the impact of paper color on processing does not appear to be mediated by mood. Furthermore, readability is not a plausible alternative explanation, given that Soldat et al. demonstrated that paper color did not affect readability.

We should point out that although Soldat et al. (1997) demonstrated that the colors used did not affect current mood, other researchers have shown small color-related mood effects. For example, Jacobs and Blandino (1992) demonstrated that red led to less reported fatigue than yellow, blue, green, and white. Furthermore, Jacobs and Suess (1975) demonstrated that red and yellow led to greater anxiety than did blue or green, and Wilson (1966) showed that red was more arousing than green. Although we chose particular colors for our study to remove the confound between item order and examination form color, it is important to note that color may have other psychological effects in other situations. Thus, regardless of the colors chosen for different forms of examinations, the potential exists for color effects on performance—a possibility apparently not recognized by many instructors.

Our results have an important implication for test situations. That is, instructors should not be cavalier about color coding different forms of examinations. In fact, we believe that it would be best if instructors did not use color-coded forms. Furthermore, people should exercise caution when they use different item orders. For example, Balch (1989) showed that different item orders can influence test performance (cf. Neely, Springston, & McCann, 1994). Thus, assigning students to different exam forms could unfairly disadvantage some students. When using different forms, one approach is to test for form effects and, if such effects emerge, apply a correction such as the Angoff (1971) correction formula, which equates forms prior to assigning grades by adjusting scores and maintaining percentile rankings within and across forms. For example, the 90th percentile score on both forms remains at the 90th percentile after adjustment. In our data, this adjustment resulted in identical means and variances across the two forms and levels of question difficulty. Finally, we point out that, in theory, factors exist that should negate our color effect; these include high motivation (though normal motivation for grades was apparently not sufficient in this study) and an explicit recognition that the affective cue provided by the color of the paper is irrelevant in the current context (Sinclair et al., 1994).

Balch, W. R. (1989). Item order affects performance on multiple-choice exams. *Teaching of Psychology, 16,* 75–77.

Clore, G. L., Schwarz, N., & Conway, M. (1994). Affective causes and consequences of social information processing. In R. S. Wyer & T. K. Srull (Eds.), *Handbook of social cognition: Vol. 1. Basic processes* (2nd ed., pp. 323–417). Hillsdale, NJ: Lawrence Erlbaum Associates, Inc.

Jacobs, K. W., & Blandino, S. E. (1992). Effects of color of paper on which the profile of mood states is printed on the psychological states it measures. *Perceptual and Motor Skills, 75,* 267–271.

Jacobs, K. W., & Suess, J. F. (1975). Effects of four psychological primary colors on anxiety state. *Perceptual and Motor Skills, 41,* 207–210.

Neely, D. L., Springston, F. J., & McCann, S. J. H. (1994). Does item order affect performance on multiple choice exams? *Teaching of Psychology, 21,* 44–45.

Sinclair, R. C. (1988). Mood, categorization breadth, and performance appraisal: The effects of order of information acquisition and affective state on halo, accuracy, information retrieval, and evaluations. *Organizational Behavior and Human Decision Processes, 42,* 22–46.

Sinclair, R. C., & Mark, M. M. (1992). The influence of mood state on judgment and action. In L. L. Martin & A. Tesser (Eds.), *The construction of social judgments* (pp. 165–193). Hillsdale, NJ: Lawrence Erlbaum Associates, Inc.

Sinclair, R. C., & Mark, M. M. (1995). The effects of mood state on judgemental accuracy: Processing strategy as a mechanism. *Cognition and Emotion, 9,* 417–438.

Sinclair, R. C., Mark, M. M., & Clore, G. L. (1994). Mood-related persuasion depends on (mis)attributions. *Social Cognition, 12,* 309–326.

Soldat, A. S., Sinclair, R. C., & Mark, M. M. (1997). Color as an environmental processing cue: External affective cues can directly affect processing strategy without affecting mood. *Social Cognition, 15,* 55–71.

Wilson, G. D. (1966). Arousal properties of red versus green. *Perceptual and Motor Skills, 23,* 947–949.

References

Angoff, W. H. (1971). Norms, scales, and equivalent scores. In R. L. Thorndike (Ed.), *Educational measurement* (2nd ed., pp. 508–600). Washington, DC: American Council on Education.

Notes

1. This research was supported by Social Sciences and Humanities Research Council of Canada operating Grant 410 970002 and a Social Sciences Research grant to Robert C. Sinclair.

Item Order Affects Performance on Multiple-Choice Exams

William R. Balch
The Pennsylvania State University, Altoona

Teachers who give multiple-choice tests often use alternate forms (i.e., different orders of the same items). This procedure is probably effective in discouraging students from copying answers from their classmates, but instructors follow this practice without considering the possible effects of item order on test performance. They seem to assume that items test separate bits of knowledge and are independent of each other.

I studied the effects of item order on test scores and completion time. Three different orders of the same items were given to different students as alternate forms of the final exam. In the S order exam, items were arranged in the same sequence in which the relevant material was presented in the course lectures and text. In the CC order exam, the items were random, except that items for any given chapter appeared together. The chapters did not appear in sequential order. Instructors often use this method for creating alternate forms. In the random (R) order exam, the same items were scrambled by a computer program; this could also be accomplished by writing items on separate index cards and then shuffling them. Many software programs for generating tests from a computerized item bank also produce random orders.

Method

Subjects

A total of 404 General Psychology students at The Pennsylvania State University, Altoona, served as subjects. Four different sections, each consisting of about 100 students, were involved. All sections came from the same student population, and the test procedures and materials were identical for each section; therefore, the data for all four sections were combined.

The study was conducted during the regular final examination. Each student was given 3 points of extra credit, out of 250 points possible in the course, to offset any reduction of test scores that might be produced by manipulating item order.

Materials

Each of the three orders contained the same 75 multiple-choice questions. Forty of these items were selected from the test bank for the course text (Benjamin, Hopkins, & Nation, 1987), and I wrote 35. Every item was based on material from a particular page of the textbook, and numerical page order was followed for the S form.

To achieve maximum contrast between the random order and the other orders, one constraint on true randomness was introduced (i.e., no two items from the same chapter were adjacent). For the CC condition, the order of items within and across chapters was randomized. However, all items within the same chapter remained adjacent. There were approximately five to six items for each of the 14 chapters.

Design and Procedure

In each of the four sections, students were randomly assigned to one condition: S, CC, or R. A sealed envelope, containing the test booklet and a standard test form for automatic scoring, was prepared for each student. The student's name and a 4-digit code were written in advance on the test booklet form as well as on the outside of the envelope. An alphabetical order was used to seat students and to

prearrange the test envelopes. This way the exams could be passed out quickly, with each student receiving the appropriate preassigned form. After all students had received their exams, a starting signal was given, and a stopwatch was started. Completion time for each student was recorded on the exam form. Debriefing sessions were held for interested students after all four exam sessions were completed.

I was concerned about the ethical problem of manipulating a variable that could cause some students to score lower than they otherwise might. In debriefing sessions, I explained to students that I did not know in advance what effects the ordering manipulation would have, and that I was trying to assess the effects of order to learn more about the common practice of giving alternate forms. Finally, I pointed out that the 3 extra credit points were intended to compensate students who may have scored a little lower due to an unfavorable order. Because grades were assigned on the basis of preset cutoffs rather than according to a normal curve, no student would be penalized by small order effects.

Results

Mean scores of 76.86%, 72.22%, and 73.19% were obtained for S, CC, and R orders, respectively. These means are based on students' scores for all sections; 134 students received each order. Two subjects' scores were randomly eliminated from the original 136 in the R group to equate the number of scores for all orders.

The effect of item order was assessed by a one-way analysis of variance (ANOVA) on the scores for the S, CC, and R forms. This effect was significant, $F(2, 399) = 4.75$, $p < .01$.

Multiple comparisons between the individual groups were performed using the Scheffé test. The sequential group performed significantly better than the chapter contiguity group, $p < .05$. The superiority of sequential over the random group was marginally significant, $p < .10$. The difference in scores between the chapter contiguity and the random groups was not significant, $p > .05$.

Mean completion times were 1,801.73 s, 1,816.66 s, and 1,830.94 s for the S, CC, and R orders, respectively. These means are based on the completion times of 134 students in each group. A one-way ANOVA revealed that the main effect of item order on completion time was not significant, $F < 1$.

Discussion

Practical Considerations

The results suggest that exam scores can be influenced by item order. Students scored slightly higher with the S form than with the CC or R forms. Such differences in scores are consequential in many course grading systems. Therefore, the small order effects found here might understandably be considered important to most students.

By using different R orders, instructors can create alternate forms that are more likely to be equivalent. Another method of reducing bias is to counterbalance S and R orders across several different tests. The instructor could assign forms to students in advance, making sure that each student receives each form equally often over a span of several tests. With the counterbalancing approach, a student's average score would be raised by taking some of the tests using the easier S form. Therefore, this method can be used by instructors who want their students to score as high as possible under an alternate form system.

Theoretical Considerations

It is useful to draw on laboratory-based memory theories in understanding certain issues in educational testing. In the present case, it is helpful to consider a multiple-choice test as providing retrieval cues for information learned earlier. Although information for a multiple-choice test does not have to be retrieved in the same way that words are recalled in a laboratory study, recognizing the correct answer to a multiple-choice question does require the access and organization of previously learned information. Therefore, theories of retrieval from memory may be useful in considering how item order affects test performance.

The easiness of the S order is generally consistent with the view of encoding specificity (Tulving & Thomson, 1973) developed from experiments on cued word recall. The information related to a given item is best retrieved in the context of surrounding information that was present during encoding. In the S ordering of questions, the context of retrieval is most similar to the context of encoding. It fol-lows, then, that test scores should be highest for the S arrangement of items.

Only three types of orders were used in this experiment. There may be other useful principles of item ordering that were not addressed here. For instance, one instructor told me that he uses item difficulty as the basis of ordering, starting with easier questions and progressing to the more challenging ones.

In discussing this research with colleagues and students, I have been gratified by their interest in these issues. In particular, I enjoyed the cooperation of the student participants. I doubt that any of them had ever before taken a final exam as part of a research project. In a situation that could have caused apprehension, most of the students responded with curiosity and enthusiasm.

References

Benjamin, L. T., Jr., Hopkins, J. R., & Nation, J. R. (1987). *Psychology*. New York: Macmillan.

Tulving, E., & Thomson, D. M. (1973). Encoding specificity and retrieval processes in episodic memory. *Psychological Review, 80,* 352–373.

Notes

1. I thank Stephanie Parks and Lauri Mohler for their assistance in conducting the exam sessions and tabulating the data.

Does Item Order Affect Performance on Multiple-Choice Exams?

Darlene L. Neely
Frederick J. Springston
Stewart J. H. McCann
University College of Cape Breton

Many instructors assume that scrambling the order of multiple-choice questions makes the exam more challenging for students. Teachers may be reluctant to give exams in which item order is sequenced according to course or text coverage, and publishers incorporate options to randomize the order of computerized test bank items.

Balch's (1989) findings suggest that students may score higher on multiple-choice exams when the items are sequenced (S). Mean exam scores of an S, a random (R), and a chapter contiguity group (in which chapters were covered in a random order and questions were randomized within each chapter) differed at the .01 level. Of most interest here, a Scheffé comparison showed that "the superiority of sequential over the random group was marginally significant, $p < .10$" (p. 76).

Given the marginal significance of Balch's (1989) sequenced-versus-random (S/R) effect, the lack of corroborating evidence, the conventional wisdom on the matter, and the practical ramifications involved, we conducted three field experiments to cross-validate the S/R effect and to determine whether the effect is moderated by test anxiety. We speculated that an S format might benefit high-anxiety students because the ordering of the items serves as a natural retrieval cue and provides greater structure to allay anxiety and to allow a clearer task focus.

Method and Results

Experiment 1

An S or an R version of a 50-item term test was randomly administered to 104 students in introductory psychology. The first 35 questions were taken from the test bank, and the last 15 were based on lecture content. The manipulation applied to the first 35 questions, which were spread evenly over approximately 120 pages of four chapters of the text (Myers, 1990). As in Balch's (1989) study, to create a maximum contrast between formats, we imposed an added constraint: In the R format, no questions from the same chapter were adjacent. Before taking the test, students completed the 20-item Test Attitude Inventory (TAI; Spielberger, 1977), a measure of test anxiety.

With test anxiety scores split at the median, the effects of item order, test anxiety, and their interaction were assessed with a 2 × 2 analysis of variance (ANOVA). There was no main effect for item order; in fact, R performance (M = 57.9%) was slightly higher than S performance (M = 56.8%). As expected, low-anxiety students tended to score higher than high-anxiety students, $F(1, 100) = 3.57, p < .10$, but the interaction between item order and anxiety was not significant.

Experiment 2

Experiment 2 was conducted during the next academic year with 149 introductory psychology students taught by the same instructor as in Experiment 1. Two 50-item tests were given on 2 consecutive class days. On each test, the first 40 questions were taken from the test bank, and the last 10 were based on lecture content. For each test, the manipulation applied to the 40 test bank questions, which were spread evenly over the same 150 pages of five chapters of the text (Myers, 1989). Again, no R-format questions from the same chapter appeared next to each other. On the first test day, 149 students were randomly given an S- or an R-format test; on the second day, students received the alternate format. The TAI (Spielberger, 1977) was completed before the first test.

Scores for the first 40 items on each test were standardized, and those of the second test were subtracted from those of the first test to form the criterion, which indicated how much better or worse each student performed on the first test than on the second test. With anxiety scores split at the median, a 2 × 2 ANOVA showed no significant effect for format; no interaction effect; and, as expected, no effect for anxiety, all $Fs < 1.00$. The relation of anxiety to performance was tested by summing the standardized scores for the first and second tests and comparing high- and low-anxiety students on this performance variable. The summed scores of low-anxiety students were significantly higher than the summed scores of high-anxiety students, $F(1, 147) = 9.10$, $p < .01$.

Experiment 3

An S or an R version of a 100-item final test was randomly given to 138 of the students studied in Experiment 2. The manipulation applied to the first 80 test bank questions, which were spread evenly over approximately 150 pages of five chapters of the text (Myers, 1989). No questions from the same chapter were adjacent. Anxiety scores were available from Experiment 2.

Using the same analysis as in Experiment 1, we found no main effect for test format; R performance (M = 67.1%) was again somewhat higher than S performance (M = 62.8%). Low-anxiety students tended to score higher than high-anxiety students, $F(1, 134) = 2.99, p < .10$, and the interaction between item order and anxiety was significant, $F(1, 134) = 7.11, p < .01$. High-anxiety students did somewhat better with the S format (M = 64.1%) than the R format (M = 61.3%); low-anxiety students did substantially better with the R format (M = 72.9%) than the S format (M = 61.5%).

Discussion and Conclusion

Results of our three experiments provide no evidence of an S item order format advantage. Furthermore, Peters and Messier (1970) found a significant effect in favor of the S format once in four replication attempts. One of their replications produced nonsignificant results favoring the R format. Therefore, including Balch's (1989) study, there have been eight tests of the S/R effect, and only two have produced results suggesting that an S-order format is easier than an R-order format.

Balch (1989) and others have underlined the practical aspects of his results. For example, a widely distributed newsletter for deans and department chairs ("Multiple-Choice Tests," 1990) reported that Balch's findings were causing a commotion among students. The article stated that "Balch recommends administering randomly ordered tests to all students" (p. 5) to remedy the discrepancy in scores that can be expected from R and S tests. It appears from our results that concern with such ramifications may be premature and unwarranted.

A significant interaction between anxiety and test format was found in only one of our three experiments. High-anxiety students appeared to profit somewhat from the S format. The advantage of the R format for the low-anxiety students was more pronounced and clearly more important to the detection of the interaction. Curiously, Peters and Messier (1970) also found a similar interaction (at the .10 level) in one of four analyses. At this time, it is probably best to view our one anxiety interaction effect as merely suggestive.

Although little support for the item order format effect exists, certain circumstances may favor an S order. For example, consider the following item:

Maslow's hierarchy provides a classification of:
a. psychological disorders.
b. human motives.
c. psychotherapies.
d. developmental stages.

This item may be more of a challenge in an R-order format than if it appeared adjacent to other items from a chapter on motivation. Another circumstance that might favor the S order may occur when items are blindly selected from a test bank and printed in an S format; such a procedure may result in direct cues being present in adjacent questions if there are several items in a row in the test bank dealing with the same concept. Rather than simply trying to establish whether or not S/R order effects generally exist, researchers should focus on delineating the structural and personological factors that may make the item order format effect most apt to occur.

References

Balch, W. R. (1989). Item order affects performance on multiple-choice exams. *Teaching of Psychology, 16,* 75–77.

Multiple-choice tests: The 3% problem. (1990, November). *Academic Leader,* p. 5.

Myers, D. G. (1989). *Psychology* (2nd ed.). New York: Worth.

Myers, D. G. (1990). *Exploring psychology.* New York: Worth.

Peters, D. L., & Messier, V. (1970). The effects of question sequence upon objective test performance. *Alberta Journal of Educational Research, 16,* 253–265.

Spielberger, C. D. (1977). *Test attitude inventory.* Palo Alto, CA: Consulting Psychologists Press.

Notes

1. We thank an anonymous reviewer for suggesting the point about the multiple-choice question concerning Maslow's hierarchy.
2. Darlene L. Neely is now a graduate student in the Department of Educational Psychology at the University of Alberta in Edmonton, Alberta, Canada.

Chapters and Units: Frequent Versus Infrequent Testing Revisited

Cathy A. Grover
Texas A&M University

Angela H. Becker
Stephen F. Davis
Emporia State University

Our students often request more tests covering less material. The most appropriate response to their pleas is not at all clear-cut. Perhaps past research can serve as a guide to solve this dilemma.

An early study by Turney (1931) reported that more frequent testing was associated with superior performance. This superiority was attributed to increased motivation engendered by frequent testing. Similar results were reported by Fitch, Drucker, and Norton (1951) who also stressed motivation in their explanation of this effect. On the other hand, Dustin (1971) demonstrated superiority for more frequently tested subjects, but downplayed the motivating effects of frequent testing.

Another early study (Keys, 1934) found that frequent testing produced significantly higher scores on exams during the semester but not on a common, comprehensive, final examination. Fulkerson and Martin (1981) reported similar findings. In both cases, the authors assumed that cramming for the previously announced final exam eliminated group differences.

Despite these discrepancies, students tested more frequently were consistent in reporting greater satisfaction with the testing procedure and the course. Subjects in all these studies were randomly assigned to the frequent and infrequent conditions. Such an arbitrary assignment might significantly affect students' satisfaction. By allowing subjects to select a preferred testing option, our study was designed to determine if the superiority attributed to more frequent testing was related to the assignment of subjects to conditions.

Method

Subjects

The subjects were 12 men and 16 women enrolled in one section of Introductory Psychology at Emporia State University in the spring semester of 1988. Fifty percent of the men were second-semester freshmen, 42% were sophomores, and 8% were juniors. The mean age of this group was 19.10 years. Thirty-eight percent of the women were second-semester freshmen, 44% were sophomores, and 18% were juniors. The mean age of this group was 19.19 years.

Materials

The textbook used for the course was *Psychology* by Benjamin, Hopkins, and Nation (1987). All exam questions were obtained from the computerized test bank supplied by the publisher.

Both chapter and unit tests consisted of 15 multiple-choice questions per assigned text chapter. The questions were selected randomly with the restriction that the material being tested had been covered in class. Of those 15 questions, a minimum of 10 were identical on both types of tests; a maximum of 5 were similar with regard to information and difficulty, but different in wording. Because most chapter tests were administered before the unit tests, these different items were included to deter cheating. All questions were given in the same order for both types of tests.

A comprehensive exam, consisting of three questions per chapter and covering chapters 1 through 12, was administered to all students during the final class session. (Because the unit test for chapters 13, 14, and 16 was administered during the scheduled final exam period following the end of classes, questions from these chapters were not included in the comprehensive exam.) Items for the comprehensive exam were selected from those used on previous tests with the restriction that only items missed with equal frequency by both chapter and unit students were included. Although the students were told which chapters would be covered on the comprehensive exam, they were unaware that the questions were to be drawn from the previous tests.

Procedure

During the first week of class, the instructor explained the two test options. Students were told to consider their schedules and determine the option that best suited their needs. The instructor also emphasized the pros and cons of both options and stressed that the one selected would obtain for the entire semester. Two class periods later, students reported the option they had chosen. Of the 28 students in the class, exactly one-half (8 women and 6 men) independently selected each option.

Students selecting the unit test (UT) option were given their tests during the class period following the completion of lecture material for the four chapters comprising each unit. Students selecting the chapter test (CT) option took the first three of every four tests at one of two prescheduled times outside of class. The fourth test was administered during the class period devoted to UT exam administration. All students, regardless of option, received the same test instructions and took as much time as needed to complete the tests.

In addition to the tests and comprehensive exam, an attitude survey concerning the test option each student had selected was completed anonymously at the end of the semester. Students indicated which test option they selected, why they selected it, and why they did not choose the other option. Students also were asked to state how well the alternative they chose suited their needs, if they felt that the option they selected had any effect on their grades, and if they would select the same option again. Suitability was measured by a 5-point scale ranging from *suited needs very well* (1) to *suited needs very poorly* (5). As just noted, the other questions asked for personal opinion and, therefore, required descriptive answers.

Results

Because the UT and CT students received common questions, we directly compared responses between the two groups. A separate repeated measures analysis of variance (ANOVA) was performed on the common items from each of the four units. To determine differences in difficulty between chapters within respective units, questions were grouped on a chapter-by-chapter basis. (Because chapters 1, 8, and 12 were represented by 14 common questions each, whereas the remainder were represented by 10 questions each, all scores were converted to a percent-correct measure prior to analysis.) Thus, the levels of the repeated measures factor for the analysis performed over the first unit consisted of chapters 1, 2, 3, and 4.

For all analyses, the type of test option factor was not significant: chapters 1–4, $F(1, 26) = .115$; chapters 5–8, $F(1, 26) = .116$; chapters 9–12, $F(1, 26) = 1.552$; and chapters 13, 14, and 16, $F(1, 26) = .036$. (Because students were not required to read chapter 15, questions covering this material were not used.) However, significant between chapter differences were found for chapters 1–4, $F(3, 78) = 8.476$, $p < .001$; for chapters 5–8, $F(3, 78) = 34.876$, $p < .001$; and for chapters 9–12, $F(3, 78) = 27.476$, $p < .001$. Table 1 presents group mean percent correct responses and standard deviations for the common questions from chapters 1–14 and 16.

Newman–Keuls tests, performed to identify the significant chapter effect for chapters 1–4 revealed that chapter 1

Table 1. Group Mean Percent Correct Responses and Standard Deviations for the Common Questions From Chapters 1–14 and 16

	Chapter														
	1	2	3	4	5	6	7	8	9	10	11	12	13	14	16
Chapter Test Group															
M	.67	.76	.73	.72	.78	.71	.72	.61	.73	.72	.70	.62	.82	.79	.76
SD	.21	.22	.22	.14	.25	.31	.23	.13	.15	.23	.22	.20	.19	.24	.25
Unit Test Group															
M	.60	.81	.72	.79	.80	.76	.69	.62	.71	.73	.76	.64	.83	.78	.73
SD	.13	.21	.21	.12	.10	.18	.17	.20	.28	.13	.19	.19	.27	.24	.13

was significantly more difficult than chapter 3, $p < .05$. Similar tests also revealed that for chapters 5–8, chapter 8 material was significantly more difficult than material from chapters 5, 6, and 7, $p < .05$. For chapters 9–12, chapter 12 was significantly more difficult than chapters 9, 10, and 11, $p < .05$.

A one-way ANOVA performed on the scores from the comprehensive exam revealed no significant differences between the CT and UT students, $F(1, 26) = 1.326, p > .05$.

Students' responses to the test-option attitude survey given at the end of the semester were also analyzed. There was no significant difference between CT and UT students in response to the question, "How well did the option you selected suit your needs?," $F(1, 26) = 1.57, p > .05$. All of the CT students indicated that they would select that option again, but only one half of the UT students indicated that they would select the UT option again. Thus, although the UT option may have served respective student needs as well as the CT option, it was not accepted as enthusiastically.

Discussion

Unlike previous findings that frequent testing resulted in better performance during the semester (e.g., Dustin, 1971; Fitch et al., 1951; Keys, 1934; Turney, 1931), our results indicate no such advantage. It is worth noting, however, that regardless of type of test taken, several chapters were more troublesome than others. These chapters included chapter 1 (Introduction to Psychology), chapter 8 (Language and Thought), and chapter 12 (Personality). Perhaps the first chapter was more difficult because of the broad scope of material covered. However, we suspect that performance on questions from the first chapter was hampered more by the fact that students were still unsure about what was expected of them and were thus less likely to pay attention to all pertinent information. It is less clear why test performance was lower for chapters 8 and 12.

More consistent with previous findings that frequency of testing makes little difference on students' comprehensive test scores (Fulkerson & Martin, 1981; Keys, 1934), we found no significant difference in comprehensive exam scores between CT and UT students. As in previous studies, our students were well aware of the impending comprehensive exam. Any long-term retention effects of frequent versus infrequent testing may have been masked by the students' propensity to cram for the final. However, the lack of any between-groups effects in our study makes this a tenuous assumption.

Fulkerson and Martin (1981) reported that students who were arbitrarily assigned to the less frequent testing condition were upset with their instructor's decision and would have preferred more frequent testing. These negative attitudes may have hindered students' performance throughout the semester. Unlike the previous research in which students were randomly assigned to conditions, students in our study were allowed to choose between CTs or UTs.

Another departure from earlier studies is that in our study, all students were enrolled in the same class section. Thus, all factors (instructor, meeting time, and lecture material) were held constant between groups. Previous studies have either divided one class into two separate sections after assignment of testing schedule or prescribed a different testing procedure to independent sections of the same course. Neither procedure adequately controls for instructor differences as did our study in which all students were taught by the same instructor in the same room at the same time.

Also unlike past research, our findings indicated no difference in performance between students who chose frequent or infrequent testing options. Analysis of student attitudes indicated that regardless of testing option selected, both groups of students felt that the option they selected best suited their needs. Because the choice of testing schedule was made before the students actually had tried the option, their selection may have reflected other than academic concerns. For example, a large number of students at our institution have part-time jobs. The working hours of the employed students in our sample may have conflicted with the CT testing times. The UT students also may have wanted to concentrate their test-studying time into a single session to minimize conflict with work schedules. The choice of the UT option would accommodate both situations. In fact, the most frequent reason given by students for choosing the UT option was that the chapter testing times did not fit their schedules. The reasons for choosing the CT option might be more academically sound. Most students chose the CT option because they felt that shorter tests over less material are easier.

When asked if they would select the same option if they could do it over, all CT students indicated that they would. The most common reasons given for this response were that students felt they learned the information better and that chapter tests were easier and more convenient. Seven of the 14 students who selected the UT option indicated that they would not choose it again. The most frequently given reasons for switching options were that studying for shorter chapter tests would be easier and that students would perform better under the CT option. Although the test scores might argue against a dramatic increase in performance, the preference to change to the CT option is consistent with previous research (e.g., Fulkerson & Martin, 1981).

Although our analyses indicated that test option did not differentially affect test performance, the majority of the students in both groups felt that the option they selected did influence their grade in the course. The CT students believed that their grades had been helped, and UT students felt that they would have done better under the CT option. A study in which students are allowed to evaluate and change their testing option at midterm would be well suited to probe such issues further. Perhaps it is not the frequency of testing that provides an advantage but the satisfaction of students in knowing that they chose their own testing procedure.

Our results may have been influenced by the small sample size available for study. However, as the groups were balanced with regard to the number of men and women and did not differ in terms of ACT scores, the specific effect of sample size is unclear. Our discrepant results may reflect an interaction between testing option and class size. In the small class, the type of testing procedure may not significantly affect performance because the instructor can attend to and motivate students on an individual basis. In the large class, testing procedure may assume a more important role because such personal attention is not possible. This possible interaction awaits experimental verification.

References

Benjamin, L. T., Jr., Hopkins, J. R., & Nation, J. R. (1987). *Psychology*. New York: Macmillan.

Dustin, D. (1971). Some effects of exam frequency. *The Psychological Record, 21*, 409–414.

Fitch, M. L., Drucker, A. J., & Norton, J. A., Jr. (1951). Frequent testing as a motivating factor in a large lecture class. *The Journal of Educational Psychology, 42*, 1–20.

Fulkerson, F. E., & Martin, G. (1981). Effects of exam frequency on student performance, evaluations of instructor, and test anxiety. *Teaching of Psychology, 8*, 90–93.

Keys, N. (1934). The influence on learning and retention of weekly as opposed to monthly tests. *Journal of Educational Psychology, 25*, 427–436.

Turney, A. H. (1931). The effects of frequent short objective tests upon the achievement of college students in educational psychology. *School and Society, 33*, 760–762.

Notes

1. Portions of these data were presented at the 5th Annual Mid-America Conference for Teachers of Psychology, Evansville, IN.

8. EXAMINATIONS: STUDENT FACTORS AFFECTING EXAM PERFORMANCE

A Reexamination of the Relationship of High School Psychology and Natural Science Courses to Performance in a College Introductory Psychology Class

Richard A. Griggs
Sherri L. Jackson
University of Florida

Many researchers have found no relationship between having completed a high school psychology course and final grades in a college introductory psychology class (e.g., Hedges & Thomas, 1980), but Carstens and Beck (1986) found that students with strong backgrounds in high school natural science (i.e., biology, chemistry, and physics) obtained higher course grades in their first college-level psychology class. Carstens and Beck's subjects were not all first-term freshmen; some may have taken or may have been enrolled in college natural science courses (C. B. Carstens, personal communication, March 25, 1988). Thus, their results may have been confounded by two factors: (a) the number of college credits completed by each subject (e.g., see Griggs & Ransdell, 1987) and (b) prior completion of or concurrent enrollment in college-level natural science courses.

Our study eliminated these possible confoundings. Subjects were freshmen enrolled in introductory psychology, but not enrolled in a natural science course. We also controlled for possible instructor effects. Our subjects were all from the same class, whereas Carstens and Beck's subjects were from five classes taught by two different instructors. In addition, we compared the performance of students whose high school psychology course covered science-oriented topics with the performance of students whose courses did not.

Method

Subjects

The subjects were 199 students (117 women and 82 men) in an introductory psychology class at the University of Florida. All were first-term students without any college credits, and none were currently registered in a college natural science course. They participated as part of the course requirements.

Materials and Procedure

During the first class meeting, the students were given a 60-item multiple-choice pretest. As in the Carstens and Beck (1986) study, the items were divided into frequent and infrequent topics subtests based on topics covered in high school psychology courses. Frequent topics were personality, disorders, therapies, assessment, learning, cognition, developmental psychology, and social psychology; infrequent topics were research methodology, statistics, physiological psychology, sensation, and perception. This classification is comparable to the one used by Carstens and Beck (1986) and is consistent with a recent survey of topic coverage in high school psychology courses (Ragland, 1987).

All items were selected from the test bank (Brink, 1986) accompanying Myers's (1986) introductory psychology text. Based on information from previous terms, we selected questions with an average item difficulty of 0.70.

During the first week of classes, students completed a questionnaire concerning their high school courses in psychology, biology, chemistry, and physics. Students who had taken a high school psychology course completed another questionnaire about topic coverage in that course. If four of the five topics—research methodology, statistics, physiological psychology, sensation, and perception—were covered, the course was classified as a more scientifically oriented course.

With the students' permission, their SAT scores were obtained from the registrar and course examination and final grades from the instructor. Course grades were coded as A = 4.0, B+ = 3.5, B = 3.0, and so on, with E = 0. Examination scores were on a scale ranging from 0 to 60 points.

Results

The intercorrelations matrix is given in Table 1. The high school natural science variable was not significantly correlated with infrequent topics subtest scores, as it was in the Carstens and Beck study. In agreement with Carstens and Beck's findings, high school psychology was positively correlated with the frequent topics subtest scores, $p < .05$, and high school natural science was positively correlated with course grades, $p < .01$.

Because SAT total score was significantly related to the frequent topics subtest score and course grade, two multiple regressions were performed using SAT total score as a co-

114

Table 1. Intercorrelations Between SAT, High School Psychology, High School Natural Science, Course Grade, Pretest Scores, and the Three Course Exam Scores

Variable	SAT	HSPSY	HSNS	Grade	FREQ	INFREQ	Exam 1	Exam 2	Exam 3
SAT	—	−.06	.05	.27**	.26*	.15**	.28**	.22**	.21**
HSPSY[a]		—	−.06	.04	.16*	.11	−.01	.08	.01
HSNS[b]			—	.20**	.05	−.03	.14c	.22**	.11
Grade				—	.15*	.07	.85**	.84**	.84**
FREQ					—	.14c	.23**	.06	.09
INFREQ						—	.15*	.08	−.02
Exam 1							—	.63**	.63**
Exam 2								—	.64**
Exam 3									—

Note. HSPSY = High School Psychology, HSNS = High School Natural Science, FREQ = Pretest Scores on Frequent Topics, INFREQ = Pretest Scores on Infrequent Topics.
[a]Students with high school psychology were coded 1; students without high school psychology were coded 0. [b]Students who had taken a high school course in each of the areas of chemistry, biology, and physics were coded 1; students without one or more of the courses were coded 0. [c]These correlations were marginally significant, $p < .06$.
*$p < .05$. **$p < .01$.

variate. High school psychology and high school natural science were the predictor variables, and scores on the frequent topics subtest and course grades were the dependent measures. Neither of the predictor variables had a significant effect in predicting the frequent topics subtest score, but high school natural science made a significant contribution to the prediction of course grades, $F(1, 165) = 15.55$, $p < .001$.

High school natural science was positively correlated with Exam 2 performance, $p < .05$, and marginally correlated with Exam 1 performance. Regression analyses with SAT total score as a covariate and Exams 1 and 2 as dependent measures showed that high school natural science contributed significantly only to the variance of the Exam 2 scores, $F(2, 164) = 10.84$, $p < .001$. Because Exam 2 covered mainly physiological psychology, sensation, and perception, one might think that the significant correlation between performance on this exam and high school natural science was due to completion of a high school biology class. This cannot be the case because all but one of the students who had not taken all three high school natural science courses had taken a high school biology course. Thus, this relationship may be due to a more general scientific preparation gained from taking all three natural science courses.

Nineteen students had taken what we operationally defined by topic coverage as a more scientifically oriented high school psychology course. We matched these students with respect to SAT total score and the high school natural science variable to 19 of the other 91 students who had taken a high school psychology course without such an orientation. There were no significant differences between the two matched groups on any of the measures. A further analysis of only the 11 pairs of subjects who had not taken all three high school natural science courses yielded no significant differences. Thus, more than coverage of the scientifically oriented topics is probably needed for the course actually to be science oriented.

Discussion

Carstens and Beck's results for precourse knowledge were not replicated. In our study, high school psychology did not contribute significantly to the variance of frequent topics subtest scores and high school natural science did not con-

tribute significantly to the variance of infrequent topics subtest scores. However, Carstens and Beck's findings for course grades were replicated. A strong background in high school natural science was associated with higher grades in the college introductory psychology course and a background in high school psychology was not. These results are also consistent with some recent findings for university graduates in the United Kingdom (Kornbrot, 1987). Kornbrot found that a higher percentage of students who had taken A-levels (roughly comparable to the last 2 years of high school in the United States) in the natural sciences, rather than in psychology and sociology, achieved "good" degrees (first or upper second-class honors) in psychology.

Our results are more understandable when the results of recent surveys of high school (Ragland, 1987) and college (Scheirer & Rogers, 1985) psychology classes are considered. The majority of high school psychology teachers believe that the most important goal of their course is self-knowledge and understanding (Ragland, 1987). In addition, most high school teachers describe their course as generally being personality–developmental or interpersonal–social in focus, as opposed to scientific–experimental.

In contrast, Scheirer and Rogers (1985) found that college instructors spend most of their time on the science of psychology and very little time on sensitivity to interpersonal situations and insight into one's own behavior. The scientific–experimental focus of high school natural science courses is more consistent with the focus of the college psychology class and, therefore, provides students with the appropriate framework for learning the material presented from the scientific perspective in the college psychology course. If most high school psychology courses had such a focus, then they might be better predictors of performance in the college class. At present, they do not and are not.

References

Brink, J. (1986). *Test bank to accompany Myers: Psychology*. New York: Worth.

Carstens, C. B., & Beck, H. P. (1986). The relationship of high school psychology and natural science courses to performance in a college introductory psychology class. *Teaching of Psychology, 13,* 116–118.

Griggs, R. A., & Ransdell, S. E. (1987). Misconceptions tests or misconceived tests? *Teaching of Psychology, 14,* 210–214.

Hedges, B. W., & Thomas, J. H. (1980). The effect of high school psychology on pre-course knowledge, midterm grades, and final grades in introductory psychology. *Teaching of Psychology, 7,* 221–223.

Kornbrot, D. E. (1987). Science and psychology degree performance. *Bulletin of the British Psychological Society, 40,* 409–417.

Myers, D. G. (1986). *Psychology.* New York: Worth.

Ragland, R. G. (1987, August). *The status of teachers and teacher education in high school psychology.* Paper presented at the annual meeting of the American Psychological Association, New York.

Scheirer, C. J., & Rogers, A. M. (1985). *The undergraduate psychology curriculum: 1984.* Washington, DC: American Psychological Association.

Self-Report Measures of Ability, Effort, and Nonacademic Activity as Predictors of Introductory Psychology Test Scores

David J. Woehr
Timothy A. Cavell
Texas A&M University

At many colleges and universities, the majority of students enrolled in introductory psychology classes are freshmen. For some, the leap into college is a difficult one: Academic tasks are demanding, extracurricular activities are wide-ranging and highly attractive, and adult supervision is virtually nonexistent. The qualitative shift from high school to college is reflected in a caution issued each year by Benjamin (1990):

> I tell the first-year students in my classes to assume that they are now in Grade 18-that they have skipped 6 years in school and have gone from being the equivalent of a sixthgrader to being the equivalent of a senior in high school. (p. v)

Difficulty making the transition from high school is evidenced by students who begin their college careers with disappointing course grades, despite academic credentials indicating they can do the work. Identifying the factors that contribute to a student's poor test performance is often a complicated matter for the student and the instructor. We are often approached by students, many of whom are in their first year of college, who are confused by their poor test performance.

In trying to understand why these students do poorly on their exams, we have recognized three areas worthy of inquiry. The first area pertains to students' academic ability to do college work—the blend of aptitude and educational skills that enables them to compete with their classmates. Students in introductory courses may do poorly on their tests because they overestimate the extent to which sheer academic ability will enable them to score well. Students whose grades and SAT or ACT scores easily surpassed those of their high school peers must learn to compete with college classmates who are equally capable. Leveling of the competition sets the stage for other, nonability variables to play a determining role in students' grades. A second area of inquiry is the amount of effort that students put into preparing for exams. Students who could easily earn top grades in high school may underestimate the effort needed to prepare for college-level examinations. The third area of inquiry concerns students' involvement in nonacademic aspects of college life. Whether that involvement translates to membership in a fraternity or sorority, a part-time job, or time in front of the television, many freshmen probably misjudge the degree to which extracurricular pursuits can interfere with academic tasks.

Previous researchers have examined some of these variables in attempting to predict students' overall college performance (Baird, 1984; Dreher & Singer, 1985; Nettles, Thoeny, & Gosman, 1986; Royer, Abranovic, & Sinatra, 1987; Schuman, Walsh, Olson, & Etheridge, 1985; White, Nylin, & Esser, 1985). However, only a few investigators have explored the contribution these factors make in predicting psychology test scores specifically (Beck, Rorrer-Woody, & Pierce, 1991; Johnson & Beck 1988; Royer et al., 1987). The variable that has received the most attention from researchers is academic ability, typically indexed by SAT scores. Johnson and Beck (1988), for example, examined the relation between SAT scores and mean test performance in an educational psychology class comprised mainly of juniors. Students with varying SAT scores earned significantly different psychology test scores. Royer et al. (1987) also assessed the relation between SAT scores and test performance among juniors and seniors in an educational psychology class. In their study, however, psychology

116

test scores were combined with test scores from a business statistics course. Correlations between SAT–Verbal (SAT–V) and SAT–Math (SAT–M) scores and this composite score were .30 and .22, respectively. In addition, Beck et al. (1991) reported a correlation of .42 between total SAT score and mean test performance in a sample of students from a general psychology class (76% freshmen). These researchers also found that students' self-reported tendency to strive for grades (as opposed to content mastery) was negatively correlated with their psychology test performance ($r = -.31$).

The total amount of variance in test scores that can be explained by academic ability, academic effort, and nonacademic activity has not been addressed empirically. Our study is an attempt to determine how these variables are related to students' psychology test performance. We hypothesized that measures of ability, effort, and activity will explain significant amounts of variance in introductory psychology test scores. We also hypothesized that information regarding academic effort and nonacademic interference will provide explanatory power over and above that attributable to academic ability alone.

Method

Subjects

Subjects were 325 students from two large introductory psychology classes (64% freshmen, 26% sophomores, and 10% juniors or seniors). Fifty-four percent of the participants were men, and 46% were women; these percentages roughly correspond to the percentages of men (56.6%) and women (43.4%) at the university in general.

Measures

Criterion variable. The criterion variable was students' scores on their first exam in the course. This criterion minimizes the influence of factors that arise as a consequence of one's test score (e.g., a drop in motivation) and that further cloud the question of why a student did poorly. The exams in each class, although not identical, overlapped substantially. Both exams used a 50-item, multiple-choice format covering the same four chapters from the same introductory psychology text (Benjamin, Hopkins, & Nation, 1990). Approximately 80% of the items on both exams were drawn directly from the test bank (King & Toglia, 1990) that accompanied the text. Test bank items were factual, conceptual, or applied in nature. For one exam, 70% of the questions were factual, 15% were conceptual, and 15% were applied. The other exam consisted of 65% factual questions, 5% conceptual questions, and 30% applied questions. Items not drawn from the test bank (approximately 20% of items for both exams) were used primarily to test material presented only in lectures. The two exams were also similar with respect to the percentage of items that covered material presented only in the text (approximately 20%).

Predictor variables. Information on several predictor variables was obtained with a brief, self-report questionnaire. All items were open-ended questions in which students simply filled in the blank with the appropriate response. The questionnaire contained items reflecting each of our three target constructs: academic ability, academic effort, and nonacademic activity.

Ability was assessed with three indicators: high school grade point average (HSGPA) indexed on a 4-point scale, SAT–V, and SAT–M. A small of students reported ACT scores rather than SAT scores; ACT scores were converted to SAT scores using conversion tables provided by the university's admissions office.

Three indicators were also used to assess effort: number of hours per week the student spent studying for the exam, number of times the student had read the chapters covered by the exam, and number of lectures the student had missed before the first exam. Note that with the first indicator subjects were instructed to estimate the average number of hours per week that they devoted to the course outside of class. This included time spent reading the text as well as engaging in any other study activity related to the course. Alternatively, with the second indicator we asked for an estimate of the number of times each subject actually read the textbook chapters covered by the exam. Although the amount of study time and number of chapter readings are not completely independent, we expected these indicators to tap different aspects of study effort.

Items measuring nonacademic activity asked students to indicate the number of hours per week they spent in each of three types of activities: school-based extracurricular activities, work, and television viewing. Because of the compensatory nature of these items (i.e., one student may spend a lot of time at work and have little time for extracurricular activities, whereas another may not work yet devote a great deal of time to extracurricular activities), reported hours engaged in each type of activity were summed to form a single nonacademic activity score.

Procedure

Participants completed the self-report questionnaire just before the start of their first exam. Data were collected in the context of a demonstration conducted over a series of classes and designed to illustrate several issues related to psychological research (e.g., the rights of subjects, measurement of variables, prediction, and correlation). As part of this demonstration, students were informed about the nature of the study and given the opportunity to participate. Although participation was entirely voluntary, nearly all students (94%) elected to participate.

Results

Preliminary analyses supported both the reliability and the comparability of the two exams. Coefficient alpha estimates of internal consistency for the two exams were .80 and .82, respectively. Also, the difference between the mean scores for each exam was not significant ($M = 73.8$; M

Variable	M	SD
Test score	73.18	12.57
Academic ability		
HSGPA	3.56	0.36
SAT–V	512.91	84.18
SAT–M	573.69	86.52
Academic effort		
Time studying[a]	4.31	3.40
Chapter readings	1.38	0.60
Classes missed	0.45	1.00
Nonacademic activity		
Total time[a]	21.19	15.35

[a]Average number of hours per week.

= 72.2, $t = .73$, ns). Because of these findings, as well as the significant overlap in test content, all subsequent analyses were performed on the combined data set from both classes.

Table 1 lists means and standard deviations for each of the variables. Mean scores for self-reported HSGPA and SAT scores in our sample paralleled figures obtained from the university for students campus-wide, thus supporting their use as a proxy for students' actual HSGPA and SAT scores. With respect to academic effort, students averaged slightly more than 4 hr per week studying introductory psychology, slightly more than one reading of the assigned chapters, and approximately one half of a class missed between the start of school and the first exam. This relatively small number of classes missed is not surprising. The exams were given in the fourth week of the semester with class meeting only twice a week; thus, there were relatively few opportunities for students to skip class. In fact, most students (74%) missed no classes, and the vast majority of those who did miss (83%) were absent on only one or two occasions. Students also reported spending an average of more than 20 hr per week in nonacademic activities. Not shown in Table 1 is the number of hours spent in each of the three activities assessed. Students reported spending most of their nonacademic hours on extracurricular activities ($M = 9.30$) or viewing television ($M = 9.02$) and relatively little time working ($M = 2.86$).

Correlations among the variables measured are presented in Table 2. Significant zero-order correlations were found between psychology test scores and each of the predictor variables except time spent studying introductory psychology. Hours of studying was significantly related, however, to

the other indicators of academic effort (i.e., number of times students read the assigned chapters and number of classes missed).

To examine how well our three target constructs predicted students' test performance, a hierarchical multiple regression analysis was conducted in which specific indicators for each construct were entered as a set. Academic ability indicators were entered first, followed in turn by indicators for academic effort and nonacademic activity. Results of this analysis are summarized in Table 3. The value of R^2 indicates the total amount of variance in test performance accounted for by the variables entered, and the change in R^2 (ΔR^2) indicates the amount of variance accounted for by each set of variables over and above previously entered sets. For the full model, R^2 was significant, $F(7, 241) = 11.74, p < .0001$, and indicated that 25% of the variance in test scores was explained when all three sets of predictors were included. Academic ability variables accounted for approximately one half (13%) of all the variance accounted for in test scores. Measures of academic effort, however, contributed significantly to the prediction of psychology test scores, accounting for an additional 10% of the variance. Involvement in nonacademic activities, although reflecting only a 2% increase in explained variance over that attributable to academic ability and academic effort, was also significant. When the order of entry for academic effort and nonacademic activity was reversed, the amount of variance explained at each step was still significant but slightly different: Nonacademic activity predicted an additional 8% in psychology test scores, whereas academic effort yielded only a 4% increment in explained variance.

To explore further the link between test scores and individual predictor variables, standardized regression coefficients that comprised the full prediction model were examined. Standardized beta weights allow for a comparison of the magnitude of effects of the different indicators on a common metric (Cohen & Cohen, 1983). As shown in Figure 1, coefficients for five of the seven variables used to predict psychology test scores were statistically significant. Only coefficients for time spent studying psychology and for SAT failed to reach significance.

Finally, analyses were conducted to examine the extent to which the inclusion of students beyond their first year (36% of the sample) influenced our results. Previous analyses were repeated using a reduced sample of participants that included only first-year students. Results of this analysis revealed that none of the coefficients obtained with the full

Table 2. Intercorrelations Among Predictor and Criterion Variables

Variables	2	3	4	5	6	7	8
1. HSGPA	.06	.09	.02	.06	−.07	−.14*	.31*
2. SAT–V	—	.05	−.07	.00	.19*	−.07	.20*
3. SAT–M		—	−.15	−.04	.11	.04	.14*
4. Time studying[a]			—	.25*	−.12*	−.06	.01
5. Chapter readings				—	−.06	−.07	.22*
6. Classes missed					—	.20*	−.22*
7. Nonacademics[a]						—	−.12*
8. Test score							—

[a]Average number of hours per week.
*$p < .05$.

Table 3. Hierarchical Regression Predicting Psychology Test Scores

	R^2	ΔR^2	ΔF
Academic ability	.13	.13	12.45*
Academic effort	.23	.10	10.28*
Nonacademic activity	.25	.02	7.74*

*$p < .01$.

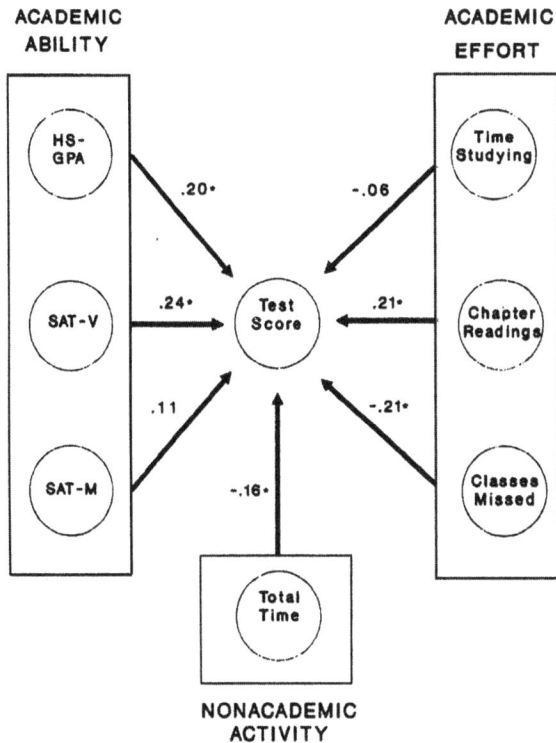

Figure 1. Standardized parameter estimates (beta weights) for each indicator predicting test performance. *$p < .05$.

sample was significantly different from those obtained with the reduced sample.

Discussion

We hypothesized that measures of students' academic ability, academic effort, and nonacademic activity would predict test scores in an introductory psychology class. Our results support this hypothesis in that a regression model containing these predictor variables accounted for a significant amount of the variance in students' first exam scores. Academic ability alone accounted for approximately 13% of the variance in test scores. This figure corresponds closely to findings obtained by our university's Office of Measurement and Research Services. Staff there consistently find that Texas A&M students' actual (as opposed to self-reported) SAT scores and high school rank account for 12% to 13% of the variance in specific course grades. In our study, the prediction of introductory psychology test scores was improved significantly by the use of self-report measures of academic

effort and nonacademic activity. These variables accounted for 12% of the variance in test scores beyond that attributable to students' academic ability.

Although our findings are based solely on correlational research and await further empirical verification, their implications are of interest to psychology students and instructors. Students whose HSGPA or SAT–V scores place them at a disadvantage relative to their more able classmates should be told the dangers of assuming that old study strategies will lead to adequate test scores in a competitive college environment (Benjamin, 1990). Students should also be advised that academic ability explains only about 13% of the variance and that other, nonability factors are also important. One such factor is the effort students devote to the course, both the amount of time and the type of effort. For example, our findings indicate that regular class attendance and multiple readings of assigned chapters are associated with higher test scores. These findings are consistent with results from previous studies in which class attendance (Schuman et al., 1985) and measures of text comprehension (Dreher & Singer, 1985; Royer et al., 1987) were found to predict college students' overall GPA as well as performance in specific courses.

Our findings do not support the strategy of simply telling students to study more; the bivariate correlation between hours spent studying psychology and psychology test scores was .01! This finding is also in line with previous results. Schuman et al. (1985) conducted a series of studies to examine the relation between amount of study time and college grades. Their findings indicate that a significant relation "can sometimes be uncovered, but it appears to be very small and largely limited to those who study well above average in terms of amount or period of the week" (p. 961). Using various estimates of study time to predict exam scores in an organic chemistry class, for example, Schuman et al. (1985) found a median correlation of .085 between study time and test scores.

As one explanation for the lack of an association between study time and test scores, Schuman et al. (1985) suggested that instructors may simply be testing students' ability to discern what material will be assessed on the test. This argument would also explain the significant association between class attendance and test performance found in our study and by Schuman et al. (1985; also see Einstein, Morris, & Smith, 1985). However, we suggest that such an explanation is insufficient because it assumes uniformity in how study time is used and it also fails to recognize the important distinction between quality and quantity of study effort (Postman, Keckler, & Schneckner, 1985). We often encounter students who attend class regularly and who claim to devote considerable time and energy to our class but do poorly on their tests. Further inquiry often reveals that these students spend much time on potentially nonproductive study activities. For example, students commonly report spending excessive amounts of time (a) recopying their lecture notes, (b) studying only their lecture notes and not the textbook, (c) writing their own chapter outlines, (d) studying only these outlines, (e) completing study guide exercises with their book open, (f) studying the study guide instead of the textbook, and (g) participating in so-called "group study." Many of these activities are very time-consuming, and most invite shallow processing of information that is incomplete and possibly inaccurate. We routinely caution our students that such activities are no substitute for careful and comprehensive reading of the text and regular class attendance. Our hypotheses about nonproductive studying are speculative, however, and need to be tested empirically. We need more research that examines in greater detail (a) students' use of various study activities, (b) the depth of processing associated with different strategies, and (c) the relation between type of study activity and students' test scores.

Our findings also shed light on students' involvement in nonacademic activities. Students' reported involvement in such activities made a unique contribution to the prediction of psychology test scores. However, the small amount of variance accounted for by the nonacademic activity variable, as well as its significant association with the number of classes missed, weakens the argument against students' pursuit of nonacademic interests. Nevertheless, test scores could conceivably suffer when nonacademic activities interfere with class attendance or consume scarce study time.

Several factors limit the conclusions we can draw from our study. Our set of predictor variables is not exhaustive; other variables may also influence students' test scores. Moreover, variables that are correlated with exam scores may not be causally linked to these scores. For example, the number of classes students missed was inversely related to test scores, but attending all future classes may not raise students' grades. Missing class may simply be more common among students who lack adequate study skills or who are indifferent about their grades. Our findings are also limited by the self-report nature of our predictor variables. Although Schuman et al. (1985) found considerable support for the use of self-reported study behavior, one could easily question the reliability of asking students to estimate the number of classes missed or the number of hours spent studying psychology or watching television. However, one could also argue that unreliability in our measures actually served to underestimate the strength of the relation between predictor variables and test scores.

Finally, our results did not change when we excluded from the analyses students who had advanced beyond their first year of college. However, given that first-year students made up a very large proportion of our sample, the similarity in findings is not surprising. Because the small number of upper level students in our sample argued against a separate set of analyses, the issue of whether these findings generalize to more experienced students enrolled in introductory psychology is still unresolved. Also unresolved is the degree to which our three target constructs predict test scores in more advanced psychology courses. Because upper level courses rarely involve first-year students or the use of multiple-choice tests, our findings may not generalize to students' performance in those courses.

References

Baird, L. L. (1984). Predicting predictability: The influence of student and institutional characteristics on the prediction of grades. *Research in Higher Education, 21,* 261–279.

Beck, H. P., Rorrer-Woody, S., & Pierce, L. G. (1991). The relations of learning and grade orientations to academic performance. *Teaching of Psychology, 18,* 35–37.

Benjamin, L. T., Jr. (1990). An open letter to college students. In B. F. Nodine, *Student study guide for* Psychology, 2nd ed. *(Benjamin/Hopkins/Nation).* New York: Macmillan.

Benjamin, L. T., Jr., Hopkins, J. R., & Nation, J. R. (1990). *Psychology* (2nd ed.). New York: Macmillan.

Cohen, J., & Cohen, P. (1983). *Applied multiple regression/correlation analysis for the behavioral sciences.* Hillsdale, NJ: Lawrence Erlbaum Associates, Inc.

Dreher, M. J., & Singer, H. (1985). Predicting college success: Learning from text, background knowledge, attitude toward school, and the SAT as predictors. *National Reading Conference Yearbook, 31,* 362–368.

Einstein, G. O., Morris, J., & Smith, S. (1985). Note-taking, individual differences, and memory for lecture information. *Journal of Educational Psychology, 77,* 522–532.

Johnson, B. G., & Beck, H. P. (1988). Strict and lenient grading scales: How do they affect the performance of college students with high and low SAT scores? *Teaching of Psychology, 15,* 127–131.

King, M. B., & Toglia, M. P. (1990). *Test bank: Psychology (2nd ed.), Ludy T. Benjamin, Jr., J. Roy Hopkins, and Jack R. Nation.* New York: Macmillan.

Nettles, M. T., Thoeny, A. R., & Gosman, E. J. (1986). Comparative and predictive analyses of Black and White students' college achievement and experience. *Journal of Higher Education, 57,* 289–318.

Postman, R. D., Keckler, B., & Schneckner, P. (1985). *College reading and study skills.* New York: Macmillan.

Royer, J. M., Abranovic, W. A., & Sinatra, G. M. (1987). Using entering reading comprehension performance as a predictor of performance in college classes. *Journal of Educational Psychology, 79,* 19–26.

Schuman, H., Walsh, E., Olson, C., & Etheridge, B. (1985). Effort and reward: The assumption that college grades are affected by the quantity of study. *Social Forces, 63,* 945–966.

White, W. F., Nylin, W. C., & Esser, P. R. (1985). Academic course grades as better predictors of graduation from a commuter-type college than SAT scores. *Psychological Reports, 56,* 375–378.

The Relations of Learning and Grade Orientations to Academic Performance

Hall P. Beck
Sherry Rorrer-Woody
Linda G. Pierce
Appalachian State University

Most investigations of college academic achievement have examined the relation between ability and academic performance. Relatively few studies have considered how differences in student motivation influence achievement. Milton, Pollio, and Eison's (1986) analysis of learning orientation (LO) and grade orientation (GO) provides an excellent framework from which to study two of the more prominent motivations of college students.

Learning-oriented students are excited by the opportunity to acquire new knowledge, and they find personal enrichment through academic experiences. Grade-oriented students base their actions on an instructor's evaluation procedures, and they work for grades. Separate LO and GO scores are obtained by administering the LOGO II Scale (Eison & Pollio, 1989).

Learning orientation and GO have been related to SAT (Harris & Harris, 1987; Johnson & Beck, 1988) and American College Test (Rogers, Palmer, & Bolen, 1988) scores. Correlations of LO and GO scores with academic ability tests suggest the possibility that analogous associations would be found between LOGO scores and course grades or classroom test results. To our knowledge, however, no studies have established significant correlations between LO or GO and class performance. Nonsignificant correlations have been reported between LOGO scores and high school GPA (Harris & Harris, 1987), college GPA (Rogers et al., 1988), and test scores in a college introductory psychology class (Kauffmann, Chupp, Hershberger, Martin, & Eastman, 1987).

Although previous studies have not found that LO or GO are related to class performance, the issue deserves further inquiry. In this investigation, we correlated LOGO II scores with two measures of academic performance: college GPAs and test scores in a General Psychology course. In addition to LO and GO, SAT was included as an independent variable to determine if the relations of LOGO II scores to GPA and psychology test scores are mediated by differences in academic ability.

Method

Subjects

Subjects were 110 undergraduates enrolled in two General Psychology sections taught by Hall P. Beck, the first author. Seventy-six percent of the students were freshmen, 19% sophomores, 3% juniors, and 2% seniors.

Procedure

LOGO II consists of 16 LO and 16 GO items rated on a 5-point Likert-type scale. The psychometric properties of LOGO II have been evaluated previously (Eison & Pollio, 1989).

Students completed LOGO II during a regular class meeting early in the semester. Students were told that the data from the questionnaire would be used in several classroom demonstrations and that their responses would be confidential.

Four multiple-choice tests were administered during the semester. Approximately half of the questions were taken from the test bank (Bootzin, Bower, & Zajonc, 1986) for the required textbook (Bootzin, Bower, Zajonc, & Hall, 1986). The remaining questions were written by the instructor and based on lecture material. When the tests were returned, students received a letter grade and were told the percentage of questions correctly answered.

The objectives of the study were explained to the students near the end of the semester. All, except five students who were absent from class, granted permission to use their LO, GO, SAT, GPA, and psychology test scores for research purposes. The data from the five absent students were not included in the analysis. The SAT scores and GPAs (based on a 4-point scale) were furnished by the registrar.

Results

Subjects' mean LO score was 47.10 (SD = 6.64), and their mean GO score was 43.82 (SD = 6.59). These values are comparable to those of other college samples (Eison & Pollio, 1989). The SATs of our subjects averaged 916.64 (SD = 118.94), and their GPAs averaged 2.43 (SD = 0.72). The mean psychology test score for the sample was 73.82% (SD = 9.57). The Spearman–Brown equation yielded split-half reliabilities ranging from .56 to .78 (median = .73) for the four psychology tests.

Learning orientation (Table 1) was negatively correlated with GO, indicating that students with high LO scores were less grade oriented than students with lower LO scores, $p <$ .05. Correlations of LO with SAT, GPA, and mean psychology test scores were not significant, all $ps >$ .05. Grade orientation was negatively correlated with SAT, GPA, and psychology test scores, all $ps <$ .01. As anticipated, SAT,

Table 1. Correlations of LO, GO, SAT, GPA, and Psychology Test Scores

Scale	GO	SAT	GPA	PSY
LO	−.23*	.10	.16	.09
GO	—	−.27**	−.26**	−.31**
SAT			.35**	.42**
GPA			—	.72**

Note. LO = learning oriented; GO = grade oriented; SAT = Scholastic Aptitude Test; GPA = grade point average; PSY = General Psychology test scores.
*$p < .05$, two-tailed. **$p < .01$, two-tailed.

GPA, and psychology test scores were positively correlated, all $ps < .01$.

Two commonality analyses (Kerlinger & Pedhazur, 1973) further explored the correlations between GO scores and the academic performance measures. The first analysis used GO and SAT scores to predict GPA. The GO variable made a significant unique contribution to the accounted for variance, $F(1, 106) = 3.97$, $p < .05$. The variance unique to SAT was also significant, $F(1, 106) = 10.36$, $p < .01$, as was the accounted for variance common to GO and SAT, $F(1, 106) = 4.72$, $p < .05$. In the second analysis, mean psychology test scores were the dependent measure and GO and SAT were the independent variables. As in the first analysis, the variances unique to GO and SAT were significant, $F(1, 106) = 5.57$, $p < .05$; and $F(1, 106) = 17.21$, $p < .01$, respectively. The variance common to GO and SAT was also significant, $F(1, 106) = 7.29$, $p < .05$.

Discussion

Commonality analyses revealed that the negative correlations of GO with GPA and psychology test scores were partially due to an element shared by GO and SAT. This result suggests that relatively low levels of academic ability contributed to the poor grades of highly grade-oriented students.

Johnson and Beck (1988) speculated that students with marginal academic skills are compelled to be highly grade oriented because they are under greater evaluative pressures than their more academically talented peers. According to this explanation, students with low SAT scores believe that they must pursue grades or jeopardize their chances for academic survival. Students with higher SAT scores do not feel that they must be highly grade oriented in order to avoid failing college. Another interpretation of the inverse relationship of GO and SAT scores is that excessive interest in grades impedes the growth of academic skills.

Even after taking into account differences in SAT scores, GO was negatively related to GPA and psychology test scores. Prior research suggests that either ineffective study habits (Eison & Pollio, 1986) or high levels of debilitating test anxiety (Eison, Pollio, & Milton, 1986) could have

contributed to the low grades earned by highly grade-oriented students. Also, informal discussions with students indicate that highly grade-oriented persons study different aspects of the course material than do less grade-oriented persons. Highly grade-oriented students concentrate only on the questions they believe will be asked on the test; less grade-oriented students study a broader spectrum of course material. If students are relatively ineffective predictors of the items professors select for test questions, then the restricted focus of highly grade-oriented students could lead to low test scores.

Although our correlational study does not demonstrate that the pursuit of grades causes substandard academic achievement, it is disconcerting that those students who are most motivated by grades are characterized by poor academic performance. We believe that this finding highlights the need for researchers to determine if grading pressures impair the performance of highly grade-oriented students. These investigations will increase our understanding of grade orientation and may produce recommendations that improve instructional effectiveness.

References

Bootzin, R. R., Bower, G. H., & Zajonc, R. B. (1986). *Test item file to accompany Psychology today: An introduction* (6th ed.). New York: Random House.

Bootzin, R. R., Bower, G. H., Zajonc, R. B., & Hall, E. (1986). *Psychology today: An introduction* (6th ed.). New York: Random House.

Eison, J. A., & Pollio, H. R. (1986). A multidimensional approach to the definition of college students' learning styles. *Journal of College Student Personnel, 27*, 434–443.

Eison, J. A., & Pollio, H. R. (1989). *LOGO II bibliographic and statistical update.* Cape Girardeau, MO: Southeast Missouri State University, Center for Teaching and Learning.

Eison, J. A., Pollio, H. R., & Milton, O. (1986). Educational and personal characteristics of four different types of learning- and grade-oriented students. *Contemporary Educational Psychology, 11*, 54–67.

Harris, C. M., & Harris, J. S. (1987, March). *Learning orientation and academic achievement.* Paper presented at the annual meeting of the Southeastern Psychological Association, Atlanta.

Johnson, B. G., & Beck, H. P. (1988). Strict and lenient grading scales: How do they affect the performance of college students with high and low SAT scores? *Teaching of Psychology, 15*, 127–131.

Kauffmann, D. R., Chupp, B., Hershberger, K., Martin, L., & Eastman, K. (1987). Learning vs. grade orientation: Academic achievement, self-reported orientations, and personality variables. *Psychological Reports, 60*, 145–146.

Kerlinger, F. N., & Pedhazur, E. J. (1973). *Multiple regression in behavioral research.* New York: Holt, Rinehart & Winston.

Milton, O., Pollio, H. R., & Eison, J. A. (1986). *Making sense of college grades.* San Francisco: Jossey-Bass.

Rogers, J., Palmer, W., & Bolen, L. (1988, March). *In pursuit of lifelong learning: A comparison of learning and grade orientation of freshmen and seniors.* Paper presented at the annual meeting of the Southeastern Psychological Association, New Orleans.

Students' Lecture Notes and Their Relation to Test Performance

Linda Baker
Bruce R. Lombardi
University of Maryland, Baltimore County

Among the many skills involved in academic success is the ability to take thorough and accurate lecture notes. This skill, like so many others that support academic endeavors, is rarely explicitly taught in the traditional classroom (Baker & Brown, 1984). Students must develop their note-taking skills on their own, deciding for themselves how much and what kinds of information they should include. It would appear, however, that these efforts are often unsuccessful, as any instructor who has ever examined students' lecture notes can attest. Nevertheless, our anecdotal observations have seldom been validated by empirical tests of either the extent of note-taking problems or of the relation between lecture note adequacy and course performance.

Although there have been several studies on the relation of note-taking to test performance, the majority have compared test scores of note-takers and non-note-takers but have not considered the contents of the notes themselves. Some of these studies have shown that note-taking facilitates performance (DiVesta & Gray, 1972; Fisher & Harris, 1973); others have shown no effect (Eisner & Rhodes, 1959; Peters, 1972); and others have shown facilitative effects under some conditions but not others (Carter & Van Matre, 1975; Peper & Mayer, 1978). Efforts to reconcile the inconsistent results have led to two different conceptions of the function of note-taking. Carter and Van Matre (1975) argue that notes are useful only to the extent that they serve as an external storage device for subsequent review. Peper and Mayer (1978) argue that the act of note-taking itself enhances test performance by promoting a richer encoding of the lecture material. Different predictions with respect to the role of note adequacy can be derived from these two perspectives. If note-taking is useful only as a means for review, then if students fail to review their notes before a test, it should not matter whether the notes were adequate or inadequate. On the other hand, if the act of note-taking itself is facilitative, better notes should promote better test performance with or without a subsequent review.

One of the few studies to relate the content of students' lecture notes to their test performance was a naturalistic investigation by Palkovitz and Lore (1980). Introductory psychology students were interviewed after taking an objective exam based on four lectures, and their lecture notes were examined for the presence and accuracy of information needed to answer eight target questions. Most of the students correctly recorded the target information in their notes; 77% of the relevant points were included. Analysis of the relation to test performance indicated that 82% of the correct test responses were associated with the presence of relevant information in the notes. Surprisingly, 66% of the

incorrect responses also were! Moreover, students who performed well on the exam and those who performed poorly did not differ in the quality of their notes. These data, supplemented by students' self-reports of study behaviors, led Palkovitz and Lore (1980) to conclude that accurate notes do not ensure good test performance; rather, students must adequately review the notes prior to the exam.

The thoroughness of the students' notes was somewhat surprising, but the target facts may have been signaled as important by Palkovitz and Lore. We know that students are more likely to remember information if the instructor tells them that it is important as opposed to unimportant (Goolkasian, Terry, & Park, 1979); and it is reasonable to assume that such information would also be more frequently included in students' lecture notes. Signals of importance may also be provided if the instructor writes anything on a blackboard or transparency since we know that they both influence note content and test performance. Locke (1975) examined the notes of nearly 200 college students enrolled in 12 different courses for inclusion of information identified as important by the instructors. Whereas 88% of the ideas that had been presented on the blackboard were included in the notes, only 52% of the non-blackboard ideas were included. Boswell (1980) compared test scores of a class that received critical information on a transparency accompanying a lecture with those of a class that received the lecture alone. Results revealed that the lower third of the class benefited from having the information presented on a transparency, whereas the upper two thirds did not. This suggests that more able students can identify the relevant information on their own, and so do not need instructor-provided cues; but the poorer students, who have more difficulty extracting the main ideas, benefit from the additional help. It may be unwise, however, for students to interpret the use of blackboards or transparencies as signals of importance. Teachers may use these devices simply to illustrate the spelling of new terms or to provide a hierarchical overview of the lecture. Under these circumstances, the burden of extracting and recording important information rests with the student, and overreliance on what the teacher has written may be deleterious.

In the present study we examined the aforementioned issues within a naturalistic setting and also examined the kinds of information students include in their notes. Introductory psychology students attended a regularly scheduled class lecture, took a multiple-choice test on the material 3 weeks later as part of a regularly scheduled exam, and submitted their lecture notes for photocopying. The lecture included four different kinds of target information: main ideas, supporting details, logical transitions, and examples. A transparency was prepared and used in order to provide a hierarchical overview of the lecture, but it contained almost none of the target information. We sought answers to the following questions: (a) Is there evidence that some students overrely on instructor-provided notes? (b) Is there a relation between lecture note quantity and test performance? (c) Are students more likely to include some kinds of information in their notes than others? (d) Is there a relation between the specific information included in the lecture notes and test performance?

Method

Subjects

The subjects were students enrolled in one section of an introductory psychology course. All students who attended class on the day the target lecture was delivered and who took the test on the material 3 weeks later were eligible to serve as subjects provided they turned in their lecture notes for photocopying. A total of 94 students out of a class of 125 met these criteria. The analyses reported in this paper were based on a randomly selected subsample of 40 students.

Materials

The lecture topic selected for the study dealt with the physiological aspects of emotion. Several factors entered into the selection of this particular topic: (a) The lecture date was midway through the semester so students were familiar with the instructor's style of teaching and testing; (b) The lecture date was 3 weeks prior to the next exam, a sufficiently long interval that students should feel the need to review their notes and not depend solely on memory; and (c) The topic was not covered exhaustively in the text so new information could be presented. As the lecture was being prepared, we incorporated information that would be the basis of the test questions. The target information included six transition points, six main ideas, six supporting details, and two examples.

Because the instructor routinely used a transparency instead of a blackboard, we did so here. Two transparencies were prepared on which key words were written in a rough hierarchical structure. To illustrate, a portion of the lecture was devoted to the disruptive effects of arousal with particular focus on Richter's work in which wild rats were stressed by forcing them to swim for many hours. Seven of the test questions were based on information presented during this part of the lecture, none of which could be answered on the basis of the rough outline alone. The transparency representation was as follows:

> Disruptive effects of arousal
>   Side effects
>   Long-term effects
>   Death
>   Voodoo
>   Richter

Procedure

The lecture was presented to the class by their regular instructor, the first author. The students had no reason to believe that there was anything special about this lecture. The lecture was attended by the second author who was unknown to the students. He tape recorded the lecture and also took notes. A transcript of the tape was later checked against the instructor's lecture notes in order to verify that the target information had been clearly presented. The test on the lecture material was given 3 weeks later. Six of the target questions (3 main points, 2 supporting details, and 1 transition) were included on the regularly scheduled 60-item multiple-choice exam, which also covered other lectures and assigned chapters in the text. The remaining 14 questions were incorporated into a separate "quiz" on the emotion lecture. These questions were substantively similar to the questions on the exam, although the "example" questions would be unlikely to appear on an actual exam. Just before taking the exam, students were informed of our interest in the relation between class notes and exam performance and were invited to participate in our study for extra credit. They were asked to remain in the lecture hall after they finished the exam in order to take the quiz. They were also asked to turn in their lecture notes to be photocopied. All students were given the opportunity to participate, regardless of whether they had attended class on the day of the emotion lecture. As long as they took the quiz and handed in *any* set of lecture notes, they received extra credit.

Results

All students' notes were first examined for degree of correspondence with the outline presented on the transparency. With but few exceptions, all sets of notes included all of the information, consisting of 35 propositions. There were vast differences among the students, however, in the amount of additional information they included in their notes. Each set of notes was scored for the number of added propositions; repetitions of the same proposition were not counted twice and propositions were counted without regard to degree of importance. The number of propositions added ranged from a low of 0 to a high of 82, with a mean of 26.6 and a standard deviation of 16.55. In order to evaluate the thoroughness of the notes, we used as our standard lecture notes taken in class by the co-investigator. Although it is true that the co-investigator had an advantage over the students in that he was familiar with the lecture material, his notes reflected what students *could* have recorded in class had they chosen to do so. The co-investigator's notes consisted of 98 propositions in addition to those presented on the transparency. The majority of the students recorded considerably less information than this experienced instructor; in fact, only 7% of the students included even half as many propositions.

Qualitative aspects of the lecture notes were examined by scoring the notes for the presence or absence of the specific information needed to answer each test question. For each type of question, the total number of items included in the notes was calculated. As expected, some kinds of information were more likely to be included than others. For main

Table 1. Intercorrelations Among the Dependent Measures

	1	2	3	4	5	6	7	8	9
1. Total No. of Propositions in Notes	—								
2. No. of Correct Main Point Questions	.47*	—							
3. No. of Correct Detail Questions	.12	.14	—						
4. No. of Correct Transition Questions	−.14	−.12	−.09	—					
5. Total No. of Correct Test Questions	.35*	.68*	.52*	.33*	—				
6. Final Grade in Course	.30*	.33*	.30*	.13	.55*	—			
7. No. of Main Points in Notes	.73*	.56*	−.07	−.15	.27*	.23	—		
8. No. of Details in Notes	.45*	.17	.32*	.10	.22	.09	.25	—	
9. No. of Transitions in Notes	.60*	.25	.17	.21	.31*	.27*	.51*	.31*	—

*$p < .05$.
Note. Measures 1, 7, 8, and 9 are derived from the students' lecture notes; measures 2, 3, 4, and 5 are based on test performance.

point questions, 47% of the target information was included in the notes, and for detail questions, 42%. However, some of the detail information was presented on the transparency. If we base the average only on those questions, which required the students to use their own initiative, the percentage decreases to 13. These data suggest that students do differentiate the main points from the supporting details in the process of note-taking. An examination of the example information revealed even more differentiation of importance level: Only 3% of the students included *any* mention of the examples in their notes. Finally, for the transition questions, 29% of the relevant information was included in the lecture notes. What this indicates is that students usually did not explicitly state the logical relations between ideas, perhaps on the assumption that the links would be readily inferable.

Each student's quiz and the relevant portions of the exam were scored for the number of target questions of each type that were answered correctly. Overall, 70% of the main point questions were correct, 59% of the details, 63% of the transitions, and 50% of the examples. (Note that two of the detail questions, unlike all others, were based directly on notes presented on the transparency, and these two questions were answered correctly 90% of the time.)

Intercorrelations among 9 variables of interest were calculated, and the resulting correlation matrix is presented in Table 1, which excludes examples because they were recorded so infrequently in the notes. Of the 36 different correlations, 19 were statistically significant, at least at the .05 level. Only those of particular interest will be discussed later. The number of propositions included in students' notes was significantly related to overall test scores, supporting the intuitively compelling but empirically undocumented expectation that the more information students include in their lecture notes, the better their test performance. Since our primary goal in lecturing is for students to learn the main ideas, it is encouraging that performance on the main point questions was related to note quantity. The correlations were not significant for the less-central detail and transition information. Note also that the total test score was significantly related to the final grade obtained in the course, suggesting that this one test was representative. The correlation between number of propositions in the notes and final course grade was also significant, suggesting that the degree of elaboration in a student's notes is a predictor of overall course performance. Also of interest was the fact that inclusion of main point information and detail information in the notes

was correlated with performance on the corresponding types of test questions; for transition information, the correlation was positive but not statistically significant.

Though suggestive, the correlational analysis does not indicate whether the presence of specific propositions in the notes was associated with correct responses to the questions based on those propositions. This issue was addressed by creating 2 × 2 contingency tables for each question based on presence or absence of target information in the notes and correctness or incorrectness of the response on the test. The cell frequencies differed somewhat from item to item, but the patterns were similar for items within question type. Accordingly, for ease of exposition and comparison across question types, the data are reported in Table 2 as average proportions for each type of question. Note that a distinction has been made between detail information that was and was not presented on the transparency. Tests of association were conducted using Yates' Corrected Chi-Square analyses and yielded significant effects for the following question types: main points, $\chi^2(1) = 18.93$, $p < .001$; details (not on transparency), $\chi^2(1) = 11.57$, $p < .001$; and transitions, $\chi^2(1) = 4.96$, $p < .05$. There are several general trends apparent in these data. First, it is clear that inclusion in the notes is not a *necessary* condition for students to answer the question correctly. It was frequently the case that there were more subjects in the notes-absent/response-correct cell than in the notes-present/response-correct cell. However, there is strong evidence that inclusion in the notes is a *sufficient* condition for students to answer the question correctly. There were very few students who fell into the notes-present/response-incorrect cell. Of all the questions answered incorrectly, only on 14% of the occasions was the relevant information included in the notes.[1]

---

[1]One additional question we were able to address concerns the relationship between a student's test performance and class attendance on the day of the lecture. If the test was in fact a valid indicator of learning, students who attended class should do better than those who did not attend class. To determine whether this was true, performance on each question was examined on the basis of lecture attendance. Overall, on 16 of the 20 questions, students who attended class were more likely to give the correct response than those who did not attend, with the difference ranging from 3% to 26% (mean = 11.17, standard deviation = 7.63). A matched pairs t-test on the difference scores for the 20 questions proved reliable, $t = 2.82$, $p < .01$; students who attended class had higher test scores than students who did not. These results are reassuring in supporting our belief that lecture attendance *does* matter!

Table 2. Relationship Between Lecture Note Contents and Responses to Test Questions for Each Type of Information[a]

Test Response	Main Points		Details (not on transparency)		Details (on transparency)	
	Notes		Notes		Notes	
	Present	Absent	Present	Absent	Present	Absent
Correct	.39	.31	.11	.38	.94	.01
Incorrect	.07	.23	.02	.49	.05	.00

Test Response	Transitions		Examples	
	Notes		Notes	
	Present	Absent	Present	Absent
Correct	.22	.42	.03	.53
Incorrect	.08	.29	.00	.45

[a]Cell entries are proportions of subjects, averaged across individual items within types.

Discussion

The present study was designed as a naturalistic investigation of the notes students take during actual classroom lectures and their relationship to performance on actual classroom exams. Some degree of control must be sacrificed in such a study (e.g., we do not know how much time students spent studying their notes before the exam), but the advantages outweigh the limitations. Because students did not know in advance that the notes taken during this lecture were to be examined, the quality of the notes should be representative of those they usually take. And because the test on the lecture was incorporated into the exam itself or given immediately afterwards, the incentives for studying and the study behaviors should also be representative.

One of our concerns was with the amount of information students included in their notes. Locke (1975) reported that students are more likely to include information presented on the blackboard than information that they must extract on their own. In the present study, virtually *all* students included *all* of the information presented on the transparencies, while recording only 27% of the additional information identified by the investigators as important. A few students were exceptionally thorough note-takers, but most did little more than copy down the key terms and topic headings provided on the transparency. A disconcerting implication is that students might take a more active role in processing the lecture material if they were given *no* assistance. On the other hand, perhaps the students would have nothing at all in their notes without these aids. As Boswell (1980) reported, it was the less successful students who benefited most by the use of transparencies.

Examination of the content of the notes revealed that students were more likely to include some types of information than others. This suggests that they selected information for recording differentially; they were more likely to include main ideas but omit details and information that could be reconstructed or inferred (transitions and examples). The fact that students did show sensitivity to importance is encouraging; the fact that they recorded less than half of the main ideas is rather less so.

Finally, the study revealed a relation between the content of the students' notes and test performance. The more information students included of a particular type, the better they did on the corresponding questions. Moreover, the presence of target information in the lecture notes appears to be a sufficient, but not a necessary, condition for correctly answering the question based on that information. Although students were able to answer many of the questions without having recorded the relevant information in their notes, they rarely answered the questions incorrectly if the information was present in their notes. This finding conflicts with that reported by Palkovitz and Lore (1980), who found that most students who answered questions incorrectly *did* include the relevant information in their notes. Palkovitz and Lore interpreted their data as support for the view that notes are useful only if they are adequately reviewed. However, the present study shows that the content of the students' notes does indeed make a difference. Nevertheless, we would not argue for a causal link, because it may be that students who take better notes in class *also* engage in more effective study strategies or have higher levels of achievement motivation.

In conclusion, the study has provided a number of important findings regarding the note-taking skills of college students. The paucity of information included in most students' notes implicates a real need for more direct information in note-taking skills, not just for the "remedial" student but for the majority of college freshmen. The frequent failures to record even the main points of the lecture further emphasize the need to help students differentiate the important information from the less important.

References

Baker, L., & Brown, A. L. (1984). Metacognitive skills and reading. In P. D. Pearson, M. Kamil, R. Barr, & P. Mosenthal (Eds.), *Handbook of reading research* (pp. 353–394). New York: Longman.

Boswell, D. A. (1980). Evaluation of transparencies for psychology instruction. *Teaching of Psychology, 7*, 171–173.

Carter, J. F., & Van Matre, N. H. (1975). Note taking vs. note having. *Journal of Educational Psychology, 67*, 900–904.

DiVesta, F. J., & Gray, G. S. (1972). Listening and note taking. *Journal of Educational Psychology, 63*, 8–14.

Eisner, S., & Rhodes, K. (1959). Note taking during or after the lecture. *Journal of Educational Psychology, 50*, 301–304.

Fisher, J. L., & Harris, M. B. (1973). Effect of note taking and review on recall. *Journal of Educational Psychology, 65*, 321–325.

Goolkasian, P., Terry, W. S., & Park, D. C. (1979). Memory for lectures: Effects of delay and distractor type. *Journal of Educational Psychology, 71*, 465–470.

Locke, E. A. (1975). *A guide to effective study.* New York: Springer.

Palkovitz, R. J., & Lore, R. K. (1980). Note taking and note review: Why students fail questions based on lecture material. *Teaching of Psychology, 7*, 159–161.

Peper, R. J., & Mayer, R. E. (1978). Note taking as a generative activity. *Journal of Educational Psychology, 70*, 514–522.

Peters, D. L. (1972). Effects of note taking and rate of presentation on short-term objective test performance. *Journal of Educational Psychology, 63*, 276–280.

Assessing the Essay Feedback Technique of Providing an Example of a Full-Credit Answer

David M. Carkenord
Longwood College

Providing students with useful feedback on graded essay test items can be challenging. Ideally the feedback should be specific enough to help students understand what type of information the instructor sought in the answer and why a particular student's response was graded as it was. One common feedback method is for instructors, on returning graded exams to the class, to verbally describe their grading criteria (major points or pieces of information sought while grading the essays). My experience with such verbal feedback is that it does not always help the students who did poorly on the essay to understand the reason for their unsatisfactory grade. A more specific method of providing feedback on essay items and other written assignments is for the instructor to select the best example from the class and (removing the student's name) distribute a copy to all students. This approach allows an instructor to describe the grading criteria with reference to an actual student response.

I incorporate this form of essay test feedback into my psychology courses, and other instructors have reported using such a feedback approach in a variety of applications. For example, in describing a technique aimed at improving writing skills, Madigan and Brosamer (1990) reported that when giving quiz feedback to students they provided two sample essay answers from among the best in the class. Wade (1995) described a set of writing assignments to enhance critical thinking skills and reported that reading some of the best student responses to the class was routinely part of the feedback procedure. Radmacher and Latosi-Sawin (1995) described a procedure of text summary writing in which they distribute copies of student summaries (at various levels of adequacy) for evaluation and assessment. Thus, this feedback technique appears to be fairly common in the teaching of psychology as well as in other academic disciplines such as English (Leahy, 1994) and economics (Pernecky, 1993). Although these authors reported that they believed the technique was an effective method of feedback, none provided any formal assessment of student attitudes regarding the approach. As such, the primary purpose of this analysis was to investigate students' attitudes regarding this type of feedback on essay test items in psychology courses.

Method

This assessment took place in four undergraduate psychology classes at a small, mid-Atlantic, liberal arts college toward the conclusion of the Spring 1996 term. The courses were two sections of introductory psychology for nonmajors, one section of social psychology, and one section of the psychology of organizational behavior. In the introductory courses, there were five tests (including the final exam) during the term. In the social and organizational behavior classes, there were four tests (including the final exam) during the term. Tests in all four of the classes were the same format; 30 multiple choice items (worth one point each), two short-answer items (worth two points each), and one essay item (worth six points) for a total of 40 possible points.

Students received their graded tests during the next class period following the examination day, and I gave the essay feedback at that time (along with feedback on the entire test). Specifically, the essay feedback consisted of a handout with a verbatim, typed copy of a student's full-credit answer (without the student's name) to the six-point essay question. I verbally described the major ideas or elements I sought in the essay answer, with reference to the handout, and responded to any student questions. The essay feedback took approximately 5 to 10 min. Students received the feedback on every test during the semester, with the exception of the final exam.

Participants

Although a total of 105 students were enrolled in and completed the four courses, 80 students were present on the day of the assessment. Sample sizes were $n = 27$ and $n = 25$ in the introductory courses, $n = 12$ in the social course, and $n = 16$ in the organizational behavior course. Forty percent of the students were freshman, 21% sophomores, 23% juniors, and 16% seniors. Sixty-four percent of the students were women.

Instrument

Students completed an eight-item survey regarding their attitudes toward the feedback technique. Students rated each item on a 5-point scale ranging from 1 (*strongly disagree*) to 5 (*strongly agree*). Students also indicated their gender and academic classification.

Procedure

Students anonymously completed the survey at the conclusion of a class period in which they received the essay feedback. This was a day late in the term, after the students had multiple experiences with the feedback technique. Specifically, students completed the assessment after the fourth test in the introductory courses and after the third test in the social and organizational behavior courses. I encouraged the students to respond honestly on the survey, and they completed the instrument in about 5 min or less.

Results

I calculated means and standard deviations for the total sample on the eight attitude items. Overall, student attitudes toward the technique were positive. In particular, students agreed that they would be flattered if the instructor chose their answer as the example ($M = 4.56$, $SD = 0.63$), that the feedback helps them understand what the instructor looks for in essay answers ($M = 4.28$, $SD = 0.70$), that this type of feedback helps them understand why the instructor graded their answer as he did ($M = 4.20$, $SD = 0.70$), and that they would like this type of feedback in other classes ($M = 4.13$, $SD = 0.75$). Students also indicated that they would not feel resentment toward the student whose answer was used as the example ($M = 1.64$, $SD = 0.93$), and they would not be embarrassed if their answer was chosen as the example ($M = 1.48$, $SD = 0.62$). Students tended to agree with the statement that the feedback made them think, "If someone else in the class was able to give a good answer, I guess that I should have been able to as well" ($M = 3.75$, $SD = 0.95$). Finally, students tended to agree that the feedback provides information on how to prepare for future tests ($M = 3.61$, $SD = 0.99$).

Discussion

Overall, the attitudinal assessment suggests that students appreciate and find useful essay feedback in the form of an actual example of a full-credit answer. This method appears to be effective in helping students understand how the instructor graded their essay response and why they received the grade they received. The results also suggest that students would be flattered (and not embarrassed) if an instructor chose their answer as the example response. This finding seems consistent with my experiences of having some students privately thank me after class for picking their essay as the example. In this vein, it is possible that the use of this technique might motivate students to strive to provide an answer worthy of being chosen as the example.

It is interesting to speculate as to why this type of feedback is effective in helping students understand their essay grades. It may be that by providing a fellow student's answer, other students see the source of the feedback information as similar to themselves and as such the information may have more persuasive power (Cialdini, 1993). It may also be possible that providing more than one example of a full-credit response, to show variations in style, would enhance the technique's effectiveness.

Some instructors may be uncomfortable with the practice of distributing a copy of a student's answer without that stu-

dent's permission. This assessment suggests that few students would be upset by having their answer chosen and displayed. Nevertheless, instructors may wish to obtain written permission from students to use their essay as an example. This might be done by explaining the feedback procedure to the class early in the term and asking students to sign a brief form indicating that they authorize the instructor to display their answer anonymously to the class (if appropriate). Another approach to obtaining student permission would be to telephone (or e-mail) the particular student prior to providing the feedback.

Although the primary goal of this assessment was to better understand student attitudes toward this feedback technique, limitations of the analysis must be noted. First, I did not compare student attitudes against a control group class that did not receive the feedback or that received some other form of feedback. Thus, this analysis does not allow the conclusion that this feedback technique is necessarily better than other possible strategies. The data do suggest, however, that students have positive attitudes about this particular approach.

A second limitation is that this analysis does not examine the relation between use of the technique and student performance on subsequent essay test items. Some information regarding the link between use of the technique and performance improvement comes from the attitude item, "This type of feedback provides me with information on how to study and prepare for the essay portion of future tests." The mean response on this item indicated mild agreement ($M = 3.61$), suggesting that students saw some utility in the technique as a means for future improvement. However, students have informally mentioned to me that because essay items change from test to test, seeing a good answer to the questions on the most recent test does not necessarily provide a direct means to increase the likelihood of providing a good answer on subsequent tests. Thus a more thorough investigation of the relation between this technique and subsequent performance appears to be worthwhile.

Finally, about 20% of the students enrolled in the courses were not present on the day the assessment occurred. This self-selection may have influenced these findings. These limitations notwithstanding, this assessment suggests that students view this essay test feedback technique favorably. The technique is also likely to be useful for other types of written assignments such as weekly journals or short papers.

References

Cialdini, R. B. (1993). *Influence: Science and practice* (3rd ed.). New York: HarperCollins.

Leahy, R. (1994). Microthemes: An experiment with very short writings. *College Teaching, 42*, 15–18.

Madigan, R., & Brosamer, J. (1990). Improving the writing skills of students in introductory psychology. *Teaching of Psychology, 17*, 27–35.

Pernecky, M. (1993). Reaction papers enrich economic discussions. *College Teaching, 41*, 89–91.

Radmacher, S. A., & Latosi-Sawin, E. (1995). Summary writing: A tool to improve student comprehension and writing in psychology. *Teaching of Psychology, 22*, 113–115.

Wade, C. (1995). Using writing to develop and assess critical thinking. *Teaching of Psychology, 22*, 24–28.

Self-Scoring: A Self-Monitoring Procedure

Lee C. Light
St. Clair Community College

Wilbert J. McKeachie
Yi-Guang Lin
The University of Michigan
National Center for Research to Improve Postsecondary Teaching and Learning (NCRIPTAL)

Students take tests; teachers score tests. Often, teachers score tests with evaluative zeal but disregard implications for improvement of teaching. Students are so involved in recalling an answer to each question that they often fail to think about the adequacy of their responses. One of the most important strategies in learning and problem solving is self-monitoring (Weinstein & Mayer, 1986). Our study describes a method of encouraging self-monitoring in test taking.

We call our technique *self-scoring*. The procedure is simple. In a typical 50-min class period, students are told that their test will be designed to take only 40 min and that they should spend the remaining 10 min self-scoring (i.e., going back over the test and scoring each question in terms of their best guess about the adequacy of their answer). If they think that an answer is inadequate, they are free to change it. Our hypothesis was that this procedure would encourage a more thoughtful, critical approach than that of simply reviewing the test. An important by-product of self-scoring is the practice that students receive in assessing their written work. In schools and in business, one's overall development and success are often determined by the ability to assess one's own work. Thus, we hoped that the procedure would improve students' test scores and help them develop a general habit of self-scoring.

Method

Subjects

The subjects were 56 General Psychology students in Light's (the first author's) classes at St. Clair County Community College. There were 31 women and 25 men; their ages ranged from 18 to 55, but the majority were 18 to 20 years old.

Tests

The achievement tests consisted of four types of questions: 8 multiple-choice (32 points), chunking (22 points), 2 short-answer essay (16 points), and 2 long-answer essay (30 to 40 points).

Chunking. Invented by Light, chunking requires the student to group or chunk 30 to 40 terms into 9 or 10 categories. Both the terms and the categories are given to the student. A term can be used in only one category. An example of chunking follows:

Terms	Categories
Gestalt	Freud
Reinforcement	
Neurosis	
Illusions	Perception
Unconscious processes	
Figure–ground	
Extinction	Conditioning
Ego	
Generalization	

Short-answer essay questions. These require a two- to three-sentence answer. A sample question: Explain how a strongly held belief or attitude may release endorphins.

Long-answer essay questions. These require a one half to one-page answer. An example: Compare and contrast three major types of psychotherapy. Students can obtain up to 10 additional points by choosing to answer one essay question designated as being more difficult by the instructor.

During the class period before the test, students were given a self-scoring form and directed to question the instructor on what they did not understand about it. The form gives the percentages for the four types of questions along with instructions for computing them. Added together, the four types of questions are worth 100 to 110 possible points, depending on whether the student chooses to answer a 15-point or a 25-point long-essay question. Self-scorers did not differ from nonself-scorers in choosing this option.

Procedure

Four tests and a final examination were given during the term. The experiment was carried out on Tests 3 and 4. Fifty-two percent of the students were self-scorers on Test 3 and served as their own control on Test 4. Forty-eight percent of the students were self-scorers on Test 4 and served as their own control on Test 3. In the experimental condition, Tests 3 and 4 were 40-min exams with 10 min added for self-scoring. In the control condition, students were allowed to spend the entire 50-min period taking or reviewing the test. In both conditions, a few students who failed to complete the test during the class period were allowed extra time.

The self-scoring forms were not seen by the experimenter until the tests had been scored. The students' self-scores were then compared to the actual grades; students who scored themselves within 5 points of the grade given by the teacher were given an extra 5% on the test. This bonus served as an incentive for students to carry out their self-scoring carefully. The extra 5% was not included in the scores reported in this study.

Results

Of the 56 students, 37 (66%) received higher scores on the test they self-scored, 18 (32%) received lower scores on the test they self-scored, and 1 (2%) received the same score with and without self-scoring. The difference between self-scored tests and nonself-scored tests (self-scoring: $M = 77.16$, $SD = 15.12$; nonself-scoring: $M = 72.91$, $SD = 14.66$) was statistically significant, $t(55) = 2.20$, $p < .03$. Students were very consistent in choosing either 100 or 110 possible points (the extra 10 points for the more difficult essay question). Of the 56 students, only 3 chose 100 points on one test and 110 points on the other.

Discussion

Our results support the original hypothesis. Self-scoring produced nearly one half a letter grade improvement in test scores. Why did students improve? We think that shifting some of the responsibility from the teacher to the student is an important factor. We produced this shift by having the students' behavior parallel that of the teacher. These students, we believe, became more aware of their own personal control in the testing situation. Carroll (1976, 1981) pointed to the self-monitoring procedure as an "executive" that is responsible for a sequence of information processing. Brown (1978) distinguished between metacognitive processes (predicting, checking, monitoring, reality testing) and cognitive processes (visual scanning, memory retrieval). Self-scoring serves the executive function of self-monitoring.

Some readers may question whether self-scoring causes improvement in test scores. Did students change answers as they self-scored, or were they simply more careful the first time through their test? Some students were observed changing answers; others may have been more careful in their initial test responses.

There may not be an exclusive cause and effect relationship between self-scoring and improved test scores. There is an inclusive relationship between self-scoring (and all that it includes) and improved test scores. This exclusive/inclusive distinction is the difference between a behavioristic or mechanical explanation and cognitive (informational) explanation of results. Also, this distinction is the difference between a content-related and a contextual explanation.

We prefer to regard self-scoring as a context that can produce possibilities for the development of responsible student behaviors. Successful teachers continually incorporate the student role in their teaching; self-scoring encourages students to take the role of teacher in reviewing their own work.

What about the future of self-scoring research? What remains to be examined in further experiments is whether students who were self-scorers on Test 3 used self-scoring on Test 4, although they were not instructed to do so. There was little evidence of such carryover on the next test given in the course. If self-scoring is an effective procedure, how can we teach students to use it on their own? In many classes, most students reread and recheck their answers, although they do not formally self-score them. For example, McKeachie (1986) instructed half of his Learning to Learn students to self-score a test and the other half to indicate how they spent the 8 min after the signal given for the self-scorers. Almost all nonself-scorers reported that they reread and rechecked their tests; the few who did not use this procedure received lower scores. Overall, however, students instructed to self-score did better. How can we facilitate the adoption of self-scoring so that students use this approach even when not instructed to do so? We believe that practicing the self-scoring procedure with explicit explanation of its potential value should increase the tendency of students to use this approach. Knowing that many people are reluctant to accept untried procedures, we suggest that teachers initially require self-scoring until continued student success produces a metacognitive transformation.

Another line of future research is to investigate individual differences in the effectiveness of this technique. Does the instruction to use self-scoring increase the anxiety of some students and result in poorer performance?

We believe that we have found an effective test-taking strategy. Now the challenge is to determine how, and by whom, this strategy can be effectively transferred to non-experimental situations.

References

Brown, A. L. (1978). Knowing when, where, and how to remember: A problem of metacognition. In R. Glaser (Ed.), *Advances in instructional psychology* (Vol. 1, pp. 77–165). Hillsdale, NJ: Lawrence Erlbaum Associates, Inc.

Carroll, J. B. (1976). Psychometric tests as cognitive tasks: A new "structure of intellect." In L. B. Resnick (Ed.), *The nature of intelligence* (pp. 27–56). Hillsdale, NJ: Lawrence Erlbaum Associates, Inc.

Carroll, J. B. (1981). Ability and task difficulty in cognitive psychology. *Educational Researcher, 10,* 11–12.

McKeachie, W. J. (1986). [Improving test scores by student self-monitoring]. Unpublished raw data.

Weinstein, C. E., & Mayer, R. E. (1986). The teaching of learning strategies. In M. C. Wittrock (Ed.), *Handbook of research and teaching* (pp. 315–327). New York: Macmillan.

Immediate Feedback, No Return Test Procedure for Introductory Courses

Herbert Friedman
College of William & Mary

The standard test procedure for large lecture courses leads to several problems:

1. To help maintain student motivation, tests should be graded and recorded quickly, preferably in time for the next scheduled class meeting.
2. Returning graded tests or answer sheets to a large number of students may be time consuming and disruptive.
3. A later class meeting, when student interest (and attendance) is generally lower than at the time of the test, is not the best time to review the test items.
4. Class time devoted to discussing the test means that a single test consumes one class meeting and a large portion of a second.

A modification of the standard procedure that deals with these difficulties has been used successfully for a number of years. The main features are:

1. For a 50-min class, the test consists of 20 to 40 multiple-choice items and, perhaps, one or two short answer items. The test is designed to allow nearly all students to finish in 30 min.
2. The test is mimeographed in one or more versions and fits on both sides of a single sheet.
3. The test and a separate answer sheet are distributed to the class. The students are instructed to mark their answers on the question sheet and on the answer sheet.
4. After 30 min, the answer sheet is collected and students retain the marked question sheet.
5. In the remaining class time, the instructor reviews the test. There is a strong student interest in the answers and in the discussion of allegedly ambiguous items.

In addition, the following features were employed, though they are not necessary for the procedure:

6. The test grades are not "curved," which allows letter grade cutoffs (in terms of the number of incorrect items) to be given at the end of the class.
7. To encourage students to review items on the retained test, they are reminded that a small portion of the final exam will consist of questions taken from each lecture test.
8. The multiple-choice items are generally two-choice, but four-choice, fill-in, and matching items are also suitable. Two-choice items work well with this procedure because they are more readily explained than four-choice items in the limited time available. Two-choice items may be derived from text test files by retaining the correct choice and the most plausible incorrect choice.

The advantages of this procedure are:

1. Students receive feedback on answers and grades immediately after the test.
2. Feedback is given when student interest and attendance are maximized.
3. Because students gain full information on their performance at the test session, there is no need to return the graded answer sheets.
4. With no answer sheets to return, there is no rush to grade the test.
5. Class time is used efficiently. Two short tests require two lecture hours, the same time absorbed for a single longer exam that is returned and discussed in a subsequent lecture. Therefore, the modified procedure makes it easier to give frequent tests.
6. Course evaluations show that student reaction to the test procedure has been positive.

Student Evaluation of Friedman's Immediate Feedback, No Return Test Procedure for Introductory Psychology

Randolph A. Smith
Randall Wight
Ouachita Baptist University

Friedman (1987) proposed a procedure for testing students in an introductory class that allows for immediate feedback about the students' performance. He recommended using a 30-min multiple-choice test and presenting the correct answers in class after students complete the test. This procedure provides immediate feedback, manages class time efficiently, and receives favorable reactions from students.

There is ample evidence to document the importance of immediate feedback on animal learning (see Renner, 1964; Tarpy & Sawabini, 1974). However, this information has not been widely applied to classroom testing. One such application is Keller's (1968) personalized system of instruction (PSI), but recent studies indicate that fewer PSI courses are being taught (Lloyd & Lloyd, 1986) and that research on PSI has declined (Lamal, 1984).

Friedman (1987) implied that immediate feedback of test information enhanced learning. Further, Calhoun (1976) demonstrated that the immediate feedback component of PSI is vital to its success. Thus, Friedman's technique seems to provide some promising educational benefits.

Designing a well-controlled classroom experiment to test the hypothesis that the immediate feedback procedure facilitates learning is difficult because of numerous extraneous variables. Nevertheless, we incorporated Friedman's procedure into our General Psychology classes in the Fall 1987 semester and assessed student reaction to it. Students in three sections of General Psychology (N = 97; one section taught by the first author and two by the second author) took four exams using Friedman's procedure. Each exam covered three or four chapters from the textbook (Benjamin, Hopkins, & Nation, 1987). Students were allowed 35 min to complete each exam. One student was allowed unlimited time (outside class) to compensate for dyslexia; all other students completed the exams in the allocated time.

The end-of-course evaluation included four questions concerning the exam procedure. Students were asked to evaluate the immediate feedback technique on a scale ranging from *poor* (1) to *great* (10). The mean rating was 9.69 (SD = .89). This evaluation is exceptionally high for any aspect of a class, indicating that the students considered the immediate feedback a welcome addition. Students were also given an opportunity to provide open-ended evaluations of the technique. Of the 84 students who made comments, 32 (38.1%) specifically stated that immediate feedback aided their learning. Remarks such as the following were common: "I thought it helped us learn the things we did not know on the test"; "It's the best way to remember for future use the material you did and didn't know on the test"; and "It allowed me to understand what was incorrect in my thinking while I was still concerned with the subject."

Students were then asked hypothetical questions about whether they learned more from immediate test review than by going over the test either during the next class meeting or during a class session 1 to 2 weeks later. The rating scale ranged from *much less* (1) through *same* (5) to *much more* (10). Students believed that they learned much more from the immediate review regardless of the comparison time. Compared to the next class meeting, immediate review was judged to result in more learning (M = 8.64; SD = 1.53). Likewise, students (N = 95 due to nonresponders) said that they learned more from immediate review than they would by reviewing a test 1 to 2 weeks later (M = 9.09; SD = 1.67).

In short, our students liked the immediate feedback approach and believed that they learned more by reviewing an exam immediately. Either one of these results is enough evidence to recommend the procedure.

References

Benjamin, L. T., Jr., Hopkins, J. R., & Nation, J. R. (1987). *Psychology*. New York: Macmillan.

Calhoun, J. F. (1976). The combination of elements in the personalized system of instruction. *Teaching of Psychology, 3*, 73–76.

Friedman, H. (1987). Immediate feedback, no return test procedure for introductory courses. *Teaching of Psychology, 14*, 244.

Keller, F. S. (1968). "Good-bye, teacher . . ." *Journal of Applied Behavior Analysis, 1*, 79–89.

Lamal, P. A. (1984). Interest in PSI across sixteen years. *Teaching of Psychology, 11*, 237–238.

Lloyd, M. E., & Lloyd, K. E. (1986). Has lightning struck twice? Use of PSI in college classrooms. *Teaching of Psychology, 13*, 149–151.

Renner, K. E. (1964). Delay of reinforcement: An historical review. *Psychological Bulletin, 61*, 341–361.

Tarpy, R. M., & Sawabini, F. L. (1974). Reinforcement delay: A selective review of the last decade. *Psychological Bulletin, 81*, 984–997.

Consequences of Missing Postexam Review Sessions

William E. Addison
Eastern Illinois University

In one of the earliest studies of the use of feedback from exams, Jones (1923) found that tests administered immediately after a psychology lecture led to improved retention among students. Jones's results supporting the value of immediate feedback were corroborated by a host of studies conducted in the 1950s (e.g., Fitch, Drucker, & Norton, 1951; Guetzkow, Kelly, & McKeachie, 1954; McKeachie & Hiler, 1954; Pressey, 1950). The consistency of these findings led McKeachie (1963) to conclude that knowledge of results clearly facilitates learning.

In the 1970s and 1980s, the emphasis on mastery learning at all levels of education led to further research on the role of feedback, although much of this research focused on specific teaching methods, such as individualized instruction and peer teaching (e.g., Good & Grouws, 1979; Kulik & Kulik, 1979; Webb, 1980). More recently, Oosterhof (1990) suggested that mastery learning must involve feedback from a test indicating what the student has and has not learned, as well as some form of remedial instruction based on this feedback.

Clearly, educators recognize the importance of providing feedback to students regarding their performance on exams. As psychologists, we also realize that feedback is valuable only if the students make use of it. With these principles in mind, I emphasize the postexam review, sometimes spending up to 30 min reviewing the items on a previous exam. This review typically covers the rationale for answering a particular question correctly as well as possible alternative interpretations by the students. Students usually respond favorably to these sessions, particularly when they view them as opportunities to improve their exam scores (i.e., to convince the instructor to give them additional points).

This approach has certain limitations. For instance, after the first exam, students realize that little new material is covered on the class day after an exam. This realization often results in low attendance on postexam review days. Assuming that the postexam review constitutes a learning experience for the students, regular attendance at the review sessions is likely to enhance the students' mastery of the course material. In addition, failure to attend these sessions may result in a decrease in overall course performance. These potential consequences are particularly relevant to courses that include a cumulative final exam.

My study examined possible negative consequences of failure to attend the postexam review in two types of psychology courses. Statistics is a required course for psychology majors, and Industrial Psychology is an elective course in which a substantial number of nonmajors are enrolled.

Design

The Statistics course is designed to be taken at the sophomore/junior level. The 33 students in this class took three regular exams and six quizzes, resulting in nine postexam (or postquiz) review sessions. The Industrial Psychology course is an upper division elective that is relatively popular among psychology majors but is also taken by students majoring in other areas, such as business and technology. Three regular exams yielded three review sessions for the 69 students in this course.

For both classes, two measures of overall course performance were used: percentage scores on the cumulative final exam and course average (also measured on a percentage basis). More than 50% of the students in both classes attended all review sessions (61% in the Statistics class and 57% in the Industrial Psychology class). Hence, two groups were formed: (a) students who missed none of the review sessions and (b) students who missed one or more of the sessions. Independent groups t tests were then used to compare the two groups on both measures of course performance.

Results

A summary of the final exam scores is presented in Table 1. In light of the evidence indicating that feedback facilitates learning, one-tailed t tests were used in making the relevant comparisons. These analyses show that, in the Industrial Psychology class, students who missed one or more of the review sessions scored significantly lower on the cumulative final exam than students who missed none of the sessions, $t(67) = 2.87$, $p < .05$. In the Statistics class, the difference was not significant, $p > .05$.

A summary of the course averages is presented in Table 2. Analyses performed on these data show that, in the Industrial Psychology class, students who missed one or more of the review sessions obtained significantly lower course averages than students who missed none of the sessions, $t(67) = 3.29$, $p < .001$. Similar results were obtained for the Statistics class, $t(31) = 2.01$, $p < .05$.

In addition, I examined differences between the two groups in their performance on the first exam. Because the first exam occurs before any postexam review, these comparisons should indicate any preexisting differences in the groups that are unrelated to attendance at review sessions (e.g., differences in ability and motivation). In the Industrial Psychology class, the scores of students who missed one or more of the review sessions ($M = 78.13$, $SD = 10.79$) did not differ significantly from those of students who missed none of the sessions ($M = 78.87$, $SD = 9.29$), $t(67) = 0.31$, $p > .05$. Similarly, in the Statistics class, the performance on the first exam of students who missed one or more review sessions ($M = 78.08$, $SD = 9.60$) was not significantly different from that of students who did not miss any review sessions ($M = 80.90$, $SD = 8.03$), $t(31) = 0.91$, $p > .05$.

Table 1. Final Exam Performance of Students Who Were Present and Students Who Were Absent at Postexam Review Sessions

Group	n	M	SD
Statistics class			
One or more absences	13	68.85	17.79
No absences	20	73.30	11.23
Industrial psychology class			
One or more absences	30	74.27	10.90
No absences	39	81.69	10.49

Table 2. Course Averages of Students Who Were Present and Students Who Were Absent at Postexam Review Sessions

Group	n	M	SD
Statistics class			
One or more absences	13	72.28	13.24
No absences	20	79.74	8.18
Industrial psychology class			
One or more absences	30	79.27	8.12
No absences	39	85.90	8.44

Discussion

Results indicate that students who miss postexam review sessions are likely to perform at a lower overall level than students who attend these sessions. The nonsignificant differences in the groups' performance on the first exam for both courses support this conclusion. The findings are consistent for both the lower division required course (Statistics) and the upper division elective (Industrial Psychology). The one exception is the nonsignificant difference in final exam scores between the two groups in the Statistics class. The relatively small sample sizes for these groups (13 and 20 subjects) and the large variability in scores for the absent group ($SD = 17.79$) compared to the present group ($SD = 11.23$) probably contributed to the nonsignificant result.

Because ethical and methodological considerations necessitate the use of a correlational design in this type of study, a direct causal link between attendance at postexam review sessions and overall course performance cannot be discerned. Perhaps the most parsimonious explanation for the findings is that the postexam review session simply provides another opportunity for students to improve their understanding of course material. And, as most instructors know, the good students are the ones most likely to take full advantage of such opportunities.

In general terms, the findings offer further support for the value of feedback in learning. More specifically, this study provides empirical evidence that instructors can cite to encourage their students to attend postexam review sessions.

References

Fitch, M. L., Drucker, A. J., & Norton, J. A., Jr. (1951). Frequent testing as a motivating factor in large lecture classes. *Journal of Educational Psychology, 42,* 1–20.

Good, T. L., & Grouws, D. A. (1979). The Missouri mathematics effectiveness project. *Journal of Educational Psychology, 71,* 355–362.

Guetzkow, H., Kelly, E. L., & McKeachie, W. J. (1954). An experimental comparison of recitation, discussion, and tutorial methods in college teaching. *Journal of Educational Psychology, 45,* 193–209.

Jones, H. E. (1923). Experimental studies of college teaching. *Archives of Psychology, 10,* 5–70.

Kulik, J. A., & Kulik, C. C. (1979). College teaching. In P. L. Peterson & H. J. Walberg (Eds.), *Research on teaching: Concepts, findings, and implications* (pp. 70–93). Berkeley, CA: McCutchan.

McKeachie, W. J. (1963). Research on teaching at the college and university level. In N. L. Gage (Ed.), *Handbook of research on teaching* (pp. 1118–1172). Chicago: Rand McNally.

McKeachie, W. J., & Hiler, W. (1954). The problem oriented approach to teaching psychology. *Journal of Educational Psychology, 45,* 224–232.

Oosterhof, A. C. (1990). *Classroom applications of educational measurement.* Columbus, OH: Merrill.

Pressey, S. L. (1950). Development and appraisal of devices providing immediate automatic scoring of objective tests and concomitant self-instruction. *Journal of Psychology, 29,* 417–447.

Webb, N. (1980). A process–outcome analysis of learning in group and individual settings. *Educational Psychologist, 15,* 69–83.

Notes

1. I thank John Best and Fred Yaffe for comments on earlier drafts of this article. I also thank Charles L. Brewer and three anonymous reviewers for their contributions.

Of Barfights and Gadflies: Attitudes and Practices Concerning Extra Credit in College Courses

John C. Norcross
Linda J. Horrocks
University of Scranton

John F. Stevenson
University of Rhode Island

Should one desire to start a barfight in a community tavern, the topics of politics, religion, and maternal heritage are likely precipitants. If one wishes to start a verbal brawl in a university faculty club, the desirability of extra credit is incendiary material. Extra credit in college is, in the words of one of our survey respondents, "the gadfly to end all gadflies." Some faculty equate extra credit with low standards and grade inflation; for others it denotes additional work and exceptional circumstances.

Apart from its acquired connotations, extra credit as a pedagogical or evaluation method is rarely discussed publicly or investigated empirically. It is not listed as an index term in *Psychological Abstracts*. Contract grading (Clark, 1978), personalized instruction (M. E. Lloyd & K. E. Lloyd, 1986), self-pacing (M. E. Lloyd & Zylla, 1981), and repeated exams (Davidson, House, & Boyd, 1984) address distantly related concerns, but not the specific topic. Moreover, we were unable to locate any articles on extra credit in the last 10 volumes of *Teaching of Psychology*.

Significantly, extra credit is not addressed in many of the standard works on college teaching (e.g., Ericksen, 1984; Guskey, 1988; Milton, 1978). Research reviews do not identify extra credit as a topic that has been studied (e.g., McKeachie, Pintrich, Yi-Guang, & Smith, 1986; Milton, 1982) or one that should be studied (Vogel & Stark, 1986). Two standard works (Eble, 1988; McKeachie, 1986) mention extra credit, but not with a research basis or any analysis beyond a subjective opinion. In a casually sympathetic manner, Eble (1988, p. 162) endorsed students' rights to inquire whether there is any "extra work" they can do to raise a grade, but said nothing specific about appropriate faculty responses. With clear disapproval, McKeachie (1986) pointed out that teachers who give extra credit to bolster poor exam performance, but give final grades that do not reflect the extra credit, will have justifiably unhappy students on their hands.

Our exploratory investigation was designed to ascertain attitudes and practices concerning extra credit in college courses by surveying faculty and students at two universities. The results are limited by the self-report methodology, response rate, and sample of institutions. Nonetheless, our findings should shed some light on this shadowy topic and perhaps prevent a few faculty barfights.

Method

Instrument

A two-page, anonymous questionnaire was constructed for this study. Respondents were asked to indicate their biological sex; major area of study; and the number of three-credit, undergraduate courses taken (for students) or taught (for faculty) last semester. Students were also asked their class year and cumulative grade point average. Seven statements regarding extra credit on the college level were offered, and participants were instructed to select the one that best reflected their general attitude. Three blank lines were provided to cite one potential advantage of extra credit and one potential disadvantage. The frequency of being offered (students) or offering (faculty) extra credit to one or more members of a class during the preceding semester was solicited. Participants who indicated one or more extra-credit opportunities were asked three additional questions concerning the most recent instance: how was the availability of extra credit made known; what were restrictions, if any, on which class members were eligible for extra credit; and what was the nature of the extra-credit assignment?

Procedure and Participants

Two universities in the northeastern United States served as survey sites in the spring of 1988. One is a medium-sized, private institution in the liberal arts tradition (University of Scranton—US); the other is a large, public facility (University of Rhode Island—URI). The 206 full-time US faculty received the questionnaire by campus mail; 106 were eventually returned (51% response rate). Five questionnaires were unusable, resulting in a final subsample of 101. The 327 full-time URI faculty members in the College of Arts and Sciences received the identical survey through campus mail. The return rate for this group was somewhat anomalous, because a number of completed ques-

Table 1. Selected Sample Characteristics

Characteristic	US Students[a]	US Faculty[b]	URI Students[c]	URI Faculty[d]
Gender:				
Female	53	16	62	33
Male	47	84	38	67
Class Year:				
Freshman	44		62	
Sophomore	33		24	
Junior	15		12	
Senior	7		2	
Other	1		0	
Major Area:				
Social–behavioral science	39	22	46	46
Natural science	17	17	9	14
Quantitative science	3	8	3	7
Humanities	8	35	11	29
Business/ management	24	14	13	0
Other	9	5	18	4

Note. All numbers shown are percentages.
[a]$n = 294$. [b]$n = 101$. [c]$n = 231$. [d]$n = 44$.

tionnaires disappeared from a collection box, possibly signaling a passive–aggressive barfight. An unknown number of the earliest returns were lost in this way. Thus, the available number of completed questionnaires was 44 (13% of the surveyed group).

Questionnaires were distributed to undergraduate students enrolled in introductory psychology courses at the same universities. Response rates were 89% ($n = 294$) for the US and 44% ($n = 231$) for the URI. Interestingly, the response rate in the URI classes was approximately two thirds, with one exception. Here, the professor expressed discomfort with missing a few minutes of class time and protested that "The students all want extra credit for doing it!" Without class time or extra credit, only 6% of the students in that class completed the questionnaire.

Selected characteristics of the two faculty samples ($n = 145$) and the two student samples ($n = 525$) are summarized in Table 1. Despite disappointing response rates from the faculty, the available evidence suggests that the US samples are demographically representative of their respective populations. Except for the prominent underrepresentation of juniors and seniors in the US student sample, return bias does not appear to be demographic in nature. Of course, motivational and interpersonal variables probably differentiate those who respond from those who do not.

Results

The participants' general attitudes toward extra credit are summarized in Table 2. As shown, one's perspective on the desirability of extra credit varied systematically as a function of whether one was the potential recipient (students) or the potential giver (faculty). Only 3% of responding students indicated that extra credit should never be offered, contrasted to an average of 21% of responding faculty. Conversely, 56% of the students said that extra credit should be offered routinely to all students, compared to 28% of the

faculty. There was a pronounced tendency for URI students and faculty to express more positive sentiments toward extra credit than did the corresponding US samples, $\chi^2(6) = 24.7$, $p < .01$, for student samples. However, the exploratory nature of the study and the low response rates for faculty preclude any broad generalizations.

Moving from attitudes to behaviors, the percentage of faculty offering extra credit in one or more of their courses during the fall 1988 semester was 20% and 30% for the two subsamples. Over two thirds of responding faculty (80%, 70%) did not offer extra credit in any of their undergraduate courses. Similarly, about half of the undergraduates (58%, 42%) did not have a single opportunity for extra-credit assignments in any of their courses that term. The percentages of students (43%, 56%) reporting extra-credit opportunities in at least one course were higher than those of faculty, which is probably attributable to the fact that they were taking more courses than faculty were teaching (means of 5.0 vs. 3.5 and 4.2 vs. 3.3, respectively). However, for both faculty and students, the number of courses taught/taken bore no significant relationship to the frequency of extra credit offered that semester.

Subsequent results are presented in terms of a ratio of the number of courses in which extra credit was offered to the number of courses taken/taught. Between 12% and 22% of undergraduate courses, on average, provided an opportunity for extra credit. These averages mask considerable variation in the frequency of offering extra credit, however. For US faculty, 80% did not offer extra credit in any of their courses and 5% offered it in all their courses; for URI faculty, 70% never offered extra credit and 9% always offered it. A small minority of faculty (15%, 21%) fell between these two extremes in offering extra credit in some but not all of their classes.

Undergraduates at these two institutions have a 50% probability of being offered extra credit in at least one course in a given semester. The probability of students being offered extra credit in all their courses in one semester is quite low (3% at both institutions). Again, prevalence of reported extra credit was consistently higher for the public than the private university.

Statistical analyses were performed on the subsamples to identify potential covariates of attitudes and practices related to extra credit. For students, grade point average was not significantly related to extra-credit attitudes in either the US ($r = -.02$) or URI ($r = -.01$) samples. Neither student gender nor major was associated with attitude in either sample.

For faculty, gender was not significantly related to extra-credit practices or attitudes in the US sample, but major

Table 2. General Attitudes Toward Extra Credit

Attitude	Students US %	Students URI %	Faculty US %	Faculty URI %
Never be offered	3.1	2.6	19.8	22.7
Offered only under exceptional circumstances	6.8	8.4	49.5	38.6
Offered to those failing	1.7	.4	1.0	0
Offered to those with D or F	4.4	1.3	3.0	0
Offered to those with C, D, or F	12.3	4.4	1.0	0
Offered to those requesting it	24.6	18.7	5.9	2.3
Offered to all students	47.1	64.3	19.8	36.4

area was marginally related. Here, faculty in the social–behavioral sciences offered extra credit significantly more often (27% of courses) than did their colleagues in the natural sciences (1%), quantitative sciences (7%), and humanities (6%), univariate analysis of variance (ANOVA), $F(5, 88) = 2.5$, $p < .05$; Newman–Keuls follow-up tests, $p < .05$. A similar but nonsignificant trend, univariate ANOVA, $F(5, 94) = 1.7$, $p = .13$, was found for attitude, with social–behavioral science faculty expressing the most positive sentiments toward extra credit on average. Parallel analyses were not conducted on the URI faculty because of the small sample size. Predictably, faculty attitudes and practices related to extra credit converged; the obtained correlations between general attitude and frequency of offering extra credit were .52 and .68 for the US and URI samples, respectively.

Students and faculty were asked to name one potential disadvantage and one potential advantage of this extra credit. The principal disadvantage, as shown in Table 3, is that it encourages a lax or irresponsible attitude among students. A typical response in this category was: "students may slack off during the semester if they know the work can be made up later." Second in popularity as a disadvantage was the inequity of offering extra credit to some students but not others: "It unfairly penalizes the majority by unbalancing the grading system." More than twice the proportion of students than faculty suggested that not all students deserve the additional chance or special consideration afforded by extra credit, whereas more than twice the proportion of faculty argued that extra credit was a disfavor to overburdened students who did not adequately comprehend the basic course material. Although obviously a favor to students' grades, extra-credit assignments may impose more work on students who are unable to handle their current workload or may require learning additional conceptual material by students who are unable to master the normally assigned material.

Faculty and students provided even more divergent perspectives on the possible advantages of extra credit. As seen in Table 4, the three most frequent reasons for faculty were to: explore a topic in greater depth, compensate for a serious student illness or problem, and motivate students to work harder. By contrast, the top three reasons for students were to: provide students with a second chance, demonstrate and reward effort, and explore a topic in greater depth. Very few faculty members acknowledged that extra credit could properly compensate for deficient ability in exam taking or rectify an atypical "bad" day, but students regularly cited these as potential advantages.

The advantages and disadvantages provided a rich harvest of sarcasm and derision on the purpose of extra credit. These responses dramatically illustrated faculty division on the topic. Among the purported advantages of offering credit were: "to make up for a lazy professor who doesn't want to teach," "to remedy a lack of (student) intelligence," "it makes the faculty members look like they are very concerned about their students," and "maybe to keep a wealthy donor's child in school." Equally hostile but less veiled sentiments were expressed as disadvantages: "faculty sell-out," "legion of mediocrity," and "this is not kindergarten!" As Dressel (1976) observed, an instructor offering extra credit is frequently seen by colleagues as weakening or destroying standards.

Finally, we were interested in the logistics of offering and assigning extra credit. Taking the four subsamples as a

whole, 288 respondents reported on their most recent experience with extra credit. Most of the time (77%) students were made aware of its availability by public announcements to the entire class. Less frequent were private offers to individual students (6%) and public announcements followed by private encouragement (17%). In two thirds of the cases, there were no restrictions on which class members were offered extra credit. When certain restrictions did apply ($n = 67$), they tended to be a course average below a certain grade (63%), almost always below a C, and a specific request by the student for extra credit (51%). The extra-credit assignment usually involved written work (56%) or oral presentation (11%). Twelve percent of the respondents indicated that the type of extra credit depended on the individual student and the reason for the grade deficiency.

Discussion

One value of this study is that it provides professors with a better understanding of the differing perspectives their students have on the issue of extra credit. "It all depends on which side of the grade book you're on," one student quipped. The basic issue is perceived fairness. How do faculty and students arrive at their judgments of fairness, and what are the implications for the choices faculty must make about extra credit?

Table 3. Potential Disadvantages of Extra Credit

	Students		Faculty	
Disadvantage	US %	URI %	US %	URI %
Encourage lax or irresponsible attitude	41	31	18	25
Unfair to offer to selected students	15	12	22	18
Some students do not deserve it	5	10	1	0
Possibility of it being abused or taken advantage of	8	7	4	9
Grades may not reflect course knowledge	3	3	4	2
Basics not understood; why give more work	4	5	14	7
Devaluation of grading standards	5	1	11	5
None known	11	24	10	16
Other	8	7	16	18

Table 4. Potential Advantages of Extra Credit

	Students		Faculty	
Advantage	US %	URI %	US %	URI %
Provides second chance	24	36	10	0
Demonstrates and rewards effort	12	9	1	2
Match student's abilities and interests	7	7	4	7
Students have bad days	6	8	0	0
Compensate poor exam takers	8	4	2	4
Explore topic in greater depth	11	5	22	18
Motivate student to work harder	4	4	10	20
Serious illness or problem	3	3	17	4
Deficient background or preparation	1	2	7	0
None known	1	1	7	14
Other	23	21	20	29

As expected, faculty were less enthusiastic about extra credit than students were. Those in power favor equity; the powerless see the virtue in compassion. There were also notable institutional differences. The US students were more ready than URI students to reward assertiveness (requesters) and undo the effects of low grades, whereas URI students were more disposed to make the benefit universally available. In a similar fashion, when URI faculty approved extra credit, they were more ready to offer universal extra credit than were their US counterparts, who preferred to use extra credit to deal with low grades and other special cases. Perhaps different perspectives on grading and fairness guide these judgments.

Are grades a reward for hard work, a quantitative estimate of ability, and/or a means of providing constructive feedback to students? These questions concerning the purpose of evaluation may fuel some of the ferocity in the faculty lounge. If grades are a reward for hard work, then it seems fair to give students additional chances to work hard in order to master the material and boost their grades—anyone willing to put in extra effort deserves some extra points. If grades are a quantitative estimate of ability, then allowing some or all students to improve their grades decreases the validity of the estimate. This practice is unfair to students of measurably high ability and is misleading to others who may use grades as a basis for judging ability. However, there is a counterargument here: If the original method for assigning grades was itself invalid, then extra credit may rectify an inequitable grading system. Those who argue that "some students just don't do well on multiple-choice exams" are making this sort of case for extra credit.

If grades are a means of providing constructive feedback to promote students' learning, then it is important to determine what kinds of learning are to be shaped. When the teacher allows individualized learning objectives, extra credit may provide students with an opportunity to receive feedback on uniquely tailored learning experiences. This point is reflected in the potential advantages of "matches student's abilities and interests" and "allows exploration of a topic in greater depth." On the other hand, if the "basics are not understood" then the feedback is misleading and the effort misplaced.

Lurking in the wings for both faculty and students is the prospect that some lazy, irresponsible, and manipulative students will be rewarded or at least go unpenalized for their dysfunctional behavior if extra credit is permitted. We are back to the equity versus compassion debate. This issue becomes a problem only if the opportunity for extra credit is offered selectively (e.g., to the poorest performing or the loudest complaining students). In the case of our respondents, most extra-credit opportunities involve public announcements to the entire class and no eligibility restrictions, thus preserving equity.

Two reasons for giving extra credit were not mentioned by our respondents but are fairly common in our experience. First, the offer defuses the anxiety and hostility occasioned by the entire evaluation process. It provides the "illusion of control" to students. Bate (1976) believed extra credit can thus increase outside reading done by students, enhance motivation and interest, and reduce withdrawal rates. If

made publicly available to all students, this could be seen as an exercise of compassion without compromising equity. Second, a common extra-credit procedure in many large schools is to reward students for participating in psychological experiments. Although student participation ostensibly has educational value, the main reason for this practice is to maintain a pool of subjects.

In conclusion, we have presented the choices involved in offering extra credit, the pros and cons as seen by the respondents, and our own thoughts on the underlying decisions concerning when and how to use extra credit. Acting as a constructively provocative stimulus in the gadfly tradition, we have tried to take a little of the heat out of this barfight and to add a little more light. We leave it to the readers to use this information in making their own choices. And we leave it to future research to examine more thoroughly the uses and meanings of extra credit on the college level.

References

Bate, B. R. (1976). Extra credit: A token reinforcement system for increasing interest, motivation, and outside reading. In J. B. Maas & D. A. Kleiber (Eds.), *Directory of teaching innovations in psychology* (pp. 64–65). Washington, DC: American Psychological Association.

Clark, T. (1978). Creating contract learning. In O. Milton (Ed.), *On college teaching* (pp. 212–235). San Francisco: Jossey-Bass.

Davidson, W. B., House, W. J., & Boyd, T. L. (1984). A test–retest policy for introductory psychology courses. *Teaching of Psychology, 11*, 182–184.

Dressel, P. L. (1976). *Handbook of academic evaluation.* San Francisco: Jossey-Bass.

Eble, K. E. (1988). *The craft of teaching* (2nd ed). San Francisco: Jossey-Bass.

Ericksen, S. C. (1984). *The essence of good teaching.* San Francisco: Jossey-Bass.

Guskey, T. R. (1988). *Improving student learning in college classrooms.* Springfield, IL: Thomas.

Lloyd, M. E., & Lloyd, K. E. (1986). Has lightning struck twice? Use of PSI in college classrooms. *Teaching of Psychology, 13,* 149–151.

Lloyd, M. E., &Zylla, T. M. (1981). Self-pacing: Helping students establish and fulfill individualized plans for pacing unit tests. *Teaching of Psychology, 8,* 100–103.

McKeachie, W. J. (1986). *Teaching tips* (8th ed.). Lexington, MA: Heath.

McKeachie, W. J., Pintrich, P. R., Yi-Guang, L., & Smith, D. A. F. (1986). *Teaching and learning in the classroom: A review of the literature.* Ann Arbor, MI: National Center for Research to Improve Postsecondary Teaching and Learning.

Milton, O. (Ed.). (1978). *On college teaching.* San Francisco: Jossey-Bass.

Milton, O. (1982). *Will that be on the final?* Springfield, IL: Thomas.

Vogel, C. D., & Stark, J. S. (1986). *Postsecondary teaching and learning issues in search of researchers.* Ann Arbor, MI: National Center for Research to Improve Postsecondary Teaching and Learning.

Notes

1. We gratefully acknowledge the participation of students and faculty in providing the data for this study and the helpful comments of three anonymous reviewers on an earlier version of this article.

Extra Credit and Peer Tutoring: Impact on the Quality of Writing in Introductory Psychology in an Open Admissions College

Nancy Oley
Medgar Evers College
City University of New York

Many authors have noted that written assignments by students in introductory psychology courses are often of poor quality (e.g., Calhoun & Selby, 1979; Costin, 1982). Such writing deficits are particularly notable in open admissions institutions. Many factors may contribute to this problem: students' lack of prior successful academic experience, insufficient library skills, poor preparation in writing before entering the course, lack of familiarity with specific psychological concepts and vocabulary, inability of the instructor to provide adequate writing instruction in the course (Meade, 1983), and students' unwillingness to seek outside help with writing.

One goal of this study was to investigate the impact of some of these factors on students' writing. A second goal was to evaluate the effectiveness of two methods in overcoming writing deficits. Many strategies have been proposed to improve psychology students' writing. These proposals range from creating a separate required psychology writing/library skills course (Calhoun & Selby, 1979) to integrating the teaching of writing into existing psychology courses (Allen, 1984; Beers, 1985; Snodgrass, 1985; Spiegel, Cameron, Evans, & Nodine, 1980). This study explores an intermediate position. The approach differs from others that relied exclusively on student peers (Beers, 1986; Levine, 1990) and library staff to teach writing. This approach was intended to minimize the anxiety students experience when their writing is judged by the professor (Scanlon, 1979), to reduce the amount of time spent in class on basic writing skills, and to allow those with more training and/or experience in teaching such skills to do so. The study also differed from others (Allen, 1984; Boice, 1982) in the method of applying operant technology. The professor offered students extra credit in two different ways to encourage their repeated participation in individualized tutoring. This procedure was intended to promote both writing productivity (increased quantity of writing) and a concern for process (cognitive functions involved in writing).

Specifically, this study assessed the relations among prior academic success (GPA), prior skill and training in writing (writing placement scores and writing courses completed), knowledge of psychology (first exam grade), willingness to seek help (voluntary tutoring only), help received (tutoring, both voluntary and involuntary), and writing quality (final paper grade).

I hypothesized that (a) students who received help, whether voluntary or required, would write better papers than those who did not; (b) students who chose help voluntarily would write better papers than those who were required to obtain help; and (c) prior academic success, knowledge of psychology, and preparation in writing before entering the course would predict quality of writing and final exam results in the course only among students who did not receive help (i.e., students who received help would do well, regardless of their prior deficits).

Method

Subjects

Four sections of Introductory Psychology students ($N = 76$), all taught by the same instructor over two semesters, served as subjects. The students ranged in age from 17 to 60+ years old; 76% were women. They ranged in rank from first-semester freshmen to graduating seniors. Eighty-two percent of the students had failed the university placement exam in writing ($M = 7.31$, $SD = 1.85$; a passing grade was 10) when they entered the college and had been placed in developmental or remedial writing courses, and 40% had not completed the college course requirement in basic English when they enrolled in Introductory Psychology. Their mean GPA in the semester preceding the course was 2.65 ($A = 4.00$, $SD = .85$); their mean grade on the first psychology exam was 3.03 ($SD = .64$). An analysis of variance (ANOVA) revealed that the four sections did not differ in prior GPA, university writing placement scores, or grade on the first psychology exam, all $Fs < 1.00$. Eleven students were excluded from the study because their papers appeared to have been plagiarized ($n = 8$) or they did not complete the paper and final exam by the end of the semester ($n = 3$).

Procedure

A between-groups design was used to study the effectiveness of two types of help with writing, voluntary and compulsory. Three class sections were randomly assigned to the voluntary-consultation group and one to the forced-consultation group.

At the first class session, all subjects were given a five-page research paper assignment on the life and works of a famous psychologist. This assignment required them to use the psychologist's own writings as well as commentaries by the psychologist's contemporaries. In an effort to ensure that students had some library skills, they were required to attend 3 hr of in-class professional instruction on how to locate and use references relevant to their paper topics.

To compensate for the instructor's inability to provide writing instruction in the course, one consultant from the library and several from the tutorial and writing center staffs were made available to students outside of class on a voluntary or compulsory basis. A professional instructional library staff member provided individualized help with the organizational and research aspects of the paper. Peer tutors (i.e., advanced students with training in English and/or psychology) provided individualized tutoring in all aspects of the writing process.

The instructor encouraged students to seek help with writing from any and all of the consultants by offering two types of extra credit for documented tutoring sessions. For the voluntary group ($n = 52$, three class sections), consultations were not required, but extra credit was given for each consultation. This group was later subdivided into two groups, the consult group ($n = 19$, consulted at least once) and no-consult group ($n = 33$, never consulted), based on the students' choice. For the forced group ($n = 13$, one class section), the initial consultation was required (without extra credit), but each subsequent consultation earned one extra credit. The forced group was later subdivided into a consult group ($n = 10$) and a no-consult group ($n = 3$). For both groups, extra credit could be earned at any point in the writing process. The paper counted 20% of the final grade in the course.

The major outcome of interest was the final grade on the paper. To assure objectivity, unidentified copies of the papers were evaluated on a traditional 4-point scale (i.e., 4.0 for A, 3.0 for B, etc.) by the instructor. A faculty member from the Writing Center helped to identify plagiarized papers. The papers were judged on the basis of the following criteria: content, clarity, organization, references, vocabulary, grammar, spelling, punctuation, and paragraphing. Content and form were weighted equally in the overall subjective evaluation of quality.

Students were also evaluated on several other criteria believed to be important in determining their writing performance: (a) Prior level of skill in writing was first evaluated by a university placement examination when the students entered the college and later by the highest level of English writing course they had completed or were taking at the time they enrolled in Introductory Psychology; (b) overall academic success was estimated by students' GPA at the time they entered the course (or at the end of the semester, for first semester students); and (c) knowledge of psychology concepts and vocabulary was assessed by a multiple-choice examination, covering the first third of the course material given before the deadline for the writing assignment.

Results

The major prediction of this study was that students who received help, voluntary or involuntary, would write better papers than those who did not. As predicted, when all students in the voluntary and involuntary groups were consid-

ered together ($n = 65$), paper grades were significantly higher for those students who consulted at least once ($M = 3.47$) than for those who never consulted ($M = 3.08$), $t(63) = 2.083$, $p < .05$. The average paper grade was 3.26 ($SD = .72$), with a range from .70 to 4.30 (A+). As shown in Table 1, there was also a significant positive correlation between the number of tutoring sessions students attended (range = 0 to 9, $M = 1.1$) and paper grades, $r = .319$, $p < .05$. However, contrary to prediction, there was no reliable effect of group assignment on paper grades, $t(27) = .436$, $p > .05$. That is, students who obtained consulation voluntarily ($n = 19$) did not receive higher paper grades than students who obtained required consultation ($n = 10$); both types of reinforcement contingencies were effective.

Differences in paper grade between the consult and no-consult groups could not be explained by prior skill or training in writing: a chi-square analysis revealed that the consult and no-consult groups did not differ significantly with respect to the proportion of students who had passed the prerequisite English course before enrolling in psychology, $\chi^2(1, N = 65) = .015$, $p > .10$, or in the proportion of students who had passed the university writing placement exam, $\chi^2(1, N = 65) = 2.976$, $p > .05$. However, prior GPA was significantly higher for students in the consult group ($M = 2.97$) than for those in the no-consult group ($M = 2.43$), $t(60) = 2.743$, $p < .01$.

Only 76% of the students in the forced group actually consulted, and 37% in the voluntary group did so. Seventy-eight percent of the tutoring sessions were with peer tutors. Seventy-two percent of the students saw only peer tutors; 12% saw only the librarian, and 25% saw both. Students were more likely to consult if they had received 3.0 or higher on their first exam, $\chi^2(1, N = 65) = 4.361$, $p < .05$. There was also a significant difference in the two groups' average grade on the first exam ($M = 3.29$ for the consult group and 2.93 for the no-consult group), $t(63) = 2.450$, $p < .05$.

The interpretation of these results is complicated by the significant intercorrelations among the variables, as shown in Table 1. Paper grades (regardless of group assignment) were correlated with prior academic success, as measured by GPA before entering the course, $r = .534$, $p < .01$, and with

Table 1. Correlations Among Selected Measures

	Paper Grade	Number of Consults	Writing[a]	Exam[b]	GPA
Paper grade	—	.319* (65)	.263 (52)	.494** (65)	.534** (62)
Number of consults		—	.396** (52)	.352** (65)	.415** (62)
Writing			—	.381** (58)	.324* (57)
Exam				—	.518** (65)
GPA					—

Note. Numbers in parentheses represent the number of subjects. Pearson product–moment correlations are based on varying sample sizes, as data were available, using pairwise deletion to handle missing cases.
[a]Score on university writing placement exam. [b]Grade on first psychology exam.
*$p < .05$. **$p < .01$.

prior knowledge of psychology, as measured by grades on the first examination, $r = .494$, $p < .01$. Contrary to prediction, these variables were important for all students, not just those who chose not to consult.

Because of the significant intercorrelations observed among the variables investigated, an exploratory stepwise multiple regression analysis was performed to better understand the contribution of some of these variables to paper grades. However, the predictor variables of interest were correlated to such a high degree with GPA that none of them produced a significant increment in explained variance when they were entered after GPA.

Discussion

This study demonstrated a significant relationship between paper grades and several variables hypothesized to influence students' writing in psychology. Students' willingness to seek outside help with writing, familiarity with specific psychological concepts and vocabulary, and prior successful academic experience were all positively correlated with paper grades.

The best predictor of paper grades was GPA, which was also highly correlated with first exam grades and number of tutoring sessions attended. Skill in handling academic demands—whether that means preparing well for the first exam, taking advantage of tutoring, or writing good papers—results in higher grades: Good students do well. These findings underscore the importance of assessing students' prior academic success and knowledge of psychology before commencing a study of intervention strategies or even before assigning a class writing project (Meade, 1983).

The results also suggest that although several other variables affect writing success, library instruction, extra credit incentives, and one-to-one assistance with writing may help students overcome some of the writing problems they face in content courses. Tutoring was correlated with greater writing success whether students consulted voluntarily or involuntarily: The more help students received, the better they did, regardless of the type of reward offered. Moreover, the success of tutoring was unrelated to students' prior skill and training in writing.

It is unclear why students were not differentially affected by the type of reward offered for participation in tutoring. One possibility is that some students from the voluntary and forced groups exchanged information about their respective class requirements and, thus, reduced any differences that might have existed between them. This is unlikely, however, because our students are commuters who spend the least possible time on campus and tend not to interact socially with their own classmates, much less students from other classes.

My experience suggests that one-on-one peer (and staff) tutoring outside of class is a useful alternative to offering a separate course in writing for psychology students (Calhoun & Selby, 1979) or integrating writing instruction into the psychology course (Spiegel et al., 1980). The effectiveness of peer evaluation in improving writing, as compared with teacher evaluation, has been documented previously (Bea-

ven, 1977; Beers, 1986). Peer tutoring was certainly more popular than staff tutoring among the students in my study. Hence, more and better individualized help sessions with students' peers might be more useful than, for example, increasing the number of writing assignments.

How to get students to take advantage of tutoring is another matter. As indicated earlier, the extra credit option did not persuade all students in the voluntary condition to consult and did not guarantee that all students in the forced condition actually consulted. The reasons for this failure to consult are unclear. Informal observations indicated that some "good" students felt that they did not need assistance with writing and did not consult, despite the course requirement. A number of students apparently preferred to plagiarize rather than to become engaged in the writing process. The overall pattern of results further suggested that students with less prior academic success or less knowledge of psychology were less likely to consult than were their classmates in the voluntary condition. Perhaps they had given up before they began. Many of these less successful students face overwhelming family and work responsibilities outside of class and view tutoring of any kind as a luxury, not a necessity.

Unpublished studies at our open admissions institution (E. Barnes-Harrison, personal communication, June 1, 1989) indicate that getting students involved in tutoring is both a difficult challenge and a worthwhile endeavor. Higher student retention rates at the college have repeatedly been linked to participation in peer tutoring. For students whose prior educational experience has been largely unrewarding, these tutors seem to provide the social support and academic mentoring that students need to stay in school. How to get students involved in the tutorial process in a psychology course remains a challenge. One possibility may be to require each student, regardless of need, to meet with a prospective tutor at the beginning of the semester. This procedure might break the ice and encourage reluctant students to seek help when they need it.

References

Allen, G. J. (1984). Using a personalized system of instruction to improve the writing skills of undergraduates. *Teaching of Psychology, 11*, 95–98.

Beaven, M. B. (1977). Individualized goal setting, self-evaluation, and peer evaluation. In C. R. Cooper & L. Odell (Eds.), *Evaluating writing: Describing, measuring, judging* (pp. 135–156). Urbana, IL: National Council of Teachers of English.

Beers, S. E. (1985). Use of a portfolio writing assignment in a course on developmental psychology. *Teaching of Psychology, 12*, 94–96.

Beers, S. E. (1986). Questioning and peer collaboration as techniques for thinking and writing about personality. *Teaching of Psychology, 13*, 75–77.

Boice, R. (1982). Teaching of writing in psychology: A review of sources. *Teaching of Psychology, 9*, 143–147.

Calhoun, L. G., & Selby, J. W. (1979). Writing in psychology: A separate course? *Teaching of Psychology, 6*, 232.

Costin, F. (1982). Some thoughts on general education and the teaching of undergraduate psychology. *Teaching of Psychology, 9*, 26–28.

Levine, J. R. (1990). Using a peer tutor to improve writing in a psychology class: One instructor's experience. *Teaching of Psychology, 17,* 57–58.

Meade, M. J. (1983, August). *Student writing in courses: Specific strategies for minimizing faculty workload.* Paper presented at the convention of the American Psychological Association, Anaheim, CA. (ERIC Document Reproduction Service No. ED 2338784)

Scanlon, L. (1979, March). *Writing groups in an interdisciplinary program or getting around the professorial block.* Paper presented at the meeting of the North–East Modern Language Association, Hartford, CT. (ERIC Document Reproduction Service No. ED 169546)

Snodgrass, S. E. (1985). Writing as a tool for teaching social psychology. *Teaching of Psychology, 12,* 91–94.

Spiegel, T. A., Cameron, S. M., Evans, R., & Nodine, B. F. (1980). Integrating writing into the teaching of psychology: An alternative to Calhoun and Selby. *Teaching of Psychology, 7,* 242–243.

Notes

1. The assistance of James Hughes, Brenda Greene, Yvonne Bennett, Elendar Barnes-Harrison, Louis Pogue, Doris Withers, Glenna Williams, and Gregory Forsythe is gratefully acknowledged.

Blood, Sweat, and Trivia: Faculty Ratings of Extra-Credit Opportunities

G. William Hill, IV
Kennesaw State College

Joseph J. Palladino
University of Southern Indiana

James A. Eison
Center for Teaching Enhancement
University of South Florida

Many college students request opportunities to earn extra credit from their instructors. After all the "blood and sweat" that students put into trying to make a good grade, they may find themselves a little short of their preferred course grade, and they turn to us for another opportunity to improve their final grade. Few colleagues have never succumbed to student pressure for an extra-credit assignment. Regardless of their tendency to give extra credit, faculty may be concerned about its use. Despite the widespread use of extra-credit assignments (if our students are to be believed), Norcross, Horrocks, and Stevenson (1989) found very little mention of them in the teaching literature. We have been unable to find any research on the topic since publication of Norcross et al. (1989). The only references to extra credit that we located were articles describing specific activities or assignments that can be used for extra credit (Bauer & Snizek, 1989; LeUnes, 1984; Oley, 1992; Sugar & Livosky, 1988).

Norcross et al. (1989) surveyed faculty and students representing several disciplines at a large, public university and a medium-size, private institution about the use of extra credit in undergraduate classes. Approximately 75% of the faculty respondents reported that they did not currently offer extra-credit opportunities, but only 21% thought that extra credit should never be offered. Among those indicat-

ing that they would offer extra credit, 28% said that it should be routinely offered to all students, and 51% favored offering extra credit only under special circumstances (e.g., a low grade or a specific student request). Norcross et al. also found that a significantly larger percentage of faculty in the social and behavioral sciences reported giving extra credit than did their colleagues in other disciplines. Social and behavioral science faculty viewed the use of extra credit more favorably than did their colleagues in other disciplines, although this difference was not statistically significant.

Norcross et al. (1989) also found that student and faculty opinions concerning the advantages and disadvantages of extra credit varied. Major disadvantages listed by the students included encouraging lax student behavior (36%), offering extra credit to selected students (14%), and offering extra credit to undeserving students (8%). Faculty, however, listed encouraging lax behavior and making the offer to undeserving students as disadvantages less frequently (22% and 1%, respectively) and offering extra credit to selected students more frequently (20%). Eleven percent of the faculty indicated that offering extra credit was a disadvantage because it requires additional work when the basics were not understood, whereas only 5% of the students listed this issue as a disadvantage. Almost all students (99%) reported at least one advantage of offering extra credit, but

11% of the faculty identified no advantages. Students emphasized the advantages of providing a second chance (30%) and rewarding effort (11%). Faculty, however, were more likely to perceive extra credit as an opportunity to explore a topic in greater depth (20%), motivate students to work harder (15%), or to accommodate a serious illness or problem (11%). The advantages and disadvantages listed by faculty reflected a negative attitude toward offering extra credit.

Norcross et al.'s (1989) findings suggest that the use of extra credit is fairly common and, despite some disadvantages, is perceived by the majority of faculty as an acceptable aspect of course grading in certain circumstances. Although Norcross et al. asked faculty to list the extra-credit opportunities they had used, the researchers did not systematically investigate faculty opinions concerning specific types of extra credit.

Our study was designed to explore psychology teachers' use of a variety of extra-credit opportunities as well as the perceived educational value of each one. Because Norcross et al. (1989) found that faculty frequently listed the opportunity to explore course content in greater depth as an advantage of extra credit, we expected to find a positive correlation between usage and educational value. In addition, a frequently listed disadvantage of extra credit previously reported by both faculty and students was the possible inequity implicit in many opportunities to earn extra credit. Inequity could result from offering extra credit to selected students (e.g., those with lower grades) or from the inability of some students to accept the opportunity due to time constraints (e.g., the student has a job and cannot attend a lecture for extra credit because it conflicts with work hours). Therefore, we also assessed the degree to which faculty believed that students could complete particular extra-credit opportunities.

Method

Questionnaire and Procedure

A questionnaire consisting of 39 extra-credit opportunities was generated from lists of actual opportunities provided by participants at the Third Southeastern Conference on the Teaching of Psychology and by psychology students and faculty at the authors' institutions. We included a wide variety of opportunities (see Table 1).

The questionnaire included a brief explanation of the study and asked respondents to rate each extra-credit opportunity as to the likelihood that they would use it in one of their classes, its potential educational value, and the likelihood that all students would have equal opportunity to complete the activity. The three categories were rated on a 5-point scale ranging from *very high* (1) to *very low* (5). In addition, respondents were asked whether they limited extra-credit opportunities to a specific population of students, either as a function of the level of the class or of the student's course grade. Respondents were invited to share extra-credit assignments that they have used in the past as well as any general comments about extra credit. The questionnaire and a preaddressed, stamped envelope were mailed to 210 randomly selected members of Division Two, Teaching of Psychology, of the APA.

Respondents

Of the 98 returned questionnaires (47%), 7 were unusable (e.g., person was no longer teaching and large portions of the questionnaire were not filled out). Although several additional respondents failed to complete one or two of the demographic information items (e.g., gender, type of institution, and years of teaching experience), these subjects were included in the overall analyses. Of the remaining respondents ($n = 91$), 29% were women and 70% were men. The mean age of the respondents was 49, and they had been teaching for an average of 21 years. The types of institutions represented by the respondents were distributed as follows: 8% taught at 2-year colleges, 29% at 4-year colleges that offered no graduate degrees, 36% at 4-year colleges offering degrees through the master's level, and 26% at institutions offering a doctoral degree.

Results

Table 2 summarizes the respondents' use of extra credit. Thirty-one percent of respondents reported that they never gave extra-credit opportunities to a whole class. Of those respondents who reported giving extra credit to their classes, the majority either offered it to all classes (36%) or limited its use to freshman or sophomore courses (30%). Only 18% of the respondents indicated that they never offered extra credit to students. Most respondents (74%) indicated that they made extra-credit opportunities available to all students in a given class; for the remaining respondents, the offer of extra credit depended on a student's grade or a specific request by the student.

Neither respondents' gender nor the type of institution at which they teach were significantly related to the offer of extra credit to classes or an offer to specific students based on their grade or individual requests. Years of teaching experience were divided into early career (under 15 years) and late career (15 years and greater) based on the assumption of an average career of 30 years. For the 89 respondents who indicated years of teaching, teaching experience was unrelated to offers of extra credit based on a student's grade or request, $\chi^2(1, N = 89) = 1.81$, $p > .05$. Respondents with fewer than 15 years of teaching experience, however, were more likely to report giving extra credit to some classes ($n = 23$, 87%) than those with more than 15 years experience ($n = 66$, 62%), $\chi^2(1, N = 89) = 4.88$, $p < .05$.

For each of the extra-credit opportunities, Table 1 shows the means and standard deviations for reported use (ordered from most to least used), educational value, and the ability of students to complete the item (access). A significant positive correlation was found between the mean rated educational value of each extra-credit item and its frequency of use, $r = .76$, $p < .001$. The correlation between use and access was also significant, $r = .39$, $p < .05$, but the correlation between educational value and access was not, $r = .24$, $p > .05$.

Similar to Norcross et al.'s (1989) findings, our survey prompted strong reactions from faculty. Written comments ranged from "You're kidding," "Are such transparent con-

Table 1. Mean (Standard Deviations in Parentheses) Ratings for Usage, Educational Value, and Student's Ability to Complete the Opportunity (Access) for Each Extra-Credit Opportunity on the Questionnaire

Opportunity	Usage[a]	Educational Value	Access
Participating as a research subject	2.76 (1.51)	2.56 (.95)	2.22 (1.11)
Doing a research paper	3.15 (1.48)	1.62 (.76)	1.69 (.97)
Completing an original research project (e.g., experiment)	3.28 (1.51)	1.36 (.71)	2.58 (1.13)
Attending class	3.29 (1.68)	1.73 (.93)	1.41 (.86)
Summarizing an article from a professional journal	3.31 (1.44)	2.13 (.85)	1.76 (.99)
Making an oral presentation to the class on a topic related to course content	3.55 (1.30)	1.80 (.84)	1.96 (1.11)
Doing an exceptional job on a required assignment	3.59 (1.47)	2.04 (1.14)	2.04 (1.19)
Turning in all out-of-class assignments on time	3.64 (1.50)	2.69 (1.20)	1.60 (.90)
Correctly answering optional essay questions on an exam	3.75 (1.19)	2.32 (.84)	1.88 (1.18)
Attending an outside of class event (e.g., lecture or play) and preparing a written summary	3.77 (1.27)	2.28 (.90)	2.77 (1.12)
Attending a professional meeting or department colloquium and writing a summary	3.82 (1.22)	2.01 (.94)	2.88 (1.05)
Watching a movie or television program related to the class and preparing a summary	3.85 (1.11)	2.56 (.85)	2.33 (1.00)
Doing extra out-of-class readings	3.88 (1.28)	2.24 (.88)	2.01 (1.13)
Submitting a newspaper or magazine article related to course content	3.89 (1.37)	2.82 (1.00)	1.84 (1.11)
Showing improved performance on later tests	3.90 (1.22)	2.60 (1.09)	2.20 (1.10)
Doing a book report	3.96 (1.27)	2.57 (.94)	1.71 (1.08)
Correctly answering bonus test questions from chapters covered in class lectures	3.96 (1.18)	2.46 (.89)	1.85 (1.25)
Completing computer simulations or exercises related to course content	4.07 (1.24)	2.23 (.86)	2.59 (1.19)
Attending an outside of class event (e.g., lecture or play) without a written summary	4.09 (1.24)	3.08 (.99)	2.75 (1.12)
Arranging for a speaker or demonstration for the class	4.09 (1.13)	2.93 (1.04)	2.94 (1.24)
Conducting an interview with a designated type of individual	4.14 (1.19)	2.56 (1.00)	2.72 (1.16)
Writing an autobiography or keeping a journal	4.14 (1.11)	2.83 (1.08)	1.71 (1.02)
Handing in questions about the text or lecture content	4.24 (1.01)	2.42 (1.02)	1.64 (1.12)
Completing assignments that complement text material (e.g., identify a notable minority psychologist when the textbook does not mention even one)	4.26 (1.06)	2.34 (.94)	2.46 (1.21)
Tutoring fellow students	4.34 (.98)	1.92 (.92)	3.20 (1.03)
Submitting misleading graphs or tables from newspapers or magazines	4.37 (.95)	2.65 (.99)	2.39 (1.17)
Taking a pop quiz	4.40 (1.11)	3.19 (1.05)	1.76 (1.25)
Volunteering to do charity or community service work	4.41 (1.10)	2.87 (.92)	2.92 (1.20)
Answering study questions at the end of a textbook chapter	4.42 (.95)	2.48 (.86)	1.58 (1.10)
Creating a scrapbook of articles, advertisements, and shows related to course content	4.43 (.91)	2.93 (.95)	2.14 (1.09)
Submitting comic strips related to course content	4.52 (.94)	3.51 (.93)	2.15 (1.12)
Retaking the exam with the lowest grade at the end of term	4.59 (.88)	2.92 (1.06)	2.35 (1.37)
Taking a career interest inventory at the placement center and writing a report	4.67 (.82)	3.16 (1.05)	2.37 (1.20)
Finding spelling errors on an exam	4.69 (.85)	4.28 (.94)	2.00 (1.44)
Preparing a written comparison between the assigned textbook and another text	4.73 (.63)	2.50 (1.10)	2.81 (1.34)
Correctly answering trivia questions unrelated to course content on exams	4.84 (.54)	4.70 (.57)	2.65 (1.57)
Attending class on the day your professor wears clothing of a specified color	4.91 (.49)	4.69 (.88)	2.11 (1.53)
Donating blood	4.96 (.26)	4.58 (.62)	3.16 (1.32)
Donating food to the needy	4.97 (.23)	4.48 (.74)	2.90 (1.28)

Note. Each item was rated on a 5-point scale ranging from *very high* (1) to *very low* (5).
[a]Usage ratings are ordered from most to least used.

trol items necessary?" (remember that all items were actual extra-credit opportunities), and "I believe extra credit de-

Table 2. Usage of Extra-Credit Opportunities

Classes With Opportunities	%
All classes	36
Freshman- and sophomore-level only	30
Junior- and senior-level only	1
No classes	31
No response	2

Students With Opportunities	%
All students	74
Only those with an F	0
Only those with a D or lower	3
Only those with a C or lower	1
Only those who ask	2
Never give extra credit to students	18
No response	2

feats the purpose of knowing the material" to expressions of gratitude for new ideas for extra credit. Respondents also provided some of their own extra-credit opportunities, such as "writing a report on applications of the material presented in the text or lecture," "attending class on bad weather days," and "getting an A or B after certain holidays."

Discussion

Our finding that 18% of faculty never offered extra credit closely matched Norcross et al.'s (1989) finding that 21% of their respondents thought that it should never be offered. Our results, however, indicated that 67% of psychology faculty offered extra credit to at least some classes compared to only 25% of Norcross et al.'s sample. This discrepancy in reported use may be partly a function of differences in the two samples. Norcross et al. sampled faculty from all arts and sciences disciplines, whereas our sample consisted only of psychology faculty who were members of APA's Division Two.

Norcross et al. (1989) found that faculty in the social and behavioral sciences offered extra credit in significantly more classes (27%) than their colleagues in the natural sciences (1%), humanities (6%), and quantitative disciplines (7%). Social and behavioral faculty also had a more positive attitude toward the use of extra credit, but the difference was not significant. These trends are supported by our data because psychology faculty were probably included in Norcross et al.'s social–behavioral category. Furthermore, our results suggest that psychology faculty may be more likely than their colleagues in other disciplines to provide extra credit, particularly during the first half of their careers. One possible explanation for the large percentage of use reported by psychology faculty is the practice of giving extra credit to students who participate in research investigations. This extra-credit opportunity received the highest rated use (M = 2.76) of all items listed. The general acceptance of extra credit among psychology faculty is also indicated by articles that describe activities specifically offered as extra-credit opportunities (LeUnes, 1984; Oley, 1992; Sugar & Livosky, 1988).

Note, however, that Norcross et al. (1989) reported that the faculty sample from one university they surveyed may have been biased because an undetermined number of faculty responses disappeared from the collection box. Because the return rate from that institution was only 13% of the arts and science faculty, any comparison of the overall usage rates between our study and Norcross et al.'s should be considered tentative.

Written comments by our respondents were less hostile toward the use of extra credit than were those reported by Norcross et al. (1989). Our respondents' most frequent comment was that these items were being or should be used as required assignments rather than as optional extra-credit opportunities. Although we received some negative responses about the use and value of a study on extra credit, very few were as negative or sarcastic as those reported by Norcross et al.

Overall, the range of means for usage (2.76 to 4.97, SD = .52) indicates that all of the extra-credit opportunities on our list are used with low to moderate frequency. Although most (80%) of our respondents indicate that they offer extra credit to classes or students, our survey did not directly measure the frequency of such offers. The obtained means for usage suggest that although faculty indicate a willingness to provide extra-credit opportunities, they do not offer any particular opportunity with a high frequency. There was greater variability, however, in the rated educational value of the listed opportunities, with means ranging from 1.36 to 4.70 (SD = .82). The significant positive correlation between usage and educational value supported our hypothesis that faculty would use extra-credit opportunities that allowed students to explore a topic in greater depth. Opportunities that received high ratings in both educational value and usage included doing a research paper, summarizing an article from a professional journal, completing an original research project, and attending class. These ratings suggest that faculty may favor extra-credit opportunities that emphasize writing and synthesis of course material. Faculty rated opportunities that were peripheral or even unrelated to course content as low in both educational value and usage (e.g., donating blood, donating food, attending class on the day the professor wears clothing of a specified color, or answering trivia questions unrelated to course content).

Two matters not addressed in our study involve the ethics of extra credit use in general and the ethics of extra-credit opportunities that are of questionable educational value in particular. Although the use of extra credit is not specifically addressed in the Ethical Principles of Psychologists (American Psychological Association, 1992), several principles could be interpreted to suggest caution in the use of certain extra-credit assignments. For example, Principle 6.03(a) states "When engaged in teaching or training, psychologists present psychological information accurately and with a reasonable degree of objectivity" (p. 1607). An extension of this principle might be that extra-credit options that reflect an instructor's unique personal interests or values (e.g., giving blood, attending a particular lecture or play, or donating food to the needy) may raise ethical questions about an instructor's objectivity.

Results of Matthews and Hill's (1992) study support questioning the ethical appropriateness of some extra-credit options. They had psychology faculty rate the ethics of specific behaviors in teaching settings. One example involved giving blood or adopting an animal for extra credit in an introductory psychology class. Although the behavior encouraged in this instance may be laudable, this item had a mean rating of 4.30 on a 5-point scale (5 representing a judgment of *completely unethical behavior*). This rating suggests that psychology faculty may perceive the use of some extra-credit opportunities investigated in our study as violating ethical standards.

Another ethical issue suggested by Norcross et al.'s (1989) results is the potential inequity in the offer of and ability to complete extra credit. Offering extra credit to selected or undeserving students was a frequently listed disadvantage by their student and faculty respondents. The significant positive correlation between ratings for use and ability of students to complete the opportunities in our study indicates that faculty are sensitive to students' ability to complete a particular extra-credit opportunity. Note that our respondents think that students have a moderate to high ability to complete any of the extra-credit opportunities on our list (mean ratings ranged from 1.41 to 3.20). Faculty responses concerning the offer of extra credit, however, suggest that some faculty (6%) offer extra credit only to individual students. Thus, faculty seem generally to be concerned that all students have the opportunity to complete a particular assignment, but some faculty are willing to offer extra-credit options only to selected students.

Although opinions about extra credit vary dramatically, the practice of using extra credit appears to be well entrenched. Our results provide some comfort in that the most commonly used extra-credit opportunities were rated as highest in educational value and as least likely to be difficult for the majority of students to complete.

References

American Psychological Association. (1990). Ethical principles of psychologists and code of conduct. *American Psychologist, 47,* 1597–1611.

Bauer, H. H., & Snizek, W. E. (1989). Encouraging students in large classes to ask questions: Some promising results from classes in chemistry and sociology. *Teaching Sociology, 17,* 337–340.

LeUnes, A. (1984). The institutional tour: Some reflections. *Teaching of Psychology, 11,* 42–43.

Matthews, J. R., & Hill, G. W., IV. (1992). *Faculty opinions concerning ethical behavior in teaching.* Manuscript submitted for publication.

Norcross, J. C., Horrocks, L. J., & Stevenson, J. F. (1989). Of barfights and gadflies: Attitudes and practices concerning extra credit in college courses. *Teaching of Psychology, 16,* 199–203.

Oley, N. (1992). Extra credit and peer tutoring: Impact on the quality of writing in introductory psychology in an open admissions college. *Teaching of Psychology, 19,* 78–81.

Sugar, J., & Livosky, M. (1988). Enriching child psychology courses with a preschool journal option. *Teaching of Psychology, 15,* 93–95.

Notes

1. We appreciate the assistance of our colleagues and the participants at the Third Southeastern Conference on the Teaching of Psychology in providing us with examples of extra-credit assignments that they have used.

Faculty Use and Justification of Extra Credit: No Middle Ground?

John C. Norcross
Heather S. Dooley
University of Scranton

John F. Stevenson
University of Rhode Island

Few topics among academics precipitate as much acrimonious debate as offering extra credit in college courses. Why such a seemingly minor matter triggers such vehement reactions is at the heart of our work.

Although offering extra-credit assignments in college courses is apparently common, systematic examination of extra-credit practices on the college level has been negligible. Extra credit is not addressed in many of the standard works on college teaching (e.g., Ericksen, 1984; Guskey, 1988; Milton, 1978) or is mentioned as a subjective opinion rather than as a research topic (Eble, 1988; McKeachie, 1986).

Norcross, Horrocks, and Stevenson (1989) surveyed by mail 145 faculty and 525 students, regarding their views and use of extra credit. They found that extra-credit assignments were available in 12% to 20% of undergraduate courses. Students were far more positive toward the practice of extra credit than were faculty.

Our study was designed to extend those preliminary findings. Specifically, by interviewing professors at the same universities, we hoped to clarify the faculty rationales for and against extra credit and to identify specific instances in which it might be seen as an appropriate pedagogical or evaluative device.

Method

Participants

Two northeastern universities served as the survey sites. One is a medium-size, private institution in the liberal arts tradition (University of Scranton [US]); the other is a large public institution (University of Rhode Island [URI]). We tried to contact all of the 213 full-time faculty at US. We reached 210 faculty members, but 29 were unusable for various reasons (6 teachers were on sabbatical, 6 taught only graduate courses, 7 had not been teaching lately, and 10 declined the interview), leaving 181 completed interviews. Because of the large size of the URI faculty, we sampled every fourth member from an alphabetical list of 914 faculty. We reached 145 faculty members within three calls, but 39 were unusable for various reasons (14 teachers were on sabbatical, 10 taught only graduate courses, 9 had been not teaching lately, 6 declined the interview), leaving 106 completed interviews. The US sample contained 24% women; the URI sample, 18% women. Respondents primarily represented the humanities (32% at US and 18% at URI), natural sciences (17% and 38%, respectively), business/management (19% and 12%, respectively), and social/behavioral sciences (12% and 15%, respectively).

Procedure

A 10-min structured telephone interview was developed for this study. Instructors were asked to provide the average size of their courses, number of undergraduate courses taught in the past two semesters, and the number of those courses in which they provided extra credit. Then they were asked to describe an instance in which they thought extra credit was appropriate and the rationale they applied in that situation. Next, instructors were presented with six situa-

| Situation | Likelihood | | % Who Would Offer Extra Credit | |
	M	SD	Never or Almost Never	Always or Almost Always
A student desires to explore a topic more extensively.	27.7	36.6	59	14
Personal problems are hurting academic achievement.	21.0	33.5	68	7
Hardworking student does poorly despite help from teacher.	21.4	32.6	65	7
English is second language. Initially, student does poorly but improves. Overall grade is still low.	27.3	35.2	57	8
Student is admitted to an academic development program. He or she writes poorly but participates.	24.1	33.9	61	8
Student consistently performs well but has one poor grade. Exam might have been unclear.	21.7	34.7	68	10

tions and asked to assign their likelihood (0% to 100%) of offering extra credit in each circumstance, assuming that the student asked them personally and in private for the opportunity to do extra-credit work. The six situations were to: stimulate exploration of a topic in greater depth, compensate for acute illness or problem, reward effort, account for cultural differences, respond to deficient preparation, and compensate for possibly faulty evaluation procedures (see Table 1).

Results

The percentage of faculty offering extra credit in their undergraduate courses was calculated as a ratio of the number of classes with extra credit over the total number of classes. During the past two semesters, 78% of the respondents had not offered extra credit; 8% had offered it in all of their classes. Extra credit was offered in 13% of undergraduate courses.

When asked to identify an instance in which extra credit was appropriate, only 41% ($n = 119$) of the respondents could describe even one such instance. Frequent nominations were as follows: only when it was offered to the entire class as part of the course structure ($n = 24$); when a student missed an exam for a legitimate reason, such as an illness or emergency ($n = 18$); when a student wanted to explore a class-related topic in greater detail ($n = 14$); when students and/or the instructor desired to boost exam grades ($n = 10$); and when the instructor provided bonus questions or problems on a required exam ($n = 9$).

Then these 119 faculty provided a rationale for offering extra credit, and a few generated several rationales, leading to 136 codable responses. The most common reasons were that extra credit offers an alternative grading method to meet individual needs ($n = 16$); motivates and challenges students ($n = 15$); allows students a second opportunity to master the material and improves ability ($n = 11$); compensates for unrepresentative student performance due to a "bad day" or "slump" ($n = 11$); improves grades ($n = 9$); rectifies an uncontrollable situation, such as a student illness or emergency ($n = 8$); encourages creativity and independence ($n = 7$); adds a learning dimension not available in the textbook or classroom ($n = 5$); and assists students, especially freshmen, in adjusting to new teachers ($n = 4$).

The 168 faculty members who could not identify an instance when extra credit was appropriate were asked why they opposed the practice. In descending order of frequency, the most common reasons were as follows: an equal opportunity must be provided for all students ($n = 67$); the course assignments on the syllabus are necessary and sufficient ($n = 43$); there is already enough to do in the class ($n = 31$); extra credit distorts the meaning of the assigned grade ($n = 17$); other available methods, such as exam curves, rewrite opportunities, and dropping the lowest grade, handle the situation ($n = 16$); and extra class work already contributes to student grades, as reflected in exam performance and class participation ($n = 12$).

Table 1 presents the likelihood of faculty offering extra credit in six specific situations. Over half of the faculty gave a probability of offering extra credit between 0% and 9% ("never or almost never") in all six instances. Conversely, less than 15% gave a probability between 91% and 100% ("always or almost always") in all cases. In other words, the chance of a student securing an extra-credit opportunity was not significantly related to the particular reasons for requesting it.

Discussion

There is little middle ground among faculty on the controversial topic of extra credit. Approximately 60% to 70% of responding college teachers were adamant about refusing to offer extra credit, and about 10% always provided extra-credit opportunities. Between these two poles were 20% to 30% who occasionally offer it, depending on the specific situation. However, our results demonstrated that an instructor's attitude toward extra credit, rather than the circumstances of the particular course or the individual student, largely determined whether it was offered.

Two major conclusions emerged from the practices of college instructors who routinely offer extra credit to their students. First, these teachers make it available to all students in the class, build it into the course structure, and describe it in the syllabus. These practices mute the criticism that extra credit is selectively and covertly provided to a few, possibly undeserving, students. Second, advocates of extra credit in this sample and elsewhere (e.g., Appleby, 1987; Bate, 1976; Gershaw, 1990; Oley, 1992) contend that it enhances student learning. Instead of being viewed largely as a means of increasing grades, extra credit is seen as facilitating hard work, course relevance, outside reading, and student enthusiasm. This application of extra credit is consistent with the growing body of work on intrinsic motivation in higher education (e.g., Deci & Ryan, 1985; Lowman, 1990).

We were surprised by the relatively undifferentiated reactions of faculty to our six situations. These described diverse roles of student evaluation (e.g., incentive for learning, reward for effort, and measure of individual differences in student achievement). We expected faculty to be more sympathetic to applications of extra credit in some circumstances than in others, consistent with the more general view of the role of student evaluation and course grades. However, such variations of this sort were too minor to support this expectation. Instead, faculty were more likely to take a global stance on the utility of extra credit, generally a negative one.

References

Appleby, D. C. (1987). Using *Psychology Today* articles to increase the perceived relevance of the introductory course. *Teaching of Psychology, 14,* 172–174.

Bate, B. R. (1976). Extra credit: A token reinforcement system for increasing interest, motivation, and outside reading. In J. B. Maas & D. A. Kleiber (Eds.), *Directory of teaching innovations in psychology* (pp. 64–65). Washington, DC: American Psychological Association.

Deci, E. L., & Ryan, R. M. (1985). *Intrinsic motivation and self-determination in human behavior.* New York: Plenum.

Eble, K. E. (1988). *The craft of teaching* (2nd ed.). San Francisco: Jossey-Bass.

Ericksen, S. C. (1984). *The essence of good teaching.* San Francisco: Jossey-Bass.

Gershaw, D. A. (1990). *Use and success of grade insurance in psychology courses.* Unpublished manuscript, Arizona Western College, Yuma.

Guskey, T. R. (1988). *Improving student learning in college classrooms.* Springfield, IL: Thomas.

Lowman, J. (1990). Promoting motivation and learning. *College Teaching, 38,* 136–140.

McKeachie, W. J. (1986). *Teaching tips* (8th ed.). Lexington, MA: Heath.

Milton, O. (Ed.). (1978). *On college teaching.* San Francisco: Jossey-Bass.

Norcross, J. C., Horrocks, L. J., & Stevenson, J. F. (1989). Of barfights and gadflies: Attitudes and practices concerning extra credit in college courses. *Teaching of Psychology, 16,* 199–203.

Oley, N. (1992). Extra credit and peer tutoring: Impact on the quality of writing in introductory psychology in an open admissions college. *Teaching of Psychology, 19,* 78–81.

Notes

1. An earlier version of this article was presented at the annual meeting of the Eastern Psychological Association, New York, April 1991.

Empowering the Marginal Student: A Skills-Based Extra-Credit Assignment

Ellen N. Junn
Department of Child Development
California State University, Fullerton

Although the topic of extra credit is familiar and often controversial for college students and faculty alike, the use of extra-credit assignments in undergraduate courses has escaped much empirical scrutiny. As Norcross, Horrocks, and Stevenson (1989) pointed out, extra credit does not appear as an index term in *Psychological Abstracts* and is rarely mentioned (e.g., Guskey, 1988; McKeachie, 1986). Indeed, only four articles in *Teaching of Psychology* addressed the topic of extra credit: Norcross, Dooley, and Stevenson (1993) and Norcross et al. (1989) assessed faculty and student attitudes and practices regarding extra-credit assignments and found that most faculty had a globally negative view of extra credit; Oley (1992) described a peer tutoring exercise to improve students' research paper writing skills; and Sugar and Livosky (1988) described a child observation and journal writing option.

Norcross et al. (1989) reported that students widely endorsed the use of extra credit in college courses, believing that it should be offered routinely to all students. Similarly, students' second most popular incentive (following "release from final examination") was extra "points toward course grade" (Bebeau, Eubanks, & Sullivan, 1977, p. 142). These positive attitudes are also reflected in students' behavior; for example, 95% of the psychology faculty at a midsized university reported that at least one student had approached them seeking extra-credit options (Junn, 1990).

In contrast to student attitudes, faculty sentiments often are markedly less positive. For example, in Norcross et al.'s (1989) survey, only 20% to 30% of instructors reported offering extra credit in their courses. Instructors' three most frequently cited reasons for disapproving of extra-credit assignments included "encourages lax or irresponsible attitude," "unfair to offer to selected students," and "basics not understood; why give more work." Despite faculty skepticism, they did, however, acknowledge that some advantages might include "explore a topic in greater depth," "compensate for a serious student illness or problem," and "motivate students to work harder" (Norcross et al., 1989, p. 201).

Faculty have also expressed negative attitudes about the effectiveness of their interventions with failing students. For example, Junn (1990) found that only 19% of faculty surveyed believed that any of their interventions (e.g., reviewing past exams and referrals to the campus learning center) actually improved the performance of their failing students. In fact, faculty attributed students' continued failure to competing time commitments and lack of intellectual or linguistic ability. Thus, many faculty may experience cynicism and powerlessness when they try to assist failing students.

Instructors who permit extra-credit options most often required additional written work (Norcross et al., 1989). Unfortunately, these assignments do little to improve weaker students' deficiencies in study or exam-taking skills. Underprepared students may be at greater risk for failure because outside written papers require additional time that may otherwise be directed toward mastering the normally assigned material. Thus, the purpose of the present study was to improve the marginal or failing student's course performance by explicitly rewarding students for using good studying strategies.

Method

Participants

The experimental group consisted of 12 students who were averaging a grade of D+ or lower after two exams (which were roughly 70% objective and 30% essay). These 12 were all the eligible students from three undergraduate psychology courses taught during the same term by the same instructor: one section of Critical Thinking and two sections of Infancy, mean $n = 20$. The remaining 47 students in these classes comprised the nonfailing control group. Also, a matched control group of 12 failing students was drawn from the same three courses that had been taught within 2 years of the experimental group's courses. These students' midterm exam scores were within 6% of the experimental group's scores.

Materials

A handout described the seven learning activities required to obtain extra credit. These activities involved learning strategies that positively relate to students' cognitive or academic performance. Item 1 required student attendance for all remaining class sessions. Item 2 required students to turn in weekly detailed, well-organized, and highlighted copies of their class notes; late notes received fewer points. Awarding points contingent on the timing and quality of work combats student procrastination (Bufford, 1976; Glick & Semb, 1978). Although students in all groups received skeletal outlines highlighting important

concepts from lecture (e.g., Boswell, 1980), students in the experimental group had to expand on these points and provide relevant examples from both class and their own experiences (Baker & Lombardi, 1985; Palkovitz & Lore, 1980). For Item 3, experimental students submitted weekly detailed notes and questions of the assigned readings by using active reading strategies such as the Survey, Question, Read, Recite, Review (SQ3R) method (F. P. Robinson, 1961) or the Preview, Question, Read, Reflect, Recite, Review (PQ4R) method (Thomas & H. A. Robinson, 1972). Item 4 requested that students submit weekly flash cards with terms or questions written on one side and explanations on the reverse side. Item 5 asked students to generate at least 12 specific mnemonic devices (e.g., their own acronyms) for each week's class and associated readings. For Item 6, students documented other forms of active learning, such as engaging in cooperative studying with others (Annis, 1983; Bouton & Garth, 1983) or delivering a minilecture (to an audience or alone onto an audiotape). Documentation was as simple as supplying an audiotaped recording of these activities. Finally, Item 7 encouraged students to participate more frequently in class. The more regularly students engaged in these activities, the more points they could earn—up to 15 extra-credit points (1.7% of the total).

Procedure

After the second exam (roughly midsemester), all students at risk for failing were given a note telling them not to feel discouraged and to meet with the instructor for a "plan to help their performance." During these short individual meetings, students were encouraged to focus on future efforts. The instructor suggested that students should attribute their poor exam performance to external factors, such as ineffective learning strategies (Anderson & Jennings, 1980).

Experimental group. The instructor discussed the extra-credit assignment and handout. Each subsequent week, students were responsible for turning in their extra-credit work without reminders from the instructor. The instructor checked their efforts (usually in time to return the materials by the next class session) and made comments and corrections either in writing or in person. Reviewing each week's materials required roughly 10 min per student. The instructor maintained a running, dated record of the quantity and quality of the work submitted for each of the seven items (e.g., noting that "class notes missed several key concepts" or "excellent flash cards"). The instructor allocated extra-credit points just before the final exam.

Matched control group. Like the experimental group, these potentially failing students were encouraged to adopt a positive, forward-looking attitude and to meet with the instructor whenever necessary. During individual meetings, the instructor encouraged these failing students to engage in the same study skills as the experimental group but did not provide a handout or the incentive of 15 points.

Nonfailing comparison group. No special interventions were directed toward passing students; they could, however, earn the usual extra-credit points by answering the extra-credit exam questions or by volunteering to participate in experiments.

Results

Exam Scores

Three *t* tests were performed to compare midterm to final exam scores for each group. Experimental students significantly increased their exam scores from the midterm (M = 57.9%, SD = 8.5) to the final (M = 70.0%, SD = 16.5), $t(11)$ = 3.27, $p < .01$. In contrast, the matched control group, without an intervention, showed no significant improvement from midterm (M = 63.8%, SD = 5.8) to the final exam (M = 66.5%, SD = 10.6), $t(11) = 1.41$, $p > .05$. The nonfailing control students also did not improve from the midterm (M = 85.5%, SD = 11.1) to the final exam (M = 85.9%, SD = 12.3), $t(46) = .48$, $p > .05$. These results suggest that the extra-credit assignment helped marginal and failing students improve their exam performance. Lack of improvement by the nonfailing control students, who were enrolled in the same courses as the experimental group, rules out the competing explanation that other features of those particular classes that semester (e.g., an easier final exam) accounted for the experimental group's improvement.

Student Retention Rates

Despite the attempt to match control students to experimental students on midterm exam scores, the experimental group actually performed significantly worse (M = 57.9%, SD = 8.5) than the control group (M = 63.8%, SD = 5.8), $t(22) = 2.80$, $p < .01$. The reason for this disparity was that six potential control students with extremely low scores (e.g., 45% and below) never took the final exam and simply "disappeared" from class after the individual meeting with the instructor. One possible explanation for their disappearance may be that students with exceptionally poor scores who were not given special extra-credit options may have felt helpless and cut their losses. In contrast, no student with the extra-credit assignment dropped out of the course or failed to show up for the final exam, despite some extremely poor scores.

A chi-square analysis, using Yates's correction for continuity for small frequencies, comparing the retention rates in the three experimental courses versus the three matched control courses approached statistical significance, $\chi^2(1, 134) = 3.50$, $p = .06$. This result suggests that the extra-credit assignment may increase retention rates among marginal and failing students.

Final Grades

Another chi-square analysis, using Yates's correction, indicated that significantly more students from the experimental group obtained final course grades of C or better (even when subtracting the points earned from the extra-credit assignment) than students from the matched control group, $\chi^2(1, 24) = 4.29$, $p < .05$. In fact, 8 of the 12 experimental students received passing final grades (1 B, 7 Cs, 3 Ds, and 1 F), whereas none of the 12 control students passed the course (10 Ds and 2 Fs). This result is all the more striking because the experimental group performed significantly worse than the control group at the midterm assessment.

Student Study Habits and Reactions

Eleven of 12 experimental students anonymously completed a questionnaire about their study habits before and after receiving the assignment and their reactions to it. Although a questionnaire regarding study habits should also have been administered at the beginning of the course, students had no reason to misrepresent the truth. All students now reported engaging in four study strategies: rewriting class notes (previously used by 64% of the students), taking notes from the readings (previously 45%), making flash cards, and generating mnemonics (both previously 36%). The rate of studying with others increased from 0% to 50%, and the rate of regular studying (at least every other day) increased from 9% to 50%.

Students rated various aspects of the extra-credit assignment on 5-point scales ranging from *very negative* (1) to *very positive* (5). They were very positive about having the opportunity to do this exercise (M = 4.8, SD = 0.4). The most useful specific feature was getting feedback from the instructor (M = 4.9, SD = 0.3). Following this, students rated reorganizing class notes as very helpful (M = 4.7, SD = 0.5) and being forced to distribute their studying, as opposed to cramming (M = 4.64, SD = 0.67). The next three most helpful strategies were making flash cards of important concepts (M = 4.5, SD = 0.8), writing notes and questions based on the readings (M = 4.5, SD = 0.7), and generating their own mnemonic devices (M = 4.4, SD = 0.7).

The least liked feature of this extra-credit exercise was the amount of time required to complete the assignment. Although two students expressed some resentment over the effort involved, the remaining students clearly understood that their newfound successes partially depended on increased commitment in time and effort. One wrote, "Not enough time—felt very pressured (but this was actually good for me in the end—it worked!)." When queried on the best features of this extra-credit assignment, students primarily focused on avoiding the perils of procrastination. For example, one wrote, "It made me sit down and study on a schedule rather than randomly studying on whichever days." On the topic of increasing study skills and motivation, comments included, "Gave me extra credit, while *encouraging* me to develop a pattern of better study habits and devices," and "I do very poorly on tests. Therefore, the extra credit gave me a positive attitude. It gave me hope."

Discussion

This innovative but simple extra-credit exercise produced positive outcomes. First, students who participated in this assignment engaged in a wider variety of effective learning and study strategies and to a greater degree than they had in the past. Second, these study skills improved students' later exam performance. Third, significant improvement on exams resulted in reducing the number of failing students. Fourth, student retention rates in courses increased as a function of providing failing students with a vehicle for maintaining higher motivation. Fifth, providing extra-credit options for poorly performing students may offset learned helplessness and enhance student interest and desire to persist (Bate, 1976). Finally, this assignment can be easily modified for any course. Unlike more traditional forms of extra credit (e.g., writing additional papers or participating in psychology experiments), this assignment directly helps students master the course material.

One important recommendation for instructors includes providing alternative extra-credit options (e.g., extra-credit exam questions) for all students in the course. Norcross et al.'s (1993) faculty survey showed that providing extra credit to select students was the most common argument against the use of extra credit. Indeed, last year, my Faculty Senate asked the Academic Standards Committee to review the university's policy on the use of extra-credit options for similar reasons. After much discussion, the Academic Standards Committee, with the approval of the Senate, recommended that, if faculty used extra-credit options, the information be presented on the course syllabus and discussed explicitly with students.

Another suggestion is to rework the items required for the exercise. For example, two students thought that making stacks of flash cards was tedious; an alternative is to require that students submit an audiocassette of themselves practicing flash card terms. More recently, I modified the assignment by including an eighth item that asked students to seek tutoring or attend workshops on study or test-taking skills at the campus learning center.

Perhaps one student's comment sums it up best when she wrote in an unsolicited personal note after completing the class:

> I want to thank you for helping me through [the class]. Never before has anyone showed me your technique of studying. . . . I used it for biology and went from an F to a C on a test. I wish I knew this technique sooner. Thanks tons!

References

Anderson, C. A., & Jennings, D. L. (1980). When experiences of failure promote expectations of success: The impact of attributing failure to ineffective strategies. *Journal of Personality, 48,* 393–407.

Annis, L. F. (1983). The processes and effects of peer tutoring. *Human Learning, 2,* 39–47.

Baker, L., & Lombardi, B. R. (1985). Students' lecture notes and their relation to test performance. *Teaching of Psychology, 12,* 28–32.

Bate, B. R. (1976). Extra credit: A token reinforcement system for increasing interest, motivation, and outside reading. In J. B. Mass & D. A. Kleiber (Eds.), *Directory of teaching innovations in psychology* (pp. 64–65). Washington, DC: American Psychological Association.

Bebeau, M. J., Eubanks, J. L., & Sullivan, H. J. (1977). Incentive preferences of introductory psychology students. *Teaching of Psychology, 4,* 141–143.

Boswell, D. A. (1980). Evaluation of transparencies for psychology instruction. *Teaching of Psychology, 7,* 171–173.

Bouton, C., & Garth, R. (1983). *Learning in groups.* San Francisco: Jossey-Bass.

Bufford, R. (1976). Evaluation of a reinforcement procedure for accelerated work rate in a self-paced course. *Journal of Applied Behavior Analysis, 9,* 208.

Glick, D. M., & Semb, G. (1978). Effects of pacing contingencies in personalized instruction: A review of the evidence. *Journal of Personalized Instruction, 3,* 36–42.

Guskey, T. R. (1988). *Improving student learning in college classrooms.* Springfield, IL: Thomas.

Junn, E. (1990). [Undergraduate psychology faculty attitudes and practices regarding extra credit assignments: Data from a state university campus]. Unpublished raw data.

McKeachie, W. J. (1986). *Teaching tips* (8th ed.). Lexington, MA: Heath.

Norcross, J. C., Dooley, H. S., & Stevenson, J. F. (1993). Faculty use and justification of extra credit: No middle ground? *Teaching of Psychology, 20,* 240–242.

Norcross, J. C., Horrocks, L. J., & Stevenson, J. F. (1989). Of barfights and gadflies: Attitudes and practices concerning extra credit in college courses. *Teaching of Psychology, 16,* 199–203.

Oley, N. (1992). Extra credit and peer tutoring: Impact on the quality of writing in introductory psychology in an open admissions college. *Teaching of Psychology, 19,* 78–81.

Palkovitz, R. J., & Lore, R. K. (1980). Note taking and note review: Why students fail questions based on lecture material. *Teaching of Psychology, 7,* 159–161.

Robinson, F. P. (1961). *Effective study.* New York: Harper & Row.

Sugar, J., & Livosky, M. (1988). Enriching child psychology courses with a preschool journal option. *Teaching of Psychology, 15,* 93–95.

Thomas, E. L., & Robinson, H. A. (1972). *Improving reading in every class: A source book for teachers.* Boston: Allyn & Bacon.

Notes

1. I thank Ruth L. Ault, Diana Guerin, and three anonymous reviewers for their helpful comments and suggestions.

Academic Dishonesty: Prevalence, Determinants, Techniques, and Punishments

Stephen F. Davis
Emporia State University

Cathy A. Grover
Texas A&M University

Angela H. Becker
Texas A&M University

Loretta N. McGregor
Southern Arkansas University

Academic dishonesty is a perennial problem in higher education. Although scholarly reports of academic dishonesty have appeared for more than 60 years, a concerted research effort was mounted only during the past 20 years. This increased interest may reflect the fact that "cheating has become one of the major problems in education today" (Singhal, 1982, p. 775). For example, Haines, Diekhoff, LaBeff, and Clark (1986) stated that "student dishonesty on college campuses throughout the nation has been widely recognized as epidemic" (p. 342).

Published accounts suggest that these statements may be accurate and that cheating has escalated recently. Drake (1941) reported a cheating rate of 23%, whereas Goldsen, Rosenberg, William, and Suchman (1960) reported rates of 38% and 49% for 1952 and 1960, respectively. Hetherington and Feldman (1964) and Baird (1980) reported cheating rates of 64% and 76%, respectively. Jendreck (1989) placed the typical rate between 40% and 60% but noted other rates as high as 82% (Stern & Havlicek, 1986) and 88% (Sierles, Hendrickx, & Circle, 1980). Clearly, we need more research designed to understand academic dishonesty and how to deal with it.

Method

Four years ago, we developed a 21-item survey. Students take 10 to 15 min to complete the questionnaire anonymously. The first three questions deal with general attitudes toward cheating. For example, Question 1 asks "Is it 'wrong' to cheat?," and Question 2 is "Should students go ahead and cheat if they know they can get away with it?" Question 3 asks "Should students try to cheat even when they know that their chances of getting away with it are very slim?"

Question 4 deals with whether the student has cheated in high school and/or college. If the answer is yes, students answer Question 5 about how they cheated. Questions 6 through 9 ask whether the student has been caught cheating, who detected the incident, the penalty involved, and if the student had knowledge of the penalty before cheating.

Questions 10 through 13 concern students' intent when allowing someone else to cheat from their exam. Questions 14 through 18 ask students to react to two hypothetical situations that entail either little or much effort and preparation for a test.

Question 19 taps students' opinions about the instructor's concern with cheating. Questions 20 and 21 concern appropriate measures for preventing cheating and dealing with offenders. This questionnaire has been administered to more than 6,000 students at large state schools ($n = 8$), medium state schools ($n = 8$), large private schools ($n = 5$), small private schools ($n = 8$), and 2-year schools ($n = 6$).

Prevalence

Most students say that it is wrong to cheat. For example, the percentage of students answering yes to the question "Is it wrong to cheat?" has never been below 90%. This opinion contrasts sharply with the mean percentage of students who report having cheated in either high school or college or both (76%). Rates of cheating in high school range from 51% reported by women at a small state university to 83% reported by men at a large state university. These high school cheating rates are to be contrasted with those reported at the collegiate level. A low of 9% was reported by one sample of women at a small private liberal arts college; a high of 64% was reported by men at a small regional university. There is a significant decrease in the incidence of cheating from high school to college, smallest $\chi^2(1, N = 183) = 3.96, p < .05$. Except for extending the range of collegiate cheating downward, our data are similar to those reported by Jendrick (1989).

Gender and institutional affiliation influence cheating. Women consistently report lower cheating rates than men in high school and college. This difference was statistically reliable, smallest $\chi^2(1, N = 167) = 4.61, p < .05$, in all but one instance. The percentages of men and women at small, private liberal arts colleges who reported having cheated in college are significantly lower, smallest $\chi^2(1, N = 218) = 4.23, p < .05$, than those reported by their counterparts at larger state and private institutions.

Determinants

What factors influence academic dishonesty? Are certain students more likely to cheat than others?

Situational Determinants of Cheating

Drake (1941) suggested that stress and the pressure for good grades are important determinants of academic dishonesty. Keller (1976) reported that 69% of the students in his study cited pressure for good grades as a major reason for cheating. Baird (1980) and Barnett and Dalton (1981) indicated that these pressures are important and that faculty members may not fully comprehend the stress experienced by their students.

Large, crowded classes that use only multiple-choice exams foster cheating (Houston, 1976). Computerized test banks that enable instructors to scramble the order of test questions may help alleviate this problem.

Answers to Question 5 suggest why students allow other students access to their answers during an exam. The most popular reason, "because he/she was a friend," was cited by a low of 76% in one sample and a high of 88% in another. On a positive note, the percentage of students allowing others to cheat for monetary considerations ranged from a low of .30% to a high of only 8.00%. A sampling of some other reasons is interesting and instructive because each statement reflects similar comments by several students.

1. He was bigger than me.
2. I knew they needed to do good in order to pass the class. I felt sorry for them.
3. I wouldn't want them to be mad at me.
4. She was damn good-looking.
5. Because they might let me cheat off of them sometime.
6. No particular reason. It doesn't bother me because I probably have it wrong and so will they.
7. I knew they studied and knew the material, but test taking was really difficult.
8. Just to do it. I didn't like the teacher, and I knew if I got caught nothing would happen.

Keith-Spiegel (1990) corroborated several of these sentiments. For example, she indicated that:

1. We put a lot of pressures on our students.
2. Young people see huge reinforcing properties in cheating. It's everywhere.
3. A new view of academic ownership appears to be emerging among our students. One student thought that buying a term paper justified his claiming somebody else's work as his own.
4. Our students have a new view about cheating. One respondent saw nothing wrong with a student cheating from another student's exam when the two had arranged a collusion.

Dispositional Determinants of Cheating

Students' beliefs that "everyone cheats" (Houston, 1976, p. 301) or that cheating is a normal part of life (Baird, 1980) encourage cheating. The adage "cheaters never win" may not apply in the case of academic dishonesty. With cheating rates as high as 75% to 87% (e.g., Baird, 1980; Jendreck, 1989) and detection rates as low as 1.30% (Haines et al., 1986), academic dishonesty is reinforced, not punished. Even when cheating is detected, swift and appropriate punishment may not follow. Singhal (1982) suggested ". . . that most educational units in a college do not pay adequate attention to cheating and moreover do not have techniques to deal with cheating if it is detected" (p. 775).

Personality research has identified some characteristics of those who cheat. For example, students with lower intelligence cheat more than students with higher intelligence (Hetherington & Feldman, 1964; Johnson & Gormly, 1971; Kelly & Worrell, 1978). Crowne and Marlowe (1964) reported a positive relation between the need for social approval and frequency of cheating. Eve and Bromley (1981) reported a negative relation between internalized social control and frequency of cheating. Eisenberger and Shank (1985) demonstrated that students with a high personal work ethic were more resistant to cheating than students with a low personal work ethic.

Results from studies of the relation between gender and academic dishonesty are inconsistent. Several authors (e.g., Hetherington & Feldman, 1964; Johnson & Gormly, 1971; Kelly & Worrell, 1978; Roskens & Dizney, 1966) reported higher levels of cheating by men, but Jacobson, Berger, and Millham (1970) reported the opposite outcome. Several others (e.g., Fischer, 1970; Houston, 1977; Karabenick & Srull, 1978; Vitro & Schoer, 1972) observed no reliable gender differences. Our data support the proposition that men cheat more than women.

Responses to the two hypothetical situations that involved cheating from another person's examination (Questions 14 to 18) indicated that women reacted more intensely than men. On a scale ranging from *that's great* (1) to *very angry* (7), women had significantly higher scores, smallest $F(1, 468) = 5.72, p < .05$, than did men. The lowest mean for women was 5.06 for Question 13: "What would your reaction be if you were to find out that a classmate has been, is presently, or plans to cheat on an exam?"

The hypothetical situations also showed that different situations engendered different degrees of emotionality. When students perceived the situation as innocuous, they reported lower anger scores. Thus, Question 15—"Given that 'You have not studied well for your exam and at best you only know the material well enough to earn a D,' how would you feel about someone else cheating off of your paper?"—yielded means from a low of 4.73 for one sample of men to a high of 5.57 for one sample of women. When cheating was perceived as having a direct bearing on or relation to the respondent, anger increased. Thus, Question 18—"Given that 'You have put many hours into studying for your test and you are certain you are going to get a very high grade,' how would you feel about a student cheating and doing better than you?"—yielded means from a low of 5.85 for one sample of men to a high of 6.63 for one sample of women.

Cheating Techniques

To catch the academic thieves, we must know their modus operandi. Our surveys indicated that approximately 80% of the cheaters copied from a nearby paper or used crib notes. The remaining 20% provided some food for thought. Items 1 to 5 represent composite statements; Items 6 to 9 are unique approaches to cheating:

1. We worked out a system of hand and feet positions.
2. Each corner of the desk top matched an answer—A, B, C, or D. We simply touched the corner we thought was the right answer.
3. I had a copy of the test and looked up the answers ahead of time and memorized them.
4. We traded papers during the test and compared answers.
5. Opened my book and looked up the answers.
6. I hid a calculator down my pants.
7. The answers were tape recorded before the test and I just took my Walkman to class and listened to the answers during the test.
8. I've done everything from writing all the way up my arm to having notes in a plastic bag inside my mouth.
9. I would make a paper flower, write notes on it, and then pin it on my blouse.

This sample of methods indicates that faculty members may not be able to afford the luxury of reading a book, writing, or grading papers during an examination. If we could only harness these students' creative energies in a more productive manner!

Faculty and Institutional Responsibility

Question 19 deals with whether faculty should be concerned with academic dishonesty. The concept of scholastic integrity provides a compelling affirmative. Paradoxically, students who cheat agree. No sample produced fewer than 90% "yes" answers to the question "Should an instructor care whether or not students cheat on an exam?"

Unfortunately, such concerns may not always be translated into appropriate actions. For example, Keith-Spiegel

(1990) reported that 21% of her faculty respondents had ignored evidence of cheating and that 30% of this number believed that this was an appropriate reaction. What prompts such reactions from faculty? Confronting students in these situations creates possibly undesirable consequences. A student's career may be ruined. The faculty member may become entangled in lengthy litigation. Like students' views about ownership of term papers and the appropriateness of cheating, faculty views about detection and intervention may have changed.

Discouraging Cheating In the Classroom

Question 20 is "What measures will deter or discourage cheating in the classroom?" Regardless of the size and type of institution, our respondents had definite ideas about what should be done. The most desirable deterrent was the use of separate forms of the test. This measure was followed closely by these preferred deterrents (in order of preference):

1. Simply informing the students why they should not cheat.
2. Arranging seating so that students are separated by empty desks.
3. Walking up and down the rows during the test.
4. Constantly watching the students.

The less preferred deterrents (in order of preference) included:

1. Announcing "do not cheat."
2. Having assigned seats.
3. Having all essay exams.
4. Requiring students to leave their belongings outside the classroom during an examination.

Preferred deterrents, such as having separate forms of the exam and separating students by an empty desk, have merit. In contrast, unless faculty do not routinely discuss cheating with each class, one must question the impact of simply informing students why they should not cheat. Common sense suggests that some of the less preferred methods might be effective, but implementing them can be difficult. For example, students dislike taking all essay tests, and faculty dislike grading them. Personal items might be left in the front of the lecture hall, but retrieving them as the students finish their examinations may cause undue commotion. Legitimate reasons for not having assigned seats are less obvious.

Punishment

Question 21 is "What should be done if someone is caught cheating?" Substantial percentages of our samples believed that nothing should be done until after the test. This way one's class is not disrupted and the culprit is not publicly humiliated. Delayed action is a less effective deterrent and may even signal tacit condonation.

The most popular "punishment" suggested by our respondents was for the instructor to tell students to keep their eyes on their own paper. The efficacy of this approach is questionable. Likewise, one might question the advisability of simply taking the test away and allowing the student to start over. Nevertheless, more than 20% of the students endorsed these two options. Perhaps the students favoring these alternatives are those who have cheated.

Another 20% endorsed giving a failing grade to someone caught cheating. This viewpoint may represent the opinion of those who have not cheated.

Conclusions

Our results indicate that several factors are important determinants of cheating. For example, in addition to pressures for good grades, student stress, ineffective deterrents, and condoning teachers, our respondents demonstrate a diminishing sense of academic integrity.

Consider also data that appeared in the October 30, 1989 issue of *Newsweek*. The Pinnacle Group, Inc., an international public relations firm, surveyed 1,093 high school seniors about how far they would stretch ethical standards to get ahead in the business world. Some results of this survey were:

1. When asked if they would be willing to face 6 months probation on an illegal deal in which they made $10 million, 59% of the students responded either "definitely yes" or "maybe."
2. Thirty-six percent indicated they would plagiarize in order to pass a certification test.
3. Sixty-seven percent said they would inflate their business-expense reports.
4. Fifty percent said they would exaggerate on an insurance damage report.
5. Sixty-six percent said they would lie to achieve a business objective.
6. Forty percent indicated they would accept a gift from a supplier worth more than $100; 23% would accept $500 in cash from a supplier; 32% would accept a free vacation.

These alarming results are consistent with statements from several of our respondents. One student said: "Generally when someone cheats, it's like adultery. What they don't know, ain't going to hurt 'em." Another student said: "I will never be caught." Still another student indicated that "cheating in high school is for grades, cheating in college is for a career." Clearly, many students in the Pinnacle Group survey and in our samples lack integrity, academic or otherwise. Hence, their behavior is influenced by external pressures.

Forsyth, Pope, and McMillan (1985) reported an attributional analysis of academic dishonesty. When they compared the causal inferences of cheaters and noncheaters, the external attributions of cheaters were significantly greater than those of noncheaters. Equally relevant is their finding that external attributions made by the cheaters for the dishonest act were significantly greater in number than those

made by a group of uninvolved observers. In short, cheaters excuse their cheating.

Although preventive measures deter cheating in specific situations, they will not succeed in the long run. Only when students develop a stronger commitment to the educational process and when they possess or activate an internalized code of ethics that opposes cheating will the problem have been dealt with effectively. Achieving this goal is unlikely as long as the educational system remains unchanged.

Before our students will internalize standards and apply them, the institutions and their faculties must openly and uniformly support such ethical behaviors. According to Fass (1986),

> Academic and professional ethics must be widely understood and supported throughout the institution if a college or university is to be regarded as a community in which it is legitimate to hold students to the highest standards of behavior in their academic works. (p. 35)

Is your college such an institution? Recent data suggest that many colleges and universities do not belong in this category. Academic dishonesty policies at various institutions were studied by collecting a sample of 200 college catalogs (Weaver, Davis, Look, Buzzanga, & Neal, in press). The catalogs containing information about responsibility indicated that faculty were obligated to inform students of academic dishonesty policies. Hence, written policies confirm the students' sentiments that faculty members should be concerned with academic dishonesty. However, the strength of this obligation may not be pervasive. Of the 200 catalogs surveyed, only 55% (63 public institutions and 47 private institutions) contained relevant policy statements. Although catalogs are not the only printed source for such policies, a disturbing message is that many institutions may not wish to become involved in such matters. Hence, responsibility is deferred to individual departments and faculty members. In addition to the mixed messages that independent policies send to students, Keith-Spiegel's (1990) report suggests how individual faculty may choose to view this situation.

According to Fass (1986),

> If a policy about academic dishonesty does not exist already, a college or university should undertake to develop one. This process will focus attention and discussion on the ethical issues involved, and will provide a basis for regular, ongoing education about academic ethics. If the institutions are reluctant to address this issue and assume responsibility, who can fault the faculty for following suit? (p. 35)

The challenge is clear. Are institutions and their faculties willing to accept it?

References

Baird, J. S., Jr. (1980). Current trends in college cheating. *Psychology in the Schools, 17*, 515–522.

Barnett, D. C., & Dalton, J. C. (1981). Why college students cheat. *Journal of College Student Personnel, 22*, 545–551.

Crowne, D. P., & Marlowe, D. (1964). *The approval motive.* New York: Wiley.

Drake, C. A. (1941). Why students cheat. *Journal of Higher Education, 12,* 418–420.

Eisenberger, R., & Shank, D. M. (1985). Personal work ethic and effort training affect cheating. *Journal of Personality and Social Psychology, 49,* 520–528.

Eve, R., & Bromley, D. G. (1981). Scholastic dishonesty among college undergraduates: Parallel test of two sociological explanations. *Youth and Society, 13,* 3–22.

Fass, R. A. (1986). By honor bound: Encouraging academic honesty. *Educational Record, 67,* 32–35.

Fischer, C. T. (1970). Levels of cheating under conditions of informative appeal to honesty, public affirmation of value and threats of punishment. *Journal of Educational Research, 64,* 12–16.

Forsyth, D. R., Pope, W. R., & McMillan, J. H. (1985). Students' reactions after cheating: An attributional analysis. *Contemporary Educational Psychology, 10,* 72–82.

Goldsen, R. K., Rosenberg, M., William, R., Jr., & Suchman, E. (1960). *What college students think.* Princeton, NJ: Van Nostrand.

Haines, V. J., Diekhoff, G. M., LaBeff, E. E., & Clark, R. E. (1986). College cheating: Immaturity, lack of committment, and the neutralizing attitude. *Research in Higher Education, 25,* 342–354.

Hetherington, E. M., & Feldman, S. E. (1964). College cheating as a function of subject and situational variables. *Journal of Educational Psychology, 55,* 212–218.

Houston, J. P. (1976). The assessment and prevention of answer copying on undergraduate multiple-choice examinations, *Research in Higher Education, 5,* 301–311.

Houston, J. P. (1977). Four components of Rotter's internal–external scale and cheating behavior. *Contemporary Educational Psychology, 2,* 275–283.

Jacobson, L. I., Berger, S. E., & Millham, J. (1970). Individual differences in cheating during a temptation period when confronting failure. *Journal of Personality and Social Psychology, 15,* 48–56.

Jendreck, M. P. (1989). Faculty reactions to academic dishonesty. *Journal of College Student Development, 30,* 401–406.

Johnson, C. D., & Gormly, J. (1971). Achievement, sociability and task importance in relation to academic cheating. *Psychological Reports, 28,* 302.

Karabenick, S. A., & Srull, T. K. (1978). Effects of personality and situational variation in locus of control on cheating: Determinants of the "congruence effect." *Journal of Personality, 46,* 72–95.

Keith-Spiegel, P. (1990, April). *Ethical conflicts between students and professors.* Paper presented at the annual meeting of the Western Psychological Association, Los Angeles.

Keller, M. (1976, August). Academic dishonesty at Miami. *Student Life Research, Miami University,* pp. 1–16.

Kelly, J. A., & Worrell, L. (1978). Personality characteristics, parent behaviors, and sex of the subject in relation to cheating. *Journal of Research in Personality, 12,* 179–188.

Roskens, R. W., & Dizney, H. F. (1966). A study of unethical behavior in high school and college. *The Journal of Educational Research, 59,* 321–324.

Sierles, F., Hendrickx, I., & Circle, S. (1980). Cheating in medical school. *Journal of Medical Education, 55,* 124–125.

Singhal, A. C. (1982). Factors in students' dishonesty. *Psychological Reports, 51,* 775–780.

Stern, E. B., & Havlicek, L. (1986). Academic misconduct: Results of faculty and undergraduate student surveys. *Journal of Allied Health, 5,* 129–142.

Vitro, F. T., & Schoer, L. A. (1972). The effects of probability of test success, test importance, and risk of detection on the incidence of cheating. *Journal of School Psychology, 10,* 269–277.

Weaver, K. A., Davis, S. F., Look, C. T., Buzzanga, V. L., & Neal, L. (in press). Academic dishonesty in college catalogs. *College Student Journal.*

Notes

1. We thank Charles L. Brewer and three anonymous reviewers for their excellent suggestions and their patience in the preparation of this article.

Additional Data on Academic Dishonesty and a Proposal for Remediation

Stephen F. Davis
Emporia State University

H. Wayne Ludvigson
Texas Christian University

Cheating has become a major concern on many college campuses (Fishbein, 1993; Haines, Diekhoff, LaBeff, & Clark, 1986; Singhal, 1982). Jendreck (1989) and Davis, Grover, Becker, and McGregor (1992) indicated that between 40% and 60% of their student respondents reported cheating on at least one examination. McCabe and Bowers (1994) corroborated these data at non-honor-code institutions, but they found that students at institutions having honor codes had lower self-reported cheating rates. In addition, Davis et al. reported that students at small, private liberal arts colleges reported lower cheating rates.

Davis et al. (1992) and McCabe and Bowers (1994) also discussed techniques used to cheat. Although the most popular techniques were copying from a nearby paper and using

157

crib notes, more unusual techniques included trading papers during the test or using intricate patterns of hand and foot position.

Most of the students in Davis et al.'s (1992) study thought that instructors should care whether students cheat. To discourage cheating during a test, students favored the instructor's use of separate forms of the test, informing students about the penalties for cheating, separating students by an empty desk, walking up and down the rows, and constantly watching the students.

Although Davis et al.'s (1992) study provided information about the percentage of cheaters, cheating techniques, and in-class deterrents, it provided no information about the number of repeat offenders or the number of repeated offenses. In this study, we corrected this deficit. The fear of being caught and the influence that this fear has on one's decision to cheat also received attention in this study, as did the effect of announcing strict penalties at the beginning of the semester. Finally, we sought to ascertain why students cheat.

Method

Participants

A total of 2,153 undergraduates (675 men and 1,478 women) enrolled in upper division courses voluntarily participated in this study. All students were classified as either juniors or seniors and were surveyed during regular class sessions.

Materials

We devised a seven-item questionnaire that takes 10 min or less to complete. The first two questions dealt with whether the respondent had cheated at least once, the frequency of cheating, and whether the person had been caught cheating in high school (Question 1) and college (Question 2). Question 3 required a yes or no answer to the question, "Do you fear being caught cheating?" If the respondents answered yes to Question 3, they rated this fear on a 7-point scale ranging from *minimally fearful* (1) to *very fearful* (7). Using a 7-point scale ranging from *minimal influence* (1) to *great influence* (7), they further indicated (Question 4) the extent to which this fear influences whether they will cheat.

Students also responded yes or no to Question 5, "If a professor has strict penalties for cheating and informs the class about them at the beginning of the semester, would this prevent you from cheating?" Question 6 requested a listing of penalties most likely to prevent the individual from cheating. The final question dealt with reasons for cheating. The respondents also provided information about their sex; age; academic major; year in school; and if they hold a job (if so, they were asked to list the number of hours they work each week). All questionnaires were completed anonymously.

Procedure

The 71 samples were obtained from private and public institutions located in 11 different states. The class size of the 71 classes surveyed ranged from 19 to 53 students. Enrollment at the institutions surveyed ranged from approximately 3,000 to more than 30,000. A faculty contact at each institution assumed responsibility for distributing, collecting, and returning the informed consent documents and completed questionnaires. All data were gathered in accord with institutional review board principles at all participating institutions.

Results

Frequency of Cheating

More than 70% in each sample (lowest = 71% and highest = 79%) reported cheating in high school, and the percentage of men and women who cheated did not differ. Self-reports of cheating in college fell within the 40% to 60% range (lowest = 42% and highest = 64%). Corroborating Davis et al.'s (1992) results, there was a consistent and reliable trend for a higher percentage of the men in each sample to report cheating in college, $t(140) = 2.07$, $p < .05$.

More than 80% of the students who reported cheating at least once in high school reported cheating on several occasions during high school (lowest = 83% and highest = 88%). Nearly 50% of those in each sample who reported cheating in college also reported doing so on more than one occasion (lowest = 45% and highest = 53%). The average number of transgressions was 7.88 in high school and 4.25 in college. In both instances, more men than women were repeat offenders, smallest $t(140) = 2.13$, $p < .05$.

Virtually all (98.64%) students who reported cheating on several occasions in college had also cheated on several occasions in high school. This result contrasts with the findings that (a) of the students who reported cheating once in high school, only 24.36% reported cheating in college on no more than one occasion; and (b) of the students who did not cheat in high school, only 1.51% reported cheating in college on no more than one occasion.

The Influence of Announced Penalties

In response to the question concerning whether the instructor's announcement of strict penalties at the beginning of the semester would deter cheating, more than 40% of each sample of men responded no (lowest = 42% and highest = 47%). Contrarily, less than 10% of each sample of women answered no to this question (lowest = 4% and highest = 7%). A closer inspection of these no respondents indicated that the majority in each sample reported cheating in college (for men, lowest = 82% and highest = 96%; for women, lowest = 93% and highest = 100%).

Reasons for Cheating

The most frequently cited reason for cheating (29.25%) was "I do study, but cheat to enhance my score." "My job cuts down on study time" (14.28%) and "usually don't study" (13.60%) also were frequently cited reasons for cheating. Other reasons included "I cheat so my GPA looks better to prospective employers" (8.16%), and "I feel pressure from parents to get good grades so I cheat" (6.80%). Various other reasons, such as "pass the class," "class is too hard," "nervous," "only if I'm not sure of my answers," and "if I blank out and someone else's paper is in clear sight," accounted for 18.36% of the reasons for cheating. The number of references to external factors/pressures is noteworthy.

Discussion and Remediation

One message from these data is clear: Although cheating in college is a major problem that needs attention, there is an equally pressing need to discourage cheaters, especially repeat offenders, in high school. The extrapolation from cheating in college to cheating in real life also has been documented (Sims, 1993). Our data contradict McCabe's contention (see Pavela, 1993) that academic dishonesty is learned during one's collegiate career and is largely determined by its social acceptability at a given institution.

Our data also indicate that, in general, professor-announced penalties have more influence on female students than male students. Moreover, the threat of strict penalties appears to have a greater impact on women who have cheated in college than men who have cheated in college.

Although measures to render cheating difficult, such as those discussed by Davis et al. (1992), should reduce cheating, they do not solve the problem. Indeed, our data suggest that external deterrents will fail in the long run. Alternatively, the existence of ethical–moral–religious systems of social control, from apparently early in our species's history, tells us that only when students have developed a stronger commitment to the educational process and an internalized code of ethics that opposes cheating will the problem be eradicated.

How do we facilitate appropriate internal controls? A Skinnerian analysis (cf. Nye, 1992, p. 65, for a useful discussion) suggests two possible strategies: (a) Manipulate the relevant contingencies of reinforcement, and (b) encourage the learning of relevant rules. In both cases, we aim to produce or strengthen dispositions that naturally resist tendencies to cheat.

Although manipulation of the contingencies of reinforcement surrounding cheating would seem, at first glance, to be difficult, the work of Eisenberger (1992) and Eisenberger and Shank (1985) is encouraging. For example, students trained on high-effort tasks, for which they received only modest reinforcement, displayed substantial resistance to cheating compared with students trained on low-effort tasks (Eisenberger & Shank, 1985). In short, Eisenberger (1992) concluded, from a rich source of data, that long-term training in effortful tasks contributes to durable industriousness, a work ethic that naturally resists cheating. In this context, the spectacle over the last 20 to 30 years of substantial grade inflation and associated pressures to reduce the necessity for effortful student behavior (e.g., through student-controlled contingencies influencing what teachers expect from students, the most obvious being universal student evaluation of teaching) is depressing. If we have an epidemic in cheating, we can apparently lay part of the blame on a deterioration of our own standards for student conduct.

Fishbein (1993) provided another view of manipulating relevant reinforcement contingencies. Here he argued that one way to "fundamentally alter [improve] the climate of academic integrity [is] by increasing the volume of cases handled by legitimate university disciplinary procedures and by making enforcement more widespread and equitable" (p. A52). Having codified penalties that take seriousness of offense and number of offenses into account, Fishbein delineated a streamlined procedure. This proposed system may have merit, but it awaits verification in the academy.

The second strategy, encouraging relevant rule learning or, even better, encouraging a world view, life theory, or philosophy that naturally resists cheating has probably seen diminished use as standards have deteriorated. Resistance to such teaching may arise from an understandable reluctance of instructors to impose their values on others. However, the values implied by a world view that naturally opposes cheating may be nearly universally accepted in all education.

Such a world view relevant to education and opposed to academic dishonesty (Ludvigson, 1992) establishes the goal of understanding as central (necessary but not sufficient) for success and general well-being. Perhaps a causal picture of the following sort would be helpful:

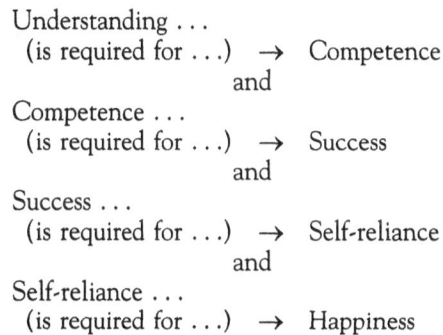

Understanding . . .
 (is required for . . .) → Competence
         and
Competence . . .
 (is required for . . .) → Success
         and
Success . . .
 (is required for . . .) → Self-reliance
         and
Self-reliance . . .
 (is required for . . .) → Happiness

Given its central role, students must learn that understanding does not entail rote memorization, although some things must be memorized, or the learning of isolated facts, although facts must be learned. In contrast, understanding requires the construction of a personal theory of what is to be understood. That is, if students are to understand something, they must build their own theories in their own heads and not just parrot others'. Such a theory will yield a new perspective that permits generalization of inferences to new situations. It will permit the student to know what is important about the subject and what is not.

Pertinent for resistance to cheating, students must be convinced that building a good personal theory, just as in science, is a continuing process of testing and revising the theory. Testing the theory is critical for a good theory. Recitation, listening to lectures, and exams are all ways of testing one's personal theory. Cheating in the process of theory construction leaves one bereft of understanding. Cheating during exams deprives students of an opportunity to test their theory. Students who aim for understanding must take every opportunity to be tested. We believe that such a philosophy of education, if taught with conviction, just may lessen cheating.

References

Davis, S. F., Grover, C. A., Becker, A. H., & McGregor, L. N. (1992). Academic dishonesty: Prevalence, determinants, techniques, and punishments. *Teaching of Psychology, 19*, 16–20.

Eisenberger, R. (1992). Learned industriousness. *Psychological Review, 99*, 248–267.

Eisenberger, R., & Shank, D. M. (1985). Personal work ethic and effort training affect cheating. *Journal of Personality and Social Psychology, 49*, 520–528.

Fishbein, L. (1993, December 1). Curbing cheating and restoring academic integrity. *The Chronicle of Higher Education*, p. A52.

Haines, V. J., Diekhoff, G. M., LaBeff, E. E., & Clark, R. E. (1986). College cheating: Immaturity, lack of commitment, and the neutralizing attitude. *Research in Higher Education, 25*, 342–354.

Jendreck, M. P. (1989). Faculty reactions to academic dishonesty. *Journal of College Student Development, 30*, 401–406.

Ludvigson, H. W. (1992, November). *Cheating: What to do?* Paper presented at the Southwest Regional Conference for Teachers of Psychology, Fort Worth, TX.

McCabe, D. L., & Bowers, W. J. (1994). Academic dishonesty among males in college: A thirty year perspective. *Journal of College Student Development, 35*, 5–10.

Nye, R. D. (1992). *The legacy of B. F. Skinner*. Pacific Grove, CA: Brooks/Cole.

Pavela, G. (1993). Donald L. McCabe on academic integrity: What the latest research shows. *SYNTHESIS: Law and Policy in Higher Education, 5*, 340–343.

Sims, R. L. (1993). The relationship between academic dishonesty and unethical business practices. *Journal of Education for Business, 68*, 207–211.

Singhal, A. C. (1982). Factors in students' dishonesty. *Psychological Reports, 51*, 775–780.

Notes

1. We appreciate the assistance of Charles L. Brewer and three anonymous reviewers on the final draft of this article.

Detection of Cheating on Multiple-Choice Tests by Using Error-Similarity Analysis

Francis S. Bellezza
Suzanne F. Bellezza
Ohio University

Cheating on tests is common in American colleges. About 75% of college undergraduates admit that they have cheated on tests (Baird, 1980). Baird found that obtaining information from another student about a test was the most common form of cheating. In a study of medical school students, 87% admitted to having cheated as undergraduates and 58% confessed to cheating while in medical school (Sierles, Hendricks, & Circle, 1980). Many students accept cheating without concern. Forty percent of the college students surveyed did not disapprove of cheating on tests, 29% did not feel guilty about cheating, and only 1% said that they would report cheating if they observed it (Baird, 1980). Certain groups are more likely to cheat: men, students with low grades, underclassmen, business majors, fraternity and sorority members, and students involved in few extracurricular activities (Baird, 1980). The two most common reasons for cheating are grade pressure and lack of time to complete class work (Barnett & Dalton, 1981).

Cheating by Copying on Multiple-Choice Examinations

We are specifically concerned with copying during multiple-choice examinations which, in large and crowded rooms with an inadequate number of proctors, favor cheating (Houston, 1976). Copying someone else's work during a test is the fifth most common form of cheating (Baird, 1980). One may assume that a large proportion of test copying involves multiple-choice tests because it is easy to copy the marks made on the answer sheet.

Instructors can discourage copying by taking precautions. Although use of multiple forms of the test is one such precaution, Houston (1983) found that rearranging the order of questions did not reduce copying, presumably because students copied only from someone with the same form. On the other hand, Houston found that rearranging the order of questions on multiple test forms, rearranging the order of alternative answers, and spreading the students out in the testing room reduced copying.

Another helpful precaution is vigilant monitoring during the test by an adequate number of proctors. Although Barnett and Dalton (1981) found that intelligent students cheated less in high-risk situations (e.g., when there were several proctors) and Baird (1980) found that women were much less likely to cheat in high-risk environments, students typically perceive proctoring as less effective than do teachers. Forty-eight percent of faculty but only 21% of students agreed that proctors watch carefully and consistently throughout tests (Barnett & Dalton, 1981).

This difference between instructors' and students' evaluations of the effectiveness of proctoring suggests that copying is difficult to detect. Although instructors think that they are vigilant, students believe that copying is undetectable, a result they attribute to inadequate supervision. Our own experience is that instructors who performed the following analysis were surprised by the amount of cheating suggested by the procedure. In addition, the analysis indicates that some students engaging in suspicious behavior, such as looking around frequently, are not cheating.

A final precaution that discourages copying is to assign seats that vary from one examination to the next and differ from students' lecture seats. This procedure ensures that students cannot plan to copy from friends or from students who are performing well in the course.

Analysis of Multiple-Choice Items Using Error Similarity

Although these precautions are reasonable, instructors do not always have the resources to carry them out. To help discourage students from cheating on multiple-choice examinations, we developed a procedure that determines the similarity of errors for any pair of examinees. The procedure is implemented by a computer program that records the items both students got wrong and whether the number of same wrong answers was above a chance level. The analysis is restricted to errors because cheating is suggested if two students consistently choose identical wrong alternatives for the same items.

Cody (1985) described a similar procedure, and both Cody's method and the one described here are closely related to Angoff's (1974) Index B developed to detect cheaters. The advantage of our procedure is that it yields a critical value indicating whether cheating is likely.

To exemplify the procedure, assume that Student X made 25 errors and Student Y made 23 errors on a 60-item multiple-choice test with 5 alternative choices for each item. Also, assume that 20 of these errors involved the same items and that for 18 of these 20 items both students chose the same wrong alternative. Even though the answer sheets are not identical, an error-similarity analysis suggests that cheating is likely because the probability of choosing by chance 18 of the same wrong alternatives for 20 wrong items is on the order of 5 in a million. One must also use a seating chart to determine whether two students were sitting close enough to cheat and which student may be copying from the other.

Probability of Same Errors Using the Binomial Distribution

The error-similarity analysis works like this: Once all of the answer sheets have been scored, the computer program counts the number of times all pairs of students chose the same incorrect alternative for all items. If all four incorrect alternatives of a five-alternative item were equally attractive, then the probability of two students choosing the same incorrect alternative for an item by chance would be 4/16 or .25. Because it is unrealistic to expect that all incorrect alternatives will be equally likely, the probability (P) of an identical error by two students on an item is computed by the program from the students' responses and typically has a value around .40.[1] Using the binomial distribution (McNemar, 1962), when the probability that errors match on any item is P, then the probability for k of N item errors matching is:

$$\frac{N!}{k!(N-k)!} P^k (1-P)^{N-k}.$$

Using the previous example of Student X and Student Y, assume that the probability (P) of any two students choosing the same wrong answer is .40. Then the probability of choosing 18 or more answers the same out of 20 wrong items is the probability of choosing 18, 19, or 20 answers the same by chance. Using the binomial distribution with $P = .40$ and $N = 20$, this probability can be represented as $(20!/18!\ 2!)$ $(.40)^{18}\ (.60)^2 + (20!/19!\ 1!)\ (.40)^{19}\ (.60)^1 + (20!/20!\ 0!)$ $(.40)^{20}\ (.60)^0$, which is equal to .000004700 + .000000330 + .000000011 = .000005031, or about 5 millionths.

Because computing binomial probabilities when N is large can be time consuming, a normal approximation to the binomial may be used if $N\,P > 5$ and $N\,(1 - P) > 5$ (McNemar, 1962). The value for the mean of this normal approximation is NP and the value of the standard deviation is $\sqrt{N}\,P\,(1 - P)$. For the binomial distribution from the just-cited example in which $P = .40$ and $N = 20$, the mean of the normal approximation is 8 and the standard deviation is 2.19. Because 18 identical answers were given for 20 wrong items, the standard normal value is $z = (X - M)/SD = (17.5 - 8)/2.19 = 4.34$. Using a standard normal table, the probability of obtaining 18 or more of the same wrong answers by chance is .000007 or about 7 millionths. This is close to the probability of 5 millionths computed previously using the binomial distribution.

The probability of choosing the same wrong answers by chance can be computed for every possible pair of students. If there are S students, then the number of comparisons is $S(S - 1)/2$. The probability computed for each pair of students indicates the probability with which their similar errors occur by chance. The error-similarity analysis is based on these probabilities. Although only probabilities need to be computed for the analysis, it is convenient to express the

---

[1]If there are only four alternative answers for each item, as is true of many items provided with introductory psychology texts, then P may be higher than .40. The program automatically takes the number of alternatives into account, and the procedure remains the same.

degree of similarity by using a z score computed using the normal approximation.

Is Cheating Occurring?

To illustrate how the detection procedure works, consider the following example. Figure 1 shows a distribution of error-similarity scores expressed as z scores for 39 students. Of the 741 possible pair-wise similarity scores, only 735 could be computed because some pairs of students had no errors in common. The 39 students were administered the same examination form and represent approximately half the students tested in an Introductory Management course at Ohio University.

The error-similarity scores form a unimodal distribution with a mean of −.63 and a standard deviation of 1.01. This distribution allows all the error-similarity scores to be inspected simultaneously; however, the exact shape of this distribution is not critical to the analysis. To generate these 735 scores, the N used in computing each score depended on the number of wrong items each pair of students had in common. The P of the same incorrect choice for any wrong item was estimated by the program from the item analysis, and for this group the value was .42.[2] Two similarity scores lie above the rest of the distribution: one at $z = 3.44$ and one at $z = 4.89$.

How can we decide whether these high error-similarity scores indicate cheating? Our procedure considers the computed z scores as z tests. If the z score is greater than some critical value, then most likely the score results from one student copying from another. In order to use this procedure, a proximity or closeness parameter (C) must be used. The parameter C represents the estimated number of other students with the same test form from whom a given student may be close enough to copy. To estimate C, we sat in a number of testing rooms and tried to read answer sheets placed on other desks. We estimated the value of C to be no larger than 3 when two forms of a test were used with a large number of test takers. That is, the average student can see the answer sheets of, at most, three other students using the same test form. So the maximum number of error-analysis scores that might actually involve cheating is C × S, where C is the proximity parameter and S is the number of students using the same form of the test.

When using a z score as a z test, the alpha level represents the probability of a Type I error. When making a Type I error, one concludes that cheating is occurring when it really is not. If we wish to have only an alpha probability of making one or more Type I errors when performing C × S tests, then an error-similarity score considered as a z test has to be significant at the level of (alpha/C S). This adjustment in the alpha level is a Bonferroni correction (Kirk, 1982). In the distribution presented in Figure 1, the alpha level was set at .05. Thus, the probability value used to test the z score for each pair of students was .05/3(39) or .00043. This probability can be looked up in a standard normal table and

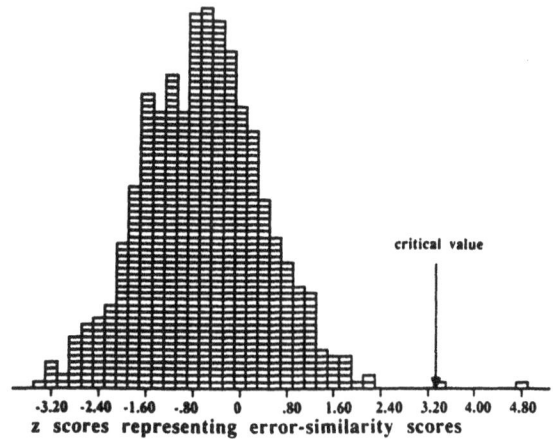

Figure 1. Distribution of error-similarity scores for all possible pairs of 39 students who took the same form of a 60-item multiple-choice examination.

shows that a z score has to exceed the critical value of 3.33 for cheating to be suspected.

The first outlying score ($z = 3.44$) falls just above the critical value. However, the seating chart for the test revealed that the two students were not sitting near each other.[3] So, this z score is not one of the C S error-similarity scores that we need to test for significance. The second outlying score ($z = 4.89$) does represent two students sitting near one another. An analysis of the 60 items shows that Student X and Student Y got 31 of the same items correct. Also, Student X got 3 items correct that Student Y got wrong, and Student X got 1 item wrong that Student Y got correct. Finally, Student X and Student Y got 25 of the same items wrong. The z score is based on these last 25 items, of which the two students answered 24 the same. Because a Bonferroni correction has been made for the number of pairs of students tested, we may conclude that there is a probability of .95 that these two students were involved in cheating.

The next question is, which student was the cheater? We usually assume that collaboration does not occur because our seating involves random assignment. Inspection of the seating chart often shows the student suspected of cheating sits behind the other. In most instances, this student copied from the student in front. Inspection of nonmatching items may also provide some evidence. In this example, Student X got only two more items correct than Student Y, but sometimes this discrepancy is larger. The student with the lower score is likely to be the student copying.

As mentioned previously, the z scores are used as error-similarity scores to represent the degree of similarity between two students' sets of errors. These z scores are more convenient to use than probabilities because they do not take on extremely small values and seem to form a unimodal, symmetric distribution. To perform the cheating analysis, however, the z scores are not necessary. Only the binomial distribution is needed to compute a probability for each pair of students tested. If the computed probability is less than the value (alpha/C S), then one may suspect cheating.

---

[2]For each pair of students, N is the number of items on which both students made an error. In addition, P can be computed using only those items on which both students made errors.

[3]Obtaining a z score this high and finding that the two students involved were not sitting close to each other is a rare event, as demonstrated in Figure 2.

Analysis of Extreme Scores From 90 Tests

Figure 2 shows 24 extreme error-similarity scores obtained by analyzing test results from 15 classes in Introductory Management at Ohio University. Each class was administered two midterm tests and a final examination, and each of these tests consisted of 60 five-alternative, multiple-choice items. Because two forms of each test were always used, there were a total of 90 analyses of the kind illustrated in Figure 1. From these 90 analyses, 24 pairs of students were found to be above the critical value computed for each analysis.

The mean number of students included in each analysis was 31.6. Note that in a class of 32 students, the number of pairs of students, regardless of proximity, is $[S(S - 1)/2] = (32 \times 31)/2 = 496$. Of these 496, $C \times S = 3 \times 32 = 96$ pairs are estimated to be sitting close to one another, and $496 - 96 = 400$ are not. Using comparable numbers from all the classes analyzed, a mean of 15% of the students were estimated to be sitting in proximity. Yet, Figure 2 shows that 19 of the 24, or 79%, of the extreme scores involved pairs of students sitting close enough to cheat. If these large error-similarity scores were due to chance factors, then only 15% rather than 79% should involve students sitting close together. Using a binomial test with $N = 24$ and $P = .15$, it can be shown that obtaining 19 or more cases of students sitting in proximity out of a total of 24 cases is a very unlikely event. The results shown in Figure 2 allow us to conclude that error-similarity scores larger than the critical value resulted largely from one student's copying answers from another.

The percentage of students in these 90 analyses suspected of copying was very low. For the first test in each course, this was .5%; for the second test, .3%; and for the final examination, 1.4%. In each of the classes, the students had been forewarned of the analysis and were cautioned against trying to cheat. However, data from classes prior to the use of the analysis suggest that the number of students copying on a test may have been as high as 5%.

Measures to be Taken Once Cheating is Suspected

Although error-similarity analysis should be used in a conservative manner, we believe that it can help control cheating. We list examples from the most to the least conservative.

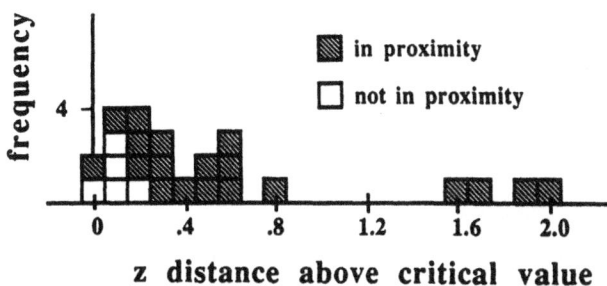

Figure 2. Distribution of extreme scores from 90 multiple-choice examinations involving students sitting in proximity versus those not in proximity.

1. General deterrent to copying. The instructor may announce in class that a computer program exists to detect cheating and that it is used whenever answer sheets are machine scored. Even if the instructor does not always perform the analysis, this policy is helpful because it discourages students from cheating. Such an announcement is most effective if students are convinced that such a computer program exists.

2. Evaluation of testing environment. Sometimes an instructor wants to determine, in general, if any copying is occurring on tests. No action against individual students is planned. After performing the analysis and inspecting the results, the instructor may decide to use more forms of a test, use random assignment of test seats, get more proctors, use a larger testing room, and so on. Also, the program can be used when doing research on the factors that influence cheating behavior.

3. Special seating assignments. As a result of the analysis, the instructor may decide to assign suspected cheaters test seats that can be closely monitored. If randomly assigning test seats is part of the course procedure, then students suspected of cheating should consider their assigned seats as resulting from chance.

4. Special counseling. The instructor may wish to speak to suspected cheaters. Such an interview provides the opportunity not only to inform the student of the instructor's suspicions but also to discuss problems the student may be having in the course. Special seating may also be assigned for the next test.

5. Disciplinary action. The instructor may wish to bring charges against the suspected cheater using the departmental, college, or university committee dealing with student misconduct. Sometimes an instructor will have corroborative evidence, such as other students who witnessed the cheating or the reports of proctors who noted suspicious behavior. Occasionally, the same individual will be repeatedly detected as cheating despite the precautions taken. In this case, the statistical evidence becomes compelling. We have observed the same students appearing as suspects in more than one course.

Limitations of the Error-Similarity Analysis

When using the error-similarity procedure, one must be aware of its limitations. First, it deals only with one kind of cheating: copying another's work on a multiple-choice examination. It cannot detect cheating by using crib sheets on tests or through out-of-class plagiarism. Furthermore, in order for copying to be detected, the test should be difficult enough for the mean number of errors to be 15 items or more when there are five alternatives for each item. Even under these optimal conditions, cheating will not be detected if a student copies only a few answers.

A second limitation is that there must be a record of where students sit during the test. The procedure works best when students are randomly assigned to different seats for each test so that any cheating discovered is probably not the result of collaboration.

A third problem is that the procedure is statistical in nature. Even if there is a probability of only 1 in 1 million that two students could have the same pattern of errors, it is still possible that cheating did not occur.

Fourth, there are questions as to how statistical evidence is interpreted legally (Buss & Novick, 1980). This last point is important because disciplinary action taken against students involves judiciary committees that often use procedures and rules of evidence similar to those of a court of law.

Fifth, many college deans and judiciary committees, even when convinced of the value of the procedure, are not familiar with evaluating statistical evidence and its associated probability values. They usually deal with physical evidence and interview witnesses of cheating. A user of the error-similarity procedure who wishes to take disciplinary action must be prepared to educate the people involved in the case.

The Computer Program

The computer program used to implement the error-analysis procedure is written in FORTRAN IV and can be obtained from the authors. The program was developed on an IBM mainframe computer but can be used with any computer that has a FORTRAN compiler, including microcomputers. For the program to be of practical value, the user must be able to read multiple-choice answer sheets with an optical scanner or some such device. The file created by this device must be available to the computer running the program. Input–output modifications of the program might be necessary to make it conform to the particular computer system being used.

The output of the program corresponds to what has been described here. A distribution of z scores is printed as well as statistics for pairs of students who have high z scores. These statistics include the probability that the error overlap could occur by chance, the item numbers for which answers are the same, and information regarding which of the two students performed better on the test. Also printed are critical z values for a variety of values for the proximity parameter (C) combined with different alpha values. The user can estimate what value of C is appropriate for a particular testing room and decide on the value of alpha. The appropriate critical z value can then be found in the output.

References

Angoff, W. H. (1974). The development of statistical indices for detecting cheaters. *Journal of the American Statistical Association, 69*, 44–49.

Baird, J. S., Jr. (1980). Current trends in college cheating. *Psychology in the Schools, 17*, 515–522.

Barnett, D. C., & Dalton, J. C. (1981). Why college students cheat. *Journal of College Student Personnel, 22*, 545–551.

Buss, W. G., & Novick, M. R. (1980). The detection of cheating on standardized tests: Statistical and legal analysis. *Journal of Law and Education, 9*, 1–64.

Cody, R. P. (1985). Statistical analysis of examinations to detect cheating. *Journal of Medical Education, 60*, 136–137.

Houston, J. P. (1976). Amount and loci of classroom answer copying, spaced seating, and alternate test forms. *Journal of Educational Psychology, 68*, 729–735.

Houston, J. P. (1983). Alternate test forms as a means of reducing multiple-choice answer copying in the classroom. *Journal of Educational Psychology, 75*, 572–575.

Kirk, R. E. (1982). *Experimental design: Procedures for the behavioral sciences* (2nd ed.). Belmont, CA: Wadsworth.

McNemar, Q. (1962). *Psychological statistics* (3rd ed.). New York: Wiley.

Sierles, F., Hendricks, I., & Circle, S. (1980). Cheating in medical school. *Journal of Medical Education, 55*, 124–125.

Detection of Copying on Multiple-Choice Tests: An Update

Francis S. Bellezza
Ohio University

Suzanne F. Bellezza
Department of Finance and Business Law
University of Wisconsin-Oshkosh

We outlined a method for the detection of cheating on multiple-choice tests (Bellezza & Bellezza, 1989). In this update, we expand on the three ideas presented therein: (a) establish a response-similarity measure and its statistical distribution under the assumption that no cheating has occurred, (b) establish a rule using that distribution to decide if cheating has occurred, and (c) use the procedure in the classroom to deter cheating or confront those suspected of cheating.

Establishing a Measure for Similarity of Responses

To detect copying on a multiple-choice test, we (Bellezza & Bellezza, 1989) adopted a measure similar to Cody's (1985) that uses only those items on which both examinees made errors. Versions of this error-similarity measure apparently have also been used by national testing organizations (Buss & Novick, 1980). Our procedure uses a binomial distribution whose parameter N is the number of items on the test for which both students in the pair made an error. The parameter P is the probability that two students will choose the same incorrect alternative and is assumed to have the same value for all items and for all students. The value of P is estimated from the group of students being tested. The main advantage of this binomial model of identical errors is its simplicity.

This error-similarity measure resembles Angoff's (1974) Index B because it uses as an index of cheating the number of identical errors between two examinees. However, instead of using a binomial model to predict the number of common errors occurring by chance, Angoff used a norming sample in which no cheating could possibly take place to predict empirically the number of common errors. His predictor was the product obtained by multiplying the number of errors made by each examinee in the pair. If a pair of examinees tested show too great a discrepancy between observed and predicted common errors, then one suspects cheating.

In Bellezza and Bellezza (1989), we described a statistical procedure for detecting cheating that we and other researchers have used, but this procedure may not be familiar to most teachers of psychology. We also described (a) a way to set a criterion probability value in the statistical test to decide whether cheating occurred, (b) some of our experiences using this statistical procedure with actual classroom data, and (c) five increasingly forceful ways to use this statistical analysis. At this juncture, we compare our measure of cheating with some others that have been proposed and emphasize that ours is somewhat different from that given by Frary (1993).

We can identify a problem with the binomial model described earlier, namely, that the same value of P is used for all items. For example, one pair of examinees may have low total scores, with their identical wrong responses consisting of popular distracters for 10 very difficult items. A second pair of examinees may have higher total scores, and their 10 identical wrong responses may include several unpopular distracters. The probability of identical responses by chance is greater for the first pair of examinees than for the second pair. We addressed this problem in footnote 2 (Bellezza & Bellezza, 1989, p. 153) by indicating that one option is to compute the value of P based only on those incorrect items from a particular pair of examinees.

In some instances, it would be appropriate to use a procedure in which the probability of an identical error was computed separately for each test item and then the probability of similar errors computed. We have used this analysis for those cases in which cheating was suspected based on the mean P value. This computation always resulted in a slightly lower probability of examinees' responses agreeing by chance than when using the mean value of P. Although we did not discuss this outcome because it did not seem to fit with our main points, we mention it here because it may be relevant to some applications.

The Measure g_2

One reason we (Bellezza & Bellezza, 1989) gave, which was also given by Angoff (1974) and Cody (1985), for using only common errors is that suspected cheaters claim that they chose correct answers because of their knowledge, not because they were copying. It is more difficult for examinees to make this argument when they selected common incorrect distracters.

Buss and Novick (1980), however, compellingly argued that all information should be used to develop a measure of cheating, including information supporting the alternative that one examinee was not copying from another. The measures we (Bellezza & Bellezza, 1989) used and those used by Angoff (1974) and Cody (1985), do not do this because they rely only on those items to which examinees responded incorrectly. The measures developed by Frary, Tideman, and Watts (1977), however, use marginal frequencies across examinees and items to estimate the probabilities of correct and incorrect responses to each item by each examinee. First, Frary et al. developed a model that predicts each examinee's choices. Then, they used this model to determine the degree to which the responses of any two examinees should be the same. One of their measures, g_2, uses these probabilities to estimate the chance probability that any Examinee A will obtain the same answers on a set of items as Examinee B. Hence, Frary et al.'s measure takes into account common responses for both correct and incorrect items, each examinee's total score, the difficulty of each item, and the probability of each incorrect alternative. Although the g_2 measure uses information from both correct and incorrect items, it is sensitive to information from incorrect items. For example, in the computer simulation of cheating reported in Table 2 of Frary et al. (1977), the g_2 measures of the 10 cheaters correlated .74 with the number of errors that cheaters made and, correspondingly, correlated $-.74$ with the number of correct responses. Yet, g_2 is a potentially valuable measure of response similarity, with outlying scores in the g_2 distribution indicating that cheating may have taken place.

To evaluate the various measures of response similarity, Hanson, Harris, and Brennan (1987) compared seven measures of cheating under different types of computer-simulated cheating (e.g., copying randomly, copying difficult items, and copying strings of items). They suggested that the most likely type of cheating was copying a string of about five items at a time. Cody's (1985) measure, similar to one we used (Bellezza & Bellezza, 1989, but Cody used different probability values for each item), was found to be the least desirable for detecting cheating. The best measure was what

Hanson et al. labeled the *CP measure*. The CP measure is Cody's measure along with the probability of an identical incorrect response computed separately not only for each item but also for different levels of examinees categorized by their total scores. The CP measure was more powerful than the g_2 measure in detecting cheaters. Also, the theoretical probabilities of the g_2 measure indicated more false positives than did the CP measure. In summarizing their results, Hanson et al. (1987) emphasized the basic similarity of the results using the various cheating measures. They stated:

> For the type of simulated copying thought to be most realistic the methods do not differ greatly in performance, and approximately 5%, 20%, 50%, 85% and 95% of the simulated copiers who copied 10%, 20%, 30%, 40%, and 50% of the items, respectively, could be detected with a false positive rate of .001. (p. 2)

Establishing a Decision Rule for Detecting Cheating

The problem of choosing a probability value for determining when cheating has taken place may seem straightforward, but it is not trivial. The choice of the criterion probability value can have a greater effect on decisions about cheating than the choice of the statistical measure of cheating. One can easily convert z scores into probabilities and probabilities into z scores, but a more important issue is how to establish a probability criterion for deciding if cheating has occurred.

Testing a large number of students results in a large number of comparisons. For example, a test of 300 students results in 44,850 similarity values or 89,700 values if nonsymmetric measures are used for each pair of examinees. Some of these similarity measures will have large values by chance. Labeling one of these large values as not part of the null distribution (no-cheating distribution) and deciding that cheating has taken place when it really has not is committing a Type I error. How can these Type I errors be minimized? Frary et al. (1977) suggested using a g_2 statistic greater than 4.5 (criterion probability approximately equal to 1 in 100,000) and checking examinees who sit in adjacent seats. Angoff (1974) mentioned a probability value of 1 in 10,000. Buss and Novick (1980) compared an examinee with the eight other examinees sitting nearest. But where do these probabilities and checking procedures come from, and how can they be justified? Remember that Type I errors cannot be completely avoided; however, one can determine the probability of at least one Type I error occurring by setting the criterion probability value to an appropriate level.

Once a value of alpha has been chosen, we (Bellezza & Bellezza, 1989) recommended a procedure for setting a probability criterion value for deciding whether cheating has taken place. Alpha, in this instance, is the probability that at least one Type I error will occur when the cheating decision is made. The value of alpha and the probability value used for setting the decision criterion are not the same numeric value. To obtain the criterion probability value, we suggested inspecting each test room to determine how many other same-form answer sheets can be seen by any student. We called this value the *proximity index*, C, and typically

used a C value of 3. By keeping a seating record, only $C \times S$ similarity measures need be considered when S examinees are tested. For example, if the alpha probability of at least one Type I error occurring should not be greater than .001, then the decision rule is that cheating should be considered to have occurred only if the similarity statistic has a chance probability less than alpha/($C \times S$). Using the earlier example, the criterion probability is .001/(3 × 300) = .00000111. This formula uses the Bonferroni correction for performing multiple statistical tests. If one erroneously used the value of alpha as the criterion value for detecting cheating, then the probability of at least one Type I error is $1 - (1 - \text{alpha})^{C \times S}$. For the earlier example, this value is $1 - (1 - .001)^{900} = .59$. So, even when using an alpha value as low as .001, one would be more likely than not to make at least one false decision that cheating has occurred. To avoid this outcome, the Bonferroni correction should be used, $1 - (1 - .00000111)^{900} = .001$. As stated earlier, Type I errors cannot be eliminated; however, they can and should be estimated.

Dealing With Cheating in the Classroom

Statistical analyses of cheating have not focused on the needs of the classroom teacher. Some of the literature deals with the problems of national testing organizations that give one-time tests of ability or professional knowledge to thousand of examinees in various locations (e.g., Buss & Novick, 1980). Other researchers have emphasized the need for physical evidence corroborating these statistical tests (e.g., Cody, 1985; Hanson et al., 1987). Problems of classroom teachers differ from those of national testing organizations, and the resources available to teachers are often limited. For example, teachers may routinely have trouble monitoring large groups of students taking tests in confined areas. Also, they may neither easily acquire corroborative evidence for suspected cheating nor have the resources to try to collect such evidence. In addition, they often believe that they have a professional responsibility to discuss suspected cheating with the students involved. If teachers act on their suspicions, they may be required to explain the statistical procedure used to detect cheating to the students, the students' parents, and members of a judiciary committee. We (Bellezza & Bellezza, 1989) suggested solutions to some of these problems associated with detecting cheating in the classroom.

References

Angoff, W. H. (1974). The development of statistical indices for detecting cheaters. *Journal of the American Statistical Association*, 69, 44–49.

Bellezza, F. S., & Bellezza, S. F. (1989). Detection of cheating on multiple-choice tests by using error-similarity analysis. *Teaching of Psychology*, 16, 151–155.

Buss, W. G., & Novick, M. R. (1980). The detection of cheating on standardized tests: Statistical and legal analysis. *Journal of Law and Education*, 9, 1–64.

Cody, R. P. (1985). Statistical analysis of examinations to detect cheating. *Journal of Medical Education*, 60, 136–137.

Frary, R. B. (1993). Statistical detection of multiple-choice answer copying: Review and commentary. *Applied Measurement in Education*, 6, 153–165.

Frary, R. B., Tideman, T. N., & Watts, T. M. (1977). Indices of cheating on multiple-choice tests. *Journal of Educational Statistics*, 2, 235–256.

Hanson, B. S., Harris, D. J., & Brennan, R. L. (1987, April). A *comparison of several statistical methods for examining allegations of* *copying*. Paper presented at the meeting of the American Educational Research Association, Washington, DC.

Notes

1. We thank two anonymous reviewers for their comments on a draft of this article.

Fraudulent Excuse Making Among College Students

Mark D. Caron
Susan Krauss Whitbourne
Richard P. Halgin
University of Massachusetts at Amherst

Most college professors have faced the dilemma of whether or not to accept excuses presented by students requesting permission to submit a paper late or postpone an examination. Many academics prefer to believe that their students are honest and that only a few would lie about the death of a grandparent in order to get special consideration regarding a deadline or a scheduled examination. Nevertheless, it seems safe to assume that questions about the truthfulness of excuses occur at least occasionally to even the most trusting of professors. Guidance for answering these questions is scarce. Even McKeachie's (1986) influential *Teaching Tips*, which addresses major concerns of college teachers, does not discuss how to deal with excuses.

Informal commentaries are occasionally published on academic excuse making (e.g., Chiodo, 1986), but we found no abstracts in the psychological literature on this topic. In an unpublished master's thesis, Beck (1985) studied excuse making and other illicit behavior, including shoplifting, cheating, and lying. Sixty percent of Beck's subjects admitted to having used a false excuse to avoid taking a scheduled test or turning in an assignment on time. This surprising statistic suggests that excuse making in academic settings should be a serious concern.

Social psychologists have occasionally studied excuse making. Snyder, Higgins, and Stucky (1983) developed an excuse-making model from the literature on attribution of responsibility for failure. They argued that people use excuses when their self-esteem is threatened by past or expected poor performance. This model, which follow Adler's (1931) theory of neurotic excuse making, has been supported by subsequent research (Basgall & Snyder, 1988; Jung, 1987; Smith & Whitehead, 1988). It does not, however, provide a source of concrete help for the college professor who must take a more pragmatic approach. Regardless of a student's reasons for making up an excuse, the professor must evaluate the legitimacy of the excuse and decide what action to take. Knowing that a student is trying to save face is not particularly helpful to the professor who is attempting to be equitable.

In this study, we expanded Beck's (1985) work by exploring in greater depth the context and correlates of fraudulent excuse making. We compared the frequency of fraudulent and legitimate excuses. A *fraudulent excuse* was defined as one that the student fabricated specifically for the purpose of avoiding an academic responsibility. A *legitimate excuse*, in contrast, was defined as one based on events beyond the student's control and that prevented the student from fulfilling the expected task. We also investigated the kinds of excuses that students fabricate. Finally, we explored the relation between excuse making and certain other factors, such as gender, year in college, grade point average (GPA), and college major.

Method

Sample

The sample consisted of 261 undergraduates from the University of Massachusetts at Amherst. There were 159 women (61%) and 102 men (39%), representing 48 different majors. The largest proportion of the sample (38%) had a GPA between 2.50 and 2.99. The ages of the subjects ranged from 18 to 29, with a mode of 21 years. The sample included 14% first-year students, 25% sophomores, 34% juniors, and 27% seniors.

Instrument

The Questionnaire on Academic Excuses (QAE) consists of 21 items. Respondents are asked to indicate how many fraudulent and legitimate excuses they have used while in college and to describe the circumstances involving a fraudulent excuse. The QAE also contains items that ask the subjects' reasons for using the fraudulent excuses, feelings about the excuse-making episode, and outcome of the situation.

Procedure

In a pilot study, 20 students were given a semistructured interview to identify the types of questions to include in the main investigation. These students, recruited through the Psychology Department's subject pool, were asked about the types of excuses they or their friends had used, why they were used, and how requests connected with the excuses were accommodated by professors (e.g., postponement of a deadline). Responses to these questions formed the basis for a two-page questionnaire of close-ended items used in the main investigation.

For the main investigation, students from many academic departments were included, because we thought that students would be more likely to respond honestly if there was no connection between the questionnaire and an academic department. Therefore, the questionnaire was administered in a location through which most students pass at some point in their daily or weekly routine (an area in the student union complex near cafeterias, lounges, and the bookstore). The sample was obtained over a 6-week period, from the beginning to the middle of the spring semester.

Results

Our respondents used fraudulent excuses frequently and in a variety of contexts. As shown in Table 1, 68% of the students who completed the QAE admitted to using at least one fraudulent excuse while in college. Some insight into the reason for this frequency can be gained from examining the reported responses made by professors to fraudulent excuses. Ninety percent of the students who used a fraudulent excuse reported having their excuse accepted. Furthermore, students reported that professors seldom requested proof. The majority (57%) stated that less than 25% of their professors demanded proof of excuses. Moreover, a substantial number (13%) of all respondents reported that their professors never asked for proof of an excuse's veracity.

The data shed little light on how professors might distinguish between legitimate and fraudulent excuses. As shown

Table 1. Percentage of Students Using Fraudulent and Legitimate Excuses

Category	Frequency				
	0	1	2	3	4+
Fraudulent, college	33	16	17	12	23
Legitimate, college	13	29	27	10	20
Fraudulent, semester	65	17	9	6	4
Legitimate, semester	47	32	15	4	2

Note. College refers to number of each type of excuse while in college, and *semester* refers to number of each type of excuse during the past semester.

Table 2. Frequency of Fraudulent and Legitimate Excuses

Given Excuse	Fraudulent	Legitimate
Personal illness	96	115
Family emergency	77	53
Did not understand assignment	45	55
Alarm failed/overslept	36	42
Left paper in dorm	33	33
Out of town	24	33
Computer failed	24	27
Grandparent death	6	21
Best friend death	0	4
Other	43	59

in Table 2, the frequency of each legitimate and fraudulent excuse is virtually equivalent. The only apparent difference is the greater number of fraudulent excuses claiming that there was a family emergency. Fewer fraudulent than legitimate excuses involved death of a grandparent. All other categories of excuses were observed with roughly equal frequency as both fraudulent and legitimate.

It is no surprise that the most common reason (91%) for fabricating an excuse was the hope of gaining more time. Several variables influence whether or not a student offers a fabricated excuse. Eighty-five percent reported that they would be more likely to make up an excuse if the professor was perceived as lenient. Other factors that contribute to fabrication were knowing the professor well (56%), having a younger professor (68%), being in a large class (58%), and being in a lower level class (70%). Male and female faculty were targeted with equal frequency.

Among the characteristics that influenced whether students presented fraudulent excuses, gender of student appeared to have the strongest relation with using a fraudulent excuse. An analysis of gender by frequency of fraudulent excuses revealed that men were more likely than women to fabricate fraudulent excuses, $\chi^2(4) = 9.38$, $p < .05$, a finding that might be expected in light of the higher percentage of men who stated that they had fabricated four or more excuses (31% of men compared to 17% of women). Thus, men are more likely to be repeat offenders in the case of academic excuse making.

GPA was also related to excuse making, with students having GPAs of 3.00 or greater (collapsed from .50 intervals) being less likely to fabricate excuses, $\chi^2(8) = 15.57$, $p < .05$. There was no relation between year in college and fraudulent excuse making.

We also asked students to describe the emotions they felt concerning one instance of giving a fraudulent excuse. In Table 3, these findings are reported in terms of the three most highly rated emotions experienced before, during, after, and now relative to the excuse-making episode. As can be seen from this table, students reported feeling moderately guilty only during the period of actually giving the excuse. The emotions most frequently and strongly experienced before the excuse-making incident were fear and desperation. Afterward, students felt relieved and happy. Although students reported feeling some shame and guilt, at no time were these emotions reported as the strongest experienced emotions. Further evidence for the painlessness of this experience came from responses to the question of whether the

168

Table 3. Reported Emotions at Each Phase of the Excuse-Making Episode

Time	Emotions	M	SD
Before	Nervous	2.60	2.04
	Desperate	2.05	2.02
	Scared	1.67	1.83
During	Nervous	2.63	2.10
	Scared	1.81	1.88
	Guilty	1.65	1.84
After	Relieved	3.09	2.05
	Happy	2.23	2.15
	Confident	1.78	1.93
Now	Calm	1.76	2.01
	Relieved	1.63	2.01
	Happy	1.50	1.92

Note. Subjects rated each emotion on a scale ranging from *not experienced at all* (0) to *highest* (5). Emotions were rated for before, during, and after an excuse-making episode as well as at the time of completing the QAE.

student would do it again. Of those who made up fraudulent excuses, 55% said they would use the same excuse again, and another 14% said they would change their excuse next time. Only 20% said they would not make up a fraudulent excuse again. Predictably, because students did not experience much shame about fabricating an excuse, they reported being likely to repeat the behavior, $\chi^2(25) = 54.39$, $p < .01$. Similarly, students who felt little guilt at the time they answered the questionnaire were more likely to state that they would make a similar excuse in the future, $\chi^2(25) = 73.33$, $p < .01$.

Discussion

Our findings suggest that professors should be cautious in evaluating students' excuses. Apparently, many students take advantage of the professor's wish to be understanding and helpful toward students who are perceived to be genuinely distraught due to some unfortunate event beyond their control. Professors rarely ask students to verify their excuses, perhaps because of their discomfort at communicating disbelief to a troubled student; for example, the professor might feel that it is intrusive to inquire about the details of a reported family emergency.

Some guidelines to help professors judge the legitimacy of excuses emerged from our study. Younger professors should be more wary, because students perceive them as more likely to accept an excuse. Professors perceived as knowing the students well should also be on guard because their attitude of trust might be exploited. In addition, the notorious grandparent death excuse is more likely to be valid than fraudulent.

Apart from judging the content of an excuse, we can offer several other recommendations to help faculty ease the burden of making this difficult determination. At the beginning of the semester, professors should clearly state their policy about accepting excuses. The number of students who will attempt to pass off a fraudulent excuse as real will probably be decreased by the professor's statement that no

excuse will be accepted without proof of its validity. It may not always be possible to obtain proof that an excuse is legitimate, but many potential excuse makers will probably be discouraged by a professor's firm stand. In any case, professors should consider asking students for details about excuses they give. Even if a student manages to describe these with apparent credulity, word that the professor does not take an excuse lightly is likely to spread, thus reducing attempts at fraudulent excuses.

Final recommendations for dealing with excuse making concern the structure of the course and grading policies. One way to reduce excuse making is to offer various options (Chiodo, 1986) that allow students to miss an exam without penalty. This strategy conveys to students the instructor's wish to be realistic and flexible in the event of unanticipated emergencies. It also provides students with some protection for their privacy in the event of an emergency that they may not feel comfortable discussing with a professor. Another suggestion is for the professor to clarify grading policies and to write exams unambiguously so that students are less pressured to resort to deception as a way of achieving desired grades (Milton, Pollio, & Eison, 1986).

The topic of excuse making warrants further investigation, both from the standpoint of instructional policy and as a source of information about the social psychological processes involved. Psychologists have a rich theoretical tradition from which to draw. Our data suggest that college teachers must first make the unpleasant admission that fraudulent excuse making is a common and successful practice.

References

Adler, A. (1931). *What life should mean to you.* Boston: Little, Brown.

Basgall, J. A., & Snyder, C. R. (1988). Excuses in waiting: External locus of control and reactions to success–failure feedback. *Journal of Personality and Social Psychology, 54,* 656–662.

Beck, L. (1985). *Prediction of socially undesirable behavior: Lying, cheating, shoplifting.* Unpublished master's thesis, University of Massachusetts, Amherst, MA.

Chiodo, J. J. (1986, August 6). The effects of exam anxiety on grandma's health. *Chronicle of Higher Education,* p. 68.

Jung, J. (1987). Anticipatory excuses in relation to expected versus actual task performance. *The Journal of Psychology, 121,* 413–421.

McKeachie, W. J. (1986). *Teaching tips: A guide for the beginning college teacher* (8th ed.). Lexington, MA: Heath.

Milton, O., Pollio, H. R., & Eison, J. A. (1986). *Making sense of college grades.* San Francisco: Jossey-Bass.

Smith, S. H., & Whitehead, G. I. (1988). The public and private use of consensus-raising excuses. *Journal of Personality, 56,* 355–371.

Snyder, C. R., Higgins, R. L., & Stucky, R. J. (1983). *Excuses: Masquerades in search of grace.* New York: Wiley.

Notes

1. This article is based on the first author's senior honor's thesis at the University of Massachusetts at Amherst.

Section II
Demonstrations and Activities
in Introductory Psychology

12. GENERAL

A Jigsaw Puzzle Approach to Learning History in Introductory Psychology

Judith Krauss
St. John's University

When students of introductory psychology open their textbooks to the first chapter, they encounter a variety of formidable topics, examples of which appear in any current textbook. Chapter 1 of an introductory textbook typically presents definitions, gives the origins and history of psychology, describes the major perspectives for studying behavior, compares and contrasts research methodology, and offers information on psychology as a profession. Names, dates, places, and terms abound. Because many universities consider introductory psychology an ideal choice for first semester freshmen, novice college students are likely to confront this chapter. Students enter the course with expectations as to what they will learn, often hoping for exciting coverage of abnormal behavior or the psychology of dating; hence, the inclusion of the history of psychology in the first chapter may come as a surprise. Studying psychology's past to understand its present state is necessary (Goodwin, 1997) but perhaps, is a daunting task for some students.

Few students are familiar with the historical terms of structuralism, functionalism, and gestalt psychology. The unique presentation of these terms in the history of psychology makes it unlikely that students studied them in another discipline. Bringing history to life (e.g., Benjamin, 1993) may be one way to engage students in the study of this important topic. There is support for using active learning and critical thinking to engage students in education (Halpern, 1998). Providing specific examples of the intersection between concepts in a discipline and their application to daily life is one strategy for strengthening critical thinking skills (Ennis, 1995).

From this perspective, and to make this introductory chapter more meaningful and enjoyable, I devised a method for teaching three of the early perspectives of modern psychology by using simple jigsaw puzzles. To conduct this activity, I use one or more jigsaw puzzles, depending on class enrollment. Each puzzle measures about 9″ × 12″ and contains 12 to 15 pieces. This size ensures that puzzle pieces are large enough for students to observe color, shape, and other characteristics and that puzzle assembly is simple. In a class of 50 students, four puzzles provide sufficient opportunities for everyone to participate. I use puzzles for children ages 3 to 5 because such puzzles are colorful and readily available.

Initially, I break each puzzle apart and distribute the pieces randomly throughout the class. I do not give adjoining puzzle pieces to adjacent students. After all students receive a piece, I invite them to tell me everything they can about their piece. I reject answers such as "it is part of a puzzle" or "it has a ninja turtle on it" because these answers assume I have prior knowledge or experience with "puzzles" and "ninja turtles." I invite the students to consider me as "an alien who has just landed from the mother ship," someone for whom everything must be reduced to a basic level and explained in terms that cannot be reduced further. Eventually, although most descriptions will still require some prior knowledge, I accept the answers "it is round," "it has color on it," "it has no odor," and others of that type because these descriptions are more fundamental than the previous ones. This dilemma in describing helps students understand the difficulty of reducing anything to its most fundamental level. When the students have nothing more to say, I introduce the word *structuralism* and teach that it is a way of knowing an object or behavior by reducing it to its most basic parts. Then I ask students to tell me how much they know about their piece, and how much they still need to know about it. The limits of structuralism become apparent as students realize there is no mention of the purpose of their piece.

Next, students figure out what their piece does. I encourage them to find another piece that might relate to their piece in some way. Because I distributed the pieces randomly, students must get up and walk around the class to find an adjoining piece. This exercise, used in either the first or second class, serves as an excellent icebreaker as students must interact. After the students see how their pieces work in conjunction with other pieces, I introduce the word *functionalism* and teach that it is a way of knowing an object or behavior by seeking to understand its function or purpose. In short, we discuss what the piece can do and what it cannot do. At this point, I ask them if knowledge of their piece is complete. Although we know its parts (structure) and we know what it does (function), is there more to know? As isolated groups of students hold their two-piece objects, they realize the limitations of this approach as well. Unless everyone continues to explore, we will not obtain larger meaning and additional knowledge.

Thus, students continue to work with their pieces to assemble all relevant parts into a whole. Again, with multiple puzzles and random piece distribution, the students must cooperate and communicate to create meaningful whole puzzles. The group that produces the first completed puzzle usually displays team pride, and a spirit of fun is present throughout the entire activity. After puzzle assembly, I introduce the words *gestalt psychology* and teach that it is a way of knowing an object or behavior by creating a whole from parts, but that the whole derives its meaning only when the parts relate and work together. I ask if anyone has heard the maxim "the whole is greater than the sum of its parts" and explain its meaning in relation to what we have just learned.

This exercise communicates three new and difficult concepts clearly and effectively. In Fall 1997, I compared the performance of first-semester freshmen who learned these concepts through the jigsaw puzzle technique to that of first-semester freshmen who learned by reading about these concepts in the textbook. There was a clear advantage for students who learned using the jigsaw puzzle technique over reading the textbook. I taught four introductory psychology classes by the puzzle method ($n = 114$) and one introductory psychology class by assigning the text reading ($n = 24$). I collected data from 3 test questions pertaining to the topics. Using the number of students who scored correctly on each of these 3 questions in each of the four puzzle method classes, I computed the average number of puzzle method students who scored correctly on those 12 questions. For the puzzle method students, an average of 24.75 per class of 28.5 (87%) scored correct answers on questions covering these topics. For the text-reading students, an average of 13 students in the class of 24 (54%) scored correct answers on the same 3 questions. The difference was significant, $t(13) = 6.06$, $p < .01$.

In addition to the advantage to learning and test performance, the students enjoyed this activity as evidenced by their remarks. For example, anonymous end-of-semester evaluations that asked what lesson(s) were memorable included the following comments about the puzzles:

"One of the very first lessons . . . sticks out in my mind. Your use of the puzzles made for a clear understanding of what the differences were. I still think of the puzzles when I need to remember."
"I enjoyed the first lesson with the puzzles. It taught me about structure and that everyone and everything can be broken down into pieces."
"I loved the puzzles . . . these things may seem silly but the concepts stayed with me."

I believe that students' evaluations are useful in determining whether to continue with a particular teaching technique. In this case, remarks about remembering the concepts influenced me to continue using this technique and to develop future techniques with an active learning format.

References

Benjamin, L. T., Jr. (1993). *A history of psychology in letters*. Madison, WI: Brown & Benchmark.

Ennis, R. (1995). *Critical thinking*. Englewood Cliffs, NJ: Prentice-Hall.

Goodwin, C. J. (1997). The vital role of psychology's history in introductory courses: An interview with Ludy T. Benjamin, Jr. *Teaching of Psychology, 24*, 218–221.

Halpern, D. F. (1998). Teaching critical thinking for transfer across domains. *American Psychologist, 53*, 449–455.

Notes

1. I thank Nicholas Luis for the generous loan of his Ninja Turtle puzzles used in gathering data for this article.
2. I am grateful to Randolph A. Smith and three anonymous reviewers for their helpful comments on earlier drafts of this article.
3. Send correspondence to Judith Krauss, Division of Social Sciences, Bent Hall–268, St. John's University, Jamaica, NY 11439; e-mail: krausj@stjohns.edu.

Student-Created Skits: Interactive Class Demonstrations

Jane P. Sheldon
Ferrum College

Teaching a wide variety of psychology courses, I have found that the use of skits works well and can be adapted to several different psychological topics. These in-class performances incorporate group learning, cooperation, creativity, multiple perspectives, and good old-fashioned fun. Although others (Balch, 1983; Sroufe & DeHart, 1988) have also suggested that role-playing can be incorporated into the classroom as a teaching tool, their suggested activities have used only a handful of student volunteers, instead of getting the entire class involved. The in-class skits I use involve all students in the writing, performing, observing, and analyzing processes. At first, many students groan and complain but are then transformed into stage actors par excellence. Even reticent and shy students are able and willing to participate, although perhaps with no speaking roles.

Toner (1978) and Brooks (1985) pointed out the usefulness of student drama productions in the psychology classroom; however, their dramatic creations were semester-long, required activities for which students received a grade. Many instructors may not desire such long-term creative projects, but they may feel comfortable devoting a single class period to student-created skits. In addition, many instructors may be reluctant to grade student drama productions for fear that introverted students may be unfairly penalized for awkward performances. In-class skits offer the shy or anxious student either an active role in the creative process or the option of adopting a nonspeaking role in the performance. Because no grades are at stake, there is also less anxiety and less group pressure exerted on shy or insecure students. Even without grades at stake, students are highly motivated to give presentations that are creative, humorous, and accurate portrayals of the concept. They seem to find the activity intrinsically motivating.

So far, I have used skits created and performed by students to demonstrate Kohlberg's moral development stages (i.e., preconventional, conventional, and postconventional), defense mechanisms (e.g., regression, sublimation, projection, displacement, and reaction formation), operant-conditioning terminology (i.e., positive reinforcement, negative reinforcement, and punishment), identity status (i.e., negative identity, foreclosure, role diffusion, and moratorium), and parenting styles (i.e., authoritarian, permissive, and authoritative). For example, one group of four students depicted the defense mechanism of displacement by performing a skit in which a young man is treated unfairly by his boss and goes home to yell at his child and kick his dog. Kohlberg's preconventional stage of moral reasoning was demonstrated by three students pretending to be children in a store deciding not to steal candy for fear of being punished by their parents.

As Thompson and Osberg (1993) pointed out in their review of articles published in *Teaching of Psychology* since 1974, more classroom activity ideas are needed for numerous psychological concepts. The need for a demonstration or activity for parenting styles was specifically mentioned by Thompson and Osberg, so student-created skits can fill that void. An activity such as in-class skits may be a much needed tool for teaching many of the specialty areas of psychology.

The procedure for the in-class skits for a class size up to 40 or 45 students is simple. The instructor divides students into groups of three or four (five or more is too many), and each group draws a slip of paper out of a box that is passed around the room. They are then required to create and eventually perform a skit that demonstrates the concept written on the piece of paper. The rest of the class tries to guess which concept is being portrayed. Usually 10 to 15 min is enough time for the scripts to be written and the actors to learn their lines or know their roles. The rest of the class time is spent performing and guessing what concept is being portrayed. Each skit generally lasts about 1 min. Now and then, the instructor may need to clarify or correct information presented in the skits, but generally any confusion is cleared up in the script-writing process, when the instructor acts as editor and creative consultant for any group needing assistance. The activity can immediately follow the instructor's brief explanation of the concepts to be learned or can be scheduled the following class day.

Guidelines may be needed to keep skits understandable and relevant to the class. A group may need to tell the audience before the skit which actor (or actors) is exhibiting the behavior to be guessed. Also, the instructor may decide that, to be relevant to the class, the skits should focus on a particular age group. For example, an instructor may decide that skits demonstrating parenting styles in a child development course must all involve 2- to 12-year-old children or that operant-conditioning skits in an adolescence course must all use adolescents as characters, instead of adults or young children.

My classes during fall 1993 used skits to demonstrate parenting styles and Kohlberg's moral development stages. End-of-semester student evaluations ($N = 68$) indicated that they enjoyed the class skits and found them helpful. On a scale ranging from 1 (*not at all enjoyable*) to 5 (*highly enjoyable*), the mean score for how much the students liked the activity was 4.2 ($SD = 1.1$). On a scale ranging from 1 (*not at all helpful*) to 5 (*very helpful*) for learning or remembering the material, students' mean rating was 4.1 ($SD = 1.2$).

Skits created and performed by students can be a successful supplement to the classroom experience. In addition, the nature of the task requires cooperation, communication, and creativity. As with any demonstration or activity, however, skits should not be overused: Once or twice per semester seems to be most beneficial.

References

Balch, W. R. (1983). The use of role-playing in a classroom demonstration of client-centered therapy. *Teaching of Psychology, 10,* 173–174.

Brooks, C. I. (1985). A role-playing exercise for the history of psychology course. *Teaching of Psychology, 12,* 84–85.

Sroufe, L. A., & DeHart, G. (1988). *The instructor's manual and testbank for Child Development.* New York: Knopf.

Thompson, W. B., & Osberg, T. M. (1993, August). Teaching of Psychology *publication patterns: Plugging the gaps in our teaching techniques.* Paper presented at the meeting of the American Psychological Association, Toronto, Canada.

Toner, I. J. (1978). A "dramatic" approach to the teaching of adolescent psychology. *Teaching of Psychology, 5,* 218–219.

Notes

1. I thank Charles L. Brewer and three anonymous reviewers for their helpful comments on an earlier version of this article.

Understanding and Applying Psychology Through Use of News Clippings

Elizabeth A. Rider
Elizabethtown College

To encourage students to apply course material to events outside the classroom, instructors have assigned interviews, letter writing, journals, and media analyses. For example, Walton (1988) described an interview assignment designed to help students in an adult development course apply theory and research to the lives of the people being interviewed. Walton noted two drawbacks: difficulty finding interview subjects and extensive time demands on the instructor in classes with more than 10 to 15 students. Junn (1989) designed a letter-writing activity to increase application of concepts to students' own lives and understanding of their family relationships, which could be a problem for students who do not want to write about personal experiences. Hettich (1990) described journal writing to develop critical thinking skills, writing skills, and understanding of course material in personal contexts. Journals have been criticized for being too personal, not scholarly enough (Jenkinson, 1988), and time consuming and difficult to grade objectively (Hettich, 1990; Junn, 1989).

Several media projects may increase students' appreciation of the relevance of course material. Ward (1985) used a media project to maintain students' interest in an adolescence course. Groups of students developed a question and collected observations from some form of media to address their question. Sorensen (1976) stimulated classroom discussion by asking students to monitor media reports (newspaper, radio, or television) for 1 week and then discuss their observations in class. This is a useful homework assignment, but because it lasts only 1 week, it may not affect students' overall learning.

An alternative media project that eliminates some of the drawbacks of other projects is for students to develop portfolios of newspaper and magazine clippings and write an explanation or interpretation of each clipping using course material. This technique encourages students to develop a scholarly understanding of the course material and to assess its relevance. Students who appreciate the value of course material may be more motivated to learn and to enjoy class, and they may be encouraged to relate current events to psychology after the course ends. Portfolios are also relatively easy to grade, can be used in large classes, and promote high student interest.

Description of Assignment

I have used this project in both general and developmental psychology courses, and it could easily be adapted to other courses. Students collected clippings that illustrated psychological concepts. For each clipping, students provided its source and wrote a brief description or explanation of how it related to a psychological concept, theory, or research finding covered in class. Students have used magazine articles, newspaper feature articles, editorials, commentaries, advice columns, medical columns, pictures, and cartoons.

At the first class meeting, I gave each student a photocopy of a completed portfolio and discussed the nature of the project by examining the types of clippings and the comments that accompanied each one. The sample portfolio contained 20 annotated entries compiled from clippings that students submitted during a previous semester and from clippings I found and annotated to illustrate the scope of the project. After this discussion, I gave each student a different clipping related to the course. This was the only clipping that students did not find on their own. With large classes, instructors could distribute one or a few clippings or ask each student to bring one clipping to the second class. Students spent about 15 min during this first class locating an appropriate section of the text, with help if needed, and drafting a sample comment. They turned in the clipping and comment at the next class for feedback. Doing this at the beginning of the semester familiarized students immediately with my expectations for the project. Students wanting additional feedback could submit other clippings at any time during the semester.

I encouraged students to maintain a folder throughout the semester with all clippings that might be relevant, even if they could not immediately write a comment. By the end of the semester when more course material had been covered, students were often able to find connections between clippings and psychological concepts. Guidelines suggested that students use the sample portfolio as an aid to the length of comments and that they should find at least 15 clippings distributed across each major unit of the course. The median number of entries in portfolios was 20, with a range from 14 to 28. The length of students' comments ranged from two sentences to two paragraphs based on content of the clipping and how much coverage the topic was given in the class.

I graded portfolios on several dimensions. One was the relevance of the clippings to the course material. For example, a clipping about schizophrenia was not appropriate for a portfolio in developmental psychology because this topic was not covered in the course. A second dimension was the accuracy of students' comments: Were their descriptions of the psychological terms, concepts, or theories correct? A third grading dimension was breadth of coverage. Each major section of the course or each chapter of the textbook should be covered. The fourth grading dimension was originality, which included overall presentation style of the portfolio as well as the students' ability to see psychology in a wide range of formats. For example, some students submitted clippings in which the author explicitly connected the material to psychology, and the student merely summarized the author's point. Other students submitted clippings that did not mention the psychological concept that the students identified. Students received a single letter grade for the portfolio and a rating sheet indicating their achievement on each dimension, as well as brief comments throughout the portfolio itself.

Examples From the Sample Portfolio

One clipping was a cartoon showing a little boy holding the stems of a bunch of grapes. The cartoon caption read: "All that's left of my grapes is the skeleton" (Keane, 1990). A student used this clipping to explain Piaget's concept of assimilation. A second clipping was a newspaper article, "Taste Makes Waste" (1988). The student's comment explained taste aversion and identified the components of classical conditioning. A third example was a "Dear Abby" (1988) question and answer about a toddler who continues to sleep in her parent's bed at night. The student's comment explained how reinforcement affected the child's behavior and the mother's tolerance of the child's behavior. The student also suggested operant conditioning techniques to change the situation. A fourth example was a short magazine article (Gibson, 1990) that described several aspects of infants' social development. A student related this clipping to research on infants' memory abilities and to Piaget's description of sensorimotor accomplishments.

Evaluation of the Assignment

Seventy-two students from two general psychology classes evaluated the project anonymously as part of the overall course evaluations. All but 7% of the students reported clearly understanding the nature of the project following its introduction during the first week of the semester. Twenty percent of the students reported some initial difficulty finding relevant clippings because they did not regularly receive or read newspapers or magazines. This was not a serious problem because students had access to papers in the school library and could photocopy these for their portfolio. As a result of this project, some students reported that they began a newspaper or magazine subscription.

Of particular importance were the findings that 89% of the students reported that the project was more valuable to them than completing an oral presentation or written term paper (typical course projects), and 96% believed that it increased their ability to think about course material outside the context of the classroom. Making this connection between the classroom and the "real world" is an important course outcome and one that is not always easy to achieve. Finally, 89% reported that the project improved their exam performance. This outcome may result because students need to clearly understand a concept in order to describe its

relevance to an example. Overall, on a 5-point scale ranging from *most favorable* (1) to *least favorable* (5), 85% of the students rated the project 1 or 2.

Some students also provided written comments about the project. Consistent with the quantitative evaluation, these comments were quite positive. Many students expressed their enjoyment of working on a project other than, as one student put it, "yet another journal or paper." Another student commented that she "liked being able to write about a variety of topics rather than a single paper topic." Students also noted that the nature of the project encouraged them to distribute their time across the semester, rather than concentrating their efforts at the end of the semester. Finally, students noted that they read the textbook more than usual because they were looking for ways to link specific clippings to the course material. This fact may have contributed to their reports that the project improved their exam performance.

This assignment can be graded quickly and thus can be used in larger classes. It can also be graded objectively because students are not using personal experiences to illustrate psychological concepts. Although students could link clippings to the course material in different ways, their explanations of psychological concepts were easily identified as either correct or incorrect. The projects are interesting to read because each one is different, and an added benefit is that the journals can help keep the instructor current on media reports relevant to the course. Finally, the project is not limited to any particular topic or course.

References

Dear Abby. (1988, October 21). *The Patriot-News*, p. C2.
Gibson, J. T. (1990, May). As they grow: 1-year-olds. *Parents*, p. 205.
Hettich, P. (1990). Journal writing: Old fare or nouvelle cuisine? *Teaching of Psychology, 17,* 36–39.
Jenkinson, E. B. (1988). Learning to write/writing to learn. *Phi Delta Kappan, 69,* 712–717.
Junn, E. N. (1989). "Dear Mom and Dad": Using personal letters to enhance students' understanding of developmental issues. *Teaching of Psychology, 16,* 135–139.
Keane, B. (1990, November 11). The family circus. *Intelligencer Journal,* p. C8.
Sorensen, J. L. (1976). Increasing the relevance of the media to psychology courses. *Teaching of Psychology, 3,* 140–141.
Taste makes waste: It's root of most food phobias. (1988, November 30). *The Patriot-News,* p. C1.
Walton, M. D. (1988). Interviewing across the life span: A project for an adult development course. *Teaching of Psychology, 15,* 198–200.
Ward, T. B. (1985). The media project: Enhancing student interest in the psychology of adolescence. *Teaching of Psychology, 12,* 87–89.

Notes

1. We thank Delbert Ellsworth and three anonymous reviewers for their helpful comments on an earlier draft of this article.
2. A preliminary version of this article was presented at the Eastern Conference on the Teaching of Psychology, Harrisonburg, VA, October 1990.

The Media Assignment: Enhancing Psychology Students' Ability to Apply Their Knowledge of Psychology

Timothy J. Lawson
College of Mount St. Joseph

Psychology instructors have used many techniques to enhance students' ability to apply their knowledge of psychology to real-world events (e.g., Hettich, 1990; Junn, 1989; Rider, 1992; Walton, 1988). Walton (1988) had students relate their knowledge of adult development to the lives of people they interviewed. To enhance students' ability to relate their knowledge of psychology to their own lives, Junn (1989) had students write semiautobiographical personal letters, and Hettich (1990) had students write journal entries that focused on the relation between course material and their personal experiences.

Each of these techniques may be impractical for some students and instructors. Students may have trouble finding interview subjects (Walton, 1988) and may be hesitant to write about personal experiences in letters or journals. Furthermore, evaluating journals may be time-consuming (Hettich, 1990).

Rider (1992) described a technique that avoids these disadvantages. Students in a general psychology course collected magazine articles or newspaper clippings for each major unit of the course and wrote brief descriptions of how these materials related to course content. This technique is superior to others because the assignments can be graded in a relatively quick and objective manner and because it helps students and the instructor stay current on media reports relevant to the course (Rider, 1992). Although Rider found that students reacted favorably to the assignment and believed that it increased their ability to apply their knowledge, their beliefs may not accurately reflect actual improvements.

In this study, I explored whether a media assignment, similar to that used by Rider (1992), increased psychology students' ability to apply their knowledge of psychological concepts to examples of real-world events. Students in different sections of an introductory psychology course collected examples from the popular media that illustrated either operant- or classical-conditioning concepts. Afterward, students took a quiz that contained factual and applied multiple-choice questions on classical and operant conditioning. Because the assignment required students to apply their knowledge to media examples, as opposed to memorizing factual information, I predicted that the media assignment would primarily affect their ability to apply their knowledge. If so, each group of students should outperform the other group on applied questions related to their assigned topic, and the difference between the two groups in performance on factual questions should be minimal.

Method

Subjects

Quiz data were collected from 88 students enrolled in four sections of introductory psychology. I taught all of these sections—two during the beginning and two during the end of 1 academic year. Students in each section had been randomly assigned to one of the two experimental conditions ($n = 44$ in each condition). However, 19 students (9 in the classical-conditioning group and 10 in the operant-conditioning group) did not complete the media assignment by the due date.

Nature of the Assignment

Students were required to complete three media assignments during the semester. For the first and last assignments, students chose a concept from one of several chapters in the text and found a related example in the popular media (e.g., newspaper or magazine articles, cartoons, or song lyrics). For the second assignment (the focus of this study), students were randomly assigned to locate an example related to either classical or operant conditioning. For all three assignments, students handed in a photocopy of the media item and wrote one or two paragraphs describing how it related to the psychological concept. The assignments were each worth 3% of the final grade and were evaluated on their relevance to the concept, the clarity of the written description, and how closely they followed the directions for the assignment.

Dependent Measures

On the day the media assignment was due—one class period before the second exam—students took a practice quiz. The quiz contained 20 multiple-choice questions obtained from an introductory psychology test bank (Galliano, 1990); 6 of these questions were revised either to make the wording consistent with the terms and examples used in class or to change applied questions to factual questions. Half of the questions were related to operant conditioning, and half were related to classical conditioning. Moreover, half of each of the two categories of questions were factual (i.e., tested knowledge of terms or concepts), and half were applied (i.e., required relating concepts to real-world

Table 1. Mean Quiz Scores and Sample Sizes by Media Assignment, Question Topic, and Question Type

		Question Type	
	n	Applied	Factual
Operant conditioning questions			
Media assignment			
Operant conditioning	34	3.47	3.65
Classical conditioning	35	2.89	3.34
M		3.17	3.49
Classical conditioning questions			
Media assignment			
Operant conditioning	34	3.91	3.53
Classical conditioning	35	4.03	3.31
M		3.97	3.42

Note. Maximum score = 5.

events). Whether a question was applied or factual was determined by its classification in the test bank and by comparing the question with the aforementioned definitions. All questions were of a similar level of difficulty, and each applied question covered a concept also covered by a factual question.

Students were also asked to rate, on a 5-point scale ranging from *strongly disagree* (1) to *strongly agree* (5), the extent to which they agreed with the statements "the homework assignments help me understand some of the concepts I am learning in class," and "the homework assignments help me see how some of the things I am learning in class apply to the real world."

Results

Quiz Performance

For each student who completed the media assignment, the total number of questions answered correctly was calculated for each of the four cells formed by question topic (operant vs. classical conditioning) and question type (applied vs. factual). The mean scores are presented in Table 1.

A $2 \times 2 \times 2$ (Media Assignment: Operant vs. Classical Conditioning × Question Topic: Operant vs. Classical Conditioning × Question Type: Applied vs. Factual) analysis of variance (the latter two variables were within subjects) was performed on students' scores. Although no media assignment effects were significant, separate analyses were performed at each level of question topic to examine the lower order effects predicted from the hypotheses. These analyses revealed a significant main effect of the media assignment on the number of operant-conditioning questions answered correctly, $F(1, 67) = 3.94$, $p = .051$. Specifically, the operant-conditioning group ($M = 7.12$) outperformed the classical-conditioning group ($M = 6.23$). There were no significant effects of the media assignment on the classical-conditioning quiz scores (all $Fs < 1.7$).

Because performance on applied questions was of central interest, the effect of the assignment on the applied operant-conditioning quiz scores was examined separately from its effect on the factual operant-conditioning quiz scores.

The results revealed that the operant-conditioning group ($M = 3.47$) scored significantly higher than the classical-conditioning group ($M = 2.89$) on the applied questions, $F(1, 67) = 5.34$, $p = .024$; but not on the factual questions ($M = 3.65$ and $M = 3.34$, respectively), $F(1, 67) = 1.14$. However, the Media Assignment × Question Type interaction was not significant, $F < 1$. Similar analyses performed on students' scores on the classical-conditioning questions revealed no significant effects involving the media assignment (all $Fs < 1.7$).

The same analyses were performed on quiz scores of the 19 students who did not complete the assignment by the due date. Results revealed no significant effects of the media assignment (all $Fs < 2.6$). These students, on the average, scored significantly lower ($M = 12.11$) than the other students ($M = 14.06$) on the quiz, $t(86) = 2.27$, $p = .026$—an unsurprising finding, given that 74% of these students had a below average grade on the first exam.

Students' Perceptions

Of the 69 students who completed the assignment, 83% reported agreement (i.e., circled 4 or 5) with the statement "the homework assignments help me understand some of the concepts I am learning in class" ($M = 4.09$), and 88% reported agreement with the statement "the homework assignments help me see how some of the things I am learning in class apply to the real world" ($M = 4.34$).

Discussion

Consistent with Rider (1992), most students in this study reported that they thought the media assignments enhanced their understanding of course material and their ability to see how that material related to the real world. This study provided some evidence that media assignments can improve students' understanding of specific concepts and their ability to apply their knowledge to real-world events, as reflected in their performance on a quiz. Specifically, students assigned to collect media examples of operant-conditioning principles performed better than students who collected classical-conditioning examples on quiz questions designed to assess their ability to apply their knowledge of operant conditioning. Moreover, students who did not complete the assignment before the quiz showed no significant benefit from the assignment.

It is somewhat puzzling, however, that no effect of the assignment was found with the students who collected media examples of classical conditioning. One possible explanation is that the applied classical-conditioning questions were not difficult enough to produce a difference between the two media assignment groups. Although the quiz questions were all classified at a similar level of difficulty in the test bank, students' superior performance on the applied classical-conditioning questions (see Table 1) suggests that these questions may have been easier to answer than the other types of questions.

In short, media assignments may enhance students' learning and their ability to apply course knowledge to real-world events. This assignment has the added advantage of getting students actively involved in learning and thinking about how psychological concepts relate to current events, and it may have a lasting effect (after the course) on students' tendency to think about how psychology relates to events described in the media.

References

Galliano, G. (1990). *Test bank*. New York: Harper & Row.

Hettich, P. (1990). Journal writing: Old fare or nouvelle cuisine? *Teaching of Psychology, 27*, 36–39.

Junn, E. N. (1989). "Dear Mom and Dad": Using personal letters to enhance students' understanding of developmental issues. *Teaching of Psychology, 16*, 135–139.

Rider, E. A. (1992). Understanding and applying psychology through use of news clippings. *Teaching of Psychology, 19*, 161–163.

Walton, M. D. (1988). Interviewing across the life span: A project for an adult development course. *Teaching of Psychology, 15*, 198–200.

Notes

1. This research was supported in part by a Faculty Development Grant from the College of Mount St. Joseph.

2. An earlier version of this article was presented at the Tenth Annual Mid-America Conference for Teachers of Psychology, University of Southern Indiana, Evansville, IN, October 1993.

3. I thank Ruth Ault, Gwen Briscoe, George Banziger, and three anonymous reviewers for their helpful comments on a draft of this article.

Psychology Is Not Just Common Sense: An Introductory Psychology Demonstration

Timothy M. Osberg
Niagara University

Numerous researchers have studied the misconceptions that students bring with them to the introductory psychology course. Beginning with the work of McKeachie (1960) and Vaughan (1977) through more recent studies (e.g., Brown, 1983, 1984; Gardner & Dalsing, 1986; Gardner & Hund, 1983; Gutman, 1979; Ruble, 1986), the nature and correlates of misconceptions and the influence that introductory psychology has on them have been examined. Although the specific nature of students' misconceptions has been inconsistent across some of these studies (Griggs & Ransdell, 1987), one point is not disputed: Students do bring misconceptions to the first course.

Many of my introductory psychology students believe that psychology is nothing more than common sense and that, therefore, the course will be easy. Countless times, in interviews with students who have failed the first course exam, I have heard the lament: "I should have studied harder! I assumed the course would be easy because psychology is just common sense!" Students taking introductory courses in other disciplines, such as chemistry, English, or accounting, seem less inclined to take the content of those courses for granted.

I developed a demonstration that curbs this misconception. During the first or second week, I simply describe one of psychology's classic experiments and then ask students to guess its outcome. Because the vast majority of the class guesses an intuitive outcome, students are surprised by the actual, counterintuitive findings. Thus, they learn early in the term that psychology is not just common sense.

I chose Festinger and Carlsmith's (1959) classic study of cognitive dissonance because I thought that it would be an engaging example and that most students would be surprised by its counterintuitive findings. Other studies could be substituted, depending on the personal inclination of the instructor.

Procedure

The demonstration takes about 10 to 15 min. The issue of intuitiveness should not be discussed before conducting the demonstration. After defining psychology and its subfields and describing the history of the discipline, and as a transition into a discussion of research methods, I engage the students in the following task:

Suppose you had volunteered to participate in a psychology experiment on campus. Upon arrival, you were seated at a table and asked to undertake a series of dull, meaningless tasks for about an hour. Afterward, the experimenter convinced you to extol the virtues of the tasks you had performed by describing them to other potential participants as highly worthwhile, interesting, and educational. You were paid either $1 or $20 to do this. Suppose you were then asked to privately rate your enjoyment of the tasks on a questionnaire.

I then pose the following question:

After which amount do you believe your actual enjoyment rating of the tasks would be higher—$1 or $20?

Responses can be obtained by show of hands or by having students hand in their written responses for tabulation. Students will nearly unanimously indicate the $20 payment, in line with their intuition, often expressing wonder at why you asked the question. At this point, the class is given feedback about their collective responses. This feedback heightens the effect of the demonstration once students are told the true outcome of the study. Finally, the class is told that Festinger and Carlsmith (1959) found that students who received $1 rated the tasks as more enjoyable than those paid $20. The authors used the concept of cognitive dissonance to explain this finding. The students who received $1 presumably had insufficient justification for their behavior, which led to dissonance that produced a change in attitude about the tasks.

Evaluation

Evaluative data from the most recent time I used this demonstration (the fall semester of 1991) suggest it achieved its aim and that students were very engaged by it. The students in this sample were drawn from two sections of introductory psychology at a small northeastern university of approximately 2,000 students. They had declared a variety of majors in the arts and sciences, business, education, and nursing. Eighty-one of the 86 students (94.2%) gave the intuitive $20 answer. Much lively discussion followed when the true findings of the experiment were revealed. Therefore, Festinger and Carlsmith's (1959) study serves well as research with counterintuitive findings.

The questionnaire to evaluate the demonstration included five items. Two open-ended items asked students to indicate what they found useful about the demonstration and to provide any additional comments about it. Three closed-ended questions assessed students' perceptions of the overall usefulness of the demonstration, their ratings of whether or not it helped them understand that psychology is not just common sense, and their recommendations concerning the future use of the demonstration.

Because 3 students failed to return their evaluation questionnaires, the data here are based on the responses of 83 students. When asked to rate the overall usefulness of the demonstration, 87.9% rated it as either *useful* or *very useful*

(56.6% and 31.3%, respectively). The demonstration was rated as *somewhat useful* by 12.1% of the students, with none rating it as *not useful*. When asked if the demonstration helped them to understand that not all of psychology's findings simply reflect common sense, 97.6% either *agreed* or *strongly agreed* (57.8% and 39.8%, respectively) and only 2.4% *disagreed* or *strongly disagreed* (1.2% and 1.2%, respectively). When asked if they recommended using the demonstration in future classes, 83.1% said *yes, definitely*; 16.9% said *maybe*; and no one said *no*. Students' open-ended comments included: "It showed me we can't always rely on intuition." "It really helped prove your point that psychology is not just common sense." "It helped me to understand that I must study in order to do well in this course because it is not just common sense but can involve surprising results." "You could have told us 'psychology does not mirror common sense' and I probably would have forgotten it. I won't forget it now." Thus, the demonstration forcefully drives home the point that psychology does not merely verify the obvious. The demonstration is a good opening gambit for the introductory course because it stimulates lively discussion and captures students' interest.

References

Brown, L. T. (1983). Some more misconceptions about psychology among introductory psychology students. *Teaching of Psychology, 10*, 207–210.

Brown, L. T. (1984). Misconceptions about psychology aren't always what they seem. *Teaching of Psychology, 11*, 75–78.

Festinger, L., & Carlsmith, J. M. (1959). Cognitive consequences of forced compliance. *Journal of Abnormal and Social Psychology, 58*, 203–210.

Gardner, R. M., & Dalsing, S. (1986). Misconceptions about psychology among college students. *Teaching of Psychology, 13*, 32–34.

Gardner, R. M., & Hund, R. M. (1983). Misconceptions of psychology among academicians. *Teaching of Psychology, 10*, 20–22.

Griggs, R. A., & Ransdell, S. E. (1987). Misconceptions tests or misconceived tests? *Teaching of Psychology, 14*, 210–214.

Gutman, A. (1979). Misconceptions of psychology and performance in the introductory course. *Teaching of Psychology, 6*, 159–161.

McKeachie, W. J. (1960). Changes in scores on the Northwestern Misconceptions Test in six elementary psychology courses. *Journal of Educational Psychology, 51*, 240–244.

Ruble, R. (1986). Ambiguous psychological misconceptions. *Teaching of Psychology, 13*, 34–36.

Vaughan, E. D. (1977). Misconceptions about psychology among introductory psychology students. *Teaching of Psychology, 4*, 138–141.

Excerpts From Journal Articles as Teaching Devices

Helen Pennington
Massey University

Several psychologists have reported their use of journal articles in teaching. Suter and Frank (1986) described how their undergraduate methodology students read original reports of classic experiments. They also described techniques for promoting critical reading of research articles, as did Chamberlain and Burrough (1985) and Anisfeld (1987). Klugh (1983) reported using journal articles to promote writing and speaking skills. Ault (1991) presented a technique for teaching students about the structure of a journal article. Chamberlain (1988) used core articles as the basis for undergraduate laboratory projects. All of these activities use entire, or almost entire, journal articles. Shorter activities involving extracts can also be helpful. This article describes my use of excerpts from journal articles in introductory and advanced courses.

A Multi-Purpose Activity for an Introductory Course

In our 1st-year laboratory–tutorial program (Pennington, 1990), students read several short excerpts from journal articles and answer questions on each one while working individually or in small groups. Discussion by the whole class usually follows. The excerpts, usually either abstracts or parts of Method sections, come from journal articles cited in the chapter of the course text under consideration.

The activity has three major purposes. First, it introduces students to the general nature and function of psychology journal articles. At the start of the activity, I tell students that: (a) The journal article is the primary way in which researchers communicate their findings, (b) textbook authors obtain most of their material directly or indirectly from journals, and (c) in advanced psychology courses they will read published research and write their own original research reports. I also describe the basic structure of journal articles, tell students where to find psychology journals in the university library, and circulate recent issues of an APA journal. For students taking further psychology courses, the activity gently introduces more demanding tasks, such as reading, evaluating, and writing entire research reports.

Second, the activity reminds students about important scientific terms and concepts that they learned at the beginning of the course. For example, the activity helps students review concepts, such as independent and dependent variables, population, sample, hypothesis, operational definition, random assignment, control group, experiment versus correlational study, demand characteristics, informed consent, and significance level. Typical questions include: Was this study an experiment or a correlational study? How do you know? What were the researcher's hypotheses? How were subjects assigned to groups? What were the operational definitions of the independent and dependent variables? How do you know that inferential statistics were used? When reading an abstract, students may answer questions about the aim of the study and how to distinguish results from conclusions.

Third, the activity exposes students to details about studies cited in their text, brings the studies to life, and shows the limitations of secondary sources. Oversimplification is more common than error in some textbooks, but errors do occur (see Herzog, 1986; LeUnes, 1983; Suter & Frank, 1986). For instance, our introductory text (Kalat, 1990) says that Farmer (1983) found "the goals that high school girls set for themselves are about as high as those of high school boys" (p. 416). Farmer's abstract actually states that "A highlight among findings is that girls in high school are aspiring to higher career levels compared to boys" (p. 40). Exposing students to limitations of secondary sources helps to accomplish our department's goal of fostering critical thinking. I tell students that introductory texts often oversimplify issues, and that one must consult primary sources to obtain a true picture of the state of knowledge.

Activities for Advanced Courses

Journal article excerpts can also be used in advanced courses. For example, excerpts and activities can be tailored to help students read research reports critically and consider specific points of methodology.

Lectures and readings in our 3rd-year Developmental Psychology course teach students about methodological issues, such as those concerning: cross-sectional, longitudinal, and sequential research designs; sampling; and choice of measuring instruments. Students later perform short individual or small-group activities based on journal article extracts to help consolidate their learning. These activities break up lectures and provide feedback to me and students about how much has been learned.

One activity involves questions about extracts from various sections of recent articles on aging. Students identify research designs; note any limitations in research design, sampling, or measuring instruments; and look for authors' acknowledgments of such limitations. A fringe benefit is that carefully chosen extracts expose students to topical areas of research on aging and to important journals in the field.

Another activity concerns issues of sampling. Many studies in the field of aging lack careful sampling and an adequate description of sample characteristics (Crandall, 1982). I illustrate this point by having students read a Method section extract in which the sampling procedure is inadequately described and revealed as dubious. I tell students that the sampling is fairly typical of earlier studies, and I ask them to comment on how the sample was chosen and reported.

Concluding Comments

Journal article extracts are versatile teaching tools in my classes. Activities based on journal article extracts may require only a few minutes; fit easily into lectures, tutorials, or laboratories; and serve various functions. Students seem to find the activities absorbing. I encourage instructors to devise and use similar activities for their courses.

References

Anisfeld, M. (1987). A course to develop competence in critical reading of empirical research in psychology. *Teaching of Psychology, 14,* 224–227.

Ault, R. L. (1991). What goes where? An activity to teach the organization of journal articles. *Teaching of Psychology, 18,* 45–46.

Chamberlain, K. (1988). Devising relevant and topical undergraduate laboratory projects: The core article approach. *Teaching of Psychology, 15,* 207–208.

Chamberlain, K., & Burrough, S. (1985). Techniques for teaching critical reading. *Teaching of Psychology, 12,* 213–215.

Crandall, R. C. (1982, November). *Characteristics of research appearing in gerontology journals between 1975–1980.* Paper presented at the 35th Annual Scientific Meeting of the Gerontological Society of America, Boston.

Farmer, H. (1983). Career and homemaking plans for high school youth. *Journal of Counseling Psychology, 30,* 40–45.

Herzog, H. A., Jr. (1986). The treatment of sociobiology in introductory psychology textbooks. *Teaching of Psychology, 13,* 12–15.

Kalat, J. W. (1990). *Introduction to psychology* (2nd ed.). Belmont, CA: Wadsworth.

Klugh, H. E. (1983). Writing and speaking skills can be taught in psychology classes. *Teaching of Psychology, 10,* 170–171.

LeUnes, A. (1983). Little Albert from the viewpoint of abnormal psychology textbook authors. *Teaching of Psychology, 10,* 230–231.

Pennington, H. (1990). A brief training program for graduate student teachers of laboratory–tutorial classes. *Teaching of Psychology, 17,* 120–121.

Suter, W. N., & Frank, P. (1986). Using scholarly journals in undergraduate experimental methodology courses. *Teaching of Psychology, 13,* 219–221.

Teaching Observational Research in Introductory Psychology: Computerized and Lecture-Based Methods

Victoria A. Kazmerski
Dawn G. Blasko
School of Humanities and Social Sciences
Penn State Erie, The Behrend College

Instructors report that two of their most important goals in the introductory psychology course are to engage students in scientific inquiry of psychological processes and to convince students that psychology is a science (Miller & Gentile, 1998). Having students conduct their own observations can be an effective way to use active and collaborative methods to meet these goals. In this article, we describe a study conducted in our introductory psychology classes using observational research as a technique to foster learning about the scientific method. We compared teaching observational research using a standard lecture format and using an interactive software program that we originally developed for the basic research methods class.

Computer-based teaching methods have become fairly common in psychology. Forsyth and Archer (1997) reported that such methods may improve knowledge transfer as well as increase enthusiasm and motivation for learning. Using these methods for teaching research methods has become common. Several commercial programs are available to demonstrate or teach experimental research methods to undergraduate psychology students. However, there is a dearth of programs available for teaching observational research. Courseware for Observational Research (COR) is a multimedia program designed to fill this void (Blasko, Kazmerski, Corty, & Kallgren, 1998).

COR is organized into three sections: "lessons" is used by an instructor during class, a "laboratory" section is used independently by students to apply to concepts learned in class, and a "library." The lessons section uses digitized video to illustrate three basic coding strategies: frequency coding, duration coding, and interval coding. It also provides instruction on how to simplify complex coding situations through the use of event, time, and individual sampling. Lessons are also included for assessing interrater reliability using percentage agreement and Cohen's kappa and for assessing statistical significance using the chi-square goodness-of-fit test (for more detail on lessons, see Blasko et al., 1998). The laboratory section provides five video clips that students can use to conduct observational research. The program guides students through each of the steps in the lessons and allows them to link back to the lessons to review the concepts. The library provides direct access to the videos, background information on the video subjects, and interviews with the caretakers of some of the video subjects.

We designed the program to improve on traditional lecture-based instruction in a number of ways. First, COR uses video clips carefully chosen to illustrate the steps of observational research methods. It goes beyond simply showing videos by presenting the video clips along with interactive coding sheets that instructors can use in at least three ways. The videos can be shown alone, allowing the students to observe behaviors and develop operational definitions. They can also be shown with sample coding sheets that students can copy and code at their desk or one student can code on the computer in front of the class. In addition, the video can be played while the computer fills in the coding sheet based on data the instructor enters before class. The second benefit of COR is that it helps students by taking them through the steps of calculating interrater reliability and chi-square. Instructors or students can input data directly into the formulas and see the output at each step of the calculation. This feature is particularly useful for the math-phobic student. Therefore, COR's primary benefit is the flexibility of use by the instructor and the precision of the presentation of concepts to the students.

To test the efficacy of the lessons component of COR, we conducted a study with two sections of introductory psychology students. One section was taught observational research using COR and the other with traditional lecture-based methods. A guest lecturer taught the unit to the two sections so that the regular class instructors, who were the authors and developers of COR, would not bias the results. Evaluation was done on three levels: a multiple-choice exam tested the key concepts in the unit, a research project where pairs of students conducted a brief hypothesis-driven naturalistic observation and wrote a research report on it, and an evaluation survey asked students' opinions of the experience.

Method

Participants

Students in two introductory psychology classes ($n = 44$; $n = 41$) at Penn State Erie participated as part of their course grade. Forty-nine percent were women. Students in the two classes had similar SAT scores. The mean verbal SAT score for the first class was 531 and for the second class was 537,

$t(69) = 0.34, p > .05$. The mean math SAT score for the first class was 546 and for the second class was 538, $t(69) = 0.67$, $p > .05$.

Procedure

The two classes met in the same classroom 2 days per week for consecutive 75-min class periods. The sections were normally taught separately by two instructors (the authors), who for the purpose of the study collaborated to use the same syllabus, texts, and course projects for the two classes. A guest lecturer, who did not participate in the development of COR, instructed the two classes on the topic of observational research. The instructors introduced the guest lecturer as an expert in the field of observational research because she often uses these methods in her own developmental psychology research. A flip of a coin determined the method of instruction for each class; the guest lecturer used the traditional lecture method (lecture-instructed class) for the first class and used COR for second class (COR-instructed class).

The students in both sections were informed at the beginning of the semester that they would be taking part in a special project. They were told they would conduct their own research project rather than take part as research participants as is traditional in the introductory psychology class. The research project was scheduled to begin 3 weeks after the semester began and the students had 4 weeks to conduct their observation. In addition to the chapter on research methods in their textbook, the students read a section on naturalistic observation from a research methods textbook (Bordens & Abbott, 1996).

The regular instructors first taught the basics of research and the scientific method over two 75-min classes. The guest lecturer taught the next two regularly scheduled class periods. In both classes she covered the concepts of hypothesis testing, operational definitions, coding schemes (frequency, duration, and interval coding), sampling techniques with a focus on individual and event sampling, and interrater reliability using percentage agreement and Cohen's kappa. She concluded the unit with a discussion of significance testing using the chi-square goodness-of-fit test.

In the lecture-instructed class the guest lecturer explained the concepts verbally and used overhead transparencies. She also used video clips of child participants from her research to help illustrate the concept of operational definitions. In the COR-instructed class, she used the lessons component of COR on a projection monitor. In both classes students practiced these concepts in small groups in class using pencil and paper. Course instructors were not present during the classes.

After the lessons, both classes received a handout describing the research assignment. They completed the assignment outside of class time. Students worked in pairs to develop a hypothesis for an observation or chose one of the sample hypotheses given by the instructors (e.g., "People who drive sports cars are less likely to come to a complete stop at a stop sign then those who drive other cars.") They operationally defined their variables and conducted the observation for at least 30 min. They assessed interrater reliability of their observations using both percentage agreement and Cohen's kappa. They tested their hypothesis using chi-square. Finally, each research team wrote up their results in a simplified American Psychological Association-format research report. Students did not need to use the laboratory component of COR to complete the assignment.

Evaluation Methods

Multiple-choice exam. Both classes answered the same 10 multiple-choice questions that asked about basic concepts and definitions in observational research as part of their first exam. All of the tested concepts were in the assigned readings.

Student research reports. To make an objective assessment, we removed the students' names from each paper and mixed the papers from the two classes. We graded the research reports using a checklist of specific criteria. The criteria included accurate title, statement of the problem investigated, clearly stated hypothesis, operational definition of the variables, explanation of the coding scheme used, description of the sampling technique used, presentation of the interrater reliability and chi-square results, summary of the data in a table, valid conclusions based on the data, and accurate format. We graded three reports together to establish a standard grading criteria. We then graded five papers using the criteria to establish reliability. We agreed on the grades of each of the five test papers to within 2 points out of 100. We then randomly divided the remaining papers for grading.

Student evaluations. The classes rated the unit using two questions. The first question was "How useful do you think it is to learn about research by actually conducting an observational study as opposed to simply reading about it?", rated on a scale of 1 (*not at all useful*) to 10 (*extremely useful*). The second question was "How well did the guest lecturer teach you about the purpose and process of observational research?", rated on a scale of 1 (*not at all*) to 10 (*extremely well*). Students were also able to provide open-ended comments.

Results

Multiple-Choice Exam

On the 10 multiple-choice questions the lecture-instructed class obtained a mean score of 76% ($SD = 12.7$) and the COR-instructed class obtained a mean score of 78% ($SD = 15.03$). These scores did not differ reliably, $t(82) = 0.51, p > 0.05$.

Student Research Reports

The COR-instructed class earned higher grades ($M = 86\%, SD = 11.75$) than the lecture-instructed class ($M = 79\%, SD = 10.91$) on the research reports. This difference was statistically reliable, $t(81) = 2.80, p < 0.01, \omega^2 = 0.08$.

Both groups of students were positive about conducting their own research in the class ($M = 7.62$ on a scale of 1 [*not at all useful*] to 10 [*extremely useful*], $SD = 2.03$). In the final course evaluations, several mentioned the project as the best part of the class. One senior commented that this was the first general education course that had provided a challenge. The few negative comments about the project focused primarily on having to work in groups, with difficulty coordinating schedules or unequal distribution of work between partners. In comparing the two teaching methods, the COR-instructed class rated the usefulness of conducting research more highly ($M = 8.2$, $SD = 1.96$) than the lecture-instructed class ($M = 7.1$, $SD = 2.29$), $t(71) = 2.17$, $p < .05$, $\omega^2 = .05$. The two classes did not differ, $t(69) = 0.83$, $p > .05$, in how they rated the guest lecturer; on a scale of 1 (*not at all*) to 10 (*extremely well*) the mean rating for the COR-instructed class was 5.8 ($SD = 2.16$) and the mean rating for the lecture-instructed class was 6.2 ($SD = 2.39$). On reflection, the guest lecturer reported spending somewhat more time working with students in small groups practicing the concepts in the lecture-instructed class.

Discussion

We draw two conclusions from these results. First, asking students to complete their own psychological research is an excellent way to illustrate how the scientific method is central to psychology. Although certainly more time consuming to develop and evaluate than multiple-choice exams, these projects actively engage students to think about alternative hypotheses and consider multiple explanations of their results, some of the hallmarks of critical thinking.

Second, although multimedia programs like COR are not necessary to meet these goals, they provide a way to capture students' attention and clarify critical concepts. Multimedia presentations offer the advantages of presenting information in an incremental manner. They offer the instructor greater precision and control and allow him or her to customize learning to the individual group of students (Goolkasian, 1996). COR offers the additional benefit of being highly interactive. The instructor can demonstrate a variety of possible outcomes using the class's actual data without additional preparation time. For example, one of the most difficult concepts to teach is the importance of precise operational definitions. Using COR we have found it useful to show a video (e.g., a gorilla) and have the students pick a behavior (e.g., feeding) to code. The class watches the video and records the number of behaviors. When we compare each student's response, there is wide disagreement. We show the video again and talk about which observable movements constitute the behavior. Through this discussion and a frame-by-frame analysis of the behavior, the class develops a precise operational definition of feeding and high interrater reliability can be demonstrated. This analysis is much simpler and more precise than would be possible by replaying a videotape. In addition, students find it amusing and engaging if the data entered before class makes the computer appear to inaccurately code the behavior.

Although these data do not allow us to determine the cause of the group difference on the laboratory reports, one explanation is that COR provided a combination of attention-grabbing graphics, precise control, and student input into the lessons that enhanced the COR-instructed students' performance. Furthermore, the COR-instructed students were more positive about the importance of actual research experience. Perhaps students in the COR-instructed group had a clearer understanding of the precision and control required to do "good" science, thus making it appear more important. Or perhaps the engaging quality of the presentation created a general halo effect having to do with research experience.

The advantages seen in the COR-instructed class are consistent with other research showing that computer technology can enhance learning, especially if it goes beyond simple drill and practice text-based approaches (e.g., Forsyth & Archer, 1997). We should note, however, that we found no difference between the two groups on the multiple-choice exam. The similar performance on the exam likely reflects that both classes studied from the same reading material and covered the same material in class as well as that the questions on the test were primarily definitional. This finding is consistent with Welsh and Null (1991), who also found no difference on a comprehension task between students taught using computer simulations and those taught using traditional methods. These mixed results confirm the importance of looking at what the instructor expects students to get from the experience when assessing effectiveness of software (Castellan, 1993). If we had based assessment solely on exam performance, we would not have seen that students who used COR were better able to apply the concepts in their research and were more convinced of the value of research.

References

Blasko, D. G., Kazmerski, V. A., Corty, E. W., & Kallgren, C. (1998). Courseware for Observational Research (COR): A new approach to teaching naturalistic observation. *Behavior Research Methods, Instruments, & Computers, 30*, 217–222.

Bordens, K. S., & Abbott, B. B. (1996). *Research design and methods: A process approach.* Mountain View, CA: Mayfield.

Castellan, N. J., Jr. (1993). Evaluating information technology in teaching and learning. *Behavior Research Methods, Instruments, & Computers, 25*, 233–237.

Forsyth, D. R., & Archer, C. R. (1997). Technologically assisted instruction and student mastery, motivation, and matriculation. *Teaching of Psychology, 24*, 207–212.

Goolkasian, P. (1996). Getting started with multimedia. *Behavior Research Methods, Instruments, & Computers, 28*, 279–281.

Miller, B., & Gentile, B. F. (1998). Introductory course content and goals. *Teaching of Psychology, 25*, 89–96.

Welsh, J. A., & Null, C. H. (1991). The effects of computer-based instruction on college students' comprehension of classic research. *Behavior Research Methods, Instruments, & Computers, 23*, 301–305.

Notes

1. Funds for the development and modification of Courseware for Observational Research came from a Faculty Technology Initiative Grant from Pennsylvania State University's Educational

Technology Center and development funds from Penn State Erie, The Behrend College.
2. We thank the Penn State Educational Technology design team for Courseware for Observational Research: Eric Corty, Carl Kallgren, Carol Dywer, Morris Weinstock, and Barbara Polka Smith; the students and faculty who gave us feedback that al-

lowed us to improve the program; and especially Charisse Nixon for being the guest lecturer in this study.
3. Instructors interested in using Courseware for Observational Research should contact Dawn Blasko, Penn State Erie, The Behrend College, School of Humanities and Social Sciences, Station Road, Erie, PA 16563; e-mail: Dawnblasko@psu.edu.

Simulating Clever Hans in the Classroom

Michael J. Marshall
David R. Linden
West Liberty State College

The case of Clever Hans, the apparently sapient horse, marks a famous success in the annals of behavioral science and provides much fodder for illustrating psychological concepts. Early in this century, a German mathematics teacher toured Europe and amazed the public with a horse that could correctly tap out the answers to algebra problems, indicate the time of day, and even spell German words using a code that converted numbers to letters. Many "experts" of the day believed Clever Hans provided clear evidence that an animal was capable of human intelligence, especially because Hans responded correctly even when questioned by others in the absence of his master. Only when the psychologist, Oskar Pfungst (1911), systematically manipulated the conditions under which Clever Hans performed was the "thinking horse" exposed as an unwitting fraud. After much careful testing, Pfungst found that Hans simply responded to a subtle visual cue. Questioners invariably tilted their heads toward the horse when he had reached the correct number of taps, a signal that Hans used to stop tapping.

Because students find this story inherently interesting, psychology instructors have effectively used it to illustrate concepts such as systematic manipulation, hypothesis testing, uncontrolled conditions, experimenter effects, parsimony, falsifiability, and the dangers of relying on testimonial evidence (Kalat, 1993; Sebeok & Rosenthal, 1981; Stanovich, 1992). We believed the Clever Hans effect would have a more powerful impact on students if we could replicate it in class using a live animal.

This article describes and evaluates a demonstration in which the instructor covertly signals a rat to press a bar, giving the impression that it responded correctly to yes or no questions posed by students. A purist may call this demonstration a *Clever Hans-like effect* because it uses an auditory rather than a visual cue, and the experimenter intentionally rather than inadvertently cues the animal. We believe the demonstration aids in learning experimental design concepts and stimulates students' critical thinking and scientific skepticism.

Method

Subjects

The human subjects were 21 women and 16 men enrolled in an introductory psychology class. The demonstration subject was a female, Long-Evans hooded rat that was 4 months old when operant discrimination training began. The animal was housed in an individual cage with water available continuously and was reduced to 80% to 85% of free feeding weight for training and demonstrations.

Apparatus

A Lafayette Instruments Co. Student Operant Conditioning System was used. The operant chamber had clear plexiglass side walls and lid and a metal lever centered in the front wall. A motorized pellet dispenser delivered 45-mg Noyes pellets to a reinforcement cup at the right of the lever. The jewel light above the lever was disconnected so that the switch on the handheld unit, which normally illuminated it, could be used to activate an interval timer. A bar press could activate the pellet dispenser only during the 4-s interval set on this timer.

The terms YES and NO were cut into separate 8- × 12-cm pieces of black construction paper backed by white paper. These signs were taped to the top of the system control console. Each could be illuminated from behind by a 6W–115 VAC light bulb. A bar press during the 4-s interval illuminated the bulb behind the YES sign and reset the timer. If the interval elapsed without a bar press, the NO sign was illuminated.

During the classroom demonstrations, the operant chamber was placed on the instructor's desk and the control console, with the YES and NO signs attached, sat on top of a cart 2.5 m from the desk. The hand control unit was given to a student volunteer who was instructed to turn on the switch to initiate a trial when the rat was to answer a question.

During training, the auditory stimulus was presented from a Lafayette Precision Signal Generator (Model ANL–916) to an 8 Ω speaker set outside the front or side of the operant chamber. During demonstrations, the auditory signal was presented from an electronic dog whistle, called a Dazzer (made by K–II Enterprises, $24.95), that was concealed on a belt beneath the instructor's jacket. Both of these instruments produced a 22,000-Hz signal of 80 db against a background of 60 db to 65 db, measured inside the operant chamber.

Procedure

In the training phase, the rat was shaped to approach and press the lever for continuous reinforcement. After a response pattern was established, discrimination training was instituted with continuous reinforcement during the auditory signal and no reinforcement when the signal was absent. The signal was set at 1,000 Hz during the first two sessions of discrimination training so that the trainers could hear it. As discriminative responding emerged, the signal was changed to 22,000 Hz, and training continued until the animal responded only during the signal. The procedure was then changed so that the first response after signal onset was reinforced and terminated the signal. The duration of the signal was then reduced until the animal responded consistently within 4 s of signal onset. Although the rat's performance was almost perfect within 10 sessions, training was continued with refresher sessions, so that the behavior was well established and would not be disrupted by distracting events during the classroom demonstrations that were conducted 4 and 6 months later.

The demonstration took place after the students learned major concepts in research methods and experimental design at the introductory level through the assigned reading (Morris, 1993) and a lecture. The instructor told the students that psychologists used selective breeding and these research methods to breed and train rats to be as intelligent as humans. Students' denunciations were met with an offer by the instructor to "prove" it was true with a rat that was brought into the classroom in a Skinner box. The class was told that the rat, named Hanzel, would be able to answer correctly almost any yes or no question that anyone in the class posed by pressing the bar to indicate an answer of yes and refraining from bar pressing to indicate an answer of no. Just after each question was asked, a student volunteer flipped the switch on the hand control unit, which activated the 4-s timer. In response to a question such as "Is the moon made out of cheese?," the instructor did not trigger the ultrasonic signal, the rat did not bar press, and the NO sign was illuminated after a 4-s delay. In response to such questions as "Is 5 the square root of 25?," the instructor covertly activated the ultrasonic tone with a surreptitious push of the wrist against the on button of the Dazzer. This tone signaled the rat to bar press, which illuminated the YES sign. (The YES and NO signs were used only for theatrical purposes. The demonstration could be performed just as easily by saying that a bar press means yes and no bar press means no.)

After demonstrating that the rat could indeed answer correctly almost any question posed to it, the students were polled to find out who was and who was not convinced that the rat had superior intelligence. The class was divided about evenly. The instructor then guided the ensuing discussion to determine which half of the class was right by assessing the evidence through the use of critical thinking. In turn, students were challenged to try to ascertain the validity of the instructor's claims by suggesting some more parsimonious explanations and checking them with testable (falsifiable) hypotheses. After awhile, the class reasoned that they could systematically manipulate the situation to assess the validity of the instructor's claims. They tested the hypothesis "The instructor is providing visual cues to the rat" by having the instructor stand out of view of the rat for a set of trials. Eventually, they figured out that the instructor was the source of the rat's sapient performance by having the instructor leave the room. After the class identified the successful experimental manipulation, the instructor related the story of Clever Hans. The instructor guided a discussion to generalize the principle of the Clever Hans effect to thinking critically about testimonial evidence provided in relevant media reports of psychological findings.

Evaluation

After the exercise, 37 students completed a 7-item questionnaire evaluating their experience on a scale ranging from *strongly disagree* (1) to *strongly agree* (5). Student responses indicated that the exercise was very interesting ($M = 4.81$, $SD = .39$), worthwhile ($M = 4.54$, $SD = .55$), and a positive experience ($M = 4.51$, $SD = .64$). They also indicated that this activity helped them better understand the concepts in experimental design ($M = 4.46$, $SD = .39$), improved their ability to think critically ($M = 4.16$, $SD = .72$), enabled them to understand better how the methods of psychology can be helpful in solving real problems ($M = 4.35$, $SD = .67$), and should be used in future classes ($M = 4.84$, $SD = .37$).

Informally, students commented that they especially liked this exercise because (a) the live animal captivated their attention, (b) the challenge to prove the rat did not have human intelligence motivated them to think critically about the situation and apply their knowledge of research methods, and (c) active involvement in an actual event was more fun than discussing it in the abstract (Benjamin, 1991). Hanzel also created a minor sensation on campus; students from all over campus came to the animal lab and requested to see Hanzel. We have had requests from nonpsychology instructors to show the demonstration to their classes, including requests for Hanzel to perform for middle school students and a class from a neighboring college.

Discussion

This exercise is appropriate for any psychology class that requires students to learn about experimental research methods. In particular, the experimental concepts of systematic manipulation, hypothesis testing, uncontrolled conditions, experimenter effects, parsimony, falsifiability, and the danger of relying on testimonial evidence can be discussed in relation to this demonstration. The instructor's original claim that psychologists could create rats with human intelligence was testimonial evidence. The students were then able to test and disconfirm this claim by generating their own falsifiable hypotheses and systematically manipulating the variables under controlled conditions to develop the more parsimonious explanation—that the rat's performance was due to experimenter effects.

In addition, this demonstration can be used as a critical-thinking exercise to help students acquire the skills necessary to assess the validity of psychological events reported in the media. Teaching critical thinking with this type of demonstration is superior to the traditional method of teaching critical thinking (i.e., as a general formula of abstractly learned steps) because students become engaged in finding an implicitly generated solution to a problem rather than studying critical thinking per se (Gray, 1983). Students initially challenge the instructor to prove that the rat is sapient, and then the instructor puts the shoe on the other foot by challenging the students to prove it is not. The switching nature of these roles nicely incorporates an active learning approach (Benjamin, 1991).

The media are replete with news reports that cry out as targets to which students can generalize this lesson. For example, a *Time* magazine cover asked, "Can Animals Think?" (Linden, 1993). Inside was a story about animals, such as chimpanzees and dolphins, that seem to use language to communicate with their trainers. Also, there are the omnipresent stories of psychic readings and paranormal communication. Other types of relevant news items are usually reported as psychological breakthroughs. A recent example involves the use of facilitated communication for profoundly retarded, autistic children who suddenly show literacy by typing on a computer with the aid of a human facilitator, whose role is to lightly support their hands over the keyboard (Wheeler, Jacobson, Paglieri, & Schwartz, 1993). Could this be just a modern equivalent of the Clever Hans effect? To the degree that this type of exercise can help students assess more critically the validity of these types of real-world claims, its value extends beyond learning the subject matter.

References

Benjamin, L. T., Jr. (1991). Personalization and active learning in the large introductory psychology class. *Teaching of Psychology, 18,* 68–74.
Gray, P. (1993). Engaging students' intellects: The immersion approach to critical thinking in psychology instruction. *Teaching of Psychology, 20,* 68–74.
Kalat, J. W. (1993). *Introduction to psychology* (3rd ed.). Pacific Grove, CA: Brooks/Cole.
Linden, E. (1993, March 22). Can animals think? *Time,* pp. 54–61.
Morris, C. G. (1993). *Psychology: An introduction.* Englewood Cliffs, NJ: Prentice-Hall.
Pfungst, O. (1911). *Clever Hans.* New York: Holt.
Sebeok, T. A., & Rosenthal, R. (1981). *The Clever Hans phenomenon: Communication with horses, whales, apes, and people.* New York: The New York Academy of Sciences.
Stanovich, K. E. (1992). *How to think straight about psychology* (3rd ed.). New York: HarperCollins.
Wheeler, D. L., Jacobson, J. W., Paglieri, R. A., & Schwartz, A. A. (1993). An experimental assessment of facilitated communication. *Mental Retardation, 31,* 49–60.

Using the Barnum Effect to Teach About Ethics and Deception in Research

Bernard C. Beins
Ithaca College

Psychologists are intensely interested in establishing ethical guidelines that help direct their professional relationships. The American Psychological Association exerts ongoing efforts to revise its guidelines (e.g., "APA Continues to Refine," 1992), and a growing corpus of relevant articles and publications exists (e.g., Tabachnick, Keith-Spiegel, & Pope, 1991).

Although professionals are acutely aware of the importance of this issue, students do not systematically learn about it at more than a cursory level (Korn, 1984). Fortunately, individual instructors have recognized the traditional gap in teaching ethics. McMinn (1988) developed a computerized approach to ethical decision making; Rosnow (1990) described an approach involving role-playing, discussion, and debate.

The approach to teaching ethics described here puts students in the role of the deceived in a classroom project. There are two main reasons why lectures and discussions about the ethics of deceit need to be supplemented by a more direct demonstration.

First, Milgram (1963) found that people are not very accurate in predicting how subjects will react when confronted with an ethically ambiguous situation. If people cannot reliably predict subjects' behavior, perhaps students might think that they know how a deceived subject would feel, but the actual experience may be much more compelling.

Second, students may not empathize initially with research subjects who are deceived. For example, student researchers who participated in some conformity studies (Beins & Porter, 1989) showed no distress about using deception in the research (the Institutional Review Board that approved the research also showed no distress). Similarly, Harcum and Friedman (1991), who expressed reservations about the ethics of using some fairly common classroom demonstrations, noted that about 93% of their subjects accepted deception as part of a legitimate research design.

The vehicle for creating this teaching activity is the *Barnum effect*, in which individuals are gulled into believing invalid results of psychological tests. This effect was originally used to teach students about testing (Forer, 1949); as a phenomenon, it is well documented (e.g., Baillargeon & Danis, 1984; Furnham & Schofield, 1987; Holmes, Buchannan, Dungan, & Reed, 1986). It can also introduce students to the pitfall of blind acceptance of test results (Palladino, 1991).

The goals of the activity described herein are to foster an appreciation of the feelings of research subjects who are lied to and an awareness of the need to avoid deception when possible. This approach complements those used by McMinn (1988) and Rosnow (1990). The demonstration combines an initial discussion of crucial ethical issues that I take from Reynolds (1982), a firsthand account of being deceived, and a final discussion.

Generating the Barnum Effect

Procedure

Students in a research methods class participated in the project as part of the course requirement. There were 28 women and 11 men; 10 were sophomores, 23 were juniors, and 6 were seniors.

Students completed a 20-item bogus personality inventory, the Quacksalber Personality Inventory for Normal Populations (Beins, 1987). They subsequently received interpretations that were identical for all students. All feedback statements were intended to be neutral or mildly positive.

One class ($n = 19$) completed the test with a version designed for Apple II computers; feedback was provided immediately. The second class ($n = 20$) took a version printed on paper and responded on a computer scoring sheet. A confederate of the teacher left the room and returned about 10 min later with printouts that had been prepared in advance with each student's name written across the top. There was no obvious reason to expect the two groups to differ in their reactions; a comparison between the two would only indicate how robust the effect might be.

Both groups then completed a form designed to access the perceived validity of the test. One question asked how well students thought the feedback described themselves. Students responded using a scale ranging from *this is the real me* (1) to *this is not like me* (10). In addition, they indicated how useful the test would be in five situations: personal adjustment, employment screening, assessment of honesty, identification of a person's minor problems, and identification of a person's major problems. Students responded using a scale ranging from *very useful* (1) to *not very useful* (10).

Assessing the Barnum Effect

Students were predictably accepting of the test results as descriptive of themselves. The mean rating was 3.6. This represented a significant departure from a neutral value of 5.5, $t(38) = 6.24$, $p < .001$. However, students felt that the test would not be particularly effective in assessing personal adjustment, employee honesty and stability, or major or minor emotional problems. Thus, students did not blindly accept the test as being a universally valid instrument.

To test the robustness of the effect, a 2 (Medium: Computer vs. Paper) × 2 (Sex) × 3 (Year in School) analysis of variance was conducted on the acceptance ratings. Only the main effect of year was significant, $F(2, 36) = 5.09$, $p = .011$. Sophomores ($M = 3.00$) and juniors ($M = 3.43$) did not differ reliably, but they were significantly less skeptical than seniors ($M = 5.67$). The small number of seniors renders the difference between them and the sophomores and juniors somewhat suspect. I have tried to generate acceptance of the results of the Quacksalber inventory for other seniors and for graduate students without much success. Even so, these students experience the deceit, their skepticism in the results of the test notwithstanding.

Generating Postdemonstration Discussion

Students discussed their feelings when I told them that they had been deceived. Their initial reaction to the deceit was to feel gullible and stupid. In general, they were mildly distressed at first. I also noted what seemed to be nervous laughter from several students during the initial stages of the discussion.

Discussion focused on the fact that they had taken the Quacksalber inventory seriously, on their feelings about being deceived, and on the idea that their reactions to being deceived were common. I also pointed out that if they used deception in research, their subjects would feel the same way. Finally, I used this situation to illustrate the importance of debriefing.

During the next class meeting, they wrote answers to questions about the suitability of this exercise to illustrate relevant points about deception in research and whether this demonstration should be repeated in future classes. We spent nearly an entire class period discussing what they had written. I made it clear that I would consider their responses seriously before deciding whether to repeat this activity with another class. I pointed out that deception was as much a problem in the classroom as in the context of experimental research.

Assessing Student Reactions to the Deception

Of the 31 students who commented anonymously about whether this demonstration was effective in teaching about both the Barnum effect and deception, 30 students responded affirmatively. Their comments generally asserted that the costs of doing the demonstration (failure to acquire prior informed consent, invasion of their privacy in asking questions about their likes and dislikes, and lying to them about the nature of the test) were outweighed by the benefits of learning that deception is not free of cost and of knowing firsthand how subjects feel when lied to. Other notable and potentially serious effects of this exercise are that students may question the instructor's credibility, they may think that psychological research is without validity or integrity, and they may develop negative feelings about psychological research. None of these unwanted eventualities emerged.

The sole dissenter suggested that it was not worth making students feel stupid and that the point about deception in research could be made simply by giving facts and examples. Several students noted that some students may be distressed (e.g., freshmen who lacked confidence in themselves) and that I should be aware of this. We had not discussed the question of individual differences regarding negative reactions, but some students spontaneously mentioned it.

Discussion

This project seems to have been effective on two levels. On one hand, the students became acquainted with the Barnum effect. More important, they also seemed quite touched at the personal level by the experience. It was clear to me that they did not enjoy the trickery when it was inflicted on them. On the other hand, they agreed that it provided a compelling message. The class discussion was tinged with a sense of empathy with research subjects who are deceived. The degree to which students objected to the procedure was as low as that reported elsewhere (Britton, Richardson, Smith, & Hamilton, 1983; Harcum & Friedman, 1991): Students may have felt some distress, but it was mild and short-lived.

The students also learned that, in some cases, deception can be tolerated. For example, in my classes, the students agreed that I should not regularly lie to them; however, the mild and short-lived discomfort about knowing that they had been lied to served to teach them an important lesson about deception in research. Thus, they asserted that the project was worth repeating with subsequent classes.

This demonstration has several advantages. It teaches about deception in the context of a social psychology phenomenon. It is more accessible than Forer's (1949) original demonstration of the Barnum effect, which was based on his Diagnostic Interest Blank and some astrological personality descriptions. This version is also quicker than Forer's, which extended over a period of 1 week. Also, the Quacksalber inventory provides the same kind of feedback Forer provided, although the personality descriptions used here are more neutral.

Furthermore, when the computer version is used, no responses are actually recorded, thus ensuring confidentiality.

(The computerized version is available only for Apple II computers, but is written in BASIC, so it should be easily convertible to GW BASIC for IBM-type computers.)

The project seems amenable either to computerized or paper application. Men and women reacted in the same way, both in generating the effect and in their responses to deception. Seniors seemed more skeptical of the feedback (as did master's level students in education in a similar situation). Even when students failed to accept the output as descriptive of themselves, they still seemed to have accepted the test as legitimate. This demonstration seems robust and pedagogically useful for a wide range of students.

References

APA continues to refine its ethics code. (1992, May). *APA Monitor*, pp. 38–42.

Baillargeon, J., & Danis, C. (1984). Barnum meets the computer: A critical test. *Journal of Personality Assessment, 48*, 415–419.

Beins, B. C. (1987). Psychological testing and interpretation. In V. P. Makosky, L. G. Whittemore, & A. M. Rogers (Eds.), *Activities handbook for the teaching of psychology* (Vol. 2, pp. 266–274). Washington, DC: American Psychological Association.

Beins, B. C., & Porter, J. W. (1989). A ratio scale measurement of conformity. *Educational and Psychological Measurement, 49*, 75–80.

Britton, B. K., Richardson, D., Smith, S. S., & Hamilton, T. (1983). Ethical aspects of participating in psychology experiments: Effects of anonymity on evaluation, and complaints of distressed subjects. *Teaching of Psychology, 10*, 146–149.

Forer, B. R. (1949). The fallacy of personal validation: A classroom demonstration of testing. *Journal of Abnormal and Social Psychology, 44*, 118–123.

Furnham, A., & Schofield, S. (1987). Accepting personality test feedback: A review of the Barnum effect. *Current Psychological Research & Reviews, 6*, 162–178.

Harcum, E. R., & Friedman, H. (1991). Students' ethics ratings of demonstrations in introductory psychology. *Teaching of Psychology, 18*, 215–218.

Holmes, C. B., Buchannan, J. A., Dungart, D. S., & Reed, T. (1986). The Barnum effect in Luscher color test interpretation. *Journal of Clinical Psychology, 2*, 186–190.

Korn, J. H. (1984). Coverage of research ethics in introductory and social psychology textbooks. *Teaching of Psychology, 11*, 146–149.

McMinn, M. R. (1988). Ethics case-study simulation: A generic tool for psychology teachers. *Teaching of Psychology, 15*, 100–101.

Milgram, S. (1963). Behavioral study of obedience. *Journal of Abnormal and Social Psychology, 67*, 371–378.

Palladino, J. J. (1991, August). *The BRPI—The Blatantly Ridiculous Personality Inventory*. Paper presented at the annual convention of the American Psychological Association, San Francisco.

Reynolds, P. D. (1982). *Ethics and social science research*. Englewood Cliffs, NJ: Prentice-Hall.

Rosnow, R. L. (1990). Teaching research ethics through role-play and discussion. *Teaching of Psychology, 17*, 179–181.

Tabachnick, B. G., Keith-Spiegel, P., & Pope, K. S. (1991). Ethics of teaching: Beliefs and behaviors of psychologists as educators. *American Psychologist, 46*, 506–515.

Notes

1. I thank Ruth Ault for her comments on a previous draft of this article.

Defying Intuition: Demonstrating the Importance of the Empirical Technique

Art Kohn
North Carolina Central University

In about 350 BC, Aristotle argued that the speed with which an object falls to earth is directly proportional to its weight (i.e., that heavier objects would fall to earth faster than lighter ones). Aristotle was wrong. But owing to the sheer force of his rhetoric, his axiom remained unchallenged for more than 2,000 years. Indeed, it was not until the Renaissance that Galileo performed his famous experiment proving gravity works with equal force on all objects. This refutation of Aristotelian physics shook the intellectual community of the time because it highlighted the limits of human intuition and emphasized the importance of inductive reasoning. This insight, in turn, helped to usher in the era of empirical exploration.

The following classroom demonstration, which is based on a puzzle that appeared in *Parade* magazine, dramatically illustrates both the limitations of intuitive judgments and the power of empirical investigation. The activity takes about 15 min of class time, and the only materials required are three identical envelopes and a $1 bill. I conduct this activity on the first day of my introductory and experimental psychology courses to set an empirical tone for the semester.

The Demonstration

The demonstration consists of three parts: presenting the probability puzzle, polling the class's intuitive judgments about the optimum solution to the puzzle, and conducting an experiment to test the accuracy of these intuitive judgments. To begin, tell your students that you plan to present a simple probability question involving three choices. Place the $1 bill into one envelope, seal all three envelopes, and then shuffle them so that no one, yourself included, knows which one contains the $1 bill. (You may want to put some folded paper into each envelope so that the students cannot see or feel the bill through the envelope.)

Now ask a volunteer to select an envelope, promising that the person will be able to keep the $1 bill if she or he guesses correctly. After the volunteer selects the envelope, announce that you plan to reveal that one of the unchosen envelopes is empty. Examine the contents of the two unchosen envelopes and, with a bit of fanfare, reveal to the class that one of them does not contain the $1 bill. (Indeed, at least one remaining envelope must be empty.) Finally, holding up the remaining unchosen envelope, present the class with the critical question: "As you can see, the volunteer and I each have an envelope. However, at this time I will offer the volunteer a chance to switch with me. In your opinion,

for the greatest chance of winning, should the volunteer stay with the initial choice or switch to my envelope?"

Following the discussion, poll the class's opinions. In my sections, typically 50% to 60% of the students favor staying, 20% to 30% favor switching, and 10% to 20% argue that, in terms of probability, it makes no difference whether the volunteer stays or switches.

Point out to the class that they are basing their opinions on intuition rather than on empirical data. Invite them to test their intuitive beliefs by conducting an experiment that will identify the best strategy.

Instruct the students to pair up, with one member acting as the experimenter and the other as the subject. Each experimenter should make a data sheet by labeling four columns "Correct Answer," "Subject's Choice," "Stay/Switch," and "Win/Lose" and by numbering the rows 1 to 20. Finally, the experimenters should fill in the correct-answer cells with a random assortment of the letters A, B, and C.

To conduct the experiment, each experimenter simply imitates the procedure I used with the class volunteer. The experimenter should (a) prompt the subject to guess either A, B, or C; (b) reveal that one of the unchosen options is incorrect; and (c) offer the subject the option of switching to the other unchosen option. On Trial 1, for example, if the correct answer is A and the subject chooses C, then the experimenter would inform the subject that B is an incorrect choice and offer the subject a chance to switch to A. On Trial 2, if the correct answer is A and the subject chooses A, then the experimenter would reveal that B (or C) is incorrect and offer the subject the chance to switch. For each of the 20 trials, the experimenter should record the subject's initial choice, whether the subject switched, and whether the subject ultimately selected the right choice. After everyone has completed the procedure, experimenters calculate the number of times that switching led to a win and the number of times that staying led to a win. Finally, the instructor should combine the results for the entire class and draw a graph comparing the percentage of wins that result from switching and from staying.

Evaluation

I evaluated this demonstration in three ways. First, I asked 140 undergraduates and 73 university faculty members which strategy they thought was most likely to result in winning. Each subject read a 150-word summary of the situation and then circled one of the following responses: "Your chances are best if you stay with your initial choice," "Your chances are best if you switch to the other choice," or "It will not matter whether you stay or switch; your chances of winning will be the same."

Fifty-five percent of the undergraduates believed that staying provided the greatest chance of winning, whereas 66% of the faculty believed that staying and switching yielded the same chance of winning. Only 28% of the undergraduates and 7% of the faculty believed that switching envelopes provided the best chance of winning.

Second, I conducted the in-class experiment with 84 introductory psychology students. I tallied the number of times the 42 subjects chose to stay or switch and the consequences of each choice.

Subjects significantly preferred the staying strategy, staying on 60% of the trials (binomial test, $N = 840$), $p < .001$. Although the subject preferred to stay, switching actually resulted in a significantly greater proportion of wins, $\chi^2(1, N = 840) = 95.9$, $p < .001$. Subjects won in 69% of the trials when they switched, whereas they won in only 34% of the trails when they stayed. I recently replicated this study with as few as 6 subjects, so the demonstration should work for all class sizes.

Finally, I asked all the students to complete the Trust in Research Survey (Kohn, in press) that measures reliance on intuition versus empirical investigation. The questionnaire consists of 10 questions such as "Your religion tells you that an event occurred, but research clearly shows that it did not happen. What will you base your opinion on?" and "You need to buy a reliable car, and your intuition tells you to buy *Brand X*. However, all the research shows that *Brand Z* is better. How will you decide which car to buy?" For each question, the subjects rated whether they would base their actions on *intuition only* (1) to *research only* (9). The students filled out the Trust in Research Survey along with several other unrelated surveys. Half the students filled out the survey immediately before participating in the demonstration, and half of them completed it 2 hr afterward.

Results of the Trust in Research Survey indicate that students who participated in the demonstration had higher trust in the empirical technique than students before the demonstration; however, this effect did not reach statistical significance. The mean for students who took the survey before the demonstration was 4.5, whereas the mean for those who took it afterward was 6.1, $t(166) = 1.53$, $p < .1$.

Discussion

This activity provides a dramatic example of the limitations of intuitive judgments and the importance of empirical testing. Although the puzzle is simple, involving only three possible answers, most subjects fail to solve it; ironically, subjects with doctorates err more often than undergraduates.

After the demonstration, you may want to explain the mathematical rationale for these counterintuitive results. In this explanation, the critical premise is that the instructor's act of eliminating an unchosen envelope does not affect the chances that the student's envelope is a winner. To illustrate this, I begin with an analogous, realistic situation. I tell my class to imagine that four teams have qualified for an up-coming Final Four basketball tournament. In the first round, Kentucky is scheduled to play Duke and Indiana is scheduled to play UCLA. Given equal quality of the teams, the chances that Kentucky, for example, will win the tournament are one in four. However, assume that the Indiana team decides to withdraw from the tournament. How will this affect Kentucky's chances? In fact, the odds of Kentucky winning do not change at all. Indiana was outside Kentucky's qualifying bracket in the first round, so Kentucky still must win two games. As a result, the chances that Kentucky will win the tournament remain one in four. For UCLA, however, the chances of winning improve to one in two. A betting person should shift from backing Kentucky to backing UCLA.

This situation is analogous to the three envelope problem. The initial probability that the instructor has the $1 bill is two chances in three, and the initial probability that the student has the $1 bill is one chance in three. Importantly, once the student selects an envelope, that envelope becomes a set that is entirely independent of the instructor's set; in effect, the envelope is placed into a separate qualifying bracket. Thus, when the instructor acts as an omniscient agent and eliminates a certain loser from within his or her set, that act in no way affects the probabilities that the student's set contains the winner. The chances that the instructor has the winner remain two out of three; the chances that the student has the winner remain one out of three. As a result, the student is better off switching envelopes.

Consider a different situation, however, in which the student selects envelope A and then accidently peeks into envelope C and realizes that it is empty. Should the student switch from A to B? The answer is no because, under these conditions, A was not segregated into a separate category; the student's insight simply eliminated an option from the set A, B, and C. Thus, the student's insight leaves two alternatives with equal probabilities of being correct. This latter situation is analogous to a student guessing A on a three-item multiple-choice exam. If the student later realizes that answer C is certainly wrong, the student gains no advantage by switching from A to B.

Your students might appreciate knowing that when mathematicians were confronted with an analogous puzzle, their intuition misled them as well. In 1990, a similar question was submitted to Marilyn vos Savant, a newspaper columnist who, according to the *Guinness Book of World Records*, has the world's highest IQ. When Ms. vos Savant answered (correctly) that switching provided the greatest chance of winning, she received a storm of protests from mathematicians around the country. See Posner (1991) for an interesting history of this controversy.

Following the discussion, you can again ask your volunteer whether he or she wants to stay with the original choice or switch to the remaining envelope. About 90% of the time, my volunteers seem convinced by the data and switch envelopes. However, if your experience is like mine, some of your students (and even some of your colleagues) will continue to insist that switching envelopes does not increase their chances of winning. Under these conditions, your only option may be to encourage them to conduct the experiment on their own, and then you may want to remind them that truth is not obliged to be consistent with intuition.

References

Kohn, A., (in press). *Communicating psychology: An instructor's resource guide to accompany Kalat's Introduction to Psychology* (3rd ed.). Belmont, CA: Wadsworth.

Posner, G. P. (1991). Nation's mathematicians guilty of 'innumeracy.' *Skeptical Inquirer, 15,* 342–345.

Notes

1. I thank the students in Experimental Psychology and in History and Systems at North Carolina Central University for their assistance with this study. I also thank Wendy Kohn, Richard Burke, Jim Kalat, Ruth Ault, and anonymous reviewers for their help in improving this article.

Teaching Hypothesis Testing by Debunking a Demonstration of Telepathy

John A. Bates
Department of Educational Foundations & Curriculum
Georgia Southern University

Many postsecondary educators are concerned about the rising tide of pseudoscientific, fundamentally anti-intellectual belief among otherwise well educated Americans. Bates (1987) reported that nearly half of a large sample of teacher education students believed that the full moon causes violent behavior. Feder (1986) found that more than one third of the students at a northeastern state university believed that ghosts are real. Miller (1987) conducted a national survey indicating that nearly two fifths of college graduates believe that the earth has been visited by aliens from other planets.

Educators combat student misbeliefs by debunking pseudoscientific claims specific to their own disciplines (e.g., Eve & Harrold, 1986; Harrold & Eve, 1986; Hoffmaster, 1986). These efforts have met with modest success: Some have demonstrated increased factual knowledge about reality without much corresponding decrease in pseudoscientific beliefs (Harrold & Eve, 1986); others have reported significant gains in scientific skepticism, but only for students with a neutral position on pseudoscientific claims (Banziger, 1983). Only a few reported attempts (notably, Gray, 1984) have demonstrated significant long-term changes in students' beliefs across a broad range of paranormal and irrational claims.

The classroom exercise described here holds some promise as a technique to debunk a specific pseudoscientific claim and to promote critical, scientific inquiry into psychological phenomena in general. An important goal of this exercise was to capture and hold students' attention. As Hoffmaster (1986) noted, "one of the driest subjects on earth to try to teach is the scientific method" (p. 432). The key to this goal, I believed, was to be found in the application of some basic principles of psychological arousal theory and of stage magic.

Format of the Activity

The Students

The activity was conducted in two different classrooms of introductory psychology. Both classrooms included about 35 students, all first-semester freshmen, about two thirds of whom were women.

The Lesson

All aspects of the activity were identical for both classrooms and proceeded in four stages.

Introductory information. The first 30 min of a class meeting was used to discuss some basic concepts of science. Initial consideration was given to the scientific belief in a physical reality that is independent of any observer. Special emphasis was given to the formulation of empirical hypotheses, in contrast to other sorts of answers to questions. Finally, it was pointed out that scientific hypotheses must be stated in such a way that evidence could be obtained to demonstrate that they are false, if they really are false. The lecture component of the presentation concluded with the assertion that all scientific endeavors, including scientific psychology, are not attempts to establish absolute truth, but rather are attempts to expose and eliminate false claims about the nature of reality.

Demonstration of psychic ability. After completing the lecture component, I announced that I had discovered a talent for transferring my thoughts telepathically into the

194

minds of other people. I offered to demonstrate my talent, but said that it was not yet refined, so I could not guarantee that everyone would receive exactly the right thought.

I told the class that I would think of a two-digit number from 1 to 50, such that both numbers would be odd and different from each other. As examples, I told them that the number could not be something like 11, but that 15 would be okay. After a moment, I wrote a number on my tablet, drew a line through it, wrote another, and commented that the second number seemed to be a better choice. Next, I stared at the number and announced that I was transmitting it to the class. Each student was to write down the first number that came to mind and that fit my description.

As soon as all students had written a number, I asked if any of them had chosen 37. To their surprise, about one third of the students had thought of that number. I looked disappointed, then asked whether any had chosen 35. I showed them my tablet and explained that I had written 35 first, then crossed it out. Some of the class thus might have picked up the wrong signal. I asked how many of them had thought of either 35 or 37, and more than half the class raised their hands.

I suggested that numbers do not always work for everyone; sometimes, a picture is better. Therefore, I told them that I would think of two simple geometric shapes, one inside the other. At this point, I drew something quickly on the tablet, grumbled about being sloppy, tore off the page, and drew something else. I informed the class that I was sending the image of the two shapes, and I asked them to draw what first came to their minds. After a moment, I held up the tablet for all to see the shapes of a triangle completely circumscribed by a circle. Again, about one third of the class indicated that they had drawn the same picture.

I asked whether any had drawn a circle inside a triangle, explaining that the images sometimes become reversed in the transmission. Another third raised their hands. I then showed them the drawing that I had rejected—one of a square not fully surrounded by a circle—and asked if anyone inadvertently had picked up a stray signal of it. Several more hands went up. Then, one student volunteered that she had put a triangle inside a square. I asked whether anyone else had received parts of both signals. By now, nearly everyone had raised a hand.

Finally, I told them we had with us a guest who shared with me an almost perfect psychic link. The guest, another member of my department, was introduced. I explained that our special mental relationship was best demonstrated by a simple playing-card guessing game. A volunteer shuffled a standard deck of cards and dealt three rows of five cards each, face up, on the table at the front of the room. My partner faced the back of the room, and I asked one of the students to point to one of the cards. When the student did, my partner turned around, and I proceeded to point to an apparently random sequence of the cards, saying after each, "Is it this one?" or "Is it that one?" Each time I did not point to the target card, my partner replied negatively. When, after five or six repetitions of this procedure, I finally pointed at the target, my partner quickly responded affirmatively.

Small-group generation of hypotheses. Several repetitions yielded successful detection of the target card. Students who were still skeptical of my ability were challenged

to develop a more parsimonious account of what they had observed. Students organized into groups of three or four and tried to produce at least two different testable hypotheses that could answer the question, "How did he do that?"

Hypothesis testing/revision. At the beginning of the next class meeting, students again organized into their groups, and a single, one-page worksheet requiring several categories of responses was distributed to each group. Students first were asked to summarize their observations of the psychic phenomena, to generate at least two alternative empirical hypotheses to account for their observations, and to design a test that could falsify each hypothesis. Thirty min were allotted for this part of the activity.

Next, my colleague and I made ourselves available for hypothesis testing. The groups took turns specifying a set of conditions under which the playing card "thought transfer" should occur. To ensure all groups sufficient time to test their hypotheses, I informed the class that if I knew it would be impossible to perform the transfer under a given set of conditions, then I would tell them so, rather than taking the time to demonstrate it.

The most common hypotheses involved either some prearranged number of cards to which I would point before reaching the target card or some mathematical formula involving the numerical values of the target and other cards. These were quickly rejected when the groups discovered that they could specify when in a sequence I should point to the target, and my colleague still would be able to identify it. The next most common hypotheses involved where on a card my finger was when I pointed to it. These were rejected when I varied the part touched or when I was not permitted to touch the card, which had no effect on the outcome.

Once all groups had tested both hypotheses once, they were given the opportunity either to retest what seemed to be the better of the two or to test a modified or new hypothesis. Most groups rejected all versions of numerical or positional hypotheses and focused on the modification of what I said to my partner or the tone or volume of my voice.

Within about 20 min, one or two groups were certain that they had determined the correct explanation for the phenomena, so I invited one of the members to take the place of my partner to see if the outcome could be duplicated. It was to their considerable delight, as well as to the consternation of some of their classmates, when these students were able to identify the target card.

Hypothesis testing, revision, and retesting continued until 15 min remained in the class period. Time was provided for the completion of the worksheet, including discussions of test outcomes, modifications of hypotheses, and final conclusions regarding my "special ability." As the students turned in their assignments and filed out, many of them looked at me with knowing smiles, some appeared less than sure of themselves, but nearly all were commenting to each other about what had occurred, using words like *falsified*, *replicate*, and *empirical*.

Postscript: How the Psychic Deeds Were Done

There were three components to the psychic demonstration, all supposedly involving the transference of thoughts from one mind into one or more other minds. The first two—transference of a number and transference of a shape—are illusions commonly performed by stage mentalists like Kreskin and may be thought of as the hook to capture student attention. Procedures for performing these feats are discussed in detail by Marks and Kammann (1980) in their critical analysis of claims of psychic ability.

Number transference and shape transference rely on poorly understood but documented and reliable population stereotypes in the construction of various categories of thought. As you recall, the demonstration involved the mental transference of a two-digit number between 1 and 50, such that both digits were odd and different from each other. Generally, few people realize that the qualifications placed on number selection have severely reduced the possible choices. There are only eight numbers that satisfy all the criteria: 13, 15, 17, 19, 31, 35, 37, and 39. Furthermore, the instructions were clarified by adding that the number could not be 11, but that something like 15 would be acceptable. Using 15 as an example of an acceptable target guarantees that virtually no one will select it, thus reducing the number of likely choices to seven. Marks and Kammann (1980) found that about 33% of a sample of adults think of 37 as the target number and that another 25% select 35. Thus, by claiming to have chosen first one then the other of these numbers as I was performing the thought transference, I was able to include nearly 60% of the class in my set of successes.

Most college students probably could discover that the limited number of possible targets made the outcome far less dramatic than it first appeared. It is important, therefore, to move on immediately to another, different demonstration of psychic ability—the transfer of an image of two simple geometric shapes, one inside the other. Population stereotypes for shape selection are as strong as those for number selection. Marks and Kammann reported that 33% will draw a combination of a triangle and a circle, 25% will draw a combination of a square and a circle, and 11% will combine triangle with square. With a little showmanship, I demonstrated to about 70% of my students that I had indeed transferred my thoughts into their minds.

The central component of the entire demonstration was the card-selection routine that my colleague and I enacted. To perform this illusion, cards are arranged randomly in three rows; the number of cards in each row is irrelevant. The confederate for this task needs only to remember that the top and bottom rows will be the *this* rows and the middle row will be the *that* row. If the "mentalist" points to a card and uses the correct adjective for that row of cards, then it is not the target card. The mentalist is pointing to the target only when the incorrect modifier is used.

For example, assume that the target card was in the middle row. I might point successively to cards in the top row, the middle row, and the bottom row, before pointing to the target. I would ask, "Is it *this* one?," "Is it *that* one?," and "Is it *this* one?," respectively. My partner would respond, with varying degrees of apparent certainty, that none of those was the target. Finally, I would point to the target and ask, "Is it *this* one?" My partner quickly would be able to respond correctly.

This routine has several advantages as an event for which students must generate empirical hypotheses. First, it is easy

to do: My colleague only had about 1 min of instruction before we entered the classroom for our performance, and he never made a mistake. Second, very few students are likely to be familiar with it. Third, the trick behind the event seems to be obvious but it is not. The unexpected difficulty that students experience in trying to explain what they have observed tends to arouse and maintain their curiosity. Most important, for its use in a classroom, the demonstration and its underlying causes are empirical events. Students can directly manipulate the variables of the demonstration and observe a variety of outcomes. Hypotheses can be tested quickly, modified, or rejected, without special equipment or training. Best of all, when students uncover the solution to their problem and are able to replicate the event as evidence of their success, they experience the same sort of satisfaction felt by scientific psychologists in their systematic study of human behavior.

An important goal of this activity is to capture student attention. I have been teaching undergraduate students the basic principles of science for about 12 years and do not recall ever having achieved the enthusiastic class participation that is maintained throughout the demonstration of my psychic powers. Whether this enthusiasm is due entirely to the mode of presentation of the lesson or to some combination of environmental and student factors, I cannot say. My experience suggests that incorporating novel, surprising, and varied (i.e., psychologically arousing) stimuli is essential if students are going to pay attention to the abstract concepts and philosophical issues central to scientific inquiry. This lesson incorporates such stimuli and captures student attention.

References

Banziger, G. (1983). Normalizing the paranormal: Short-term and long-term change in belief in the paranormal among older learners during a short course. *Teaching of Psychology, 10*, 212–214.

Bates, J. A. (1987). Degrees of scientific literacy and intellectualism among students in a college of education. *The Foundations Monthly Newsletter, 4*, 7–9.

Eve, R. A., & Harrold, F. B. (1986). Creationism, cult archaeology, and other pseudoscientific beliefs: A study of college students. *Youth and Society, 17*, 396–421.

Feder, K. L. (1986). The challenge of pseudoscience. *Journal of College Science Teaching, 26*, 180–186.

Gray, T. (1984). University course reduces belief in paranormal. *The Skeptical Inquirer, 8*, 247–251.

Harrold, F. B., & Eve, R. A. (1986). Noah's ark and ancient astronauts: Pseudoscientific beliefs about the past among a sample of college students. *The Skeptical Inquirer, 11*, 61–75.

Hoffmaster, S. (1986). Pseudoscience: Teaching by counterexample. *Journal of College Science Teaching, 26*, 432–436.

Marks, D., & Kammann, R. (1980). *The psychology of the psychic.* Buffalo: Prometheus Books.

Miller, J. D. (1987, June). The scientifically illiterate. *American Demographics*, pp. 26–31.

Notes

1. I thank Leigh Culpepper for his help in preparing this article.

Using Astrology to Teach Research Methods to Introductory Psychology Students

Roger A. Ward
Anthony F. Grasha
University of Cincinnati

Teaching the principles of research methodology to introductory psychology students is not an easy task. Such students are interested in learning about human behavior but are seldom enthusiastic about learning research methodology. We use a classroom exercise to test several assumptions of astrology in order to capture their interest and to introduce them to concerns psychologists face in doing research. The following activity is based on a "quasiexperimental" design and can be used to illustrate several concepts: differences between science and nonscience, the scientific method, the role of theory in developing and testing hypotheses, making comparisons among groups, probability and statistical significance, biases in self-report data, the identification of the dependent variable, and how empirical research leads to accurate information about the world.

Flow of Classroom Activity

Introduction to Activity

Students are asked whether they know anything about astrology and if they know their astrological sign. An informal poll of the class is taken. Individuals who do not know their zodiac sign are given a copy of the morning newspaper to refer to. Those individuals in class who are familiar with astrology are asked to suggest the assumptions they think astrologers make about human behavior. Student comments are listed on the blackboard. Student responses generally focus on how astrologers believe that the position of the stars and planets help to determine our personalities and behavior. This introduction usually takes about 10 min.

Generating a Hypothesis

A brief (10 to 15 min) explanation of the nature of science, nonscience, and the scientific method is presented. In particular, the role of theory and hypothesis testing in scientific research is emphasized. Students are then placed in small groups for 10 min and asked to generate a hypothesis based on an assumption they believe astrologers make about human behavior. The class is polled and ideas for hypotheses are listed on the blackboard. The student responses give the instructor an opportunity to mention that hypotheses should be testable and that a research study should allow them to be disconfirmed. Problems with a couple of the hypotheses that students generate are mentioned.

If students have not suggested it, we raise a hypothesis based on an assumption of astrologers that our personalities

are associated with certain zodiac signs. The class is then asked to accept the challenge of testing whether this is accurate, and in the process, to learn a little more about gathering and interpreting data.

The Personality Profiles

Students receive a set of six personality profiles based on personality traits that astrologers believe people with certain zodiac signs possess (cf. March & McEvans, 1982). Each set of profiles was formed by dividing the astrological year in half. Thus, students born between March 21 and September 22 receive the six sets of traits appropriate for that period and those born after September 22 and before March 21 receive the second set of profiles. Students are given 6 instead of 12 profiles to save time, to make the task more manageable, and to illustrate a potential flaw in the design when the data are later analyzed. A sample of two of the personality descriptions appear in Table 1 (and a complete list can be obtained from the authors upon request).

Instructions Given to Students

Students are asked to select the personality profile that best describes them and to mark the letter code corresponding to that profile on a separate sheet of paper. They are told to read each profile carefully and not to accept or reject a particular profile on the basis of one or two traits. Instead, they are asked to concentrate on the overall personality pattern when making a decision.

Data Analysis

After students make their choices, the correct zodiac signs for each letter code are placed on the board. Students

Table 1. Two Examples of Personality Profiles

Profile for Aries	
Impulsive	Intolerant
Courageous	Quick-tempered
Independent	Arrogant
Domineering	Blunt

Profile for Taurus	
Patient	Self-indulgent
Conservative	Stubborn
Domestic	Possessive
Sensual	Materialistic

are asked to indicate whether they correctly or incorrectly chose their zodiac sign. The number of correct and incorrect choices for each zodiac sign is then listed. We examine the data in several ways to illustrate points about data analysis and interpretation.

We note that the number of correct and incorrect responses are the dependent variable and mention that if the hypothesis is accurate, then the number of correct choices should exceed the number of incorrect choices. We explain that under ideal conditions there should be no incorrect responses.

Next, we begin to modify this simplistic way of examining the data by introducing the concepts of chance responding, probability, and statistical significance. Because everyone responded to six personality profiles, we explain that people have a one in six chance of selecting a correct profile on the basis of chance. Thus, on the basis of chance, correct choices should account for 16.6% and incorrect choices for 83.4% of the choices. The extent to which the observed data differ from these figures is noted. At this point we mention that giving everyone only 6 profiles from which to select is a potential flaw in the procedure, and that having 12 profiles would make it more difficult to select the correct profile by chance.

In addition, the concept of statistical significance is raised by having students focus on the number of correct zodiac identifications and those we expected to see occur by chance. We explain that it is important to be sure that any differences favoring astrology are not due to chance. We then note that certain statistical procedures can help us to do this. To illustrate the latter point, we use the chi-square test to analyze the overall number of correct and incorrect responses against what one would expect based on chance. Chi-square is quickly computed using a calculator programmed to do the test. A brief explanation of what it suggests is given. It is important to note that we do not teach students the intricate details of the chi-square test. The test is only used as an example of how a statistical procedure can help determine whether an event exceeds chance expectancy.

After testing for statistical significance, additional complications in interpreting research data are raised. For example, students are told that our procedure assumes people know what they are like and can accurately select personality profiles that describe themselves. We suggest that this is not always the case and is one of the reasons psychologists use objective personality inventories to determine differences among people. We also point out that individuals may select a given personality profile because it is much more flattering and/or socially acceptable, or because they are familiar with astrology and thus know what profile they should pick. Thus, the biases in self-report data like social acceptability, personal validation, and self-fulfilling prophecies can be pointed out.

We also indicate that if certain personality profiles are more popular, and if the subject pool is composed mainly of people who were born under those zodiac signs, an incorrect conclusion about the validity of astrology can be drawn. The latter point is a good way to introduce students to the idea that the level of chance responding may underestimate the popularity of each zodiac sign. This latter point allows a discussion of how such problems are handled by random selection of subjects or by randomly selecting as participants an equal number of people with each zodiac sign.

Specific biases present in selecting zodiac signs in the activity are shown by counting how many people correctly and incorrectly selected a particular zodiac sign as most like them. Our data analyses reveal that certain profiles are more socially acceptable than others. Profiles for Taurus, Leo, Libra, Pisces, and Sagittarius are selected 2 to 3 times more often than those of other zodiac signs. As one would expect, more people correctly selected the popular zodiac signs. We use the latter data to show students that correct selections are due to the popularity of certain personality descriptions and are not evidence for the validity of astrology. The latter analysis is beneficial because there have been times when the mix of birthdates in the class produced results that suggested people were selecting correct zodiac signs at a rate that was statistically significant.

Amount of Time for Activity

Depending upon how much time is allocated to each of the phases, the activity as previously outlined takes about 75 min to complete. We have run it in a 50-min session by shortening the introduction to the activity, not mentioning the distinction between science and nonscience, and not placing students in small groups to generate hypotheses. In the latter case, we have introduced astrology, indicated several of the assumptions it makes, and suggested a hypothesis that could be tested in class. The general manner in which a hypothesis is tested is noted and the other phases of the demonstration are conducted as already presented.

Prior Preparation of Students

What to emphasize and how much time to spend depends in part on what information students have had in previous class sessions and textbook assignments. We typically use this activity after the students have had a textbook assignment and an 80-min classroom session on the nature of research in psychology and the types of research methods psychologists employ (e.g., controlled experiment, case study, surveys). Thus, they are generally familiar with concepts like independent and dependent variables, hypotheses, control and experimental groups, correlational research, random sampling, statistical significance, and related terms.

Evaluation of Activity

During the current academic year, 147 students have participated in the activity. An overall indication of how much students liked and disliked the activity was assessed on a 7-point rating scale. A rating of 1 represented the worst classroom activity they had ever participated in and a rating of 7 represented the best classroom activity they had ever participated in. The mean rating was 5.46. When asked to list 2 or 3 things they liked about the activity, the most frequent responses (i.e., endorsed by at least 5 students) included: (a) the ability of the activity to hold their interest on potentially boring material, (b) seeing results from a research project immediately, (c) recognizing how deceptive research findings sometimes could be, and (d) learning that there were different ways to look at research findings. When asked to list 2 or 3 things they disliked, frequent responses (i.e., endorsed by at least 5 students) included: (a) it was somewhat long, (b) the activity tended to oversimplify astrology, (c) it was boring in places, and (d) there was nothing they disliked. Overall, evaluations suggested that the advantages of the exercise outweigh the disadvantages.

We recommend that teachers pilot test this activity with a small group of students before using it in a large class. Timing is important in order to complete the activity in a reasonable amount of time. Teachers vary in how much additional information they prefer to present and which parts of the activity to emphasize. A trial run will help to resolve these issues.

Reference

March, M. D., & McEvans, J. (1982). *The only way to learn astrology*. San Diego: Astro Computer Services.

Reaction Time as a Behavioral Demonstration of Neural Mechanisms for a Large Introductory Psychology Class

E. Rae Harcum
The College of William and Mary

Psychologists make inferences about the internal structure and states of an organism by studying the time required for subjects to make a specific response to a given stimulus under varying conditions (cf. Kantowitz, Roediger, & Elmes, 1988). This procedure, as Kantowitz et al. said, "gives psychologists a window into the mind" (p. 202).

The purpose of my demonstration is to illustrate for a large introductory psychology class the use of behavioral tests of RT to infer unobservable physiological mechanisms. The demonstration shows a delay in responding when the subject has more choices of responses (cf. Hyman, 1955). If one assumes that a more difficult choice of responses would involve more neurons and thus more synapses, then a RT requiring such a choice would be slower because of delays in crossing synapses plus the time for the spike potential to traverse individual neurons (Kalat, 1988).

As many students as is practical are recruited from the class and divided into two equal groups, with members of each group standing together at the front of the room. They are told that the instructor is going to say the name of a former United States president and that their task is to raise their hands as quickly as possible in response to the name. The subjects are then given additional written instructions according to their group, so that neither group knows the instructions given to the other. Members of the experimental group are told to raise their right hands if the president served before Abraham Lincoln and to raise their left hands if the president served after Lincoln. Members of the control group are told to raise their left hands when the instructor says the president's name.

The rest of the class is asked to note which group reacts faster. When each subject is ready, with each hand held next to the shoulder, the instructor says "Ready" and then "Ford." The control subjects, with the simple RT task, are clearly faster in raising their hands than the experimental subjects, as judged by the other students in the class, voting by a show of hands.

The hypothesis and design of the experiment are then explained to the class. The hypothesis is that more difficult tasks, requiring a choice among responses, involve longer neuronal paths and more synapses, both of which slow transmission of the neural signal. Therefore, it was predicted that the experimental group would be slower because their task required a choice. The class observations of the RTs clearly confirm the prediction and support the hypothesis.

Therefore, a behavioral experiment has been used to test a physiological hypothesis.

As an exercise in scientific logic, it should be pointed out that the results of the demonstration were predicted on the basis of synaptic delay and additional numbers of neurons, but they also could have been predicted on the basis of slower neural conduction rates for the disjunctive situation. Until this alternative possibility can be discounted, this demonstration alone does not prove the existence of synaptic delay, although such synaptic delay has been demonstrated by physiological research.

One might use microswitches and timers for more elegance. The use of timers would, of course, permit quantitative comparison of less robust independent variables. For example, the RT to a less familiar presidential name, such as *Polk*, might be compared with the response to *Ford*. A more difficult task could be achieved by asking the subjects to discriminate between a word of more or fewer than six letters and could be made even more exotic by using homophones like *through* and *threw*.

Finally, the demonstration could be expanded to illustrate a way to determine the difficulty of discriminating among several stimuli (e.g., a method for sensory scaling of preferences). For example, the disparity in preference between two foods (e.g., potato and spinach) could be determined by the differences in the disjunctive RTs. The left-hand RTs for potato would give the degree of preference for potato over spinach. The shorter RTs would indicate an easier decision process, presumably reflecting a greater degree of preference for one stimulus over the other. Other related applications might include determinations of the semantic relatedness of words or their personal significance. For example, in the former case, the left-hand response would indicate if the comparison word was a mammal or, in the second case, if a comparison adjective represented a trait that applied to the subject. Although I have not actually developed and used these extensions of the demonstration, they should work if the proper stimuli are chosen. When the choices depend on personal preference or opinion, an independent measure of the differences could be correlated with the RT differences.

This demonstration has the additional benefit of illustrating an experiment with a meaningful outcome. The students enjoy the break from lecture and easily understand the teaching objective. Nevertheless, it requires just a few minutes of class time and entails little disruption of the class to set up and complete.

References

Hyman, R. (1955). Stimulus information as a determinant of reaction time. *Journal of Experimental Psychology, 45*, 188–196.

Kalat, J. W. (1988). *Biological psychology* (3rd ed.). Belmont, CA: Wadsworth.

Kantowitz, B. H., Roediger, H. L., III, & Elmes, D. G. (1988). *Experimental psychology* (3rd ed.). St. Paul, MN: West.

The Colossal Neuron: Acting Out Physiological Psychology

Scott B. Hamilton
Thomas A. Knox
Colorado State University

While university resources are diminishing, instructors are faced with increasingly large classes. This is especially true for those who teach such popular survey courses as Introductory Psychology where classes of 200, 500, or even 1,000 students are not uncommon. Thus, instructors must use limited educational resources to maximize an important learning experience for students.

The difficulties involved in effectively teaching large classes have been addressed by using a variety of approaches, including videotape (e.g., Rosenkoetter, 1984), dramatization (Older, 1979), and the creative use of teaching assistants (Silverstein, 1982). In addition, in-class demonstrations have been advocated to maintain student interest and enhance the retention of information by exploiting the relationship between course material and the everyday life experiences of students (Caudle, 1979; Rosenkoetter, 1984; Silverstein, 1982).

More specifically, demonstrations have been found to be beneficial in teaching such diverse content as cognitive psychology (Chaffin & Herrmann, 1983; Shaffer, 1982; Thieman, 1984), social psychology (Banziger, 1982; Smith, 1982), personality (Benjamin, 1983), learning (Gibb, 1983), sensation and perception (Beins, 1983), psychotherapy (Balch, 1983), and statistics (Levin, 1982). Brain structure (Daniels, 1979) and nerve impulse speed (Rozin & Jonides, 1977) have also been addressed, but demonstrations of neuron activity that are applicable to large introductory classes have not been presented in the teaching of psychology literature.

Therefore, the purpose of this article is to describe a demonstration concerning neuron anatomy and physiology that has been used as part of a large (i.e., 300 to 400 students) Introductory Psychology course at Colorado State University over the past 5 years. In addition, data from students will be provided to support its value as both a pragmatic aid to comprehension and as an entertaining educational technique.

Predemonstration Preparation

The topic of physiological psychology is introduced with two, 50-min lectures on the nervous system. These lectures are traditional in format and cover such basic information as types of neurons, glial cells, speed of neuronal transmission, neuron firing, the action potential, and neurotransmitter activity. At the close of the second lecture, students are informed that a demonstration will be presented during the next class period that will involve 30 students joining to construct a "functioning" colossal neuron.

Before the day of the demonstration, the instructor compiles what may, at first glance, appear to be a rather bizarre set of items. Table 1 presents the list of props to be used and the signs that will identify participants during the demonstration. Readers are encouraged to modify this list to suit their own resources and needs. Although the list may appear rather long, 15 min the night before should be sufficient time to procure the necessary props. The identification signs, made by printing on standard typing paper with a large felt-tipped marker, can be stored and reused each time the demonstration is conducted.

With the preparatory lectures accomplished and the equipment and identification signs collected, the instructor is ready for "Demonstration Day." The demonstration takes approximately 30 min, including the neuron review, casting, dress rehearsal, and demonstration proper.

Neuron Review

The neuron review is accomplished in about 10 min and is used to consolidate information imparted over the previous two lectures as well as to link abstract content from the text with the concrete demonstration to follow. The knee-jerk reflex is used as the primary example because of its neurological simplicity, and an overhead transparency is used to point out such anatomical components as the receptor dendrites, the synapse in the spinal cord, and the motor neuron innervating the thigh muscle. A diagram illustrating the anatomy and physiology of an afferent and efferent neuron is also distributed (see Fig. 1).

After describing the knee-jerk reflex (with the aid of the first transparency), the instructor explains each step of the afferent-efferent diagram (which is also on a transparency), with reference to the knee-jerk reflex. For example, the stu-

Props (generic)	Identification Signs	
Bicycle air pump (1)	Activating Stimulus (1)	Soma (2)
Child's space gun (1)	Dendrite (3)	Sodium Ion + (3)
Garbage bags (4)	Action Potential (1)	Synaptic Knob (4)
Cape (1)	"A" (2)	Neurotransmitter (3)
Lightning-bolt hat (1)	"X" (2)	Deactivating Enzyme (1)
	"O" (2)	Receptor Site (3)
	"N" (2)	Muscle (1)

Note. Numbers in parentheses indicate the quantity of each prop and identification sign needed. The preferred space gun emits noises that can be heard by all class members. The lightning-bolt hat is the soft plastic or cloth variety that can be obtained from most gag and department stores; worn by the runner, it helps in emphasizing the speed of neuronal transmission.

dents are shown how the activating stimulus is the same as the hammer that strikes the area below the kneecap, how the action potential is generated on stimulation of the dendrites, and how the action potential skips from node to node if the axon is myelinated. It is also emphasized that typically there is only one neurotransmitter in each neuron, and that a particular neurotransmitter fits into only one specific kind of receptor site. The roles of potassium and calcium ions are also reviewed, although they are eliminated from the diagram for the sake of simplicity. Once the neuron review is completed, casting begins.

Casting

The neuron review ends with the announcement that 30 volunteers will be needed for the "Colossal Neuron Demonstration." The call for volunteers (especially in classes of 300 or more students) is first met with silence, and then with whispers, giggles, and other uncooperative noises. To encourage participation, several sealed envelopes are held up as the instructor indicates that volunteers can have whatever is inside (usually they contain play money). Slowly, the first few volunteers come forward and are asked to stand near the stage in the front of the class while two "specialized" volunteers are sought. The students are first asked, "Who in the class is a track star or was a track star in high school?" If no one responds, the instructor asks, "Who has someone sitting near you who is a runner or a jogger?" (several are now pointing to a few students). A runner can now be fairly easily cajoled into joining the steadily-growing group of volunteers. Using the same technique, a weight-lifter/body-builder is added. By now there are a fairly large

number of people milling about near the front of the class and the noise level is high throughout the room. Although for the moment it looks like pandemonium, the casting to form the colossal neuron is ready to proceed.

While Figure 1 is kept on the overhead projector, students are chosen to play each of the 30 parts and are arranged at the front of the room in the same position as in Figure 1. First the body builder is assigned to play the part of the muscle and is placed on the far right with the "MUSCLE" sign attached to the person's chest with cellophane tape. Four students are then chosen to play the efferent axon, and the appropriate signs are attached, lining them up so that they spell "AXON" when viewed by the rest of the class. A student is chosen to be the soma, then three males are selected to be receptor sites and three females to be neurotransmitters. A volunteer is now assigned the role of the deactivating enzyme and is given the space gun to hold. Next, the synaptic knobs are chosen, and then, the sodium ions. Each student is placed into position according to Figure 1, which remains projected overhead throughout the demonstration. The runner/jogger is assigned the role of the action potential, is given the lightning-bolt hat and cape to wear, and is placed into position. Four more students are chosen to be the afferent axon and are given plastic garbage bags to wear because of their myelinated status. Another student is assigned the role of the soma of the afferent neuron and is given the air pump to hold. Three males are chosen to be dendrites, and a female is assigned the part of the activating stimulus.

At this point, 30 students, some with props or costumes, and each wearing an identification sign, are arranged across the front of the room to match the overhead projection of

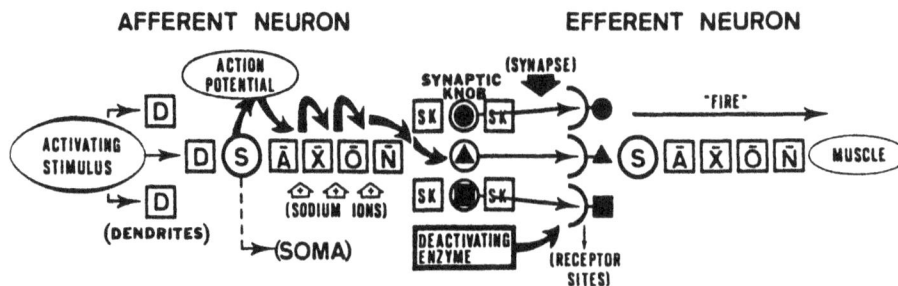

Figure 1. Diagram of neuron anatomy and physiology used during the colossal neuron demonstration. (The black circle, triangle, and square in the middle of the figure represent three different types of neurotransmitters.)

Figure 1. Dress rehearsal for the activation of the colossal neuron can now begin.

Dress Rehearsal

The class is informed that the action of the nerve impulse will be performed in slow motion. First, a final check is made to ensure that everyone is in proper position and that the students comprising both axons are holding hands or locking arms in order to keep the sodium ions on the outside of the axon. The activating stimulus is then asked to "do whatever you would like to do to stimulate these dendrites." Although this instruction prompts various reactions from the audience, the instructor quickly directs the males playing the dendrites to "make the sound you usually make when stimulated." After the dendrites make noises, the soma is told to yell "fire," and immediately the runner/action potential, complete with lightning-bolt hat and cape, begins darting in and out along the axon between the myelinated students. As this action occurs, each student/axon in turn yells "fire" and drops hands, allowing each sodium ion to rush in sequentially. Thus, the permeability of the axon changes with respect to sodium ions, and depolarization takes place.

Depolarization is followed immediately by the soma "pumping" the sodium ions back out, via the action of the bicycle (sodium/potassium) pump. Meanwhile, the action potential bumps the neurotransmitters, which respond by moving across the synapse toward their respective receptor sites. Each neurotransmitter has either an "A," "B," or "C" on her sign, and each receptor site has the same on his sign. Thus, the "lock and key" specificity of neurotransmitters and receptor sites is again emphasized. (Students are reminded, however, that there would typically be only one neurotransmitter per neuron.) The receptor sites are told to hold their arms out in a receptive position and to "bind-on" (i.e., hug) their neurotransmitter as she arrives. Immediately, the deactivating enzyme shoots the neurotransmitters with the electronic space gun, they collapse to the floor, and return on hands and knees to the area surrounded by synaptic knobs. Simultaneously, the efferent soma has yelled "fire" and the student/axons have each dropped hands and sequentially yelled "fire." Finally, as the last student yells "fire," the weight-lifter (muscle) is asked to strike a bodybuilder's pose, to the delight of all.

The class is then asked if they need one more dress rehearsal. Because they typically do, the performance is rehearsed in slow motion one more time, and then the announcement is made that it is time for "action."

Demonstration Proper

The instructor moves to the back of the room and to the call of "ready . . . roll 'em," the sequence occurs with three consecutive repetitions. The instructor stands back and the audience watches as the activating stimulus "stimulates" the dendrites, the action potential starts running, the soma and subsequently each student/axon yell "fire," sodium rushes in

and is quickly pumped back out, neurotransmitters migrate and then become deactivated, the muscle flexes, and the process begins again.

Wrap-Up

After the laughter subsides and a round of applause is given to the "Colossal Neuron Players," the instructor quickly retrieves all props and signs and responds to any questions and comments from the class. The role of sodium, potassium, and calcium ions is again emphasized. The transition from the molecular to the molar aspects of the nervous system is accomplished during the final 20 min of class. This traditional lecture content on the central and peripheral nervous systems provides an appropriate introduction to later lectures on cortical function and the endocrine system.

Evaluation

During the past 5 years, it has been apparent that students have enjoyed the colossal neuron demonstration and have found it to be helpful. In order to obtain a more formal evaluation, data were collected via an anonymous 6-item questionnaire immediately following the fall, 1984 demonstration. Students were asked to rate on a 5-point Likert scale (0 = not at all; 4 = extremely) how helpful they found the 10-min neuron review, as well as the demonstration, in increasing their understanding of neuron anatomy and physiology. They were also asked to rate how entertaining they found the demonstration to be, and to indicate whether or not they thought the review and demonstration together would aid them in remembering neuronal content, whether the review should be retained as part of the course, and whether the demonstration itself should be retained. Comparisons were made between the responses of the 30 participants and the 311 nonparticipants.

Results

The authors' impression that the demonstration appealed to students was supported by the finding that 99.1% of all students favored retention of the demonstration (100% of the participants and 99% of the observers). In addition, 99.7% indicated that both the review and demonstration assisted in their retention of the material, thus supporting the notion that the colossal neuron is not only entertaining but also educational.

Two-tailed t tests for independent samples indicated that there were no differences between participants and observers in terms of helpfulness of the review, helpfulness of the demonstration, and how entertaining the demonstration was (all $ps > .30$). These results suggested that participation was not necessary for self-reported benefits to occur and that participation did not interfere with perceived learning. The t tests for correlated measures suggested that students found the demonstration (M = 3.37; SD = 0.64) to be significantly more helpful in their understanding of neuron anatomy and operation than was the review ($M = 2.50$; $SD = 0.89$). Interestingly, however, 97.9% of all students favored retention of the review. These findings suggested that, although the demonstration was seen as being more helpful than the traditional lecture/review method, students perceived the educational relevance of the review in combination with the demonstration.

Concluding Comments

Recently, two business students who had taken Introductory Psychology 3 years earlier approached the first author to request assistance in setting up a demonstration for a management class using student participation. The gratifying nature of this encounter was that the students could recite the basic components and operation of the neuron by conjuring up an image of "... all those funny people running around on stage," and that they were interested in applying this active teaching method to another field of study.

Although neither the preceding anecdote nor the subjective evaluations of students proves that the active demonstration method enhances learning and retention, the colossal neuron appears to have been well received by introductory students over the past 5 years. Because the anatomical and electro-chemical aspects of neuronal activity are often seen as abstract and irrelevant to students' everyday experience, the colossal neuron combines the visual, auditory, and humorous aspects of live drama to allow difficult content to become anchored to concrete events. Although some instructors may prefer to spend less time on the molecular aspects of physiological psychology, the importance of neuronal activity in understanding such phenomena as schizophrenia, habituation, the effects of drugs, and other content areas, may justify the 2½ class periods devoted to this issue. Regardless of teacher preference, the colossal neuron may provide an effective alternative to the traditional presentation of physiological content in the large undergraduate classroom.

References

Balch, W. R. (1983). The use of role-playing in a classroom demonstration of client-centered therapy. *Teaching of Psychology, 10,* 173–174.

Banziger, G. (1982). Teaching about crowding: Students as an independent variable. *Teaching of Psychology, 9,* 241–242.

Beins, B. (1983). The light box: A simple way of generating complex color demonstrations. *Teaching of Psychology, 10,* 113–114.

Benjamin, L. T., Jr. (1983). A class exercise in personality and psychological assessment. *Teaching of Psychology, 10,* 94–95.

Caudle, F. M. (1979). Using "demonstrations, class experiments and the projection lantern" in the history of psychology course. *Teaching of Psychology, 6,* 7–11.

Chaffin, R., & Herrmann, D. J. (1983). A classroom demonstration of depth of processing. *Teaching of Psychology, 10,* 105–107.

Daniels, C. E. (1979). Should a psychology student have a brain of clay? *Teaching of Psychology, 6,* 175–177.

Gibb, G. D. (1983). Making classical conditioning understandable through a demonstration technique. *Teaching of Psychology, 10,* 112–113.

Levin, J. R. (1982). Modifications of a regression-toward-the-mean demonstration. *Teaching of Psychology, 9,* 237–238.

Older, J. (1979). Improving the introductory psychology course. *Teaching of Psychology, 6,* 75–77.

Rosenkoetter, J. S. (1984). Teaching psychology to large classes: Videotapes, PSI and lecturing. *Teaching of Psychology, 11,* 85–87.

Rozin, P., & Jonides, J. (1977). Mass reaction time: Measurement of the speed of the nerve impulse and the duration of mental processes in class. *Teaching of Psychology, 4,* 91–94.

Shaffer, L. S. (1982). Hamilton's marbles or Jevon's beans: A demonstration of Miller's magical number seven. *Teaching of Psychology, 9,* 116–117.

Silverstein, B. (1982). Teaching a large lecture course in psychology: Turning defeat into victory. *Teaching of Psychology, 9,* 150–155.

Smith, G. F. (1982). Introducing psychology majors to clinical bias through the adjective generation technique. *Teaching of Psychology, 9,* 238–239.

Thieman, T. J. (1984). A classroom demonstration of encoding specificity. *Teaching of Psychology, 11,* 101–102.

Demonstrations of the Size–Weight Illusion

David T. Horner
K. Desix Robinson
University of Wisconsin, Oshkosh

Charpentier (1891) first introduced the size–weight illusion. When lifting two objects that are identical in weight but different in size, the larger object seems to be lighter than the smaller object. Several cues affect the strength of the illusion including cutaneous information (McCloskey, 1974), haptic information (cues obtained when the hand lifts an object; Amazeen & Turvey, 1996; Ellis & Lederman, 1993), and visual information (for a review, see Jones, 1986). Because different cues affect illusion strength, demonstrations of the illusion provide excellent opportunities to discuss how theories must account for different facts and the importance of experimentally controlling for extraneous variables. Demonstrations of the illusion also illustrate the importance of designing experiments to generate empirical evidence that differentiates between competing theories.

There are many methods for presenting the size–weight illusion in the classroom; the best method depends on which topic the instructor wishes to emphasize. This article gives several scenarios, each focusing on a particular topic related to the size–weight illusion: Actual demonstrations may involve a combination of these procedures.

Scenario 1: The Roles of Vision and Haptics

Preparation

Obtain two small and two large identical-brand coffee cans. Fill them to equal weights with stones wrapped in rags and seal them. Label each of the two large cans A and each of the small cans B. Center rubber bands around one large can and one small can to provide anchors, and tie a string 15 cm long to each rubber band.

Presentation

Students in a no-haptics group lift the cans with strings using their thumb and forefingers (Ellis & Lederman, 1993), whereas students in a haptics group use their hands to lift the plain cans. Each group further divides into a sighted subgroup that looks at the cans and a blindfolded subgroup. Leaders in each group present cans in random order (or simultaneously) to each student. Students judge which can feels lighter and the leader records the responses for each subgroup.

Discussion

When students lift the cans with strings, no haptic size information is available. In the sighted condition, the observed size difference between objects leads to more "lighter" judgments for the large can. In the blindfolded condition, with no size information available, students judge the cans to be identical in weight.

Lifting the cans using the hands provides haptic size information. Including both visual information and haptic information produces a strong illusion. The performance of the blindfolded subgroup demonstrates that vision augments the illusion, but is not necessary for it. Haptic cues provide size information and the illusion persists, but may be weaker.

One theory for the size–weight illusion that students seem to understand readily is that expectations drive the perception of weight (Ross, 1969). Based on past experience, observers expect large objects to weigh more than small objects. This expectation causes the observer to exert more force initially when lifting the large can, with the result that the large can feels easier to lift than the small can. The observer judges the large can to be lighter because it is easier to lift than the small can. The illusion is absent without knowledge of the size of the cans. Instructors can introduce competing theories and ask students to design procedures to differentiate between them (Amazeen & Turvey, 1996; Anderson, 1970, 1972; Stevens & Rubin, 1970).

Scenario 2: The Importance of Relative Size

Preparation

Obtain several equal-diameter cardboard tubes (e.g., from paper towel or aluminum foil rolls). Cut them to create four different-length tubes (12, 19, 33, and 46 cm), fill the tubes with rags to equal weights, and seal the ends with tape. The length of the smallest tube should extend beyond the edges of the observer's palm. Label each of the two largest tubes A and each of the two smallest tubes B.

Presentation

All observers use vision. Give one group of students the smallest and largest tubes and give the other group the intermediate tubes. Have a leader test each group member by placing one tube centered in each hand of the observer without the observer feeling the edges. Observers judge how much heavier B feels relative to A (or vice versa, which would be unusual) and the leader records a proportion (e.g., equal, 1.5 times as heavy as A, twice as heavy as A, etc.). The average proportion for each group provides a measure of the "strength" of the illusion.

Discussion

The average proportion should be larger for the group that held the largest and smallest tubes than for the group that held the intermediate tubes. The greater the difference in size, the greater the effect.

Scenario 3: Active Versus Passive Touch

Preparation

Cut two rectangular blocks of Styrofoam with bases of equal size, but different heights. Make sure the bases will fit against an observer's palm. Equalize their weights by inserting pieces of metal coat-hanger wire into each block. Distribute the added weight as evenly as possible throughout the Styrofoam. You may have to increase their weights somewhat to achieve the proper effect.

Presentation

The active-touch group of students lifts the blocks and judges which is lighter. The passive-touch group of students rests their extended arms motionless and palm up on a table and judges which block is lighter only after someone places each block on their palm.

Discussion

The active-touch group should perceive a stronger size–weight illusion than the passive-touch group, which may report no illusion at all. If there is no difference in reports for the groups, have each student perform the task using active touch and passive touch. Students may also close their eyes to explore the role of vision.

Conclusions

Students appreciate several aspects of these demonstrations. First, they experience the effects of vision, haptics, and passive touch on weight perception directly rather than reading about them or receiving the information auditorily. Second, they actively participate in collecting data and testing hypotheses. Third, they contribute ideas and suggestions for further exploration and some of these suggestions may

even provide continuity between scenarios. For example, after discussing Scenario 1, some students may wonder how the relative size of the objects affects illusion strength, leading to the demonstration in Scenario 2.

The demonstrations have several practical advantages in addition to their pedagogical uses. The stimuli are easy to construct and the materials are cost effective and readily available. Preparation time is short and limited to the time required to construct the stimuli. Presentation and discussion time for each demonstration varies depending on class size and the amount of discussion following each demonstration.

These demonstrations were presented in a 1-hr class meeting of an upper division Sensation and Perception course. Following the demonstrations, 14 students responded to three questions about the effectiveness of the demonstrations using a 10-point scale, ranging from 1 (*low*) to 10 (*high*). The mean ratings were calculated for the questions: "How interesting were these demonstrations?" ($M = 8.4$, $SD = 1.1$), "How useful were these demonstrations for learning each topic?" ($M = 9.0$, $SD = 1.0$), and "Should these demonstrations be used in future classes?" ($M = 9.3$, $SD = 1.1$). Clearly, students found the demonstrations worthwhile for learning concepts related to the size-weight illusion.

References

Amazeen, E. L., & Turvey, M. T. (1996). Weight perception and the haptic size–weight illusion are functions of the inertia tensor. *Journal of Experimental Psychology: Human Perception and Performance, 22,* 213–232.

Anderson, N. H. (1970). Averaging model applied to the size–weight illusion. *Perception & Psychophysics, 8,* 1–4.

Anderson, N. H. (1972). Cross-task validation of functional measurement. *Perception & Psychophysics, 12,* 389–395.

Charpentier, A. (1891). Analyse experimentale de quelques elements de la sensation de poids [Experimental study of some aspects of weight perception]. *Archives de Physiologie Normales et Pathologiques, 18,* 79–87.

Ellis, R. R., & Lederman, S. J. (1993). The role of haptic versus visual volume cues in the size–weight illusion. *Perception & Psychophysics, 53,* 315–324.

Jones, L. A. (1986). Perception of force and weight: Theory and research. *Psychological Bulletin, 100,* 29–42.

McCloskey, D. I. (1974). Muscular and cutaneous mechanisms in the estimation of the weights of grasped objects. *Neuropsychologia, 12,* 513–520.

Ross, H. E. (1969). When is a weight not illusory? *Quarterly Journal of Experimental Psychology, 21,* 346–355.

Stevens, J. C., & Rubin, L. L. (1970). Psychophysical scales of apparent heaviness and the size–weight illusion. *Perception & Psychophysics, 8,* 225–230.

Notes

1. A poster version of this material was presented at the Council of Teachers of Undergraduate Psychology's Creative Classroom Session at the Midwestern Psychological Association meetings, Chicago, May 1995.

A Computer-Assisted Difference Threshold Exercise for Introductory Psychology

Thomas Brothen
General College
University of Minnesota

The *difference threshold* is a difficult concept for introductory psychology students to understand. Introductory textbook authors usually explain it in two steps. First, they cover the technical aspects, often leaning heavily on the mathematics of Weber's law. Second, they present examples from everyday life. For instance, the textbook I use (Myers, 1992) briefly describes Weber's law and then gives students an example comparing 10% price increases for a 50¢ candy bar with a $50,000 Mercedes-Benz. In my experience, as reasonable as this approach is, it does not deal effectively with students' confusion about and avoidance of the technical aspects of the concept and probably causes them to focus too much on interesting examples. One result is that they often miss the element of threshold; they think the differences are all or nothing—failing to incorporate the central notion of "just noticeable." In the Mercedes-Benz example, for instance, they have a difficult time noticing a $5,000 difference. I once asked a student if he thought Ross Perot would notice it, and he said that noticing such things is probably how Perot amassed his fortune.

Experience has convinced me that simply lecturing and giving yet more examples of the difference threshold does not help very much. My solution was to use an active-learning approach (Older, 1979; Schomberg, 1986). I have students work actively with the threshold concept instead of just reading or hearing about it. In addition, because a major focus of introductory psychology is research methodology, I give students experience first producing data as a "subject" and then analyzing the same data as an "experimenter." This approach helps them understand how psychologists do research. Specifically, I present pairs of stimuli to students and ask them to indicate whether these stimuli are different or the same. Students produce the very data they later analyze to illustrate the difference threshold concept.

My first attempt to use this procedure involved a crude device consisting of two household light bulbs, two dimmer switches, and an ammeter to calibrate the dimmer switch settings. I presented two light stimuli that differed either well below, well above, or approximately at the difference threshold. Brightness levels of the two bulbs were laboriously set before each trial behind a screen that was then lifted to show the lights in a darkened lecture hall. Students indicated on worksheets whether they thought the lights were the same or different. Later, they analyzed the resulting data in groups and drew conclusions as to which pairs of stimuli were closest to the difference threshold.

In this article, I describe an exercise using computer technology that improves on the original technique. It is part of a computer-assisted model for teaching introductory psychology that incorporates several similar active-learning exercises (Brothen, 1991). Students enrolled in my courses spend each class day in a computer classroom in which they work individually at networked microcomputers to complete programmed-learning exercises, study questions, and take chapter quizzes and a final exam. They also conduct actual studies of behavior, of which this is one.

Classroom Procedure

Overall Procedure

Students hear sound pairs of different pitch levels on 42 trials. The instructor runs a computer program that automatically creates two sounds for about 1 s each 2 s apart, and students indicate whether the pitch levels in each sound pair seem the same or different by typing an "s" or a "d" on their computers. The pitch levels differ between pairs over a moderate range of about one octave. Pitch levels within pairs differ either much less than .3%, much more than .3%, or about .3%. (The percentage differences were only a rough starting point in the design of this exercise. Given the vagaries of the software and hardware described later, they were empirically derived.) Once all sound pairs are presented, students proceed individually through a computer-assisted instructional program that explains thresholds, asks questions in a branching format, and has them interpret their individual data. Later, students work in six-person groups to analyze the class data using worksheets containing instructions and 21 blanks for entry of the class data for each trial pair.

The 42 sound pairs are counterbalanced. For example, on Trial 1, a lower pitch sound is presented first, and the higher pitch sound presented second. Trial 1 is counterbalanced with Trial 22, in which the same two sounds are presented in reverse order. Thus, each sound pair is presented twice. Once the data gathering is concluded (after about 10 min), I activate a computer program to tabulate students' data and then write the total number of student indications of "different" on the board for each of the 21 trial pairs. Students calculate the percentage of judgments of "different" for each trial pair using these class data. Thus, if all students thought the sounds were always different over both presentations of a sound pair, the number of "ds" written on the board for the corresponding trial pair would be double the number of students in class, and the correct calculation would be 100%. If exactly half the student judgments of a sound pair were "different," the value for the corresponding trial pair would be 50%, and it would be defined as precisely at the difference threshold. Once they calculate the class percentages for each of the 21 trial pairs, students work in groups to decide (based on the textbook's definition) which pairs were "close" to the difference threshold and why. This process results in much discussion among students about just what it is they are supposed to be looking for and what it means to be "close" to the difference threshold. It also provides many opportunities for instructor intervention in students' misconceptions about the concept and how the experiment was conducted. Finally, students work in their groups to write (on the computer) research reports that summarize the results and include original examples of the concept (e.g., cooking examples involving the use of seasonings are popular), which they turn in with their worksheets.

Materials and Apparatus

The stimulus presentation and student data-recording/instruction computer programs are written in the Pilot programming language (Barker, 1987). Pilot allows values to be entered in the program that control the pitch levels of a computer's sound-generating capability. For the sound-generating presentation program, the values of each pair of sound frequencies were set approximately .3% different (as noted in Myers, 1992, p. 135) for those intended to be at the difference threshold and greater or less than .3% different for those intended to be above or below the difference threshold. Then, the values were pilot tested, adjusted, and retested with a group of students recruited from other classes to ensure that they were indeed below, above, or approximately at (i.e., as indicated by pilot students as different 50% of the time) the difference threshold. The presentation program runs on an IBM Model 25 computer hooked through its speaker jack to a Realistic SA–150 Stereo Amplifier and two Realistic Minimus 7 speakers. The students' data-recording/instructional program runs on the computer network described in Brothen (1991). The sound-generating presentation program was adjusted further, based on the class data for the first several times it was used. The objective was to have students say that nearly none of the sound pairs below the difference threshold were different, nearly all the sound pairs above the difference threshold were different, and approximately half of those at the difference threshold were different.

Results

Seven trial pairs each were designed to be below, above, and at the difference threshold. As one may expect, there is variation. But, in every 1 of the 10 classes using this experiment in its current form during three academic terms, at least one trial pair was exactly at the 50% level, and several usually were within a few percentage points of 50%. If students applied the definitions strictly, they found at least one instance of each. They also had to decide whether a few percentages were "close" or not (e.g., is 38% close—compared to 2% or 98%?). The average percentage of "ds" (i.e., students saying they heard a difference) for sounds below the difference threshold was 1.67%, the average percentage for sounds above was 98.72%, and the average percentage for sounds at the threshold was 49.30%. The average percentages for all trial pairs for the 10 classes (available from the author) revealed a consistent pattern—students perceived one third of the sound pairs as below, one third above, and one third near the difference threshold.

Discussion

The active-learning procedure described in this article meets its objectives. First, it provides a way for students to interact actively with a basic concept in psychology—the difference threshold. Second, it provides students the experience of participating as subjects and as experimenters. Observations of students working in class and informal interviews conducted with them have convinced me that the exercise improves their understanding of the difference threshold and how psychologists investigate human behavior. I now use the exercise in a classroom equipped with a computer network. However, the presentation software and hardware apparatus are sufficient for it to be useful to most instructors. Students could record each response on a worksheet and then tabulate and analyze their data in groups of 5 to 10.

As now used, the exercise takes approximately 90 min of class time to provide an overview (10 min) and to have students complete the data gathering (10 min), work through the instructional program (20 min), analyze the class data (recording total "ds" and calculating proportions for 21 trial pairs; 20 min), decide which pairs were closest to the difference threshold, and then write group research reports (30 min). For a traditionally equipped classroom, simply presenting the stimuli via the apparatus described earlier, having student groups record and analyze their data by hand, and having them make decisions as to which trial pairs were at the difference threshold could be done in approximately 30 min. This procedure could be supplemented by instructor explanation and class discussion.

The approach of having students first serve as subjects and then switch to the role of experimenter is a fruitful one (Brothen, 1984). Students experience an important concept as they are learning about it, and they gain an understanding of the research process by actually engaging in it. For introductory psychology to be more than a collection of concepts for students to memorize, occasional forays into in-class research are useful for students and instructors.

References

Barker, P. (1987). *Authoring languages for CAL*. London: Macmillan.

Brothen, T. (1984). Three computer-assisted laboratory exercises for introductory psychology. *Teaching of Psychology, 11,* 105–107.

Brothen, T. (1991). Implementing a computer-assisted cooperative learning model for introductory psychology. *Teaching of Psychology, 18*, 183–185.

Myers, D. (1992). *Psychology* (3rd ed.). New York: Worth.

Older, J. (1979). Improving the introductory psychology course. *Teaching of Psychology, 6*, 75–77.

Schomberg, S. (1986). *Strategies for active teaching and learning in university classrooms*. Minneapolis: University Of Minnesota Communication Services.

Notes

1. Requests for reprints or further information may be sent to Thomas Brothen, 346 Appleby Hall, University of Minnesota, Minneapolis, MN 55455; e-mail: broth001@maroon.tc.umn.edu. Those wishing a copy of the presentation program should send an MS–DOS formatted disk with sufficient return postage.

The Janus Illusion

Dale Klopfer
Michael E. Doherty
Bowling Green State University

The Roman god Janus, having two faces, could look both forward and backward at the same time; whether one stood in front of or behind Janus, one was face-to-face with the god. In the Janus illusion, a mask appears to face the observer not only when it does, but also when it is placed at a 180° angle. The illusion was described by Gregory (1970, 1980), Gogel (1990), and Ramachandran (1988) and was recently investigated by Klopfer (1991). The Janus illusion is less well known than the Muller–Lyer, Ponzo, and moon illusions that commonly appear in introductory textbooks, but it nicely complements the more familiar static illusions. It is inexpensive to construct and provides a compelling demonstration.

Equipment

A reasonably rigid, plastic mask of a face, commonly sold in toy stores or in costume and novelty shops, is adequate. We have used opaque, smooth, white masks and translucent masks of smiling male and female faces, complete with laugh lines and forehead wrinkles. Guidelines for buying and preparing masks include:

1. Make sure that the mask is sufficiently rigid to withstand slow rotation without losing its shape. Grasp the chin of the mask between your thumb and forefinger and rotate the mask to the right and left. If the mask wiggles or changes shape, then look for a sturdier one.

2. Make certain that the textures of the inner and outer surfaces of the mask are the same. This is not likely to be a problem with molded plastic masks; however, with some material, the inside may be smoother than the outside. The demonstrations may be less compelling if students can identify the inner and outer surfaces of the mask on the basis of surface differences.

3. If the mask is not already opaque, make sure that both surfaces of the mask can be painted; we spray painted ours a flat gray. If you show the illusion in a large room, a flat gray will make the features of the mask more readily discriminable from the back when the mask is of intermediate reflectance. With a black mask, features would be lost to the observer due to absorption of light; with a white mask, features would be lost due to excessive reflection.

4. Trim the edges of the mask, if necessary, to make the effects demonstrable at a wide variety of viewing angles. Consider the arc of the face from earhole to earhole to be 180°. Trim the mask so that it covers roughly 120° of arc. We trimmed the mask so that the edges were just behind the cheekbones of the mask, but not all masks will have cheekbones.

How you mount the mask will depend on the viewing situation. When the mask is static, a stand fashioned from a 1.25-cm diameter wooden dowel mounted perpendicular to a flat wooden base will suffice. The stand's height will depend on the classroom size. Make the stand sturdy enough to support the mask but small enough to carry. The mask can be attached to the dowel with a thumbtack or screw through the base of the chin. Be sure that the line of sight of the mounted mask is parallel to the ground plane, not tilted up or down.

For a rotating mask, mount the mask on the spindle of a LaFayette Model 14015 Illusionator, bolting it through a hole drilled in the base of the chin. Or you can use any variable speed motor with a vertical shaft on which to mount the mask, such as those used to demonstrate Ames's trapezoidal window illusion. You can also gear down an unused record player, so that it will spin at 2 or 3 rotations per minute (rpm).

In one of the viewing conditions described later, perceptions of the rotating mask are compared to those of an unfamiliar object. One unfamiliar object could be the molded plastic packaging attached to cardboard that is often used for toys and that approximates the shape of one half of the enclosed toy. Make sure the molded plastic is sufficiently rigid to withstand rotation without undue deformation and it has a flat part that can be attached to the spindle of the variable speed motor. (See Figure 1 of Klopfer, 1991, for examples of unfamiliar objects.) As with the mask, we spray painted our unfamiliar objects gray.

Conditions

Static Mask–Static Viewers

Instructors of fairly large introductory courses would most likely use this situation. Place the mask in the front of the room, as close to the center as possible, facing the students (the 0° position). Light the room normally, but provide more light coming from the back of the room. In a large (225-seat) classroom, turning off the overhead row of lights at the front of the room yielded quite satisfactory results. If you cannot create differential lighting or if your classroom is extremely deep, try dimming the room lights and focusing the light from a slide projector on the mask.

Have students close one eye and raise their hands if they think that the mask is looking in their direction. Then shield the mask from student view, move it 45° to the right, and repeat the request. Next shield the mask, move it 45° to the left of 0°, and ask for hands. Repeat with students using both eyes; the results should be the same as with one eye. The unremarkable result should be that students sitting in the center section of the class should raise their hands when the mask is set to face 0°, followed by those sitting on both sides.

Again shield the mask and set it at 180° (i.e., facing directly away from the students sitting in the center). Now nearly everyone should think that the mask is looking in their direction, regardless of where they are sitting. (Students at the extreme sides in the front row or two might not see the mask looking at them.)

Static Mask–Moving Viewers

This situation is best used in a standard classroom, but it could be adapted for a large lecture hall. Place the mask in the front of the room in the 0° orientation. Have students walk back and forth along the back of the classroom (i.e., in the frontal plane of the mask) and have them report the direction in which the mask faces as they walk. They should report that the mask maintains a constant orientation, facing toward the back of the room. Shield the mask, set it at 180°, and again have students walk back and forth in the frontal plane of the mask. They should report that the face follows them as they traverse the room, turning as they move from one side to the other. Some students may report that the mask appears to turn through a greater arc than that described by their path. For example, a student standing to the left of the mask may report that the mask appears to be looking over his or her left shoulder.

Rotating Mask–Static Viewers

In this situation, which is suitable for both standard classrooms and large lecture halls, the mask is rotated about its vertical axis. The procedures described later will enable students to compare perceptions of an unfamiliar rotating object with the perception of a rotating mask, but simply rotating the mask alone without a comparison object still provides a demonstration as stunning in its own way as Ames's trapezoidal window illusion.

Mount the unfamiliar object on the motor, and set it with the convex side facing the students. Tell the students that you will turn on a motor that will rotate the object slowly in one direction, and ask them to raise their hands if they see the object appear to change its direction of rotation. Rotate the object at 2 or 3 rpm for at least 1 min. A few students may see the unfamiliar object change direction, but the majority will see it rotate continuously in the same direction— the one in which it is in fact rotating. Then mount the mask on the spindle, so that the convex side faces the students (the 0° orientation). After a few complete rotations of the mask, nearly all students will see the mask oscillating twice during each complete physical rotation, changing its direction of rotation to maintain an apparent orientation facing the students. For the few who continue to see complete rotations even after 3 or 4 rotations, reduce the rotation rate to 1 or 2 rpm.

Videotape of a Rotating Mask

If a variable speed motor is not readily available but a VHS videocassette recorder and television or projection screen are, then the rotating mask can be shown from a videotape of the rotating objects used in Klopfer (1991). (For a copy of the videotape, send a blank ½-in. VHS tape to either author.) The experiences associated with the static situations can be reproduced via videotape, but not those associated with moving viewers or binocular vision.

Discussion

The phenomena described earlier allow students to ponder some issues in perception and to be exposed to some aspects of experimental methodology.

Discussion for Introductory Psychology

These demonstrations can be used, paradoxically, to argue that perception is normally highly veridical. Why else would illusions be so striking? This argument can be presented in a way to dispel the common notion that knowledge about the world is completely subjective. Although students are tricked in this unusual situation, they can see that their experience of something out of the ordinary is just that—out of the ordinary.

An important point to make is that the static, monocular retinal image is fundamentally ambiguous. Moreover, although viewing with two eyes often helps to disambiguate percepts, the retinal image cannot be completely disambiguated by binocular information; the Janus illusion would not be present with both eyes open. The retinal image cannot be completely disambiguated by motion information; mask rotation and observer motion would destroy the illusion.

Another important point is that past experience influences perception. We have millions of experiences with retinal images in which two eyes, a nose, and a mouth turn out to be a face. We have many fewer experiences with such objects turning out to be the inside of a mask. Consequently, we are likely to interpret the inside of a mask as a face. With an unfamiliar object, neither the inside nor the outside of the object is more familiar; hence, we tend to see the object in its true orientation.

The Janus illusion illustrates a general principle discussed in many introductory textbooks: Perception is not a simple, passive copying of external reality; rather, it is an active, constructive process that resembles hypothesis testing.

Discussion for Sensation and Perception

The static retinal image is inherently ambiguous; yet, when we look at the world, we experience a single arrangement of objects and surfaces; despite ambiguity in stimulation, our perceptions are generally unambiguous. Two general approaches offer explanations for the uniqueness of our experience. The first asserts that retinal information is insufficient to explain perception, so cognitive processes must aid the interpretation of sensory input. That is, our perceptual experience is based in part on what we think may have created our retinal image. This *constructivist* view, stated clearly by John Stuart Mill and by Hermann von Helmholtz over 100 years ago, has modern adherents (e.g., Gregory, 1980; Hochberg, 1986; Rock, 1983). It does not hold that we consciously weigh alternative interpretations of the retinal image, but that we make rapid unconscious inferences about reality.

The second approach holds that, under normal viewing conditions, stimulus information available to the viewer accounts fully for veridical perceptual experience (Gibson, 1966, 1979). This *ecological* approach holds that perception is not mediated by inferences, unconscious or otherwise, and that illusions result from artificial viewing conditions of the laboratory. In normal viewing, people are free to move about and look at objects with two eyes, thereby picking up a full complement of information from motion and binocular vision.

The Janus illusion allows the merits of both approaches to be explored. For the static mask, it is important for students to realize that no single experiment or set of experiments will adjudicate between the two general approaches, because aspects of both have merit. But the phenomena described earlier allow both approaches to be explored.

In the static mask–static viewer situation, when all students look at the 0° mask both monocularly and binocularly, only those sitting in the center of the room should indicate that the mask is facing them. The ecological view might claim that information about where the mask is facing is provided by shading, by texture, and, for those who are close enough, by accommodation. The same claim can be made when the mask is facing the left and right sides of

the classroom. The constructivist view is that perceivers unconsciously infer that the object producing the retinal image is a mask facing the class. A similar argument applies when the mask faces the left and right sides of the room.

When the mask faces away from students, regardless of where they are sitting, they see the mask facing themselves. According to the ecological view, this should not happen, because information about where the mask is facing has been provided. The constructivist view can explain the illusion: The retinal image could have been created by a mask facing away, which looks like an inside-out face, or by a normal face looking at the perceiver. Because we are more likely to encounter normal faces than inside-out ones, we infer that the retinal image was created by a normal face, and that is what we see. The fact that the illusion persists when viewers use two eyes suggests that binocular depth information can be overpowered by our unconscious inferences.

In the static mask–moving viewer situation, with the mask at 0°, the mask is correctly seen to face the students. Here, motion parallax, which specifies depth relations among the parts of the mask, provides additional information for veridical perception. With the mask at 180°, however, the mask appears to face the viewer and to follow the viewer's movements. The inference that the mask faces the viewer seems to overpower the information specifying where the mask is actually facing, even to the point where a stationary object is seen as moving. The ecological view cannot readily account for this.

The rotating mask situations, both live and videotaped, yield a full complement of motion information specifying the mask's true orientation. If the object-based motion information allowed the viewer to see the mask in its true orientation, the mask should appear to rotate. Instead, it appears to oscillate, owing to the viewers' differential familiarity with normal and inside-out faces. With an unfamiliar object, differential familiarity does not apply, and the object is accurately seen as rotating.

We believe that the data favor a constructivist view of the nature of perception. Two interesting intellectual challenges are for students to produce this explanation themselves and to attack the constructivist explanation and reinterpret the data from an ecological perspective.

The Janus illusion demonstrations illustrate the intricacies of perception and show that perception is a proper field of investigation. Perhaps because perceptual experience is usually veridical, arising instantaneously and effortlessly, students naively believe there is nothing to study. They respond to the question "How do we see?" with an incredulous "We open our eyes and look, of course." As is true in many disciplines, teaching about perception requires disabusing students of their naive beliefs. Because visual illusions lack veridicality, students must confront their beliefs. Moreover, students can experience and explore compelling, theoretically relevant perceptual phenomena.

References

Gibson, J. J. (1966). *The senses considered as perceptual systems.* Boston: Houghton-Mifflin.

Gibson, J. J. (1979). *The ecological approach to visual perception.* Boston: Houghton-Mifflin.

Gogel, W. C. (1990). A theory of phenomenal geometry and its applications. *Perception and Psychophysics, 48,* 105–123.

Gregory, R. L. (1970). *The intelligent eye.* New York: McGraw-Hill.

Gregory, R. L. (1980). Perceptions as hypotheses. *Philosophical Transactions of the Royal Society of London, B 290,* 181–197.

Hochberg, J. (1986). Visual perception. In R. C. Atkinson, R. J. Herrnstein, G. Lindsey, & R. D. Luce (Eds.), *Stevens' handbook*

of experimental psychology (Vol. 1, pp. 195–276). New York: Wiley.

Klopfer, D. (1991). Apparent reversals of a rotating mask: A new demonstration of cognition in perception. *Perception and Psychophysics, 49,* 522–530.

Ramachandran, V. S. (1988). Perceiving shape from shading. *Scientific American, 259*(2), 76–83.

Rock, I. (1983). *The logic of perception.* Cambridge, MA: MIT Press.

Oh Say, Can You See?

Frederick J. Kozub
University of Richmond

Many introductory psychology textbooks (e.g., Carlson, 1990; Morris, 1990; Rathus, 1990) present information about Gestalt psychology's principles of visual perception by using lines, dots, and squiggles. Although these are appropriate abstractions, I neither "see" the world nor assume that my students see the world in that fashion. Rather, we are bombarded with images from catalogs, magazines, posters, and t-shirts that compete for our attention. I wondered if I could take advantage of these readily available sources of visual stimulation to help my Introductory Psychology students understand the application of Gestalt principles involved in visual perception.

After an in-class discussion of the principles involved using the standard lines, dots, and squiggles, I showed slides, transparencies, and posters of everyday advertisements taken from a wide range of sources. I used advertisements from popular magazines, record jackets, posters from the school bookstore, and catalogs from mail-order houses and major department stores. We discussed each example with respect to the use of changes in luminosity and hue that define edges and contours; the use of proximity and similarity of size, shape, and color; and the use of the law of Prägnanz, including symmetry and closure. Where possible, I either used a transparent overlay or drew directly on the item to abstract and highlight the basic principle. A line drawn through some items separated them into symmetrical components. For others, simple measurements of the angle of limbs in human figures showed similarities of bends (e.g., forearm–upper arm and thigh–lower leg). For still others, repetition of images was shown, as was similarity in the use of color and meaning.

Students were asked to locate and bring to class examples of these organizing principles from their own visual worlds. They were told that several organizing principles could be operating in the same advertisement but to pick the best one they could find to illustrate each principle. They were required to highlight (via an overlay, tracing, or sketch) the

principle involved and to describe it. They were told not to damage any item that was not theirs and that should they desire it, items would be returned to them (e.g., record jackets, t-shirts, buttons, posters, etc.).

I was delighted with the quality and range of the students' submissions. All were good examples; many were superb. The materials included sew-on patches, pins, t-shirts, student-produced photographs, reproductions of favorite paintings and/or posters, and a wide range of advertisements.

I offer student comments and some examples about the efficacy of this exercise. Some comments were, "I never realized that this was going on"; "I look at ads a bit differently now"; "Gosh, ads are more complicated than I thought"; and "Maybe that's why I like that painting so much."

The students appeared excited about some of their discoveries. For example, in the painting *American Gothic* by Grant Wood, the repetition of the three-prong design in the pitchfork, cactus, seams on the overalls, and the male face (outer edge of face and chin cleft) were noted; symmetry was expressed in corporate graphic symbols (e.g., Chrysler and Chase Manhattan Bank); mirror image symmetry was noted in advertisements for cameras, shirts, and jewelry. One student presented an advertisement for woolen clothing that showed a hat, scarf, and sweater in warm shades of brown, orange, and yellow worn by a female model holding an orange and brown tabby cat. The student used two copies of the advertisement, the original and one in which she painted the cat black with sleek fur. She commented that the use of the orange and brown cat conveyed warmth, softness, and fuzziness (like wool), whereas the black sleek cat did not appear to convey the same meaning as the intended selling points for the use of wool.

In one unusual submission, a student took photographs of a television commercial in which the image was black and white but the product was in color. This example was a good illustration of a figure–ground relationship.

Several students kept bringing new material 2 or 3 months later when they found better examples. Students' reactions are not hard evidence, but it seems fair to conclude that the exercise achieved its goal of using contemporary materials to illustrate Gestalt principles of organization in visual perception.

References

Carlson, N. R. (1990). *Psychology: The science of behavior* (3rd ed.). Boston: Allyn & Bacon.

Morris, C. G. (1990). *Psychology: An introduction* (7th ed.). Englewood Cliffs, NJ: Prentice Hall.

Rathus, S. A. (1990). *Psychology* (4th ed.). Fort Worth: Holt, Rinehart & Winston.

Notes

1. This exercise was developed as part of the exercise/experiment component of the Introductory Psychology course.

Negative Reinforcement and Positive Punishment

James V. McConnell
University of Michigan

There probably is no concept more difficult to teach to introductory students than that of negative reinforcement (Tauber, 1988). There are at least four reasons why this is so: (a) the surplus meaning carried by such terms as negative and punishment; (b) the fact that Skinner (1938, 1953) described two types of reinforcement (positive and negative), but only one type of punishment; (c) the tendency that most students have to perceive reinforcement and punishment in terms of their effects on the organism's emotions rather than on overt behaviors; and (d) Skinner's (1938, 1953) habit of using the words *reinforcement* and *punishment* in at least two different ways. Finding a more effective way to teach the concept of negative reinforcement requires resolving all four problems.

Surplus Meaning of *Negative* and *Punishment*

Webster's New Collegiate Dictionary defines reinforcement as "the act of strengthening," clearly a behavioral definition. However, the dictionary also defines *negative* as "disagreeable" and *punishment* as "suffering, pain, or loss," words that appeal to inner feelings or emotions, rather than to measurable behaviors. Little wonder, then, that most students (and some psychologists) believe that negative reinforcement refers to the act of punishment—that is, to the onset of pain or dissatisfaction—rather than an action that strengthens a response by reducing or terminating an aversive stimulus.

Two Types of Reinforcement but Only One Type of Punishment?

Although Skinner (1953) mentioned two types of reinforcement—positive and negative—he described but one type of punishment. *Positive reinforcement* is the technical term he used in place of *reward*; however, he did not supply a technical term to replace *punishment*.

Given that *reward* is a synonym for *positive reinforcement* and that *negative* is defined as "something disagreeable," many students assume that negative reinforcement should be the technical term that is synonymous with punishment (Tauber, 1988). Had Skinner provided us with a technical term for *punishment*, this confusion might not exist.

Feelings Rather Than Behaviors

To avoid discussing what goes on inside the organism when reinforcement or punishment occurs, Skinner defined these concepts in terms of their behavioral consequences. He (1953) noted, for example, that organisms tend to approach positive reinforcers and escape from punishers. However, it is difficult to convince most students that the organism's emotions do not mediate the behavioral changes that Skinner spoke of. Indeed, one question students frequently ask is, "But why does the organism approach or avoid the stimulus?" They know full well that they like rewards and dislike punishers and presume that their consequential behaviors are motivated by their feelings. Most students also assume that other organisms feel and respond as they do.

Skinner's Definitions

Most of the time, Skinner (1938, 1974) defined *reinforcement* as a behavioral consequence that increases the probability that a response will be repeated in the future. He (1971) put it this way: "When a bit of behavior is followed by a certain kind of consequence, it is more likely to occur again, and a consequence having this effect is called a reinforcer" (p. 27).

Most of the time, too, Skinner spoke of punishment in terms of its behavioral consequences. Suppose an organism is punished for making a certain response. The effects of this punishment are threefold; he said: First, there is a time-limited reduction in the rate at which the organism emits the undesirable response; second, there is an increase in escape or avoidance behaviors; and third, if the punishment is strong enough, the undesirable response actually increases in strength once punishment is terminated. In describing one of his own experiments, Skinner (1953) said: "The effect of punishment was a temporary suppression of the behavior, not a reduction in the total number of responses" (p. 184).

At first glance, it would appear that Skinner successfully defined both *punishment* and *reinforcement* in terms of their behavioral consequences. However, an analysis of Skinner's writings suggests that he also used the terms *reinforcement* and *punishment* in quite a different way—to describe the onset and offset of certain classes of stimuli under the experimenter's control. This conflict in Skinner's definitions shows up most clearly in his discussion of negative reinforcement. According to Skinner, "You can distinguish between punishment, which is making an aversive event contingent upon a response, and negative reinforcement, in which the elimination or removal of an aversive stimulus, conditioned or unconditioned, is reinforcing" (cited in Evans, 1968, p. 183). Here, surely, Skinner defined both *punishment* and *negative reinforcement* as the onset or offset of a noxious stimulus, not as consequential behaviors.

One reason, perhaps, why it is difficult to explain negative reinforcement to students is that most psychologists tend to use the term in Skinner's second sense—as "the elimination or removal of an aversive stimulus"—not as an increase in the organism's response rate. It is also true, of course, that the words *noxious* and *aversive* appeal as much to emotional mediators as they do to behavioral reactions.

Positive and Negative Punishment

Fortunately, there is a fairly simple way of overcoming the difficulties associated with teaching our students what negative reinforcement actually is. More than 2 decades ago, Catania (1968) noted that there are actually two types of punishment: "Like reinforcement, punishment can be positive or negative" (p. 241). In a subsequent publication, he (1979) defined *positive punishment* as that associated with the presentation of an aversive stimulus, whereas negative punishment results from the withdrawal of a positively reinforcing stimulus. Rachlin (1970) took a similar position, although he did not adopt the terms *positive* and *negative punishment* until several years later (Rachlin, 1976). Redd, Porterfield, and Anderson (1979) also spoke of two types of punishment in their text on behavior modification.

Despite the logic of Catania's assertion that there must be both positive and negative punishment, the terms seldom appear even in operant-oriented journals. A search of *Psychological Abstracts* since 1966—the earliest date that the *Abstracts* are available in computerized form—turned up but 18 references for each term. However, in 14 of these articles, the authors actually referred to the positive or negative consequences of using punishment as a means of controlling behavior. In only 4 of the articles did the authors use the terms as Catania defined them (Jackson & Molloy, 1983; Scott & Wood, 1987; Whitehurst & Miller, 1973; Zirpoli & Lloyd, 1987). The fact that punishment can be either positive or negative is discussed in two recent books on learning and memory (Gordon, 1989; Hall, 1989) and in one introductory text (Wade & Tavris, 1987).

Presenting These Concepts in Class

When I discuss reinforcement and punishment in my introductory classes, I make two small changes in Catania's terminology. First, I substitute the terms *stimulus onset* and *offset* for *stimulus presentation* and *withdrawal*, because the latter phrases imply that reinforcement and punishment are limited to situations in which an experimenter does something to a subject. Second, I use the Thorndikean terms *satisfying* and *dissatisfying* rather than their operant equivalents, *positively reinforcing* and *aversive*.

Once students have mastered information in Table 1, they appear more receptive to the Skinnerian belief that

Table 1. A Comparison of Positive and Negative Reinforcement and Punishment

	Positive	Negative
Reinforcement	ON +	OFF –
Punishment	ON –	OFF +

Note. ON or OFF denotes onset or offset of a stimulus; the symbols + and – denote the subjective quality associated with the stimulus, either satisfaction (+) or dissatisfaction (–).

feelings can be defined as external behaviors. Use of the table also helps students appreciate the fact that a given stimulus input may be both positively and negatively reinforcing. Food, for example, is a positive reinforcer because it tastes good (ON +; see Table 1), but it is also a negative reinforcer because it reduces hunger pangs (OFF –; see Table 1). Before I began presenting the table in class, most students assumed that food was only a positive reinforcer.

Conclusions

I draw two conclusions from my attempts to clarify the concept of negative reinforcement for my students. First, it would be simpler if we spoke of onset and offset reinforcement and punishment rather than positive and negative reinforcement and punishment. However, the older terms are so ingrained in the literature that it probably would be easier to add the adjectives *positive* and *negative* to punishment than to remove them from reinforcement.

Second, perhaps it is time to abandon Skinner's fuzzily defined concepts of reinforcement and punishment and return to Thorndike's (1935) terminology, namely *satisfiers* and *dissatisfiers*. Thorndike defined a *satisfier* as a stimulus or situation that the organism either approached or did nothing to avoid; he defined a *dissatisfier* as a stimulus or situation that the organism either avoided or did nothing to approach. These definitions are not only behavioral in viewpoint, they are simple to comprehend because Thorndike presumed that the organism's emotions mediate many of its behaviors. Furthermore, because Thorndike's terms are not widely used, adding the adjectives *onset* and *offset* to satisfier and dissatisfier should be a less formidable task than trying to do so with punishment and reward.

References

Catania, A. C. (Ed.). (1968). *Contemporary research in operant behavior*. Glenview, IL: Scott, Foresman.

Catania, A. C. (1979). *Learning*. Englewood Cliffs, NJ: Prentice-Hall.

Evans, R. I. (Ed.). (1968). *B. F. Skinner: The man and his ideas*. New York: Dutton.

Gordon, W. C. (1989). *Learning and memory*. Pacific Grove, CA: Brooks/Cole.

Hall, J. F. (1989). *Learning and memory* (2nd ed.). Boston: Allyn & Bacon.

Jackson, H. J., & Molloy, G. N. (1983). Tangible self-consequation and arithmetic problem-solving: An exploratory comparison of four strategies. *Perceptual and Motor Skills, 57,* 471–477.

Rachlin, H. (1970). *Introduction to modern behaviorism.* San Francisco: Freeman.

Rachlin, H. (1976). *Behavior and learning.* San Francisco: Freeman.

Redd, W. H., Porterfield, A. L., & Anderson, B. L. (1979). *Behavior modification.* New York: Random House.

Scott, D. W., & Wood, R. L. (1987). The role of food substitutes in a token economy system. *British Journal of Psychiatry, 150,* 864–867.

Skinner, B. F. (1938). *The behavior of organisms: An experimental analysis.* New York: Appleton-Century-Crofts.

Skinner, B. F. (1953). *Science and human behavior.* New York: Free Press.

Skinner, B. F. (1971). *Beyond freedom and dignity.* New York: Knopf.

Skinner, B. F. (1974). *About behaviorism.* New York: Knopf.

Tauber, R. T. (1988). Overcoming misunderstanding about the concept of negative reinforcement. *Teaching of Psychology, 15,* 152–153.

Thorndike, E. L. (1935). *The psychology of wants, interests and attitudes.* New York: Appleton-Century-Crofts.

Wade, C., & Tavris, C. (1987). *Psychology.* New York: Harper & Row.

Whitehurst, C., & Miller, E. (1973). Behavior modification of aggressive behavior on a nursery school bus: A case study. *Journal of School Psychology, 11,* 123–128.

Zirpoli, T. J., & Lloyd, J. W. (1987). Understanding and managing self-injurious behavior. *Remedial and Special Education, 8,* 46–57.

An Objective and Functional Matrix for Introducing Concepts of Reinforcement and Punishment

Stephen R. Flora
William B. Pavlik
University of Georgia

The operant approach to psychology applies "the methods of a natural science to its investigation" (Skinner, 1984, p. 462). Subjective terminology is not used in a scientific explanation of behavior, but the field of psychology is replete with subjective terminology. This situation produces confusion over basic operant concepts, which have proper meaning only in an objective, functional framework.

Examples of this confusion are widespread. Tauber (1988) pointed out that 37% of his Introductory Psychology students consider *negative reinforcement* and *punishment* to be synonyms. Confusion over basic operant concepts exists among psychologists as well. We have seen psychologists narrate videotapes in which the punishment of self-injurious behavior is erroneously described as negative reinforcement.

A Proposed Solution

Emphasis on the words *any time* and *always* is important in stressing the objective, functional nature of the terms. Four sentences properly describe the basic concepts of reinforcement and punishment. The four sentences are:

1. Any time a behavior precedes the presentation of a stimulus into the environment, the first word of the procedure is always *positive*.
2. Any time a behavior precedes the removal of a stimulus from the environment, the first word of the procedure is always *negative*.
3. Any time a change in the environment results in an increase in the probability or rate of the preceding behavior, the second word of the procedure is always *reinforcement*.
4. Any time a change in the environment results in a decrease in the probability or rate of the preceding behavior, the second word of the procedure is always *punishment*.

These objective definitions should clarify the functional meanings of the terms *positive reinforcement*, *negative reinforcement*, *positive punishment* (often referred to simply as *punishment*), and *negative punishment* (often called *omission training* or *time-out*). These four sentences show that *positive* and *negative* refer only to the presentation or removal of stimuli in the environment, not to some inherent quality of the stimuli. *Reinforcement* and *punishment* refer only to the probability or rate of a behavior being increased or decreased by manipulating environmental stimuli. Reinforcement and punishment in no way suggest that the behavior involved is "good" or "bad."

Students may find this terminology unnecessarily rigorous. They may argue that common knowledge indicates reinforcers are "good" and punishers are "bad." To correct this fallacy, the instructor can point out that the same environmental stimulus may serve as either a reinforcer or punisher. Shock, for example, functions as a negative reinforcer when it is removed after a response in escape conditioning, but it also functions as a positive punisher in many laboratory studies when it is presented contingent on some behavior.

Table 1. Basic Operant Concepts

	Behavior Probability or Rate	
	Increases	Decreases
Present stimulus	Positive reinforcement	Positive punishment
Remove stimulus	Negative reinforcement	Negative punishment (Omission, Time-out)

Furthermore, shock may even function as a positive reinforcer (see Morse & Kelleher, 1977). In human society, money often functions as a positive reinforcer when a particular behavior produces money (e.g., piece work), but it may also function as a negative punisher for behaviors that produce its removal (e.g., fines contingent on traffic violations).

Several authors presented a 2 × 2 matrix to introduce the operant concepts described by our four sentences, but their labels used subjective terminology. For example, Tauber (1988) used *desired* and *dreaded*; Pettijohn (1987) used *good* and *bad*; Mazur (1986) used *pleasant* and *unpleasant*. Benjamin, Hopkins, and Nation (1987) used *positive* and *negative* as synonyms for *pleasant* and *unpleasant* to describe subjective stimulus qualities in their matrix, thereby confusing the emotional tones of the words with their operational definitions of presenting and removing stimuli.

Table 1 presents an objective, functionally correct matrix for introducing the concepts of positive and negative reinforcement and punishment. This matrix covers all instances of reinforcement and punishment; it does not rely on subjective interpretation of the terms.

There are no advantages to using subjective terminology to introduce the concepts of positive and negative reinforcers and punishers, as in, for example, Tauber's (1988) matrix. The disadvantages are revealed in the results of a simple one-question survey. We asked a graduate class in learning and motivation and an undergraduate introductory psychology class the following question: "Which do you consider more dreaded, loud or soft reprimands?" Loud reprimands were considered more dreaded by 66% of the graduate students and 62.5% of the introductory psychology students. Yet, O'Leary, Kaufman, Kass, and Drabman (1970) showed that, for disruptive behavior in school children, loud reprimands function as positive reinforcers and soft reprimands function as positive punishers. Because

Tauber's (1988) matrix uses *dreaded* to define negative reinforcement and positive punishment, it cannot account for this result. Instead, Tauber's subjective terminology may lead to student expectations that are at variance with observed results.

Using subjective terminology to help students grasp the "sense" of concepts is of no advantage if having a sense of the concepts produces incorrect conclusions. Our four sentences and matrix encourage students to ask whether the behavior produces or removes the stimulus and whether the behavior is increasing or decreasing in probability or rate. Correct identification of the concepts at this point is virtually automatic.

References

Benjamin, L. T., Jr., Hopkins, J. R., & Nation, J. R. (1987). *Psychology*. New York: Macmillan.

Mazur, J. E. (1986). *Learning and behavior*. Englewood Cliffs, NJ: Prentice-Hall.

Morse, W. H., & Kelleher, R. T. (1977). Determinants of reinforcement and punishment. In W. K. Honig & J. E. R. Staddon (Eds.), *Handbook of operant behavior* (pp. 174–200). Englewood Cliffs, NJ: Prentice-Hall.

O'Leary, K. D., Kaufman, K. F., Kass, R. E., & Drabman, R. S. (1970). The effects of loud and soft reprimands on the behavior of disruptive students. *Exceptional Children, 37*, 145–155.

Pettijohn, T. F. (1987). *Psychology: A concise introduction*. Guilford, CT: Dushkin.

Skinner, B. F. (1984). Operant behavior. In R. J. Corsini (Ed.), *Encyclopedia of psychology* (Vol. 2, pp. 462–463). New York: Wiley.

Tauber, R. T. (1988). Overcoming misunderstanding about the concept of negative reinforcement. *Teaching of Psychology, 15*, 152–153.

Using a Spatial System for Teaching Operant Concepts

Kenneth A. Kiewra
University of Nebraska–Lincoln

Nelson F. DuBois
State University of New York at Oneonta

We agree with Flora and Pavlik (1990) that instructors should teach operant concepts using functionally correct terminology presented in a matrix form. Although our research (e.g., Kiewra, DuBois, Christian, & McShane, 1988; Kiewra et al., in press) strongly supports the use of a matrix for learning comparative information, we dispute the assertion that their matrix encourages students to ask relevant questions (e.g., whether the behavior produces or removes the stimulus and whether the behavior increases or decreases in probability or rate) and virtually assures correct identification of the concepts. We believe that Flora and Pavlik's (1990) matrix falls short in four ways. It does not: (a) clarify the superordinate–subordinate relations among the operant concepts, (b) adequately represent the coordinate relations among the concepts, (c) show the sequential nature of each concept, and (d) facilitate concept learning. We developed a system for representing information spatially that uses hierarchies, sequences, and matrices. Our system overcomes the aforementioned limitations.

Superordinate–Subordinate Relations

Flora and Pavlik's (1990) matrix fails to show that there are two major operant techniques—reinforcement and punishment—each of which contains two subtypes. The representation in Figure 1 makes the superordinate–subordinate relations apparent. The hierarchy appearing in the top three rows indicates two types of operant concepts (i.e., reinforcement and punishment), each subsuming two subtypes (i.e., positive and negative).

Extending this hierarchy forms a matrix that includes the concept features (i.e., behavior and stimulus) and the attributes of those features within the matrix's cells. Concept

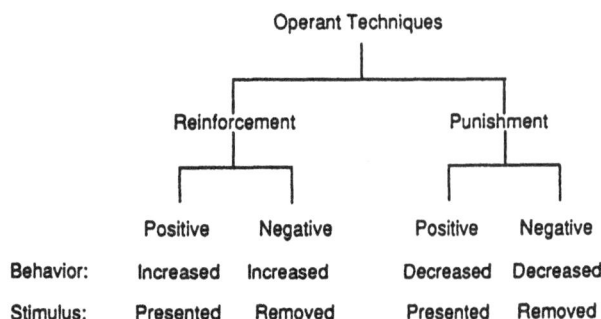

Figure 1. Matrix representation of operant concepts showing superordinate–subordinate and coordinate relations.

definitions appear when the matrix is examined vertically (e.g., positive reinforcement involves increased behavior and a presented stimulus).

Coordinate Relations

Concepts are best learned collectively within a family rather than separately (e.g., Tennyson & Park, 1980). The concepts of conservative, moderate, and liberal, for example, are learned better as a family of political ideologies than as discrete concepts. A collective approach is parsimonious because the concept features are common to all the concepts, and similarities and differences among the attributes are potentially comparable. Because it emphasizes the coordinate relations among concepts, Figure 1 makes apparent that the four operant concepts (i.e., positive reinforcement, negative reinforcement, positive punishment, and negative punishment) are defined by the features of behavior and stimulus and that attributes of these features are comparable across concepts. Thus, Figure 1 is better than Flora and Pavlik's (1990) matrix. A student reading across the matrix should note that behavior increases for both types of reinforcement but decreases for both types of punishment; positive techniques involve the presentation of a stimulus, whereas negative techniques involve the removal of a stimulus.

Sequential Nature of the Concepts

For many concepts, the relationship among the attributes is as important as the identification of those attributes (e.g., Bassok & Holyoak, 1990). Each of the four operant concepts contains attributes pertaining to the features of stimulus and behavior; however, the sequence of these attributes actually defines each concept. For example, positive reinforcement is more than the presentation of a stimulus and the increase in behavior; it is the presentation of a stimulus following a response that leads to an increase in that behavior. The top line of Figure 2 represents the sequential relations among the attributes for the concept of positive reinforcement. The other concepts (e.g., negative punishment) can be represented in the same manner. Flora and Pavlik's (1990) matrix does not represent the attributes' sequence for the operant concepts.

218

Positive Reinforcement

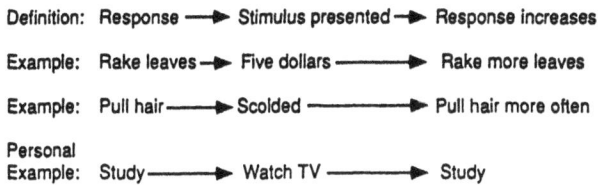

Definition:	Response	→	Stimulus presented	→	Response increases
Example:	Rake leaves	→	Five dollars	→	Rake more leaves
Example:	Pull hair	→	Scolded	→	Pull hair more often
Personal Example:	Study	→	Watch TV	→	Study

Figure 2. Matrix representation for teaching the concept of positive reinforcement.

Concept Learning

Concept learning is demonstrated when students correctly classify previously unencountered examples (Gagné, 1985). Concept learning is facilitated when students are provided with a range of concept examples whose parts are matched to the related attributes in the concept (see Cheng, Holyoak, Nisbett, & Oliver, 1986; Glick & Holyoak, 1983; Tennyson & Park, 1980). Therefore, we disagree with Flora and Pavlik's (1990) contention that their matrix makes concept learning "virtually automatic" (p. 122).

To teach the operant concept of positive reinforcement, develop a matrix (e.g., Figure 2) that includes a range of examples provided by the instructor and the students. The other concepts can be represented in the same manner.

The matrix in Figure 2 allows the student to follow horizontally the sequence of the attributes in the concept and in each example and follow vertically how attributes of the concept match attributes in the examples (e.g., scolding is a presented stimulus). A student given novel examples on a test can now simply "map out" the sequence in the novel example and compare it to the definitions and/or examples previously represented along the lines of those shown in Figure 2. Without instruction in identifying attributes, their order, and their correspondence with examples, students often use an inferior default strategy wherein they learn simply the definition of the concept (e.g., Reder & Anderson, 1980; Reder & Ross, 1981). Learning the definition only is inadequate for classifying previously unencountered examples (e.g., Nitsch, 1977).

Conclusion

When teaching about reinforcement and punishment, the representation in Figure 1 and ones similar to Figure 2 are necessary. Figure 1 shows the superordinate–subordinate and coordinate structures of the concepts and their attributes for easy comparison. A series of matrices similar to Figure 2 helps students learn the order of the attributes and identify new examples of the concepts.

The types of representations used to teach operant concepts appear useful in many situations. The hierarchy represents superordinate–subordinate information; the sequence represents temporal information; and the matrix, a downward extension of a hierarchy or sequence, represents the features and attributes of coordinate topics. These knowledge patterns help represent text (Kiewra & Sperling, 1991), plan writing (Benton, Kiewra, Whitfall, & Sperling, 1991), and solve problems (Day, 1988). Use of these knowledge patterns for concept learning (e.g., operant concepts) appears promising but awaits empirical testing.

References

Bassok, M., & Holyoak, K. J. (1990, April). Conceptual structure and transfer between quantitative domains. Paper presented at the annual meeting of the American Educational Research Association, Boston.

Benton, S. L., Kiewra, K. A., Whitfall, J., & Sperling, R. A. (1991, April). Encoding and external-storage effects of note taking on writing performance. Paper presented at the annual meeting of the American Educational Research Association, Chicago.

Cheng, P., Holyoak, K. J., Nisbett, R. E., & Oliver, L. M. (1986). Pragmatic versus syntactic approaches to training deductive reasoning. Cognitive Psychology, 18, 298–328.

Day, R. S. (1988). Alternative representations. In G. H. Bower (Ed.), The psychology of learning and motivation (Vol. 22, pp. 261–305). New York: Academic.

Flora, S. R., & Pavlik, W. B. (1990). An objective and functional matrix for introducing concepts of reinforcement and punishment. Teaching of Psychology, 17, 121–122.

Gagné, R. M. (1985). The conditions of learning. New York: Holt, Rinehart & Winston.

Glick, M. L., & Holyoak, K. J. (1983). Schema induction and analogical transfer. Cognitive Psychology, 15, 1–38.

Kiewra, K. A., DuBois, N. F., Christian, D., & McShane, A. (1988). A comparison of three types of notes for review. Journal of Educational Psychology, 80, 595–597.

Kiewra, K. A., DuBois, N. F., Christian, D., McShane, A., Meyerhoffer, M., & Roskelley, D. (in press). Notetaking functions and techniques. Journal of Educational Psychology.

Kiewra, K. A., & Sperling, R. A. (1991, April). How supplemental representations affect learning from a research article. Paper presented at the annual meeting of the American Educational Research Association, Chicago.

Nitsch, K. E. (1977). Structuring decontextualized forms of knowledge. Unpublished doctoral dissertation, Vanderbilt University, Nashville, TN.

Reder, L. M., & Anderson, J. R. (1980). The role of elaboration in the comprehension and retention of prose. Review of Educational Research, 50, 5–53.

Reder, L. M., & Ross, B. H. (1981). Integrated knowledge in different tasks: The role of retrieval strategy on fan effects. Journal of Experimental Psychology: Human Learning, Memory, and Cognition, 9, 55–72.

Tennyson, R. D., & Park, O. C. (1980). The teaching of concepts: A review of instructional design research literature. Review of Educational Research, 50, 55–70.

Notes

1. We thank Charles L. Brewer and three anonymous reviewers for their detailed comments and suggestions.

219

Demonstrating Differential Reinforcement by Shaping Classroom Participation

Gordon K. Hodge
Nancy H. Nelson
University of New Mexico

Principles of operant conditioning are easily presented in classroom demonstrations. For example, descriptions of students operantly shaping their instructors' behaviors have been reported (Chrisler, 1988; Melvin, 1988). As a variation on this theme, we devised a demonstration in which the instructor shapes the students' level of class participation using a differential reinforcement procedure.

In our experience, uneven distribution of student participation in the classroom is common. In large lecture sections of 400 to 600 students, opportunities for participation are sometimes limited by time constraints and the intimidating atmosphere. But in small classes, such as seminars, labs, or discussion sections, the ideal scenario is one in which all students contribute, and discussions dominated by the assertive few are minimized.

We strive to foster creative exchange and discussion of ideas in the introductory psychology labs. As stated in the syllabus, students receive a grade for class participation. They are encouraged and, presumably, motivated to take part in discussions; still, many students do not participate.

In one lab section, we noted that three students overly participated in discussions at the expense of other students who rarely spoke. We believed it would be advantageous to foster more equitable interactions. We also saw an opportunity to implement an educationally valuable demonstration that would enhance previously learned class material.

Method

Subjects

Subjects were 8 women and 6 men enrolled in an introductory psychology lab at the University of New Mexico.

Materials

Two weeks before the actual demonstration, students circled the value on a 7-point scale that best indicated their own level of class participation. The scale ranged from *I never participate* (1) to *I always participate* (7). These ratings provided a baseline level of self-perceived participation for each student.

After the demonstration and before debriefing, each student completed an anonymous questionnaire consisting of the following three items:

1. In your own words, describe the demonstration implemented during today's class. Include whether or not you believe the demonstration influenced your level of class participation.
2. Was the demonstration useful in illustrating how reinforcers may be used in an operant conditioning procedure? Explain how the demonstration was useful and possible ways it may be changed and/or improved.
3. Any additional thoughts concerning this demonstration.

Design and Procedure

One week after the lecture on learning, the lab instructor distributed the scale assessing each student's perceived level of class participation. To avoid biasing the demonstration, students were not told the reason for filling out the questionnaire. The scale was used to assist the instructor in determining the appropriate differential reinforcement schedule to be implemented during the demonstration.

The demonstration using differential reinforcement to shape classroom participation was implemented 2 weeks after the rating scales were distributed. Each student's initials were placed on the top of the chalkboard at the front of the class. The reinforcer consisted of a plus mark placed underneath a student's name whenever the desired behavior (increased or decreased participation) was emitted. The instructor determined before the demonstration which students would receive a reinforcer for either participating or not participating, based on the rating scales and familiarity with class dynamics.

Among the 14 students, 3 were judged as overparticipators; they were reinforced only when they did not participate or interrupt or when specifically called on by the instructor after raising their hands. The 5 students who rarely participated were reinforced for making even the slightest effort to participate; for example, hand raising, saying anything (correct or not) when called on, and, in one instance, making eye contact with the instructor. These students were then reinforced less frequently as they began to emit more responses according to general shaping procedures (Gordon, 1989). The remaining 6 students normally participated in a moderate fashion and were reinforced on a variable ratio schedule to maintain their active participation.

Following the demonstration and before debriefing, a short questionnaire was given to assess whether the students caught on to the demonstration and to get their feedback and suggestions. Debriefing consisted of discussing the items on the questionnaire in a classroom forum and reemphasizing the principles of operant conditioning, shaping, and differential reinforcement.

Results

Student responses on the rating scale reflected the instructor's perceptions of participation levels. Only one student, rated by the instructor as a 1 (I never participate), placed a rating of 2 on his scale. The scales, therefore, appeared to complement the ratings made independently by the instructor, providing a reasonably reliable tool for devising a differential reinforcement schedule for each student.

Based on the instructor's subjective observation, class participation seemed noticeably more balanced after the technique was implemented. Overparticipators contributed much less; underparticipators contributed more often and enthusiastically. Only one of the identified underparticipators remained reticent. This balance in participation was noticed by 5 of the students on their questionnaires. One wrote that "people like an upbeat situation and are encouraged to join in," and another student noted that "students that [sic] don't normally contribute began to participate."

Based on the responses to the first item on the questionnaire, 12 of 14 students identified the demonstration as an example of operant conditioning or the use of a shaping procedure or both. One student identified it as a motivational study (the demonstration was implemented during a lecture on motivation), and one student did not answer the question.

In response to the second part of Item 1 (whether or not the demonstration influenced their level of class participation—either increasing or decreasing it), 10 of 14 students believed that the demonstration affected their class participation. One student stated "I think some people talked a lot more than usual," and another stated "many students gave input that usually do not." The other 4 students did not believe the demonstration affected their participation.

In response to Item 2, 12 of the 14 students found the demonstration useful in illustrating the role of reinforcers in an operant conditioning procedure, noting that the demonstration was "closely related to our computer assignment" (which dealt with shaping) and better "integrated our lecture notes." Four students mentioned that they would prefer a more potent reinforcer, such as extra credit, rather than "just a plus mark."

Discussion

The demonstration was a valuable and worthwhile way to illustrate differential reinforcement in shaping classroom participation. The usefulness of the demonstration, based on responses to the questionnaire, is evident, although there are obvious limitations. The demonstration is limited to a small class size (approximately 20 students) in order for the instructor to implement an effective differential reinforcement procedure tailored for each student. With larger groups, it would be difficult to keep track of the target responses and dispense reinforcers in a timely fashion.

Of some concern was how students, particularly overparticipators, perceived the fairness of the procedure. For example, overparticipators might have wondered why others received plus marks and they did not. On the questionnaires, two students expressed frustration for not receiving reinforcement of their active participation. One student wrote that the activity was "quite frustrating, considering that I didn't get a plus until the latter portion of the demonstration after participating considerably." That overparticipators experienced frustration when their normally high participation levels went unrewarded was not surprising. In general, overparticipators seem frustrated whenever the instructor fails to call on them or limits their comments. The concern is whether frustration elicited by the demonstration was notably different from feelings ordinarily elicited during routine classroom management.

Some frustration was probably due to initial misperceptions that the goal was to increase everyone's participation equally, rather than differentially. As the demonstration progressed, however, overparticipators responded by curtailing their behavior in order to earn plus marks. One student's strategy provided insight into the process: "I initially increased participation to ascertain whether I would receive points. This attempt was to no avail so I proceeded to lessen my degree or amount of participation" (for which the student was then reinforced). Although frustration occurred, there were no indications from questionnaire responses or discussions during debriefing that overparticipators thought the experience was unfair. Both students who expressed initial frustration reported that the demonstration was interesting and useful. Nevertheless, instructors should be alert for signs of unusual discomfort or frustration and be ready to end the demonstration and initiate debriefing as necessary.

In discussing the demonstration with students, it is worthwhile to point out that the changes in participation frequencies probably reflected a real-life application of an operant conditioning procedure. Moreover, even though students became aware of the purpose of the demonstration while it was ongoing, their behavior nevertheless changed in response to the procedures (cf. Blanchard & Johnson, 1982). Discussion could then focus on students' ideas of how similar procedures could be applied in other situations (e.g., encouraging more balanced communication in a personal relationship).

Although not quantified, some positive effects on class participation appeared to remain throughout the semester. This pleasant residual effect may have occurred because students and instructor were now more aware of their class behavior. Students who normally did not participate may have felt more comfortable about contributing after their first experience in speaking, or, possibly, the class dynamics became less threatening and more comfortable to these students.

Ways to improve this demonstration include developing a more objective, less intrusive assessment of class participation in addition to the questionnaire. One possibility would be to use a hidden tape recorder or video camera to record a baseline session before the demonstration, record the demonstration, and then have an objective third party score the tape(s).

The demonstration is a useful technique for illustrating differential reinforcement and for encouraging more equitable participation in small classes.

References

Blanchard, K., & Johnson, S. (1982). *The one minute manager*. New York: Berkley.

Chrisler, J. C. (1988). Conditioning the instructor's behavior: A class project in psychology of learning. *Teaching of Psychology, 15*, 135–137.

Gordon, W. C. (1989). *Learning and memory*. Pacific Grove, CA: Brooks/Cole.

Melvin, K. B. (1988). Rating class participation: The prof/peer method. *Teaching of Psychology, 15*, 137–139.

Notes

1. We thank Frank A. Logan, Charles L. Brewer, and the anonymous reviewers for their helpful comments.

Name Seven Words: Demonstrating the Effects of Knowledge on Rate of Retrieval

Jacqueline E. Muir-Broaddus
Departments of Psychology and Education
Southwestern University

The relation between domain-specific knowledge and memory is commonly addressed in introductory psychology, cognition, and cognitive development courses. One aspect of this relation is that knowledge enhances the speed with which one processes information (Roth, 1983). Cognitive psychologists typically conceptualize the effect of knowledge on retrieval using modified network models of semantic memory (Bjorklund, Muir-Broaddus, & Schneider, 1990; Schneider & Bjorklund, 1997). According to this view, features of concepts are represented as a network of interconnected "nodes" that are accessed through spreading activation (Collins & Loftus, 1975). Associative priming, which refers to the activation of related concepts in response to a cue, is often interpreted as behavioral evidence of spreading activation (Meyer & Schvaneveldt, 1971). For example, for most people, the cue *music* activates concepts such as *note*, *song*, and *band*, before, and more quickly than, unrelated concepts such as *plant* or *banana*. As expertise increases, representations of domain-specific concepts become increasingly elaborated, organized, and interconnected, thereby enhancing the automaticity with which these concepts and their associative relations are activated in response to a cue (Bjorklund et al., 1990).

Simple and effective demonstrations of the relation between knowledge and memory abound, including the role of context and meaningfulness (e.g., Fernald & Fernald, 1981; Jenkins, 1981; Klein, 1981). However, demonstrations showing specifically how knowledge enhances the rate of retrieval of domain-specific information do not exist. In response, I developed a simple 10-min class demonstration of this relation, in which two (or more, if desired) relative experts and novices in a specific domain name any seven words that relate to that domain as quickly as possible. Reliably, the relative experts complete the task more quickly than the novices.

Description of Demonstration

Four students volunteer for the demonstration, 2 who report knowing little about music and 2 who report having some expertise (e.g., music majors or minors, or students with at least several years of private music instruction). Al-

though any number of content domains are appropriate, music has proven successful as it is one for which an appropriate range of expertise can usually be found in any class.

The 4 volunteers leave the room, at which time the instructor briefs the remaining students as to the nature of the task and asks them to generate predictions. This helps the student observers to focus their attention on the relevant behavior. Each volunteer then enters the room, one at a time, and is given the same instructions: "As fast as you can, as soon as I say 'go,' tell me ANY seven words that relate to *music*. Go!" It is important that the topic, music, is mentioned last because the process of spreading activation begins as soon as the instructor states the cue. The instructor times the latency to name the seventh word with a stopwatch and records the results (in seconds) on a blackboard or overhead. Each successive volunteer enters the room until all 4 have completed the task.

The instructor can calculate the mean response time for each pair of students. However, the results are often dramatic enough (e.g., the ranges do not overlap) that this is not necessary. Although the time to completion varies greatly from student to student, past experience shows that experts typically take about 7 to 10 sec and novices typically take about 12 to 16 sec.

One reason for having 2 students (rather than 1) at each level of expertise is to prepare for the possibility that 1 of the students implements a retrieval strategy, such as naming a series of notes (e.g., A, B, C, D, E, F, G). Although this has only occurred two or three times in the approximately 24 volunteers who have completed the demonstration, it is important to be prepared because such strategies can shorten response times enough to obscure (in the case of novices) or inflate (in the case of experts) the expected knowledge base effect. It is advisable to warn the observing students of the power of strategies in advance so that the successful use of a strategy, especially to shorten the response time of a novice, is not perceived as a post hoc explanation. Then, if a student uses a strategy, discuss each volunteer's response time separately (e.g., the novice who used a strategy vs. the novice who did not, vs. the mean of the 2 experts who did not).

In the event that a relative expert discovers a strategy, instructors may wish to segue to a discussion of how expertise facilitates not only nonstrategic organization and item-specific activation, but strategy use as well (see review by

Schneider & Bjorklund, 1997). One explanation is that faster processing of information from a rich knowledge base leaves more mental resources remaining for strategic and metacognitive processes (Bjorklund et al., 1990). For example, automatically activated associative relations may be noticed, and subsequently consciously exploited in the form of an organizational strategy, during retrieval (e.g., Bjorklund & Zeman, 1982). In the context of this demonstration, the cue *music* may activate the word *note*, which activates A, which activates B, which leads to the realization that one can continue to list the names of notes.

Evaluation of the Demonstration

Seven men and 18 women enrolled in an upper-level cognition course at a small liberal arts college evaluated the demonstration. Each student completed an anonymous three-item questionnaire.

First, students rated the degree to which the demonstration achieved its primary purpose, which was to "illustrate how one's level of expertise in a content domain affects accessibility (that is, the speed with which the information can be retrieved)." Using a 7-point scale ranging from 1 (*very unsuccessful*) to 7 (*very successful*), the students positively endorsed this statement ($M = 5.60$, $SD = 1.00$, range = 3–7).

Second, students rated the degree to which the demonstration successfully illustrated the more subtle theoretical point that "the reason why information in one's area of expertise is more accessible (i.e., more quickly retrieved) is that the greater quality and quantity of knowledge facilitates spreading activation through the semantic network." Using the same scale as for Question 1, the students also positively endorsed this statement ($M = 5.24$, $SD = 0.97$, range = 4–7).

Third, students rated the degree to which the demonstration was "enjoyable" and "interesting" using a 7-point scale that ranged from 1 (*not at all*) to 7 (*very much*). The students gave their highest endorsement to this statement ($M = 6.17$, $SD = 0.76$, range = 5–7).

Thus, students responded favorably to the demonstration, assigning an overall mean rating of 5.67 across the three 7-point scales. Furthermore, an examination of individual responses revealed that every student found the experience to have value, in that every student assigned a rating of at least 4 to at least one dimension.

Discussion

Students positively endorsed this demonstration of how content knowledge facilitates the rate of retrieval of domain-specific information for both its educational value and its interest value. Moreover, it has proven to be one of the easiest and most reliable demonstrations in my repertoire.

That is, even with such small sample sizes, I have yet to experience a failure to capture the effect. And, although the effect size can vary widely depending on the specific students involved, it is often dramatic. To enhance the impact of the demonstration, I remind the students at its conclusion that even the most novice among them knows many times more than the seven music-related words requested (e.g., *singers*, *bands*, *songs*, *instruments*, *notes*, *music halls*, etc.), so one cannot simply attribute the novices' difficulty to insufficient knowledge. Furthermore, I remind them that the range of expertise in a college classroom is usually relatively truncated, so that the effects in the population at large would likely be even greater. This demonstration can be followed by a discussion of how the modified semantic network model of memory, as described earlier, can account for the observed results.

References

Bjorklund, D. F., Muir-Broaddus, J. E., & Schneider, W. (1990). The role of knowledge in the development of strategies. In D. F. Bjorklund (Ed.), *Children's strategies: Contemporary views of cognitive development* (pp. 93–128). Hillsdale, NJ: Lawrence Erlbaum Associates, Inc.

Bjorklund, D. F., & Zeman, B. R. (1982). Children's organization and metamemory awareness in their recall of familiar information. *Child Development, 53*, 799–810.

Collins, A. M., & Loftus, E. F. (1975). A spreading activation theory of semantic processing. *Psychological Review, 82*, 407–428.

Fernald, P. S., & Fernald, L. D., Jr. (1981). Meaningfulness and memory. In L. T. Benjamin, Jr., & K. D. Lowman (Eds.), *Activities handbook for the teaching of psychology* (Vol. 1, pp. 84–85). Washington, DC: American Psychological Association.

Jenkins, J. (1981). Meaning enhances recall. In L. T. Benjamin, Jr. & K. D. Lowman (Eds.), *Activities handbook for the teaching of psychology* (Vol. 1, pp. 81–82). Washington, DC: American Psychological Association.

Klein, M. (1981). Recall versus recognition. In L. T. Benjamin, Jr. & K. D. Lowman (Eds.), *Activities handbook for the teaching of psychology* (Vol. 1, pp. 79–80). Washington, DC: American Psychological Association.

Meyer, D. E., & Schvaneveldt, R. W. (1971). Facilitation in recognizing pairs of words: Evidence of a dependence between retrieval operations. *Journal of Experimental Psychology, 90*, 227–234.

Roth, C. (1983). Factors affecting developmental changes in the speed of processing. *Journal of Experimental Child Psychology, 35*, 509–528.

Schneider, W., & Bjorklund, D. F. (1997). Memory. In W. Damon (Series Ed.) & D. Kuhn & R. S. Siegler (Vol. Eds.), *Handbook of child psychology: Vol. 2. Cognition, perception, and language* (5th ed., pp. 467–522). New York: Wiley.

Notes

1. This work was supported by the Cullen Faculty Development Program at Southwestern University.

Coming to Terms With the Keyword Method in Introductory Psychology: A "Neuromnemonic" Example

Russell N. Carney
Southwest Missouri State University

Joel R. Levin
Department of Educational Psychology
University of Wisconsin

As in many survey courses, introductory psychology presents extensive new terminology to beginning students—a lexicon that may prove difficult to master. A potential solution to such memory difficulties lies in the use of the mnemonic (memory-enhancing) keyword method. Although the technique is applicable to a variety of paired-associate learning tasks (e.g., Levin, 1993), textbook examples have historically focused on the acquisition of foreign vocabulary (Atkinson, 1975). Hence, students and instructors may not readily see the relevance of the keyword method for learning new terms in psychology. Our goal is to help make that connection.

In the central nervous system, for example, the medulla is that part of the brain that controls such functions as heartbeat and respiration. To apply the keyword method, one first recodes the term *medulla* into an acoustically similar and concrete keyword, such as *medal*. Then, *medal* and the *effects of the medulla* are made to interact in an image. For example, imagine that a runner has just won a race. *Breathing heavily* and with his *heart pounding*, he bends to have a *medal* hung round his neck. With the information encoded in this manner, the retrieval path is as follows: *Medulla* cues *medal*; *medal* cues the interactive image of the heart-pounding, out-of-breath medal winner; and the image brings back the medulla's functions, controlling such things as heartbeat and respiration. Table 1 shows examples of the keyword method applied to terminology related to the central nervous system. We developed a complete set of "neuromnemonic" materials for use in an introductory psychology course at a metropolitan community college.

We then conducted an experiment to provide empirical evidence regarding the effectiveness of these materials. Participants were undergraduates enrolled in educational psychology classes who had just completed a separate experiment that involved learning foreign vocabulary words using the keyword method (Carney & Levin, in press). In that experiment, random assignment was used to place students in one of the same three study strategy conditions included here: repetition, keyword, or keyword plus image. A 6-min "your strategy" section in the study booklets provided described their study strategy along with five practice items. Following study of 24 foreign vocabulary words, students took a test to see how many definitions they could remember. To examine delayed recall, we also tested students 2

and 5 days later. This experiment took place immediately following the second delayed test of the prior experiment. Because students kept the same condition assignment for this experiment, study booklets simply directed students to use the same strategy as before, only this time applying it to terms in psychology. Students in the prior experiment were directed not to discuss the experiment with others until the conclusion of the study. In effect, the prior experiment may be viewed as brief training in students' use of their respective study techniques.

Method

Participants and Design

Ninety-one undergraduates (19 men, 72 women) participated in the experiment. Repetition students studied by saying each psychology term and its meaning over and over to themselves. Using provided keywords ("word clues"), keyword students associated terms and their meanings through an image of their own making. Keyword plus image students additionally used experimenter-provided verbal descriptions of images that related keywords and meanings. The participants were upper-class students enrolled in educational psychology classes, and they received extra credit for their participation. Although the students may have studied such terms in first-year introductory psychology, these terms were not part of their educational psychology curriculum, and the use of random assignment is sufficient to argue for comparable groups with respect to students' prior knowledge.

Materials and Procedure

On entering the classroom, students received a study booklet corresponding to one of the three conditions. In Part I, a generic introduction directed students to use their same strategy "to associate psychology terms and their meanings" and to proceed through their study booklet in a manner similar to the procedure in the previous study. Part II represented a familiarization stage for repetition students. Here, a tape recording paced students through a list of 18

Table 1. Example Neuromnemonic Study Materials for the Keyword Plus Image Condition

Term	Keyword	Meaning	Your Mental Picture
Medulla	Medal	Controls heart rate, respiration, and blood pressure	Imagine the winner of a race. *Heart pounding* and *breathing* heavily, a *medal* (medulla) is hung round the winner's neck.
Pituitary glands	Pit	Regulates growth	Imagine a young child down in a *pit* (pituitary). The child *grows* and *grows* (growth) until he's big enough to climb out!
Reticular formation	Retickle	Attention	Imagine *tickling* someone to get her *attention*. Then, she loses interest again so you have to *retickle* (reticular) her!
Parasympathetic nervous system	Parachute	Calms the body	Imagine the peace and *calming* effect of watching a *parachute* (parasympathetic) drift slowly downward.
Sympathetic nervous system	Symphony	Excites the body	Imagine a *symphony* (sympathetic) playing loudly in the room next door! The music *excites* you and you can't sit still.
Cerebellum	Cereal bell	Facilitates movement	Imagine someone hearing the *cereal bell* (cerebellum). That's the signal to *move* to the breakfast table and begin *moving* the cereal to his mouth (movement) with his spoon.
Thalamus	Thermos	Relay station for incoming information	Imagine a *relay* race. The first runner hands a *thermos* (thalamus), instead of a baton, to the next runner.

psychological terms by sounding a tone at 10-sec intervals. Simultaneously, this tape recording paced students in both mnemonic conditions through a list of the 18 terms and their corresponding keywords. Part III presented a review page, where students reviewed their respective strategies and a recording paced them through two final practice items to give them a feel for the 20-sec intervals. They were now ready for the actual study section.

This time, a tape recording paced students through the 18 terms and their meanings at 20-sec intervals. Repetition students studied the 18 items using repetition. Students in the keyword condition studied the 18 items using the provided keywords and images of their own making. Additionally, students in the keyword plus image condition used experimenter-provided images relating the keywords to the meanings (e.g., see Table 1). Following this and a 2-min filler task (i.e., an unrelated crossword puzzle), students completed a definition-matching test on the 18 terms. Students in the two mnemonic conditions also wrote down the corresponding keywords. Next, students turned the page to complete a test consisting of 10 multiple-choice application items (e.g., "The loss of physical coordination and balance is most likely to result from damage to the: A. hypothalamus B. cerebellum C. corpus callosum D. amygdala."). We permitted the students to refer back to their definition-matching responses when taking the application test. The application questions were representative relevant items selected from the ancillary test materials accompanying an introductory psychology text (Myers, 1993). Our goal in selecting these 10 items was to measure students' higher order learning, as reflected by their ability to go beyond the information given and apply the just-learned terms (e.g., Levin & Levin, 1990).

Results

Definition Matching

A one-way ANOVA yielded statistical differences among the three conditions in students' mean definition-matching performance, $F(2, 88) = 14.41$, $p < .001$. Subsequent Fisher LSD comparisons based on $\alpha = .05$ revealed sizable nonchance differences between the means for both mnemonic conditions (91% and 90%, for keyword and keyword plus image, respectively) and the repetition condition (72%, resulting in an effect size of more than 1 within-conditions standard deviation in each case), with no mean difference between the two mnemonic variations.

Application

A similar one-way ANOVA on the multiple-choice application test produced statistically parallel, though educationally weaker, effects, $F(2, 87) = 3.97$, $p < .025$. Again, both of the mnemonic conditions (77% and 78%) statistically surpassed the repetition condition (65%), but by a smaller margin on this measure (by about 0.6 of a within-group standard deviation in each case).

Discussion and Educational Implications

Our simple experiment demonstrates that the keyword method can help students "come to terms" with new terminology in psychology. For example, on the definition-matching test, students using a mnemonic approach statistically outperformed those using a repetition approach. Likewise, on a multiple-choice test that tapped concept application, the same statistical mnemonic advantage was present. This latter finding is important in that it underscores the notion that using a mnemonic strategy can lead to something more than verbatim fact recall. Furthermore, the success of the students in the keyword condition suggests that only terms, keywords, and meanings need be provided (i.e., interactive images can be left to the student's own making).

We recommend that psychology instructors both describe the keyword method to their students and then go on to provide course-related mnemonic study materials such as those listed in Table 1. Applying the method to the learning of these terms should not only facilitate the acquisition of new terminology, but also help to convince the students of the potency and personal relevance of mnemonic techniques (Carney, Levin, & Levin, 1994).

References

Atkinson, R. C. (1975). Mnemotechnics in second-language learning. *American Psychologist, 30,* 821–828.

Carney, R. N., & Levin, J. R. (in press). Do mnemonic memories fade as time goes by?: Here's looking anew! *Contemporary Educational Psychology.*

Carney, R. N., Levin, J. R., & Levin, M. E. (1994). Enhancing the psychology of memory by enhancing memory of psychology. *Teaching of Psychology, 21,* 171–174.

Levin, J. R. (1993). Mnemonic strategies and classroom learning: A 20-year report card. *Elementary School Journal, 94,* 235–244.

Levin, M. E., & Levin, J. R. (1990). Scientific mnemonomies: Methods for maximizing more than memory. *American Educational Research Journal, 27,* 301–321.

Myers, D. G. (1993). *Exploring psychology* (2nd ed.). New York: Worth.

Notes

1. This experiment was presented at the 1996 annual meeting of the American Educational Research Association. We are grateful to Mary E. Levin and Christine M. Cook for her assistance with this project.

Piagetian Conservation in College Students: A Classroom Demonstration

Eliot Shimoff
University of Maryland Baltimore County

One of the central themes of many introductory psychology descriptions of intellectual development is to remind us (and our students) that young children are cognitively different and not simply small adults. The Piagetian concept of conservation (e.g., Piaget & Inhelder, 1969)—that volume or mass remains the same despite changes in shape, form, or distribution—provides some of the most dramatic demonstrations of such cognitive differences. For example, if you pour water from a short, wide glass into a narrow, tall one, a 5-year-old who has not mastered conservation of volume is likely to say that there is more water in the narrow glass "because it [the water level] is higher." Similarly, when you roll one of two identical balls of clay into a sausage shape, the 5-year-old who has not mastered conservation of mass is likely to say that there is now more clay in the latter "because it is longer."

Introductory psychology students who read about (or see) a child who has not yet mastered conservation are often amazed how easy it is to mislead the child. I have discovered an instructive (and entertaining) demonstration showing that a conservation of area task strikingly similar to the classical Piagetian conservation task can mislead even college students.

I use the power cord of an overhead projector to make a circle and ask the students to note the area of the circle. Next, I squeeze the top and bottom of the loop, so that the circle deforms into an ellipse; as the top and bottom are squeezed together, the sides move out. Almost all students agree that the area has not changed; the top and bottom of the circle have "flattened," but the sides have compensated by moving out slightly.

Now, I go to the chalkboard and draw a square with sides marked as 2 units; the students generally agree that the area of the square is 4 square units. Next, I redraw the 2 × 2 square as a 1 × 3 rectangle (i.e., with the same 8 unit perimeter); almost all the students agree that "flattening" the square to a rectangle changes the area. Having seen that deforming the square to a rectangle changes the area, most students recant their earlier judgment that the area of the circle was unchanged when deformed into an ellipse.

In the standard Piagetian conservation task, a child believes that physical properties (e.g., volume) change even when they are in fact conserved. In this demonstration, college students believe that a physical property (area) is conserved, even though it really changes. (Skeptical students

will, to some extent, be convinced if the ellipse is further deformed into a U-shaped figure. A formal mathematical demonstration is also possible but is unlikely to be as compelling as deforming the square into a rectangle.)

I have used this demonstration in 10 classes, with enrollments ranging from fewer than 20 to more than 200 undergraduates. All the students report that they took high school geometry, and almost all (the rare exceptions are engineering students) initially agree that deforming the circle does not change the area. When I point out the error (and deform a square into a rectangle), the most common reactions are smiles, insightful "Ahas," and bemused puzzlement.

The demonstration, with no further explanation, reminds students of the subtle complexity of what superficially appears to be a simple task. For some instructors, that lesson may be sufficient. But other instructors, with more lecture time to devote to Piagetian concepts, may wish to expand on some of the issues. In such cases, the demonstration sets the occasion for more detailed discussion of some aspects of Piagetian developmental analyses.

Why are preoperational children fooled by conservation tasks? One feature of a 5-year-old's thought is centration, or focusing on only one aspect of a problem (e.g., the height of the water in the glass or the length of the piece of clay). As children enter the Piagetian concrete operations stage, they learn to *decenter* and take into account more than just one dimension. A second feature of preoperational thought is *irreversibility*, the inability to imagine doing and undoing a sequence of operations. A child entering the concrete operational stage learns reversibility: "The two glasses have the same amount of water, because you can always pour it back from the tall glass to the shorter one."

Just as the lack of decentering and reversibility describe why a preoperational child is misled by a conservation task, the presence of these operations may describe how college students are misled by this demonstration. College students have learned to decenter; when a circle is deformed into an ellipse, they note that as the top and bottom are flattened, the sides extend. College students have also learned about reversibility and note that the ellipse can be undeformed back into a circle.

This demonstration also shows what Piaget called *horizontal decalage*. Children acquire different kinds of conservation at different ages, even though the underlying centration and reversibility are the same. Children first learn to conserve number, then length and liquid quantity. Similarly, college students who have learned that the area of a square is not maintained when it is deformed into a rectangle usually continue to assume (at least until the inconsistency is explicitly pointed out) that the area of a circle is maintained when it is deformed into an ellipse.

One possible reason for horizontal decalage may be experience; most middle-class U.S. children learn to conserve number before they conserve liquid quantity, perhaps because they have relatively little experience pouring water from one glass to another. Price-Willams, Gordon, and Ramirez (1969) found that Mexican children from pottery-making families conserved mass (e.g., deforming a ball of clay into a sausage-shaped piece) earlier than children from nonpottery-making families. An analogous explanation may be appropriate for college students' recognition that the area of a square deformed to a rectangle changes but not the area of a circle deformed to an ellipse; college students who have taken high school geometry have had more experience with squares and rectangles than with circles and ellipses.

An alternative explanation focuses on the role of formal mathematical training rather than on informal experience. College students have learned a readily available algorithm for calculating the areas of squares and rectangles in high school geometry classes, based on graphic demonstrations of the number of squares of graph paper covered by squares and rectangles. Calculating the area of a circle, on the other hand, involves pi and is not so intuitively clear; furthermore, most college students have no experience calculating the area of an ellipse. Thus, the deformed square (for which there is a familiar algorithm) does not mislead these students, but they are misled by the deformed circle. Young children, on the other hand, do not have any algorithm available for calculating area, and must rely on intuition; thus, they are misled by both the deformed square and circle. (This account is consistent with the suggestion that children master conservation of number before other forms of conservation because these children have mastered the simple numerical concept of one-to-one correspondence.)

A demonstration such as this sensitizes students to limitations of children's cognitive ability. Most students initially view a 5-year-old's inability to master conservation with some smugness; after seeing this demonstration, undergraduates often report having more respect for children's developmental tasks.

References

Piaget, J., & Inhelder, B. (1969). *The child's conception of space*. New York: Basic Books.

Price-Willams, D. R., Gordon, W., & Ramirez, M. (1969). Skill and conservation: A study of pottery-making children. *Developmental Psychology, 1*, 769.

Using Feature Films to Teach Social Development

Chris J. Boyatzis
California State University, Fullerton

Psychology instructors have used feature films to foster students' learning (e.g., Bolt, 1976; Dorris & Ducey, 1978; Kinney, 1975). More recently, Fleming, Piedmont, and Hiam (1990) discussed the effective use of film in a course on psychopathology, and Anderson (1992) described the value of film in a course on psychology and law. These authors described many values of film in psychology classes. Students responded positively to the films, perhaps because they offer entertaining, concrete examples of course topics. Students also seemed to become engaged directly with film themes, thereby becoming more involved with course content (Fleming et al., 1990). Film may also improve students' critical thinking and perspectives (Anderson, 1992).

For several years I have used feature films, mostly European, in an undergraduate course, Middle Childhood, covering development during the elementary school years. European films were emphasized because they capture children's experiences and development more genuinely than do American films. The major purpose of the assignment was to elucidate social development topics that we studied in the course via scientific research and theory.

The Film Analysis Assignment

The timeline for this assignment spans several classes (about 2 weeks) during coverage of social development and peer relations. Students complete the assignment during the latter portion of this coverage. During this time, students continue to learn about social development through lecture, readings, and educational films. Sources that I present in class and assign in readings include those by Buhrmester and Furman (1987); Dodge (1983); Hartup (1983); Thorne (1986); and Zarbatany, Hartman, and Rankin (1990).

Students select a film from a list I provide. They watch the movie at home, usually over a weekend, for several reasons. Showing a film in class would require excessive time and would allow students to watch only one film for the assignment. The take-home assignment allows students to watch a film of their own choice, probably one they had not yet seen. Home viewing also allows the luxury of watching the film or certain scenes more than once, which could help students better understand how theory and research are exemplified by the character's experience (Anderson, 1992). Although a film rental may pose logistical problems for some students (e.g., those not owning a videocassette recorder), students may watch a movie with a classmate, sharing the costs and equipment. Students are also encouraged to contact local libraries, which often have varied and inexpensive movie selections.

After watching the movie, students write an essay (of two to four pages), analyzing some aspects of the film characters' social development. Students are instructed to "use the psychological theory and research from the course as a framework in which to understand the social development of the children in the movie." Students are told to "make connections between the characters and their experiences with ideas we have read or discussed in class." Students write their essay in about 1 week and submit it around the time I finish the topic.

To facilitate their analysis, students are given the following questions on a handout: (a) How does the film capture the way a child's peer group makes up a subculture or "society of children"? How does the child's experience in this society differ from his or her experience with adults? (b) How does the film illustrate psychological benefits of having friends and being in a peer group? Conversely, how does the film illustrate the dangers of being socially rejected or isolated? (c) How does the film convey how peers contribute to the child's acquisition of new skills (e.g., cognitive, social)? (d) How does the film illustrate horizontal, bilateral peer relations as compared to vertical, unilateral relations with adults? (e) Does the film offer examples of how peers provide a protective function that compensates for dysfunctionality or abuse in the child's home? (f) How does the film illustrate how peers provide a looking-glass self that enhances the child's self-concept and self-esteem? (g) How does the film illustrate how peers help children develop intimacy and perspective-taking? In addition to these issues, students may generate others that arise in their film.

Papers were graded on how thoroughly and accurately they addressed these questions and how well they integrated specific examples from their film with theory and research from the course.

Selection of Films

Without guidance, students might choose popular American movies that may not offer optimal material for this assignment. Therefore, students choose from a list of films I provide (see Table 1).

Most films on the list are European. There are some important differences between European and American films about children that are relevant to the learning experience. Most European filmmakers use a style of realism that is usually lacking in American movies. This realism is achieved

Table 1. Choices for Film Analysis Assignments

Title	Year	Nationality
Alan and Naomi	1992	American
Au Revoir, les Enfants [Goodbye, Children]	1987	French
Cinema Paradiso	1990	Italian
Cross My Heart [La Fracture du Myocarde]	1991	French
Distant Voices, Still Lives	1989	British
Fanny and Alexander	1983	Swedish
Hope and Glory	1989	British
Il Ladro di Bambini [Stolen Children]	1993	Italian
Le Grand Chemin [The Grand Highway]	1987	French
My Girl	1992	American
My Life as a Dog	1987	Swedish
Olivier, Olivier	1993	French
Pelle the Conqueror	1988	Danish
Pocket Change [L'Argent de Poche]	1976	French
Sandlot	1993	American
Stand by Me	1986	American
The 400 Blows	1959	French
The Secret Garden	1993	American

through several means: Real-world settings are used rather than sets, nonprofessional actors are typically used, films often rely on documentary-style cinematography, background music is used infrequently, and camera shots change less often than in American films. Also, many European films are imbued with a strong social or moral conscience, as compared to American films' more mass-market appeal that tends to be superficially glib or sentimental. In addition, European filmmakers tell stories from the perspective and experience of the children themselves, providing an authenticity that is missing from most American films. American films' depictions of children in adventurous, fantastic, or violent romps are highly popular with the public, both in the United States and abroad. However, in these outlandish adventures children do, say, or think things that typical children are unlikely to do, say, or think. Therefore, American films are less appropriate as learning tools than films that capture the fidelity of children's actual experience.

Perhaps as a result of the contrast between American and European films, American students often find the latter too solemn. Discussing these issues before students choose their film may prompt students to question their tastes and prejudices and lead some to select a European film "despite its subtitles," as several students remarked.

Student Evaluation of the Assignment

After using the assignment for several years, I recently collected evaluation data. At the end of a Middle Childhood course, students rated each assignment in terms of how "valuable, interesting, and/or effective" it was. There were five graded assignments: a collaborative exercise on cross-cultural issues in math education, two mixed-format exams, a written analysis of a childhood autobiography (see Boyatzis, 1992), and the film assignment. Of 26 students in the class, 23 (88%) gave the film assignment the highest rating and the remaining 3 students gave it the next highest rating, for a mean rating of 3.88 of a possible 4. When asked to choose their "favorite assignment," 10 students (38%) selected the film.

Many students claimed the assignment helped them understand and integrate developmental concepts and course materials. One student claimed the assignment was "applicable to our studies of middle childhood growth, needs, values, and perceptions . . . (My Life as a Dog [Hallstrom, 1987]) allowed such a wonderful view of the richness of play and peer interaction." Based on the richness of students' connections between their film and course topics, I believe the assignment promoted students' critical thinking. One student said the assignment "helped me apply everything I've learned about children the past three years."

Most students chose American films, the most frequent selection being Stand by Me (Evans, Gideon, Scheinman, & Reiner, 1986). Both students and I believed the movie was especially appropriate for this assignment. Students who chose European films, in particular My Life as a Dog (Hallstrom, 1987), Au Revoir, les Enfants (Malle, 1987), and Le Grand Chemin (Chaouche & Hubert, 1987), spoke in superlative terms not only of the films' suitability for the assignment but of their artistry and authenticity in capturing children's experience.

Conclusion

Movies tell a story and offer a powerful aesthetic experience. Perhaps for these reasons alone they can be effective teaching tools. Requiring an analysis of the film's psychological concepts may enhance students' comprehension of theory and research. The assignment may help students become more sophisticated consumers of psychological content in film and other media. Finally, instructors can modify this assignment to analyze other topics in their courses.

References

Anderson, D. D. (1992). Using feature films as tools for analysis in a psychology and law course. Teaching of Psychology, 19, 155–158.

Bolt, M. (1976). Using films based on literature in teaching psychology. Teaching of Psychology, 3, 189–190.

Boyatzis, C. J. (1992). Let the caged bird sing: Using literature to teach developmental psychology. Teaching of Psychology, 19, 221–222.

Buhrmester, D., & Furman, W. (1987). The development of companionship and intimacy. Child Development, 58, 1101–1113.

Chaouche, F. (Producer), & Hubert, J-L. (Director). (1987). Le grand chemin [Film]. Beverly Hills: Pacific Arts.

Dodge, K. A. (1983). Behavioral antecedents of peer social status. Child Development, 54, 1386–1399.

Dorris, W., & Ducey, R. (1978). Social psychology and sex roles in films. Teaching of Psychology, 5, 168–169.

Evans, B., Gideon, R., Scheinman, A. (Producers), & Reiner, R. (Director). (1986). Stand by me [Film]. Burbank, CA: Columbia.

Fleming, M. Z., Piedmont, R. L., & Hiam, C. M. (1990). Images of madness: Feature films in teaching psychology. Teaching of Psychology, 17, 185–187.

Hallstrom, L. (Producer & Director). (1987). My life as a dog [Film]. Los Angeles: Skouras/Paramount.

Hartup, W. (1983). Peer relations. In E. M. Hetherington (Ed.), Handbook of child psychology: Vol. 4. Socialization, personality, and social development (pp. 103–196). New York: Wiley.

Kinney, D. K. (1975). Cinema thrillers: Reviews of films highly rated by psychology students. Teaching of Psychology, 2, 183–186.

Malle, L. (Producer & Director). (1987). Au revoir, les enfants [Film]. New York: Orion.

Thorne, B. (1986). Girls and boys together . . . but mostly apart: Gender arrangements in elementary schools. In W. W. Hartup & Z. Rubin (Eds.), Relationships and development (pp. 167–184). Hillsdale, NJ: Lawrence Erlbaum Associates, Inc.

Zarbatany, L., Hartman, D. P., & Rankin, D. B. (1990). The psychological functions of preadolescent peer activities. Child Development, 61, 1067–1080.

Notes

1. I thank Robin Jarrell for her encouragement and assistance, and I thank Ruth Ault and the reviewers for their contributions.

Bringing Piaget's Preoperational Thought to the Minds of Adults: A Classroom Demonstration

Jane Ewens Holbrook
University of Wisconsin Center–Waukesha

Students who study Piaget are often captivated by his descriptions of children's reasoning, learning that children do not simply know less than adults but actually think differently. Many instructors demonstrate conservation tasks because they draw students into the child's world. Students begin to appreciate the complexities of the child's reasoning and view of reality. In addition, these demonstrations can sometimes strengthen the conviction that adults are clearly more reasonable than children. To indicate that adult thinking is not always reasonable and that inability to solve a conservation task is not unique to childhood, two tasks are demonstrated. The first is a standard conservation task (water pouring). The second is a conservation-like task too difficult for many students to solve. Students analyze their ways of problem solving by applying the same Piagetian concepts used to understand the nonconserving child; they are thus encouraged to ponder their own thinking.

For the water conservation task, place two identical glasses, each filled to the same point, in front of a 5 year old. Ask, "Do these two glasses contain the same amount of water?" When the child agrees, pour all the water from one glass into a taller, thinner glass. Now ask, "Do these two glasses contain the same amount of water, or does one glass have more?" The typical 5 year old will answer that the taller glass has more water. Ask the child to explain why. This demonstration can be made more elaborate by having the child do the pouring and by varying the wording and asking more questions.

According to Piaget (1952), the nonconserving child's reasoning can be explained by referring to the characteristics of preoperational thought. *Centration* describes the child's tendency to focus on only one aspect (height of water). *Irreversibility* describes the child's inability to imagine reversing the physical action; in this case, it is the pouring process that would return the water to its original glass. The preoperational child is said to be *concrete* and *perceptually bound*, reaching conclusions by how the world looks rather than by systematic reasoning; perceptual cues supercede logical principles.

Students are usually surprised by the child's first response to the task; they are even more surprised that, after repeating demonstrations and explanations of water pouring, the typical 5 year old will hold firm to the belief that the taller glass contains more water. For many students, the child's refusal to see what seems obvious is strong evidence that children do not reason like adults.

The second demonstration should be used after students are familiar with Piaget's stages. In addition, familiarity with some of the questions about the validity of the conservation tasks (e.g., the effect of the wording of the questions) would be useful background for the second part of the demonstration. Introduce the second task as a conservation-like problem for adults. Place two identical jars on a table, explaining that one jar contains exactly 200 red jelly beans and that the other contains exactly 200 black jelly beans. The scoop on the table will hold exactly 15 jelly beans. Tell the students that you are going to fill the scoop with 15 red jelly beans and pour them into the jar containing the black jelly beans. Then, you are going to shake that jar to mix the jelly beans. You will then scoop 15 jelly beans (any 15) from the jar containing the black jelly beans and pour them into the jar containing the red jelly beans. (The description of this process should probably be repeated so students are sure of the procedure.) Then ask, "Will the number of red jelly beans in the jar that initially contained only black jelly beans be the same as the number of black jelly beans in the jar that originally contained only red jelly beans?" Some students will immediately realize that the answer to the question must be "the same," but most students, like children, will examine the demonstration as a new problem.

If you are interested in keeping track of students' initial responses, distribute a questionnaire, including a place to check "yes" or "no," and a space to explain their answers. Begin the discussion after collecting their responses. Most students will argue that there will not be the same number of black beans in the jar that initially contained only red jelly beans as there are red beans in the jar that originally contained only black jelly beans; some students will answer "yes" but give an incorrect reason. Because most people do not enjoy being wrong, it is important to comment that the reason some people get the wrong answer is because they have too much information rather than too little. To let the students know that failure is usual, but temporary, it is helpful to discuss the research that suggests that 40% to 60% of college students have difficulty solving formal operations problems (Neimark, 1975) and that children and adults think more reasonably about familiar tasks (Chi, 1978; Siegler, 1986). Use the list of reasons given by the students who answered incorrectly to begin the discussion of how sensible thought patterns can lead to incorrect answers. To dramatize the solution, repeat the actual scooping–mixing–scooping process several times to demonstrate that the answer is indeed always "the same."

Of 54 students in two introductory psychology classes, 6 answered correctly after the first presentation of the problem. After the discussion accompanied by the actual pouring of jelly beans, 11 students still answered "no." They could see that the numbers remained the same but could not reason why. For weeks after the demonstration, students reported on how their friends responded to the problem and continued to argue among themselves about how to understand the demonstration. They also suggested more dramatic ways of setting up the demonstration (e.g., using crates of easter eggs or giant cookie jars).

Why do college students have such difficulty solving this problem? How does their difficulty help them understand Piaget's theories about preoperational children? Centration is a useful concept; people focus on one aspect of the task and lose sight of the whole context. Typical student comments are "But the probability of getting the same number of red jelly beans the second time is very low," "If you've mixed them up, you just can't end up with the same number," "The chances of getting the same number might be 1 in 10 million." By centering on the mixing of the red and black beans, students turn the task into a probability problem. Focused on the probability of scooping exactly the same numbers of red and black beans, they cannot see that the actual numbers are irrelevant. Other examples of centering include focusing (a) on the colors, (b) on certain words like *mix* or *same*, and (c) on the process of scooping or pouring or mixing. Like the children who are sure that the height of the water proves their point, these adults are sure that the detail they have selected is the key to the solution. In the child, the centration is perceptual; in the adult, the centration is conceptual. Some may argue, however, that the first step for those adults who turn the task into a probability problem is to focus on color or number cues. These are perceptual cues; the concept of probability is what the adult applies to these cues. The adult subject is more likely to be misled by the conceptual cues, but the way in which the concept misleads the adult is analogous to the way in which the percept misleads the child. Only by decentering, by giving up the focus on the chosen detail, can the solution be seen.

Irreversibility also illustrates reasoning that leads to an incorrect solution. A person who cannot imagine reversing the scooping process (by which any single jelly bean must be replaced by a jelly bean from the other jar) often fails to see that the two jars together provide the whole context simultaneously. The person who sees the solution understands that it does not matter how many jelly beans of each color are removed each time as long as the total number in the scoop is the same. Moving the jelly beans (and pouring the water) could be repeated endlessly without changing the answer.

The person worried about the mixing, the colors, and the probability of coming up with equal numbers of red and black jelly beans can also be described as being concrete, or perceptually bound. Like the child who is perceptually caught by the height of the water, the adult is trapped by the significance of the colors and particular words. These detailed aspects of the demonstration are distracting enough to prevent the observer from seeing the larger context.

The process of solving the problem can be very instructive. Students may learn how one can get stuck on irrelevant details, see new approaches to a problem, and gain fresh insight into the need to relinquish a particular viewpoint for greater comprehension. It is difficult to predict what will cause the decentering process. Students' descriptions of their decentering process suggest that it involves attention shifts similar to those that Gelman and Baillargeon (1983) taught to promote conservation in preoperational children. The catalyst to decentering may be a verbal suggestion, for example, "It's a spatial, not a probability problem," or watching the actual scooping and mixing of the jelly beans. Many students who watch the process will acknowledge that the final numbers are the same, but they remain mystified about why. They are like the child who pours the water back into the shorter glass and declares that magic accounts for the result. For students struggling with the problem, the decentering process is often gradual, taking

several days. Once they understand, they are amazed at how they missed the obvious. If time permits, the experience of coming to understand the jelly bean task can be tied to discussions of critical thinking, general problem-solving techniques, and functional fixedness.

Some students claim that they have a new appreciation for children's thinking and a new interest in thinking about their own thinking. In the long run, being wrong may encourage students to examine their certainties and to listen to other perspectives before reaching conclusions. These demonstrations are simple and short but bring important puzzles to the classroom. Both use a straightforward question with a single correct answer to raise questions about answers, show how language may hinder and help reasoning, and suggest that a comprehensive focus entails letting go of limited points of view.

References

Chi, M. R. H. (1978). Knowledge structures and memory development. In R. Siegler (Ed.), Children's thinking: What develops? (pp. 73–95). Hillsdale, NJ: Lawrence Erlbaum Associates, Inc.

Gelman, R., & Baillargeon, R. (1983). A review of some Piagetian concepts. In J. H. Flavell & E. M. Markman (Eds.), Handbook of child psychology: Vol. 3. Cognitive development (pp. 167–230). New York: Wiley.

Neimark, E. D. (1975). Longitudinal development of formal operational thought. Genetic Psychology Monographs, 91, 171–225.

Piaget, J. (1952). The child's conception of number. London: Routledge & Kegan Paul.

Siegler, R. S. (1986). Unities across domains in children's strategy choices. In M. Perlmutter (Ed.), Perspectives on intellectual development. The Minnesota symposia on child psychology (Vol. 19, pp. 1–48). Hillsdale, NJ: Lawrence Erlbaum Associates, Inc.

The Nature–Nurture Issue: Lessons From the Pillsbury Doughboy

David B. Miller
Department of Psychology and
Center for the Ecological Study of Perception and Action
University of Connecticut

One of the most difficult concepts to teach is the intricate transaction that takes place between genes and experience throughout development. This is hardly surprising, given that the nature–nurture problem has engrossed the minds of scientists for centuries. Recent literature is replete with claims for innateness (e.g., Herzog & Hopf, 1984; Marler & Pickert, 1984), genetic programs (e.g., Mayr, 1982; Moltz, 1984), and attempts to assess how much of a given trait is influenced by genes and how much by the environment

(e.g., Marler & Sherman, 1985; Owens & Owens, 1984). The problem with claims of innateness and genetic programs is that they merely label rather than explain the developmental process. The problem with attempting to assess the extent to which a given behavior is caused by genes and how much by the environment relegates the developmental process to a simplistic interaction between two entities (i.e., genes and environment), neither of which seems capable of affecting the other (see Hebb's, 1953, critique of this point of view). It is, therefore, no wonder that students share the confusion expressed by their teachers and textbooks.

During the last several years, I have tried to explain the intricate transaction (i.e., a complex interaction in which the interactants are inseparable and constantly changing; see Miller, 1988) of genes and experience by using the metaphor of cooking, which is a microcosm of development. In this metaphor, flour is analogous to genes. Genes, of course, have their own environments that will influence their activity throughout development. Genetic activity is also influenced by (and influences) other components unique to any organism. Such is the case with flour in the cooking process.

As I explain the analogy to my students, I take four different food items (i.e., developmental outcomes) that use flour as a base (i.e., genetic factors), but that also have other ingredients that will interact with the flour in unique ways (i.e., yielding different developmental trajectories). Also, different cooking methods (i.e., experiential factors) influence these developmental trajectories and yield different developmental outcomes.

In the first case, FLOUR + SALT + WATER fried in shortening "develop" into a FLOUR TORTILLA. In the second case, we take precisely the same ingredients and provide them with a "baking" experience (without shortening). The developmental outcome is entirely different as a function of this alteration in experience, for now these ingredients yield a MATZO. In the third case, we keep these three ingredients and add YEAST to them. While baking, these develop into BREAD. Finally, we retain the FLOUR and SALT, but add to them BUTTER, COCOA, and SUGAR. Again, bake them, and the result is a BROWNIE.

I have tried two different methods of presenting this metaphor to my classes, each with equal impact (as far as I could judge). The less dramatic method involves preparing and showing a sequence of slides of: (a) the ingredients, (b) the frying or baking process (i.e., the ingredients, still boxed, sitting in a frying pan atop a stove or in a baking dish inside an open oven), and (c) the developmental outcomes. The more dramatic method is rather messy and requires a bit of theatrics; specifically, bring the ingredients to class and mix them on paper plates before the students, explaining what the developmental process will entail (either frying or baking). Then, pull out of a paper bag the developmental outcome of each. Students in both large and small classrooms have found the latter demonstration particularly informative (if not amusing). I prefer it because it enables me to have the ingredients and the outcomes laid out on the table as I continue to explain the metaphor with behavioral development (discussed next). (Flour, when tossed exuberantly on small paper plates in a fashion that would rival that of Julia Child, can make quite a mess. I caution that students may find this amusing, but most janitors do not!)

The growing literature showing dramatic effects of different developmental contexts on the expression of behavioral as well as morphological outcomes provides a good example of this cooking metaphor. For example, it has often been assumed that physical variations within a species are due solely to genetic variation. However, James (1983) transplanted red-winged blackbird eggs between nests located hundreds of miles apart and found that nestlings were, in some respects, more similar in physical appearance to their foster parents than to their biological parents. Thus, common ingredients (i.e., shared genes between parent and offspring) yielded different developmental outcomes due to different cooking methods (i.e., different environments). With respect to behavior, I have shown how rearing and observing domestic mallards in a species-typical environment (i.e., a natural pond) results in the expression of species-typical social courtship displays (Miller, 1977). Prior to this research, it had been believed that these behaviors were genetically altered or entirely bred out of domestic breeds (Lorenz, 1974). Rather, my study showed that such behaviors are inhibited due to the unfavorable species-atypical environments (e.g., barnyards) in which domestic animals are reared. Again, the developmental outcome is primarily a function of the cooking process.

This cooking metaphor illustrates several important developmental principles. First is the concept of developmental constraints. That is, there is a range of possible outcomes constrained by nature of the ingredients and the types of developmental interactions that take place. For example, in no way will the ingredients described before yield vanilla pudding or duck à l'orange. Accordingly, genetic and environmental factors that develop into some form of primate cannot give rise to amphibians. Second, flour does not "code" for any specific outcome, nor do genes code or contain programs for developmental outcomes. The developmental outcome is a complex transaction involving the flour (genes), other ingredients, and the nature of the developmental process (cooking method). Altering the environment yields very different outcomes, even with the same set of ingredients (e.g., flour tortilla vs. matzo as a function of frying vs. baking the same three ingredients). Third, as development proceeds (or, as you get further along in the cooking process), the organism (or food item) achieves greater form, more closely approximating the developmental outcome (see Oyama, 1985). Fourth, one cannot partition a developmental outcome into heritable and environmental components. It would be entirely arbitrary to quantify the degree to which bread is a function of flour (i.e., heritability) as opposed to baking (i.e., environment). Accordingly, heritability quotients and assertions about environmental variance are highly arbitrary estimates and yield little information about the development and expression of behavior. Finally, when you have reached the developmental "endpoint" or outcome, you cannot easily identify the earlier constituent elements. That is, you cannot look at the brownie and see the individual ingredients or the nature of the transactions of those ingredients that occurred throughout the brownie's ontogeny. The same is true of behavioral and morphological development. If the individual factors leading up to the developmental outcome were apparent, developmental psychologists, psychobiologists, and ethologists would have rather boring jobs and little to quarrel about.

References

Hebb, D. O. (1953). Heredity and environment in mammalian behaviour. *British Journal of Animal Behaviour, 1*, 43–47.

Herzog, M., & Hopf, S. (1984). Behavioral responses to species-specific warning calls in infant squirrel monkeys reared in social isolation. *American Journal of Primatology, 7*, 99–106.

James, F. C. (1983). Environmental component of morphological differentiation in birds. *Science, 221*, 184–186.

Lorenz, K. (1974). *Civilized man's eight deadly sins.* New York: Harcourt Brace Jovanovich.

Marler, P., & Pickert, R. (1984). Species-universal microstructure in the learned song of the swamp sparrow (*Melospiza melodia*). *Animal Behaviour, 32*, 673–689.

Marler, P., & Sherman, V. (1985). Innate differences in singing behaviour of sparrows reared in isolation from adult conspecific song. *Animal Behaviour, 33*, 57–71.

Mayr, E. (1982). *The growth of biological thought.* Cambridge, MA: Belknap.

Miller, D. B. (1977). Social displays of mallard ducks (*Anas platyrhynchos*): Effects of domestication. *Journal of Comparative and Physiological Psychology, 91*, 221–232.

Miller, D. B. (1988). The development of instinctive behavior: An epigenetic and ecological approach. In E. M. Blass (Ed.), *Handbook of behavioral neurobiology: Vol. 9. Developmental psychobiology and behavioral ecology* (pp. 415–444). New York: Plenum.

Moltz, H. (1984). Why rat young respond to the maternal pheromone. In G. Greenberg & E. Tobach (Eds.), *Behavioral evolution and integrative levels* (pp. 277–288). Hillsdale, NJ: Lawrence Erlbaum Associates, Inc.

Owens, M., & Owens, D. (1984). *Cry of the Kalahari.* Boston: Houghton Mifflin.

Oyama, S. (1985). *The ontogeny of information: Developmental systems and evolution.* New York: Cambridge University Press.

Notes

1. I thank Charles F. Blaich and Gloria Hicinbothom for many fruitful discussions about behavioral development. Devising this exercise depended on a reevaluation of past and present developmental theories, which came about largely through their insights. I also thank the editor and three reviewers for helpful suggestions. One of the reviewers suggested the point about heritability quotients, and I am grateful for that insight.

A Life Stress Instrument for Classroom Use

Michael J. Renner
R. Scott Mackin
West Chester University

Most introductory psychology textbooks discuss the Holmes and Rahe (1967) approach to stress and its effect on health, and many texts include Holmes and Rahe's Social Readjustment Rating Scale (SRRS) instrument, which generates stress scores as *life change units*. Although students seem willing to entertain the possibility that stressors can affect their health, the teaching process is sometimes impaired by the actual SRRS instrument. The SRRS does not include many common events that act as stressors affecting traditional-age college students (e.g., final examinations). It also includes many items that are not meaningful to the typical entry-level college student or that have lost their meaning because of the nearly 30 years that have passed since the original research (e.g., "mortgage over $10,000"). This article describes a similar instrument, which is intended for classroom use in teaching these concepts. Finally, we offer a local set of norms to illustrate the types of scores generated by this instrument and to aid in planning its effective classroom use.

Development of the Instrument

We gave the College Life Stress Inventory, included in the *Instructor's Manual To Accompany Kalat's Psychology* (Kohn, 1993), to a large general psychology class. At the same time, students received Holmes and Rahe's (1967) original instrument. We asked students to suggest additional items. The instructions also asked students to indicate which of the described events had happened to them within the past 12 months. We collected these responses and condensed them into a draft form, with the goal that the instrument would include major and minor stressors affecting contemporary college students. In two subsequent semesters, we revised the resulting item list through an iterative process. In each semester, we added items and revised and deleted others based on student suggestions and frequency of occurrence. We eliminated items describing infrequent events that were not among the most stressful events on the list. In some cases we combined descriptions of two or more specific events into single, more general items.

The final version of the scale included 51 items, as shown in Table 1. We made two attempts to develop and assign relative stress values using an anchoring method. This method, however, produced inconsistent scalings. In addition, it was clear from student questions that they did not fully understand the task we had asked them to perform. Finally, we gave the list of items to 149 general psychology students who had not previously seen any form of the instrument and asked them to rate each item using a Likert scale ranging from 1 (*not at all stressful*) to 7 (*extremely stressful*). We used two forms of the scale, with items in alphabetical and reverse-alphabetical order. We ordered the items by mean ratings and scaled their stress values so that the most stressful item had a stress value of 100.

Empirical Evidence and Local Norms

We named the resulting instrument the College Undergraduate Stress Scale (CUSS). We administered the CUSS to 257 students in three sections of an Introductory Psychology course. The participants were students at a state-assisted comprehensive university of approximately 12,000 students in the eastern United States. Students ranged in age from 17 to 45 (M = 19.75, Mdn = 19, 90th percentile = 22). Approximately two-thirds of the participants were women (160 women, 79 men; 18 did not report their gender), which reflects recent enrollment patterns for this course.

The three sections of the course did not differ significantly in mean total stress scores, $F(2, 256) < 1$, so we pooled the data for these sections. The mean total stress rating was 1247 (SD = 441). Scores ranged from 182 to 2571.

There was a small but significant negative correlation between stress score and age ($r = -0.175$, $p = .007$). Although female students were significantly more stressed than male students, $t(237) = 2.24$, $p = .026$, this may be an artifact: Items that cause stress for female students may be overrepresented or may be assigned excessive weight in the instrument because most of the students in sections used for item development and scaling of the instrument were women.

Discussion

We developed a questionnaire instrument illustrating life stress and its cumulative nature using events that are likely to be familiar to traditional-age college students and using data from students concerning the relative perceived stressfulness of these events. We have used it successfully as a demonstration, as have several colleagues. In the classroom, we distribute copies of the instrument while presenting the topic of health psychology and stress. We explain that it may give students a personally relevant way to understand the SRRS and the research literature on life stress. After

Table 1. College Life Stress Inventory

Copy the "stress rating" number into the last column for any item that has happened to you in the last year, then add these.

Event	Stress Ratings	Your Items
Being raped	100	
Finding out that you are HIV-positive	100	
Being accused of rape	98	
Death of a close friend	97	
Death of a close family member	96	
Contracting a sexually transmitted disease (other than AIDS)	94	
Concerns about being pregnant	91	
Finals week	90	
Concerns about your partner being pregnant	90	
Oversleeping for an exam	89	
Flunking a class	89	
Having a boyfriend or girlfriend cheat on you	85	
Ending a steady dating relationship	85	
Serious illness in a close friend or family member	85	
Financial difficulties	84	
Writing a major term paper	83	
Being caught cheating on a test	83	
Drunk driving	82	
Sense of overload in school or work	82	
Two exams in one day	80	
Cheating on your boyfriend or girlfriend	77	
Getting married	76	
Negative consequences of drinking or drug use	75	
Depression or crisis in your best friend	73	
Difficulties with parents	73	
Talking in front of a class	72	
Lack of sleep	69	
Change in housing situation (hassles, moves)	69	
Competing or performing in public	69	
Getting in a physical fight	66	
Difficulties with a roommate	66	
Job changes (applying, new job, work hassles)	65	
Declaring a major or concerns about future plans	65	
A class you hate	62	
Drinking or use of drugs	61	
Confrontations with professors	60	
Starting a new semester	58	
Going on a first date	57	
Registration	55	
Maintaining a steady dating relationship	55	
Commuting to campus or work, or both	54	
Peer pressures	53	
Being away from home for the first time	53	
Getting sick	52	
Concerns about your appearance	52	
Getting straight A's	51	
A difficult class that you love	48	
Making new friends; getting along with friends	47	
Fraternity or Sorority rush	47	
Falling asleep in class	40	
Attending an athletic event (e.g., football game)	20	
Total		

students have had time to complete the instrument and to-tal their personal score, we show students the local norms (reported earlier) and offer general guidelines on interpreting individual scores based on these values. Although we have not gathered systematic data on students' reactions to the scale, student comments have been both frequent and uniformly positive, most often variations on the theme of "*now* I understand that stuff!"

Although we have provided a set of approximate norms for the CUSS, local circumstances and the characteristics of the student population would probably influence these

norms. Instructors who use the instrument should gather data at the institution where they use the instrument.

References

Holmes, T. H., & Rahe, R. H. (1967). The social readjustment rating scale. *Journal of Psychosomatic Research, 11*, 213–218.

Kohn, A. (1993). *Instructor's manual to accompany Kalat's Psychology* (2nd ed.). Belmont, CA: Wadsworth.

Notes

1. R. Scott Mackin is now at Pennsylvania State University.

2. A preliminary version of the instrument was presented at the second annual American Psychological Society Institute on the Teaching of Psychology, New York, June 1995.

A Humorous Demonstration of In Vivo Systematic Desensitization: The Case of Eraser Phobia

Timothy J. Lawson
Michael Reardon
College of Mount St. Joseph

Systematic desensitization (SD) is a common topic covered in general, abnormal, and clinical or counseling psychology courses. Developed by Wolpe (1958), SD involves associating a relaxed state with graduated exposure to anxiety-provoking stimuli. SD typically involves three steps. During the first step, the therapist teaches the client to relax, creating a response that is incompatible with anxiety. For the second step, the therapist and client work together to create an anxiety hierarchy, ordering anxiety-provoking stimuli from lowest to highest (related to a common fear dimension, such as proximity to a snake). The therapist ensures that there is not a large difference in anxiety ratings between any two adjacent hierarchy items. For the third step, the therapist (starting at the bottom of the hierarchy) guides the progressive association of each hierarchy item with relaxation, until the client is able to remain relaxed in response to each item. The therapist may accomplish this association by asking the client to imagine hierarchy items (traditional SD) or by actually presenting the feared items (in vivo SD). Therapists sometimes combine traditional SD and in vivo SD, using the former technique first.

Although Balch (1983) acknowledged the need for more creative ways of teaching therapeutic techniques, few authors have discussed methods for teaching SD. Sprecher and Worthington (1982) tried having general psychology students experience SD for seven 30 min sessions. However, they concluded that this teaching method was too lengthy and produced few therapeutic benefits.

We present a technique for demonstrating in vivo SD in an engaging, humorous, and informative manner that uses relatively little class time. Our technique involves brief role playing similar to that recommended by Balch (1983) for teaching client-centered therapy (see also Low, 1996).

Nature of the Demonstration

The second author, Michael, conducted the demonstration in three sections of general psychology. Prior to the demonstration, he explained the three steps of SD (see the first paragraph for a similar explanation). He explained that he would demonstrate the technique with a student who was ostensibly currently in therapy with him because of a phobia of chalkboard erasers. Before the beginning of the class period, the course instructor had selected a student who always sat at the back of the room and quietly asked the student to play along with the demonstration.

To start the demonstration, Michael explained that the student always sat at the back of the room because of a phobia of chalkboard erasers. He stated that he had already taught progressive relaxation to the student, worked with the student to develop an anxiety hierarchy, and desensitized the student to a photograph of a chalkboard eraser. Michael then showed the class the photograph and moved it toward the student to show that the student had indeed been desensitized to it.

Then, Michael explained that he planned to desensitize the student to items higher in the anxiety hierarchy. He took a caged eraser out of his briefcase and showed it to the student. The toy metal cage was slightly larger than the eraser and was locked with a small toy padlock. As Michael moved closer to the student with the caged eraser, the student acted anxious and Michael asked the student to take some deep breaths and to invoke the relaxation training.

Once the student was relaxed, Michael removed the eraser from the cage and showed it to the student until the student became relaxed once again. He moved the uncaged eraser closer and closer to the student until, finally, the student could touch the eraser without becoming overly anxious. At each step, Michael asked if the student was feeling anxious and progressed only after the student reported low anxiety. Michael then ended the demonstration and explained that the student did not really have an eraser phobia, but that the procedure he demonstrated was similar to that used with real phobias. He also noted that SD usually takes more than one session (10–12 sessions may be more typical).

Evaluation of the Demonstration

At the end of the class sessions in which Michael performed the demonstration, the instructors gave students a questionnaire for evaluation. We asked students to rate, on

238

a scale ranging from 1 (*strongly disagree*) to 5 (*strongly agree*), the extent to which they agreed with the statements, "This demonstration increased my understanding of how systematic desensitization is used to treat phobias," and "I enjoyed watching this demonstration." The questionnaire also contained space for students to provide additional comments. Fifty-nine students provided ratings, but one was excluded from statistical analyses because the ratings and comments were not consistent with each other, suggesting the student misunderstood the rating scales. Students indicated a high level of agreement with the former ($M = 4.41$, $SD = .75$) and the latter ($M = 4.40$, $SD = .86$) statements.

Fifty-six students provided open-ended comments, and they were overwhelmingly positive. Typical comments included: "It was funny . . . showed, in detail, the steps used to desensitize a person," "it was a creative way to teach something and made it very interesting to learn," "funny and explained to me what systematic desensitization was in terms that I could really understand," "Words don't describe it as well as the demonstration," and "entertaining way to facilitate learning." Only 4 students had negative comments, all of which indicated that they thought the demonstration was "silly," or it could have involved better acting on the part of the student.

Conclusions

We have found this demonstration to be an easy, engaging, and humorous way to teach students about SD. Although fictitious, eraser phobia is consistent with actual phobias in that it focuses on a frequently encountered object and causes avoidance of the feared object (i.e., by sitting in the back of the room). The demonstration provides students with a live example of a therapeutic technique, yet it does not require the amount of time involved in the technique discussed by Sprecher and Worthington (1982). Moreover, students appreciate the fact that it is entertaining and that it goes beyond what they would get from the text or a typical lecture.

Although this demonstration has proved valuable for our purposes, variations on it may better suit particular courses or instructor preferences. For a course in counseling, for example, the instructor may give a longer demonstration by presenting the complete anxiety hierarchy along with a detailed description of how it was developed and by having the student actor report subjective units of discomfort at each hierarchy step. Another way to provide students with more detail may be to use the demonstration to spur a discussion about the advantages and disadvantages of traditional versus in vivo SD or about the essential components of SD (see Spiegler & Guevremont, 1993). Instructors may also want to select the student actor prior to the day of the demonstration to coach the student on how to play the role of an SD client.

Although we emphasize to students that SD is more complex than the demonstration, instructors may also want to warn students that what they have learned from the demonstration does not qualify them to conduct therapy with others. Finally, instructors may also point out that conducting therapy with one's student would create a multiple relationship that would violate the ethical principles of the American Psychological Association.

References

Balch, W. R. (1983). The use of role-playing in a classroom demonstration of client-centered therapy. *Teaching of Psychology, 10,* 173–174.

Low, K. G. (1996). Teaching an undergraduate seminar in psychotherapy. *Teaching of Psychology, 23,* 110–112.

Spiegler, M. D., & Guevremont, D. C. (1993). *Contemporary behavior therapy* (2nd ed.). Monterey, CA: Brooks/Cole.

Sprecher, P. L., & Worthington, E. L., Jr. (1982). Systematic desensitization for test anxiety as an adjunct to general psychology. *Teaching of Psychology, 9,* 232–233.

Wolpe, J. (1958). *Psychotherapy by reciprocal inhibition.* Stanford, CA: Stanford University Press.

Notes

1. We thank Randolph A. Smith and the anonymous reviewers for their helpful comments.

Participant Modeling as a Classroom Activity

Dolores Hughes
Iona College

Participant modeling is a behavioral technique in which the therapist models approach and coping responses, encouraging and guiding the client to take a progressively active role in interacting with anxiety-provoking stimuli. Its major goals are the extinction of avoidance responses and the conditioning of appropriate approach responses. This technique has also been called *contact desensitization, demonstration plus participation,* and *guided participation* (Redd, Porterfield, & Andersen, 1979).

Many studies have demonstrated the effectiveness of participant modeling in the treatment of fears and phobias (e.g., Bandura, Adams, & Beyer, 1976; Bandura, Blanchard,

& Ritter, 1969; Ritter, 1969). The classic study of modeling for this purpose used young adults whose fear of snakes was severe enough to restrict some of their everyday activities (Bandura et al., 1969). Although all subjects in three treatment groups showed improvement in comparison with a control group, the subjects who imitated the behavior of a live model with guided participation demonstrated the most improvement. Several subsequent studies have demonstrated that this type of participant modeling is the most effective method of reducing snake phobias (e.g., Bandura et al., 1976).

Bandura (1977) suggested that participant modeling is effective because it provides individuals with experiences that enhance their perceptions of self-efficacy. Efficacy expectations are governed by information from a variety of sources. The most reliable source of information derives from performance accomplishments. Because participant modeling requires these accomplishments, it is particularly effective for inducing behavioral, affective, and attitudinal changes (Bandura, Adams, Hardy, & Howells, 1980).

The following activity was designed to: (a) demonstrate participant modeling as a technique for reducing fear and avoidance of nonpoisonous snakes, (b) illustrate the concept of self-efficacy, (c) illustrate some of the problems encountered when evaluating the effectiveness of therapeutic techniques, (d) actively engage students in the learning process, and (e) encourage critical thinking.

Procedure

This activity was conducted in the context of a unit on behavior therapies in my Introductory Psychology course. Approximately 1 week before the activity, students completed a questionnaire about their fear of nonpoisonous snakes. I told them that an expert in wildlife biology, James Rod of the National Audubon Society, would be visiting class to help with this activity.

He began the activity with a brief lecture about the biology of snakes and their ecological importance. He answered several questions about snakes before uncovering an aquarium containing a red rat snake, *Elaphe quttata*, commonly known as a corn snake. He removed the snake and handled it with obvious competence and a complete lack of fear.

Students were invited to hold the snake, and some always did so. I then selected students, based on their scores on the fear questionnaire, who were moderately afraid. I requested, but did not insist, that they try to do some or all of the following steps in sequence as the expert held the snake: (a) approach the snake within a radius of 6 ft, (b) gradually approach the snake more and more closely, (c) lightly touch its tail, (d) lightly touch the middle of its body, (e) touch the middle of its body more firmly, and (f) help the expert hold the snake. Then, students were asked to hold the snake by themselves.

Each of these steps was done slowly for each moderately afraid student with encouragement and reassurance from the expert, other students, and me. Students were asked to report what they were feeling as they went through these steps. Finally, I asked students who had scored high on the fear questionnaire if they were willing to do some or all of these steps, and some were always willing to try.

Students' Evaluations

Evaluations were obtained from 406 students in 14 sections of my Introductory Psychology course from 1976 to 1988. Class sizes ranged from approximately 20 to 40 students.

Using a 5-point scale, students were asked two questions: (a) How interesting was the activity? (1 = *not at all*, 5 = *extremely interesting*), and (b) How helpful was the activity for understanding the technique of participant modeling? (1 = *not at all*, 5 = *extremely helpful*). Combining all sections, the mean rating for interest was 4.33, and the mean rating for helpful was 4.21.

Discussion

The students' evaluations and comments were very favorable. Many students stayed after class to talk with the expert and touch or hold the snake. I am always struck by the combination of fear and fascination that students exhibit toward snakes.

Many students said they never believed they could touch or hold any snake. They seemed very proud that they were able to approach the snake and actually touch or hold it. Some students later reported that they had told their parents and friends about being able to touch or hold the snake. All of the students' comments were consistent with Bandura's (1984, 1986) concept of self-efficacy or sense of mastery, which has been emphasized as a component of all effective therapeutic techniques.

This activity is very interesting and helpful to students. It provides an excellent introduction to behavior therapies and introduces students to the difficulties involved in identifying the specific factors that are effective in therapeutic techniques. It also encourages students to think critically.

I ask students to think of the factors that were part of this activity. They usually report: (a) characteristics of the snake, such as size and color; (b) characteristics of the expert model and the peer models; (c) encouragement and reassurance from the expert model, other students, and me; (d) motivation to cooperate; and (e) participation in front of a classroom of peers. They understand that we did not isolate which factors may have been most strongly influencing behavior, and we did not use a control group. It is possible that all, some, one, or none of the factors were effective, and there may have been unidentified variables operating.

Students should realize that those who participated were probably not phobic. These students, therefore, were not representative of clients who enter treatment for phobias. This limitation leads to a discussion of the problem of treatment analogues (e.g., Bernstein & Paul, 1971; Borkovec & Nau, 1972). Much of our knowledge about the effectiveness of behavioral approaches for reducing anxiety derives from college students who volunteer for studies; they may not be typical of clients who share some specific problem.

Furthermore, we do not know if students' attitudes and behaviors will be permanently changed and will transfer to situations outside of the classroom. Some of the students who participated expressed doubts about touching a snake in other circumstances. These doubts lead to a discussion about the obstacles encountered in measuring the observable and permanent effects of any therapy.

I have always included an expert model as well as peer models, but the activity may be effective without the expert model. When modeling is used in the treatment of phobias, a distinction is often made between coping and mastery models. Coping models initially exhibit fearful performances and gradually become increasingly competent as modeling proceeds. Mastery models, in contrast, exhibit fearless performances from the beginning. Kazdin (1974) and Meichenbaum (1972) suggested that coping models may be more effective than mastery models. Coping models can, however, be ineffective. Geer and Turteltaub (1967), for example, found that models who demonstrated nonfearful behaviors toward snakes improved subjects' attitudes toward snakes. In contrast, fearful models did not produce attitudinal changes.

In my activity, some students served as coping models, and other students, who were not afraid of snakes, served as mastery models. If instructors prefer to include an expert model, and I do recommend using one, they may ask faculty or students in biology departments for help. Or they may check with pet stores, zoos, nature centers, and environmental organizations. Staff members of nature centers will probably help, because they want to educate people about wildlife.

The need to educate people about wildlife and help them overcome their fears of wildlife, especially snakes, was cogently addressed by Morgan & Gramann (1989). They successfully used a variety of behavioral techniques, including participant modeling, to help students change their attitudes toward snakes.

My experience suggests that people who are knowledgeable about snakes are eager to help others overcome their fears of snakes. They want people to appreciate that nonpoisonous snakes are harmless and ecologically important. I also discovered that some of my students have positive attitudes toward snakes before this activity.

This activity or modifications of it should be useful in courses such as abnormal psychology, behavior modification, learning, or research methods. It lends itself to a variety of modifications and applications that can engage students in the learning process. Students understand that participant modeling can be used in a variety of anxiety-provoking situations. The concept of participant modeling and its broad applications are easy for students to understand and appreciate. Students find this activity interesting, helpful, and enjoyable.

References

Bandura, A. (1977). Self-efficacy: Toward a unifying theory of behavioral change. *Psychological Review, 84,* 191–215.

Bandura, A. (1984). Recycling misconceptions of perceived self-efficacy. *Cognitive Therapy and Research, 8,* 231–255.

Bandura, A. (1986). *Social foundations of thought and action: A social cognitive theory.* Englewood Cliffs, NJ: Prentice-Hall.

Bandura, A., Adams, N. E., & Beyer, J. (1976). Cognitive processes mediating behavioral change. *Journal of Personality and Social Psychology, 35,* 125–139.

Bandura, A., Adams, N. E., Hardy, A. B., & Howells, G. N. (1980). Tests of the generality of self-efficacy theory. *Cognitive Therapy and Research, 4,* 39–66.

Bandura, A., Blanchard, E. B., & Ritter, B. (1969). Relative efficacy of desensitization and modeling approaches for inducing behavioral, affective, and attitudinal changes. *Journal of Personality and Social Psychology, 13,* 173–199.

Bernstein, D. A., & Paul, G. L. (1971). Some comments on therapy analogue research with small animal "phobias." *Journal of Behavior Therapy and Experimental Psychiatry, 2,* 225–237.

Borkovec, T. D., & Nau, S. D. (1972). Credibility of analogue therapy rationales. *Journal of Behavior Therapy and Experimental Psychiatry, 3,* 257–260.

Geer, J. H., & Turteltaub, A. (1967). Fear reduction following observation of a model. *Journal of Personality and Social Psychology, 6,* 327–331.

Kazdin, A. E. (1974). Covert modeling, model similarity, and reduction of avoidance behavior. *Behavior Therapy, 5,* 325–340.

Meichenbaum, D. H. (1972). Examination of model characteristics in reducing avoidance behavior. *Journal of Behavior Therapy and Experimental Psychiatry, 3,* 225–227.

Morgan, J. M., & Gramann, J. H. (1989). Predicting effectiveness of wildlife education programs: A study of students' attitudes and knowledge toward snakes. *Wildlife Society Bulletin, 17,* 501–509.

Redd, W. H., Porterfield, A. L., & Andersen, B. L. (1979). *Behavior modification: Behavioral approaches to human problems.* New York: Random House.

Ritter, B. (1969). Treatment of acrophobia with contact desensitization. *Behaviour Research and Therapy, 7,* 41–45.

Hindsight Bias and the Simpson Trial: Use in Introductory Psychology

George J. Demakis
Elmhurst College

In introductory psychology, providing a rationale for psychology as the scientific study of behavior is critical. Many students enter their first psychology course with "folk" theories of behavior, and they see psychology as simply intuitive and commonsensical. To help students appreciate the need for the scientific method in the study of behavior, teachers can discuss cognitive biases, such as the overconfidence phenomenon, the confirmation bias, and the hindsight bias (Myers, 1995; Wood, 1984). The focus of this article is how to demonstrate the hindsight bias in the classroom and how it illustrates critical points about psychological science.

The *hindsight bias* is a tendency to exaggerate one's ability to have foreseen the outcome of an event, after learning the outcome. More simply, on learning the outcome of an event, individuals may claim that they "knew it all along." For instance, Leary (1982) had participants estimate prior to or after an election the percentage of votes candidates would receive. Consistent with a hindsight bias, ratings made after the election were more accurate than ratings made before the election. Similarly, more accurate hindsight versus foresight judgments have been observed with the outcome of football games, medical diagnoses, and legal decisions (Hawkins & Hastie, 1990). Such events, with discrete outcomes, provide an excellent opportunity to illustrate the hindsight bias.

The recent adjudication in the Simpson criminal trial also provided an excellent opportunity to illustrate the hindsight bias and to provide an active-learning experience about cognitive biases. In October 1995, Simpson was found not guilty of murdering Nicole Brown Simpson and Ronald Goldman. Consistent with the hindsight bias, I predicted that participants who estimated the outcome of the trial postverdict would be more accurate (i.e., more likely to indicate that Simpson was not guilty) than participants who made preverdict judgments.

Method

Participants

Three classes of introductory psychology students participated ($N = 66$). One class ($n = 24$) made preverdict predictions regarding the outcome of the Simpson trial, and two classes ($n = 42$) made postverdict predictions about what they would have predicted the outcome to have been. Age and sex characteristics of the groups were equivalent. Sixty-five (98%) participants were White and 1 (2%) was Native American.

Procedures

One week prior to the Simpson verdict, the pretrial group predicted the outcome of the trial (guilty, not guilty, or hung jury). One month after the verdict, I requested that the postverdict group to "think back before the jury reached a verdict . . . [and] recall what you would have predicted the outcome to have been."

Results and Discussion

There was a significant difference between pre- and postverdict predictions $\chi^2(2, N = 66) = 9.38, p < .009$. Participants who made posttrial ratings were more likely to predict a not guilty verdict (57% vs. 25%) and less likely to predict a hung jury verdict (14% vs. 46%) than participants who made pretrial predictions. There was no change in predictions about guilty verdicts (29%). These data indicate the presence of the hindsight bias.

In introductory psychology, I focus first on the possible motivational and cognitive mechanisms by which the hindsight bias might operate and then on how notions of psychology as common sense might be fostered. Motivationally, the hindsight bias may operate because individuals desire to present themselves in a positive fashion (Hawkins & Hastie, 1990). One can easily think of many social and personal pressures to claim that one "knew it all along" (see Taylor & Brown, 1988). Cognitively, the tendency for individuals to automatically incorporate new information into their knowledge base makes delineation of old and new information difficult (Fischhoff, 1975). Once new information is incorporated, individuals are likely to overestimate how much they knew in advance. In addition to the Simpson findings, several examples can illustrate this phenomenon (Wood, 1984). For example, jurors may be unable to ignore information even when instructed to do so by a judge, because once this information is incorporated into their knowledge base, they may perceive that they knew it all along. In all, after a discussion of the mechanisms by which the hindsight bias may operate, I discuss how reasoning about behavior might be affected.

The hindsight bias may lead students to view research findings, particularly those in social and personality psychology, as commonsensical. I suggest that commonsensical or "folk" approaches to psychology are simply the use of the hindsight bias to make retrospective "explanations" about behavior (Stanovich, 1992). Specifically, I discuss many commonly used and occasionally contradictory proverbs and clichés used to explain behavior (e.g., "Birds of a feather flock together" vs. "Opposites attract"). I indicate that these proverbs are typically invoked only after a behavior has occurred and that, with their wide applicability, any behavior may be "explainable." At this juncture, students typically perceive the difficulty in relying on intuitive approaches to understanding behavior and are receptive to the need for the scientific method in psychology. Issues important for scientific analysis (e.g., empiricism, falsifiability) may be presented here, followed by specific discussion of research methods in psychology.

According to students, this demonstration assisted comprehension of the hindsight bias and the larger issue of the scientific method in psychology. Similar demonstrations can be conducted with other events that have a discrete outcome (e.g., athletic events and elections). As in this demonstration, I recommend use of participants from different classes to make pre- and postevent predictions. Other attempts to demonstrate this bias have failed when participants from the same class made both pre- and postevent predictions. This failure is not surprising because participants

are likely to recall a single prediction and to respond similarly later. Although this issue may be circumvented by having participants make predictions about multiple events, I have found that the most effective demonstration of this bias is to have different classes make pre- and postevent predictions.

References

Fischhoff, B. (1975). Hindsight ≠ foresight: The effect of outcome knowledge on judgment under uncertainty. *Journal of Experimental Psychology: Human Perception and Performance, 1,* 288–299.

Hawkins, S., & Hastie, R. (1990). Hindsight: Biased judgments of past events after the outcomes are known. *Psychological Bulletin, 107,* 311–327.

Leary, M. (1982). Hindsight distortion and the 1980 presidential election. *Personality and Social Psychology Bulletin, 8,* 257–263.

Myers, D. (1995). *Psychology* (4th ed.). New York: Worth.

Stanovich, K. (1992). *How to think straight about psychology* (3rd ed.). New York: HarperCollins.

Taylor, S., & Brown, J. (1988). Illusion and well-being: A social psychological perspective on mental health. *Psychological Bulletin, 103,* 193–210.

Wood, G. (1984). Research methodology: A decision-making perspective. In A. Rogers & C. Scheirer (Eds.), *The G. Stanley Hall lecture series* (Vol. 4, pp. 189–217). Washington, DC: American Psychological Association.

Notes

1. I thank Jane Jegerski for helpful comments on earlier drafts of this article.

Demonstrating a Self-Serving Bias

Dana S. Dunn
Moravian College

The presentation and discussion of particular attributional biases in introductory social psychology courses frequently engage student interest. Students readily recognize the overuse and abuse of dispositional attributions, for example, through the "fundamental attribution error" (L. Ross, 1977). I noticed, however, that self-serving attributional biases are not as readily recognized by students. As first time readers in social psychology, students seem to take note of their inferential failings when making attributions about others, but may be less likely to do so when making attributions about themselves. Self-serving or "hedonic" biases should be intrinsically interesting because they raise issues involving individual information processing as well as motivations to enhance self-esteem.

When attention is drawn to them, the differing roles for success and failure attributions seem obvious and familiar: Students accept personal credit for high scores on exams, for example, but are reluctant to accept responsibility for failing performances. Yet the recognition that such self-serving biases may extend beyond the internal–external dimension of success and failure often escapes students. My impression is that students frequently fail to consider other ways in which they seek to portray themselves in a favorable light. To broaden the understanding of self-serving attributions and to place them firmly in the realm of students' experience, I used a simple, in-class demonstration that both captures their interest and illustrates the impact of self-serving attributions.

I used two approaches. One method involves having students anonymously list what they consider to be their individual "strengths" and "weaknesses." I do not reveal the purpose of the exercise but, as I pass out a one-page questionnaire, I inform the students that the psychology of the self will be one of the topics discussed during the next class. The questionnaire simply asks students to first write down what they believe are their personal strengths and then list their weaknesses. I emphasize that anonymity must be maintained and remind students not to put their names on the questionnaires.

After collecting their lists, I promise to report the results in the next class. I tabulate the number of strengths and weaknesses, recording the mean for each category. Not surprisingly, students tend to report almost twice as many positive as negative attributes about themselves. In addition to eliciting a number of sheepish grins, the presentation of results usually prompts a discussion concerning the processes underlying self-serving biases. Do we tend to list more positive than negative self-descriptions due to some motivational bias such as self-esteem maintenance? Or, is our information processing the origin of the bias? Perhaps we recall more easily those situations in which we displayed positive rather than negative traits. Further, this differential recall may confirm existing expectations about ourselves; we simply spend more time thinking about our perceived positive attributes. The discussion allows me to introduce the egocentric bias (i.e., people overestimate their contributions to a jointly produced outcome, M. Ross & Sicoly, 1979). This may be another instance of differential recall influencing self-attribution.

In an alternative exercise, I have students verbalize their strengths and weaknesses during class. I write a heading for strengths on one half of a chalkboard and weaknesses on the other, while asking the class members to think about themselves in these terms. Student participation in this version of the exercise is voluntary; only those students who indicate a willingness to offer self-descriptions are called on. Instructors should be extremely cautious not to embarrass students by requiring them to participate in an exercise involving self-disclosure.

After students' responses are recorded on the chalkboard, I note that the number of strengths outweighs the weaknesses. Then, I turn exclusively to the weaknesses list, discussing each item individually. Usually, several (if not most) of the weaknesses show another example of self-enhancement. For example, "lazy" can be deemed a relatively negative trait, but descriptions like "too trusting," "workaholic," and "sensitive" still maintain some positive

connotations. Indeed, many of the weaknesses students offer resemble the negative-yet-still-positive traits they might use to describe themselves to a prospective employer during an interview. I point out that because these descriptions were collected in a public setting, some self-presentational concerns were probably operating. The discussion of self-presentational issues allows for a careful consideration of how presenting ourselves to observers may differ from the manner in which we reflect on our perceived self-images. A motivation toward modesty may have a role in the former situation; however, an informational bias better accounts for the latter situation. I discuss the aforementioned role of differential recall in emphasizing the positive rather than the negative aspects of our characters.

Regardless of which method I use, after considering the results in some detail, I try to guide class discussion toward the implications of self-serving biases. Are these biases adaptive or troublesome for our views of ourselves? When do they cease to aid us and, instead, become a potentially dysfunctional aspect of the attribution process? In response to these questions, students frequently raise the issue of individual differences, pointing out that extremes exist: Some people are truly narcissistic; others tend toward self-disparagement.

Students seem to enjoy this exercise because it makes discussing inferential bias and attribution theory more personal. It also presents a novel way of thinking about the self, one that offers some explanation for our tendency to see ourselves favorably. Comments of several students indicate that it is something of a revelation to discover that such self-reflection is susceptible to error and open to doubt.

Additional demonstrations of self-serving biases are included in Wood (1984). These exercises may lead students to scrutinize thoughts about themselves a bit more and to broaden their appreciation for potential bias in self-perception.

References

Ross, L. (1977). The intuitive psychologist and his shortcomings: Distortions in the attribution process. In L. Berkowitz (Ed.), *Advances in experimental social psychology* (Vol. 10, pp. 173–220). New York: Academic.

Ross, M., & Sicoly, F. (1979). Egocentric biases in availability and attribution. *Journal of Personality and Social Psychology, 37,* 322–336.

Wood, G. (1984). Research methodology: A decision-making perspective. In A. M. Rogers & C. J. Scheirer (Eds.), *The G. Stanley Hall lecture series* (Vol. 4, pp. 189–217). Washington, DC: American Psychological Association.

On Seeing Oneself as Less Self-Serving Than Others: The Ultimate Self-Serving Bias?

James Friedrich
Willamette University

Research has shown that, in a wide range of contexts and on a variety of measures, people exhibit what has been termed a *self-serving bias* in judgment. For example, we tend to attribute our successes to internal causes and our failures to external forces, overestimate our likelihood of engaging in socially desirable behaviors, misremember our behavior in self-enhancing ways, overestimate the accuracy of our judgments, show unrealistic levels of optimism about experiencing positive events and avoiding negative events in our future, overestimate the degree to which others share our views and opinions, and underestimate the degree to which others share our skills and positive attributes (see Myers, 1990, for a review).

Another way we exhibit this self-serving bias is by seeing ourselves as being better than average on many socially desirable dimensions—a phenomenon sometimes referred to as the *Lake Wobegon effect* after Garrison Keillor's fictitious town where all the children are above average. Although some people necessarily are average on any given quality, not everyone can be. I once read the results of a faculty survey conducted as part of an accreditation self-study in which 100% of the faculty rated their teaching performance as better than the average performance at the institution. This notion is illustrated more formally in a study reported by Myers (1990), based on data collected by the College Entrance Examination Board. Over 800,000 students taking the Scholastic Aptitude Test (SAT) were asked to indicate how they felt they compared to others their own age in terms of several abilities. For leadership ability, 70% rated themselves above average, and only 2% rated themselves below average. For the ability to get along with others, 60% rated themselves in the top 10%, and 0% rated themselves below average—results that may explain why nearly every student who has spoken to me about a roommate conflict has reported the same difficulty (their roommate's poor skills in getting along with others).

Experimental work has also demonstrated that we generally perceive our own behavior to be fairer and more moral than the behavior of others. Interestingly, however, this same work has shown similar self-enhancing perceptions to be weak or absent for the socially desirable dimension of intelligence (Allison, Messick, & Goethals, 1989; Van Lange, 1991). This and other research (e.g., Dunning, Meyerowitz, & Holzberg, 1989) indicates that self-enhancement in judgments of relative standing seems to be greatest on dimensions that are not only socially desirable but also ambiguous (open to idiosyncratic definition by the respondent), more controllable (and thus more self-revealing), and less easily verified or objectively scaled.

Several of the examples already noted—teaching performance, leadership ability, and skill at getting along with others—fit this description. Another quality that falls into this domain is self-servingness itself. The tendency to be self-serving in one's judgments is likely to be perceived as an undesirable quality that we may expect to be exhibited less strongly in ourselves than in other people. The tendency to be modest (or at least accurate) in one's self-assessments represents the desirable pole of this dimension, complete with the value overtones associated with humility and lack of conceit. Moreover, misperceptions of one's own self-servingness would be difficult to define, quantify, and verify objectively. Finally, self-serving judgment is likely to be perceived as a largely voluntary, controllable quality (although researchers in the area argue that the truth of the matter is quite the opposite).

In a sense, research on self-serving biases in judgment suggests that we should be somewhat conceited in our perceptions of our own humility. That is, we should see ourselves as somewhat better than average at not thinking ourselves to be better than average. Ironically, such a tendency would likely work against any prophylactic effects associated with raising people's awareness of the problem. As Myers (1990) noted in concluding his discussion of this literature, "perhaps some readers have by now congratulated themselves on being unusually free of the self-serving bias" (p. 93). The two studies reported here, designed for use as classroom demonstrations, test the hypothesis that even people informed about this bias will see themselves as less frequently self-serving in their judgments than the average person.

Study 1

Method

Participants. Forty-seven upper level undergraduates participated in the study. Thirty-three were enrolled in an Elementary Statistics course, and 14 were enrolled in an Industrial/Organizational (I/O) Psychology course; I taught both courses. Enrollments were nonoverlapping, and results of the study were analyzed and discussed with each class as part of the ongoing instructional activities.

Materials and procedure. At the beginning of regular class periods several weeks into the term, students in each class were asked to fill out an anonymous survey. This one-page questionnaire began with a quote from Myers (1990, p.

84)—the entire paragraph in which he describes the results of the SAT survey mentioned earlier. Immediately following this attributed quote, students read one of two versions of the following:

Research such as this has led psychologists to conclude that when people rate themselves in terms of socially desirable qualities or performance, they tend to see themselves as being better than average when they are really not. This tendency is often referred to as a "self-serving bias" in judgment. How often do you think (you; the average person) make this kind of mistake when judging or evaluating (yourself; him- or herself)?

The self and average person versions were randomized before distribution. Students indicated their answers by circling the appropriate number on a scale ranging from 1 (*almost never*) to 9 (*nearly all the time*).

Results and discussion. A 2 (Statistics vs. I/O students) × 2 (Self vs. Average Person Phrasing) analysis of variance (ANOVA) on these responses produced only the expected main effect for the phrasing of the question (all other $ps \geq$ .2). Students who responded to questions about their own tendency to fall prey to this bias gave significantly lower ratings (M = 5.13) than did those who rated the same tendency for the average person (M = 6.54), $F(1, 43) = 18.71, p < .01$, $\eta^2 = .20$. Note that the quoted research explicitly called attention to the nature and prevalence of self-serving bias effects in a national population of SAT-takers presumably perceived as similar to the respondents themselves. Nevertheless, students tended to see themselves as being significantly less likely than others to distort their self-perceptions in this manner.

Study 2

Method

Participants. Thirty-eight introductory psychology students (one entire section that I taught) participated in the study during a regular class period approximately 2 weeks into the term. Data were analyzed in class, with results and possible interpretations discussed as illustrations of principles covered in lectures.

Materials and procedure. During the last third of a regularly scheduled class period, I lectured on research related to the self-serving bias—material presented in connection with the concurrently assigned chapter on social psychology. At the beginning of the next class period, students were handed a questionnaire and asked to complete it anonymously. This one-page survey read as follows:

I'm conducting an anonymous survey for my Industrial/Organizational Psychology class. One of the topics for the course is whether or not people's own self-ratings should be used in the evaluation of their work performance. [The survey results were, in fact, discussed in that course.]
Some research has suggested that people tend to rate themselves as better than average on most desirable quali-

ties even when they are really not. How often do you think (you; the average person) makes this kind of mistake when describing (yourself; him- or herself)?

The self and average person versions of the surveys were randomized before distribution. Students indicated their responses on the same 9-point scale used in Study 1.

Results and discussion. As predicted, students who responded to questions about their own tendency to fall prey to this bias gave significantly lower ratings (M = 4.95) than did those who rated the same tendency for the average person (M = 6.62), $t(36) = 2.78, p < .01$, $\eta^2 = .18$. Although the context of the question (SAT example vs. employment example), the type of students surveyed (upper level vs. introductory), and even the institution at which the experiments were conducted differed for Studies 1 and 2, the absolute values of the means for the self and average person groups (and thus their differences) were nearly identical across the two investigations. Students referring to themselves seemed to locate their own tendency at the scale midpoint (5) and the tendency of others somewhat above the midpoint. In this sense, students as a whole did not seem to be denying that they make this mistake. Rather, they simply indicated their belief that others are even more likely than themselves to do so.

General Discussion

The tendency for people to be self-serving in their judgments of self-serving tendencies, documented in both of these studies, is fairly robust. These experiments represent only two of many replications I have conducted with variations of the procedure (e.g., out-of-class surveys, student experimenters, and different courses). Across variations, results have been consistent, and the moderate effect sizes reported in the present studies (roughly equal to point-biserial $rs \geq .4$) are typical. One advantage of this broader replicability is that the demonstration can be adapted to fit the needs and particular instructional goals of different courses. For example, in the studies reported earlier, results were used to discuss the self-serving bias with introductory students reading a chapter on social psychology and to discuss a variety of measurement issues in the use of judgmental ratings of work performance with I/O psychology students. In the Elementary Statistics course, the demonstration was used both as an illustration of significant issues in experimental design (random assignment, equivalent conditions except for the manipulated variable, and use of between-subjects designs to control for demand characteristics) and as a quick way to generate an interesting in-class data set for computing statistics (e.g., ANOVAs, *t* tests, and Pearson or point-biserial correlations).

Some of the best discussions have been in my Social Psychology classes, due in part to the students' greater familiarity with models of self-presentation, self-justification, and information processing that may account for the findings (Myers, 1990). The demonstration also raises an important question about how personal knowledge of particular social psychological processes (e.g., from material taught in the course) affects an individual's behavior. Results obtained in class can serve as a springboard for examining the debate over the historically bound nature of social psychological research (Gergen, 1973) versus the field's claims of identifying transhistorical principles and mechanisms (Schlenker, 1974).

Data reported in this article also point to new empirical work that may further explore this tendency toward self-servingness in estimates of one's self-servingness. For example, no data on sex of participant were collected for the studies. Although past studies on self-serving biases have typically failed to obtain or report significant sex effects (e.g., Allison et al., 1989; Dunning et al., 1989; Van Lange, 1991), the possibility deserves further exploration. For example, when asked to think of an average person, do men and women differ in terms of the sex of the exemplar or prototype they envision? Does the use of gender-neutral pronouns in the stimulus materials influence this process (cf. Hamilton, 1988)? Another methodological question centers on the use of a between-subjects design. Although I typically use such a design in these demonstrations to avoid the demand characteristics associated with explicit self–other comparisons, other researchers (e.g., Allison et al., 1989) have obtained self-serving biases even when the self–other comparisons are made directly. Would the effects documented in the present study be obtained with a within-subjects design? If not, would this call into question the claim that people are in fact seeing themselves as being better than others?

The present data also leave open the question of whether the effects are attributable to a tendency to (a) overestimate others' vulnerability to the self-serving bias while judging one's own vulnerability accurately, (b) underestimate one's own vulnerability while judging others' vulnerability accurately, or (c) both underestimate one's own vulnerability and overestimate others'. Research on *false uniqueness* and *false consensus* effects (e.g., Goethals, 1986) has shown that people tend to see their own desirable behaviors as less common than they actually are and their undesirable behaviors as more common than they are, respectively. That is, in an absolute sense, people appear to be meeting self-esteem needs by misperceiving typical others. This research paradigm has not, however, tended to examine possible distortions in perceptions of one's own behavior; the participant's own attitude or behavior is specified or taken as a given, and the resulting effect on perceptions of others is then examined. In contrast, research on the better-than-average effect has typically been interpreted as revealing objective distortions in perceptions of oneself. Although research findings on the better-than-average effect and the false uniqueness effect have emerged somewhat independently, these phenomena are in several respects variations on a common theme and should be considered jointly in future attempts to explore the relative accuracy of perceptions of self versus others.

In the common debriefing I provide for all my classes, I point out to students that self-serving tendencies like the one illustrated in the demonstration are widespread and that their own responses are not unique. (Students seem to enjoy hearing about the faculty survey noted earlier, for which I was one of the respondents.) I also note that such self-esteem-enhancing perceptions may be adaptive, appearing commonly in people judged to be psychologically healthy by several criteria (Myers, 1990; Taylor & Brown, 1988, 1994). For teachers and students interested in pursuing this last issue more deeply, some researchers have questioned whether such judgments constitute distortions or biases at all and whether true, significant distortions would necessarily be adaptive in mental health terms (Colvin & Block, 1994; Shedler, Mayman, & Manis, 1993). Although the purposes served by the demonstration are different in each of my courses, these in-class studies have been consistently well received, with the irony of their results providing a humorous context for discussing a variety of important issues.

References

Allison, S. T., Messick, D. M., & Goethals, G. R. (1989). On being better but not smarter than others: The Muhammad Ali effect. *Social Cognition, 7,* 275–296.

Colvin, C. R., & Block, J. R. (1994). Do positive illusions foster mental health? An examination of the Taylor and Brown formulation. *Psychological Bulletin, 116,* 3–20.

Dunning, D., Meyerowitz, J. A., & Holzberg, A. D. (1989). Ambiguity and self-evaluation: The role of idiosyncratic trait definitions in self-serving assessments of ability. *Journal of Personality and Social Psychology, 57,* 1082–1090.

Gergen, K. (1973). Social psychology as history. *Journal of Personality and Social Psychology, 26,* 309–320.

Goethals, G. R. (1986). Fabricating and ignoring social reality: Self-serving estimates of consensus. In J. M. Olson, C. P. Herman, & M. P. Zanna (Eds.), *The Ontario symposium on personality and social psychology* (Vol. 4, pp. 135–157). Hillsdale, NJ: Lawrence Erlbaum Associates, Inc.

Hamilton, M. (1988). Using masculine generics: Does generic "he" increase male bias in the user's imagery? *Sex Roles, 19,* 785–799.

Myers, D. G. (1990). *Social psychology* (3rd ed.). New York: McGraw-Hill.

Schlenker, B. (1974). Social psychology and science. *Journal of Personality and Social Psychology, 12,* 564–578.

Shedler, J., Mayman, M., & Manis, M. (1993). The *illusion* of mental health. *American Psychologist, 48,* 1117–1131.

Taylor, S. E., & Brown, J. D. (1988). Illusion and well-being: A social psychological perspective on mental health. *Psychological Bulletin, 103,* 193–210.

Taylor, S. E., & Brown, J. D. (1994). Positive illusions and well-being revisited: Separating fact from fiction. *Psychological Bulletin, 116,* 21–27.

Van Lange, P. A. M. (1991). Being better but not smarter than others: The Muhammad Ali effect at work in interpersonal situations. *Personality and Social Psychology Bulletin, 17,* 689–693.

Notes

1. I thank students at Hobart and William Smith Colleges (Study 1) and Willamette University (Study 2) for their assistance with this project.

Bringing Cognitive Dissonance to the Classroom

David M. Carkenord
Joseph Bullington
Georgia Southern University

The concept of cognitive dissonance (Festinger, 1957) is often difficult for instructors to explain and students to understand. Instructors in our department frequently express something akin to dread over an impending "cognitive dissonance" lecture.

Explanation of the concept often begins in a straightforward manner: If a person's thoughts and behaviors are inconsistent, the person is motivated to change attitudes or behaviors to reestablish consistency. After all, we do not want to appear to be hypocritical, either to ourselves or others. Students can generally follow the argument to this point. The problem begins when one then attempts to explain the experimental tests of cognitive dissonance theory, most notably Festinger and Carlsmith's (1959) classic study. In this study, a group of students completed a boring task and were later paid either $1 or $20 to tell a potential "subject" (actually a confederate) that the same task was really interesting. Subjects in each group, then, told the subject that the experiment was very interesting. On a later measure of their attitudes toward the task, subjects in the group that received $1 reported more favorable attitudes toward the boring task than subjects in the group that received $20. The $1 group, according to Festinger and Carlsmith, experienced more dissonance than the $20 group because $1 provided insufficient justification for their attitude-discrepant behavior (telling a person something they themselves did not believe).

In explaining this study to a class, we have noticed that the discussion typically gets bogged down over the notion of how dissonance, a psychological state, provides the motivation for a change in attitude. Many students fail to understand that it is the experience of dissonance that directly motivates the change in Festinger and Carlsmith's (1959) experiment, not the amount of money received (although the amount of money does induce the dissonance). It is as if students forget about the notion of dissonance and focus solely on the money variable. (Our students often state that subjects in the $20 condition should rate the task more favorably because they received more money!) We hypothesized that providing students with an opportunity to experience a state of dissonance resulting from discrepancies between their own attitudes and behaviors might better enable them to understand the concept of cognitive dissonance and, consequently, the subtleties of Festinger and Carlsmith's experimental manipulation. Thus, we developed a simple but effective in-class exercise that induces dissonance by comparing students' personal attitudes and behaviors on a number of social issues. Our findings suggest that a majority of students agree or strongly agree with a series of attitudinal statements, but only a minority perform behavior consistent with their reported attitudes.

Method

Materials

The stimulus material for the exercise consists of one double-sided page. Side 1 is titled "Attitude Survey" and contains four items to be rated on a 5-point scale ranging from *strongly disagree* (1) to *strongly agree* (5). The items are: (a) World hunger is a serious problem that needs attention, (b) Our country needs to address the growing number of homeless, (c) The right to vote is one of the most valuable rights of American citizens, and (d) Our government should spend less money on nuclear weapons and more on helping citizens better their lives. Instructions at the top of the page read, "Please indicate your attitudes on the four statements below."

Side 2 is titled "Behavioral Survey" and is headed with instructions reading, "Please indicate whether or not you perform the stated behavior on a regular basis." Below the instructions are four items corresponding to the attitudinal items on page 1: (a) Do you personally do anything to lessen world hunger (e.g., donate money or food or write your representative)?, (b) Do you personally do anything to help the homeless (e.g., volunteer at homeless shelter or donate money)?, (c) Did you vote in the last election for which you were eligible?, and (d) Do you personally convey your feelings to the government (e.g., write your representatives or participate in protests/marches)? Response options of "yes" and "no" are offered for each item.

Procedure

Prior to any discussion of cognitive dissonance, distribute copies of the handout to students with instructions to complete Side 1 (Attitude Survey) before Side 2 (Behavioral Survey). Then ask the class (by a show of hands) how many agreed or strongly agreed with attitudinal Item 1. Next, ask the students to turn to Side 2 and again raise their hands if they responded "yes" to the corresponding behavioral item. Repeat the process of comparing the attitudinal responses with the corresponding behavioral responses for the remaining three items. Most students will quickly get the point of the exercise.

A subsequent discussion of cognitive dissonance can begin with a simple question like, "How does it make you feel when these inconsistencies are pointed out to you?" Our students responded, "hypocritical," "guilty," or some related remarks. Further discussion can focus on formal definitions of cognitive dissonance and cognitive consonance, research studies on cognitive dissonance (e.g., Aronson & Mills, 1959; Festinger & Carlsmith, 1959), and dissonance reduction strategies.

Table 1. Attitudinal and Behavioral Responses

Item and Course[a]	Attitudes (% Agree and Strongly Agree)	Behaviors (% Yes)
World hunger a problem		
Social	87	17
Introductory	90	7
Must address homeless problem		
Social	96	32
Introductory	95	33
Right to vote important		
Social	94	47
Introductory	85	40
Government should better people's lives		
Social	91	11
Introductory	88	3

[a]$n = 53$ for social, $n = 72$ for introductory.

For purposes of this article, we asked students to return their completed forms, but instructors would typically not need to collect the forms unless they plan to report the specific results to the class later. Table 1 displays the responses of 125 students; 53 were enrolled in two social psychology classes and 72 in two introductory psychology classes. These responses highlight the large discrepancies between students' attitudes and behaviors.

Only one student reported complete attitude–behavior consistency on all items. The remaining 124 students (99.2%) reported attitude-discrepant behavior on at least one of the four items. Twenty-nine students (23%) reported attitude–behavior inconsistencies on all four items. These findings demonstrate that the exercise highlighted inconsistencies in virtually all students in our sample.

Student Assessment

After the discussion, students evaluated their experiences on a 5-point scale ranging from *strongly disagree* (1) to *strongly agree* (5). For all four items, students' reactions were quite positive. They reported that (a) the exercise helped in understanding cognitive dissonance ($M = 4.5$), (b) they experienced dissonance ($M = 4.1$), (c) the exercise provided self-insight ($M = 4.0$), and (d) the exercise was a useful learning experience ($M = 4.3$).

Eight students also wrote comments, all of which were positive. One response was particularly interesting: "[The exercise] works well, even to the point where I 'fudged' on the second sheet [Behavioral Survey] to try to relieve some cognitive dissonance." Not surprisingly, this response was from the lone student who reported complete attitude–behavior consistency. Evidently, the exercise was especially effective for this individual.

Discussion

We believe the exercise is very useful for introducing and explaining the concept of cognitive dissonance, because virtually all students actually experience cognitive dissonance. Thus, students learn and understand the concept in direct relation to their own attitudes and behaviors. Later discus-

sions of research on cognitive dissonance take on more meaning because students have recently experienced such a psychological state. Nevertheless, a number of related issues must be addressed.

First, some instructors may be concerned about the ethical nature of our exercise. Asking students to publicly admit to certain attitudes and behaviors may be considered too intrusive for a classroom demonstration. One strategy to avoid this problem would be to collect the completed surveys, shuffle them, and redistribute them to the class. At this point, proceed through the item-by-item comparisons, again by a show of hands. In this situation, students would be expressing the attitudes and opinions of anonymous fellow students. Although our data were not obtained in this manner, we believe such an approach would alleviate any ethical concerns while maintaining the overall usefulness of the exercise.

A second and related issue is whether the public admission of attitude–behavior inconsistencies may have induced the reported dissonance rather than (or in addition to) the inconsistencies themselves. Although this situation is possible, we believe students experienced dissonance before the public admission. We have no empirical data to support our belief, but our subjective appraisal of student responses during the exercise provides some evidence. As students completed Side 2 of the survey, extensive murmuring and mild laughter occurred. We interpret such activities as the behavioral manifestation of the students' dissonance resulting solely from completing the exercise instrument.

A final concern is whether the dissonance induced by our exercise ultimately results in any attitude or behavior changes, as predicted by cognitive dissonance theory. Such evidence, although interesting, would be difficult to obtain and is beyond the intended scope and purpose of our exercise. The goal of our procedure is to induce dissonance so that students can directly experience such a psychological state. The exercise is not intended as a test of cognitive dissonance theory or dissonance reduction strategies. Those topics could be addressed in the discussion following the exercise. Thus, although possible attitude or behavior changes resulting from our exercise would be an intriguing topic, lack of such information does not detract from the usefulness of the procedure. Future users of the exercise may want to devise a means to deal more extensively with this issue.

References

Aronson, E., & Mills, J. (1959). The effects of severity of initiation on liking for a group. *Journal of Abnormal and Social Psychology, 59,* 177–181.

Festinger, L. (1957). *A theory of cognitive dissonance.* Stanford, CA: Stanford University Press.

Festinger, L., & Carlsmith, J. M. (1959). Cognitive consequences of forced compliance. *Journal of Abnormal and Social Psychology, 58,* 203–210.

Notes

1. We thank Bill McIntosh, Michael Zuschlag, and three anonymous reviewers for their helpful comments and suggestions on earlier drafts of this article.

Prisoner's Dilemma as a Model for Understanding Decisions

Janet D. Larsen
John Carroll University

When will people cooperate, and when will they decide to take advantage of others? Introductory and social psychology textbooks present the prisoner's dilemma (PD) as a framework for understanding the decisions people make when they have the choice of taking advantage of others or cooperating with them. It has been used to explain panic behavior in crowds (Gleitman, 1987) and the choices people make in labor union negotiations (Worchel & Cooper, 1983).

PD is best explained by a story about two men who are arrested on a minor charge and placed in separate rooms. Although the authorities believe that both men are guilty of a more serious crime, there is no proof of their guilt. The following options are explained to each man. He can continue to claim his innocence and, if his friend also continues to maintain his own innocence, they will both receive short sentences. The man can turn state's evidence and give the authorities the information they want. If he does, his friend will receive the maximum sentence but he will go free. However, the same options are offered to his friend. If his friend also confesses, both men will receive intermediate sentences. What will the men do?

It would be to the prisoners' mutual advantage for both to remain silent, but each takes a risk in doing so. Choosing to remain silent requires that the man be confident that his friend will not turn state's evidence. If he thinks his friend will confess, it is to his advantage to confess. Then, if his friend confesses, he assures himself of a lighter sentence; if his friend does not confess, the man will get off with no penalty.

This same analysis can be applied to the behavior of people when there is a fire in a theater. Common sense suggests that everyone has the best chance of escaping if people file out, taking turns to get through the door. However, we do not trust others to take turns. Like the prisoner, we make the exploitive choice and look out for ourselves first, because we expect others to act the same way. Rather than taking the chance of being pushed out of the way and burned to death, most people push ahead and many are hurt.

The following class activity allows students to experience the dilemma. If PD is discussed in your textbook, you may want to conduct this activity before students read that assignment; however, the demonstration is effective even if students have already read about PD.

Dollars, Dimes, or Doughnut Holes

Tell your class that you would like to give away some money, but only under certain conditions. Each student may ask for $1.00 or 10¢. You will give all of the students what they ask for if fewer than 20% of the students ask for $1.00. Ask students to write their choices on a slip of paper, along with their name or some identification code if they ask for $1.00. In addition, ask them to indicate the percentage of the class they expect to ask for $1.00. These choices should be made without consulting other members of the class, just as the prisoners made their decisions to confess or not confess without talking to each other.

Collect the slips, and read the choices. Sort the slips into $1.00 or 10¢ requests and, within each category, whether the person expects over or under 20% of the class to ask for $1.00. About half the students usually ask for $1.00. Some of the students in this group expect 20% or less of the class to make the same request (corresponding to the prisoner who decides to confess in the hope of going free). Most of those who ask for $1.00 expect a large proportion of the class to do the same. (These students correspond to the prisoner who confesses because he expects his friend to confess.) After students have had a real experience of choosing to exploit others or to trust that others will not take advantage of them, similar situations are easier to understand. The PD model can be applied to diverse situations such as: driving, where you must decide whether to get in line or stay in the lane that is about to end; infant inoculation, where parents must decide whether their child will receive a shot for diphtheria, pertussis, and tetanus and risk the rare but deadly reaction; and cheating on a test where, if everyone cheats, the curve will be raised and no one will benefit.

This activity can also be used to introduce the ideas in Hardin's (1968) article, "The Tragedy of the Commons." He argued that people behave selfishly in group situations because they expect others to make selfish choices. This analysis can be applied to problems such as trying to get manufacturers to stop polluting the environment or trying to get countries to limit fishing in international waters.

The Matching Game

PD can also provide the basis for understanding how people behave when they know they will relate to one another in the future. The iterated version of PD, or playing the game over and over with the same person, can serve as a model for understanding some of the features of labor union bargaining and international treaty negotiations.

Each student needs a coin for this game. Pairs of students play PD 20 times, indicating their choices by placing a coin on the desk heads up or tails up. If Player A and Player B choose heads, each gets 6 points. If both choose tails, both lose 6 points. However, if one chooses heads and the other chooses tails, the player choosing heads loses 8 points and the player choosing tails gets 8 points. Have students keep track of the number of points each person earns and report to the class the number of points earned by each player. When the pairs play cooperatively, both players have high scores. If one player chooses tails frequently, the other player usually does the same, and both end the game with low or even negative scores.

One of the factors that determines how people will play this game is how they define the goal. One way of viewing the goal of the game is to obtain the most points possible. In this case, players consistently make the cooperative play. As the 20th trial approaches, however, a player may succumb to the temptation to "defect" and earn a few more points than the other player. You should be aware of such defections because they may cause an emotional reaction on the part of the person who has been exploited. Many people define the goal as earning more points than their partner. In this case, both players will often choose tails and will have low scores, compared to people who have played cooperatively.

In the iterated version of PD, the way to get the highest score possible is to be consistently cooperative, but not a fool. Computer simulations have been used to test the success of various strategies for playing this version of the game (Campbell, 1985). The strategy that consistently led to the highest scores was a Tit for Tat strategy in which the player began by making a cooperative choice and continued to be cooperative as long as the other player did not make the exploitive move. If the other player failed to cooperate, the Tit for Tat program began to follow the play of the opponent, continuing to copy what the opponent did on the last move. In this way, as soon as the other player signaled a willingness to cooperate by making the cooperative move, Tit for Tat responded by returning to cooperative play.

This iterated version of PD is similar to what occurs in labor union bargaining and in the negotiations of treaties between nations. One issue is whether the other party can be trusted to play the game cooperatively. The other issue is how the parties define the goal. For example, if labor and management define the situation as one in which there will be a winner and a loser, they will follow the equivalent of the "all tails" strategy. If they see the situation as one in which both parties can benefit, more cooperative strategies may be used. This model can also be applied to arms limitation talks, school rivalries, and dealing with unfriendly neighbors. By playing the game and discussing their strategies, students get a better view of the kinds of thinking that lead to different behaviors in situations where people have to deal with one another repeatedly.

Student reactions to these demonstrations are almost universally positive. A typical comment written by a student is, "At first I thought it was just a game, but I saw that it applied to many serious subjects in life." Students recognize different implications of the demonstration. For example, "If each would cooperate with each other, everyone would be better off. But because some wish to get ahead of others, we all get hurt"; "Being cooperative, one can get ahead"; and "People always want to get ahead, regardless of the other person." Both activities lead to lively discussions; they provide a model for helping students to understand some human behaviors that seem, at first glance, to be irrational.

References

Campbell, R. (1985). Background for the uninitiated. In R. Campbell & L. Sowden (Eds.), *Paradoxes of rationality and cooperation: Prisoner's dilemma and Newcomb's problem* (pp. 3–41). Vancouver, British Columbia, Canada: University of British Columbia Press.

Gleitman, H. (1987). *Basic psychology* (2nd ed.). New York: Norton.

Hardin, G. (1968). The tragedy of the commons. *Science, 162,* 1243–1248.

Worchel, S., &. Cooper, J. (1983). *Understanding social psychology* (3rd ed.). Homewood, IL: Dorsey.

Robbers in the Classroom: A Deindividuation Exercise

David K. Dodd
Saint Mary College

A deindividuation demonstration, which I have developed and evaluated over the past 5 years, has yielded excellent results. The objective of the exercise is to illustrate deindividuation by asking students to imagine and anonymously report those behaviors in which they might engage if they were actually in such a deindividuated state. The idea for this demonstration is taken directly from Zimbardo (1979a), and is based more generally on Zimbardo's (1970) theory of deindividuation. Zimbardo defined deindividuation as "a complex process in which a series of social conditions lead to changes in perception of self and of other people," consequently "behavior that is normally restrained and inhibited is 'released' in violation of established norms of appropriateness" (1979b, p. 702). A major contributing factor to deindividuation, according to Zimbardo (1979b), is perceived anonymity, which psychologically protects individuals from being held responsible for their actions.

The primary purpose of this classroom demonstration is to illustrate the concept of deindividuation, and to reveal that even "normal, well-adjusted" college students are capable of highly inappropriate, antisocial behavior, given certain social and situational conditions. In the present study, 312 responses were generated from 229 undergraduate psychology students. Because 26 of the respondents were students in prison college programs, a secondary objective was to compare the responses of prisoners to nonprisoners in terms of the proportion and kinds of antisocial responses.

Method and Results

The deindividuation demonstration was used with 13 undergraduate psychology classes, including 11 general and 2 social psychology classes. Three classes (hereafter "prison") were conducted in maximum security prison settings: one of these classes was exclusively female and consisted of five respondents; the other two were exclusively male and consisted of 10 and 11 respondents. These students, all convicted of felonies, generally fell in the age range of 24–32, came from lower socioeconomic backgrounds, and were evenly divided between Caucasians and non-Caucasians. The remaining 203 respondents (hereafter "campus") were enrolled in on-campus programs and were predominantly female, Caucasian, middle-class, and traditional college age (17–24).

The stimulus question for the demonstration was "If you could be totally invisible for 24 hours and were completely assured that you would not be detected, what would you do?" Because this instruction tended to yield many responses that were not humanly possible, such as "walk on the ocean" and "fly around at a party pinching people," the instruction was modified to, "If you could do anything humanly possible with complete assurance that you would not be detected or held responsible, what would you do?"

Students quickly recorded their responses and were asked to turn them in to the instructor, with no identifying information included. After receiving all the responses, the instructor outlined the basic premises of deindividuation theory and read the responses aloud to the class. The entire demonstration was usually completed in about 15 minutes.

In order to examine the deindividuation hypothesis, it was necessary to categorize and rate each response according to content and social desirability. After examining the data, the author established 11 content categories of responses: aggression, charity, academic dishonesty, crime, escapism, political activities, sexual behavior, social disruption, interpersonal spying and eavesdropping, travel, and a catch-all "other" category. To rate the social desirability of responses, the following terms and definitions were employed. *Prosocial* behavior was defined as intending to benefit others; *antisocial* behavior as injuring others or depriving them of their rights; *nonnormative* behavior as clearly violating social norms and practices, but without specifically helping or hurting others; and *neutral* behavior as meeting none of the above three definitions.

Three raters, blind to the specific deindividuation hypothesis and to the backgrounds of the individual respondents, independently categorized each response according to its content and rated its social desirability. A criterion of at least two-thirds agreement among the trio of raters was established, and this criterion was met for 97% of the responses for content and 98% for social desirability. Responses for which the criterion was not met were excluded from the relevant analyses.

Results revealed that 36% of the responses were antisocial, 19% nonnormative, 36% neutral, and only 9% prosocial. There was no significant difference between the social desirability of the responses of prison versus campus students, χ^2 (3) = 3.67, ns. Regarding response content, the most frequent responses were criminal acts (26%), sexual acts (11%), and spying behaviors (11%); here again, the prison and campus students did not differ significantly, χ^2 (5) = 6.22, ns. The most common single response was "rob a bank," which accounted for 15% of all responses, and jewel theft and counterfeiting were also popular responses under the "crime" category. Responses categorized as "sexual" were evenly divided among: sex with a famous person, stranger or casual acquaintance; sex with a lover; exhibitionism and public nudity; and voyeurism. Infrequent but notable responses from campus students included murder, rape, and political assassination.

Discussion and Evaluation

This is a highly educational and entertaining demonstration. When the instructions for this demonstration are given, there is invariably an immediate reaction of excitement and anticipation of the results. Indeed, the results provoke much laughter and surprise at such "murderous thoughts," as one student put it.

Evaluation data were collected from 53 subjects representing three different campus classes. On a 7-point scale (7 = *high value*, 1 = *little or no value*), the demonstrations received mean ratings of 5.5 and 5.8 for educational and entertainment value, respectively. These high ratings are corroborated by written and spontaneous comments from students, who frequently describe the demonstration as "fascinating," "funny," and "hard to believe!"

In addition to illustrating the concept of deindividuation, this exercise can also be used to demonstrate the strengths and weaknesses of statistical prediction. After collecting the responses from a class, but before examining them, I can boldly predict the kinds of responses that have just been turned in based on analyses of previous data. For example, it is safe to predict that responses involving bank robbery, spying, and sexual behavior will be quite frequent. Academic cheating and vandalism, although infrequent, will usually draw at least one or two responses from even a small class. Likewise, charitable responses, also infrequent, appear to be reliable in content, and usually include freeing hostages or solving international conflicts, alleviating social inequities such as poverty and hunger, and being kind to one's enemies.

Of course, I point out to my classes that my statistical predictions are based entirely on data obtained from previous demonstrations, and the issue of generalizing from one sample to another naturally arises. Furthermore, I emphasize that the data do not permit me (nor is it my intention) to predict the responses of individual students, and it is explained that this inability to predict the behavior of individuals is true of most social psychological research at this time.

Students are also impressed by the fact that no significant differences were found between my prison and campus students, regarding either the kinds of responses or the extent of their antisocial content. In this respect, the deindividuation demonstration emphasizes the important role of situational conditions, such as perceived anonymity, rather than personal traits or characteristics, in antisocial behavior. Therefore, the demonstration can be effectively used in conjunction with lecture or discussion of such social psychological studies as Milgram's (1974) obedience studies or Zimbardo's Stanford prison study (Haney, Banks, & Zimbardo, 1973), both of which also emphasize the crucial role of situational determinants of antisocial behavior.

Finally, whether or not my students fully appreciate the "moral of the story," that is, the educational value of the exercise, they quite obviously delight in observing the antisocial and nonnormative responses that are elicited from their own classmates!

References

Haney, C., Banks, C., & Zimbardo, P. (1973). Interpersonal dynamics in a simulated prison. *International Journal of Criminology and Penology, 1,* 69–97.

Milgram, S. (1974). *Obedience to authority.* New York: Harper & Row.

Zimbardo, P. G. (1970). The human choice: Individuation, reason, and order versus deindividuation, impulse, and chaos. In W. J. Arnold & D. Levine (Eds.), *Nebraska symposium on motivation, 1969* (pp. 237–307). Lincoln, NE: University of Nebraska Press.

Zimbardo, P. G. (1979a). *Instructor's resource book to accompany Psychology and Life (10th ed.).* Glenview, IL: Scott, Foresman.

Zimbardo, P. G. (1979b). *Psychology and life (10th ed.).* Glenview, IL: Scott, Foresman.

APPENDIX: CITATION INFORMATION

All articles in this book appeared originally in the journal, *Teaching of Psychology*. This appendix provides the year and volume of original publication, plus page numbers, to facilitate proper citation of these articles.

1. Approaches to the Introductory Course
   McAdam, 1987, *14*, 29–31
   Appleby, 1987, *14*, 172–174
   Ferguson, 1986, *13*, 217–218
   VanderStoep, Fagerlin, & Feenstra, 2000, *78*, 89–92
2. Students' Interests, Perceptions, and Motives
   Perlman & McCann, 1999, *26*, 277–279
   Becker & Calhoon, 1999, *26*, 6–11
   Perlman & McCann, 1998, *25*, 201–203
   Laffitte, 1986, *13*, 89–91
   Messer & Griggs, 1989, *16*, 187–191
   Weiten, Deguara, Rehmke, & Sewall, 1999, *26*, 19–21
3. Students' Knowledge about Psychology
   Griggs & Ransdell, 1987, *14*, 210–214
   Rickard, Rogers, Ellis, & Beidleman, 1988, *15*, 151–152
   Barnett, 1986, *13*, 62–64
   Barnett, Knust, McMillan, Kaufman, & Sinisi, 1988, *15*, 195–197
   Lamal, 1995, *22*, 177–180
   Miller, Wozniak, Rust, Miller, & Slezak, 1996, *23*, 215–219
4. Introductory Textbooks: Objective Features
   Griggs, 1999, *26*, 248–253
   Zechmeister & Zechmeister, 2000, *27*, 6–11
   Marek, Griggs, & Christopher, 1999, *26*, 11–19
   Griggs, Jackson, Marek, & Christopher, 1998, *25*, 254–266
5. Introductory Textbooks: Problems
   Windholz & Lamal, 1985, *12*, 165–167
   Griggs, 1988, *15*, 105–106
   Letourneau & Lewis, 1999, *26*, 253–258
6. Examinations: Questions
   Kerkman, Kellison, Piñon, Schmidt, & Lewis, 1994, *21*, 104–106
   Foos, 1989, *16*, 77–78
   Gurman, Holliman, & Camperell, 1988, *15*, 149–151
   Nield & Wintre, 1986, *13*, 196–199
   Dodd & Leal, 1988, *15*, 37–38
   Wollen, Quackenbush, & Hamlin, 1985, *12*, 136–139
7. Examinations: Test Factors Affecting Exam Performance
   Sinclair, Soldat, & Mark, 1998, *25*, 130–132
   Balch, 1989, *16*, 75–77
   Neely, Springston, & McCann, 1994, *21*, 44–45
   Grover, Becker, & Davis, 1989, *16*, 192–194
8. Examinations: Student Factors Affecting Exam Performance
   Griggs & Jackson, 1988, *15*, 142–144
   Woehr & Cavell, 1993, *20*, 156–160
   Beck, Rorrer-Woody, & Pierce, 1991, *18*, 35–37

   Baker & Lombardi, 1985, *12*, 28–32
9. Examinations: Feedback
   Carkenord, 1998, *25*, 190–192
   Light, McKeachie, & Lin, 1988, *15*, 145–147
   Friedman, 1987, *14*, 244
   Smith & Wight, 1988, *15*, 209–210
   Addison, 1995, *22*, 121–123
10. Extra Credit
   Norcross, Horrocks, & Stevenson, 1989, *16*, 199–203
   Oley, 1992, *19*, 78–81
   Hill, Palladino, & Eison, 1993, *20*, 209–213
   Norcross, Dooley, & Stevenson, 1993, *20*, 240–242
   Junn, 1995, *22*, 189–192
11. Academic Dishonesty
   Davis, Grover, Becker, & McGregor, 1992, *19*, 16–20
   Davis & Ludvigson, 1995, *22*, 119–121
   Bellezza & Bellezza, 1989, *16*, 151–155
   Bellezza & Bellezza, 1995, *22*, 180–182
   Caron, Whitbourne, & Halgin, 1992, *19*, 90–93
12. General
   Krauss, 1999, *26*, 279–280
   Sheldon, 1996, *23*, 115–116
   Rider, 1992, *19*, 161–163
   Lawson, 1994, *21*, 157–159
   Osberg, 1993, *20*, 110–111
   Pennington, 1992, *19*, 175–177
13. Research Methods and Statistics
   Kazmerski & Blasko, 1999, *26*, 295–298
   Marshall & Linden, 1994, *21*, 230–232
   Beins, 1993, *20*, 33–35
   Kohn, 1992, *19*, 217–219
   Bates, 1991, *18*, 94–97
   Ward & Grasha, 1986, *13*, 143–145
14. Biopsychology
   Harcum, 1988, *15*, 208–209
   Hamilton & Knox, 1985, *12*, 153–156
15. Sensation and Perception
   Horner & Robinson, 1997, *24*, 195–197
   Brothen, 1995, *22*, 136–138
   Klopfer & Doherty, 1992, *19*, 37–40
   Kozub, 1991, *18*, 180–181
16. Learning
   McConnell, 1990, *17*, 247–249
   Flora & Pavlik, 1990, *17*, 121–122
   Kiewra & DuBois, 1992, *19*, 43–44
   Hodge & Nelson, 1991, *18*, 239–241
17. Memory and Cognition
   Muir-Broaddus, 1998, *25*, 119–120
   Carney & Levin, 1998, *25*, 132–134
18. Developmental Psychology
   Shimoff, 1998, *25*, 48–49
   Boyatzis, 1994, *21*, 99–101

SUBJECT INDEX

A

Abnormal psychology, 236–238; participant modeling, 239–241; systematic desensitization, 238–239

Academic dishonesty, cheating on multiple-choice tests, 153–157, 157–160, 160–164; determinants, 153–157, 157–160; fraudulent excuse making, 167–169; prevalence, 153–157, 157–160; punishments, 153–157, 157–160; techniques, 153–157

Applying psychology, effect on test performance, 93–95; finding Gestalt organizing principles, 212–213; media assignment, 178–180; news clippings, 176–177; *Psychology Today* articles, 5–6; to students' lives, 3–4

B

Barnum effect, and ethics and deception in research, 189–191

Behavior analysis, differential reinforcement, 216–217; negative reinforcement and positive punishment, 214–216; representational systems for teaching reinforcement and punishment, 218–219, 220–222; student misperceptions of, 40–43

Brain, neuron anatomy and physiology, 201–204; neuromnemonic for central nervous system, 225–227; neuronal mechanisms, 200–201

C

Cheating, determinants, 153–157, 157–160; discouraging, 153–157; on multiple-choice tests, 153–157, 160–164, 164–167; reasons for, 157–160; techniques, 153–157

Child sexual assault, 83–88

Clever Hans, 187–189

Cognitive development, 228–229, 231–233

Color-coded exams, and performance, 104–106

Cognitive dissonance, 248–249

Common sense, and research findings, 35–37, 38–40

Computer-assisted activities, 184–187, 207–209

Counterattitudinal advocacy, as a means of enhancing instructional effectiveness, 43–48

Course syllabus, and what students attend to, 14–19

Critical thinking, and Bloom's taxonomy, 6–8; coverage in introductory texts, 68–79; and experimental design, 187–189; in text supplements, 68–79

D

Deception, in research, 189–191

Decision making, 250–251

Deindividuation, 251–253

Developmental psychology, common sense and research findings, 38–40; nature–nurture issue, 233–235; Piaget's preoperational thought, 231–233; Piagetian conservation in college students, 228–229; using feature films to teach social development, 229–231

Difference threshold, 207–209

D (continued)

Differential reinforcement, 216–217

E

Empirical technique, and its importance, 192–194

Enhancing student interest, 3–4, 5–6

Essay exams, effects of providing full-credit answer examples, 128–129; student-generated questions, 6–8, 91–93

Ethics in research, 189–191

Experimental design, the story of Clever Hans, 187–189

Extra credit, advantages and disadvantages, 136–139; faculty ratings of extra-credit opportunities, 143–147; faculty use, 136–139, 143–147, 147–149; helping the marginal student, 149–152; impact on quality of writing, 140–143; justification, 147–149

F, G

First day of class, 12–14

Fraudulent excuse making, 167–169

Frequency of testing, and performance, 110–113

Gestalt organization principles, 212–213

Grade orientation, and performance, 121–122

H

Helping the marginal student, a skills-based extra-credit assignment, 149–152

High school natural science courses, relationship to performance in introductory course, 114–116

High school psychology, relationship to performance in introductory course, 114–116

Hindsight bias, and the Simpson trial, 242–243

History in introductory psychology, 173–174

Homunculus illustrations, 82–83

Hypothesis testing, 192–194, 194–196, 197–199

I

Illusions, size–weight illusion, 205–206; Janus illusion, 209–212

Interactive class demonstrations, student-created skits, 174–175

Introductory psychology course, content coverage, 54–60; course syllabus, 14–19; critical thinking, 6–8; effects of topic order, 21–22; individualized learning experiences, 3–4; relevance to academic majors and career areas, 5–6; student participation, 6–8; students' memory for the course, 8–11; student achievement, 8–11, 21–22, 23–27, 34–35, 89–91, 91–93, 93–95, 95–99, 99–100, 101–103

J, K, L

Janus illusion, 209–212

Journal articles, use as teaching devices, 182–183

Keyword memory method, 225–227

For Product Safety Concerns and Information please contact our EU
representative GPSR@taylorandfrancis.com
Taylor & Francis Verlag GmbH, Kaufingerstraße 24, 80331 München, Germany